I0815951

Praise for the *Lexham Geographic Commentary on the Historical Books*

"The role of geography is the most significant dimension of any of the realia found in the early historical books, above all in Joshua. This review, update, and significant contribution to the geographical study of these biblical books and to the value of that study for interpretation of their message is a welcome addition to current scholarship. Every serious interpreter of Israel's story, from its entrance into the land at the fords of Jericho to the love story of Ruth and its picture of early Israelite village life in Bethlehem, will find this work an essential asset for understanding these biblical texts."

—Richard S. Hess, distinguished professor of Old Testament and Semitic Languages, Denver Seminary, Colorado

"Historical record or folktale including poetry or prophecy—opinions may differ over how best to evaluate the books covered by this commentary. But their geographical setting remains fixed and constant, and a galaxy of specialists here unpacks those details with full attention to texts and archaeology in a manner not paralleled in any other available resource. Ease of reference is aided by a plethora of exceptionally clear maps and other illustrations. It helpfully serves to remind us that biblical literature of all kinds is firmly grounded in space and time."

—H. G. M. Williamson, Emeritus Regius Professor of Hebrew, University of Oxford, United Kingdom

"This volume properly highlights the foundational, though often overlooked reality of the physical settings upon which the events recorded in the biblical text unfolded and which influenced the biblical authors' narratives and poetry. By providing layered approaches to discreet corpora of texts from Joshua through Ruth, the contributors ground theological claims, provide guidance and parameters for text-critical interpretations, and offer much needed nuance that corrects more dogmatic and/or text-only studies that fail to appreciate the importance of geography for the biblical authors' truth claims. This volume tackles the biggest issues in the historicity of ancient Israel's story by integrating detailed understanding of the region's geography, the available archaeological remains, and philologically informed discussions of the Hebrew language. The results are nuanced, refreshing, and, at times, novel interpretations of the biblical texts that are attuned to text-critical and theological matters."

—Kyle Keimer, honorary senior research fellow in the archaeology, history, and language of ancient Israel, Macquarie University, Australia

"Geography often seems to be the weak step-sister of archaeology in biblical studies, so this thoroughgoing study of the geography of the Old Testament historical books is certainly in order. It will add perspective to any study of the biblical books covered here. And a welcome serendipity is that it is also a valuable resource for matters of archaeology, backgrounds, apologetics, and even exegesis. I recommend it highly!"

—David M. Howard, Jr., professor of Old Testament,
Bethlehem College and Seminary, Minnesota

"The *Lexham Geographic Commentary on the Historical Books* continues the important approach to biblical interpretation found in the previous volumes of this project. The geographic setting in historical context is a crucial element in the interpretation of the biblical narratives, since the stories assume the implied readers' knowledge of locations, topography, etc., as these impact the events that the stories narrate. This commentary successfully addresses this concern. Throughout the volume, the understanding of the individual narrative episodes is greatly enriched through a solid analysis of the geographic and cultural data. Readers will benefit from its wonderful maps, photos, and illustrations. It is an important contribution to the understanding of this portion of Scripture."

—K. Lawson Younger, Jr., professor emeritus of Old Testament,
Semitic languages, and ancient Near Eastern history,
Trinity Evangelical Divinity School, Illinois

LEXHAM GEOGRAPHIC COMMENTARY

on the Historical Books

VOLUME 1: JOSHUA–RUTH

LEXHAM GEOGRAPHIC COMMENTARY

on the Historical Books

VOLUME 1: JOSHUA–RUTH

Barry J. Beitzel, General Editor

Lexham Geographic Commentary on the Historical Books, Volume 1: Joshua–Ruth
Edited by Barry J. Beitzel

Lexham Press, 1313 Bay St., Bellingham, WA 98225
LexhamPress.com

Print ISBN 9781683597919
Digital ISBN 9781683597926

Lexham Editorial: Douglas Mangum, Amy Balogh, Jessica Parks, Jonathan Gardner, Lynsey Stepan, Katy Smith, Abigail Stocker, Mandi Newell
Cover Design: Bryan Hintz
Typesetting: ProjectLuz.com

25 26 27 28 29 30 31 / IN / 12 11 10 9 8 7 6 5 4 3 2 1

CONTENTS

ABBREVIATIONS

AB	Anchor (Yale) Bible Commentary
ABD	*Anchor (Yale) Bible Dictionary*. Edited by David Noel Freedman. 6 vols. New York: Doubleday, 1992
ABL	*Assyrian and Babylonian Letters Belonging to the Kouyunjik Collections of the British Museum*. Edited by Robert F. Harper. 14 vols. Chicago: University of Chicago Press, 1892–1914
AEL	*Ancient Egyptian Literature*. Miriam Lichtheim. 3 vols. Berkeley: University of California Press, 1971–1980
ANET	*Ancient Near Eastern Texts Relating to the Old Testament*. Edited by James B. Pritchard. 3rd ed. Princeton: Princeton University Press, 1969
ANRW	*Aufstieg und Niedergang der römischen Welt: Geschichte und Kultur Roms im Spiegel der neueren Forschung*. Edited by Hildegard Temporini and Wolfgang Haase. Berlin: de Gruyter, 1972–
Ant.	*Jewish Antiquities* (Josephus)
b.	Babylonian Talmud
BA	*Biblical Archaeologist*
BAR	*Biblical Archaeology Review*
BASOR	*Bulletin of the American Schools of Oriental Research*
BBR	*Bulletin for Biblical Research*
BDAG	Bauer, W., F. W. Danker, W. F. Arndt, and F. W. Gingrich, eds. *Greek-English Lexicon of the New Testament and Other Early Christian Literature*. 3rd ed. Chicago: University of Chicago Press, 2000
BDB	Brown, Francis, S. R. Driver, and Charles A. Briggs. *A Hebrew and English Lexicon of the Old Testament*. Oxford: Clarendon, 1906
BRev	*Bible Review*
BTB	*Biblical Theology Bulletin*
CAD	*The Assyrian Dictionary of the Oriental Institute of the University of Chicago*. 21 vols. Chicago: The Oriental Institute of the University of Chicago, 1956–2010
CAH	The Cambridge Ancient History
CBQ	*Catholic Biblical Quarterly*
COS	*The Context of Scripture*. Edited by William W. Hallo and K. Lawson Younger Jr. 4 vols. Leiden: Brill, 1997–2016
CRIPEL	*Cahier de Recherches de l'Institut de Papyrologie et d'Egyptologie de Lille*
CT	*Cuneiform Texts from Babylonian Tablets in the British Museum*
DANE	*Dictionary of the Ancient Near East*. Edited by Piotr Bienkowski and Alan Millard. Philadelphia: University of Pennsylvania Press, 2000

DCH	*Dictionary of Classical Hebrew*. Edited by David J. A. Clines. 9 vols. Sheffield: Sheffield Phoenix Press, 1993–2016
DDD	*Dictionary of Deities and Demons in the Bible*. Edited by Karel van der Toorn, Bob Becking, and Pieter W. van der Horst. 2nd rev. ed. Leiden: Brill, 1999
DOTP	*Dictionary of the Old Testament: Pentateuch*. Edited by T. Desmond Alexander and David W. Baker. Downers Grove, IL: InterVarsity Press, 2003
DOTHB	*Dictionary of the Old Testament: Historical Books*. Edited by Bill T. Arnold and H. G. M. Williamson. Downers Grove, IL: Intervarsity Press, 2005
DULAT	*A Dictionary of the Ugaritic Language in the Alphabetic Tradition*. Edited by Gregorio Del Olmo Lete and Joaquín Sanmartín. Translated and edited by W. G. E. Watson. 3rd ed. 2 vols. Leiden: Brill, 2015
EA	El-Amarna tablet
EBC	*The Expositor's Bible Commentary*. Edited by Frank E. Gaebelein. 12 vols. Grand Rapids: Zondervan, 1979–1992
EBR	*Encyclopedia of the Bible and Its Reception*. Edited by Constance M. Furey, Joel Marcus LeMon, Brian Matz, Thomas Römer, Jens Schröter, Barry Dov Walfish, and Eric Ziolkowski. 22 vols. Berlin: De Gruyter, 2009–
EDB	*Eerdmans Dictionary of the Bible*. Edited by David Noel Freedman. Grand Rapids: Eerdmans, 2000
EEC	Evangelical Exegetical Commentary
EJ	*Encyclopaedia Judaica*. Edited by Fred Skolnik and Michael Berenbaum. 2nd ed. 22 vols. Detroit: Macmillan Reference USA, 2007
HALOT	*The Hebrew and Aramaic Lexicon of the Old Testament*. Ludwig Koehler, Walter Baumgartner, and Johann J. Stamm. Translated and edited under the supervision of Mervyn E. J. Richardson. 5 vols. Leiden: Brill, 1994–2000
HTR	*Harvard Theological Review*
IBC	Interpretation: A Bible Commentary for Teaching and Preaching
ICC	International Critical Commentary
IEJ	*Israel Exploration Journal*
ISBE	*International Standard Bible Encyclopedia*. Edited by Geoffrey W. Bromiley. 4 vols. Grand Rapids: Eerdmans, 1979–1988
JBL	*Journal of Biblical Literature*
JCS	*Journal of Cuneiform Studies*
JETS	*Journal of the Evangelical Theological Society*
JNES	*Journal of Near Eastern Studies*
JSOT	*Journal for the Study of the Old Testament*
J.W.	*Jewish War* (Josephus)
KRI	Kitchen, K. A. *Ramesside Inscriptions, Historical and Biographical*. 8 vols. Oxford: Blackwell, 1969–1990
KTU	*Die keilalphabetischen Texte aus Ugarit*. Edited by Manfried Dietrich, Oswald Loretz, and Joaquín Sanmartín. Münster: Ugarit-Verlag, 1976, 1995, 2013
LBD	*The Lexham Bible Dictionary*. Edited by John D. Barry. Bellingham, WA: Lexham Press, 2016
LCL	Loeb Classical Library

LEM	*Late Egyptian Miscellanies*. Alan H. Gardiner. Brussels: Édition de la Fondation Égyptologique, 1937
LES	*The Lexham English Septuagint: A New Translation*. 2nd ed. Bellingham, WA: Lexham Press, 2019
LSJ	Liddell, Henry George, Robert Scott, Henry Stuart Jones. *A Greek-English Lexicon*. 9th ed. with revised supplement. Oxford: Clarendon, 1996
LXX	Septuagint
m.	Mishnah
MAB	*The New Moody Atlas of the Bible*. Barry J. Beitzel. Chicago: Moody Press, 2009
MT	Masoretic Text
NAC	New American Commentary
NBD	*New Bible Dictionary*. Edited by D. R. W. Wood, Howard Marshall, J. D. Douglas, and N. Hillyer. 3rd ed. Downers Grove, IL: InterVarsity Press, 1996
NEA	*Near Eastern Archaeology*
NEAEHL	*New Encyclopedia of Archaeological Excavations in the Holy Land*. Edited by Ephraim Stern. 5 vols. Jerusalem: Israel Exploration Society, 1993, 2008
NETS	*A New English Translation of the Septuagint*. Edited by Albert Pietersma and Benjamin G. Wright. Oxford: Oxford University Press, 2007
NIB	*The New Interpreter's Bible*. Edited by Leander E. Keck. 12 vols. Nashville: Abingdon, 1994–2004
NICOT	New International Commentary on the Old Testament
NIDB	*New Interpreter's Dictionary of the Bible*. Edited by Katharine Doob Sakenfeld. 5 vols. Nashville, TN: Abingdon, 2006–2009
NIDOTTE	*New International Dictionary of Old Testament Theology and Exegesis*. Edited by Willem A. VanGemeren. 5 vols. Grand Rapids: Zondervan, 1997
NIVAC	New International Version Application Commentary
OEANE	*The Oxford Encyclopedia of Archaeology in the Near East*. Edited by Eric M. Meyers. 5 vols. New York: Oxford University Press, 1997
Onom.	*Onomasticon* (Eusebius)
OTL	Old Testament Library
OTP	*The Old Testament Pseudepigrapha*. Edited by James H. Charlesworth. 2 vols. Garden City, NY: Doubleday, 1983–1985
PEQ	*Palestine Exploration Quarterly*
RA	*Revue d'assyriologie et d'archéologie orientale*
RINAP	The Royal Inscriptions of the Neo-Assyrian Period
RITA	Kitchen, K. A. *Ramesside Inscriptions Translated and Annotated: Translations*. 7 vols. Oxford: Blackwell; Chichester: Wiley-Blackwell, 1993–2014
RlA	*Reallexikon der Assyriologie und Vorderasiatischen Archäologie*. Edited by Erich Ebeling et al. 15 vols. Berlin: de Gruyter, 1928–2017
SBL	Society of Biblical Literature
SJOT	*Scandinavian Journal of the Old Testament*
TA	*Tel Aviv*
TDOT	*Theological Dictionary of the Old Testament*. Edited by G. Johannes Botterweck and Helmer Ringgren. Translated by John T. Willis et al. 15 vols. Grand Rapids: Eerdmans, 1974–2006

TLOT	*Theological Lexicon of the Old Testament*. Edited by Ernst Jenni, with assistance from Claus Westermann. Translated by Mark E. Biddle. 3 vols. Peabody, MA: Hendrickson, 1997
TOTC	Tyndale Old Testament Commentary
TWOT	*Theological Wordbook of the Old Testament*. Edited by R. Laird Harris, Gleason L. Archer Jr., and Bruce K. Waltke. 2 vols. Chicago: Moody Press, 1980
TynBul	*Tyndale Bulletin*
UF	*Ugarit-Forschungen*
VT	*Vetus Testamentum*
WBC	Word Biblical Commentary
WTJ	*Westminster Theological Journal*
y.	Jerusalem Talmud
ZAW	*Zeitschrift für die alttestamentliche Wissenschaft*
ZDPV	*Zeitschrift des deutschen Palästina-Vereins*
ZECOT	Zondervan Exegetical Commentary on the Old Testament
ZIBBCOT	*Zondervan Illustrated Bible Backgrounds Commentary (Old Testament)*. Edited by John H. Walton. 5 vols. Grand Rapids: Zondervan, 2009

SERIES PREFACE

To adapt a line from Ecclesiastes 12, "Of the writing of commentaries there is no end." Today's practitioners of biblical studies axiomatically regard the enterprise to be richly multi-faceted—even multidisciplinary. As a result of such breadth of inquiry, no one commentary series is capable of straddling the entire intellectual waterfront. When we see a "Layman's Commentary" series or a "Critical Commentary" series or an "Expositor's Commentary" series, we implicitly recognize and accept the fact that certain aspects of the biblical text will be emphasized while others may be treated more selectively or not at all. The same largely holds true for a "Theological Commentary" series, an "Exegetical Commentary" series, or a "Bible Backgrounds Commentary" series. Perhaps even more narrowly focused but still in this same tradition, one thinks of an "Arminian Commentary" series, a "Lutheran Commentary" series, and possibly even a "Woman's Commentary" series or a "South Asia Commentary" series. It has become understandably acceptable to us that no one commentary source can or should attempt to cover everything inherent in this widely diverse field. Accordingly, to refer to a "Geographic Commentary" series is merely to echo this same sentiment, while at the same time to attempt to delineate something of a distinctive approach and to define a particular focus of textual explication.

The conceptual premise of this commentary holds that geography is a legitimate, if commonly overlooked, hermeneutical category. Even cursory reflection leads one to the inescapable conclusion that words from God have been revealed in *real time* about *real people* in *real places*. And we think it *highly significant* that authors who spell out for us the biblical storyline in terms of "Who," "Why," "When," "How," "What," or "So What," frequently add the element of "Where," whether explicitly or implicitly. This fairly common tendency to weave the spatial dimension into the fabric of the Bible's narrative storyline actually sets the Scriptures apart from most other ancient holy writings. And it does this in quite striking and dramatic ways!

To be sure, sacred writings of each of the world's religions are designed to guide and nurture their devoted followers. But it must be stressed, other sacred writings do this in markedly different ways, insofar as geography is concerned. Let us take a glimpse at the sacred writings of the world's five largest religions. Thus, for example, the *Rigveda* (or *Rig-Veda*) of Hinduism is a complex of more than one thousand holy hymns, poetically expressing interest in establishing or maintaining cosmic/pantheistic order, which will bring to its faithful adherents a life of balance, bounty, and fertility on earth. The hymns reference a myriad of deities but few places. The *Rigveda* makes repeated mention of "seven rivers," but most are of uncertain or fluctuating identifications. It is noteworthy that the mention of these rivers relates thematically to the slaying of the god Vrdra, the dragon, thus releasing vast reservoirs of celestial water so that these seven rivers can be free to surge and to inundate the thirsty plains and deserts and to establish fertility across the land.

Likewise, in Buddhism's *Tripiṭaka* (or *Tipiṭaka*)—where concern focuses on Enlightenment and on its four noble truths designed to point out the way of morality, concentration, and knowledge—geography can be said to play a negligible, almost nonexistent role. The *Tripiṭaka* makes mention of fewer than three dozen place names, a great majority of which appear pragmatically in the text only to identify where Buddha stayed during the rainy season, where he gave a particular *sutta* (teaching), or where he spent a night during one of his itinerant journeys. Few places are found in these writings, and even these few seem to have neither narrative nor religious function of any sort.

Taoism's *Daodejing* (or *Dao De Jing*), from a quantitative perspective, is probably the least geographically-conscious ancient religious expression. The religion's essentially ascetic core priorities are focused elsewhere. I have found the Yangtze river identified twice in the text, in the context of ruling over kings, and the *Daodejing* may likewise make passing reference to an unnamed and unsituated river, stream, ravine, valley, or road. There is not much more.

Finally, Islam's *Qu'ran* (or *Koran*) bears the closest affinity to the Bible in terms of its spatial priorities. At the end of the day, however, the entire *Qu'ran* contains fewer geographical citations than can be found in Genesis 1–20 alone. Moreover, many of its locational referents appear ultimately to derive *from* the Bible: e.g., the Garden of Eden; Egypt; Mt. Sinai; Babylon; Media/Midian; and Gog and Magog. In fact, the *Qu'ran* tends to display a sharp antipathy towards towns and cities, where in its view sin abounds, people disobey God, and from where true believers have been evicted (doubtless reflecting Muhammad's own story in this regard). Islam's writings mention Mecca and Medina, as well as several people groups spread across the Arabian Peninsula (Russ; Yathrib; Tubba; Aad; Thamood), but not much more. Little wonder that an OCLC WorldCat bibliographic search for the entry "Atlas: Qur'an/Koran" yields but one entry.[1]

In vivid contradistinction to these other sacred writings, the Bible in all its canonical segments is replete with references to place names (by my rough count, nearly nine hundred distinct names, many attested multiple times), in addition to scores of names for mountains, bodies of water, deserts/wildernesses, regions, territories, provinces, and the like—including at times when geography is tellingly employed as a nexus of interpretation.

It is this distinctive and rather common *integration* of place names into the narrative by the biblical authors I wish to stress, not just the sheer quantity of references. Often an incident will be said to have occurred on a certain identified hill, in a particular designated valley, on a discrete named plain, or at a given denominated town. There are

1. Shawqī Abū Khalīl, *Atlas of the Qur'ân* (Riyadh and New York: Darussalam, 2003), appearing in four language editions. I am making a formal distinction here between an Atlas of the *Qur'an* and an Atlas of Islam. The latter bibliographical category, describing and portraying the growth of Islam throughout the Arabian Peninsula, across the Middle East and the Mediterranean world, and into Europe and to points beyond, is well represented in literature and is very useful.

times when the name of the place itself becomes an important part of the revelation, frequently including a wordplay or a pun on the name, so as to reinforce the event's explicit location in public consciousness and memory. Occasionally, an aspect of geography becomes a theological axis around which a major theme and/or a large portion of a book revolves such as fertility and the book of Deuteronomy, forestation and the book of Isaiah, hydrology and the book of Psalms, or agriculture and the book of Joel. Sometimes it is precisely a geographical reference or allusion that enables scholars to assign a book to a place of origin (e.g., Amos in Israel's northern kingdom; James in the eastern Mediterranean basin). Geography can be found as a significant component of biblical prophecy, whether a prophecy both given and realized in the Old Testament or fulfilled later in a New Testament narrative.

As I have argued elsewhere, many crucially important aspects of biblical history are said to have transpired *in very precise places* on earth—not just in empty space nor even in heaven.[2] In the Old Testament, covenantal faith is inextricably tied to place, and "land" becomes the prism of this faith. Land is the arena in which God acts mightily on behalf of his people. The ancestral narratives of the biblical patriarchs tell a story of place and offer spatial detail: early Israelite forebears lived in a named city within a given region (Ur of the Chaldeans), and they moved from there to take up residence at another place (Harran). While living at this latter location, the patriarch Abraham was singled out by God and commanded to move to yet another particular place (Canaan), where we are told he lived and worshiped in specified locations. And significantly, one must recall that many aspects of this primeval story are later rehearsed in the biblical text, often also precisely in the context of space.

Once in Canaan, Abraham and his descendants are promised definable land (הארץ, *ha'arets*), further qualified with geographical boundaries. Many of the subsequent narratives are shaped in a certain trajectory because of this promise of land: the years in Egypt, the Exodus motif, the Sinai covenantal formulation, the conquest/settlement of the land, the Israelite kingdoms in the land, the captivity away from the land, the return to the land, and the New Israel in the land. It is not an overstatement to declare that during its later years of history, Israel's rootage in this covenantal "land" provides its faithful their foundational identity, security, and even prosperity.

When they were not in possession of their land, Israelites are often described by the biblical writers in terms that reflect the precarious connotations of landlessness, aimlessness, and estrangement. At such times they are called "sojourners," "wanderers," or "exiles." And whether removed to Egypt, Babylonia, or elsewhere, landlessness became tantamount to hopelessness. At the same time, it is a remarkable reality that biblical writers normally give us an indication of where Israel was, even when relocated outside their land: they were in Egypt, they were in Goshen, they journeyed to Sinai to receive the law, they lived for the better part of forty years at Kadesh Barnea,

---

2. Barry J. Beitzel, *The New Moody Atlas of the Bible* [*MAB*] (Chicago: Moody Press, 2009), 14–17; Beitzel, *Biblica, the Bible Atlas: A Social and Historical Journey Through the Lands of the Bible* (London: Viking/Penguin, 2006), Foreword. Parts of this preface draw from sections of these works. Used with permission.

and so forth.[3] Later, when their kingdoms collapsed, they fled to Egypt or were taken captive to Transjordan, to Assyria, to Babylon, to Elam, or to Media.[4] While such information may seem extraneous to the modern reader, it is worth noting that this information is sometimes repeated in the text or is rehearsed in a later text. It is also from many of these same locations that Israel will come to settle in their land or later will be regathered to their land.

Israel's covenantal faith was very much based on and grounded in events that occurred *in certain places* in the world. There was an acute consciousness of a national home, a definable geographic domain in which even the soil was divinely consecrated, what one may call the "holy land" (Zech 2:12 [MT 2:16]—אדמת הקדש, *admath haqqodesh*; Ps 78:54—גבול קדשו, *gevul qodsho*; see also Dan 11:16, 41—ארץ־הצבי, *erets-hatsevi*; compare Heb 11:9—εἰς γῆν τῆς ἐπαγγελίας, *eis gēn tēs epangelias*). It must be concluded that space/place plays an integral role in the whole of Old Testament history and theology.

Similarly, in the New Testament Gospels, one thinks of the location of Jesus' birth, his crucifixion, his resurrection, and his ascension. Also, much of the teaching of Jesus was clearly correlated to where he was situated at the time. He speaks of "living water" at Jacob's well (John 4:10), he calls himself the "bread of life" at Capernaum, where basaltic grain mills were manufactured (John 6:48); he declares Peter to be the "rock" against which not even the "gates of Hades" could prevail while at Caesarea Philippi, a site known for its associations with the underworld (Hades or hell) in ancient Near Eastern, Jewish, and Greek literature (Matt 16:18). In a same manner, while situated at certain locations, Jesus speaks of various kinds of soil, of thorns and thistles, of the strong east wind, of the flowers of the field, and of branches abiding in vines, and more.

Following the Gospels, one observes an unmistakable geographical correlation between the uniquely centrifugal form of the Great Commission (Acts 1:8: *from* Jerusalem, *then to* all of Judea and Samaria, and *finally to* the ends of the earth) and the way in which the early apostolic movement and the expansion of the early church are presented pervasively in both Acts and the Epistles. Once again geography is found to play a pivotal role in the biblical storyline.

So, is there a place for a "Geographic Commentary" in today's world? Consider this illustration. A patient begins to awaken from the anesthesia of an outpatient surgery. The attending physician soon happily discovers that the patient has become fully conscious and is quite aware of her circumstances: the patient can recall her name and address, if married the name of her spouse, if a parent the number and names of her children (and perhaps grandchildren), and, if quizzed, she can recite the password for her iPhone or the security code for her house. One might say this patient has regained full cognizance—except in one critical way. This patient has awakened in a new place, the unfamiliar location of a recovery room, and therefore she is unaware of her wider spatial surroundings. The patient cannot identify exactly where she is and, without

3. Refer to such texts as Gen 12:10; 13:1; 45:10; 46:34; 50:8; Exod 19; Num 10:11–12; 13:26; Deut 2:14. This segment of Israel's history is addressed in *MAB*, 106–14 (and maps 33–35).

4. Refer to such texts as 2 Kgs 15:29; 17:6; 18:11; 24:12–17; 25:6–12; 1 Chr 5:26; 8:6.; Ezra 2:59–63; Esth 2:6; Jer 52:28–30; Ezek 3:15; Dan 1:2–7. This segment of Israel's history is addressed in *MAB*, 194–95 (and map 81).

assistance, she would be unable immediately to locate the hospital's exit door or to find her car parked outside.

This patient, unmindful of her spatial surroundings, can be said to be suffering from a condition called "atopia." Atopia derives from a Greek word—actually the combination of a Greek negative particle prefixed to a noun referencing space or place (ἄ + τοπος = ἄτοπος, *atopos*)—and it means literally "no space/place" or "out of place."[5] Our patient lacks awareness of her spatial environs; she has atopia.

Behind this simple and inconsequential illustration lies a more profound reality. We can discover atopia at work in more than just recovery rooms. In America, what I will call "cultural atopia" can be observed across our educational systems, and, more generally, it has insinuated itself into our culture. Some twenty years ago, the widely-recognized educational authority, Alexander B. Murphy, asserted that from the 1960s through the 1980s, in the wake of the triumph of the social sciences and humanities, most academics in the United States considered the subject of geography to be a marginal discipline.[6] By the late 1980s, Murphy observed, Americans' general ignorance of geography, when compared to most other western countries, had become too widespread to ignore any longer. To the degree that Murphy's assessment is accurate, and there is an abundance of literature to support his claims, it seems we moderns, particularly in America, continue to some extent to live in a state of cultural atopia. Thus, for example, in a 1993 Gallup poll taken for the National Geographic Society, one in six Americans could not identify the continent of North America on an unmarked map of the world, and one in five could not identify on an unmarked map the particular state in which they resided. Feeling that somehow I must have misread or misunderstood these results in an article in the *Chicago Tribune*, I corresponded directly with George Gallup, who kindly confirmed in a personal letter that, in fact, these were the actual findings.

Nearer to our own time, Roper Public Affairs conducted a nationwide survey for the National Geographic Society, between the dates of December 17, 2005 and January 20, 2006. Among their findings were the following: After two Gulf wars, 63% of adult respondents could not identify Iraq on an unmarked map of the Middle East. Perhaps

---

5. For the etymology and meaning of "atopia" in several semantic fields, including medicine, see *The Oxford English Dictionary*, 2nd ed., suppl. vol. 1 (Oxford: Oxford University Press, 1993), 146c; *Webster's Third New International Dictionary, Unabridged* (Springfield, MA: Merriam-Webster, Inc.), 139b. Prefixing this privative to Greek lexemes can produce other words with a negative denotation, such as *a*gnostic, *a*theist, *a*millennial, or *a*symmetry. Adding other prefixes to this same Greek noun can produce words such as *u*topia (= "perfect space/place") or *dys*topia (= "bad/wicked space/place"). This Greek word occurs in the New Testament, either describing someone/something that is morally or behaviorally out of place (i.e., wrong, perverse, evil, degenerate; e.g., Luke 23:41; Acts 25:5; 2 Thess 3:2) or physically unusual, improper, unexpected, abnormal or out of place (e.g., Acts 28:6). The same word appears in very similar contexts in the works of Thucydides, Polybius, Philo, Dio Chrysostom, and Josephus, just as it appears in Ignatius' *Letter to the Magnesians*.

6. Alexander B. Murphy, "Rediscovering the Importance of Geography." *The Chronicle of Higher Education* 45.10 (October 30, 1998), A64–65. This situation has shown signs of some improvement over the past fifteen years; see "Geography's Place in Higher Education in the United States," *Journal of Geography in Higher Education* 31.1 (2007): 121–41, though atopia is still alive and well in today's culture.

more pertinent, with so many jobs leaving America for places like India, 47% of the respondents were unable to locate that country where their jobs may go. Still closer to home, 50% could not identify the State of New York (after the events of 9/11), and 34% could not identify Louisiana (after Hurricane Katrina). When told in the survey that escape from an approaching hurricane was possible only by evacuating to the northwest, 34% were unable to indicate correctly which way was northwest on a map. A wide array of other, more current, survey materials exist, and their findings generally follow this same cultural pattern.

I suppose results like these may evoke comments having to do with the need for a more robust understanding of world affairs or of what it means to be living in a global society with numerous globally-affected realities, but that is not where I wish to go. Rather, it seems to me that, as a consequence of this spatial malady or disquieting trend, if I may call it that, a rational argument can be adduced according to which this kind of spatial deficiency will inevitably carry over and bear tellingly upon *how we educate ourselves and others in biblical matters*: how we read and study our Bible, how we assess various elements found in a given biblical text, how we question and what sorts of questions we pose to the text, and the like. Those tutored in the American educational system are far more likely to follow their training and to ask questions of "Who," "Why," "How," "What," "When," but they are far less likely to ask questions of "Where." And, to the degree there is continuing validity to this line of reasoning, modernity and the modern church have now inherited what I shall call "biblical atopia," a lack of awareness of the spatial realia of the Bible, a malady in our contemporary world that may actually worsen as a result of certain tools of technology available in the computer age.

Biblical atopia, in my view, can manifest itself in different ways. It can appear, for example, as innocent exclusionism, simply failing to pose questions of "Where" and thereby failing to discern what must be seen as a conspicuous and deliberate geographical pattern found in the writings of the inspired biblical authors. It can also appear as ignorant romanticism. Some years ago I had a student in seminary who was joining the Trinity Middle Eastern Studies Program and was going to join us for a study tour of Israel and Sinai. She added that she could hardly wait to go home at Christmas and to share this good news with an elderly saint, a lady she much adored in her local church. When she returned after the holidays, she said to me, "I told my friend that I was going to be able to visit Mt. Sinai, Judea, Galilee, Jericho, Jerusalem, Bethlehem, Capernaum, and many other places associated with the lives of Abraham, Moses, David, Peter, and Jesus, thinking she would be delighted to hear such news." Instead, my student reported, the saintly woman had replied: "Well now, I know all those places are in the Bible, but I never thought of them as being on the earth."

Beyond innocent exclusionism or ignorant romanticism, biblical atopia can appear as idealized sentimentalism. Centuries of medieval art or poetry, or layers of preaching or meditation, can so idealize and sanctify the biblical storyline that one is led to imagine the land of promise as a veritable paradise, a glorious, magnificent, sacred, and utopian place of almost mythical proportions. This form of biblical atopia is likewise misguided and is out of step with the realistic presentation of biblical authors.

Finally, biblical atopia can appear today in the form of overt skepticism. Wanting perhaps quick and easy answers, some Bible readers may ask, "What difference does it *really* make where this or that biblical event took place? After all, it was very long ago and very far away."

As a response, I would strenuously argue that one must guard against *any* tendency to tacitly disregard what appears to be the priority of the inspired biblical writers, simply because of possible competing priorities in our modern world: Not only with names or discussions of places found in the biblical text, but also with names of persons, or identifiable conversations, or recorded dates, or narrative scenes and sequences, or even particular names for God, any of which may at times seem to us to be extraneous to a given plot and are therefore unworthy of our consideration in interpreting a text. Stated otherwise, in our search for answers to textual questions, or in our quest to discover meaning, relevance, and application in a biblical verse, paragraph, or chapter, we must be sure to exercise caution, lest we unwittingly create contemporary interpretative priorities that may, in fact, not align with those of the biblical authors, who, in the economy of biblical inspiration, can hardly be accused of including meaningless and trivial subject matter. We may not always be able to discern why a text reads as it does, but we *can* be certain that the text was not written to veil meaning or to add what the text's author regarded as extraneous and irrelevant details.

If the Christian gospel were simply a matter of otherworldliness, or if it were concerned only with applying spiritual or moral values, gaining an appreciation of the spatial dimension of the Bible would hardly matter, and seminal events in the Bible would hardly have been geographically encoded in the text by inspired biblical writers. But it is neither of these! Central to the *kerygma* of the New Testament is the foundational claim that God became Man at a definite moment in time and at a precise point in space. To be unaware of or to neglect the geographical DNA of the Bible or the biblical world will therefore often mean that one may run afoul of the biblical argument or that reality may dissolve into sentimentalism. The *Lexham Geographic Commentary* [LGC] seeks to address many "Where" questions.

Barry J. Beitzel
Bannockburn, Deerfield, IL
October 2018

VOLUME PREFACE

The history of the Israelite nation developed within a fixed, specific geographical context and, for that reason, the Bible takes geography seriously. It records events that took place in a particular temporal and spatial setting: history is forever connected to the geography of the land.

The Historical Books of the Old Testament commence with the Israelites crossing the Jordan River and settling in their land of promise. They end with the Persian Empire, with Cyrus the Great, his decree permitting dispossessed peoples—including Jewish refugees—to return to the native lands, and the story of some of those Jews who returned. Between those two pivotal bookends, the Historical Books present—*inter alia*—the tribal distribution of the land; the assignment of Levitical cities; the era of the judges; the domestic and international wars of Saul and David; the rise and dominion of the kingdoms of Saul, David, and Solomon; the fracture and division of the United Monarchy; the period of Israel's prophets; the destruction of the northern kingdom by the Assyrians; the fall of Judah and Jerusalem to the Babylonians; the Jewish deportations to lands abroad; and the regathering of Jewish people under the direction of Zerubbabel and Ezra, after the completion of the seventy years captivity. Also, woven into these historical narratives is the corollary historical concerns of Egyptian campaigns into the land, the rise and extent of Philistine control over the land, and the kingdoms of Syria, Assyria, and Babylon with the delicate interplay these nations had upon the rise and fall of Israel. The vast scope of history for this period, and the attendant slate of topics to cover, dictated that two Historical Books volumes would be necessary in this series. So, this volume covers only Joshua, Judges, and Ruth, and a second volume addressing the remaining Historical Books will follow shortly.

As one might imagine, I was keenly interested in recruiting contributors who possess a high level of geographical knowledge and competence. Towards that end, the reader will observe that some thirty-seven scholars have been invited to contribute to the Historical Books volumes. Those scholars display great skill in their research and writing, and I am pleased to present their work here.

Within such an expansive span of time, the Historical Books record hundreds of discrete historical incidents, mentioning many town names and locating them in the text, many associated with a particular tribe or, in some cases, with certain movements of part or all of the people of Israel or Judah (not to mention water names, mountain names, valley names, region names, and the like). Over one thousand such names are given, but the exact location of most of these towns remains uncertain. The possible location of some of these places is taken up in these volumes.

But there are larger historical questions in the Historical Books that must be addressed too: What evidence is there that "Israel" existed in the thirteenth century BC? Or in the tenth century? If it *did* exist, what did Israel look like? What extrabiblical evidence exists to address whether David and/or Solomon were actual historic/monarchic figures? If they *did* exist, over what and from where did they reign? How important were they *really?* And what would have been the shape and the extent of their rule? Why were Israelites and Judahites subjected to deportation, and how many people were deported and to what regions were they taken? What did Judea look like in the post-exilic era? And there are many other similar questions. Many of these questions are addressed in these volumes.

For myself, the study of the geography of the Historical Books culminates in doxology. I confess to resonating with the declaration of the psalmist:

Come, let us sing for joy to the LORD;
let us shout aloud to the Rock of our salvation.

Let us come before him with thanksgiving
and extol him with music and song.

For the LORD is the great God,
the great King above all gods.

In his hand are the depths of the earth,
and the mountain peaks belong to him.

The sea is his, for he made it,
and his hands formed the dry land.

Come, let us bow down in worship,
let us kneel before the LORD our Maker;

for he is our God
and we are the people of his pasture,
the flock under his care.

(Psalm 95:1–7a NIV)

Barry J. Beitzel
February 2025

CHAPTER 1

"THE PLACE THE LORD YOUR GOD WILL CHOOSE" (DEUT 12:5): WHERE WAS IT IN ANCIENT ISRAEL?

Josh 1:1–11; 4:18–20; 5:10; 8:30–35; 18:1–10; 19:51; 24:1–28; Judg 18:31; 20:26–28; 1 Sam 1:1–7:2; 21:1–9; 2 Sam 6:1–19; 1 Kgs 6:1–38; 8:4; 1 Chr 13:1–14; 15:1; 16:39; 21:29; 2 Chr 1:3

Benjamin A. Foreman

KEY POINTS

- The tabernacle, the ark, or the temple were housed in at least six cities in the land of Israel throughout the nation's history.
- All these cities were in Benjamin, except for Shiloh, which was in Ephraim.
- For nearly one hundred years, the tabernacle and the ark resided in separate cities.

INTRODUCTION

Few Christians today would have difficulty naming the city in which Israel's first and second temples resided. It is well known that the house of the Lord stood on the Temple Mount in Jerusalem for nearly one thousand years. The location of Israel's successive central places of worship prior to the construction of the temple, however, is less familiar. This chapter traces the movement of the chosen place of worship throughout the nation's history. Although this a large subject and deserves a book-length treatment, in this essay, I offer a brief overview of this oft-neglected topic. Before diving into some of the specifics, a brief comment on the history and concept of centralized worship in Israel is necessary.

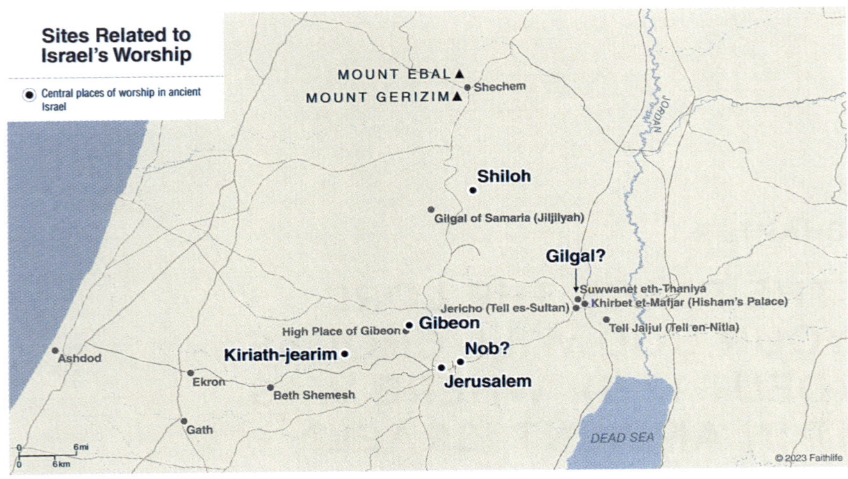

THE CENTRALIZATION OF ISRAEL'S WORSHIP

On the surface, the Old Testament seems clear: as opposed to the Canaanites who worshiped their gods "on the high mountains" and "under every green tree" (Deut 12:2), Israel was to worship Yahweh at only one central location when they entered the land (Deut 12:4–7). While these verses may seem plain enough at first sight, there is much disagreement among the scholarly community about the extent and timing of the centralization requirements in Deuteronomy.

Many scholars assume Deuteronomy limits all worship and all sacrifice to one location, but also believe the book was written near the end of the First Temple period (seventh century BC). In their view, the centralization of Israel's worship occurred very late in Israel's history (i.e., the time of Josiah).[1] Others assert Deuteronomy is older than the seventh century, but believe the command for centralized worship came into effect only when Solomon built the temple.[2] Still others believe Deuteronomy may or may not be older than the seventh century, but in any case, does not call for the centralization of Israel's worship.[3]

I take a mediating position. In my view, the Old Testament requires centralized worship from the time of the exodus onward but does not forbid the Israelites from offering sacrifices on special occasions outside the central place of

1. Julius Wellhausen argued for this in the first chapter of his *Prolegomena to the History of Ancient Israel* (Gloucester: Peter Smith, 1878), 18–51. He argued his case so powerfully that this theory, known as the Documentary Hypothesis, became the scholarly consensus for nearly a century.

2. E.g., Richard E. Averbeck, "Sacrifices and Offerings," *DOTP*, 728–32; Eugene H. Merrill, *Everlasting Dominion: A Theology of the Old Testament* (Nashville: Broadman & Holman, 2006), 346–47.

3. Fredrick E. Greenspahn, "Deuteronomy and Centralization," *VT* 64.2 (2014): 227–35. See also Adam C. Welch, "The Problem of Deuteronomy," *JBL* 48 (1929): 291–306; Baruch Halpern, "The Centralization Formula in Deuteronomy," *VT* 31.1 (1981): 20–38.

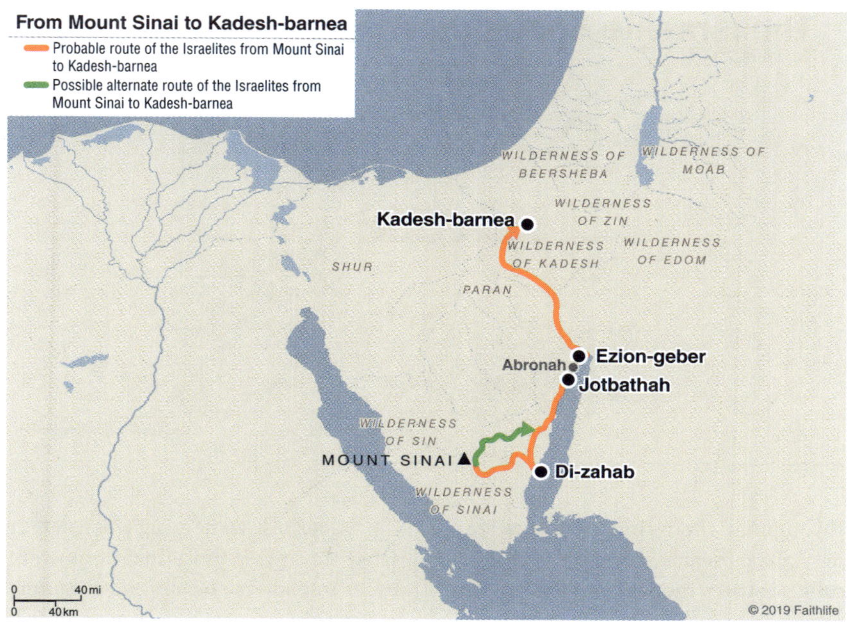

worship.[4] Since our goal here is to trace the movements of the chosen place, this is an important foundation for this study. Not every instance of sacrifice offered by a righteous individual implies it was sacrificed at the central sanctuary.

PLACES ASSOCIATED WITH THE ARK AND THE TABERNACLE

1. MT. SINAI AND THE WILDERNESS

Our study begins outside the land of Israel.[5] Mount Sinai was the first place where the people of Israel gathered as a community to worship Yahweh.[6] This was where the instructions for corporate worship were given (Exod 19:1–Deut 34:12), and it was also where the tabernacle was constructed and first erected (Exod 25–30; 37–40).

According to the narrative, the tabernacle was completed and set up about ten months after the people arrived at Mount Sinai (Exod 19:1; 40:17). Approximately one month later (Exod 40:17; Num 10:11) they set out for the promised land, and

4. For the full argument, see Benjamin A. Foreman, "Sacrifice and Centralisation in the Pentateuch: Is Exodus 20:24–26 Really at Odds with Deuteronomy?," *TynBul* 70.1 (2019): 1–21.

5. The Bible gives no details about the Israelites' worship practices during their Egyptian sojourn. They clearly worshiped Yahweh, but presumably on an individual basis, as did the patriarchs. For more on the meaning of Exod 6:3 where God says he did not reveal himself as Yahweh prior to Moses' time, see Austin Surls, *Making Sense of the Divine Name in Exodus: From Etymology to Literary Onomastics* (Winona Lake, IN: Eisenbrauns, 2017), 83–115.

6. I locate Mount Sinai in the southern Sinai Peninsula, though an argument in support of this is outside the scope of this chapter.

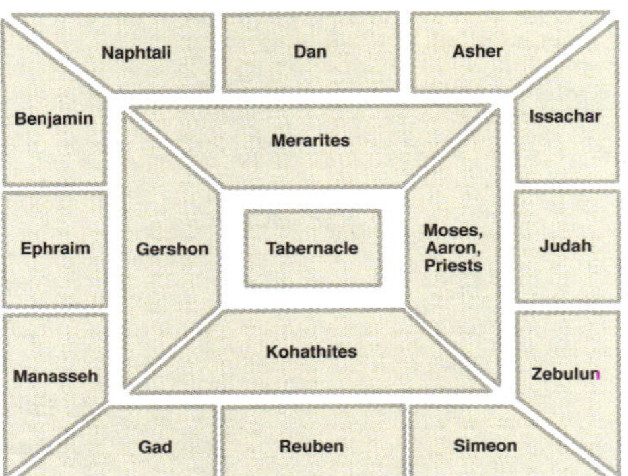

throughout their time in the wilderness, the moveable sanctuary was physically located in the center of the Israelite nation, in both their camping and marching formations (Num 10:11–28). This arrangement made two implicit theological points: (1) there was to be only one sanctuary for formal worship; and (2) God was to be the center of all activity.[7]

Although a detailed examination of Israel's stopping points in the wilderness would be an interesting study, it is not necessary to explore this here. The goal of the exodus was to settle in the promise land (Exod 3:8), and since the wilderness wandering was a detour from that goal, those locations were never intended to be long-term centers of worship.

2. Gilgal

After wandering in the wilderness for forty years, the Israelites finally came to Gilgal on the west side of the Jordan (Josh 4:19) and began taking the land. The conquest lasted seven years,[8] and throughout that time Gilgal functioned as the administrative center of the nation (Josh 9:6; 10:6, 15, 43; 14:6, 13). But was it the central place of worship?[9]

7. See Benjamin A. Foreman, "Israel's Camping Pattern and Marching Arrangement" in *Lexham Geographic Commentary on the Pentateuch*, ed. Barry J. Beitzel (Bellingham, WA: Lexham Press, 2023), 598–610.

8. According to Josh 14:7, 10, Caleb was forty when Moses sent him to spy out the land of Israel and eighty-five at the end of the conquest. Because Caleb and the rest of the spies were sent from Kadesh Barnea into the land in the second year after they left Egypt (Num 10:11; 13:26), Caleb was thirty-eight at the beginning of the exodus and seventy-eight at the beginning of the conquest. Since Caleb was eighty-five when the conquest ended, it must have lasted seven years.

9. The national administrative center and central place of worship were not always one in the same. Early in David's reign, for example, the capital was at Hebron (2 Sam 2:1–7), but the tabernacle and ark were at Nob (probably) and Kiriath Jearim.

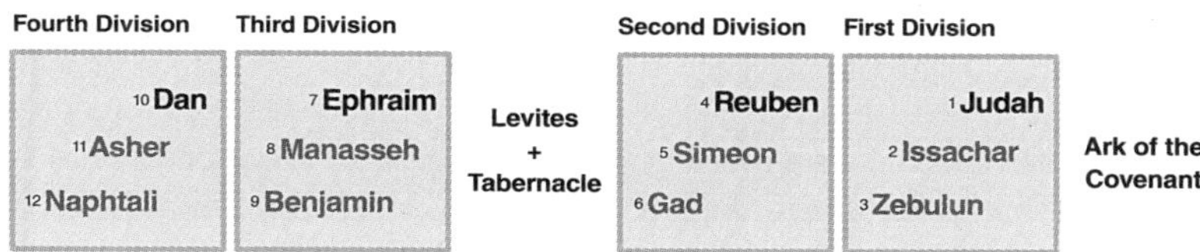

The First Central Place of Worship in the Land?

Although the book of Joshua affirms the ark was at Gilgal (Josh 4:18; 7:6), it never states the tabernacle was set up there. Moreover, Jer 7:12 seems to imply *Shiloh* was where Israel's central sanctuary was first located: "Go now to my place that was in Shiloh, *where I made my name dwell at first*." To some, these two factors suggest that Shiloh was Israel's first national center of worship in the promised land.[10]

But the evidence points in the other direction. First, according to Josh 18:1–19:51, seven tribes received their land allotments at Shiloh. Joshua 19:51 explicitly says the division occurred "at the entrance to the tent of meeting." This is significant because prior to this, Judah, Ephraim, and Manasseh (Josh 15–17) were given their territorial allotments at Gilgal (see 14:6). Since the partition of the land at Gilgal was carried out in the same way that it was in Shiloh (i.e., by casting lots; 17:4–5; 18:10; 19:51), it is likely the allocation at Gilgal occurred in the tabernacle as well. Second, Josh 5:10 notes that the Israelites celebrated the Passover at Gilgal. Since Deut 16:2 stipulates this festival is to be celebrated at the chosen place, it is reasonable to assume the Israelites had set up the tabernacle for that purpose, especially since this was their first Passover in the land. Finally, if the tabernacle was not set up at Gilgal during the conquest, where was it throughout that time and what was the ark housed in while it resided at Gilgal?

As for Jer 7:12, the Hebrew word frequently translated "first" (רִאשֹׁנָה, *rishonah*) can also mean "formerly" (e.g., Josh 8:33). The reason Jeremiah mentions Shiloh and not Gilgal is because the latter does not illustrate the point Jeremiah is making in that chapter. Jeremiah's main point in chapter 7 is to warn the people of Jerusalem that God's presence in the temple is not a guarantee for Jerusalem's survival, as they believed. Shiloh is the best case in point for this message. It, like Jerusalem, was Israel's central place of worship, yet it was destroyed by the Philistines (see below). Gilgal, on the other hand, was not destroyed by Israel's enemies. In short, although Joshua does not explicitly say the tabernacle was set

10. Gordon J. Wenham, "Deuteronomy and the Central Sanctuary," *TynBul* 22 (1971): 107; Jeffrey Niehaus, "The Central Sanctuary: Where and When?," *TynBul* 43.1 (1992): 17.

up at Gilgal, this seems to be the most logical conclusion.

The Location of Gilgal

The name Gilgal occurs forty times in the Bible, and at least three—perhaps even five—sites in Israel were called by this name.[11] One Gilgal was in the hill country of Samaria near Bethel (2 Kgs 2:1).[12] Deuteronomy 11:30 seems to indicate there was another city with this name near Shechem.[13] Two verses in the Bible may imply there was a Gilgal on the Sharon Plain and another one near Jerusalem, although these latter two are less certain.[14] The most frequently referenced Gilgal, however, is the site in the Jordan Valley near Jericho (Josh 4:19). This is the city from Joshua's day.

Joshua 4:19 notes that the city was "on the east border [i.e., district] of Jericho," on the western side of the Jordan River. As for where exactly in that region it was located, two main candidates have been suggested. This first is Tell Jaljul, also known as Khirbet en-Nitla, three miles (5 km) southeast of Jericho (Tell es-Sultan). This identification goes back to Edward Robinson in 1838 and has found the support of numerous scholars since.[15] Although this might be a tempting suggestion since the site has a toponymic connection (Jaljul/Gilgal) and also roughly fits Eusebius's description (c. AD 325) that Gilgal is at a "deserted place" two miles (3 km) from "Jericho" (the tell), excavations in 1950 did not reveal any remains there prior to the fourth century AD.[16] The lack of LB material, therefore, does not make Tell Jaljul a viable option for Joshua's Gilgal.

The second candidate is Khirbet el-Mafjar. This was first suggested in 1931, but excavations there revealed it is a palace from the eighth century AD known as "Hisham's Palace."[17] Two hills nearby have slightly more potential. In 1955 James Muilenburg excavated a site several hundred yards to the north and found numerous potsherds from the

11. See Wade R. Kotter, "Gilgal," *ABD* 5:1022–24.

12. Since 2 Kgs 2:2 says Elijah and Elisha "went down" from Gilgal to Bethel, Gilgal must have been higher in elevation than Bethel and therefore not in the Jordan Valley. This Gilgal is commonly identified with Jiljilyya, seven and a half miles (12 km) north of Bethel (James Muilenberg, "Gilgal," in *Interpreter's Dictionary of the Bible*, ed. George A. Buttrick [New York: Abingdon Press, 1962], 2:398).

13. The Hebrew is difficult; however, it seems to indicate Mount Ebal and Mount Gerizim are in the Jordan Rift (the "Arabah"). Gilgal, however, is near the Oak of Moreh, which according to Gen 12:6 is near Shechem.

14. The MT of Josh 12:23 mentions a Gilgal in the Sharon Plain. The Hebrew is probably corrupt, however. The LXX reads "Galilee," and given the other cities listed in the verse, this seems more likely. According to Josh 15:7 another city by this name (called Geliloth in 18:17) was located on the northern border of Judah. It is unclear if this should be identified with the Gilgal near Jericho or with Khan el-Ahmar, the traditional site of the Good Samaritan Inn, halfway between Jericho and Jerusalem.

15. See James Muilenburg, "The Site of Ancient Gilgal," *BASOR* 140 (1955): 13–14.

16. *Onom.* 311/64:24 (R. Steven Notley and Ze'ev Safrai, *Eusebius, Onomasticon: A Triglott Edition with Notes and Commentary* [Leiden: Brill, 2005]). Muilenburg, "The Site of Ancient Gilgal," 20.

17. Robert W. Hamilton, "Mafjar, Khirbet El-," *NEAEHL* 3:922–29.

Iron I period (c. 1200–1000 BC).[18] Another mound nearby known as Suwwanet eth-Thaniya was excavated in 1968 and revealed Iron II remains, but no conclusive pottery from Iron I.[19] While these latter two sites may be of more interest since they were settled in the Israelite period (see 1 Sam 15:12), neither have LB remains and therefore are also not convincing candidates for the Gilgal of Joshua's day. Although the city was somewhere near Jericho, its exact location is still a mystery today.

The Covenant Renewal Ceremonies at Shechem?

After conquering the inner swath of the hill country (i.e., Jericho, Ai, and their environs), Joshua led the Israelites to Mount Ebal to renew the covenant (Josh 8:30–35). At the end of the conquest, the Israelites once again returned to that region for another covenant renewal ceremony (Josh 24).[20] These two events raise an important question for our study: did the area of Shechem function at times as the central place of worship during the conquest? (For a map featuring Jericho, a supposed location of Gilgal, Shechem, and Mount Ebal see the "Map of the Battle of Ai" on page 53).

Some scholars believe the answer is yes, since the ceremonies seem to allude to the centralization texts in Deuteronomy: both were national gatherings (Josh 8:32; 24:1; compare with Deut 16:16), involved the reading of the law (Josh 8:34; 24:26; compare with Deut 31:11), and the offering of sacrifices (Josh 8:31; compare with Deut 12:5–6).[21] Additionally, the ark is explicitly mentioned in the first ceremony (Josh 8:33), and Josh 24:26 mentions a "holy place" (מִקְדָּשׁ, *miqdash*), the term frequently used for the tabernacle.[22]

A closer look at the text, however, reveals this was not the case. According to Josh 8:31, the Israelites built an altar on Mount Ebal "of uncut stones, upon which no man has wielded an iron tool." This reference harks back to the command in Deut 27:1–8, which itself is based on the altar instruction in Exod 20:24–26. As I have shown elsewhere, Exod 20:24–26 does not relate to the altar of the central sanctuary, but to altars built for special occasions.[23] The altar of the tabernacle (and later the temple) was made of bronze (Exod 27:1–8; 2 Chr 4:1).

As for the term *miqdash* ("holy place") in Josh 24:26, this word is not always synonymous with "tabernacle." In Jer 51:51, for example, the prophet laments that the Babylonians have come into "the holy places of the temple." Since the word "temple" also appears in the verse, *miqdash* refers to a location, not the building itself.

---

18. Muilenburg, "The Site of Ancient Gilgal," 20–27.

19. Boyce M. Bennett, "The Search for Israelite Gilgal," *PEQ* 104 (1972): 116–17.

20. Some commentators believe Josh 8 and 24 refer to the same event (e.g., Robert Boling and G. Ernest Wright, *Joshua*, AB [New York: Doubleday, 1982], 533). In my opinion, however, the placement of the two chapters in the narrative (at the middle and end of the conquest) and the differences between the two events suggest that they were two separate events.

21. E.g., Martin Noth, *The History of Israel*, 2nd ed. (New York: Harper & Row, 1960), 92–93; Arthur E. Cundall and Leon Morris, *Judges and Ruth*, TOTC (Downers Grove, IL: InterVarsity Press, 1968), 194–95.

22. Compare with the NLT: "tabernacle."

23. Foreman, "Sacrifice and Centralisation," 6–16.

Two related reasons suggest this is the best way to understand the word in Josh 24:26.[24] First, the ceremony at Shechem was a special event. It is unlikely the Israelites would have moved the tabernacle from Shiloh to Shechem just for this occasion. Second, the ceremony in Josh 24 was clearly a repetition of the event in Josh 8:30–35. Since the tabernacle was not moved to Shechem for the first covenant renewal (see paragraph above), there is no reason to believe it was fetched for this ceremony at the end of the conquest. Most likely then, the "holy place" in Josh 24:26 was the area where the ceremony occurred. In the ancient world, sacrifices were typically part of covenant ceremonies (e.g., Gen 8:20–9:17; 15:7–21; Exod 24:3–8), and since they are specifically mentioned in Josh 8:31, the Israelites most likely offered sacrifices in Josh 24 as well. The "holy place," therefore, was probably the area around the altar where Joshua and the other leaders stood.

3. Shiloh

The Bible does not explicitly say when the tabernacle was moved to Shiloh. Although, since the city is first mentioned in Josh 18:1, after the three campaigns of the conquest, and since that verse says the land lay subdued before them at the time, it is reasonable to assume the tabernacle was moved sometime shortly after the conquest.

The Location of Shiloh

In contrast to Gilgal, the location of ancient Shiloh is certain. Its location seems to have been known throughout the Middle Ages, but the first person in

24. Compare with the NIV: "holy place."

modern history to identify it was Edward Robinson in 1838. He correctly located it at the Arab village of Seilun, which is no longer in existence today, approximately nineteen miles (31 km) north of Jerusalem.[25] This identification fits the Bible's description that Shiloh was "north of Bethel, on the east of the highway that goes up from Bethel to Shechem, and south of Lebonah" (Judg 21:19). It also accords with Eusebius's note that the city is twelve miles (19 km) south of Shechem.[26] Archaeological excavations have revealed the city was in existence in the LB,[27] and no scholar today contests its identification.

We are not told why the Israelites decided to set up the tabernacle at Shiloh. Josephus alleges it was selected because it was a beautiful site (*Ant.* 5.68). Israel Finkelstein, who excavated the site from 1981–1984, speculates the Israelites chose it because it was an ancient Canaanite cultic site and was deserted at the time of the conquest.[28] More likely, the tabernacle was moved to Shiloh for a more pragmatic reason. Geographically, Gilgal is not an ideal location for a central sanctuary—it is not centrally located, nor is it easily accessible.[29] Shiloh, on the other hand, is in the heartland of the country, roughly in the middle of the Israelite-controlled area of the promised land.[30]

Where in Shiloh Was the Tabernacle Located?

Given the certainty of the location of ancient Shiloh, scholars are naturally curious about where the tabernacle was set up in the Israelite period. Topographically, there are three options.

(1) The northern end of the tell. Approximately three hundred fifty feet (107 m) north of the summit, the tell levels out and forms an east-west runway. In 1873, Sir Charles Wilson proposed that this was where the tabernacle stood.[31] Wilson based his hypothesis on the dimensions of the platform, which closely parallel those of the tabernacle, and the topography of the tell. This suggestion took deep root over the next century, and in 1988, Asher Kaufman made a robust attempt to buttress this theory. He listed seven reasons why the tabernacle was likely located on the northern fringe of the tell.[32] Visitors to the site today are presented this option as fact.

(2) The top of the tell. Since cultic centers were frequently built on hilltops,

25. Edward Robinson and Eli Smith, *Biblical Researches in Palestine, Mount Sinai and Arabia Petraea: A Journal of Travels in the Year 1838* (Boston: Crocker & Brewster; London: John Murray, 1841), 3:86–89.

26. *Onom.* 847/156:28.

27. Israel Finkelstein, "Shiloh: Renewed Excavations," *NEAEHL* 4:1367.

28. Israel Finkelstein, "Shiloh Yields Some, But Not All, of Its Secrets: Location of Tabernacle Still Uncertain," *BAR* 12.1 (1986): 40.

29. It sits on the eastern border of the promised land at nearly the lowest point on earth, approximately a thousand feet below sea level.

30. See Daniel I. Block, *Judges, Ruth,* NAC (Nashville: Broadman & Holman, 1999), 513; Jacob Milgrom, *Leviticus 1–16*, AB (New York: Doubleday, 1991), 32.

31. Charles W. Wilson, "Shiloh," *PEQS* 5–6 (1873): 38.

32. See Asher Kaufman, "Fixing the Site of the Tabernacle at Shiloh," *BAR* 14.6 (1988): 42–49.

Aerial View of Shiloh from the East

some believe the tabernacle sat on the summit of the tell.[33] Finkelstein argues that the archaeology supports this suggestion. On the western side of the tell, he uncovered several large Iron I buildings that he believes were storerooms for the tabernacle. Since the storerooms would presumably have been built close to the tabernacle they serviced, he concludes the latter must have been located on the top of the tell.[34] In 2017, the Associates for Biblical Research began a multi-year archaeological expedition to the site, and Scott Stripling, the director of the excavations, has recently argued in support of this theory.[35] Two years after publishing an article on the topic, his team uncovered a ceramic pomegranate on the top of the tell, which he tentatively dates to Iron I (i.e., the period of the judges).[36] Although this by no means settles the issue, the find *might* support this theory since pomegranates were frequently used in cultic contexts.[37]

(3) South of the tell. Another possibility is on the plateau outside the city, just south of the tell. Two considerations might support this suggestion. First, this theory has the oldest tradition: Byzantine Christians built four churches

33. As Stripling notes, sacred precincts are found on the acropolises of Gibeon, Hazor, Megiddo, Malha, and Jerusalem (Scott Stripling, "The Israelite Tabernacle at Shiloh," *Bible and Spade* 29.3 [2016]: 93).

34. Finkelstein, "Shiloh," 40–41.

35. Stripling's view is slightly different, however, as he argues the tabernacle was originally erected on the summit of the tell then later moved to another location when it was replaced by a more permanent building (cf. 1 Sam 3:15; see Stripling, "The Israelite Tabernacle at Shiloh," 89–94).

36. Tim Lopez, Scott Stripling, and David Ben-Shlomo, "A Ceramic Pomegranate from Shiloh," *Judea and Samaria Research Studies* 28.1 (2019): 38–56.

37. Pomegranates were used as decorations for the high priest's robe (Exod 28:33) and lined the top of the temple pillars (1 Kgs 7:18).

View of the Tabernacle Plateau at Shiloh

there, and the Muslims also erected several holy places in the area.[38] Second, the area south of the tell is flat, open, and could more easily have accommodated the large crowds that would have congregated around the structure during the festivals.

Which option seems most likely? A definitive answer is hard to give. However, since the tabernacle was *the* central sanctuary for the entire nation of Israel, it seems most logical to assume the tent was set up in an accessible and spacious location. If this was the case, then the location to the south seems most probable. One point frequently missed in this discussion is 1 Sam 4:18, which implies Eli's seat was near the city gate.[39] Although the gate has not yet been found, it most likely was on the southern side of the city based on the topography of the tell. If this was the case, then Eli's seat, which must have been in the tabernacle area, was near the gate on the south side of the city.

The Tabernacle's Sojourn at Shiloh

The word usually translated "tabernacle" (מִשְׁכָּן, *mishkan*) does not appear in the book of Judges, though 18:31 refers to the "house of God" (בֵּית־הָאֱלֹהִים, *bet-haelohim*) at Shiloh. Since Josh 18:1 (end of conquest), Judg 18:31 (period of judges), and 1 Sam 1:3 (end of period of judges) all imply that the tabernacle was at Shiloh, the natural conclusion seems to be that Shiloh served as the central place of worship throughout the period of the judges.

Judges 20:26–28, however, states that during the Benjamite War, probably near the beginning of the period of the judges, the ark was at Bethel and Phineas the priest was there ministering before the Lord.[40] Since the Israelites also sac-

38. Aharon Kempinski, "Shiloh," *NEAEHL* 4:1364–65.

39. The Hebrew reads *bead yad hashaar* (בְּעַד יַד הַשַּׁעַר) but probably should be read *al yad hashaar* (עַל יַד הַשַּׁעַר) (BHS) "near the gate"—compare with verse 13.

40. Block, *Judges, Ruth*, 561–62. Since Bethel means "house of God" in Hebrew, some believe the text is not referring to the city of Bethel but to the house of God (e.g., KJV). According

rificed burnt and peace offerings there, some commentators conclude the tabernacle had moved from Shiloh to Bethel shortly after the conquest. In their view, the central place of worship was at Bethel throughout most of the period of the judges, but then moved back to Shiloh sometime before Samuel was born.[41]

This theory, however, is unconvincing. First, if the tabernacle was at Bethel in those days, why does Judg 20:27 say the *ark* was there? Second, Judg 18:31 refers to the house of God at Shiloh. Since it is not mentioned in Judg 19, readers would naturally assume it was still there in Judg 20. This assumption makes the most sense of the aside in 20:27—since the ark was not where readers would expect it to be at that time (in Shiloh), the author felt the need to say so. Third, although describing Shiloh as being in the land of Canaan is odd (Judg 21:12), the verse also states the women taken from Jabesh Gilead were brought to the camp at Shiloh.[42] Since procuring wives for the Benjaminites was a national emergency (21:6–7), it would have been odd for the Israelites to bring the women to Shiloh if the city played no essential role in the nation at that time.[43] Finally, the reference in Judg 21:19 to a yearly festival at Shiloh seems to be an allusion to the pilgrimage festivals in Deut 16:16, which were meant to be celebrated at the central place of worship. In short, the ark seems to have been brought from Shiloh to Bethel for consultation prior to the battle. How long it remained there is matter of speculation, but it likely was brought there only for the Benjamite War then promptly returned to Shiloh.

Sometime during the period of the judges, modifications were made to the tabernacle that gave it the appearance of a more permanent building. Not only does the author of Samuel refer to it as the "house of the Lord" (בֵּית יְהוָה, *bet YHWH*; compare to Judg 18:31), he even calls it a temple (הֵיכָל, *hekhal*) and says it had "doorposts" (מְזוּזוֹת, *mezuzot*; 1 Sam 1:9), a word usually associated with buildings (e.g., Exod 12:7). Unfortunately, the Bible does not give any details about when this transformation took place or what the structure looked like. Two clues, however, suggest it was still essentially a tent. First, 2 Chr 1:3 notes that the tabernacle was set up at the high place of Gibeon in Solomon's day, and there it is called the *tent* of meeting (אֹהֶל מוֹעֵד, *ohel moed*). Second, when David brought the ark to Jerusalem, he placed it in a *tent* (2 Sam 6:17). This suggests David believed a tent was still the proper

---

to Rabbi David Kimchi (twelfth century AD), the events of verses 26–28 occur in the house of God, which was at Shiloh (see Rashi on Judg 19:18).

41. According to Cundall and Morris, Judg 21:12 conclusively proves the central sanctuary was at Bethel in the period of the judges since Shiloh is there said to be "in the land of Canaan." In their mind, such a description (i.e., Shiloh in Canaan rather than Shiloh in Israel) would not be appropriate if the city housed the tabernacle at that time (Cundall and Morris, *Judges and Ruth*, 203).

42. Block convincingly argues the reference to Canaan in Judg 21:12 is a rhetorical device—by saying Shiloh is a Canaanite site, the author "invites the reader to generalize the characterization to the entire land and to evaluate all the activities that transpire at Shiloh in this chapter as essentially Canaanite in character and intent" (Block, *Judges, Ruth*, 576).

43. Note also the reference to the *camp* at Shiloh. This is how Gilgal was described in Josh 9:6; 10:6, 43.

house for the ark prior to the construction of the temple. All of this implies that while the tent was still in existence in Samuel's day, a more permanent structure had probably been built over it for added protection.

Motivated by previous instances in which the ark seemingly played a role in securing an Israelite victory (Num 10:33–34; Josh 3:11; 6:6; 20:27, 36), the Israelites once again removed the ark from the tabernacle at the end of the period of the judges and brought it to the battlefront at Ebenezer (1 Sam 4:3). To teach the Israelites the ark was not meant to be used as a talisman, God allowed the Philistines to capture it and keep it for seven months (1 Sam 6:1). Although the author of Samuel carefully follows the ark through Philistine territory and back into Israelite hands (1 Sam 4:11–7:2), he never returns to Shiloh to tell us what happened to the tabernacle. Shiloh's fate is only alluded to in later biblical texts. Jeremiah 7:14 and Ps 78:60–64 imply the city was destroyed by the Philistines, and this is confirmed by the archaeology of the site, which reveals that the city was destroyed by fire in the mid-eleventh century—the time of Samuel.[44] The tabernacle, however, escaped the flames of destruction (see below).

Depending on one's preference for the date of the exodus, Shiloh functioned as Israel's central place of worship for either one or three hundred years.[45] With the capture of the ark and the destruction of the city, Shiloh's significance greatly diminished. Although it was later resettled and even produced a prophet (1 Kgs 11:29; Jer 41:5; Neh 11:5), it is rarely mentioned in the Bible after this. The capture of the ark and the move of the tabernacle initiated a major change in the history of Israel's chosen place of worship. For the next century, the ark and the tabernacle were housed in separate locations and were not reunited until Solomon built the temple in Jerusalem.

4A. THE ARK: KIRIATH JEARIM

The ark of the covenant proved to be somewhat of a loose cannon for the Philistines. In a highly ironic and slightly humorous chapter, the author of 1 Sam 5 informs us that the ark afflicted the inhabitants of Ashdod, Gath, and Ekron for seven months (1 Sam 6:1). Desperate to rid themselves of the Israelite shrine, the Philistines sent it back to Beth Shemesh, a Levitical city (1 Chr 6:59) just inside Israelite territory (1 Sam 6:9). Surprisingly, the ark devastated the Israelite population in Beth Shemesh as well (6:19), and they swiftly sent it off to Kiriath Jearim, where it finally found a more permanent residence in the "house of Abinadab on the hill" (7:1).

In Joshua's day, Kiriath Jearim was one of four cities belonging to a Hivite enclave in the hill country, the largest of which was Gibeon (Josh 9:7, 17).[46] At some point in the period of the judges, however, Kiriath Jearim came into Israelite hands (Judg 18:12). According to the border descriptions in Josh 15 and 18, the city sat right on the boundary between Judah (south), Benjamin (east), and Dan (west).

44. Israel Finkelstein, "Seilun, Khirbet," *ABD* 5:1072.

45. Late date: c. 1200–1100 BC; Early date: c. 1400–1100 BC.

46. See the section on the Hivites in Benjamin A. Foreman, "The 'Seven Nations' of Canaan," in *Lexham Geographic Commentary on the Pentateuch*, ed. Barry J. Beitzel (Bellingham, WA: Lexham Press, 2023), 796–814.

In 1838, Edward Robinson located Kiriath Jearim at Kuryet el-Enab, which today is the Israeli-Arab village of Abu Ghosh. Although a few have criticized this view, a variety of textual, geographical, and archaeological factors confirm this basic identification. The ancient biblical site, however, is not in Abu Ghosh, but above the city at Deir el-Azhar, where the Our Lady of the Ark of the Covenant (Notre Dame de l'Arche d'Alliance) church sits today.[47] Surprisingly, the site has only recently begun to be systematically excavated.[48]

First Samuel 7:2 states that the ark remained at Kiriath Jearim for twenty years. This number should not be understood to relate to the entire time the ark remained there. The twenty years, rather, is a reference to the amount of time that elapsed between the arrival of the ark and the Israelites' repentance in 1 Sam 7:3–14. Since David brought the ark to Jerusalem from the house of Abinadab on the hill (2 Sam 6:3), it remained at Kiriath Jearim for approximately one hundred years.[49]

Before moving on, a short word on 1 Sam 14:18 is necessary. According to the Hebrew of that verse, Saul asks for the ark of God to be brought to Gibeah for consultation (compare with NIV, KJV, NKJV, NASB, ESV, NRSV). In the Greek Septuagint (LXX), however, Saul summons the ephod (compare with NLT, Message). Commentators are split on which is the better reading.[50] In the final analysis, the LXX is probably the best reading for several reasons. First, the Hebrew is awkward as it stands.[51] Second, the ephod—not the ark—was consulted for decisions (e.g., 1 Sam 2:28). Third, Saul's demand to "bring near" (נָגַשׁ, *nagash*) the ark is used two other times in 1 Samuel for the ephod (1 Sam 23:9;

47. See Chris McKinny et al., "Kiriath-Jearim (Deir El-'Âzar): Archaeological Investigations of a Biblical Town in the Judean Hill Country," *IEJ* 68 (2018): 30–49.

48. Under the direction of Israel Finkelstein of Tel Aviv University. He and his team plan to excavate the site every other summer, the first of which was in 2017. See https://kiriathjearim.wordpress.com/.

49. Around 1104–1000 BC. It is impossible to determine the exact number of years. If Eugene Merrill's chronology is followed, then the ark arrived at Kiriath Jearim around 1104 BC and remained there until around 977 BC (Eugene Merill, *Kingdom of Priests: A History of the Old Testament*, 2nd ed. [Grand Rapids: Baker Academic, 2008], 192–97, 255–65). Merrill believes the ark was transferred to Jerusalem near the end of David's life; However, as Bolen convincingly argues, the biblical text suggests this happened at the beginning of his reign over all Israel (c. 1004 BC; Todd Bolen, "Date of the Davidic Covenant and Its Implications for Messianic Psalms" [paper presented at the Annual Meeting of the Evangelical Theological Society, San Diego, CA, 22 November 2019]). I would like to thank Dr. Bolen for showing me a preliminary copy of his paper, which has now been published (Bolen, "The Date of the Davidic Covenant," *JETS* 65.1 [2022]: 61–78).

50. E.g., MT: David Toshio Tsumura, *The First Book of Samuel*, NICOT (Grand Rapids: Eerdmans, 2006), 365–66; David G. Firth, *1 & 2 Samuel*, Apollos Old Testament Commentary (Downers Grove, IL: InterVarsity Press, 2009), 160. LXX: Robert P. Gordon, *I & II Samuel: A Commentary* (Exeter: Paternoster Press, 1986), 137–38; J. Robert Vannoy, *1–2 Samuel*, Cornerstone Biblical Commentary (Carol Stream, IL: Tyndale House, 2009), 129.

51. The Hebrew literally reads: "And Saul said to Ahijah, 'Bring the ark of God.' For the ark of God was in that day and the children of Israel."

30:7).[52] This being the case, the ark presumably was not removed from Kiriath Jearim until David brought it Jerusalem (2 Sam 6:16).

4B. THE TABERNACLE: NOB

The Bible does not tell us what happened to the tabernacle after the Philistines captured the ark. Jewish tradition, however, fills in some of the details. According to the Talmud, the tabernacle was set up at Shiloh, Nob, and Gibeon, and remained at Nob and Gibeon for a combined total of fifty-seven years (b. Zevahim 118b–119a).

Although the Talmud does not give us a source for its assertion that the tabernacle moved from Shiloh to Nob, 1 Sam 21:1–9 strongly supports this. The tabernacle is not mentioned in the passage, but several clues in the passage make it clear the tabernacle was set up at Nob at that time. First, when David comes to Nob, he is greeted by Ahimelek *the* priest (1 Sam 21:1). References to the high priest are rare in the Old Testament, and the designation "the priest" usually refers to the high priest (e.g., 1 Sam 1:9). This is significant since we would expect the high priest to be in the tabernacle area. Second, Ahimelek gives David the bread of the presence, which was taken from "before the Lord" (21:6). Third, Ahimelek also gives David Goliath's sword (21:9). This also is significant since 1 Sam 31:10 demonstrates that the weaponry of vanquished enemies was sometimes placed in a temple. Fourth, 1 Sam 2:28 notes the sword was hidden behind the ephod, a priestly garment connected to the tabernacle (Exod 28). Fifth, Nob seems to have had an unusually high number of priests living in the city (22:18–19). Sixth, the author records that Doeg the Edomite was "detained before the Lord" at Nob. This implies that the presence of God, usually associated with the tabernacle (Exod 40:34–38), was connected to the city. Finally, Jesus himself, when mentioning this story, says David entered the house of God to eat the bread of the presence (Matt 12:4; Mark 2:26; Luke 6:4).

As for when the tabernacle was brought to Nob, some suggest it was temporarily located at Mizpah or Gilgal prior to its arrival at Nob.[53] However, there is no evidence for this, and it is probably best to assume it was brought straight to Nob just before Shiloh was destroyed. Why this site was selected is unclear.

The exact location of Nob is uncertain. The description of the advancing army in Isa 10:32 indicates it was south of Anathoth, but north of Jerusalem. Since that verse also mentions shaking one's fist at Jerusalem from Nob, this may mean the site overlooked Jerusalem. Based on this limited evidence, the best guess is a location somewhere on the Mount of Olives, perhaps Mount Scopus where the Hebrew University is today.[54]

Aside from the references in 1 Sam 21–22 and Isa 10, Nob only appears one

---

52. See further Stephen Hre Kio, "What Did Saul Ask for: Ark or Ephod? (1 Samuel 14.18)," *Bible Translator* (1996): 240–46.

53. Merrill, *Kingdom of Priests*, 257–58.

54. See Jan Simons, *The Geographical and Topographical Texts of the Old Testament* (Leiden: Brill, 1959), 696. For a few other suggestions, see Joseph Blenkinsopp, *Gibeon and Israel: The Role of Gibeon and the Gibeonites in the Political and Religious History of Early Israel* (Cambridge: Cambridge University Press, 1972), 127 n. 59. Note also his comment that Nob has roughly the same meaning as "Scopus."

more time in the Bible (Neh 11:32). The inspired record, therefore, does not indicate when the tabernacle was relocated from Nob, though Chronicles does tell us that by David's time it was located at Gibeon.

5A. THE TABERNACLE: GIBEON

Unfortunately, the Bible does not discuss the circumstances that led to the tabernacle's movement from Nob. The next reference in the historical books to the tent is in David's day: "And he [David] left Zadok the priest and his brothers the priests before the tabernacle of the LORD in the high place that was at Gibeon" (1 Chr 16:39). Evidently, the tabernacle remained there until Solomon built the temple; the tabernacle's presence at Gibeon is noted several other times in Chronicles (1 Chr 21:29; 2 Chr 1:3).

When did this move occur? According to Jewish tradition, Nob was destroyed when Samuel died, and at that time the tabernacle was moved to Gibeon (b. Zevahim 118b). While this is theoretically possible, nothing in 1 Sam 25:1 (Samuel's death) suggests this.[55] One possibility, perhaps more likely, is that the tabernacle was moved to Gibeon after Saul slaughtered the eighty-five Nobian priests. Since 1 Sam 22:19 records that Doeg, Saul's agent, also decimated the city of Nob, this is a plausible explanation for what may have triggered the tabernacle's move. Details are lacking, but in the absence of evidence to the contrary, it is best to assume the tabernacle was moved directly to Gibeon just after the debacle at Nob.

According to one widely accepted chronology, Shiloh was destroyed in 1104 BC and Saul began to pursue David around 1020 BC.[56] If this is correct, then the tabernacle may have remained at Nob for approximately eighty years. Since it took Solomon seven years to complete the temple, the tabernacle was moved to Jerusalem in 959 BC, meaning it sat at Gibeon for about sixty years.

As for the location of Gibeon, Edward Robinson (1838) was the first modern scholar to link the ancient city to el-Jib, an Arabic village eight miles (13 km) north of Jerusalem. This identification was contested by some in the 1920s, but James Pritchard's excavations in the 1950s proved this location beyond a doubt. Over five seasons of excavation, he and his team found some thirty jar handles with the name Gibeon inscribed on them. The context of the discoveries and other finds associated with them made it clear that the jars originated at that site.[57] The archaeologists also found evidence of occupation from the biblical period (LB–Iron II), and thus the archaeology lines up well with the biblical picture.[58]

5B. THE ARK: A TENT IN JERUSALEM

After a stay of approximately one hundred years at the border city of Kiriath Jearim, David decided to move the ark of the cov-

55. The biblical text does not mention Samuel's activity at Nob. He seems to have distanced himself from the tabernacle after it was moved from Shiloh.

56. Merrill, *Kingdom of Priests*, 261.

57. See James B. Pritchard, *Gibeon, Where the Sun Stood Still: The Discovery of the Biblical City* (Princeton: Princeton University Press, 1962), 24–52.

58. Pritchard, *Gibeon*, 145–65.

enant to Jerusalem (2 Sam 6:2; 1 Chr 13:6),[59] presumably to prepare for the building of the temple. Tragically, the ark was mishandled on the way and diverted to the house of Obed-Edom the Gittite for three months (2 Sam 6:10; 1 Chr 13:14).[60]

We are not told where Obed-Edom's house was. The passage does say, however, that Obed-Edom was a Gittite. Since this word is derived from Gath, some suggest Obed-Edom was a Philistine from Gath—Goliath's hometown (1 Sam 17:4).[61] This is incorrect. First Chronicles 15:17–19 (compare with 16:5, 38) states Obed-Edom was a Levite and therefore the description "Gittite" must derive from an Israelite village with that toponym. Possibly, therefore, Obed-Edom was from Gath Rimmon in Dan (Josh 19:45; compare with 21:24). Alternatively, and perhaps more likely, he may have been a native of Gittaim (see 2 Sam 4:3). Since Neh 11:32–33 lists Gittaim with other cities in central Benjamin, this city may have been located in Benjamin as well.[62] Geographically, this would fit the story quite well since the easiest route to Jerusalem from Kiriath Jearim is northeast through the central Benjamin plateau (i.e., through Gibeon).[63] On the other hand, 2 Sam 4:3 may indicate that Gittaim was west of Beeroth, and therefore some scholars locate the city on the Sharon Plain near Gezer.[64] At present, the evidence for the location of Gittaim is inconclusive, as is the question of whether Obed-Edom was even in his hometown when he cared for the ark.

In any event, after a three-month hold, David brought the ark to Jerusalem and placed it in a tent he had pitched for it (2 Sam 6:7; 7:3; 1 Chr 15:1). Most likely, this was intended to be a temporary shelter for the ark prior to the construction of the temple, but since the building of the temple was delayed until Solomon's day (2 Sam 7; 1 Chr 17), the ark remained in the Jerusalem tent for several decades.[65]

For reasons not stated in the text, David chose to leave the tabernacle at Gibeon (1 Chr 16:39). By the end of his life, the Jerusalem tent had attained an important status: when Solomon was anointed king, this was where the special anointing oil was kept (1 Kgs 1:30; compare with Exod 30:22–28), and by that time an altar for sacrifice had also been built there (1 Kgs 2:28).[66] The Jerusalem tent, however, never fully replaced the

59. Although the verse notes the ark was taken from Baalah in Judah, this was another name for Kiriath Jearim. The city is also called Baalah in Josh 15:9 and Kiriath Baal in 18:14. Evidently the city was an ancient locus of Baal worship.

60. Using a cart to transport the ark was the same way that the Philistines sent it back to the Israelites (1 Sam 6). Old Testament law, however, required that the ark be carried by Kohathites (Num 4:4–6, 15, 17–20).

61. Gordon, *I & II Samuel*, 233.

62. Gordon, *I & II Samuel*, 222.

63. Although it is more direct to travel southeast to Jerusalem from Kiriath Jearim, the Sorek Valley makes travel in that direction quite difficult.

64. See Benjamin Mazar, "Gath and Gittaim," *IEJ* 4.3/4 (1954): 227–35. This, however, does not seem to fit the description of the city in Neh 11:32–33.

65. It was nearly removed from Jerusalem during Absalom's rebellion but was returned to the city at David's request (2 Sam 15:24–29).

66. Although "tent of the Lord" may sound like a reference to the tabernacle, it is a reference to the tent David pitched in Jerusalem. This is the only place in the Old Testament where

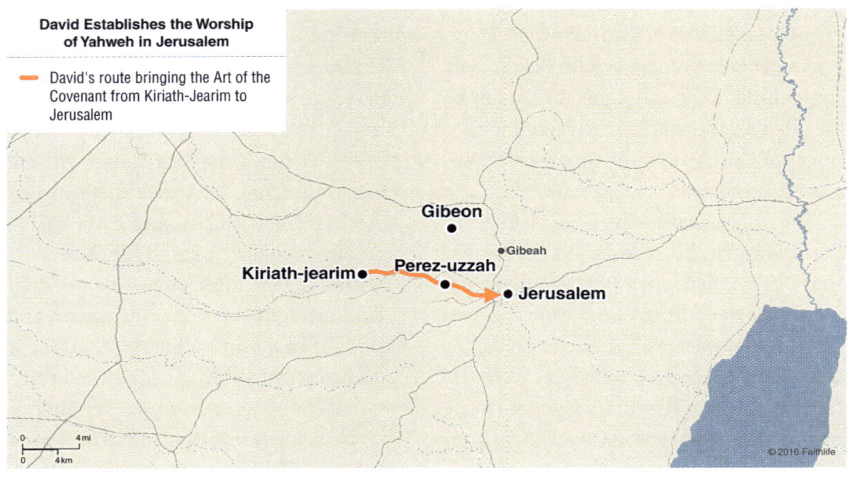

tabernacle at Gibeon—the daily burnt offerings continued to be offered on the bronze altar at Gibeon, not in Jerusalem (1 Chr 16:39–40). This changed when Solomon built the temple.

6. THE JERUSALEM TEMPLE(S)

The final stage in the history of Israel's chosen place of worship came when Solomon built the temple in Jerusalem. Although much could be said about Jerusalem and the subsequent role it played in Israel's worship, the discussion here will be kept short.

According to 1 Kgs 6:1, Solomon began to build the temple in the fourth year of his reign (966 BC) and took seven years to complete it (959 BC; 1 Kgs 6:38; 9:10). The Bible says Solomon brought the tabernacle to Jerusalem (1 Kgs 8:4; 2 Chr 5:4) for the temple's inauguration. This probably was to show that, from that point forward, Jerusalem was now Israel's only central place of worship. Dismantling the tabernacle at Gibeon permanently removed the temptation to venerate the site as a rival worship center. Unfortunately, the author does not say what happened to the tabernacle after it was brought to Jerusalem.

Although the temple is mentioned frequently throughout the period of the divided monarchy, there are surprisingly few references to the ark. After Solomon's day, it is only mentioned once in the historical books, in the reign of Josiah (2 Chr 35:3). The lack of reference to the ark has led to a host of theories about its fate.[67] For a variety of reasons, however, it most likely was destroyed by Nebuchadnezzar in 586 BC (see Jer 3:16–17; Lam 2:1).

The construction of a permanent place of worship in Jerusalem tied the nation to that location in an unprecedented way. The First Temple stood in Jerusalem for some 373 years (959–586 BC), and the Second Temple, built on

the expression "tent of the Lord" occurs, and when referring to the tabernacle the author of Kings uses the usual phrase "the tent of meeting" (1 Kgs 8:4; 2 Chr 5:5).

67. See John Day, "Whatever Happened to the Ark of the Covenant?," in *Temple and Worship in Biblical Israel*, ed. John Day (London: T&T Clark, 2005), 250–70.

the very foundations of the first (Ezra 6:3), existed for 586 years (516 BC–AD 70). Although the coming of Jesus distanced the city from future generations of worshipers (John 4), Jerusalem continues to be a symbol of the ultimate Christian hope: one day the people of God will commune with Him in his dwelling place—the new Jerusalem (Rev 21:3).

SUMMARY

One of the more surprising discoveries that emerges from this study is that the central sanctuary was never located in the tribe of Judah. Given the redemptive role Judah played as the tribe from which the messiah would come (e.g., Gen 49:8–11; Isa 9:2–7; Micah 5:2), we may have expected the Israelites to select a site for the chosen place of worship somewhere in that territory but, aside from Shiloh, which is in Ephraim, all the other cities housing the ark, the tabernacle, or the temple, are in Benjamin.[68]

It is also unexpected that the Old Testament does not systematically trace the movement of Israel's chosen place of worship. Some of the details are cloudy at best, and thus the historical reconstruction is only tentative at points. Perhaps there is an implicit lesson here: although Israel's worship was centralized in the Old Testament period, the actual location of the chosen place was not of primary importance. This seems to be supported by the fact that the Pentateuch itself does not state where the central place of worship was to be located.

In the end, true worship has never been about location, but about the One worshiped. God is not bound by geographical borders, and the centralization of Israel's worship was only one chapter in the story of redemption. For New Testament believers, geography plays little or no formal role in worship, for as Jesus said, "The hour is coming, and is now here, when true worshipers will worship the father in spirit and truth" (John 4:23).

BIBLIOGRAPHY

Averbeck, Richard E. "Sacrifices and Offerings." *DTOP*, 706–32.

Bennett, Boyce M. "The Search for Israelite Gilgal." *PEQ* 104 (1972): 111–22.

Blenkinsopp, Joseph. *Gibeon and Israel: The Role of Gibeon and the Gibeonites in the Political and Religious History of Early Israel*. Cambridge: Cambridge University Press, 1972.

Block, Daniel I. *Judges, Ruth*. NAC. Nashville: Broadman & Holman, 1999.

Bolen, Todd. "The Date of the Davidic Covenant and Its Implications for Messianic Psalms." Paper presented at the Annual Meeting of the Evangelical Theological Society. San Diego, CA, 22 November 2019.

———. "The Date of the Davidic Covenant." *JETS* 65.1 (2022): 61–78.

Boling, Robert, and G. Ernest Wright. *Joshua*. AB. New York: Doubleday, 1982.

Cundall, Arthur E., and Leon Morris. *Judges and Ruth*. TOTC. Downers Grove, IL: InterVarsity Press, 1968.

Day, John. "Whatever Happened to the Ark of the Covenant?" Pages 250–70 in *Temple and Worship in Biblical Israel*. Edited by John Day. London: T&T Clark, 2005.

68. Although Kiriath Jearim is said to be in Judah in Josh 15:60, it is located in Benjamin in Josh 18:28. Since it sat on the border, it in essence was in both tribes. In any event, the tribe of Judah would have been hard-pressed to claim exclusivity to the site.

Finkelstein, Israel. "Seilun, Khirbet." *ABD* 5:1069–72.

———. "Shiloh: Renewed Excavations." *NEAEHL* 4:1366–70.

———. "Shiloh Yields Some, But Not All, of Its Secrets: Location of Tabernacle Still Uncertain." *BAR* 12.1 (1986): 22–41.

Firth, David G. *1 & 2 Samuel*. Apollos Old Testament Commentary. Downers Grove, IL: InterVarsity Press, 2009.

Foreman, Benjamin A. "Israel's Camping Pattern and Marching Arrangement." Pages 598–610 in *Lexham Geographic Commentary on the Pentateuch*. Edited by Barry J. Beitzel. Bellingham, WA: Lexham Press, 2023.

———. "Sacrifice and Centralisation in the Pentateuch: Is Exodus 20:24–26 Really at Odds with Deuteronomy?" *TynBul* 70.1 (2019): 1–21.

———. "The 'Seven Nations' of Canaan." Pages 796–814 in *Lexham Geographic Commentary on the Pentateuch*. Edited by Barry J. Beitzel. Bellingham, WA: Lexham Press, 2023.

Gordon, Robert P. *I & II Samuel: A Commentary*. Exeter: Paternoster Press, 1986.

Greenspahn, Fredrick E. "Deuteronomy and Centralization." *VT* 64.2 (2014): 227–35.

Halpern, Baruch. "The Centralization Formula in Deuteronomy." *VT* 31.1 (1981): 20–38.

Hamilton, Robert W. "Mafjar, Khirbet El-." *NEAEHL* 3:922–29.

Kaufman, Asher. "Fixing the Site of the Tabernacle at Shiloh." *BAR* 14.6 (1988): 42–49.

Kempinski, Aharon. "Shiloh." *NEAEHL* 4:1364–66.

Kio, Stephen Hre. "What Did Saul Ask for: Ark or Ephod? (1 Samuel 14.18)." *Bible Translator* (1996): 240–46.

Kotter, Wade R. "Gilgal." *ABD* 5:1022–24.

Lopez, Tim, Scott Stripling, and David Ben-Shlomo. "A Ceramic Pomegranate from Shiloh." *Judea and Samaria Research Studies* 28.1 (2019): 37–56.

Mazar, Benjamin. "Gath and Gittaim." *IEJ* 4 (1954): 227–35.

McKinny, Chris, Oron Schwartz, Gabriel Barkay, Alexander Fantalkin, and Boaz Zissu. "Kiriath-Jearim (Deir El-'Âzar): Archaeological Investigations of a Biblical Town in the Judean Hill Country." *IEJ* 68 (2018): 30–49.

Merrill, Eugene H. *Everlasting Dominion: A Theology of the Old Testament*. Nashville: Broadman & Holman, 2006.

———. *Kingdom of Priests: A History of Old Testament Israel*. 2nd ed. Grand Rapids: Baker Academic, 2008.

Milgrom, Jacob. *Leviticus 1–16*. AB. New York: Doubleday, 1991.

Muilenburg, James. "The Site of Ancient Gilgal." *BASOR* 140 (1955): 11–27.

———. "Gilgal." Pages 398–99 in vol. 2 of *Interpreter's Dictionary of the Bible*. Edited by George A. Buttrick. New York: Abingdon Press, 1962.

Niehaus, Jeffrey. "The Central Sanctuary: Where and When?" *TynBul* 43.1 (1992): 3–30.

Noth, Martin. *The History of Israel*. 2nd ed. New York: Harper & Row, 1960.

Notley, R. Steven, and Ze'ev Safrai. *Eusebius, Onomasticon: A Triglot Edition with Notes and Commentary*. Leiden: Brill, 2005.

Pritchard, James B. *Gibeon, Where the Sun Stood Still: The Discovery of the*

Biblical City. Princeton: Princeton University Press, 1962.

Robinson, Edward, and Eli Smith. *Biblical Researches in Palestine, Mount Sinai and Arabia Petraea: A Journal of Travels in the Year 1838*. Vol. 3. Boston: Crocker & Brewster; London: John Murray, 1841.

Simons, Jans. *The Geographical and Topographical Texts of the Old Testament*. Leiden: Brill, 1959.

Stripling, Scott. "The Israelite Tabernacle at Shiloh." *Bible and Spade* 29.3 (2016): 89–94.

Surls, Austin. *Making Sense of the Divine Name in Exodus: From Etymology to Literary Onomastics*. Winona Lake, IN: Eisenbrauns, 2017.

Tsumura, David Toshio. *The First Book of Samuel*. NICOT. Grand Rapids: Eerdmans, 2006.

Vannoy, J. Robert. *1–2 Samuel*. Cornerstone Biblical Commentary. Carol Stream, IL: Tyndale House, 2009.

Welch, Adam C. "The Problem of Deuteronomy." *JBL* 48 (1929): 291–306.

Wellhausen, Julius. *Prolegomena to the History of Ancient Israel*. Gloucester: Peter Smith, 1878.

Wenham, Gordon J. "Deuteronomy and the Central Sanctuary." *TynBul* 22 (1971): 103–18.

Wilson, Charles W. "Shiloh." *Palestine Exploration Quarterly Statement* 5–6 (1873): 37–38.

CHAPTER 2

THE JORDAN CROSSING: A GEOGRAPHICAL AND THEOLOGICAL ASSESSMENT

Josh 3–4

Thomas Middlebrook

KEY POINTS

- The Jordan River is the traditional boundary of Canaan, the original promised land.
- The Jordan crossing strongly alludes to the exodus event when Israel also crossed over on "dry ground." Both events are constitutive of Israel's identity.
- The rituals surrounding the Jordan crossing emphasize Israel's unity and the vital role of God's presence.
- The Jordan crossing signals a liminal zone between the wilderness generation and the conquest/settlement generation, between Moses' leadership and Joshua's, between Israel's reception of the law and their long struggle to keep it in the land.
- Like Moses and Joshua, the coordinated prophetic missions of Elijah and Elisha, and John the Baptist and Jesus of Nazareth utilized the Jordan River as an evocative stage for their ministries and as a stage for transferring the mantles of their authority.

INTRODUCTION

The nineteenth-century American abolitionist Frederick Douglass once wrote, "A keen observer might have detected in our repeated singing of 'O Canaan sweet Canaan/I am bound for the land of Canaan,' something more than a hope of reaching heaven. We meant to reach the north—and the north was our Canaan."[1] Douglass assumes his readers understand

1. Frederick Douglass, *My Bondage and My Freedom* (Chicago: Johnson Publishing Company, 1970), 215.

that Canaan usually signifies heaven (and not Palestine), but he must clarify the northern states as a new "land of promise" for these hymn-singing abolitionists. Relatedly, "crossing the Jordan" often transcends its literal interpretation as a river and becomes any boundary between hardship and God's future blessings. With such a rich history in theology and hymnology, this essay takes another look at the historical geography of the Jordan River crossing and its theological import.

SUMMARY OF JOSHUA 3–4

The Jordan crossing is "the single most important event" in the book of Joshua, according to Gordon McConville.[2] The first five chapters relate to the crossing. The event itself consumes all of chapters three and four. In them, Joshua's narrator slows down the tempo and utilizes a series of flashbacks in order to focus the reader's attention on the event from three different vantage points: from Shittim in Josh 3:1–13; from the Jordan in 3:14–4:10; and from the plains of Jericho in 4:11–24.[3]

The central section (Josh 3:14–4:10) describes the moment of the crossing. The narrative pays close attention the movements of the ark of the covenant and the priests who carry it. As soon as the priests stand (עמד, *'md*, 3:8, 17) in the water, the river stands up (*'md*, 3:13, 16) and dries up.[4] This focus reinforces that Israel's presence in Canaan should recognize and reflect the holy presence that has traveled in their midst since the creation of the tabernacle at Sinai (Exod 40). The impending conquest must be a *holy* war, or it will be a miserable defeat as in Josh 7.

GEOGRAPHIC ASSESSMENT OF THE JORDAN CROSSING

THE JORDAN RIVER

The modern geographer has a cluster of toponyms from the text (below) that help anchor the Jordan crossing near where the river empties into the Dead Sea. In ancient times, this section of the river could swell up to ninety-eight and a half feet wide and eleven and a half feet deep (30 m by 4 m).[5] In the modern period, much of the river is diverted due to water shortages that threaten the surrounding population.[6] The primary course of the Jordan River spans the sixty-five miles (105 km) of the Jordan Valley (i.e., the *Ghor*) between the Sea of Galilee and the Dead Sea. In ancient times, it dropped roughly seven hundred feet (175 m) in the process, all of it below sea-level. The smaller "upper course" of

2. J. Gordon McConville and Stephen N. Williams, *Joshua*, Two Horizons Old Testament Commentary (Grand Rapids: Eerdmans, 2010), 18.

3. David G. Firth, *The Message of Joshua: Promise and People*, The Bible Speaks Today (Downers Grove, IL: InterVarsity Press, 2015), 54. The use of repetition in this passage reflects a pattern in Hebrew narrative which compares a divine commission with its human conveyance and, finally, its fulfillment. The repetition highlights human obedience to royal and divine commands.

4. For this and other wordplays, see Richard S. Hess, *Joshua: An Introduction and Commentary*, TOTC (Downers Grove, IL: InterVarsity Press, 1996), 105.

5. Hess, *Joshua*, 104. The Jordan is easily the most prominent of the few year-round rivers in Israel.

6. Peter Schwartzstein, "Biblical Waters: Can the Jordan River Be Saved?," *National Geographic* (blog), February 22, 2014, https://www.nationalgeographic.com/news/2014/2/140222-jordan-river-syrian-refugees-water-environment/.

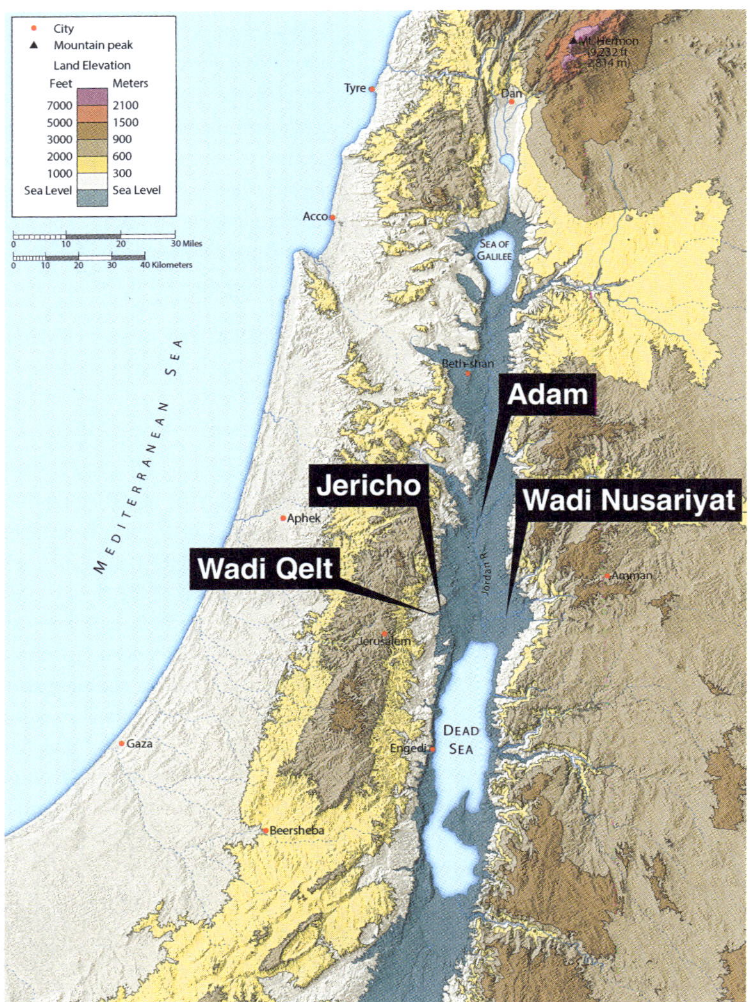

The Elevation of Palestine

the river drains the Huleh Valley north of the Sea of Galilee.

THE FORDS OF THE JORDAN

For the Israelites, the closest natural crossing of the Jordan lies twenty-three miles (37 km) north of the Dead Sea near the town of Adam (Tell ad-Damiyya).[7] This location should be identified with the "fords of the Jordan" that were used during the military actions of judges Ehud and Jephthah (Judg 3:28; 12:5–6) as well as king

7. The men of Jericho pursued the Israelite spies for three days (Josh 2:22). This may reflect the time required for a round trip to the fords near Adam.

Aerial View of Adam

David (2 Sam 17:22; 19:16–18, 31).[8] It was at this spot that some historical records have confirmed blockages of the Jordan's flow due to earthquakes: (1) in AD 1267 for ten hours, (2) in AD 1546/7 for two days, (3) in AD 1906 for ten hours, and (4) in AD 1927 for a day.[9] The text of Joshua does not record any such seismic activity.

THE PLAINS

The story of the Jordan crossing in Josh 3–4 traces the short, but miraculous, transfer of Israel from an alluvial plain on the east side of the Jordan to another alluvial plain on the west side. The erosion of sediment down the canyons—the Wadi Nusariyat in the east and the Wadi Qelt in the west—from the highlands above provides enough water and nutrients for basic farming in this arid region of the Jordan Valley. The text calls these the "plains of Moab" (Num 22:1; Deut 34:8) and the "plains of Jericho" (Josh 4:13; 5:10), respectively. Israel's story of territorial integrity began in the plains of Jericho and, incidentally, also ended in the same place when King Zedekiah was captured there by the Babylonians (2 Kgs 25:5).

TOPONYMS

Before the conquest, Israel stayed at the sites of Shittim in the east and Gilgal in the west (Josh 2:1; 4:19). The prophet Micah urges Israel to remember what happened "from Shittim to Gilgal" (Mic 6:5). The former is identified tentatively with Tell Hamman due its prominence in the plains of Moab and the presence

8. See Yohanan Aharoni, *The Land of the Bible: A Historical Geography*, trans. Anson F. Rainey, rev. and enl. ed. (Philadelphia: Westminster, 1979), 34.

9. *MAB*, 50–51; Carl Rasmussen, *Zondervan Atlas of the Bible*, rev. ed. (Grand Rapids: Zondervan, 2010), 61.

Tel es-Sultan, Jericho

of artifacts from this time period.[10] The latter is said to rest "on the eastern border of Jericho (Tel es-Sultan)," but its precise location remains unidentified, because no permanent occupation was established at Gilgal.[11] A mere eleven miles (18 km) separates Shittim and Jericho. The river blocks this path of travel in normal conditions, but the day of the Jordan crossing was anything but normal.

TIME OF CROSSING

The peculiar temporal setting of the Jordan crossing affects its geographical and theological assessment. Joshua describes how Israel set off at the river's "flood stage during [the spring] harvest" and more specifically, "on the tenth day, the first month [Nissan]" (Josh 3:15; 4:19).[12] Clearly, this was the most improbable season and an unlikely location for crossing the Jordan, not unlike Israel's unlikely exodus through Egypt's "front door" near Migdol (lit: "fortress") in Exod 14:2. In each case the Bible offers this purpose: that the nations might know the Lord, his power, and his glory (Exod 14:4; Josh 4:24; compare Mic 6:5).

---

10. Tell Kefrein is also suggested. Burton MacDonald, *"East of the Jordan": Territories and Sites of the Hebrew Scriptures* (Boston: American Schools of Oriental Research, 2000), 90; Joel C. Slayton, "Shittim," *ABD* 5:1222. It is alternatively known as Abel Shittim as in Num 33:49.

11. MacDonald, *East of the Jordan*, 90.

12. Unless otherwise indicated, Scripture quotations are the author's own translation.

THE AMBIVALENCE OF THE JORDAN

Close readers of the biblical text will notice ambivalence regarding the significance of the Jordan River. This is not surprising. Rivers both divide and unify, serving both as military impediments and as connective tissues in commerce. They are dead ends and highways. Rivers cut the landscape but also hold it together in a network of life-giving waterways, making the watershed one type of natural political boundary.[13]

DIVIDED BY NAMES

The Jordan River carves an imposing dividing line in the southern Levant. The Jordan Valley can be quite arid and its cliffs treacherous to traverse. These geographical realities likely influenced the socio-linguistic divide between the ancient Cisjordan and Transjordan polities.[14] Before his death, Moses traced the eastern borders of the promised land along the Jordan (Num 34:12). On one side would lie Israel's inheritance of Canaan.[15] On the other lies the inheritance of Israel's kindred: the Ishmaelites (Ishmael), the Edomites (Esau), the Ammonites and Moabites (Lot), and the Arameans (Aram/Nahor, Gen 10:22; 22:20–24). The tribal groups adjacent to the Jordan River are *divided* by it.[16]

Despite the Jordan's divisiveness, Israel's history complicates a simplistic separation. The addition of the territories of Sihon and Og extended the boundaries of the promised land *ex post facto* into the Transjordan (Num 32; Deut 2–3). These surprising additions to Israel's inheritance complicate the traditional boundary at the Jordan. Tellingly, the Reubenites, the Gadites, and the half-tribe of Manasseh were compelled to build a monument, lest the other tribes of Israel say, "The LORD has made the Jordan a boundary between us" (Josh 22:24–25). In other words, blood should be

---

13. Barham notes that knowledge about the vital watershed management is passed down in "traditional societies" (Elizabeth Barham, "Ecological Boundaries as Community Boundaries: The Politics of Watersheds," *Society and Natural Resources* 14.3 [2001]: 184). Havrelock also notices the ambivalent function—as unifier or divider—of the Jordan River within the Bible and premodern, European maps. From 1920 to 1923 under the British Mandate for Palestine, the territory that would become modern Israel saw the stabilization of the Jordan as its boundary, which, according to Havrelock, was inherited more from the British Empire than the Bible and earlier maps of Palestine (Rachel S. Havrelock, "The Jordan River in Ancient and Modern Maps," in *Art and Identity at the Water's Edge*, ed. Tricia Cusack [Burlington, VT: Ashgate, 2012], 108).

14. Note that even our modern designations of "cis-" and "trans-" reveal an orientation to the land that is fundamentally divided by the Jordan.

15. The boundary line of the Jordan would later be maintained by Ezekiel's eschatological vision of the land in Ezek 47:18, perhaps reflecting the original, ideal placement of the Transjordan tribes amidst their Cisjordan kin. See further on the extent and history of "Canaan" in the first half of K. Lawson Younger Jr., "Another Look at 'Early' Ideologies of the Land in the Hebrew Bible in Light of Recent Study," *Ex Auditu* 35 (2019): 39–79.

16. Although the groups did share familial connections. The biblical text bemoans that Edom, Moab, and Ammon lapsed in their familial obligations during Israel's migrations in Num 20:14–21 and Deut 23:3–4.

thicker than water.[17] But if the dividing line of the Jordan threatened to fracture the unity of God's people in Josh 22, then Judg 12:1–6 demonstrates how devastating such a fracture could become. In this episode, the Gileadites (under Jephthah) captured the fords of the Jordan and murdered any Ephraimites who failed to pronounce "Shibboleth"—a marker of Jordanian socio-linguistic separation—killing a total of forty-two thousand or forty-two fighting units.

UNITED BY RITUAL

Importantly, then, *the story of the Jordan crossing stood against division*, mainly by recounting several ritual acts of Israel's unity. Below, we will cover three of these rituals. The first ritual is the actual crossing of the Jordan River. Surely it was a ritualized act, as is demonstrated by (1) the divine command for Israel to consecrate themselves beforehand in Josh 3:5, by (2) the divine command for Israel to walk a prescribed distance away from the ark in 3:4, and by (3) Joshua's command to commemorate the event in perpetuity in 4:21. Note the similar calls for consecration, a prescribed distance, and a perpetual commemoration in the previous generation (Exod 19:10–15 and 19:12, 23 and 13:10, 14 respectively). Joshua, once again, assumes a leadership role similar to Moses which had unified the "mixed multitude" exiting Egypt (Exod 12:38). The young nation's river crossing was a single, ritualized event, and it included the *Trans*jordanian Reubenites, Gadites, and half-tribe of Manasseh, armed and ready to do their part in the conquest (Josh 4:12–13).

The second ritual that highlights Israel's unity is the raising of twelve stones at Gilgal (4:20).[18] The number of stones relates to the number of Israel's tribes in a similar fashion to the twelve pillars that Moses erected at Mt. Sinai in Exod 24:2 or the twelve stones fashioned onto Aaron's breastplate in Exod 28:21. Again, Israel is unified. Joshua would go on to call Israel to be unified in their commitment to the Mosaic covenant by setting up more stones at Mt. Ebal (Josh 8:32) and a large stone at Shechem (24:26).

The third ritual that unified Israel at the time of the Jordan crossing (the tenth of Nissan) was the celebration of the Passover in Josh 5:9 (the fourteenth/fifteenth of Nissan). At some point in the days before the Passover, Joshua circumcised the new generation (Josh 5:2–9), for God had strictly commanded: "No

---

17. For different readings, see Douglas A. Knight, "Joshua 22 and the Ideology of Space," in *"Imagining" Biblical Worlds: Studies in Spatial, Social and Historical Constructs in Honor of James W. Flanagan*, ed. David M. Gunn and Paula M. McNutt (London: Sheffield Academic, 2002), 51–63; David Frankel, *The Land of Canaan and the Destiny of Israel: Theologies of Territory in the Hebrew Bible* (Winona Lake, IN: Eisenbrauns, 2011).

18. A second set of stones appears to have been erected on the spot where the ark rested in the river and could be seen in the years that followed (Josh 4:9). Was Gilgal, then, a copy of the stones (an altar?) set up in the Jordan? This may have strengthened their memorial function. In a contrasting explanation, McConville and Williams comment that "the curious duplication [of stone memorials] has been widely seen as evidence of the complicated prehistory of the present text" (McConville and Williams, *Joshua*, 23). Dozeman believes the two sets of stones each relate to the two catechisms (Josh 4:6b–7 and 21–24) within his interpretation of Joshua's redactional history (Thomas B. Dozeman, "The *yam-sûp* in the Exodus and the Crossing of the Jordan River," *CBQ* 58 [1996]: 411–14).

INTERTEXTUAL CONNECTIONS BETWEEN
THE EXODUS AND JORDAN CROSSINGS

Intertextual Connections	Exodus Crossing & Sinai	Jordan Crossing & Gilgal
pass over (עבר, *'br*)	Exod 12:12; 15:16	Josh 1:2, 11; 3:6, 11, 17
dry land (*yabbashah* / *ybsh*)	Exod 14:16, 21–22; 15:19c; Josh 2:10; Ps 66:6	Josh 4:22–23; 5:1
waters in a heap (נֵד, *ned*)	Exod 15:8	Josh 3:13, 16
consecration	Exod 19:10–15	Josh 3:5
prescribed distance	Exod 19:12, 23	Josh 3:4
twelve stones	Exod 24:2	Josh 4:20
when your children ask	Exod 13:10, 14	Josh 4:21
theological purpose	Exod 14:4	Josh 4:24
foreigners' fear	Exod 15:14	Josh 2:9

uncircumcised person shall eat of [the Passover meal]" (Exod 12:48).[19] Israel feasts before they fight. Victor Turner argues that such festivals produce a sense of unity and *communitas*—a condition in contrast to the normal hierarchy and structures of society, i.e., "an unstructured or rudimentarily structured and relatively undifferentiated [community] of equal individuals who submit together to the general authority of ritual elders."[20] Israel's political and religious unification, therefore, emerges as a major theme in the narrated events of the Jordan crossing.

BIBLICAL ALLUSIONS TO THE JORDAN CROSSING

The previous section highlighted a number of literary allusions to events in Exodus: the consecration of Israel, the perpetual commemoration of a divine miracle, and the erection of stones. Indeed, the Jordan crossing has numerous allusions within the Hebrew Bible.

The most compelling of them relates to the crossing of the Reed Sea. Joshua 4:23 makes this explicit: "The LORD your God dried up the waters of the Jordan for you until you passed over, *just as* the LORD your God did to the Reed Sea." The

19. A folk etymology for Gilgal is connected with this circumcision in Josh 5:9, which explains that the reproach of the wilderness generation was rolled away (גלל, *gll*) at Gilgal. The resulting site, Gibeath Haaraloth, "Hill of the Foreskins," was like Gilgal, a mere camp/worksite.

20. Victor Turner, *The Ritual Process: Structure and Anti-Structure* (Ithaca, NY: Cornell University Press, 1969), 96.

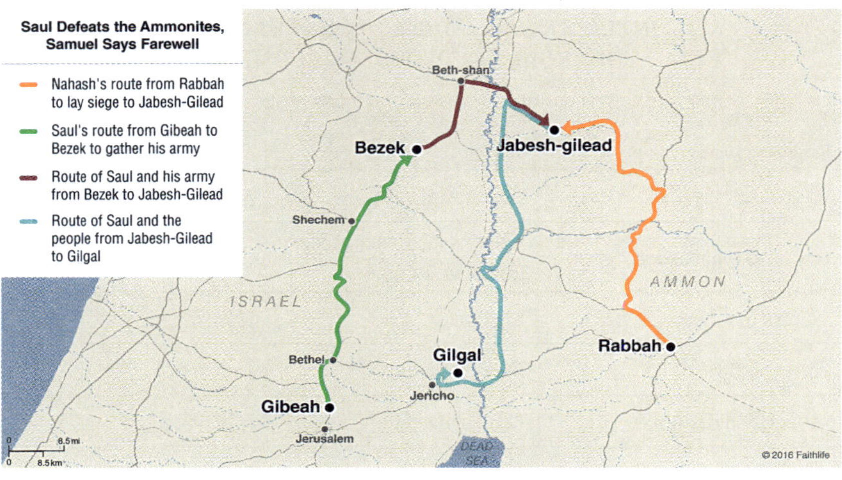

appearance of "dry land" (as the noun יַבָּשָׁה, *yabbashah*, and in its verbal form יבשׁ, *ybsh*) creates a strong lexical connection. Rahab reveals in Josh 2:10 that news of the "dry land" of the exodus crossing had spread in Canaan. The term soon reappears in Josh 4:22–23 and 5:1 to describe the Jordan crossing. In the exodus, *yabbashah* appears in both the prose (Exod 14:16, 21–22) and the poetic narration of events (15:19c). Joshua does not record a poem, but we do hear of the Jordan crossing in Ps 66:6 "[God] turned the sea into dry land; through the river they passed on foot."

Markedly absent in this exodus/Jordan crossing comparison is the activity of God's Spirit (רוּחַ, *ruah*). Even though the exodus features unique allusions back to the creation and the flood in Genesis through its mention of water and the Spirit (Gen 1:2; 8:1; see also Exod 14:21; 15:8–10), Joshua is silent on the matter of *ruah*. This restriction helpfully focuses the interpretation of the Jordan crossing and situates its relative importance. The story is derivative of the exodus event, or better, an express continuation of it.

Later in biblical history, the national memorial of the Jordan crossing at Gilgal was exploited by Israel's first king. The tribes were summoned there to "renew the kingdom. So all the people went to Gilgal, and there they made Saul king before the LORD in Gilgal" (1 Sam 11:14–15). This crucial moment in Saul's political and military career required a dramatic stage to unify the tribes under his authority. Not without irony, Gilgal would later become the stage of his loss of authority—God "tore the kingdom" from Saul there (1 Sam 15:26–28).[21]

21. If Saul's Ammonite and Amalekite campaigns were in the spring "when kings go to war" (2 Sam 11:1), then the time of year may also have corresponded well to the Jordan crossing. Gilgal's stage was also exploited by the tribe of Judah as they curried the favor of David there when he was returning from the Transjordan and had quelled Absalom's insurrection (2 Sam 19:15). This reaffirmation of David's authority demonstrates the on-going royal significance of Gilgal even after the establishment of Jerusalem as the capital of the united monarchy.

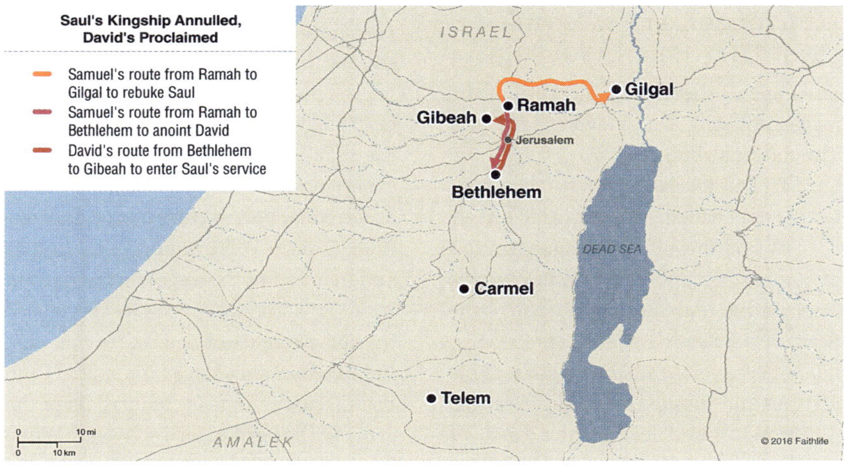

The Bible records numerous crossings of the Jordan River. Jeremy Hutton traces a distinction between those crossings that served a more pragmatic purpose (e.g., the political and military actions of the judges and kings of Israel) and the crossings that served a transformational purpose.[22] The latter is exemplified by the twin crossings of Elijah and Elisha in 2 Kgs 2:1–18. In this account, Elijah was translated to heaven by a windstorm/fiery chariot (2:11). Elisha then inherited Elijah's cloak along with his prophetic anointing and office. This cloak symbolized the presence of God with his prophet and, thus, could miraculously part the river as if it were the ark of the covenant in Joshua's day. In these accounts, the Jordan assumes a liminal position in this process of personal and corporate transformation.

The biblical meaning of the Jordan crossing can be summed up as a revelation of God's power, as a symbol of Israel's corporate unity, and as a transformational process that separates one way of being from another. In the New Testament, we find similar threads. John the Baptist and his cousin Joshua (i.e., Jesus) also take advantage of the Jordan as a poignant stage for their ministries (Matt 3:5–6; John 10:40–42). Their emphasis upon cleansing, repentance, and a renewed commitment to God's ethical demands compares well with Israel's consecration in Joshua's day as well as their ritual transformation of identity.[23]

22. It seems the source critical explanation for Josh 3–4 is that it (retroactively) functions as an etiology for the later transformational crossings (Jeremy M. Hutton, *The Transjordanian Palimpsest: The Overwritten Texts of Personal Exile and Transformation in the Deuteronomistic History* [Berlin: de Gruyter, 2009], 376). A key to Hutton's descriptions of these transformation events is one's separation from community, following a theory of ritual (17).

23. Cyril of Jerusalem (among others) argues that Joshua was a type of Jesus. Origen argues that the first Jordan crossing was a type of baptism. Those who turn away from their baptismal commitments become bitter, like the waters that flow into the Salt Sea (John R. Franke, ed., *Joshua, Judges, Ruth, 1–2 Samuel*, Ancient Christian Commentary Series [Downers Grove, IL: InterVarsity Press, 2005], 15–24). Moreover, Jesus' wilderness wanderings in Matt 4//

THEOLOGICAL ASSESSMENT OF THE JORDAN CROSSING

The explicit theological message of the Jordan crossing is provided by Josh 4:24: The nations shall "know" (ידע, *yd'*) the Lord and Israel shall "fear" (ירא, *yr'*) the Lord. Israel had already acquired knowledge of God through his demonstration of compassion and power in the exodus. Their initial reaction was worship—the Song of the Sea in Exod 15. Their subsequent task was to remain obedient to his statutes and submissive to his direction.

Knowing and fearing the Lord, of course, are repeated themes in the Psalter and are closely tied to worship. Psalm 46:10 says, "Be still, and know (*yd'*) that I am God. I will be exalted among the nations." Psalm 2:11 advises, "Serve the LORD in fear (*yr'*), and rejoice with trembling," and Ps 5:7 claims, "I will bow down to your holy temple in fear (*yr'*) of you." In light of this, the fearful reaction of the Canaanites (Josh 2:9) and the great disobedience of the Israelites (Josh 7:1) are truly ironic and truly tragic. Psalm 95:3–6 expresses the hoped-for reaction: "For the LORD is ... a great king above all gods ... The sea is his, for he made it; and his hands formed the dry land (*yabbashah*). O come, let us worship and bow down; let us kneel before the LORD, our maker!" Israel should have been an exemplar in their reaction to the mighty presence of their Creator and Savior.

The revealed presence of God appears at strategic moments in order to catalyze the shape of Israel's history. Moses first experienced the holy presence of the Lord at Mt. Sinai before confronting the pharaoh (Exod 3–4). He removed his sandals and listened to the angel of the Lord in Exod 3:2–6. Likewise, Joshua experienced the holy presence of God before confronting Jericho. He removed his sandals and listened to the angelic commander of the army of the Lord in Josh 5:13–6:5.[24] When the ark of the covenant crossed the Jordan River, it was sure proof of God's *enduring* presence in Israel's story.

In the wider arc of salvation history, however, the Jordan crossing also represents a transition point. As Leonard Thompson argues, God's intervention at the Jordan inaugurates a new epoch, a "transition from the time of promise to the time of fulfillment."[25] The primary promise in view is the possession of land in the Abrahamic covenant (Gen 15:7; 17:8). The river is a liminal zone between the rootless and the rooted. Moving into the land of Canaan signals a *settled* existence for Israel, which the line of promise had not known since their expulsion from Eden.[26]

A secondary promise in view is the abundance of the land in the Mosaic

---

Luke 4 seem to recapitulate the wanderings of Israel though *after* passing through the Jordan instead of before.

24. Chambers's article offers a compelling model ("creature-control") for understanding the commander of the Lord's army as a divine theophany (note his dependence upon Sarah Hall's *Conquering Character* (2010) in order to defend the continuation of this theophany into Josh 6:2f; Nathan J. Chambers, "Reading Joshua with Augustine and Sommer: Two Frameworks for Interpreting Theophany Narratives," *JSOT* 43.3 [2019]: 273–83).

25. Leonard L. Thompson, "The Jordan Crossing: *Ṣidqot* Yahweh and World Building," *JBL* 100 (1981): 355.

26. Gen 3:23–24; Walter Brueggemann, *The Land: Place as Gift, Promise, and Challenge in Biblical Faith*, 2nd ed. (Minneapolis: Fortress, 2002), 15–20.

covenant (Deut 28:1–14; 30:1–10), which was conditional upon obedience to the law. After leaving Egypt, Israel's wilderness wanderings are bookended by two phases of the receiving of the law—from Mt. Sinai (Exod 20–Num 9) to Mt. Nebo (Deuteronomy). *The crossing of the Reed Sea and the Jordan create a wider bookend around the whole era of law-giving*. After crossing into Canaan, Israel would wrestle with their compliance to the law and how to be faithful amidst blessing (Josh 7; Deut 8:17–18).

Finally, the account of the Jordan crossing actively engages one of the most important practices in the theological formation of Israel—intergenerational dialogue. In Josh 4:6, 12, we see the commandment for all Israelites to entertain the curiosities of their children regarding the stones of Gilgal: "What do these stones mean?" This practice fits, in fact, a pattern that is promoted in the book of Deuteronomy's "rhetoric of remembrance."[27] Each generation is to witness to the next concerning God's person and ways, exemplified in the Shema: "You must teach [these words] to your children, and speak of them as you sit in your house" (Deut 6:7; 4:9–10; 11:19; 31:13; 32:46). Joshua's command to remember the Jordan crossing through intergenerational dialogue effectively makes this event an identifying feature of Israel's social fabric.

CONCLUSION

As in Frederick Douglass's era of abolition, Israel's crossing of the Jordan River held a significance that transcended the idea of a merely physical obstacle to be overcome. The act of crossing became a potent symbol of Israelite unity and identity. The ritualized crossing was further memorialized as a critical moment in salvation history, a moment that later prophets would build upon. Modern hymns and theology show how the legacy of the Jordan crossing continues to inspire and instruct.

BIBLIOGRAPHY

Aharoni, Yohanan. *The Land of the Bible: A Historical Geography*. Translated by Anson F. Rainey. Rev. and enl. ed. Philadelphia: Westminster, 1979.

Barham, Elizabeth. "Ecological Boundaries as Community Boundaries: The Politics of Watersheds." *Society and Natural Resources* 14 (2001): 181–91.

Brueggemann, Walter. *The Land: Place as Gift, Promise, and Challenge in Biblical Faith*. 2nd ed. Minneapolis: Fortress, 2002.

Chambers, Nathan J. "Reading Joshua with Augustine and Sommer: Two Frameworks for Interpreting Theophany Narratives." *JSOT* 43 (2019): 273–83.

Douglass, Frederick. *My Bondage and My Freedom*. Chicago: Johnson Publishing Company, 1970.

Dozeman, Thomas B. "The *yam-sûp* in the Exodus and the Crossing of the Jordan River." *CBQ* 58 (July 1996): 407–16.

Firth, David G. *The Message of Joshua: Promise and People*. The Bible Speaks Today. Downers Grove, IL: InterVarsity Press, 2015.

Franke, John R., ed. *Joshua, Judges, Ruth, 1–2 Samuel*. Ancient Christian Commentary Series. Downers Grove, IL: InterVarsity Press, 2005.

27. Jerry Hwang, *The Rhetoric of Remembrance an Investigation of the "Fathers" in Deuteronomy* (Winona Lake, IN: Eisenbrauns, 2012).

Frankel, David. *The Land of Canaan and the Destiny of Israel: Theologies of Territory in the Hebrew Bible*. Winona Lake, IN: Eisenbrauns, 2011.

Havrelock, Rachel S. "The Jordan River in Ancient and Modern Maps." Pages 107–22 in *Art and Identity at the Water's Edge*. Edited by Tricia Cusack. Burlington, VT: Ashgate, 2012.

Hess, Richard S. *Joshua: An Introduction and Commentary*. TOTC. Downers Grove, IL: InterVarsity Press, 1996.

Hutton, Jeremy M. *The Transjordanian Palimpsest: The Overwritten Texts of Personal Exile and Transformation in the Deuteronomistic History*. Berlin: de Gruyter, 2009.

Hwang, Jerry. *The Rhetoric of Remembrance an Investigation of the "Fathers" in Deuteronomy*. Winona Lake, IN: Eisenbrauns, 2012.

Knight, Douglas A. "Joshua 22 and the Ideology of Space." Pages 51–63 in *"Imagining" Biblical Worlds: Studies in Spatial, Social and Historical Constructs in Honor of James W. Flanagan*. Edited by David M. Gunn and Paula M. McNutt. London: Sheffield Academic, 2002.

MacDonald, Burton. *"East of the Jordan": Territories and Sites of the Hebrew Scriptures*. Boston: American Schools of Oriental Research, 2000.

McConville, J. Gordon, and Stephen N. Williams. *Joshua*. Two Horizons Old Testament Commentary. Grand Rapids: Eerdmans, 2010.

Rasmussen, Carl. *Zondervan Atlas of the Bible*. Rev. ed. Grand Rapids: Zondervan, 2010.

Schwartzstein, Peter. "Biblical Waters: Can the Jordan River Be Saved?" *National Geographic* (blog), February 22, 2014. https://www.nationalgeographic.com/news/2014/2/140222-jordan-river-syrian-refugees-water-environment/.

Slayton, Joel C. "Shittim." *ABD* 5:1222.

Thompson, Leonard L. "The Jordan Crossing: *Ṣidqot* Yahweh and World Building." *JBL* 100 (1981): 343–58.

Turner, Victor. *The Ritual Process: Structure and Anti-Structure*. Ithaca, NY: Cornell University Press, 1969.

Younger, K. Lawson, Jr. "Another Look at 'Early' Ideologies of the Land in the Hebrew Bible in Light of Recent Study." *Ex Auditu* 35 (2019): 39–79.

CHAPTER 3

THE BATTLE OF JERICHO: A GEOGRAPHICAL ANALYSIS

Josh 2:1–24; 6:1–27

S. Cameron Coyle

KEY POINTS

- The southern Jordan Valley was an important area for Joshua's conquest, as it served as the staging ground for the effort to conquer lands in the Cisjordan.
- The city of Jericho was a strategic first target for Joshua, as it controlled access to important roads leading westward into the central hill country.

INTRODUCTION

Joshua's narrative of the battle of Jericho, the opening strike in the story of Israel's aggressive entrance into the land of Canaan, is set within the rich geographical context of the southern Jordan Valley. This article will illuminate this vital region through a discussion of its physical features, and the ways in which the biblical authors use those features to shape the powerful imagery found in the text. Jericho itself plays an important role in the region, a fact reflected in the names used to refer to the area, as well as the city's control of roadways in and out of the valley. An understanding of Jericho's strategic position within this geographical context serves as foundational for a discussion of the biblical description of the battle of Jericho. As we shall see, this discussion offers intriguing insights into the details of the Joshua narrative.

THE SOUTHERN JORDAN VALLEY

Jericho was the chief city located within the southern Jordan Valley. The valley is sometimes referred to as the Jordan Rift and constitutes a portion of the northern end of the much larger Great Rift Valley that stretches well into the African continent. The Jordan Valley spans approximately sixty-five miles (105 km) between the Sea of Galilee in the north and the Dead Sea in the south.[1] Despite the tradi-

1. The Dead Sea is referred to in Hebrew as the *yam hammelah* (יָם הַמֶּלַח), often rendered into English more literally as "the Salt Sea." Compare, for example, the translations of Josh 15:2

tional use of the English term "sea," both bodies of water are inland lakes fed by freshwater rivers. The Sea of Galilee drains into the Jordan River, which follows a meandering path southward through the valley until it reaches the Dead Sea, about ten miles (16 km) southeast of Jericho. The Dead Sea is located at the lowest land elevation on the planet and, as a result, has no outlet for its waters. Instead, the lake loses water through evaporation alone, resulting in an abnormally high mineral content. Due to the high salinity of the water, the Dead Sea does not support life either in its waters or along its shores, apart from certain microscopic organisms. Thus, life in the arid region is limited to those areas with access to regular freshwater sources.

The biblical text associates several names with this geographical region. While the term Arabah is used today to refer to the stretch of the Great Rift Valley that runs from the Dead Sea southward to the Gulf of Aqaba, in the biblical text, the term also includes those portions of the valley located north of the Dead Sea. In Josh 12:3, for example, the Jordan Valley along the eastern side of the river between the Sea of Galilee and the Dead Sea is referred to as the "Arabah."[2] The "plains of Moab," in which the Israelites camped from Num 22 through the book of Deuteronomy, are known in Hebrew as the *arevoth moav* (עַרְבוֹת מוֹאָב). The use of the plural form of Arabah, identifies the area as the Moabite (or eastern) side of the Arabah, across the river from Jericho (e.g., Num 26:3).[3] In like manner, Josh 4:13 refers to the western side of the Jordan River, across from the plains of Moab, as the *arevoth yeriho*; "plains of Jericho" (עַרְבוֹת יְרִיחוֹ). Much of this region is a desert landscape where soil conditions are too dry and salty to support vegetation.[4] As such, the Arabah was sometimes used as a negative image in poetic passages: "The land mourns and languishes; Lebanon is confounded and withers away; Sharon is like a desert [*aravah*], and Bashan and Carmel shake off their leaves" (Isa 33:9).[5]

This same region, however, is also described positively at times. In Gen 13, Lot chooses to settle in the Jordan Valley when he sees that it "was well watered everywhere like the garden of the LORD, like the land of Egypt" (13:10). The comparison here is most likely based on the Jordan River's flood cycle. Fueled by winter rains drained through the wadi systems from both east and west of the river, in pre-modern times the Jordan would annually flood its banks and fill a

in the NASB, ESV, and NKJV with those of the NIV, HCSB, and NLT. The Dead Sea is also occasionally referred to as the "Sea of the Arabah" (יָם הָעֲרָבָה, *yam haaravah*); e.g., Deut 3:17; 4:49; Josh 3:16; 12:3; and 2 Kgs 14:25.

2. The term was equally applicable to the western side of the river but was limited to the eastern side in this text because of the context of the passage. Here, and in numerous other passages, the term appears with the definite article: "the Arabah."

3. All biblical quotations are taken from the English Standard Version (ESV) unless otherwise noted.

4. Compare the description of the Jericho area in 2 Kgs 2:19–22.

5. Compare also Jer 2:6; 17:6; 50:12; 51:43; and Job 24:5. The ESV renders *aravah* as "desert" in each of the Jeremiah passages, and as "wasteland" in Job 24:5.

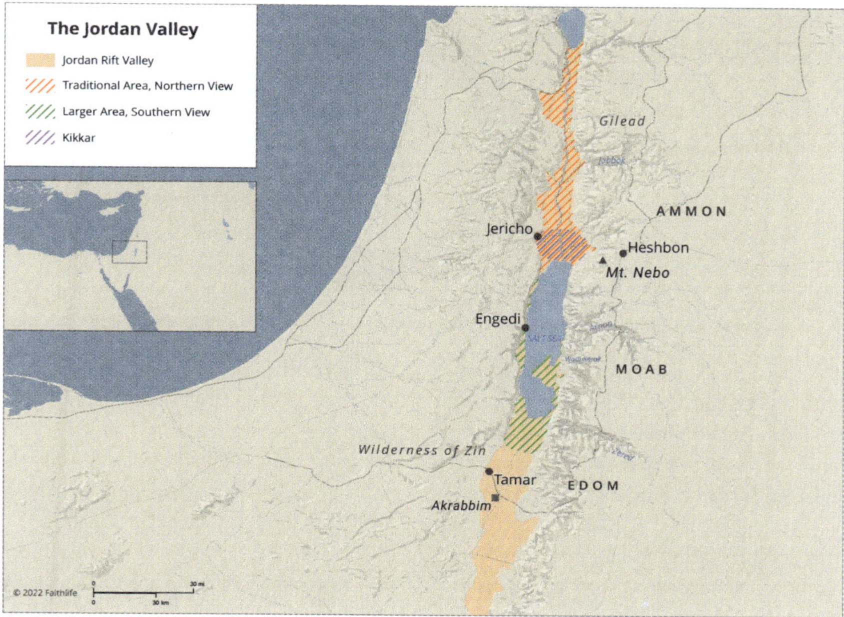

floodplain ranging in width from half a mile to a mile (0.8–2 km).[6] This floodplain supported lush vegetation, in contrast to the rest of the valley. Agriculture in Egypt benefited from the same cycle with the Nile River, and Gen 2:6 suggests a similar phenomenon associated with the primordial waters of the garden of Eden, leading to the narrator's comparison in Gen 13:10.[7] The floodplain of the Jordan is elsewhere termed the *geon hayyarden* (גְּאוֹן הַיַּרְדֵּן), rendered by the ESV as the "thicket of the Jordan" (Jer 50:44; Zech 11:3) and "jungle of the Jordan" (Jer 49:19). *Geon* refers to "pride" or "majesty," and the imagery behind the phrase seems to view the bountiful vegetation of the floodplain as a sort of jewel adorning the Jordan Valley (e.g., Zech 11:3 NKJV, "For the pride of the Jordan is in ruins").[8] The dense vegetation would also have attracted abundant wildlife, some of which is hinted at in the

6. Claude R. Conder and H. H. Kitchener, *The Survey of Western Palestine: Memoirs of the Topography, Orography, Hydrography and Archaeology* (London: Palestine Exploration Fund, 1882), 2:79.

7. The Hebrew אֵד (*ed*) of Genesis 2:6 is a *hapax legomenon* whose precise meaning is uncertain. Suggestions include "mist" (ESV), "streams" (NIV), and "water" (HCSB). There is an Akkadian cognate term *edû* which refers to the high flood waters of a river (*CAD* 4, s.v. "*edû*"). This may support a similar meaning for the Hebrew *ed*. Whatever the exact meaning of the term, the process of the *ed* moving up from the land and watering the surface of the ground is reminiscent of a cyclical flood pattern, perhaps one associated with the river that watered the garden (Gen 2:10).

8. Compare Menashe Har-El, "The Pride of the Jordan: The Jungle of the Jordan," *BA* 41 (1978): 68–69.

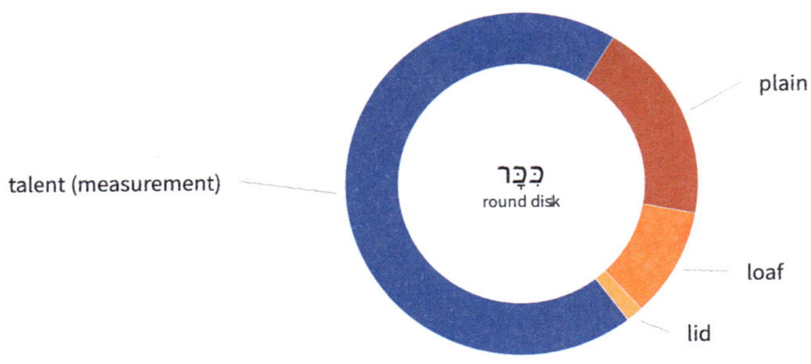

biblical text. Lions in particular are associated with the area: "like a lion coming up from the *geon hayyarden*" (Jer 49:19); "The sound of the roar of lions, for the *geon hayyarden* is ruined!" (Zech 11:3).

The term used in Gen 13:10–11 for the Jordan Valley is *kikkar hayyarden*; "circle of the Jordan" (כִּכַּר הַיַּרְדֵּן). In addition to indicating a geographical feature, *kikkar* is commonly used in reference to a measure of precious metal (e.g., כִּכַּר זָהָב, *kikkar zahav*; "talent of gold," 2 Sam 12:30) and a round loaf of bread (e.g., כִּכַּר לֶחֶם, *kikkar lehem*, "loaf of bread," Exod 29:23). Comparison of these usages with the observation that the southern Jordan Valley is the only geographical area to be described as a *kikkar* suggests that the name may be derived from the shape of the valley, the southernmost portion of which widens into a roughly circular area that is notably distinct from the rest of the valley. Thus, the term *kikkar hayyarden* would refer specifically to this southernmost section of the valley. At times the area is simply called *hakikkar*, "the circle," using the definite article, as in 2 Sam 18:23.[9] Deuteronomy 34:3 refers to *hakikkar* in a list of geographical zones, and then specifies that the reference is to *biqat yereho ir hattemarim* (בִּקְעַת יְרֵחוֹ עִיר הַתְּמָרִים), "the Valley of Jericho the city of palm trees." The phrase *biqat yereho* is used only here as a term for the area.

The *kikkar* region is defined on its eastern side by the steep ascent to the Transjordanian plateau. A similar feature lines the western side of the *kikkar*, where the hills leading up to the Cisjordanian central hill country begin to rise less than a mile (2 km) west of Jericho. Travel across the *kikkar* required traversing the Jordan River, which could be managed relatively easily during most of the year at any number of shallow fords. Such locations may have shifted through time as floodwaters rearranged the riverbed, but surveyors in the nineteenth century identified at least five fords in the general vicinity of Jericho.[10] Routes connecting the *kikkar* with the Cisjordanian hill country followed the limited number of continuous east-west ridges that allowed for unimpeded travel up to the watershed ridge. Movement in a north-south direction could be easily

9. Genesis 19 refers to the area of Sodom as *hakikkar* four times without indicating more precisely which area is in view. Given the usage of the definite article and the author's lack of any attempt to further clarify his meaning, it seems that the term was specific enough to be used as a stand-alone reference to the area. E.g., Neh 3:22.

10. Condor and Kitchener, *Survey*, 3:170.

Aerial View of the Ascent of Adummim and Wadi Qelt near Jericho

accomplished on the watershed ridge or in the *kikkar* below but was effectively prevented between the two by the deep wadis that drain the watershed. Several of these routes entered the *kikkar* at a location that allowed Jericho to control access to them.

Southwest of Jericho is the ascent of Adummim, mentioned in Josh 15:7 and 18:17. This route passed south of the large Wadi Qelt and reached the watershed ridge at Jerusalem. A more northerly route that approached Jericho from the same direction led westward to Michmash, located some five miles (8 km) southeast of Bethel. This may be the "border road" of 1 Sam 13:18.[11] Northwest of Jericho, a route led westward toward Ai and Bethel, approaching those sites from the southeast. This was likely the primary route utilized by the Israelites in their attack on Ai (Josh 7–8). An offshoot of this road turned northwest towards Ophrah. Together these routes gave Jericho easy access to a large swath of the hill country, spanning from Jerusalem in the south to the Shiloh area in the north.

THE SITE AND BATTLE OF JERICHO

Jericho has long been identified with Tell es-Sultan. The site is located on an almost ten-acre mound situated on the far western edge of the *kikkar*, just east of the hills leading up to the watershed ridge. Jericho had access to a regular water source via the Ein es-Sultan, a spring on the eastern side of the tell. The site benefited from a second spring, the Ein Duq, located less than two miles to the northeast, during periods when the population undertook efforts to divert the water of the spring toward Jericho. Although the area of Tell es-Sultan receives very little annual rain-

11. Many versions, including the ESV, render *derek haggevul* (דֶּרֶךְ הַגְּבוּל) as "toward the border." However, "road of the border" is a more literal reading and is possibly the name the route was known by to the biblical author. Compare David A. Dorsey, *The Roads and Highways of Ancient Israel* (Baltimore: Johns Hopkins University Press, 1991), 204.

Aerial View of Modern-Day Jericho

fall, these springs were capable of supporting extensive agriculture around the site. This unique feature is reflected in the biblical description of Jericho as a "city of palm trees" (Deut 34:3; 2 Chr 28:15).

Archaeological attempts to characterize the Jericho of Joshua's conquest have been notoriously plagued by difficulties. However, the text of Joshua provides sufficient description of the site to allow for a basic reconstruction from the narrative. Jericho is described using the common term *ir* (עִיר). The word is typically translated as "city" in most versions, but *ir* can be used to refer to a settlement of any size, and does not necessarily designate a large population center.[12] In similar fashion, the leader of Jericho is referred to as a *melek* (מֶלֶךְ), a term which is consistently rendered into English as "king," though the word is used to designate individuals with a broad range of authority, not all of whom would fit the usual definition of a "king."[13] While the English term "king" is suggestive of a larger "kingdom," the Hebrew *melek* does not necessarily imply such a situation. Neither of these terms require an interpretation of the narrative that views Jericho as a large and powerful city with a substantial population.[14]

12. Avraham Faust, "Cities, Villages, and Farmsteads: The Landscape of Leviticus 25:29–31," in *Exploring the Longue Durée: Essays in Honor of Lawrence E. Stager*, ed. J. David Schloen (Winona Lake, IN: Eisenbrauns, 2009), 105.

13. Compare the discussion of these terms in S. Cameron Coyle, "The Battle of Ai: A Geographical Analysis," in this volume.

14. Compare Richard S. Hess, "The Jericho and Ai of the Book of Joshua," in *Critical Issues in Early Israelite History*, ed. Richard S. Hess, Gerald A. Klingbeil, and Paul J. Ray Jr. (Winona Lake, IN: Eisenbrauns, 2008), 33–46.

Joshua 2:15 describes the house of Rahab as having been built into the city wall. As a result, the spies were able to access the exterior of the city wall by way of a window within her home. Such a situation was not out of place in the region. Settlements were sometimes encircled by a ring of adjacent structures whose exterior walls formed a defensive barrier for the settlement itself.[15] Enclosed settlements of this type often featured a large open area in the center that could serve as a livestock pen when needed.[16] Such an area may have been used at Jericho for the oxen, sheep, and donkeys encountered by the Israelites (Josh 6:21). That the spies would seek refuge in the house of a prostitute is not surprising as few alternatives would have been available for foreign strangers seeking lodging. This is especially true in light of Rahab's characterization of the people of Jericho as being afraid of the Israelites (2:9–11), which would likely have resulted in a tendency to suspend the cultural norms regarding hospitality.

The mission of the spies did not remain secret; both their presence and purpose were discovered and reported to the leader of the settlement (Josh 2:2). The text does not indicate whether the report was based on knowledge or presumption, but it was correct regardless. Anticipating the subsequent search for the spies, Rahab took it upon herself to hide the Israelite men on the roof of her house beneath stalks of flax that she had previously laid out. Rooftops were regularly used as an extension of the home in the ancient Near East, both as a living area and a workspace. The practice was so common, in fact, that the Mosaic Law required homes to be built with a parapet surrounding the roof to prevent individuals from accidentally falling off (Deut 22:8).[17] The Israelite spies remained on Rahab's roof while she falsely reported that they had slipped out of the settlement just before the gate was shut at dark (Josh 2:5). The practice of the gate being open during daylight hours and closed after dark is not in itself noteworthy, except in contrast to the situation that transpired after Israel was encamped at Gilgal, at which point "Jericho was shut up inside and outside. ... None went out and none came in" (6:1).

In pursuit of the spies, the men of Jericho made the assumption that the Israelites would move east from Jericho, back toward the Israelite camp on the opposite side of the river. They searched the road as far as the fords, unaware that the spies had remained in the settlement. In the meantime, Rahab advised the spies to journey in the opposite direction, into the hill country, and to hide for three days until the search was abandoned. The text reports that they followed Rahab's advice, although no mention is made of how or where they spent the three days. Given how quickly they had been discovered in Jericho, the men may have avoided the settlements in the hill country, opting instead to camp in the open field. It is possible that they took advantage of the

15. Ze'ev Herzog, "Settlement and Fortification Planning in the Iron Age," in *The Architecture of Ancient Israel: From the Prehistoric to the Persian Periods*, ed. Aharon Kempinski and Ronny Reich (Jerusalem: Israel Exploration Society, 1992), 233.

16. The containment of herds would require the pen to be closed at night. It is worth noting in this context that Rahab indicates that the gate of Jericho was closed at dark (Josh 2:5).

17. Compare also Judg 16:27; 1 Sam 9:25; 2 Sam 11:2; 2 Kgs 4:10; 23:12; Neh 8:16; and Jer 19:13.

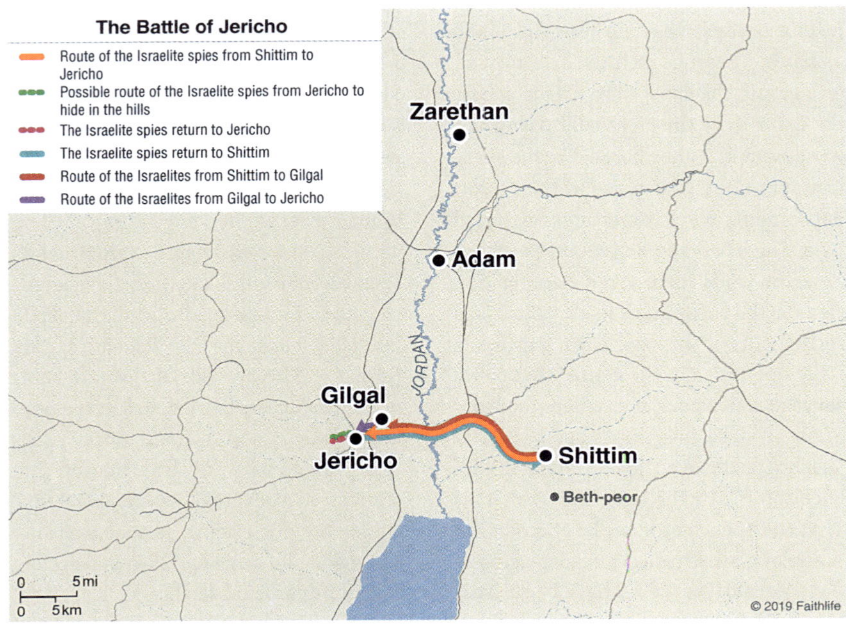

opportunity to surveil the hill country area as well. The relatively quick decision to target Ai following the victory at Jericho may have been influenced by information provided by these men. Once sufficient time had passed, the spies returned to the camp at Shittim to give their report to Joshua. The only recorded portion of their report focuses not on the logistical intelligence they had been sent to gather, but rather on their conclusion that "the Lord has given all the land into our hands" (2:24).

Following the spies' report, and prior to the movement against Jericho, Joshua moved the Israelites across the Jordan and established the camp at Gilgal (Josh 4–5). The exact location of Gilgal is uncertain. It is said to be on the "east border of Jericho" (4:19), suggesting a point just far enough from Jericho to be beyond the city's territory, yet still on the western side of the river. Proximity to the river would have provided the camp with abundant water, a necessary consideration given that Gilgal would remain the Israelite base of operations throughout the conquest period. Thus, Gilgal was likely somewhere in the open field just west of the Jordan River, perhaps five miles or less (8 km or less) from Jericho.

The divine intervention involved in the fight against Jericho resulted in a battle strategy that could not be justified apart from Israel's dependence on God. Joshua was instructed to march Israel's warriors around the city once daily for six days, then seven times on the seventh day (6:3–4). Such a march would not have been too demanding, courage notwithstanding. The mound of Tell es-Sultan has a perimeter of about half a mile (0.8 km), and one could maintain a distance of one hundred yards (92 m) from the tell itself and still circumnavigate the entire mound in the span of about one mile (2 km). Assuming a distance of five miles (8 km) between Jericho and Gilgal, this would mean a round trip journey of about eleven miles (18 km) on each of the first six days and a march of twelve miles (19 km) prior to the start of the battle on the seventh day. For a population accustomed to traveling everywhere on foot, these distances would be quite manageable. Contemporary armies could travel an average of twelve and a half miles (20 km) per day with their full supply chain, while the Israelite maneuver against Jericho could have maintained a quicker pace, given that only the "men of war" took part in the march from Gilgal (6:3).[18] Following the final circuit around the site, the priests blew their trumpets, the men shouted, "and the wall fell down flat" (6:20). The literal meaning of the last phrase is "the wall fell under itself," suggesting that the collapsed portion of the wall may have fallen down the slope of the tell, so that the collapsed stones came to rest at an elevation lower than the founding level of the wall. Evidently the collapse did not involve the full length of the wall, as Rahab's house remained standing afterward. The structure did not survive for long, however, since the text states that the city and everything in it were destroyed by fire (6:24). As such, Jericho is one of only three sites described in Joshua as having been destroyed by fire.[19]

CONCLUSION

The battle of Jericho serves as a pivotal event in the history of Israel, and a key moment in the narrative of Israel's emergence in the land of Canaan. While much of the significance of the victory for Joshua's Israel is found in the theme of God's provision for his people, the success at Jericho also provided Joshua with a strategic foothold in the land of promise, one which paved the way for Israel's subsequent forays into the Canaanite heartland. Failure at Jericho would have left all the routes into the Cisjordanian hill country too well defended for Israel to consider attacking other cities from their location in the southern Jordan Valley. Jericho's true importance is found in the city's status as the gatekeeper to these routes, the first line of defense for the land of Canaan against the Israelites. Triumph at Jericho enabled Israel to continue pushing into Canaan by opening the doors to additional targets.

BIBLIOGRAPHY

Coyle, S. Cameron. "The Battle of Ai: A Geographical Analysis." In vol. 1 of *Lexham Geographic Commentary on the Historical Books*. Edited by Barry J. Beitzel. Bellingham, WA: Lexham Press, 2025.

———. "The Battle at Gibeon—Makkedah: A Geographical Analysis." In vol. 1 of *Lexham Geographic Commentary on the Historical Books*. Edited by Barry J. Beitzel. Bellingham, WA: Lexham Press, 2025.

18. Anthony Spalinger, *War in Ancient Egypt: The New Kingdom* (Malden, MA: Blackwell Publishing, 2005), 212. Compare the Israelites' eighteen mile (29 km) overnight march from Gilgal to Gibeon (Josh 10), followed by a thirty mile (48 km) pursuit of the enemy from Gibeon to Makkedah. See S. Cameron Coyle, "The Battle at Gibeon–Makkedah: A Geographic Analysis," in this volume for a discussion of the movements recorded in Josh 10.

19. The two other sites destroyed by fire are Ai (8:19) and Hazor (11:11).

Conder, Claude R., and H. H. Kitchener. *The Survey of Western Palestine: Memoirs of the Topography, Orography, Hydrography and Archaeology*. 3 vols. London: Palestine Exploration Fund, 1881–83.

Dorsey, David A. *The Roads and Highways of Ancient Israel*. Baltimore: Johns Hopkins University Press, 1991.

Faust, Avraham. "Cities, Villages, and Farmsteads: The Landscape of Leviticus 25:29–31." Pages 103–12 in *Exploring the Longue Durée: Essays in Honor of Lawrence E. Stager*. Edited by J. David Schloen. Winona Lake, IN: Eisenbrauns, 2009.

Har-El, Menashe. "The Pride of the Jordan: The Jungle of the Jordan." *BA* 41 (1978): 65–75.

Herzog, Ze'ev. "Settlement and Fortification Planning in the Iron Age." Pages 231–74 in *The Architecture of Ancient Israel: From the Prehistoric to the Persian Periods*. Edited by Aharon Kempinski and Ronny Reich. Jerusalem: Israel Exploration Society, 1992.

Hess, Richard S. "The Jericho and Ai of the Book of Joshua." Pages 33–46 in *Critical Issues in Early Israelite History*. Edited by Richard S. Hess, Gerald A. Klingbeil, and Paul J. Ray Jr. Winona Lake, IN: Eisenbrauns, 2008.

Spalinger, Anthony. *War in Ancient Egypt: The New Kingdom*. Malden, MA: Blackwell Publishing, 2005.

CHAPTER 4

THE BATTLE OF AI: A GEOGRAPHIC ANALYSIS

Josh 7–8, Num 1

S. Cameron Coyle

KEY POINTS

- The cities of Ai and Bethel were targeted first after the fall of Jericho as a means of gaining access to the important central hill country.
- The initial skirmish at Ai was perhaps the smallest target and battle of Joshua's conquest, but the initial defeat suffered by the Israelites makes it one of the most significant events in the narrative.
- Common misconceptions about the portrayal of Ai in the narrative have often led to a rejection of the historicity of the text.

INTRODUCTION

The battle at Ai, literally "the ruin" in Hebrew, was a significant and unexpected defeat for Israel early in Joshua's conquest narrative. The site itself was of little importance as illustrated by the fact that the name alone was insufficient to identify the location, leading to the description in Josh 12:9 of "Ai, which is next to Bethel."[1] Additional place names that appear throughout the narrative serve not only to locate the events, but to subtly characterize the story as well. Israel suffers defeat at "The Ruin" (Ai), located near the "House of Iniquity" (Beth Aven), in the highlands west of the "Valley of Trouble" (Valley of Achor). In their initial devastating loss, they are pursued by the enemy to the "Place of Crushing" (שְׁבָרִים, *Shevarim*). Adding insult to injury, the defenders of "The Ruin" are aided by men from the "House of God" (Bethel) in a subtle, yet painful, reminder that Israel's defeat was a result of God's anger over the

1. Unless otherwise noted, all Scripture quotations are taken from the New Revised Standard Version (NRSV).

sin of Achan. The very landscape upon which these events unfold reflects the darkness of this moment in Israel's story.

The study of the battle of Ai by biblical scholars and archaeologists has often ended with negative conclusions about the historicity of the event.[2] In particular, the absence of any evidence of occupation at the site of Ai during the Late Bronze Age (1550–1200 BC), the period of Joshua's conquest, has led many to either deny the historicity of the account altogether, or to view the text as ascribing to the time of Joshua events which took place during a later period.[3] These conclusions reflect the failure of the available archaeological data to match the expectations that scholars have often developed from their reading of the Joshua narratives.[4] However, a careful reading of the narrative suggests that the real problem may reside with the *expectations* drawn from the text. The following analysis will attempt to demonstrate that the narrative of the battle of Ai found in Josh 7–8 is not nearly as inconsistent with the archaeological data as it is commonly accused of being.

AI AND BETHEL IN THE TEXT

The text of Joshua characterizes Ai as a "city" (עִיר, *ir*) with a "people" (עַם, *am*) and a "king" (מֶלֶךְ, *melek*). When taken together with the summary statement of Josh 8:25 that "all the people of Ai" numbered twelve thousand, these descriptors could be understood to indicate that Ai was a city of impressive size. However, there are a number of mitigating factors within the narrative that call this interpretation into question. Foremost among these is the report from the scouts sent by Joshua to survey Ai prior to the initial attack. The report as recorded focuses entirely upon the size of the defending force and is noteworthy for its assessment that "[the people of Ai] are few" (Josh 7:3). So few, in fact, that the scouts recommended that only two or three thousand (or two or three אֶלֶף [*eleph*]; see below) men be sent to fight against the city. When compared with forty thousand—the total number of men ready for war presented in Josh 4:13—the scouts' recommended detachment represents less than eight percent of the full Israelite force.

At first glance, the scouts' characterization of Ai's size may seem at odds with the later statement that "all the people of Ai" numbered twelve thousand (Josh 8:25). However, the lexical range of the Hebrew *eleph*, typically translated into

---

2. As Richard Hess has observed, the accumulated archaeological data from Jericho and Ai have "led to a widespread rejection of the biblical account as envisioned by archaeologists and biblical scholars," (Hess, "The Jericho and Ai of the Book of Joshua," in *Critical Issues in Early Israelite History*, ed. Richard S. Hess, Gerald A. Klingbeil, and Paul J. Ray Jr. [Winona Lake, IN: Eisenbrauns, 2008], 34).

3. The latter view was advocated by Joseph Callaway, one of the excavators of Ai (et-Tell) (Callaway, "Ai [Place]," *ABD* 1:130). Concerning the location of Ai, and its association with the modern site of et-Tell, see the section below titled "Site Identification."

4. Compare David Merling, "The Book of Joshua, Part II: Expectations of Archaeology," *Andrews University Seminary Studies* 39 (2001): 209–21; Leonard Allen, "Archaeology of Ai and the Accuracy of Joshua 7:1–8:29," *Restoration Quarterly* 20 (1977): 41–52; Ziony Zevit, "Archaeological and Literary Stratigraphy in Joshua 7–8," *BASOR* 251 (1983): 23–35. For a summary of the common responses to this problem, see Richard Hess, *Joshua: An Introduction and Commentary*, TOTC (Downers Grove, IL: InterVarsity Press, 1996), 157–59.

English as "thousand" in this context, offers a potential solution to this difficulty. In the biblical text, *eleph* conveys a number of meanings. It is often the case that "thousand" is the best translation of the term, as, for example, in Gen 20:16, where Abimelek tells Sarah, "Look, I have given your brother a thousand (*eleph*) pieces of silver."

However, in other contexts, *eleph* is used not as a number, but as a reference to a subgroup within a particular tribe. This is the most likely meaning of Gideon's statement in Judg 6:15 when he protests to the angel of the Lord: "But sir, how can I deliver Israel? My clan (*eleph*) is the weakest in Manasseh, and I am the least in my family." English translations have consistently rendered *eleph* in this passage as "clan" or "family," and no major English translation uses "thousand." While Gideon's intended meaning may or may not have had a militaristic nuance (note the explicit context of an armed conflict), several scholars have viewed the term as referring to a military unit of one sort or another.[5]

It may be that the word combines the sense of "family" with that of "military unit," possibly as a group of military-age men drawn from a particular extended family. Such a nuance seems to fit well within the context of the census data from Num 1 and 26, where "all who were able to go to war" are counted according to family groupings: "their generations, by their clans, by their father's houses" (1:20, ESV; compare with Num 26). In his helpful mathematical analysis of the Numbers census passages, Colin Humphreys prefers to render *eleph* as "troop," resulting in a reading such as "those listed from the tribe of Reuben: forty-six troops, [consisting of] five hundred men" (Num 1:21).[6] According to this reading, the census of Num 1 tallies 598 "troops" comprised of 5,550 men.[7] From these numbers, Humphreys calculates that the average *eleph* at the time of the first and second census consisted of about ten individuals, representing perhaps as few as two families. Not every *eleph* was of equal size; during the first census, the range was from five to fourteen men per *eleph*, while the numbers from the second census range from five to sixteen. While these numbers may seem small for a military unit, Humphreys correctly observes that they correspond well with similarly sized contingents in Canaan described in the El-Amarna correspondences from the fourteenth century BC.[8]

---

5. See George E. Mendenhall, "The Census Lists of Numbers 1 and 26," *JBL* 77 (1958): 52–66; Colin J. Humphreys, "The Number of People in the Exodus from Egypt: Decoding Mathematically the Very Large Numbers in Numbers I and XXVI," *VT* 48 (1998): 96–113.

6. Humphreys, "Number," 96–113.

7. The 598 "troops" are derived from totaling the *eleph* count for each tribe (the "thousands" in English translations), while the 5,550 men are the sum of the "hundreds" listed for the tribes. Reading the 598 *eleph* as "thousands" instead of "troops" would arrive at the following equation: 598,000 + 5,550 = 603,550, the latter number being the total headcount preserved in Num 1:46.

8. The El-Amarna correspondence is a corpus of diplomatic letters between the Egyptian pharaoh and other rulers of the ancient Near East, primarily the pharaoh's vassals who ruled over the city-states of Canaan. Most of the letters were written during the reign of the Pharaoh Akhenaten, who ruled c. 1353–1336 BC. In letters EA 148 and 149, ten and twenty soldiers, respectively, are requested for the defense of the city of Tyre. See Anson F. Rainey,

Humphreys's analysis provides not only an attractive solution to the apparent difficulties of the large numbers reported in the census passages but also a useful tool for characterizing the battle of Ai. When the scouts recommended a detachment of two or three *eleph* be sent to Ai because of the city's small size, they may have in mind a force of only twenty to thirty individuals. The text states that "about three *eleph*" were ultimately sent to the engagement, of which "about thirty-six" men were killed by the defenders of Ai (Josh 7:4–5). The notice that thirty-six Israelites were killed in the battle indicates that the "about three *eleph*" totaled at least that number, which is slightly more than the average from Humphreys's study. However, the upper limit of the range of men per *eleph* in the second census (Num 26) was sixteen, indicating that three of the larger groups could have included as many as forty-eight men. Thus, we can reasonably reconstruct the Israelite force in the ill-fated attack to have likely consisted of between thirty-six and forty-eight men, drawn from perhaps as few as six extended families.

Arguing for the lower end of this range is the observation that the text does not explicitly mention any survivors of the initial attack. In fact, if the attacking force was completely, or very nearly wiped out, the subsequent reaction seems much more understandable. The narrator describes the men of Ai as pursuing the Israelite force "as far as *Shevarim*" (Josh 7:5). Whether this is intended as a place name is uncertain, but if so, the meaning of the name translates as "the place of crushing," a name which likely could have been derived from this event. Alternatively, the phrase may mean that the Israelites were pursued "until they were crushed."[9]

When the rest of Israel learned the outcome of the battle, "the hearts of the people melted and turned to water" (Josh 7:5b), echoing the reaction the Canaanites had experienced when Israel first entered the land (5:1). As for Joshua himself, he tore his clothes, covered his head with dust, fell before the ark, and demanded to know why the Lord had brought Israel into the land "to destroy us" (7:7). These reactions constitute a natural response to a total loss of the attacking force, especially if that loss was concentrated within a small group of Israelite families who would have been left bereft of adult men.

This understanding of *eleph* also sheds light on the summary statement in Josh 8:25 that twelve thousand men of Ai were killed in the second battle. Reading this statement as twelve family or military units drastically lowers the population numbers of Ai. Using Humphreys's average of ten men per *eleph*, we can understand the enemy losses as numbering around one hundred twenty. Since Josh 8:17 informs the reader that the men of Ai were joined by the men of Bethel, to the point that "there was not a man left in Ai or Bethel who did not go out after Israel," we can assume that the tally of enemy dead likely included the populations of both cities, despite the mention of only

The El-Amarna Correspondence: A New Edition of the Cuneiform Letters from the Site of El-Amarna Based on Collations of All Extant Tablets, ed. William M. Schniedewind (Leiden: Brill, 2015), 1:749–57.

9. Compare Trent C. Butler, *Joshua*, WBC (Waco: Word Books, 1983), 77; Richard D. Nelson, *Joshua: A Commentary*, OTL (Louisville: Westminster John Knox, 1997), 97.

Ai in Josh 8:25. This assumption is supported circumstantially by the fact that the king of Bethel is included in the list of defeated kings in Josh 12, despite the absence of any other narrative recounting a battle at that site. Joshua does not comment directly on the size of Bethel, but it was likely the larger of the two cities. It is Bethel, and not neighboring Ai, that is utilized as a landmark in the description of boundaries in Josh 16:1–2 and 18:13, and in Josh 12:9 Ai is identified by its association with Bethel: "the Ruin which is beside Bethel." When Josh 18:21–28 lists the cities and villages allotted to the tribe of Benjamin in the territory that would have included both Bethel and Ai, Bethel is listed (18:22), but Ai is not. Additionally, the initial belief of the scouts that Ai could be overpowered with only two or three *eleph* suggests that they deemed the population of the site to be equal to or less than that number, which in turn suggests that the majority of the twelve *eleph* of Josh 8:25 were from Bethel, rather than Ai. The reader is thus left with the impression that Ai—the Ruin—was a very small settlement indeed.

This conclusion is not incompatible with the text's characterization of Ai as a "city" with a "king." While the Hebrew term *ir* is typically translated as "city," a more precise rendering in this instance may be "settlement," i.e., a place where people dwell, without reference to size, fortifications, permanence, or other factors. As Avraham Faust has observed, the term simply differentiates "between a settlement and something that is not a settlement."[10] This broad usage is well illustrated by Num 13:19, where Moses instructs the spies going into Canaan to determine "whether the cities that they dwell in are camps or strongholds" (ESV). A camp was a temporary settlement that could have existed for a period as short as one night. A stronghold, or fortification, on the other hand, implies permanence, although it does not speak to size. A fortification could include the entire settlement or just a particular structure. Either can be referred to as an *ir*.[11] Thus, the narrative's description of Ai as an *ir* should not be assumed to say anything more about the nature of the settlement than the simple fact that people were occupying it.

A similar argument can be made for understanding the Hebrew word *melek*, typically translated as "king." *Melek* can refer to individuals with a broad range of authority. Imperial sovereigns who ruled over vast territories like the kings of Egypt (1 Kgs 14:25), Assyria (2 Kgs 15:29), and Babylon (2 Kgs 24:1) are referred to as *melek*, but so too are the rulers of smaller kingdoms who were subjugated to their more powerful neighbors. Such is the case with the rulers of Israel and Judah (1 Kgs 22:10), as well as other territories in the region, like Moab (Judg 3:12) and Edom (Gen 36:31). But the authority of a *melek*

10. Avraham Faust, "Cities, Villages, and Farmsteads: The Landscape of Leviticus 25:29–31," in *Exploring the Longue Durée: Essays in Honor of Lawrence E. Stager*, ed. J. David Schloen (Winona Lake, IN: Eisenbrauns, 2009), 105.

11. Joshua 19:29, for example, refers to the city of Tyre as an *ir mivtzar* (עִיר מִבְצָר), typically translated as "fortified city." Second Samuel 5:9, on the other hand, reports that after conquering the city of Jerusalem, David lived in the stronghold, a fortified structure, and called the stronghold the *ir David* (עִיר דָּוִד). Slightly later, Solomon would have the ark of the covenant taken "out of the *ir David*" (1 Kgs 8:1) and into the newly constructed temple, though both the *ir David* and the temple were located within the city of Jerusalem.

Aerial View of Et-Tell and Deir Dibwan from the West

could be more limited than the rulers of even these small territorial kingdoms.

The word *melek* is often applied to the ruler of a particular city, even in cases where the *melek*'s authority did not extend beyond the territory of the one settlement where he ruled. A number of examples can be found in the biblical text (e.g., Gen 14:2; 20:2; Num 21:1), but this use of the word is most common in the book of Joshua. Joshua 12:9–24 lists thirty-one cities whose *melek* was defeated by Israel under Joshua's leadership. Richard Hess has argued that comparative usage of the same root in other Near Eastern languages of the Late Bronze Age shows that the word could also refer to an administrator authorized by and responsible to an official of higher rank.[12] One such example comes from letter EA 131 of the Amarna correspondence, where the term is applied to Piwuri, an Egyptian representative of the pharaoh operating in Canaan.[13] Thus, while *melek* clearly refers to someone with authority, the nature and extent of that authority can vary greatly, and in ways that are not always consistent with the English term "king."

What, then, are the expectations a reader might reasonably draw from the biblical description of Ai in light of the preceding discussion? First, the settlement was quite small, with probably no more than a few dozen individuals occupying it. The proximity to and close association with Bethel suggests that Ai was likely a satellite settlement of the former, and it may have served as a defensive position protecting the approach to

12. Hess, "Jericho and Ai," 40–41.

13. Concerning the Amarna correspondence, see note 8 above. For the text and translation of EA 131, see Rainey, *El-Amarna*, 1:678–79.

Bethel from the east.[14] While there was a gate of some sort at the site (Josh 7:5; 8:29), no mention is made of a city wall, and the settlement may have been limited to a single fortified structure. Given that the settlement is consistently referred to as "the Ruin," this fort may have been hastily constructed among the exposed ruins of an earlier settlement in response to the Israelite encroachment in the Jordan Valley.[15] That the gate opened towards the valley, and not towards Bethel, suggests it was designed to respond to threats approaching from that direction.[16] Those manning the outpost were quite possibly residents of Bethel, and their *melek* was a fellow Bethelite who commanded the personnel stationed at Ai and operated under the authority of the ruler of Bethel. The Israelite maneuver against Ai was, in all likelihood, intended as a precursor to an attack on the larger site of Bethel, but the focus of the narrative is on Ai due to the Israelite defeat and its unique circumstances.

SITE IDENTIFICATION

Ancient Bethel has been firmly identified with the modern city of Beitin, and this identification has been rarely challenged since Edward Robinson first proposed it in the nineteenth century.[17] The proposal is well-supported by the linguistic relationship between the Hebrew Bethel and Arabic Beitin, the topography surrounding the site, the excavated remains, and descriptions of Bethel's location found in ancient texts.[18] Beitin is located approximately ten and a half miles (17 km) north of Jerusalem, along the main north/south route through the hill country, and roughly five miles (8 km) west of the descent to the Jordan Valley. To the east of Beitin by less than two miles (3 km) lies the site of et-Tell, which has long been identified as Ai. The mound of et-Tell is on the northwestern edge of the modern settlement of Deir Dibwan. It is perched above the deep Wadi Jaya, which is part of the larger Wadi Makkuk, and runs from the area east of Beitin down to the

---

14. For similar relationships between settlements, compare the statement "Ekron, with its towns and its villages" (Josh 15:45, ESV). Similar examples can be found in Josh 15:47; 17:11, 16; and 21:12.

15. Compare the comments in Hess, *Joshua*, 158–59.

16. During the second battle, Joshua stationed an ambush force to the west of Ai, between Ai and Bethel (Josh 8:9, 12). This location is described as "behind" the city (8:4, 14), implying that Ai was situated so that it faced the east. If so, the gate—the primary physical feature distinguishing the front and rear sides of the settlement—must have been located on the eastern side.

17. Edward Robinson, *Biblical Researches in Palestine and in the Adjacent Regions* (Boston: Crocker and Brewster, 1856), 1:449.

18. Anson F. Rainey, "Bethel is Still Beitîn," *WTJ* 33 (1971): 175–88; Rainey, "Looking for Bethel: An Exercise in Historical Geography," in *Confronting the Past: Archaeological and Historical Essays on Ancient Israel in Honor of William G. Dever*, ed. Seymour Gitin, J. Edward Wright, and J. P. Dessel (Winona Lake, IN: Eisenbrauns, 2006), 269–73. The identification was challenged by David Livingston, "Location of Biblical Bethel and Ai Reconsidered," *WTJ* 33 (1970): 20–44; Livingston, "Traditional Site of Bethel Questioned," *WTJ* 34 (1971): 39–50. However, Livingston's rejection of Beitin and et-Tell was primarily motivated by a dissatisfaction with the apparent compatibility of these sites with his reconstruction of the biblical conquest. Compare his comments in Livingston, *Khirbet Nisya: The Search for Biblical Ai 1979–2002* (Manheim: Associates for Biblical Research, 2003), 4.

Jordan Valley, passing along the north side of et-Tell.

Excavations at et-Tell uncovered remains of an extensive Early Bronze Age (3300–2200 BC) city that was destroyed and abandoned c. 2400 BC. No evidence of reoccupation at the site was found until the establishment of an early Iron Age (1200–1000 BC) village, possibly associated with Israelite settlers.[19] The absence of a Late Bronze Age (1550–1200 BC) occupation that can be correlated with the events of the book of Joshua has been viewed by many scholars as evidence against the historicity of the text, while others have sought to locate Joshua's Ai elsewhere.[20] However, these opinions are based on a reading of Joshua that understands Ai to be a large, fortified city at the time of the conquest, and the discussion above illustrates that such an interpretation is far from certain. In short, the lack of Late Bronze Age remains is not sufficient reason to discard either the historicity of the narrative or the association of Bethel and Ai with Beitin and et-Tell, respectively.

GEOGRAPHY AND STRATEGY

The battle of Ai took place in two stages, the first of which followed shortly after the fall of Jericho. Ai (et-Tell) is located some eleven miles west-northwest of Jericho, at an elevation of about 3,800 feet (1,158 m) above the Jordan Valley. Connecting Jericho with et-Tell and Bethel was a road that followed a ridge route westward from the Jordan Valley and approached Ai from the southeast. This road, referred to as the "Way of the Wilderness" (Josh 8:15, KJV), would have been the most direct route available to the Israelites and was likely utilized in both stages of the battle. Little is recorded regarding the initial encounter. The Israelite men are simply reported to have gone up to Ai, and then fled (7:4). The subsequent pursuit stretched "from the gate" at Ai to *Shevarim*, located somewhere along the descent from the highlands. As noted above, *Shevarim* may be a reference to an event rather than a location, and the intended meaning of the phrase may be that the Israelites were pursued until they were crushed. James Monson suggests a third possibility, that the term could refer to an area of rocky scarps cut by the wadi.[21] Such terrain may have slowed the pace of the retreat, allowing the men of Ai an opportunity to overtake the Israelites.

The second attempt at taking Ai was more carefully planned (Josh 8). The amount of geographic detail in the text allows for a fairly specific reconstruction of the event. Joshua and the main force of fighters established a camp to the north of Ai, on the opposite side of the Wadi Jaya (8:11), while a smaller group of five *eleph* laid in ambush to the west of the settlement, between Bethel and Ai (8:12). The latter group was likely hidden somewhere in the northern reaches of the Wadi Suwenit, which runs southward

19. Joseph A. Callaway, "Ai," *NEAEHL*, 1:39–45.

20. Compare, for example, Amihai Mazar, *Archaeology of the Land of the Bible: 10,000–586 B.C.E.* (New York: Doubleday, 1990), 331–32; Bryant G. Wood, "The Search for Joshua's Ai," in *Critical Issues in Early Israelite History*, ed. Richard S. Hess, Gerald A. Klingbeil, and Paul J. Ray Jr. (Winona Lake, IN: Eisenbrauns, 2008), 205–40.

21. James M. Monson, *The Land Between: A Regional Study Guide to the Land of the Bible* (Rockford, IL: Biblical Backgrounds, Inc., 1991), 168.

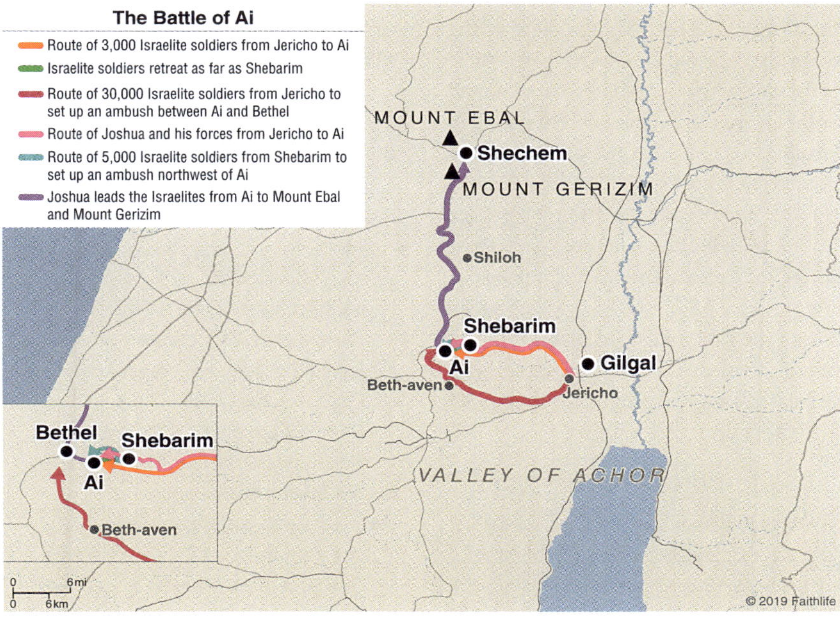

from Bethel before turning east towards the valley. This location is described by Joshua as being behind the settlement (8:4), suggesting that the gate of Ai opened toward the east. The positions of both groups, the main force and the ambush force, were established the night before the battle (8:3). The purpose of the main camp, located close enough to Ai to command attention and yet safely separated from the settlement by the deep wadi, may have been to distract the men of Ai from the preparatory movements of the ambushing force.

By the early morning, Joshua had maneuvered the main force into the plain east of the settlement, where the men of Ai engaged them in battle (8:14). Joshua then led the main force in a feigned retreat, back down the Way of the Wilderness toward the Jordan Valley, recreating the circumstances from the first engagement (8:15). In pursuit were the men of both Ai and Bethel, who left the settlement unguarded believing they had routed Israel a second time (8:17). When a sufficient distance had been achieved between Ai and its defenders, Joshua raised his javelin as a sign for the ambushing force to enter the settlement and burn it (8:18). This sign required men lying in wait who could relay the message from the eastern side of the plain back to the Wadi Suwenit.

Once the sign was received, the ambushing force entered Ai and set the settlement ablaze, making Ai one of only three settlements in the conquest narratives to have been explicitly burned by the Israelites (8:19).[22] With the settlement burning, the ambushing force

22. Also burned with fire in the Joshua narrative are the cities of Jericho (6:24) and Hazor (11:11).

then joined the battle in the plain as the main force turned westward again to confront the enemy (8:21). The men of Ai and Bethel were caught between the divided Israelite forces with no safe means of retreat, leading to the Israelite victory. Having decimated the enemy fighters, Joshua then led the Israelites back to Ai, destroyed the settlement, and buried the commander of Ai under a pile of rocks where the gate had stood (8:24–29). As a result of the decisive battle, Israel now possessed a staging ground for their push into the central hill country.

CONCLUSION

As suggested above, while the battle of Ai narrative of Josh 7–8 has often been read with the assumption that Ai was a large and formidable city, a careful reading of the text reveals that the narrative characterizes the settlement as being notable for its small size. Overshadowed by its larger neighbor Bethel, Ai's importance is found not in its size or strength, but in the failure that it handed to Israel early in Joshua's conquest. The sin of Achan during the preceding battle of Jericho had resulted in a situation wherein Yahweh would not fight for Israel. On their own, Israel proved unable to defeat the Ruin, even though they had deemed it to be unworthy of their full strength. Israel's experience at Ai, both the initial defeat and the ultimate triumph, demonstrated that their success in conquering the land—from the mighty city of Hazor to the little Ruin that was beside Bethel—was entirely dependent upon their faithfulness to Yahweh. It was through obedience and faithfulness to their covenant with Yahweh that Israel would find "good success wherever you go" (Josh 1:7 ESV).

BIBLIOGRAPHY

Allen, Leonard. "Archaeology of Ai and the Accuracy of Joshua 7:1–8:29." *Restoration Quarterly* 20 (1977): 41–52.

Butler, Trent C. *Joshua*. WBC. Waco: Word Books, 1983.

Callaway, Joseph A. "Ai (Place)." *ABD* 1:125–30.

———. "Ai." *NEAEHL* 1:39–45.

Faust, Avraham. "Cities, Villages, and Farmsteads: The Landscape of Leviticus 25:29–31." Pages 103–12 in *Exploring the Longue Durée: Essays in Honor of Lawrence E. Stager*. Edited by J. David Schloen. Winona Lake, IN: Eisenbrauns, 2009.

Hess, Richard. *Joshua: An Introduction and Commentary*. TOTC. Downers Grove, IL: InterVarsity Press, 1996.

———. "The Jericho and Ai of the Book of Joshua." Pages 33–46 in *Critical Issues in Early Israelite History*. Edited by Richard S. Hess, Gerald A. Klingbeil, and Paul J. Ray Jr. Winona Lake, IN: Eisenbrauns, 2008.

Humphreys, Colin J. "The Number of People in the Exodus from Egypt: Decoding Mathematically the Very Large Numbers in Numbers I and XXVI." *VT* 48 (1998): 96–113.

Livingston, David. "Location of Biblical Bethel and Ai Reconsidered." *WTJ* 33 (1970): 20–44.

———. "Traditional Site of Bethel Questioned." *WTJ* 34 (1971): 39–50.

———. *Khirbet Nisya: The Search for Biblical Ai 1979–2002*. Manheim: Associates for Biblical Research, 2003.

Mazar, Amihai. *Archaeology of the Land of the Bible: 10,000–586 B.C.E.* New York: Doubleday, 1990.

Mendenhall, George E. "The Census Lists of Numbers 1 and 26." *JBL* 77 (1958): 52–66.

Merling, David. "The Book of Joshua, Part II: Expectations of Archaeology." *Andrews University Seminary Studies* 39 (2001): 209–21.

Monson, James M. *The Land Between: A Regional Study Guide to the Land of the Bible*. Rockford, IL: Biblical Backgrounds, Inc., 1991.

Nelson, Richard D. *Joshua: A Commentary*. OTL. Louisville: Westminster John Knox, 1997.

Rainey, Anson F. "Bethel is Still Beitîn." *WTJ* 33 (1971): 175–88.

———. *The El-Amarna Correspondence: A New Edition of the Cuneiform Letters from the Site of El-Amarna Based on Collations of All Extant Tablets*. Edited by William M. Schniedewind. 2 vols. Leiden: Brill, 2015.

———. "Looking for Bethel: An Exercise in Historical Geography." Pages 269–73 in *Confronting the Past: Archaeological and Historical Essays on Ancient Israel in Honor of William G. Dever*. Edited by Seymour Gitin, J. Edward Wright, and J. P. Dessel. Winona Lake, IN: Eisenbrauns, 2006.

Robinson, Edward. *Biblical Researches in Palestine and in the Adjacent Regions*. 2 vols. Boston: Crocker and Brewster, 1856.

Wood, Bryant G. "The Search for Joshua's Ai." Pages 205–40 in *Critical Issues in Early Israelite History*. Edited by Richard S. Hess, Gerald A. Klingbeil, and Paul J. Ray Jr. Winona Lake, IN: Eisenbrauns, 2008.

Zevit, Ziony. "Archaeological and Literary Stratigraphy in Joshua 7–8." *BASOR* 251 (1983): 23–35.

CHAPTER 5

THE COVENANT RENEWAL CEREMONIES AT SHECHEM: A GEOGRAPHICAL AND THEOLOGICAL ASSESSMENT

Josh 8:30–35; 24:1–33

John A. Beck

KEY POINTS

- Shechem occupied a key location within the promised land and Israel's history.
- Shechem made vital contributions to the narration of two covenant renewal ceremonies.
- Shechem linked the two covenant renewal ceremonies to the past, to one another, and to future events that occurred in this location.

INTRODUCTION

The book of Joshua presents battle stories. Some of these stories entail fighting for possession of the promised land, and others entail battling for the hearts and minds of Israel. The latter were battles fought against flagging memories of their national history, and a lagging commitment to their covenant obligations. Here we will examine two covenant renewal ceremonies that are linked to Israel's past, and to each another by the place they occurred—the city of Shechem. We will consider the physical qualities of the pass between Mounts Ebal and Gerizim at Shechem, contemplate the roles that this location plays in the covenant renewal ceremonies, and weigh the cumulative impact of these stories on our reading of the larger plan of salvation.[1] In

1. There are many issues that remain under discussion concerning the relationship between these two accounts in Joshua which include their historicity, composition history,

Shechem Between Mount Gerizim and Mount Ebal

the end, we will come to appreciate that long before Shiloh or Jerusalem became the focus of divine attention and worship in the Holy Land, Shechem was the place to receive and contemplate the revelation of God.

PHYSICAL QUALITIES OF THE SETTING

Both covenant renewal ceremonies in the book of Joshua occur at the same location. The first setting is staged at the two mountains Ebal and Gerizim (8:30, 33), while the second is anchored in the same location by the mention of Shechem, the city that resided in the pass between those mountains (24:1, 25; see map on page 53).[2]

GEOGRAPHY

Shechem (Tel Balatah) is located in the mountain pass (1,800 ft., 548 m elevation) between Mount Ebal (3,084 ft., 940 m) and Mount Gerizim (2,891 ft., 881 m). It enjoyed a pleasant climate, plentiful rainfall, and fertile soil that combined to promise good living. Shechem's greatest contribution, however, to Samaria

form, structure, and literary integrity. These conversations are well documented in the literature. See Trent C. Butler, *Joshua 13–24*, WBC (Dallas: Word, 2014), 297–316; Sarah Lebhar Hall, *The Conquering Character of the Characterization of Joshua in Joshua 1–11* (New York: T&T Clark, 2010), 140–44; William T. Koopmans, *Joshua 24 as Poetic Narrative* (Sheffield: Sheffield Academic, 1990), 418–33; Pekka M. A. Pitkänen, *Joshua*, Apollos Old Testament Commentary (Downers Grove, IL: InterVarsity Press, 2010), 185–90; J. Alberto Soggin, *Joshua: A Commentary*, OTL (Louisville: Westminster John Knox, 1972), 222–26. In this essay, we will address the literary relationship between these two Shechem accounts as they are related to one another in the final form of the text.

2. Septuagint manuscripts of the Old Testament substitute Shiloh for Shechem in both verses. This may be an attempt to harmonize the second covenant renewal ceremony with the location of the tabernacle at Shiloh. For a discussion, see Butler, *Joshua 13–24*, 293.

Altar on Mount Ebal

was as an overland transportation hub.[3] This mountain pass provided a link to the coastal plain by Wadi Shechem and to the Jordan River Valley through the Salim Valley and Wadi Farah, making it the best route for transitioning laterally through Samaria.[4] In addition, the pass hosted the "ridge route," the north-south road that passed through nearly all of the important the cities and villages on the central mountain spine from Hebron to the Jezreel Valley.

ARCHAEOLOGY

These settlement factors predict that an ancient city would be established here, and it was. The twelve-acre site of Shechem was founded around 1900 BC and became one of the major city-states in Canaan.[5] The city was well fortified with a glacis, wall, and gate structure whose remains can still be seen on the site today. Shechem experienced a hiatus in its occupation from 1540–1450 BC. After that, the city was reoccupied and rebuilt, including its massive fortress temple. In the fourteenth century BC, Shechem's trouble-making king, Labayu, repeatedly attempted to expand the influence of his city, earning him and Shechem repeated mention in the Amarna Letters.[6] The archaeological heritage of the city-state continued without interruption well into the twelfth century BC.[7]

---

3. Paul H. Wright, *Greatness, Grace, and Glory: Carta's Atlas of Biblical Biography* (Jerusalem: Carta, 2008), 24.

4. David A. Dorsey, *The Roads and Highways of Ancient Israel* (Baltimore: Johns Hopkins University Press, 1991), 140–42; 174, 180.

5. LaMoine F. DeVries, *Cities of the Biblical World* (Peabody, MA: Hendrickson, 1997), 235.

6. *ANET*, 263–66, 268, 271, and 274.

7. Amihai Mazar, *Archaeology of the Land of the Bible, 10,000–586 B.C.E.* (New York: Doubleday, 1992), 251.

Also of archaeological interest is the altar which Adam Zertal discovered on top of Mount Ebal. While the surviving altar dates later than the one built there by Joshua (8:30), its unique position and associated qualities distinguish it as an Israelite worship site that likely marks the spot of the earlier altar built for the covenant renewal ceremony.[8]

JOSHUA 8:30–35

SUMMARY

The previous chapter, Joshua 7, opens with foreboding. Israel had been unfaithful to the Lord and experienced their first defeat in Canaan. This called for bold action on Joshua's part. Although it would allow the Canaanite city-states to regroup, Joshua paused operations and led all Israel to Mount Ebal for a recommitment service (8:30). When they arrived, Joshua built an altar of uncut stones on top of the mountain on which both burnt and fellowship offerings were made (8:30–31). He copied the law of Moses on plastered covered stones (8:32). He then directed half of the people to stand on Mount Gerizim and half on Mount Ebal for antiphonal recitation of the blessings and curses that offered a summary of the law in advance of Joshua's reading of the entire Mosaic code (8:33–35).

PURPOSE OF THE CEREMONY

Israel faced challenging battles against Canaanite city-states but, in many ways, the passage of time had become Israel's most potent enemy. The adults who crossed the Jordan River into Canaan (Josh 3:1–17) were not the adults who walked through the Red Sea (Exod 14:1–15:21) and responded to the Lord's covenant at Mount Sinai (Exod 24:1–18). Given Israel's unfaithfulness and their most recent defeat, it was time for them to reconnect to their founding story as a nation, to hear the agreement that bound them to the Lord, and to recommit themselves to their divinely appointed mission.

IMPACT OF THE LOCATION

The story carefully defines the location for this event, the pass between Mounts Ebal and Gerizim.[9] First, consider the way it addressed practical needs. There had to be room for thousands of people to gather in sight of one another with acoustics that would foster the antiphonal exchanges that were part of the event. It is hard to think of another place in ancient Canaan that met both needs in the way this mountain pass did.[10]

---

8. For a discussion of those qualities, see Richard S. Hess, *Israelite Religions: An Archaeological and Biblical Survey* (Grand Rapids: Baker Academic, 2007), 218–19; Ralph K. Hawkins, *How Israel Became a People* (Nashville: Abingdon, 2013), 187.

9. One of the great mysteries associated with this location is the absence of a battle report either in Joshua 8 or mention in the summary of conquered city-states in 12:9–24. The archaeology of Shechem also shows no evidence of destruction in this era (Mazar, *Archaeology of the Land of the Bible*, 251). So how was it possible that Israel gained access to this vital crossroads within Samaria? It is possible that the people of Shechem, like the people of Gibeon (Josh 9), feared Israel and relied upon an earlier agreement made with either or both Abraham and Jacob who purchased land here. See Iain Provan, V. Philips Long, and Tremper Longman III, *A Biblical History of Israel* (Louisville: Westminster John Knox, 2003), 153.

10. Hess, *Israelite Religions*, 217.

Aerial View of Shechem from the North

Second, this mountain pass had hosted one of the great founding stories of ancient Israel. Abraham and Sarah left Harran with a vague land promise (Gen 12:1; Heb 11:8). It was only when they arrived in Shechem that the Lord said, "To your offspring I will give this land" (Gen 12:6–7).[11] Abraham quickly built an altar in this location to memorialize the event. Jacob also purchased land in Shechem, built an altar, and subsequently challenged his family to rededicate itself to the Lord by burying their pagan worship paraphernalia at Shechem (Gen 33:19–20; 35:4).[12] Given these stories, Shechem was the perfect place to capture the larger backstory that informed the battles Israel fought. They were not just fighting for a national homeland. They were advancing a story begun at the time of Abraham.

Beyond all of that, Israel was living out the instructions that the Lord had given this nation in Deut 11:29 and 27:1–28:68. Prior to crossing the Jordan River, the Lord told Israel to travel to this very spot where they were to inscribe the law of Moses on plastered-covered stones and build an altar of uncut stones (Deut 27:1–6). The Lord went so far as to assign positions on the two mountains for individual tribes and the curses and blessings that were to be recited (Deut 11:29; 27:12–13). That made this mountain pass not just a feasible location for this public event. It was *the* location for this public event. The obedience to the divine plan is highlighted in Josh 8 where formal

11. Unless otherwise indicated, Scripture quotations come from the New International Version (NIV).

12. The lexeme "Shechem" appears twelve times in Gen 34. But in every one of those instances, the reference is to a person, the son of Hamor, rather than to the place. Although the clan and city are linked in Gen 33:18–19, the author makes an intentional effort to background the connection to the city throughout Gen 34 by repeatedly marking its "Shechem" as a person using language like "son of Hamor," "Shechem's father Hamor," or "Shechem's house."

mention of fidelity to divine instruction occurs three times (8:31, 33, 35). Furthermore, the location captured the full backstory of Israel's arrival in and conquest of the land. By placing Israel in a mountain setting that recalls Mount Sinai and the stories of Abraham's family, the place becomes a vital contributor in accomplishing the purpose of the event.[13]

JOSHUA 24:1–33

SUMMARY

The final chapter of Joshua records an event that is very similar to the one we have just narrated. By the time we return to the mountain pass between Mounts Ebal and Gerizim, Joshua and the Israelite army had defeated all of the major city-states in Canaan (Josh 21:43–45). Subsequently, the Israelite army disbanded, with each tribe headed for their own land parcel on which they built their homes, pastured their livestock, and planted their fields, including the tribes east of the Jordan River (Josh 22:1–9). After the passage of about thirty years (Josh 23:1), it was time for the new generation to make its commitment to the Lord at Shechem (Josh 24:1).

Once there, Joshua began by rehearsing their shared national story in which the Lord had consistently acted to bring them to this place. He spoke of Terah's family who lived "beyond the Euphrates and worshiped other gods" (24:2). The Lord appeared to his son, Abraham and brought him to Canaan. Subsequent episodes of their national story took place in Egypt, the wilderness, and east of the Jordan River. What transpired there showed how capable the Lord was in caring for his people and this plan. The review's grand climax brings the crowd to the present moment. "So I gave you a land on which you did not toil and cities you did not build; and you live in them and eat from vineyards and olive groves that you did not plant" (24:13).

Following the review of their national story, Joshua moved the focus to God's identity. In the years between the covenant ceremony performed by Moses (Exod 24) and that performed by Joshua (Josh 24), a uniform understanding of the Lord had eroded. Joshua challenged Israel to throw away its "gods" and follow the example of his family. "But as for me and my household, we will serve the Lord" (24:15). Israel quickly joined in making the same commitment, but Joshua immediately challenged them. "You are not able to serve the Lord. He is a holy God; he is a jealous God. He will not forgive your rebellion and your sins. If you forsake the Lord and serve foreign gods, he will turn and bring disaster on you and make an end of you, after he has been good to you" (24:19–20). Israel was not dissuaded. They restated their willingness to join Joshua in serving the Lord.

The event closed when Joshua reviewed the Mosaic covenant and set up a large stone. "This stone will be a witness against us. It has heard all the words the Lord has said to us. It will be a witness against you if you are untrue to your God." (24:27)

PURPOSE OF THE CEREMONY

The purpose behind this narrated gathering becomes clear when we see the relationship between the outline of this story and the structure of ancient Hittite

13. *MAB*, 117.

vassal treaties from the second millennium BC.[14] This kind of treaty defined the relationship between a vassal and suzerain. They typically began by recounting the story of the past relationship between the two, highlighting the benefits the suzerain had offered the vassal. This historical prologue was followed by a section of stipulations, regulations that governed the behavior of the vassal. Then came the call for witnesses and finally a set of curses that would follow non-conformity and blessings that followed conformity. Furthermore, it was customary in the ancient Near East for each generation to hear and commit themselves to the terms of such a covenant as their forebearers had.[15] That is what happened here.

Three decades after their parents declared their allegiance to the Lord, their children did the same. Life had become more local as the focus of this generation turned to growing their own food, securing water resources, and intermarriage within one's tribe. National matters and mission took a backseat. So, Joshua called for this new generation of Israel to formalize its relationship to the Lord and the Mosaic covenant.

IMPACT OF THE LOCATION

The author again takes us to Shechem for this event (24:1, 25) because of the con-

14. For a discussion of the individual elements of such a treaty and their correspondence to Josh 24, see Richard H. Hess, "Joshua," *ZIBBCOT* 2:84–85.

15. Eugene H. Merrill, *Kingdom of Priests: A History of Old Testament Israel* (Grand Rapids: Baker, 1987), 139.

tributions it makes to storytelling. As with the earlier convocation, Shechem met the event's practical needs, but it also hosted founding stories from the life of Abraham and Jacob related to the promised land (Gen 12:6–7; 33:19–20). Additionally, it was the location at which Jacob's family buried and abandoned pagan paraphernalia that had fostered their worship of other gods (Gen 35:4). These founding stories gave context and motivation for the very rededication to the Lord that was underway. Plus, this is the same geographical setting for the earlier covenant recommitment ceremony conducted some thirty years earlier (Josh 8:30–35). In retrospect, this group can calculate how the covenant faithfulness of their ancestors yielded divine blessing in the form of the homes, farm fields, pastures, water sources, and rest in a land of their own.

THE CUMULATIVE IMPACT OF THESE EVENTS

Given the similarity in purpose and location, we need to consider the cumulative impact of these stories both on our understanding of the plan of salvation and on the subsequent stories that engage this mountain pass. First, these Shechem stories confirm the Lord's faithfulness to his promises. Here the Lord told Abraham that his family would possess Canaan and here we find that the land of Canaan is firmly in Israelite hands.

Second, Shechem creates a bridge between the Abrahamic and Mosaic covenants. The Abrahamic covenant is the focus of attention in Genesis while Exodus through Deuteronomy largely puts our focus on the Mosaic Covenant. Both are vital to our understanding of the plan of salvation. At Shechem, we see how those two covenants come together to define the Lord's plan to reverse the curse of Eden.

Third, these two events firmly establish Shechem as a national religious site whose backstory will inform our reading of any subsequent story that occurs at Shechem (e.g., Judg 9). The infrastructure left behind for subsequent generations served to remind them of this fact. Both Abraham and Jacob built altars here. Joshua built an altar on top of Mount Ebal. Joshua wrote the law of Moses on plastered covered stones here and set up a witness stone to commemorate the rededication of the Lord's people to the covenant. All of this culminates in the narrator's bold words, calling this sanctuary "the holy place of the Lord" (24:26).

From this point forward, any story set in this mountain pass must be read against this backstory. Just a few verses later, the narrator reports that the bones of Joseph were buried here (24:32). This links the close of Genesis with the close of Joshua. At the close of Genesis, Joseph made his family swear that when the Lord brought Israel out of Egypt and back to Canaan his remains would be carried from Egypt and buried in the promised land (Gen 50:24–25).

The recognition of Shechem and its environs as sacred space lives well beyond Joshua. Consider the impact of Shechem's backstory on the division of Israel into two kingdoms at the time of Rehoboam (1 Kgs 12:1–17). The son of Solomon asked the northern tribes to meet him at Shechem to declare their loyalty to him as king. Because it is a Shechem story, we expect it to illustrate the expectations of covenant interest and national mission. But the story we get is focused on royal prerogative, abuse of power, and tax burdens, not once men-

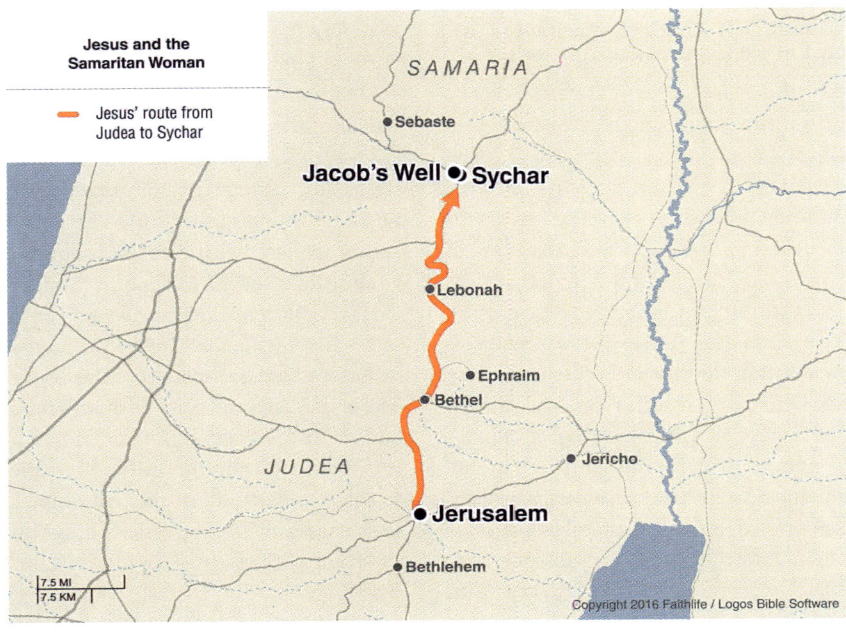

tioning the important religious heritage of Shechem.[16]

Then consider Jesus' visit to the mountain pass. Before telling us the story of Jesus and the woman at the well of Sychar (i.e., Shechem), John tells us that Jesus "had to go through Samaria" (John 4:4). This obligation was not imposed by travel considerations. Jesus had other ways he could have traveled between Judea and Galilee. I am inclined to think the imperative was theological. When he arrived at Sychar, Jesus did something the Gospels report him doing only one other time. He verbally identified himself as the Messiah.[17] Why here? Shechem/Sychar had waited longer than any other place in the Holy Land to hear it.

CONCLUSION

Shechem is an impactful place because it hosts key stories that advance the plot of the larger Old Testament storyline from the fall into sin to anticipated redemption. Here, we have explored the physical qualities of the pass between Mounts Ebal and Gerizim, contemplated the roles that this location plays in the stories it hosted, and seen the cumulative impact of its stories grow from the time of Abraham to the time of Jesus. Later, God's people would think of Shiloh and Jerusalem as the focal point of the promised land. But before either of these takes center stage, Shechem was the place to receive and contemplate the revelation of God.

16. John A. Beck, *Discovery House Bible Atlas* (Grand Rapids: Discovery House, 2015), 157–59.

17. John A. Beck, *Along the Road: How Jesus Used Geography to Tell God's Story* (Grand Rapids: Discovery House, 2018), 107–13.

BIBLIOGRAPHY

Beck, John A. *Along the Road: How Jesus Used Geography to Tell God's Story*. Grand Rapids: Discovery House, 2018.

———. *Discovery House Bible Atlas*. Grand Rapids: Discovery House, 2015.

Butler, Trent C. *Joshua 13–24*. WBC. Dallas: Word, 2014.

DeVries, LaMoine F. *Cities of the Biblical World*. Peabody, MA: Hendrickson, 1997.

Dorsey, David A. *The Roads and Highways of Ancient Israel*. Baltimore: Johns Hopkins University Press, 1991.

Hall, Sarah Lebhar. *The Conquering Character of the Characterization of Joshua in Joshua 1–11*. New York: T&T Clark, 2010.

Hawkins, Ralph K. *How Israel Became a People*. Nashville: Abingdon, 2013.

Hess, Richard S. *Israelite Religion: An Archaeological and Biblical Survey*. Grand Rapids: Baker, 2007.

———. "Joshua." *ZIBBCOT* 2:2–93.

Koopmans, William T. *Joshua 24 as Poetic Narrative*. Sheffield: Sheffield Academic, 1990.

Mazar, Amihai. *Archaeology of the Land of the Bible 10,000–586 B.C.E.* New York: Doubleday, 1992.

Merrill, Eugene H. *Kingdom of Priests: A History of Old Testament Israel*. Grand Rapids: Baker, 1987.

Pitkänen, Pekka M. A. *Joshua*. Apollos Old Testament Commentary. Downers Grove, IL: InterVarsity Press, 2010.

Provan, Iain, V. Philips Long, and Tremper Longman III. *A Biblical History of Israel*. Louisville: Westminster John Knox, 2003.

Soggin, Alberto J. *Joshua: A Commentary*. OTL. Louisville: Westminster John Knox, 1972.

Wright, Paul H. *Greatness, Grace, & Glory Carta's Atlas of Biblical Biography*. Jerusalem: Carta, 2008.

CHAPTER 6

THE BATTLE AT GIBEON-MAKKEDAH: A GEOGRAPHIC ANALYSIS

Josh 9–10

S. Cameron Coyle

KEY POINTS

- The alliance with the Hivite cities of the hill country gave Israel control over the strategic central Benjaminite plateau.
- Victory over the Jerusalem coalition opened the door for Joshua's conquest of southern Canaan.

INTRODUCTION

The Israelite victory against the cities of Ai and Bethel (Josh 7–8) resulted in a unifying fear among the kings of Canaan, who began aligning themselves against the threat posed by Israel (9:1–2). Interestingly, the first conflict to result from these alliances was directed not against Israel, but against the Hivite population centered at Gibeon in the central Benjaminite plateau. Israel, however, would be drawn into the battle as a result of their newly forged covenant with the Hivites (9:15). At stake for Israel was control of the strategic central Benjaminite plateau, a territory that would give them access to both the central hill country and the lowlands to the west. A review of the geopolitical situation in the region and the events of the battle will illustrate how Joshua's victory over the coalition led by Jerusalem stretched well beyond those five cities and helped to establish Israel's position in southern Canaan.

THE GEOPOLITICAL SITUATION

Israel's alliance with the Hivites of the central Benjaminite plateau, though acquired through deception on the part of the people of Gibeon (Josh 9), was a strategic territorial gain for Israel that forced the rulers of the southern hill country to take defensive action. Joshua 9:17 lists four cities of the Hivites: Gibeon, Kephirah, Beeroth, and Kiriath Jearim. Together, these four cities controlled access to the Kiriath Jearim and Beth Horon ridge routes leading down to the

Aerial View of Gibeon and the Central Benjaminite Plateau

Aijalon Valley, two of a limited number of routes connecting the central hill country with the coastal and Shephelah ("western foothills," NIV) regions to the west.

The chief city of this lot was Gibeon, located at modern el-Jib, some six and a half miles (11 km) southwest of Bethel and Ai, and about six miles (10 km) northwest of Jerusalem. No other major settlements were located between Gibeon and Bethel during the Late Bronze Age, a fact that underscores the urgency of the Gibeonite attempt to forge a peace treaty with Israel after the latter's victory at Ai and Bethel (8:1–29).[1] The Hivite territory in the central Benjaminite plateau was suddenly on the front lines of the Israelite invasion. Despite the negative reaction of the Israelites to the alliance (9:18), the union provided Israel with effective control of the important central Benjaminite plateau. The plateau is situated along the main north-south route through the hill country and gives access to both the Kiriath Jearim and Beth Horon ridge routes. By controlling the central Benjaminite plateau, Israel possessed ready access to the lowland regions west of the hill country and could isolate the regions to the north and south of the plateau.

This new geopolitical situation moved the front line of Israel's advance to the area south of the central Benjaminite plateau, into the territory controlled by the king of Jerusalem, Adoni-Zedek (Josh 10:1). Jerusalem is situated along the watershed ridge of the central hill country, a mere five miles (8 km) or so from Beeroth and the Hivite enclave now aligned with Israel. Its location on the

1. The Late Bronze Age in Canaan is known as a period of general decline in urbanization, with fewer numbers of settlements than other historical periods. This general state of affairs is also applicable to the specific case of the central hill country, which was home to far fewer settlements during the Late Bronze Age (the period of Joshua) than it was during the subsequent Iron Age. Compare the discussion in Amihai Mazar, *The Archaeology of the Land of the Bible: 10,000–586 B.C.E.* (New York: Doubleday, 1992), 239–41.

watershed ridge means that north-south travel from Jerusalem was relatively easy, while routes leading east or west into the lowlands were more difficult to come by. The western edge of the hill country is characterized by high ridges regularly cut by deeply eroded wadis. Routes traversing this transition zone must follow the small number of continuous ridge lines that allow for unimpeded movement into or out of the highlands. The rarity of such routes made their control strategically important for the cities of the hill country in all periods.[2] For Adoni-Zedek and Jerusalem, the only major route leading eastward was the Ascent of Adummim, which led directly to Jericho and the vicinity of the Israelite camp at Gilgal. Israel's control of the central Benjaminite plateau had cut Jerusalem off from both the region to the north and the ridge routes at Kiriath Jearim and Beth Horon that served as Jerusalem's primary paths westward. Adoni-Zedek was left increasingly isolated and desperately needed to reestablish his route to the Shephelah and coastal regions.

JERUSALEM'S RESPONSE

King Adoni-Zedek's concern in the face of the Israelite advance was significant not only because of the logistical problems that had been created, but because Gibeon was a "great city ... and all its men were warriors" (Josh 10:2).[3] Israel, which had already experienced success against Jericho, Bethel, and Ai, now had a geographical advantage and an influx of fighters. In response, Adoni-Zedek needed to retake the pass at Kiriath Jearim and address the Gibeonite alignment with Israel. To that end, he put together a coalition of Amorite cities from the southern hill country and Shephelah to take the fight to Gibeon.

The cities of Jerusalem's coalition included Hebron, Eglon, Lachish, and Jarmuth (10:3). Hebron is located approximately twenty miles (32 km) south of Jerusalem along the watershed ridge, while Jarmuth, Lachish, and Eglon are all to be found in the Shephelah region just west of the hill country. Eglon was possibly located at Tel Eton, which lies just off of a ridge route leading from Hebron and is at a distance of about eleven miles (18 km) from the latter. Some seven miles (11 km) to the northwest was the city of Lachish, firmly identified with Tell ed-Duweir. Lachish, too, was connected with Hebron by way of a ridge route. This route passed by Khirbet el-Qom, which some have identified as Makkedah, on its way into the highlands. This is where the kings of the Amorite alliance would eventually seek refuge from the Israelites, as discussed later in this article. Jarmuth was further north, approximately twelve miles (19 km) northeast of Lachish and fifteen miles (24 km) northwest of Hebron, at Tel Yarmut. Jarmuth's position just north of the Elah Valley provided the city with easy access to a ridge route of its own, one that reached the watershed ridge near Bethlehem, a few miles south of Jerusalem.

One point of commonality between the cities of Adoni-Zedek's coalition is that each is connected to the others via the ridge routes that tied these two

2. For a full discussion of ancient roadways in this region see David A. Dorsey, *The Roads and Highways of Ancient Israel* (Baltimore: Johns Hopkins University Press, 1991).

3. Unless otherwise noted, all Scripture quotations are taken from the English Standard Version (ESV).

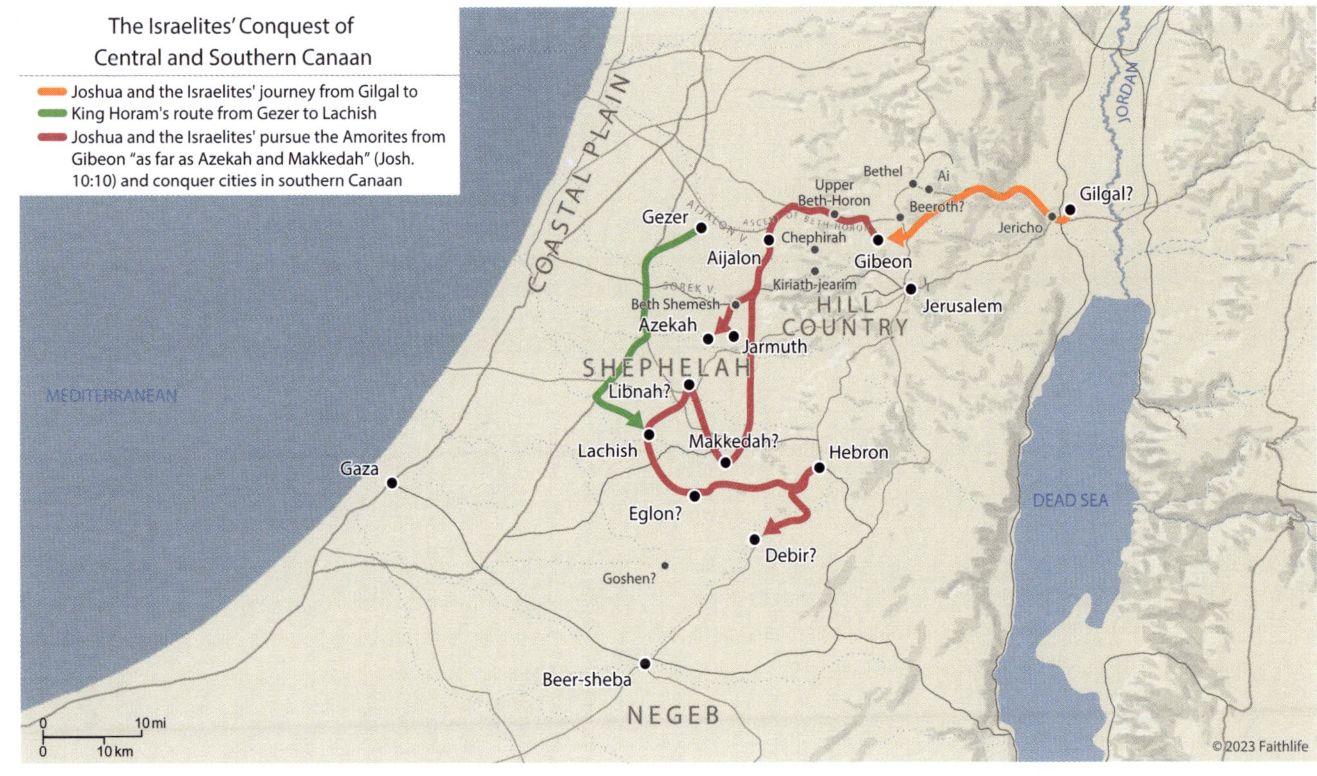
The Israelites' Conquest of Central and Southern Canaan
Joshua and the Israelites' journey from Gilgal to
King Horam's route from Gezer to Lachish
Joshua and the Israelites' pursue the Amorites from Gibeon "as far as Azekah and Makkedah" (Josh. 10:10) and conquer cities in southern Canaan
COASTAL PLAIN
MEDITERRANEAN
SHEPHELAH
HILL COUNTRY
NEGEB
DEAD SEA
JORDAN
Gezer
Aijalon
Sorek V.
Beth Shemesh
Azekah
Jarmuth
Libnah?
Lachish
Makkedah?
Hebron
Eglon?
Debir?
Goshen?
Gaza
Beer-sheba
Upper Beth-Horon
Chephirah
Kiriath-jearim
Gibeon
Bethel
Ai
Beeroth?
Jericho
Gilgal?
Jerusalem
0 10 mi
0 10 km
©2023 Faithlife

regions together. Another is their shared cultural tradition. The text refers to the inhabitants of these cities as Amorites. This term is occasionally used in Joshua as a generic reference to the inhabitants of Canaan (e.g., Josh 24:15), but typically refers to the inhabitants of either the Transjordanian kingdoms of Sihon and Og, or the Cisjordanian hill country area.[4] Joshua 5:1 summarizes all the rulers of Canaan with the statement "all the kings of the Amorites who were beyond the Jordan to the west, and all the kings of the Canaanites who were by the sea," again associating the Amorites with the area just west of the Jordan, in apparent distinction to the peoples living further west by the Mediterranean coast.

Given their cultural affinity and connections via the ridge routes, the cities of Adoni-Zedek's coalition were likely allied with one another in some form even prior to the Israelite threat.[5] Regardless, the text provides no indication of hesitation on the part of the other cities to heed Jerusalem's call to arms. The rulers joined forces and marched on Gibeon to lay siege to the Hivites' chief city. The staging area for this assault was likely Jerusalem, from which the combined forces could easily march northwest along the watershed ridge to Gibeon. The lack of any mention of Beeroth in this context, despite the site's closer proximity to Jerusalem, reflects Gibeon's superior strength within the Hivite settlements.

THE ISRAELITE RESPONSE

With the Amorite coalition encamped against their city, the inhabitants of Gibeon sent word to Joshua requesting Israel's aid. Despite Israel's recent success at Ai and Bethel, the Israelite camp remained at Gilgal in the Jordan Valley. Such was Israel's practice throughout Joshua's conquest narrative; after each engagement Israel would return to Gilgal rather than occupy the newly conquered territory (Josh 4:19; 10:6, 43; 14:6). Gilgal's exact location is unknown, but it is most likely somewhere between Jericho and the Jordan River.[5]

The journey on foot between Gilgal and Gibeon would have been significant. As the crow flies, the distance between the two would have been around eighteen miles (29 km), with significant changes in elevation. The area of Gilgal lies at an elevation of around one thousand feet (305 m) below sea level, while Gibeon is

4. The term Amorite appears five times in a list of peoples of Canaan (Josh 3:10; 9:1; 11:3; 12:8; 24:11), seven times in reference to the Transjordanian kingdoms of Sihon and Og (2:10; 9:10; 12:2; 13:10, 21; 24:8, 12), three times in reference to unspecified inhabitants of the Cisjordanian hill country (5:1; 7:7; 13:4), and three times to describe the coalition forces that attacked Gibeon (10:5, 6, 12). The two occasions on which the term is used in a generic sense for pre-Israelite inhabitants of Canaan (24:15, 18) may also be intended to refer to residents of the Cisjordanian hill country and the former kingdoms of Sihon and Og. Compare the discussion in John Van Seters, "The Terms 'Amorite' and 'Hittite' in the Old Testament," *VT* 22 (1972): 72.

5. The ruler of Jerusalem was involved in similar geopolitical maneuvers during the fourteenth century BC. As evidenced by a collection of letters sent between the Egyptian pharaoh and his vassal kings in Canaan, known as the Amarna correspondence, Jerusalem often quarreled with Shephelah sites such as Gezer and Gath over control of smaller settlements positioned along the ridge routes. See, for example, the discussion in Anson F. Rainey and R. Steven Notley, *The Sacred Bridge: Carta's Atlas of the Biblical World* (Jerusalem: Carta, 2006), 85–86.

6. Compare the discussion in Robert L. Hubbard Jr., "Gilgal," *DOTHB*, 334–36.

around two thousand five hundred feet (762 m) above sea level, leaving a difference of three thousand five hundred feet (1,067 m) in relative elevations for the two sites. It is, therefore, quite impressive that Joshua and Israel marched overnight from Gilgal to Gibeon to engage the Amorite coalition (Josh 10:9). One implication of this temporal marker is that the battle began in the early morning. This point is made more significant by the text's claim that the day was divinely lengthened to provide Israel with the necessary time to defeat the Amorites (10:12–14).[7]

The extra time from the Lord was necessary because of the Amorite flight from battle and the ensuing Israelite chase. The text provides no details regarding the Amorite positions around Gibeon or the events of the initial encounter upon Israel's arrival, but some reasonable inferences can be made. Gibeon was located on the western side of the main north-south route along the watershed. Thus, if Adoni-Zedek's forces were encamped near the city, they would likely have been somewhere between Gibeon and the main north-south road. When Joshua arrived from the east, Israel could have easily cut off the Amorites from their presumed escape route, namely the road back to Jerusalem, especially given their arrival under the cover of darkness was at an unexpected hour. Israel's sudden appearance to the Amorites' rear would have contributed to the panic Jerusalem's forces experienced, enabling Israel to strike a "great blow" in the field outside the city (10:10). An Israelite position between the Amorites and the watershed route would have then forced the enemy coalition to retreat in the opposite direction, toward the descent to the Shephelah.

The text states in summary fashion that Israel chased the Amorites along the route of the Ascent of Beth Horon and "struck them as far as Azekah and Makkedah" (Josh 10:10). The Ascent of Beth Horon was a ridge route connecting the central Benjaminite plateau with the Aijalon Valley below. This was the northernmost of two ridge routes that converged at Gibeon. The southern route traveled through the heart of the Hivite territory and directly past the city of Kiriath Jearim. As such the northern route was the only viable option, though it was a longer journey that took the coa-

7. While the interpretation most commonly taken is that the miracle in this passage is a temporary cessation of the movement of the sun and moon across the sky (along with the concomitant implications regarding the earth's rotational spin, the orbit of the moon around the earth, the earth's orbit around the sun, etc.), it is not the sole possibility. One alternative takes Joshua's command to the sun and moon not as to be "still" (from *damam* [דָּמַם] , "to stand still") but "silent," and views Joshua's words as a plea for shade rather than time. Such a request would fit the circumstances of the narrative well. After an arduous all-night march from Gilgal, Israel overcomes the enemy in battle at Gibeon only to see them retreat westward towards the open road. Facing a potentially drawn-out pursuit into the Shephelah in the early summer heat (there does not appear to be a significant passage of time between the Passover of Josh 5:10 and the battle at Gibeon), Joshua requests relief from the sun and receives a divine reply in the form a hailstorm that would have included cloud cover. The biblical author notes that the significance of the moment is not the sun and moon, but rather the fact that "the Lord heeded the voice of a man" (10:14). For discussion of this interpretation, compare *MAB*, 118–20. For a summary of other views, see Richard S. Hess, *Joshua: An Introduction and Commentary*, TOTC (Downers Grove, IL: IVP Academic, 1996), 196–99.

lition forces even further from their home territories. The descent from Gibeon to the Aijalon Valley is a difference of around one thousand eight hundred feet (549 m) in elevation. The valley itself comprises the far northern end of the Shephelah region, where the topography changes to the rolling hills that separate the central hill country from the coastal plain. It was on the descent that the Amorites first encountered the hailstones from the Lord (10:11). The Hebrew text refers simply to "large stones" (אֲבָנִים גְּדֹלוֹת, *avanim gedolot*), but these have been understood as a reference to hail at least as early as the Greek Septuagint (λιθους χαλαζης, *lithous chalazes*, "hail stones").[8] The hail would continue to fall upon and kill soldiers from the coalition until they reached the area of Azekah, more than ten miles (16 km) south of where they entered the valley.

Upon descending into the valley, the coalition's route turned southward, passing by the city of Aijalon before continuing towards the area of the Amorite cities. The text's statement that Israel chased the Amorites "as far as Azekah and Makkedah" (Josh 10:10) suggests that the group may have broken up and followed divergent routes through the Shephelah. The route leading south from Aijalon divides into eastern and western paths as it approaches the Sorek Valley just north of Beth Shemesh. The western option passes by Beth Shemesh and Jarmuth before reaching Azekah at the Elah Valley. Azekah was perched atop Tell Zakariya, some three hundred eighty feet (116 m) above the surrounding valley. It is unlikely that the Amorite survivors were attempting to reach and enter Azekah; the site probably serves simply as a landmark along the journey. Some of the men, however, may have taken refuge at Jarmuth (10:20), although there is no explicit mention in the narrative of them doing so.

The eastern path through this region bypasses these cities and travels through a north-south depression separating the hill country from the Shephelah known as a trough valley. Located along this route is Khirbet el-Qom, commonly thought to be Makkedah on the basis of the site's close correspondence with the ancient city's geographic position as described in both biblical and extrabiblical sources.[9] Continuing along this eastern trough valley route one would arrive at Tel Eton, likely the site of ancient Eglon.[10] Similarly, after passing Azekah, the western route leads southward to Lachish. It is possible that the Amorite fighters separated and made use of both routes in an effort to reach their respective cities, although the five kings evidently remained together (Josh 10:17). Another option for interpreting the phrase "as far as Azekah and Makkedah" (10:10) would be that the bulk of the group stayed together, fleeing south-

8. Compare the comments in Robert B. Y. Scott, "Meteorological Phenomena and Terminology in the Old Testament," *ZAW* 64 (1952): 19–20. Hess notes similar passages in other ancient Near Eastern sources involving deities using hailstones as a weapon against men (Joshua, 196).

9. David A. Dorsey, "The Location of Biblical Makkedah," *TA* 7 (1980): 185–93.

10. Compare Anson F. Rainey, "The Administrative Division of the Shephelah," *TA* 7 (1980): 197; Avraham Faust and Hayah Katz, "A Canaanite Town, a Judahite Center, and a Persian Period Fort: Excavating Over Two Thousand Years of History at Tel 'Eton," *NEA* 78 (2015): 88–102.

Relief of Tiglath-Pileser III with His Foot on the Neck of an Enemy

ward to Azekah, then turned eastward through the Elah Valley before continuing southward in the trough valley, perhaps intending to circle back to the hill country for Hebron or Jerusalem.

These movements would have taken a significant amount of time. Following a fairly direct route from Gibeon to Makkedah via the Ascent of Beth Horon, the journey would have been more than thirty miles (38 km) on foot. While the pursuing Israelites no doubt provided the motivation to keep moving, the Amorite forces would have been slowed by the hail that was falling along the way. They probably sought cover as the opportunity presented itself. This may be why the five kings of the coalition first entered the cave at Makkedah (Josh 10:16). Caves are a common feature of the Shephelah region, the prevalent soft, chalky limestone being prone to both naturally eroded and man-made caverns. The presence of a cave large enough to serve as a hiding place for five or more men would not be out of place, nor would there be a problem finding "large stones" (10:18) to block the entrance of a cave. The irony of "large stones" constituting both the need for the kings to be in the cave and the means by which they were trapped within it may explain why Josh 10:11 does not make use of the more common term *barad* (בָּרָד), "hail."

With the Amorite kings trapped in the cave at Makkedah, and the Israelite soldiers in pursuit of the remaining Amorite troops, Joshua established a temporary camp. All who were caught in the field were killed, but the cities themselves were not attacked at this time (Josh 10:20–21). The battle finally ended with the execution of the Amorite kings in the Israelite camp at Makkedah. The execution itself was both a final end to the leaders of the coalition and a symbolic performance for the Israelites. While Joshua himself dealt the lethal blow to each king, he had the leaders of the people place their feet upon the necks of the Amorites. In doing so, the men were physically enacting an image of victory common across the ancient Near East (compare 1 Kgs 5:3; Pss 18:38; 47:3; 110:1).[11] The purpose of this pageantry is conveyed through Joshua's words in 10:25: the men were to take courage from this moment "for thus the LORD will do to all your enemies against whom you fight." The performance did not end with the execution of the kings. Their bodies were subsequently impaled and left on display, probably for the watchful eyes of the inhabitants of Makkedah who would soon be targeted as well, before being taken down at sunset and buried in the same cave in which they had earlier sought refuge (compare with Deut 21:22–23).

VICTORY IN THE SOUTH

After the execution of the Amorite kings, Joshua turned his attention to the cities of the Amorite territory. With the Israelite camp already at Makkedah, this city was the natural starting point for the southern campaign (Josh 10:28). The destruction mentioned in this context was directed toward the inhabitants rather than the city itself. Most of the cities defeated by Israel during the conquest were left intact while their populations were targeted. Only the cities of Jericho (6:24), Ai (8:19), and Hazor (11:11) are specifically described as having been burned. This observation illustrates the problematic nature of attempts to associate archaeologically excavated destruction levels at various sites with conflicts recorded in Joshua's narratives.[12]

From Makkedah, Joshua proceeded to move counterclockwise through the southern Shephelah and into the southern hill country. The next target was the city of Libnah, likely located at modern Tel Burna, roughly nine miles (15 km) northwest of Makkedah.[13] The victory at Libnah is reported in Joshua's typical stylized fashion: "he struck it with the edge of the sword, and every person in it; he left none remaining in it. And he did to its king as he had done to the king of Jericho" (Josh 10:30). No details of the battle are recorded. From Libnah, Joshua led the

11. One example of this imagery comes from an Assyrian wall relief that once decorated the Northwest Palace at Nimrud. The relief depicts the king, Tiglath-Pileser III, standing before a prostrate foe, with the heel of his foot pressed firmly against the defeated enemy's neck. In his right hand the king holds a spear that appears ready to execute the captive at any moment. See image on page 73.

12. It can be tempting to assume an association between excavated destruction levels dated to the approximate time of biblical events and the same events as described in the biblical narratives. However, identifying the cause of a destruction layer with certainty is often not possible. Archaeologists must make inferences from limited and fragmented evidence regarding the historical circumstances that brought about the destruction event. Those who would like to infer connections between destruction layers at various sites and events in the book of Joshua should bear in mind that the narratives themselves make very few claims about the events that would result in such destruction layers. To associate the events of Joshua with such destruction layers at any site other than Jericho, Ai, or Hazor is to assume more about the events than the narratives themselves claim.

13. Compare Rainey, "Administrative Division," 194–202; Chris McKinny and Amit Dagan, "The Explorations of Tel Burna," *PEQ* 145 (2013): 294–305.

Israelites southward five miles (8 km) to Lachish. The battle at Lachish required a siege that went into a second day (10:32). During the siege the leaders of Lachish were able to send word to their ally at the northern Shephelah site of Gezer, whose king brought fighters to Lachish in a bid to aid the beleaguered city. The defensive effort was unsuccessful, however, and both Lachish and the warriors from Gezer were defeated. Interestingly, Lachish served a role within the Egyptian imperial system during this period and was possibly the base of operations for a small number of Egyptian personnel, yet the book of Joshua makes no mention of the site's Egyptian connections.[14]

Seven miles (11 km) to the southeast of Lachish lies Eglon at Tel Eton. Here, too, Israel laid siege to the city before capturing it, though no timeframe is provided by the narrative (Josh 10:34). After achieving victory at Eglon, Israel marched eleven miles (18 km) east to the hill country site of Hebron. Once more the victory is narrated with little detail. However, the mention of Hebron's king in this context (10:37) may be an indication that a sufficient amount of time had passed since Joshua executed the Amorite kings at Makkedah, including the king of Hebron, for the city to have established a new leader. This new king's tenure was short-lived, however, as the flow of the text suggests that little more than a week may have elapsed between the two events.

The final recorded target of the campaign was the southern hill country site of Debir, associated with Khirbet Rabud some eight miles (13 km) south of Hebron along the watershed route. Both Hebron and Debir are noteworthy for the inclusion of their associated settlements among the list of defeated foes. The mention of the "towns" belonging to these cities (Josh 10:37, 39) underscores the regional impact achieved by the Israelite victory. This point is amplified by the closing verses of the chapter, which describe the effect of the campaign in the broadest possible terms. The description of the conquered territory is hyperbolic, including areas well beyond the specific regions described in the narrative: "the whole land, the hill country and the Negev and the lowland [i.e., the Shephelah] and the slopes, and all their kings ... from Kadesh Barnea as far as Gaza, and all the country of Goshen, as far as Gibeon" (10:40–41). Not only does this description include areas omitted from the narrative, but later narratives within Joshua demonstrate the exaggerated nature of the destruction of the local populations.[15] For example, while Josh 10:37–39 describes Israel as having "left none remaining" in both Hebron (10:37) and Debir (10:39), Josh 15:13–19 narrates

14. Compare Ann E. Killebrew, *Biblical Peoples and Ethnicity: An Archaeological Study of Egyptians, Canaanites, Philistines, and Early Israel 1300–1100 B.C.E.* (Atlanta: Society of Biblical Literature, 2005), 82.

15. For example, the phrase "from Kadesh Barnea as far as Gaza" (Josh 10:41) describes an area well to the southwest of any of the other localities mentioned in the narrative. There is no hint in the narrative prior to this summary statement that the Israelite efforts ventured so far from the central hill country. Similarly, the subsequent phrase "all the country of Goshen" introduces another new toponym to the narrative. This latter location should not be confused with the land of Goshen in which the Israelites dwelt while in Egypt; it refers to an otherwise unknown location in southern Canaan. On this point, compare William A. Ward, "Goshen," *ABD* 2:1076.

subsequent efforts to once again remove inhabitants from these same cities.

CONCLUSION

Hyperbole aside, the campaign that began as an *ad hoc* response to the call for help from Gibeon proved to be instrumental in furthering Israel's territorial aims in southern Canaan. The victory over the Jerusalem coalition not only answered the immediate threat to the Hivites, but it opened the door for Joshua to launch a broader campaign against the population of southern Canaan. The impact of this campaign helped to solidify Israel's position within the region, a point which serves to justify the hyperbolic description of the campaign's outcome in Josh 10:40–43 and sets the stage for the conflict of chapter eleven, wherein Israel faces a new coalition of kings from another region of Canaan.

BIBLIOGRAPHY

Dorsey, David A. "The Location of Biblical Makkedah." *TA* 7 (1980): 185–93.

———. *The Roads and Highways of Ancient Israel.* Baltimore: Johns Hopkins University Press, 1991.

Faust, Avraham, and Hayah Katz. "A Canaanite Town, a Judahite Center, and a Persian Period Fort: Excavating Over Two Thousand Years of History at Tel 'Eton." *NEA* 78 (2015): 88–102.

Hess, Richard S. *Joshua: An Introduction and Commentary*. TOTC. Downers Grove, IL: IVP Academic, 1996.

Hubbard, Robert L., Jr. "Gilgal." *DOTHB*, 334–36.

Killebrew, Ann E. *Biblical Peoples and Ethnicity: An Archaeological Study of Egyptians, Canaanites, Philistines, and Early Israel 1300–1100 B.C.E.* Atlanta: Society of Biblical Literature, 2005.

Mazar, Amihai. *The Archaeology of the Land of the Bible: 10,000–586 B.C.E.* New York: Doubleday, 1992.

McKinny, Chris, and Amit Dagan. "The Explorations of Tel Burna." *PEQ* 145 (2013): 294–305.

Rainey, Anson F. "The Administrative Division of the Shephelah." *TA* 7 (1980): 194–202.

Rainey, Anson F., and R. Steven Notley. *The Sacred Bridge: Carta's Atlas of the Biblical World.* Jerusalem: Carta, 2006.

Scott, Robert B. Y. "Meteorological Phenomena and Terminology in the Old Testament." *ZAW* 64 (1952): 11–25.

Van Seters, John. "The Terms 'Amorite' and 'Hittite' in the Old Testament." *VT* 22 (1972): 64–81.

Ward, William A. "Goshen." *ABD* 2:1076–77.

CHAPTER 7

THE NORTHERN CAMPAIGN AND THE BATTLE OF HAZOR: A GEOGRAPHICAL ANALYSIS

Josh 11:1–15; 12:19–23

Benjamin A. Foreman

KEY POINTS

- The goal of the Canaanite confederation in the north was to prevent Joshua from advancing into the Jezreel Valley and beyond.
- Most likely, the city of Maron should be identified with Tell el-Khurbeh near Marun er-Ras in southern Lebanon and thus the Waters of Maron might be a reference to the Dishon River on the northern border of modern Israel.
- At present, it is still unclear how the archaeological findings at Hazor relate to Joshua's conquest.

INTRODUCTION

Joshua's strategy for taking the land of Canaan consisted of three major offensives. His first thrust focused on the central swath of the hill country and had the objective of driving a wedge between the Canaanite cities in the central highlands. The tactic worked, and with Jericho and Ai smoldering behind them, most of the central and northern hill country (i.e., Benjamin, Ephraim, and Manasseh) lay open for the taking (Josh 5:13–10:28).

The second push concentrated on the southern part of the land. Fewer details about this campaign are recorded in Joshua (see Josh 10:29–43), but it covered the southern hill country, the biblical Negev, and the land stretching down to Kadesh Barnea, Gaza, and Goshen. Much of this region, it seems, fell with little difficulty, and with nearly all the hill country and the Negev in Israel's pocket, Joshua led his forces back to Gilgal (Josh 10:43) to formulate their plan for the final attack on the Jezreel Valley and the territory beyond.

Although the general course of Joshua's campaign in northern Canaan might be clear, Josh 11:1–15 references several sites whose identifications have been contested. This essay will investigate the Israelites' northern offensive from a geographical perspective. Specifically, I will clarify the extent of the Canaanite alliance, the location of their staging ground, and the line of their retreat. In the final section, I will review some of the archaeological findings at Hazor and reflect on how these might relate to the biblical text.

THE CANAANITE LEAGUE IN THE NORTH

Word of Joshua's successes in the south and in the heartland prompted the kings of the north to forge a defensive alliance. Although only five cities of the coalition are explicitly named, the axis of powers stretched out over a tract of land that covered approximately sixteen hundred square miles (2,575 sq. km).

The sponsor and leader of the league was Jabin, king of Hazor. Nestled on the southwestern rim of the Huleh Valley along the main route leading to the major empires of the east, Hazor was the largest city of Canaan. It was first identified with Tell el-Qedah in 1875 by the explorer Josias Wesley Porter, and a cuneiform text with the name Hazor etched on it was subsequently found on the tell, thus confirming Porter's identification.[1] Throughout the Late Bronze Age (hereafter LB), the city fanned out over approximately two hundred acres and boasted of a population of fifteen thousand or more.[2] Proportionally, this is comparable to a modern metropolis like Chicago or New York. It is not surprising, therefore, that Josh 11:10 notes that Hazor "was the head of all those kingdoms." Hazor's sponsorship of this northern partnership is a testament to God's faithful execution of his promise to give his people the land of Canaan. Such a large and powerful city in the far north would not have felt threatened by the ragtag group had not "the LORD God of Israel fought for Israel" (Josh 10:42).[3]

With war drums beating just over the horizon, Jabin of Hazor was able to secure the support of Jobab, king of "Madon" (Josh 11:1). Based on the name similarity, some associate Madon with Khirbet Madin, near the Horns of Hattin.[4] Aside from Josh 12:19, however, this toponym does not occur anywhere else in the Old Testament or in any extrabiblical source. The Greek Septuagint (LXX) reads *Marron* (Μαρρων) in both 11:1 and 12:19 (LXX 12:20), and since 11:5 states the confederation assembled at the Waters of Merom, *Maron* is probably the original reading.[5] This slight emenda-

1. Yigael Yadin, *Hazor: The Schweich Lectures 1970* (London: Oxford University Press, 1972), 13. Porter's proposal was ignored or forgotten by scholars since the site was not excavated or investigated until fifty years later (1928) by John Garstang, who believed he was the first to have discovered the city in 1926. He was unaware of Porter's identification five decades earlier. See John Garstang, *Joshua-Judges: Foundations of Bible History* (London: Constable, 1931; repr., Grand Rapids: Kregel, 1978), 184 n. 1.

2. Amnon Ben-Tor, *Hazor: Canaanite Metropolis, Israelite City* (Jerusalem: Israel Exploration Society, 2016), 45.

3. Unless otherwise noted, all biblical quotes are from the English Standard Version (ESV).

4. E.g., J. Alberto Soggin, *Joshua: A Commentary*, OTL (Philadelphia: Westminster, 1972), 135.

5. The change from "d" to "r" is very minor since the two letters are very similar in Hebrew (ד and ר). Some, nevertheless, believe the Hebrew Masoretic Text (MT) should be retained. Woudstra, for example, maintains the MT and attempts "to give it a reasonable

Aerial View of Hazor

tion is supported by extrabiblical evidence. Thutmose III (fifteenth century BC), for example, mentions conquering the city of *m-r-m-i-m* on his expedition into Canaan (no. 85 in his topographical list).[6] After his near defeat at Kedesh on the Orontes, Ramesses II (thirteenth century) claims to have destroyed the city of *ma-r-ma*.[7] The Assyrian king Tiglath-Pileser III (eighth century) also mentions this city, indicating he extorted prisoners from *ma-ru-um* after ransacking most of Galilee.[8] All three of these inscriptions clearly refer to this city in upper Galilee—variously called Merom/Meron/Marom/Maron (hereafter Maron).[9] Since Maron is probably the correct reading, locating it at Madin near the Horns of Hattin is unlikely since this is based solely on the toponym. The best candidate is a large Canaanite fortress just inside modern-day Lebanon called Tell el-Khurbeh. Since the location of Maron is connected to the gathering point of the alliance (i.e., the "Waters of Maron"), I will discuss the support for this identification in the next section.

The Israelite threat in the south persuaded the king of Shimron to participate in the defensive bloc as well. This city, apparently, was originally called "Shim'on" (Simeon), and is identified with Tel Shimron, eight kilometers west

sense," but gives no suggestion as to where Madon might have been located (Marten H. Woudstra, *The Book of Joshua*, NICOT [Grand Rapids: Eerdmans, 1981], 188–89).

6. See chart in Anson F. Rainey and R. Steven Notley, *The Sacred Bridge* (Jerusalem: Carta, 2006), 72–73.

7. See Rainey and Notley, *Sacred Bridge*, 98.

8. See Rainey and Notley, *Sacred Bridge*, 230.

9. Anson F. Rainey, *Handbook of Historical Geography* (Jerusalem: Institute of Holy Land Studies, 1984), 192.

of Nazareth.[10] Sitting on the northwestern edge of the Jezreel Valley, it was near the route that connected the Carmel passes of the International Highway to the Plain of Akko.[11] It also overlooked the east-west route that ran through the Beth Netofa Valley. Its strategic location, along with its multiple references in Egyptian sources, suggests it played an important geopolitical role in the Jezreel Valley. At its height in the Middle Bronze Age (hereafter MB), it was quite large, spreading out over approximately forty-eight acres (194,249 m^2).[12] The city began to shrink in size toward the end of the LB and its power and influence continued to diminish in the Iron Age. Unfortunately, the site has only recently begun to be excavated and therefore our archaeological understanding of the site is still basic.[13]

Also backing the northern confederation was the king of Akshaph. According to a document from the reign of Ramesses II, this city was situated south of Akko on an important road.[14] More specific geographical details are lacking in both biblical and extrabiblical sources, and thus its location is uncertain.[15] At least three candidates have been suggested, all on the plain of Akko: (1) Tell Keisan, approximately nine kilometers southeast of Akko; (2) Tel Regev (Khirbet el-Harbaj) in the southeastern extremity of the plain of Akko; and (3) Tell an-Nahal (and its harbor at Tell Abu Hawam), at the foot Mount Carmel near the modern-day port of Haifa.[16] LB remains have been found at these three sites and thus the three are suitable candidates from an archaeological perspective. A Phoenician text from the fourth century BC (Pseudo-Scylax §104), however, lists all the coastal cities on the Syro-Phoenician coast from Tripoli to Ashkelon, and because Akshaph is included in the register (no. 14), it must be on the coast as well. Tell Keisan and Tel Regev are too far inland and therefore Akshaph is best identified with Tell an-Nahal/Abu Hawam.[17]

The final city named in Josh 11:1–2 is "Naphoth Dor on the west" (נָפוֹת דּוֹר מִיָּם,

10. Anson F. Rainey, "Toponymic Problems (Cont.)," *TA* 3.2 (1976): 57–69; Rainey, "Toponymic Problems (Cont.)," *TA* 8.2 (1981): 146–51.

11. David A. Dorsey, *The Roads and Highways of Ancient Israel* (Baltimore: Johns Hopkins University Press, 1991), 91–92.

12. Yuval Portugali, "A Field Methodology for Regional Archaeology (The Jezreel Valley Survey, 1981)," *TA* 9.2 (1982): 187.

13. The archaeological expedition is in part sponsored by the Museum of the Bible. The first full-scale season of excavation was in 2017, the second in 2019. A helpful preliminary summary of what we currently know about the site can be found on their website: http://www.telshimronexcavations.com/research-design.

14. See *ANET*, 477.

15. It is mentioned only in Josh 11:1; 12:20; and 19:25.

16. For Tell Keisan, see Garstang, *Joshua-Judges*, 354; Jacques Briend, "Akshaph et Sa Localisation a Tell Keisan," *Revue Biblique* 79 (1972): 239–46. For Tel Regev, see Benjamin Maisler (Mazar), *Palestine at the Time of the Middle Kingdom in Egypt* (Cairo: Institut Français D'Archéologie Orientale, 1946), 48. For Tell an-Nahal, see Jacqueline Balensi, Maria D. Herrera, and Michal Artzy, "Abu Hawam, Tell," *NEAEHL* 3:7–14.

17. Lipiński proposes the name was transferred from Tell an-Nahl to Tell Abu Hawam c. 500 BC (see Edward Lipiński, *Itineraria Phoenicia* [Leuven: Peeters, 2004], 309–14).

Aerial View of Excavations at Dor

naphoth dor miyam). This is the city of Dor (Khirbet el-Burj), just south of Haifa.[18] Although the city's location is certain, it is not clear what the extra word *naphath* (or *naphoth*) means. Some scholars connect it to an Arabic root meaning "to be high" and therefore understand *Naphoth Dor* to mean "the heights of Dor."[19] But since Dor sits on the coast in the Sharon Plain, this does not fit topographically.[20] Another explanation is to associate *naphath* with the Arabic word for "yoke" and understand the phrase to mean something like "the district of Dor."[21] Yet another understanding connects *naphath* to an archaic Greek cognate meaning "wooded country." Since *naphath* occurs only with the city of Dor (see Josh 12:23; 1 Kgs 4:11), the word may be linked to the language of the Sea People, who settled in the area. In Archaic Greek, from which the Sea People's language is derived, the word means "wooded country," and thus might be a semantic equivalent of "Sharon." "Naphath-Dor," therefore, might mean "Dor of the Sharon."[22] Either of the latter two explanations is possible, but in any

18. See Ephraim Stern, "Dor," *NEAEHL* 3:357–69; Stern, "Dor," *NEAEHL* 3:1695–1703.

19. BDB, s.v. "נוף"; compare NASB; NET; CSB ("Slopes of Dor").

20. Jan Simons, *The Geographical and Topographical Texts of the Old Testament* (Leiden: Brill, 1959), 279.

21. *HALOT*, s.v. "נָפָה"; compare KJV ("borders of Dor").

22. Yohanan Aharoni, *The Land of the Bible: A Historical Geography*, trans. Anson F. Rainey, rev. and enl. ed. (Philadelphia: Westminster, 1979), 313.

case, it is clear the reference is to the city of Dor on the coast, south of Akshaph.

Although no other cities are explicitly listed in Josh 11:1–2, the coalition was more extensive than just the five that are mentioned. Joshua 11:2 states the cities in the "northern hill country" also contributed their support to the Canaanite league. These undoubtedly included the important cities of Jokneam, Megiddo, and Taanach. Sitting on the border between the hill country and the Jezreel Valley, these cities guarded the three important passes through the Carmel ridge.

Although Beth Shan is not mentioned in Josh 11 or 12, it most likely joined the syndicate as well since Josh 11:2 states the bloc of forces included cities in the "Arabah south of Kinnereth." This is a reference to the Jordan Rift south of the Sea of Galilee.[23] How far south the line extended is impossible to say for certain, but it is reasonable to assume it stretched at least down to Beth Shan, since the eastern entrance to the Jezreel Valley would have been an important route to defend.

Finally, Josh 11:2 states that the alliance also included kings from the Shephelah. This regional term frequently refers to the lowlands between the hill country of Judah and the coastal plain (e.g., Josh 10:40), but a similar topographical region exists in Galilee as well. These are the low-rolling foothills that extend from the Nazareth ridge in western Galilee all the way up to the coastal plain of Tyre.[24] Cities in this region that may have joined the resistance might have included Akko and Tyre.

In summary, the defensive web of the northern confederation stretched from the Jezreel Valley in the south to Akko, Tyre, and perhaps even Sidon (see 11:8) in the north.[25] Their goal was to secure the north by preventing the Israelites from penetrating into the Jezreel Valley (more on this below). With a large conglomeration of infantry, horses, and chariots following in their wake, the Canaanite generals assembled at the Waters of Maron to crystalize their tactic (Josh 11:5). The location of this meeting has been the subject of much speculation.

THE LOCATION OF THE WATERS OF MARON

Eusebius (c. AD 325) associated Maron with a city called Merrus in northern Samaria and wrote, "[it] is a village twelve miles (19 km) from Sebaste near Dothan" (*Onom.* 669/128:4).[26] His reference is to an Arabic village called Qasr

23. In the Bible, the term Arabah can refer to the entire Jordan Rift from the Sea of Galilee to the Red Sea (Deut 3:17), and the Sea of Galilee is called the Sea of Kinnereth (e.g., Num 34:11), after the city on the northwestern shore of the lake (see Deut 3:17; Josh 19:35).

24. Rainey and Notley, *Sacred Bridge*, 129.

25. The reference to the six nations of Canaan in verse 3 should not be taken too literally. The Jebusites, for example, are always associated with Jebus/Jerusalem (e.g., Josh 15:8, 63; 18:28), and from a geographical perspective it is highly unlikely they were actual participants in the confederation. Since the registers of the nations of Canaan are stylized lists intended to indicate the indigenous peoples of the land, the list here is probably the biblical author's way of saying the coalition was a mixed bag of Canaanite residents from the north. See Benjamin F. Foreman, "The 'Seven Nations' of Canaan," in *Lexham Geographic Commentary on the Pentateuch*, ed. Barry J. Beitzel (Bellingham, WA: Lexham Press, 2023), 796–814.

26. R. Steven Notley and Ze'ev Safrai, *Eusebius, Onomasticon: A Triglott Edition with Notes and Commentary* (Leiden: Brill, 2005), 121.

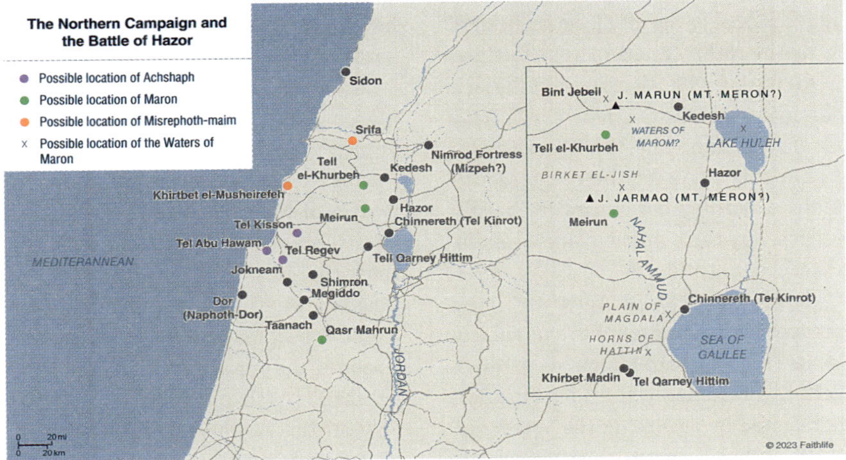

Mahrun, no longer in existence today, in the southeastern corner of the Dothan Valley. Although this site has a toponymic connection and would conform to the military strategy of the league (i.e., to restrict Joshua to the hill country), it is unlikely. First, Eusebius incorrectly identified nearly all the cities listed in Josh 11:1–2 and therefore is unlikely to have had solid information on this location.[27] Second, the extrabiblical references to the site suggest it is further north, in Galilee (see above).

Some scholars believe Maron should be associated with the modern city of Meiron, at the bottom the eastern slope of Jebel Jermuk (Mount Meiron in modern Hebrew).[28] If Maron of Josh 11:1 is located here, the Waters of Maron might be found on the plain two miles (3 km) to the north near Birket el-Jish, where Dalton Lake sits today, near the upper recesses of Nahal Ammud.[29] Another possibility would be to identify the Waters of Maron on the Plain of Magdala. This might be an attractive proposal since the international highway passes through the plain. Also, the large Ammud gorge, which drains the runoff from Mount Meiron into the Sea of Galilee, crosses the Plain of Magdala, and thus there could be a toponymic connection in this region.

Though promising, neither of these suggestions seem plausible since recent excavations at Meiron reveal the city was first settled only in 200 BC.[30] This

27. He located Hazor near Ashdod (*Onom.* 51/20:1), Akshaph near Mount Tabor, (*Onom.* 59/22:3), Mizpah (Josh 11:3) in Judah (*Onom.* 668/128:1), and made no attempt to identify Madon (*Onom.* 667/126:26). He did, however, correctly locate Naphoth Dor at Dor (*Onom.* 376/78:8; 727/136:16).

28. E.g., Robert G. Boling and G. Ernest Wright, *Joshua*, AB (New York: Doubleday, 1982), 307; Woudstra, *Joshua*, 190.

29. Hartmut Rösel, *Joshua* (Leuven: Peeters, 2011), 185.

30. On the slopes below the ruins of the synagogue, Albright claims to have found "numerous characteristics of the Late Bronze," in the spring of 1929, and thus believed this was Meron

site is probably the city Josephus refers to as Ameroth/Mero, which he fortified in AD 66 (*Life* 188; *J.W.* 2.573), but the lack of remains prior to the Hellenistic period means it cannot be the Maron from Joshua's day.[31] As for the name Mount Meiron, Rainey concludes it "hardly reflects any early nomenclature" and is "a modern invention."[32]

From the Middle Ages until the present, commentators have popularly located the Waters of Maron in the Huleh Valley.[33] Presumably, this identification is reached by assuming the Waters of Maron refers to one of the streams that drains Mount Meiron into the Huleh Valley. The name Maron, however, has never been associated with this valley, and since the Meiron in the hills just east of the valley was founded in the Hellenistic period, this identification lacks support.[34] Moreover, Garstang rightly notes that if the confrontation occurred in the Huleh Valley, Joshua would have had to march past Hazor to engage the Canaanite forces and this would have placed the Israelites at a significant disadvantage.[35] Joshua's strategy, rather, was to catch the Canaanites off-guard (Josh 11:7) and this element would have been completely eliminated if the battle occurred in the Huleh Valley.

Nadav Na'aman proposes identifying Maron (Josh 11:1) with Tel Qarney Hittin, approximately one kilometer south-east of Khirbet Madin, and locates the Waters of Maron at Wadi el-Hamam—the stream which flows through the Arbel pass and onto the Plain of Magdala. According to Na'aman, "One would expect Marom/Maron to connect Hazor on the one side, with Shim'on and Achshaph [Akshaph] on the other."[36] The only site that fits this requirement, in his view, is Tel Qarney Hittin. Additionally, Tiglath-Pileser III records in his annals that he took Maron along with several other sites in that area, and Na'aman's experimental dig at the tel revealed LB pottery, meaning it could fit as a site in Joshua's day.[37] He concludes, "The four Canaanite kingdoms of Hazor, Marom, Shim'on and Achshaph [Akshaph], situated along the borders of Galilee, were deliberately used by the writer to demonstrate that it only required a single victory over their league to conquer the whole region."[38] His identification has also won the support of some recent commentators.[39]

---

from Joshua's day (William Foxwell Albright, "New Israelite and Pre-Israelite Sites: The Spring Trip of 1929," *BASOR* 35 [1929]: 8). More recent excavations, however, have not revealed any remains prior to 200 BC. See Eric C. Meyers, "Meiron," *NEAEHL* 3:1024–27.

31. Rainey, *Handbook*, 192.

32. Rainey and Notley, *Sacred Bridge*, 129.

33. Simons, *Geographical*, §505.

34. See Rainey, *Handbook*, 192.

35. Garstang, *Joshua-Judges*, 192.

36. Nadav Na'aman, *Borders and Districts in Biblical Historiography* (Jerusalem: Simor Ltd., 1986), 123.

37. Na'aman, *Borders*, 119–27.

38. Na'aman, *Borders*, 126.

39. E.g., Richard S. Hess, *Joshua*, TOTC (Downers Grove, IL: IVP Academic, 1996), 211; and more recently Hess, "Joshua," *ZIBBCOT* 2:51.

Although Na'aman's theory might initially seem promising, it fails to be convincing for numerous reasons. First, it is unclear why Na'aman believes Josh 11:1 implies Maron is between Hazor, Shim'on, and Akshaph. Nothing in the text implies this. Second, one wonders how Maron fits this requirement even if it did. Kinnereth (Tel Kinrot; Josh 19:35), for example, could just as easily fulfill this condition.[40] Third, Hazor, Tell Qarney Hittin, Shimon, and Akshaph are not really "on the borders of Galilee." Jokneam, Megiddo, and Taanach are further south and outline the true southern border of Galilee. Additionally, Kinnereth would have been a more obvious city for the western border since it is larger than Tell Qarney Hittin and further west. Fourth, even if these cities could be seen in some way to represent Galilee, Na'aman overlooks the fact that Dor is mentioned in the following verse, which is outside of Galilee. Fifth, the lack of a toponymic connection greatly diminishes the likelihood of this suggestion. Finally, the Canaanites' line of retreat toward Sidon, Misrephoth Maim, and Mizpah (Josh 11:8), rather than toward Akko or Hazor, makes any identification south of Akko or Hazor unlikely (see below for more details).

The best location for Maron of Joshua's day is Tell el-Khurbeh in southern Lebanon. Although the site has not yet been excavated, John Garstang found LB and Iron Age pottery there in the late 1920s. The mound was a large Canaanite fortress in Joshua's day, and in his words, "The city which stood upon it [the tell] was without rival in this part of Galilee."[41] The site also has a toponymic connection: the tell sits one and a half miles (2 km) to the southwest of the modern village of Marun er-Ras, and even the tall mountain east of the city was referred to by the locals as Jebel Marun in the 1880s.[42] Finally, Tell el-Khurbeh lies nine miles (15 km) northeast of Hazor and therefore also fits the geographical requirement implied in the text that it is north of Hazor.

If Maron is located at Tell el-Khurbeh, the "Waters of Maron" could either be the perennial spring at the base of the tell or an area somewhere near the wells of the Wadi Farah (Nahal Dishon).[43] The latter seems more likely since a similar phrase, "Waters of Megiddo," appears in Judg 5:19 and is a reference to a river, the Kishon. The "Waters of Maron," therefore, could very well be a reference to the large Dishon gorge that flows down from Tell el-Khurbeh.

The Canaanite forces would not have met in the canyon and thus the phrase is probably used to designate the area nearby. The ground just northeast of Marun er-Ras, where the border between Israel and Lebanon runs today, levels out and is one possibility. This is just a guess, however, and the section of land north of Marun er-Ras near Bint Um el Jebeil is even more open and might be an option as well. According to Garstang, the roads leading into upper Galilee all converge at the bottom of Jebel Marun at Bint Um el Jebeil. In his days (1929) a large market was set up there once a week which attracted crowds from all over Galilee and

40. For a convenient summary of the site, including an extensive bibliography, see http://kinneret-excavations.org/.

41. Garstang, *Joshua-Judges*, 102.

42. Note the reference to Jebel Marun on the Palestinian Exploration Fund map of 1882–88.

43. Rainey, *Handbook*, 193.

southern Lebanon.[44] An area near Maron, therefore, would have been a convenient meeting point for the Canaanite generals to organize their defense.

Some commentators object to locating the Waters of Maron in the mountains of upper Galilee because Josh 11:4 remarks the Canaanites gathered with a large number of horses and chariots.[45] But if Garstang is correct and multiple routes ran through upper Galilee and converged at Maron, this problem is diminished. In any case, Canaanite chariots were sometimes taken apart and hand-carried through rough territory. As Boling and Wright note, "The lightweight chariot, in contrast to the heavier Hittite chariot which also carried a shield-bearer, to make a three-man team, could be disassembled easily and transported for reassembly in suitable terrain."[46] This is illustrated in an Egyptian text which speaks of a warrior climbing a mountain with his chariot "laced with ropes" and resting on his shoulder.[47] Recognition of this helps to explain how, for example, Ahab could ride in a chariot through the mountainous terrain of Ramoth Gilead down to Samaria (1 Kgs 22:34–38), or Sennacherib's boast in 2 Kgs 19:23 (=Isa 37:24): "With many chariots I have ascended the heights of the mountains, the utmost heights of Lebanon" (also Zech 6:1; see also Joel 2:5). The topography of the land of Canaan undoubtedly would have necessitated the frequent hand-transportation of their chariots.

THE LINE OF RETREAT

Geographically, it makes no sense to assume the intention of the Canaanites was to engage the Israelite troops at the Waters of Maron. A battle at this location would have left the entire Jezreel Valley and most of upper Galilee (e.g., Taanach, Megiddo, Jokneam, Akshaph, Shimron/Shimon, and Hazor) exposed and vulnerable to Israelite forces. The purpose of their assembly, rather, was to hammer out the strategy to prevent Joshua from taking the Jezreel Valley or any land further north.[48]

Since the Israelites had retreated to Gilgal after their successes in the south (Josh 10:43), the Canaanites would probably have presumed a confrontation with the Israelites was still a way off.[49] Hoping to exploit the element of surprise, Joshua came "suddenly" (פִּתְאוֹם, *pithom*) upon the Canaanites at the Waters of Marom (Josh 11:7). The tactic worked, and the Canaanites were routed in three directions. One group was pushed thirty-five miles (56 km) north to the region of Sidon.[50] Another band was forced toward Misrephoth Maim. This location is uncertain since it occurs only here (11:8) and in Josh 13:6. Some suggest it was located along the Litani River in upper Galilee, possibly at Srifa—fifteen miles (24 km)

44. Garstang, *Joshua-Judges*, 193–94.

45. E.g., Rösel, *Joshua*, 185.

46. Boling and Wright, *Joshua*, 307.

47. See *ANET*, 477.

48. Compare with Boling and Wright, *Joshua*, 306.

49. Coming up the Jordan Rift, Gilgal is approximately ninety miles (145 km) from Maron.

50. The term "Great Sidon" (צִדוֹן רַבָּה, *tsidon rabbah*) is mentioned only one other time in the Bible (Josh 19:28) and probably refers to the district of Sidon.

north of Maron.[51] Another possibility is Khirbet el-Mesherifeh, due west of Maron on the northern rim of the plain of Akko near Rosh HaNikra.[52] This identification seems more likely since Srifa is on the way to Sidon and would therefore be along the same line of retreat as the company that fled to Sidon. The third faction was driven eastward to the "Valley of Mizpah." The only valley east of Maron is the Huleh Valley (not mentioned by this name in the Bible) and given that Mizpah means "overlook" in Hebrew, the Canaanites presumably took to the higher hills overlooking the Huleh Valley. Since the text does not say they took refuge in Kedesh, the Canaanites were probably forced toward the northern part of the Huleh Valley. Certainty is impossible, but they may have escaped to some of the slopes of Mount Hermon which overlook the Huleh Valley to the east.

In short, Joshua's lightning strike at the Waters of Maron effectively cut off the Canaanites from their fortified cities of Hazor, Kedesh, and those in the Jezreel Valley. Their flight to the west, north, and northeast clearly indicates the Waters of Maron must have been north of Hazor. With the Canaanites splintered into three groups and kept in check a safe distance from their cities, Joshua and his forces were able to turn back (Josh 11:10) and take Hazor, the *pièce de résistance*.

THE DESTRUCTION OF HAZOR

Hazor is one of only three cities explicitly said to have been burned by the Israelites in the conquest.[53] Apparently its incineration made an impression on the biblical author since he mentions it three times in the narrative (Josh 11:11, 13 [2x]). The archaeological stratum dating to Joshua's day, therefore, should reveal evidence of burning.

The topography of Hazor naturally divides the city into two sections: an upper (c. 30 acres) and a lower city (c. 180 acres), both of which were inhabited in the MB and LB. The city reached its zenith in c. 1700 BC (MB) and continued to be a commercial and political powerhouse until its decline at the end of the LB (Joshua's day). Its strategic position in the north along the international highway enabled its kings to maintain close ties with the major powers of the ancient Near East, and numerous references to Hazor in Egyptian and Akkadian documents attest to these connections.[54] After the city's destruction in the thirteenth century, its size and influence diminished significantly. Throughout the Iron Age (i.e., the Israelite period, c. 1200–586 BC), settlement was restricted to the acropolis.

Archaeological exploration of the site began in 1928 under the directorship of John Garstang. He excavated the tell for only three weeks, however, and never fully published his findings. In the 1950s and 60s, Yigael Yadin led the next archaeological expedition to Hazor. Thanks to generous funding from the Rothchild Foundation, he conducted five major seasons of excavation (1955–1958, 1968), each of which involved nearly two hundred people digging for three months

51. Na'aman, *Borders*, 48–50.

52. Garstang, *Joshua-Judges*, 396; Rainey and Notley, *Sacred Bridge*, 129.

53. The other two were Jericho (Josh 6:24), and Ai (8:28).

54. For a summary see Ben-Tor, *Hazor*, 62–77.

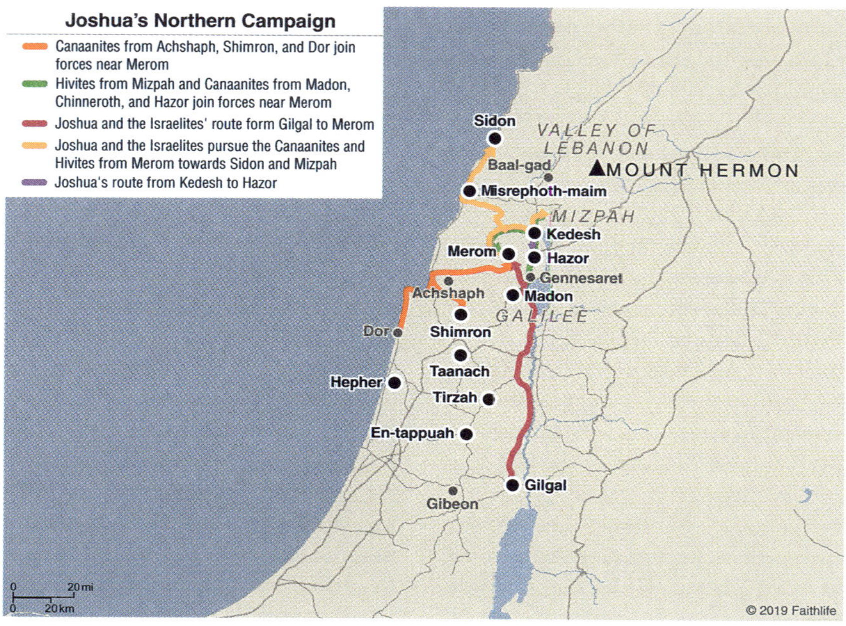

at a time compared to four to six weeks today.[55] Twenty-two years later, Amnon Ben-Tor brought a new archaeological team to the site with the goal of clarifying some of the questions raised by Yadin's team. Ben-Tor and his crew have been digging at Hazor for the past twenty-nine consecutive summers (1990–present) and have overturned some of the conclusions reached by Yadin in the 50s and 60s.

Ninety years of muscle and sweat have exposed many impressive remains at Hazor. The most important question we must address here, however, is when the city was destroyed and how this might relate to the story in Josh 11:10–13. The difficulty with answering this question is Yadin and Ben-Tor seem to have changed their minds on this issue over the years, but do not always clearly say so when they do. Collectively, Yadin and Ben-Tor have referenced at least four destruction levels from the end of the MB to the end of the LB:

(1) Fiery destruction in 1550 BC (end of the MB). In the 1960s, Yadin uncovered a thick layer of ash covering a temple in stratum 3 of the lower city (=stratum XVI of the upper tel) and concluded the entire city was destroyed at the end of the MB (c. 1550 BC). He believed a short interval of time elapsed between the city's destruction in 1550 and its rebuilding in the beginning of the LB age (LB I).[56]

55. These excavations functioned as a school of field archaeology for Yadin's students and produced prominent archaeologists such as Yohanan Aharoni, Claire Epstein, Trude and Moshe Dothan, and Ruth Amiran. See Ben-Tor, *Hazor*, 13–14.

56. Yadin, *Hazor: The Schweich Lectures*, 124–125; Yadin, "The Fifth Season of Excavations at Hazor (1968-1969)," *BA* 32.3 (1969): 55.

(2) Fiery destruction sometime in the fifteenth century (c. 1450 BC, LB I). As Douglas Petrovich notes, Ben-Tor apparently believed he found evidence of a fifteenth century destruction by fire (stratum 2/XV) in his 2000 and 2001 summer excavations.[57] In an internet digest summarizing their discoveries in 2000, Ben-Tor mentioned finding an "accumulation of fallen mud-bricks and ashes" and states "this is the only clear indication found so far for an earlier destruction, still in the Late Bronze Age, pre-dating the final destruction of [the last Canaanite] city."[58] The next year, Ben-Tor noted the following in his internet summary: "This earlier phase [LB I] ended in a conflagration similar to the one that brought an end to the later phase. The ceramic assemblage ... seems to place the date of this ... destruction somewhere in the Late Bronze Age I (fifteenth century BC)."[59]

(3) Destruction in c. 1300 BC (LB II). Yadin believed stratum 1b (=stratum XIV of the upper tel) also ended in a destruction, though he did not say anything about it being burned. He assigned this destruction to Seti I in c. 1300 BC.[60]

(4) Massive conflagration in 1230 BC (LB III). Finally, Yadin and Ben-Tor both found substantial evidence of a massive conflagration in stratum 1A of the lower city and stratum XIII of the upper tel. Based on the ceramics found in this level, Yadin dated this destruction to c. 1230 BC (LB III), and Ben-Tor later found an inscription in this level from the time of Ramesses II, which confirmed this dating.[61]

Which of these destructions should be assigned to the time of Joshua? Since the answer depends on one's view of when the conquest occurred, a variety of proposals have been given. John Bimson, for example, believes the fiery destruction of stratum 3/XVI (#1 above) relates to Joshua's time. But rather than assigning the destruction to 1550 BC, he lowers the date and argues the city of stratum 3/XVI was destroyed around 1400 BC.[62] Petrovich, subscribing to a more traditional early date of the conquest, believes Josh 11:10–15 should be dated to 1406 BC and correlates the destruction of stratum 2/XV (#2) to this event.[63] Yadin, Ben-Tor, and others who advocate a thirteenth century conquest, attribute the massive

57. Douglas Petrovich, "The Dating of Hazor's Destruction in Joshua 11 By Way of Biblical, Archaeological, and Epigraphical Evidence," *JETS* 51.3 (2008): 499–502.

58. Amnon Ben-Tor, "2000 Excavation Report," The Tel Hazor Excavation Project (website), archived February 8, 2001, https://web.archive.org/web/20010208110025/http://unixware.mscc.huji.ac.il/~hatsor/2000.htm.

59. Amnon Ben-Tor, "2001 Excavation Report," The Tel Hazor Excavation Project (website), archived December 3, 2022, https://web.archive.org/web/20221203080318/http://unixware.mscc.huji.ac.il/~hatsor/2001.htm.

60. Yigael Yadin, *Hazor II* (Jerusalem: Magnes Press, 1960), 159.

61. Yigael Yadin, *Hazor: The Rediscovery of a Great Citadel of the Bible* (London: Weidenfeld and Nicholson, 1975), 145; Ben-Tor, *Hazor*, 113–17.

62. See John J. Bimson, *Redating the Exodus and Conquest* (Sheffield: JSOT Press, 1978), 172–87.

63. Petrovich, "Hazor's Destruction," 499–510; Cambria Jones, "Contested Conflagration: Joshua and the Conquest of Hazor," *Bible and Spade* 24.3 (2011): 79–84.

conflagration in stratum 1A/XIII to Joshua (#4).[64] Advocates for both the early and the late date of the conquest, therefore, claim to have found evidence for their view.

Amnon Ben-Tor's more recent conclusions, however, overturn some of Yadin's earlier views, and even conflict with several of Ben-Tor's own previous statements. Regarding Yadin's 1550 BC destruction (#1), Ben-Tor writes: "The renewed excavations established that the transition from the Middle Bronze Age to the Late Bronze Age was a gradual process and not the result of a violent destruction. This conclusion contradicts that reached by Yadin's expedition, which maintained that Hazor was destroyed at the end of the Middle Bronze Age and that this destruction was followed by a brief gap in the site's occupation."[65] Speaking of the supposed destructions in the fifteenth (#2) and fourteenth centuries (#3), Ben-Tor notes he and his team "did not uncover evidence of destruction or of any settlement gap between the Middle and Late Bronze Ages."[66] This contradicts his own reports about his team's findings in 2000 and 2001.[67] Nevertheless, Ben-Tor concludes quite definitively: "The archaeological finds at Hazor clearly indicate that Bronze Age Hazor underwent a single destruction, sometime in the course of the thirteenth century BCE, presumably at the hands of the tribes of Israel that had come to settle the land."[68]

Although this is not the place to fully engage with the debate, Ben-Tor's latest conclusions—if they are correct—place strain on an early dating of the conquest (i.e., fifteenth century) since Josh 11:11–13 repeatedly states the city was burned by fire. In fact, the thirteenth century destruction of the city fits quite nicely with the description in the Bible. Regarding this destruction, Ben-Tor writes: "Hazor in its entirety went up in flames, in a destruction that could perhaps be described as the 'mother of all destructions' because of the intensity of the conflagration: the fire devasted the Ceremonial Palace, melting the bricks in the walls of the hall, as well as some of the ceramic vessels found inside it."[69] Interestingly, many of the hands and heads of the city's statues of their deities were cut off by the destroyers of the city.[70] Advocates of a thirteenth century conquest might see this as clear evidence of the Israelites, who rejecting the worship of the Canaanite gods, thoroughly destroyed their images.

On the other hand, attributing the thirteenth century destruction of the city to the time of Joshua creates another difficulty. According to Ben-Tor, after the

64. E.g., James K. Hoffmeier, "What Is the Biblical Date for the Exodus? A Response to Bryant Wood," *JETS* 50.2 (2007): 243–46.

65. Amnon Ben-Tor, "The Ceremonial Precinct in the Upper City of Hazor," *NEA* 7.2 (2013): 82.

66. Ben-Tor, *Hazor*, 79.

67. In all of Ben-Tor's subsequent internet summaries (2002–2019 seasons) I did not find any reference to the fifteenth century fiery destruction he alluded to in his 2000 and 2001 digests. His opinion must have changed.

68. Ben-Tor, *Hazor*, 126.

69. Ben-Tor, *Hazor*, 113.

70. Ben-Tor, *Hazor*, 115–16.

Late Bronze Palace Mudbricks at Hazor

city was destroyed in 1230, it "remained derelict until it was re-settled in the mid-eleventh century BCE [i.e., c. 1050 BC]."[71] This is a problem for a thirteenth century conquest because Judg 4–5 states that during the period of the judges, which would correspond to Ben-Tor's settlement gap, Hazor was a living city, whose king (Jabin) was killed by Deborah and Barak (Judg 4:24).

How the archaeology of Hazor relates to the conquest of Joshua is an issue that advocates of both the early and the late date of the conquest must deal with. Both views present difficulties. Unfortunately, the conundrum cannot be resolved here. For now, it is best to recognize our knowledge is limited. Archaeology is a dynamic field, views change (even those of the archaeologists!), and it is possible that further excavations will clarify the issue.

CONCLUSION

With the Canaanite league fractured into three companies and "the head of all the kingdoms" engulfed in flames, the Israelite forces were now free to set their sights on the other powers of the north. According to Josh 12:21–22, Joshua's men also smote the kings of Taanach, Megiddo, Kedesh, Jokneam, and Dor. Their initial ascendency, however, was short-lived—as even the book of Joshua attests (see Josh 13:13; 15:63; 16:10; 17:12–13, 16). Although Joshua's militia was able to subjugate the Canaanites to their rule, they were not able to fully occupy the land Yahweh had promised them.[72] In

71. Ben-Tor, *Hazor*, 126, see chart on pp. 19-20.

72. For the important distinction between subjugation and occupation, see Iain Provan, V. Philips Long, and Tremper Longman III, *A Biblical History of Israel* (Louisville: Westminster John Knox, 2003), 166–68.

time, the Canaanites returned to many of the cities in the north (e.g., Taanach, Dor, Megiddo, and Hazor; see Judg 1:27; 4:2), for as the book of Judges indicates, the Lord did not completely drive out the Canaanites from the land because his people had failed to follow him wholeheartedly (Judg 2:2–3, 20–23). This situation nicely illustrates the relationship between divine sovereignty and human responsibility. Although God sovereignly fulfills his promises to his people, his people have always been called to faithful obedience.

BIBLIOGRAPHY

Aharoni, Yohanan. *The Land of the Bible: A Historical Geography*. Translated and edited by Anson F. Rainey. Rev. and enl. ed. Philadelphia: Westminster, 1979.

Albright, William Foxwell. "New Israelite and Pre-Israelite Sites: The Spring Trip of 1929." *BASOR* 35 (1929): 1–13.

Balensi, Jacqueline, Maria D. Herrera, and Michal Artzy. "Abu Hawam, Tell." *NEAEHL* 3:7–14.

Ben-Tor, Amnon. "2000 Excavation Report." *The Tel Hazor Excavation Project* (website). Archived February 8, 2001. https://web.archive.org/web/20010208110025/http://unixware.mscc.huji.ac.il/~hatsor/2000.htm.

———. "2001 Excavation Report." *The Tel Hazor Excavation Project* (website). Archived December 3, 2022. https://web.archive.org/web/20221203080318/http://unixware.mscc.huji.ac.il/~hatsor/2001.htm.

———. "The Ceremonial Precinct in the Upper City of Hazor." *NEA* 7.2 (2013): 81–91.

———. *Hazor: Canaanite Metropolis, Israelite City*. Jerusalem: Israel Exploration Society, 2016.

Bimson, John J. *Redating the Exodus and Conquest*. Sheffield: JSOT Press, 1978.

Boling, Robert G., and G. Ernest Wright. *Joshua*. AB. New York: Doubleday, 1982.

Briend, Jacques. "Akshaph et Sa Localisation a Tell Keisan." *Revue Biblique* 79.2 (1972): 239–46.

Dorsey, David A. *The Roads and Highways of Ancient Israel*. Baltimore: Johns Hopkins University Press, 1991.

Foreman, Benjamin F. "The 'Seven Nations' of Canaan." Pages 796–814 in *Lexham Geographic Commentary on the Pentateuch*. Edited by Barry J. Beitzel. Bellingham, WA: Lexham Press, 2023.

Garstang, John. *Joshua-Judges: Foundations of Bible History*. London: Constable, 1931. Repr., Grand Rapids: Kregel, 1978.

Hess, Richard S. *Joshua*. TOTC. Downers Grove, IL: IVP Academic, 1996.

———. "Joshua." *ZIBBCOT* 2: 2–93.

Hoffmeier, James K. "What Is the Biblical Date for the Exodus? A Response to Bryant Wood." *JETS* 50.2 (2007): 225–48.

Jones, Cambria. "Contested Conflagration: Joshua and the Conquest of Hazor." *Bible and Spade* 24.3 (2011): 79–84.

Lipiński, Edward. *Itineraria Phoenicia*. Leuven: Peeters, 2004.

Maisler (Mazar), Benjamin. *Palestine at the Time of the Middle Kingdom in Egypt*. Cairo: Institut Français D'Archéologie Orientale, 1946.

Meyers, Eric C. "Meiron." *NEAEHL* 3:1024–27.

Na'aman, Nadav. *Borders and Districts in Biblical Historiography*. Jerusalem: Simor Ltd., 1986.

Notley, R. Steven, and Ze'ev Safrai. *Eusebius, Onomasticon: A Triglott Edition with Notes and Commentary*. Leiden: Brill, 2005.

Petrovich, Douglas. "The Dating of Hazor's Destruction in Joshua 11 by Way of Biblical, Archaeological, and Epigraphical Evidence." *JETS* 51.3 (2008): 489–512.

Portugali, Yuval. "A Field Methodology for Regional Archaeology (The Jezreel Valley Survey, 1981)." *TA* 9.2 (1982): 170–88.

Provan, Iain, V. Philips Long, and Tremper Longman III. *A Biblical History of Israel*. Louisville: Westminster John Knox, 2003.

Rainey, Anson F. *Handbook of Historical Geography*. Jerusalem: Institute of Holy Land Studies, 1984.

———. "Toponymic Problems (Cont.)." *TA* 3.2 (1976): 57–69.

———. "Toponymic Problems (Cont.)." *TA* 8.2 (1981): 146–51.

Rainey, Anson F., and R. Steven Notley. *The Sacred Bridge: Carta's Atlas of the Biblical World*. Jerusalem: Carta, 2006.

Rösel, Hartmut. *Joshua*. Historical Commentary on the Old Testament. Leuven: Peeters, 2011.

Simons, Jan. *The Geographical and Topographical Texts of the Old Testament*. Leiden: Brill, 1959.

Soggin, J. Alberto. *Joshua: A Commentary*. OTL. Philadelphia: Westminster, 1972.

Stern, Ephraim. "Dor." *NEAEHL* 1:357–68.

———. "Dor." *NEAEHL* 5:1695–1703.

Woudstra, Marten H. *The Book of Joshua*. NICOT. Grand Rapids: Eerdmans, 1981.

Yadin, Yigael. *Hazor II*. Jerusalem: Magnes Press, 1960.

———. *Hazor: The Rediscovery of a Great Citadel of the Bible*. London: Weidenfeld and Nicholson, 1975.

———. *Hazor: The Schweich Lectures 1970*. London: Oxford University Press, 1972.

———. "The Fifth Season of Excavations at Hazor (1968–1969)." *BA* 32.3 (1969): 50–71.

CHAPTER 8

THE ARCHAEOLOGY AND HISTORICAL GEOGRAPHY OF THE SLAIN KINGS OF JOSHUA 12

Josh 12; Num 21; Josh 5–10

Chris McKinny

KEY POINTS

- A historical and geographical assessment of all the toponyms mentioned in Josh 12 reveals many sites can be identified with some certainty.
- The textual relationship between Josh 12:1–16 and the narratives of Num 21 and Josh 5–10 is analyzed.
- The textual relationship between Josh 12:17–24 and the narrative of Josh 10–11 is analyzed, and a group of towns in central Canaan that are not mentioned in the book of Joshua is discussed.
- The archaeological profile of the towns mentioned in Josh 12 fits well with what is known of Late Bronze Age Canaan.

INTRODUCTION

Not every town in Josh 12 can be conclusively identified with an archaeological ruin, but most sites have been identified with a fair degree of certainty.[1] Despite a few exceptions, most of these identified sites have been either surveyed or excavated. Because of this, the current state of the archaeology of Israel and Jordan allows for a deeper investigation of both

1. Sections of this chapter have been adapted from the author's dissertation and the Joshua volume of the *Photo Companion to the Bible*. See Chris McKinny, "A Historical Geography of The Administrative Division of Judah: The Town Lists of Judah and Benjamin in Joshua 15:21–62 and 18:21–28" (PhD diss., Bar-Ilan University, 2017); Chris McKinny et al., *Photo Companion to the Bible: Joshua* (BiblePlaces, 2019).

the historical geography and archaeological settlement patterns of the town list of the slain kings in Josh 12.[2] This chapter analyzes the historical geography and the archaeology of each of the sites mentioned in Josh 12. Thus, it covers a group of towns unconnected to a conquest narrative in the book of Joshua as well as the towns connected with the northern campaign (Josh 11:1–16) and concludes with my archaeological and historical conclusions on all of the places noted in Josh 12 (see tables 1–2).

The historicity of the Hebrew Bible's account of the Israelite conquest and settlement (i.e., Joshua and Judges) has long been a "flashpoint" debate in biblical and archaeological discussions.[3] Most archaeologists today, as well as many biblical scholars, doubt that the book of Joshua is a reliable historical witness for reconstructing the emergence of Israel in Canaan.[4] The purpose of this chapter is not to rehash or engage in this ongoing conversation, but rather to discuss an issue that is fundamental to many of these reconstructions, namely the archaeology of the "map" of Canaan as presented in the town list of Josh 12.[5]

The fundamental nature of the list to the conquest/settlement discussion is underscored by the fact that every town mentioned in Josh 1–11 (i.e., the main narrative of the Israelite conquest) also occurs in Josh 12:7–24. Therefore, a historical geographical and archaeological analysis of Josh 12 reflects Josh 1–11, although the possibility of different textual traditions between Josh 1–11 and Josh 12 arising from different periods should also be considered. It is also worth noting that most of the towns appear in the subsequent tribal allotments.

Accordingly, a historical, geographical, and archaeological analysis of the towns of Josh 12 should enable us to determine whether the list and the related narrative of Josh 1–11 is reflective of the Late Bronze Age or a later period, such as the Iron Age. As we will see over the course

2. This chapter adopts the following archaeological periodization (only biblical periods included and all dates are approximate): Middle Bronze II (c. 2000–1550 BC), Late Bronze (c. 1550–1200 BC), Late Bronze I (c. 1550–1400 BC), Late Bronze IIA (c. 1400–1300 BC), Late Bronze IIB (c. 1300–1200 BC), Iron I (c. 1200–1000 BC), Early Iron IIA (c. 1000–900 BC), Late Iron IIA (c. 900–800 BC), Iron IIB (c. 800–701 BC), Iron IIC (c. 701–586/539 BC), Persian (c. 539–332 BC), Hellenistic (332–63 BC), and Early Roman (63 BC–AD 70).

3. E.g., William F. Albright, "The Israelite Conquest of Canaan in the Light of Archaeology," *BASOR* 74 (1939): 11–23; Martin Noth, *Das Buch Josua* (Tubingen: Mohr Siebeck, 1953); Yohanan Aharoni, "Nothing Early and Nothing Late: Re-Writing Israel's Conquest," *BA* 39.2 (1976): 55–76; Volkmar Fritz, "Conquest or Settlement? The Early Iron Age in Palestine," *BA* 50.2 (1987): 84–100; Israel Finkelstein, *The Archaeology of the Israelite Settlement* (Jerusalem: Israel Exploration Society, 1988); William G. Dever, *Who Were the Early Israelites, and Where Did They Come From?* (Grand Rapids: Eerdmans, 2003); Koert van Bekkum, *From Conquest to Coexistence: Ideology and Antiquarian Intent in the Historiography of Israel's Settlement in Canaan* (Leiden: Brill, 2011).

4. See Israel Finkelstein and Neil Asher Silberman, *The Bible Unearthed: Archaeology's New Vision of Ancient Israel and the Origin of Its Sacred Texts* (New York: The Free Press, 2001), 72–96; Thomas B. Dozeman, *Joshua 1–12: A New Translation with Introduction and Commentary*, AB (New Haven, CT: Yale University Press, 2015), 15–16; but see Bekkum, *From Conquest to Coexistence*.

5. Yigal Levin, "Conquered and Unconquered: Reality and Historiography in the Geography of Joshua," in *The Book of Joshua*, ed. Edward Noort (Leuven: Peeters, 2012), 361–62.

0 40 mi
0 40 km
VALLEY OF LEBANON
MT. HERMON
HIVITES
MAACATHITES
Kedesh
Maron?
Hazor
GESHURITES
BASHAN
Achshaph
SEA OF CHINNEROTH
Ashtaroth
KINGDOM OF OG (AMOREITES AND REPHAIM)
Shimron
Jokneam
Dor
Megiddo
Taanach
Goiim of Galilee?
Hepher
Edrei
HALF OF GILEAD (NORTHERN)
JORDAN RIVER
Tirzah
Goiim of Gilgal?
JABBOK
Tappuah
Aphek
HALF OF GILEAD (SOUTHERN)
CAANITES & PERIZZITES
AMMONITES
ARABAH
Gezer
Bethel
Ai
Jericho
HIVITES
JEBUSITES
Heshbon
Azekah
Jarmuth
Jerusalem
Adullam
AMORITES
Libnah
Geder
SHEPHELAH
HILL COUNTRY
Lachish
KINGDOM OF SIHON (AMORITES)
Eglon
Makkedah
Hebron
MIDBAR
SEA OF THE ARABAH
HITTITES
ARNON
Debir
MOABITES
NEGEV
Arad
Hormah?
MT. HALAK
SEIR
© 2023 Faithlife
Sites Related to Joshua 12
Town with slain king
Region mentioned
Political entity mentioned
Body of water mentioned

of this chapter, Josh 12 is comprised of Canaanite settlements, most of them significant cities, that were occupied both in the Late Bronze and the Iron II. This contrasts with the town lists of Judah and Benjamin (Josh 15:21–62; 18:21–28), which clearly reflect Iron II realities from the era of the monarchy. While I will not argue for the dating of the composition of the book of Joshua, I will challenge the claim that "the earliest territorial reality echoed in the Bible is that of the late Iron I and early Iron IIA, in the 10th and early 9th centuries BCE."[6]

The fact that virtually all of the towns listed in Josh 12 seem to have been occupied in the Late Bronze Age does not seem to be a coincidence. Among those who hold to any degree the historicity of the Israelite conquest and settlement as reflected in the books of Joshua and Judges, there is a debate about the timing—whether it occurred in the late fifteenth, thirteenth, or twelfth century BC. There is also a related debate about the process of the "conquest"—i.e., whether Israel's emergence involved a widespread series of destructions of Canaanite cities by the Israelites. For the purposes of this chapter, the question of "early" or "late" dates is not essential to my point (I hold to a thirteenth century BC date), as my main contention is that Josh 12 does seem to depict a "map" that is reflective of Late Bronze realities, regardless of when it was composed. In the conclusion of the chapter, once we have compiled all the archaeological data, including various archaeological strata and related destruction levels, we will briefly address the related questions of dating and settlement process.

The text of Josh 12 presents several textual critical and historical problems, most notably with regards to the different readings in the Hebrew Masoretic Text (MT) and the Greek Septuagint (LXX) versions. However, from an interpretive standpoint, the meaning and purpose of the text is straightforward. Joshua 12 serves as a summarized conclusion of the events of Num 21 (see also Deut 2:26–3:22) and Josh 1–11 by presenting a list of thirty-three kings, and their associated towns, that were defeated by Moses and Joshua during the conquest of Amorite and Canaanite territories in the Transjordan and Cisjordan.[7] In essence, this section is meant to detail how "Joshua took the whole land according to all that Lord had spoken to Moses" (Josh 11:23).[8]

In what follows, I discuss the archaeology of each town in the list with a special emphasis on the Late Bronze and early Iron Age remains at each site. When the identification of the town is in question, I discuss the proposed identification(s) for these towns. As commentators have often noted, the towns seem to be grouped according to their occurrence in the biblical narrative.[9]

---

6. Israel Finkelstein, "What the Biblical Authors Knew about Canaan before and in the Early Days of the Hebrew Kingdoms," *UF* 48 (2017): 192.

7. E.g., Dozeman, *Joshua 1–12*, 482–500. The second half of the book of Joshua (13–24) largely consists of the land allotments of the tribes (Josh 13–21).

8. Unless noted otherwise, all biblical quotations are from the English Standard Version (ESV).

9. See Robert G. Boling, *Joshua: A New Translation with Notes and Commentary*, AB (New York: Doubleday, 1982), 322; Dozeman, *Joshua 1–12*, 482; Richard Hess, "Joshua," *ZIBBCOT* 2:2–93.

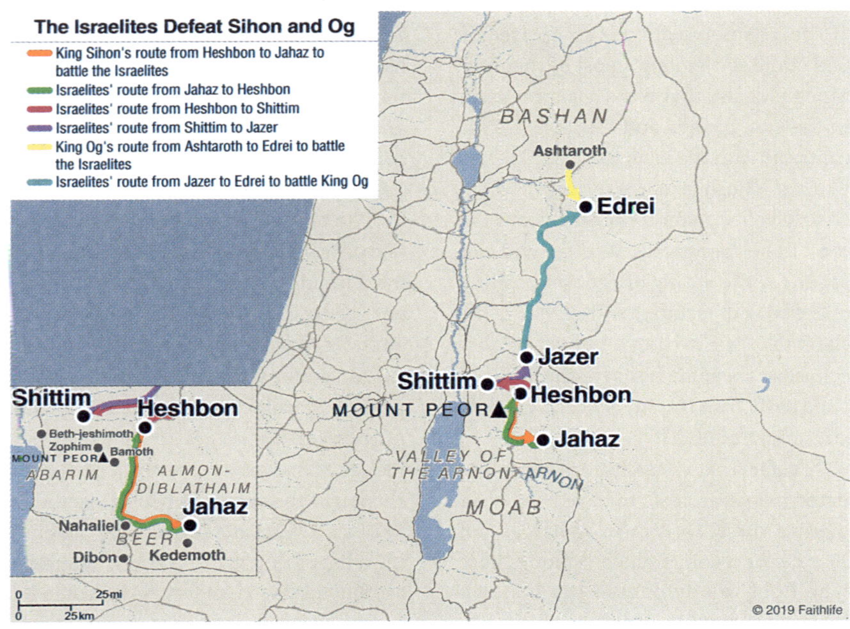

THE DEFEAT OF THE AMORITE KINGDOMS OF SIHON AND OG (JOSH 12:2–5; NUM 21:21–35)

Moses' defeat of Sihon and Og is one of the most repeated events in the Hebrew Bible (e.g., Num 32:33; Deut 1:4; 29:7; 31:4; Josh 2:10; 9:10; 1 Kgs 4:19; Neh 9:22; Ps 135:11). According to the text, the territory of Sihon and Og included the entire western portion of the Transjordan, including upper and lower Gilead, the Medeba plateau, and all of Bashan, including the Golan Heights and parts of southwestern Syria. Specifically, the towns of Heshbon (Hesban, but see below), Ashtaroth (Tell Ashtarah), and Edrei (Dera) are mentioned as the main towns of Sihon and Og that were defeated by Moses (e.g., Deut 1:4; Josh 12:2–5; 13:12, 31). Each of the towns have been identified with a suitable ruin, and each ruin has been archaeologically investigated to varying degrees.[10]

10. Besides the cities ruled by Sihon (Heshbon) and Og (Ashtaroth and Edrei), Josh 12:1–6 includes the following regional terms and toponyms: the Valley of Arnon (Wadi Mujib), Mount Hermon (Jebel esh-Sheikh), Arabah (the Jordan Valley from the Sea of Galilee to the Dead Sea and probably also from the Dead Sea to the Red Sea, as the term is used in modern times), Aroer (Arair), Jabbok River (Nahr ez-Zerqa or Wadi Zerqa), Gilead (the region north of the Jabbok River unto Bashan), Sea of Kinneroth (Sea of Galilee), Beth Jeshimoth (Tell el-Azeimeh), the Sea of the Arabah/the Salt Sea (the Dead Sea), Pisgah (Ras es-Siyagha), Bashan (the Syrian tableland including the Golan Heights), Salecah (Salkhad), and the Geshurites and Maakathites (Aramean groups apparently centralized in the Huleh Valley around et-Tell [north] and Abel Beth Maakah respectively). For a detailed discussion, see Chris McKinny, "The Historical Geography of the Settlements of the Transjordanian Tribes of Reuben, Gad, and Manasseh," in *Lexham Geographic Commentary on the Pentateuch*, ed. Barry J. Beitzel (Bellingham, WA: Lexham Press, 2023), 660–704.

A. Heshbon: The Kingdom of Sihon (Josh 12:2–3)

The ancient name of Heshbon is preserved in the name Hesban,[11] where excavations revealed remains from the twelfth century BC until modern times, including strata from the Iron I, Iron IIA, Iron IIB, Iron IIC, Persian, and the Late Hellenistic-Byzantine periods.[12] Despite the large size of the tell and the nearly continuous occupational history, the site of Hesban has no Bronze Age remains and fragmentary Iron Age remains until the seventh and sixth centuries BC.[13] On account of this, some scholars have suggested that the term "Heshbon" during the time of Moses was a regional term and the main city was actually located at Tell Jalul (6 mi., 10 km south of Hesban). This remains a distinct possibility, and it seems possible that the ancient name of Tell Jalul (Jeljul) was actually "Gilgal," which might reflect a tradition of the Israelite conquest of the site.[14] While Middle and Late Bronze remains are clearly present at Tell Jalul, the excavators have yet to reach these occupational layers to determine their character.[15]

B–C. Ashtaroth and Edrei: The Kingdom of Og (Josh 12:4–5)

Tell Ashtarah and Dera were very briefly surveyed by William F. Albright, who found that both sites were inhabited from the Early Bronze Age until the Iron II, Dera also possessing remains from the Persian-Byzantine periods.[16] Both towns also appear in Egyptian New Kingdom inscriptions and in a text found in the Canaanite city of Ugarit (KTU 1.108).[17] The topographic features of Tell Ashtarah indicate a maximum size of eighty-five dunams (21 acres).[18] Dera is more difficult to access using topographic satellite measurements as it remains populated.

The Conquest of Jericho and Ai (Josh 12:9; see also Josh 5–8)

Joshua 12:9–24 is obviously related to the conquest of the Transjordan by Moses (Josh 12:2–5), but it is also distinct in that

11. Lawrence T. Geraty, "Heshbon," *NEAEHL* 2:626–30.

12. E.g., Geraty, "Heshbon"; Paul J. Ray Jr., *Tell Hesban and Vicinity in the Iron Age* (Berrien Springs, MI: Andrews University Press, 2001); James A. Sauer, Larry G. Herr, and Paul J. Ray Jr., eds., *Ceramic Finds: Typological and Technological Studies of the Pottery Remains from Tell Hesban and Vicinity* (Berrien Springs, MI: Andrews University Press, 2012).

13. Geraty, "Heshbon," 626–30.

14. McKinny, "Transjordanian Tribes."

15. Randall W. Younker, Constance C. Gane, and Reem Al-Shqour, "The Madaba Plains Project: Excavations at Tall Jalul," in *The Madaba Plains Project: Forty Years of Archaeological Research into Jordan's Past*, ed. Douglas R. Clark et al. (London: Routledge, 2011), 66.

16. William F. Albright, "Bronze Age Mounds of Northern Palestine and the Hauran: The Spring Trip of the School in Jerusalem," *BASOR* 19 (1925): 15–16.

17. Shmuel Ahituv, *Canaanite Toponyms in Ancient Egyptian Documents* (Jerusalem: Magnes Press, Hebrew University, 1984), 72–73, 90–91.

18. A dunam is equivalent to about a quarter acre (1,000 m^2). Thus, a ten dunam site would be about two and a half acres (10,000 m^2) or one hectare. For reference, the city of David is roughly ten acres in size, which equals four hectares or forty dunams.

the two conquests are separated by a geographical description (Josh 12:7–8) and accumulated with a different accounting system.[19] The total of either twenty-nine (LXX) or thirty-one (MT) slain kings in Josh 12:24 seems to consist only of the kings killed by Joshua, as these totals match the number of kings in Josh 12:9–24 in both textual traditions (see table 1).[20] The territorial power of Hazor has been made evident through excavations, and it certainly qualified the city, along with its vassal cities, the prestige of modern usage of the term "kingdom" (Josh 11:10) and "king" (Jabin in Josh 11:1). However, the term "king" (Hebrew: מֶלֶךְ, *melek*; Greek: *βασιλεα*, *basilea*) can simply be understood as the main ruler of a city, irrespective of the relative power of the city or ruler over other regions.[21] The Amarna correspondence of the mid-fourteenth century BC are a set of nearly three hundred letters written in Akkadian cuneiform to Pharaoh Akhenaten in Tell el-Amarna (i.e., the city of Akhetaten) from the rulers of cities and kingdoms to the north of Egypt. A large number of these texts come from the warring Canaanite city-states, which were led by powerful chieftains (e.g., Labayu of Shechem). These represent a very clear parallel to the prevailing geopolitical system that existed in Canaan during the Late Bronze and early Iron Age (see table 2).

1. Jericho (Josh 12:9; see also Josh 6)

Jericho (Tell es-Sultan) and Ai (et-Tell?) are the most controversial towns in the list due to the presumed lack of correlation between the conquest narratives of Josh 6–8 and the archaeological remains for either a fifteenth or thirteenth century BC conquest. The numerous excavations at Tell es-Sultan (Warren, Sellin and Watzinger, Garstang, Kenyon, and Nigro) and et-Tell (Garstang, Marquise-Krause, and Callaway) did not reveal significant Late Bronze remains.[22] This has led some scholars—led most prominently by Bryant Wood—to offer alternative suggestions regarding the identification of Ai (see below), as well as suggest a later date of destruction of Jericho "City C" to

---

19. Baal Gad in the Valley of Lebanon (Baal Gad's location is uncertain, but it must have been located in the Beqa Valley or its southern extension, the Ijon Plain, between the Lebanese and Anti-Lebanese ranges, which seems to be identical with the "Valley of Lebanon"), Mount Halak (Jebel Halaq—just north of Nahal Zin/Wadi el-Murra), Seir (the southern Transjordan mountains and southeastern Negev highlands), hill country (the northern and southern mountains of the land of Israel), the Shephelah (low lying hills between the western coast and the Judean hill country—known as the Judean Shephelah), the Arabah (the Jordan Valley north and south of the Dead Sea), the slopes (probably the southwestern zone of the southern hill country of Judah north of the Negev), the wilderness (Judean wilderness located between the Dead Sea and the Judean hill country), and the Negev (southern desert region).

20. The LXX version is missing Bethel and does not include the two scribal errors in the MT. The actual number of towns present in Josh 12:9–24 seems to be thirty. See table 1 at the end of this chapter. For a reconstruction of the list, see Anson F. Rainey and R. Steven Notley, *The Sacred Bridge: Carta's Atlas of the Biblical World* (Jerusalem: Carta, 2006), 129.

21. *HALOT*, s.v. "מֶלֶךְ."

22. See Robert A. Mullins, "The Emergence of Israel in Retrospect," in *Israel's Exodus in Transdisciplinary Perspective: Text, Archaeology, Culture, and Geoscience*, ed. Thomas E. Levy, Thomas Schneider, and William H. C. Propp (New York: Springer, 2015), 218–19.

fit an "early date" (i.e., c. 1400 BC) of the conquest.[23] Despite Wood's argument, the final Bronze Age destruction of Tell es-Sultan (City C) should clearly be dated to the end of the Middle Bronze (c. 1550 BC) as opposed to c. 1400 BC. Radiocarbon dates place the destruction "during the late seventeenth or the sixteenth century BC," fitting Kathleen Kenyon's initial suggestion of c. 1550 BC.[24] While there is some evidence of Late Bronze remains in tombs, occupation on the mound was present only in a few places on the mound itself, including John Garstang's "Middle Building" which dates to the fourteenth and thirteenth centuries BC.[25] Despite all this, Kenyon's assessment is worth looking at as she is often derided by early date proponents for rejecting the biblical account.[26] Kenyon wrote the following (emphasis added):

> Of the defenses of the period (Late Bronze), nothing at all survives. The double wall ascribed to the Late Bronze Age in the 1930–1936 excavations is composed in part of two successive walls from the Early Bronze Age. For most of the circuit, only stumps survive. Even of these walls and of the Middle Bronze Age glacis that buried them, only the part on the slopes of the mound was intact. At the highest preserved point of the mound, the northwest corner, the glacis was intact, but of the wall that crowned it, only the bare foundations were still in position. There is not the slightest trace of any later wall. Jericho, therefore, was destroyed in the Late Bronze Age II. *It is very possible that this destruction is truly remembered in the Book of Joshua, although archaeology cannot provide the proof. The subsequent break in occupation that is proved by archaeology is, however, in accord with the biblical story. There was a period of abandonment, during which erosion removed most of the remains of the Late Bronze Age town and much of the earlier ones.* Rainwater gulleys that cut deeply into the underlying levels have been found.[27]

Regarding Kenyon's note about the lack of a post-Middle Bronze II fortification wall, a preliminary report from the new excavations at Jericho indicates that the destroyed Middle Bronze fortifi-

23. Bryant G. Wood, "Did the Israelites Conquer Jericho? A New Look at the Archaeological Evidence," *BAR* 16.2 (1990): 44–59; Wood, "The Rise and Fall of the 13th-Century Exodus-Conquest Theory," *JETS* 48.3 (2005): 475–89; see also Thomas A. Holland and Ehud Netzer, "Jericho (Place)," *ABD* 3:723–37.

24. Hendrik J. Bruins and Johannes Van Der Plight, "Tell Es-Sultan (Jericho): Radiocarbon Results of Short-Lived Cereal and Multiyear Charcoal Samples from the End of the Middle Bronze Age," *Radiocarbon* 37.2 (1995): 213–20. In addition, new excavations by Nigro support this date as well, see below.

25. Piotr Bienkowski, *Jericho in the Late Bronze Age* (Oxford: Aris & Phillips, 1986), 71, 90, 102; Kathleen M. Kenyon and Thomas A. Holland, *Excavations at Jericho: The Architecture and Stratigraphy of the Tell* (Jerusalem: British School of Archaeology in Jerusalem, 1981), 3:371.

26. See Wood, "Conquer Jericho?," 44–59.

27. Kathleen M. Kenyon, "Jericho: Tell Es-Sultan," *NEAEHL* 2:680. See also analysis by Kenneth A. Kitchen, *On the Reliability of the Old Testament* (Grand Rapids: Eerdmans, 2003), 187–88.

Jericho (Tell es-Sultan) Mudbrick Wall

cations were reused from the Late Bronze Age through the Iron II. A portion of a mudbrick wall dates to the Late Bronze IIB (i.e., thirteenth century BC). This is significant. If these fortifications can be related to Garstang's "Middle Building," whose destruction was dated to the end of the thirteenth century BC, it would provide evidence of a fortification and destruction level that would date to the timeframe of the thirteenth century, or the late date view.[28] It is also worth noting that the chronological problem between the biblical text and the archaeology of Jericho does not end with Joshua. The Bible mentions Jericho in numerous Iron IIA–B contexts (2 Sam 10:5; 1 Kgs 16:34; 2 Kgs 2:4–5, 15, 18; 1 Chr 19:5; 2 Chr 28:15), but the remains are sparse until Iron IIC/seventh century BC (see 2 Kgs 25:5; Jer 39:5; 52:8).[29] The Persian period (Ezra 2:34; Neh 3:2; 7:36) was likewise scantly represented

28. See Lorenzo Nigro, "Tell Es-Sultan 2015: A Pilot Project for Archaeology in Palestine," *NEA* 79.1 (2016): 4–17; Nigro, "The Italian-Palestinian Expedition to Tell Es-Sultan, Ancient Jericho (1997–2015): Archaeology and Valorisation of Material and Immaterial Heritage," in *Digging Up Jericho: Past, Present and Future*, ed. Rachael Thyrza Sparks et al. (Oxford: Archaeopress, 2020), 198–206; John Garstang, *The Story of Jericho* (London: Hodder & Stoughton, 1940), 147–48. It is worth noting that Nigro does not regard Josh 6–8 as historical, but, nevertheless, his own work supplements that of Kenyon's and clearly demonstrates that Jericho was occupied and likely fortified in the thirteenth century BC and suffered abandonment following the thirteenth century BC.

29. Manfred and Helga Weippert have shown that Jericho was continuously inhabited, albeit somewhat insignificantly, from the eleventh to the early sixth century BC (Manfred Weippert and Helga Weippert, "Jericho in Der Eisenzeit," *ZDPV* 92.2 [1976]: 105–48). For a

at Tell es-Sultan.[30] In particular, these later disconnects could be related primarily to erosion, as argued both by Kenyon and Lorenzo Nigro (the current excavator).

2. AI (JOSH 12:9; SEE ALSO JOSH 7:2–5; 8:1–29)

Ai (et-Tell) is best-known as the second city that Joshua conquered (Josh 7–8). However, the town is also mentioned as "Ayyah" in a geographical description of the region of Ephraim (1 Chr 7:28), and as "Aiath" in connection with the route of the Neo-Assyrian army as it passed through Benjamin in the late eighth century BC (Isa 10:28). Finally, the site is mentioned in association with the postexilic returnees to Bethel and Ai (Ezra 2:28; Neh 7:32), which underscores the connection between Bethel and Ai (see Gen 12:8; 13:3). The absence of Late Bronze Age remains at et-Tell was taken to be conclusive evidence of the lack of historicity of the biblical account of Josh 7–8. However, et-Tell also did not produce remains from the Iron II and Persian periods, which are the other two periods associated with Ai.[31] Garstang noted Late Bronze remains at the site.[32] Recent excavations along the ridge north of et-Tell and Khirbet el-Maqatir have revealed several Middle Bronze and perhaps also Late Bronze structures, as well as extensive sherds from the Iron II period.[33] Beyond the possible toponymic connection between et-Tell and Ai, the large amount of geographic detail in the Joshua narrative strongly suggests that et-Tell and its immediate vicinity are the location of Ai.[34] The Iron II and Persian site of Ai is difficult to determine. Khirbet Haiyan is a small site approximately 0.62 miles (1 km) south of et-Tell in the village of Deir Dibwan. Iron II occupation was noted at Deir Dibwan and Khirbet Haiyan.[35]

---

discussion of Israelite Jericho and the Iron Age remains, see John R. Bartlett, *Jericho* (Guildford, UK: Lutterworth Press, 1982), 99–114.

30. E.g., Holland and Netzer, "Jericho," 736.

31. For the scholarly consensus of the etiological origins of the conquest narrative of Josh 7–8, see Callaway's discussion in Joseph A. Callaway, "Ai," *ABD* 1:128–130. For an alternative to this view, that sees nearby Khirbet el-Maqatir as the Late Bronze (and Iron I) site, see Bryant G. Wood, "Excavations at Kh. El-Maqatir 1995–2000, 2009–2013: A Border Fortress in the Highlands of Canaan and a Proposed New Location for the Ai of Joshua 7–8," *Bible and Interpretation* (2014) 1–16.

32. John Garstang, *Joshua, Judges: Foundations of Bible History* (London: Palestine Exploration Fund, 1931; repr. Grand Rapids: Kregel, 1978), 149–61; see also Joseph A. Callaway, "Ai," *NEAEHL* 1:39.

33. Personal communication from Kramer, who has excavated on the ridge just north of et-Tell. Personal communication from Tavger, who has excavated the hill known as "E.P. 914" just north of Khirbet el-Maqatir and east of Beitin. See earlier discussion in Aharon Tavger, "E.P. 914 East of Beitin and the Location of the Ancient Cult Site of Bethel," *In the Highland's Depth: Ephraim Range and Binyamin Research Study* 5 (2015): 49–69 [Hebrew with English Abstract (pp. 34*–35*)].

34. Wood's excavation of Khirbet el-Maqatir demonstrates that at least part of the region's population shifted from et-Tell in the Middle Bronze II–Late Bronze (I?) to a site one kilometer to the west (Wood, "Excavations at Kh. El-Maqatir," 1–16).

35. This appears to be the site that Eusebius notes was three milestones east of Bethel, which he wrongly identifies with the Aijalon Valley (*Onom.* 48/18:13). The *Onomasticon* (*Onom.*)

THE FIVE-KING COALITION: JERUSALEM, HEBRON, JARMUTH, LACHISH, AND EGLON (JOSH 12:10–12A)

3. JERUSALEM: KING ADONI-ZEDEK (JOSH 12:10; SEE ALSO JOSH 10:1–3, 23)

The archaeology of Bronze and Iron Age Jerusalem remains elusive, but it seems likely that early Jerusalem was located around the Gihon Spring on the southern end of the eastern hill, also known as the city of David.[36] Jerusalem appears as a major player in the Amarna correspondence of the fourteenth century BC,[37] and fragments of two cuneiform tablets from the city of David might also relate to this period.[38] Joshua 11, reflected in Josh 12:10, does not indicate that Jerusalem was destroyed by Joshua. Other texts indicate that the Jebusites persisted to live in Jerusalem (Josh 15:63; Judg 1:21), but also that Judah defeated a king known as "Adoni-Bezek" and burned Jerusalem with fire (Judg 1:7–8). To date, the scant Late Bronze remains of the city of David do not allow us to determine whether destruction brought an end to Late Bronze Jerusalem.

4. HEBRON: KING HOHAM (JOSH 12:3; SEE ALSO JOSH 10:3, 5, 23, 36; 11:21; JUDG 1:10)

Hammond abandoned his excavations at Hebron (Tell er-Rumeide) following the outbreak of the Six Day War in 1967.[39] While the significance of Late Bronze Hebron has often been minimized, recent treatments by Chadwick, who is publishing Hammond's excavations, show that Late Bronze Hebron was a significant city of twenty-eight to thirty-three dunams (seven to eight acres) that was occupied during the entire period.[40] The

---

is a list of biblical place names prepared by Eusebius who provided contemporary identification during the early fourth century AD; it was later translated by Jerome. All quotations of Onom. are from R. Steven Notley and Ze'ev Safrai, Eusebius, Onomasticon: A Triglott Edition with Notes and Commentary (Leiden: Brill, 2005). Eusebius states that the site was near Geba (Jeba) and Ramah (er-Ram). Jerome adds a note about the correct biblical Aijalon, which he locates two miles east of Emmaus (Imwas).

36. Contra Israel Finkelstein, Ido Koch, and Oded Lipschits, "The Mound on the Mount: A Possible Solution to the Problem with Jerusalem," *Journal of Hebrew Scriptures* 11 (2011): art. 12, pp. 1–24, https://doi.org/10.5508/jhs.2011.v11.a12.

37. See William L. Moran, *The Amarna Letters* (Baltimore: Johns Hopkins University Press, 1992).

38. Perhaps contemporary with the letters of Abdi-Heba. Eilat Mazar et al., "A Cuneiform Tablet from the Ophel in Jerusalem," *IEJ* 60.1 (2010): 4–21; apparently "Ramesside" in date, see Eilat Mazar et al., "Jerusalem 2: A Fragment of a Cuneiform Tablet from the Ophel Excavations," *IEJ* 64.2 (2014): 129–39. For further illumination on Late Bronze Jerusalem, see Joel Uziel, Yuval Baruch, and Nahshon Szanton, "Jerusalem in the Late Bronze Age: The Glass Half Full," in *The Late Bronze and Early Iron Ages of Southern Canaan*, ed. Aren M. Maeir, Itzhaq Shai, and Chris McKinny (Berlin: de Gruyter, 2019), 171–84; see also Johanna Regev et al., "Absolute Dating of the Gihon Spring Fortifications, Jerusalem," *Radiocarbon* 59.4 (2017): 1171–93.

39. See Jeffrey R. Chadwick, "The Archaeology of Biblical Hebron in the Bronze and Iron Ages: An Examination of the Discoveries of the American Expedition to Hebron" (PhD diss., University of Utah, 1992); Avi Ofer, "Hebron," *NEAEHL* 1:606–9; Emmanuel Eisenberg and David Ben-Shlomo, *The Tel Ḥevron 2014 Excavations: Final Report* (Ariel: Ariel University Press, 2017).

40. For the importance of Late Bronze Hebron, see Nadav Na'aman, *Canaan in the Second Millennium B.C.E.* (Winona Lake, IN: Eisenbrauns, 2005), 77–78; David Ussishkin, "Was

Canaanite Walls at Hebron, Aerial View from the South

site was also destroyed at some point in the thirteenth century BC, which might be a reflection of Josh 10:36 or perhaps one of the other traditions connected with defeats of Hebron (Josh 11:21; Judg 1:10, 20).[41] It is also worth noting that, to date, the only three sites in the southern hill country that revealed extensive Late Bronze Age remains were Hebron (Tell er-Rumeide), Debir (Rabud, see below), and Anab (Khirbet Anab el-Kabir)[42]—the three towns from which Joshua "cut off the Anakim" (Josh 11:21; see also Judg 1:10, 20). Some scholars conclude that the name "Hebron" also appears alongside the towns of Janum, Drbn (Debir?), and Aphekah (see Josh 15:52–54) in a topographical list by Ramesses II that was likely copied by Ramesses III on the walls of the Egyptian mortuary temple of Medinet Habu.[43]

Jerusalem a Fortified Stronghold in the Middle Bronze Age? — An Alternative View," *Levant* 48.2 (2016): 135–51. For Hammond's excavations, see Jeffrey R. Chadwick, "Hebron in Early Bronze Age III and Middle Bronze Age II: Fortification Walls in Area I.3 of the American Expedition to Hebron (Tell Er-Rumeide)," in *Tell It in Gath: Studies in the History and Archaeology of Israel: Essays in Honor of Aren M. Maeir on the Occasion of His Sixtieth Birthday*, ed. Itzhaq Shai et al. (Münster: Zaphon, 2018), 167–86; Chadwick, "Hebron in the Late Bronze Age: Discoveries of the of the American Expedition to Hebron (Tell Er-Rumeide)," in *The Late Bronze and Early Iron Ages of Southern Canaan*, ed. Aren M. Maeir, Itzhaq Shai, and Chris McKinny (Berlin: de Gruyter, 2019), 185–216.

41. Chadwick, "Hebron in the Late Bronze Age," 203, fig. 10.12.

42. Moshe Kochavi, "The Land of Judah," in *Judaea, Samaria and the Golan: Archaeological Survey 1967–1968*, ed. Moshe Kochavi (Jerusalem: Archaeological Survey of Israel and Carta, 1972), site 234, 235; Avi Ofer, "The Highland of Judah during the Biblical Period" (PhD diss., Tel Aviv, Tel Aviv University, 1993), site 21, 22, 25, T1, T2, T3; Yoab Peleg and Ibrahim Shruch, "Rujum el-Qaṣr," *Hadashot Arkheologiyot: Excavations and Surveys in Israel / חדשות ארכיאולוגיות: חפירות וסקרים בישראל* 112 (January 1, 2000): 109*; Yitzak Magen, Yoab Peleg, and Ibrahim Sruh, "The Church at 'Anab el-Kebir," *Qadmoniot* 125 (2003): 47–54.

43. Charles R. Krahmalkov, "Exodus Itinerary Confirmed by Egyptian Evidence," *BAR* 20 (1994): 54–62, 79; Peter James, "The Levantine War-Records of Ramesses III: Changing Attitudes, Past, Present and Future," *Antiguo Oriente* 15 (2017): 110–12.

5. JARMUTH: KING PIRAM (JOSH 12:11; SEE ALSO JOSH 10:3, 5, 23)

Except for Jerusalem (see Judg 1:8), Jarmuth is the only city from the five-king coalition that was not subsequently conquered in Josh 10. Jarmuth has been conclusively identified with Khirbet el-Yarmuk based on the similarity between the names, the geographical location (see Josh 15:35; Neh 11:29), and the details from *Onomasticon* that place the site "ten miles from Eleutheropolis" (*Onom.* 540/106:24).[44] Miroschedji's excavations revealed an extensive Early Bronze Age urban settlement with an acropolis and a lower city.[45] Late Bronze and later settlements were relegated to the acropolis (24 dunams; 6 acres).[46] It is worth noting that the excavators only uncovered remains from the Late Bronze IIB (Acr-6). The Iron I acropolis city was well-established (Acr-5-3) and destroyed with fire.[47]

6. LACHISH: KING JAPHIA (JOSH 12:11; SEE ALSO JOSH 10:3, 5, 23, 31–35)

Lachish (Tell ed-Duweir) was one of the largest Late Bronze settlements in the Shephelah, occupied throughout the entire Late Bronze sequence (Lachish VII) including the continuation of the Canaanite city into the twelfth century BC (Lachish VI, sometimes referred to as Late Bronze III).[48] Both the Late Bronze IIB/thirteenth century BC city (Lachish VII) and the mid-twelfth century BC city (Lachish VI) were destroyed by fire.[49] Besides the well-known earlier excavations led by Starkey, Aharoni, and Ussishkin, the recently concluded "Fourth Expedition" led by Garfinkel, Hasel, and Klingbeil exposed extensive Late Bronze remains, including a temple near the ancient well.[50] The ongoing excavations led by Höflmayer and Streit in Ussishkin's Areas S and P have also exposed Late Bronze and earlier levels.[51]

---

44. On the *Onomasticon*, see note 35 above. On Jarmuth, see Victor Guérin, *Description Géographique, Historique et Archéologique de la Palestine*, 3 vols. (Paris: Impériale, 1869); Pierre de Miroschedji, "Jarmuth," *ABD* 3:645–46; Miroschedji, "Jarmuth, Tel," *NEAEHL* 5:1792–97.

45. Pierre de Miroschedji, "Yarmuth: The Dawn of City-States in Southern Canaan," *NEA* 62.1 (1999): 2–19; and see recently Omer Shalev and Amir Golani, "Tel Yarmut," *Hadashot Arkheologiot* 130 (2018), http://www.hadashot-esi.org.il/report_detail_eng.aspx?id=25508&mag_id=126.

46. de Miroschedji, "Jarmuth, Tel," 1797; Yehuda Dagan, *The Ramat Bet Shemesh Regional Project: The Gazetteer* (Jerusalem: Israel Antiquities Authority, 2010), site 189.1; Dagan, *The Ramat Bet Shemesh Regional Project: Landscapes of Settlement: From the Paleolithic to the Ottoman Periods* (Jerusalem: Israel Antiquities Authority, 2011), 256–58.

47. de Miroschedji, "Jarmuth, Tel," 1797.

48. On the identification of Tell ed-Duweir with Lachish, see William F. Albright, "The American Excavations at Tell Beit Mirsim," *ZAW* 47 (1929): 3. For the Late Bronze city, see David Ussishkin, "A Synopsis of the Stratigraphical, Chronological and Historical Issues," in *The Renewed Archaeological Excavations at Lachish (1973–1994)*, ed. David Ussishkin (Tel Aviv: Tel Aviv University, 2004), 1:57–76.

49. Ussishkin, "Synopsis," 57, Table 3.3.

50. Benjamin Sass et al., "The Lachish Jar Sherd: An Early Alphabetic Inscription Discovered in 2014," *BASOR* 374 (2015): 233–45; Yosef Garfinkel et al., "First Impression on the Urban Layout of the Last Canaanite City of Lachish: A View from the Northeast Corner of the Site," in *The Late Bronze and Early Iron Ages of Southern Canaan*, ed. Aren M. Maeir, Itzhaq Shai, and Chris McKinny (Berlin: de Gruyter, 2019), 122–35.

51. Katharina Streit et al., "Between Destruction and Diplomacy in Canaan: The Austrian-Israeli Expedition to Tel Lachish," *NEA* 81.4 (2018): 259–68.

7. EGLON: KING DEBIR (JOSH 12:12; SEE ALSO JOSH 10:3, 5, 23, 34–37)

The town of Eglon is mentioned only in the book of Joshua. Besides references to its participation in the five-king coalition (Josh 10:3, 5, 23, 34–37; 12:12), it also appears as a Judahite town of the Zenan district (Josh 15:39), presumably near Lachish. During the battles recorded in Josh 10, Joshua attacked Eglon after defeating Libnah, Lachish, and Horam king of Gezer who came to the aid of Lachish (Josh 10:31–37).

Eglon has previously been identified with Tell el-Hesi based on a similarity between the biblical name and Khirbet Ajlan, which is located just north of Tell el-Hesi, and Eusebius's mention of a place called Agla "at the tenth mile on the descent from Eleutheropolis to Gaza" (*Onom.* 221/48:18) in connection with Beth Hoglah of Josh 15:6.[52] However, the connection between biblical Eglon and Khirbet Ajlan has been largely abandoned.[53] Rainey, following the logic of Elliger, argued that Eglon must be located between Lachish and Hebron due to the itinerary described in Josh 10:34–36.[54] In light of this, he identified Eglon with Tell Aitun, which is situated between Lachish and Hebron. Faust, the current excavator of Tell Aitun, has tentatively followed Rainey's identification of Tell Aitun with Eglon.[55] It should be noted that in making this identification, Rainey rejected the idea that Tell Aitun reflects biblical Etam of the second Simeonite district (1 Chr 4:3; see also Josh 19:7), which is the more likely identification due to the correspondence of the names and the geographical position.[56]

Rainey's logic on the identification of Eglon is flawed on two points. First, Khirbet Ajlan is situated exactly ten Roman miles from Eleutheropolis on the way to Gaza and, thus, matches the site of Agla mentioned by Eusebius (*Onom.* 221/48:18), even if he conflated Eglon with Adullam in a different entry (*Onom.* 414/84:22; see also 77/24:21). Therefore, if Eusebius provides an earlier mention of the name Agla in the fourth century AD, it makes no difference that "at the time of the first conquest by the Arabs (i.e., mid-7th century AD), 'Amr ibn al-'Aṣ ... had at

52. William F. Albright, "Researches of the School in Western Judaea," *BASOR* 15 (1924): 7–8; Yohanan Aharoni, *The Land of the Bible: A Historical Geography*, trans. Anson F. Rainey, rev. and enl. (Philadelphia: Westminster, 1979), 353. A Roman mile (4,860 ft. or 1,481 m) is 0.92 of an English mile.

53. Anson F. Rainey, "The Biblical Shephelah of Judah," *BASOR* 251 (1983): 9–10. Contra Rainey, James W. Hardin, Christopher A. Rollston, and Jeffery A. Blakely, "Biblical Geography in Southwestern Judah," *NEA* 75.1 (2012): 20–22.

54. Following the logic of Karl Elliger, "Josua in Judäa," *Paliistinajahrbuch* 30 (1934): 66–68. Rainey rejected Elliger's proposal for identifying Eglon with Tell Beit-Mirsim as he believed that it was "too far to the south," see Elliger, "Josua," 66–67; Rainey and Notley, *Sacred Bridge*, 128.

55. Avraham Faust, "The Excavations at Tel 'Eton (2006–2009): A Preliminary Report," *PEQ* 143.3 (2011): 198–224.

56. Aharoni, *Land of the Bible*, 353–54; Aharoni and Michael Avi-Yonah, *The Carta Bible Atlas*, trans. Anson F. Rainey, 3rd ed. (Jerusalem: Carta, 2002), map 130.

Beit Jibrîn a domain, called 'Ajlân, after one of his freedmen."[57] Second, while there is obviously a logical geographical sequencing to the "southern campaign" of Josh 10:28–39 (i.e., Makkedah to Libnah to Lachish to Gezer offering aid of Lachish to Eglon to Hebron to Debir), there is no reason to conclude that Eglon must be located between Lachish and Hebron.[58] Leaving aside historical questions concerning the passage, it is clear that close proximity or a logical route is not the only rationale for the itinerary.[59] Otherwise, why did they not go to Lachish before going to Libnah, since Lachish is between Makkedah and Libnah? Therefore, it is entirely possible to interpret Eglon as being west of Lachish, as opposed to east. Accordingly, past suggestions to connect biblical Eglon with Khirbet Ajlan should be reconsidered.[60] In fact, according to Sayce, it seems that Tell el-Hesi itself may have even been known as Tell Ajlan.[61] While it cannot be stated with certainty, it seems that Eglon should be associated with Tell el-Hesi.

The Late Bronze layers at Tell el-Hesi were first excavated by Petrie and then Bliss, and, thus are difficult to determine with certainty.[62] According to the later assessment of the Joint Expedition, Tell el-Hesi's Late Bronze occupation can be broken down into the following: City II dated to the LB I; City III associated with the LB IIA, which yielded the only known Amarna tablet to be found in Canaan and was burned with a massive conflagration; and City IV related to the fourteenth and perhaps thirteenth centuries BC, after which the site was abandoned until the Iron Age.[63] The Joint Expedition found abundant ceramic evidence for the Late

57. Given the wide variety of spellings and corrupted toponyms, the difference between Ajlan and the presumed Ajlun is not unexpected (contra Jeffery A. Blakely and Fred L. Horton, "On Site Identifications Old and New: The Example of Tell El-Hesi," *NEA* 64.1/2 [2001]: 32; Rainey and Notley, *Sacred Bridge*, 128). Moreover, it is possible that Ajlun/Eglon/Agla became Ajlan during the seventh century AD on account of Amr ibn al-As. It is impossible to know, however, if the existence of Agla in the fourth century AD indicates the antiquity of the toponym. Le Strange quotes Yaqut II.19, written in the mid-thirteenth century AD (Guy Le Strange, *Palestine under the Moslems. A Description of Syria and the Holy Land from A.D. 650 to 1500* [London: Palestine Exploration Fund, 1890], 413,). Blakely and Horton indicate that Yaqut may have been quoting an earlier ninth century AD writer named Baladhurri (Blakely and Horton, "Site Identifications," 32; see also Rainey and Notley, *Sacred Bridge*, 128). For a discussion of Ajlan in the later periods, see Jeffery A. Blakely, "Ajlan: Locating the Estate of Amr b. al-As," *NEA* 73.4 (2010): 210–22.

58. Contra Rainey and Notley, *Sacred Bridge*, 128.

59. See recent discussion in Dozeman, *Joshua 1–12*, 424–58.

60. See Blakely and Horton, "Site Identifications," 26, 30 for a summary of these suggestions.

61. Archibald H. Sayce, "Excavations in Judaea," *The Contemporary Review* 58 (1890): 427; Blakely and Horton, "Site Identifications," 25–26.

62. William M. F. Petrie, *Tell El Hesy (Lachish)* (London: Palestine Exploration Fund, 1891); Frederick J. Bliss, *A Mound of Many Cities; or Tell El Hesy Excavated*, 2nd ed. (London: The Committee of the Palestine Exploration Fund, 1898); Valerie M. Fargo, "Hesi, Tell El-," *NEAEHL* 2:631–32.

63. Fargo, "Hesi, Tell El-" 631; see also Ralph W. Doermann and Valerie M. Fargo, "Tell El-Hesi, 1983," *PEQ* 117.1 (1985): 1–24; see also studies in Bruce T. Dahlberg and Kevin G. O'Connell, eds., *Tell El-Hesi: The Site and the Expedition* (Winona Lake, IN: Eisenbrauns, 1989).

Bronze in their excavations of the acropolis and lower city.[64]

THE ALLIES OF THE FIVE-KING COALITION AND THE NEGEV CAMPAIGN: GEZER, DEBIR, GEDER, HORMAH, ARAD, LIBNAH, ADULLAM, AND MAKKEDAH (JOSH 12:12B–16A)

The "southern campaign" continues the battle against the five Amorite kings and their allies— Gezer, Debir, Libnah, and Makkedah. The slain kings' list includes these towns but in a slightly different order, probably due to the fact that the tradition connected with the defeat of the cities of Hormah and Arad are also listed (Josh 12:14; Judg 1:16–17; Num 21:1–3; 33:40; see tables 1–2). In addition, the sites of Geder and Adullam are included even though they do not appear in the narrative of Josh 10. It is worth noting that the LXX does not include the return to Gilgal (MT Josh 10:15) following the pursuit to Azekah, which seems to make more logical geographical sense.

8. GEZER: KING HORAM (JOSH 12:12; SEE ALSO JOSH 10:33)

Gezer is universally identified with Tell Jazar, which preserves the name and has substantial remains from the Late Bronze, including the recent discovery of a thirteenth century BC destruction which seems to fit with the attack of Merenptah, king of Egypt.[65] Late Bronze Gezer was one of the main city-states in southern Canaan as reflected in numerous Egyptian texts.[66]

9. DEBIR (JOSH 12:13; SEE ALSO JOSH 10:38–39; 11:21)

The city plays a prominent role in the southern campaign of Joshua (10:38–39; 11:21–23; 12:13), the traditions associated with Caleb's settlement (Josh 15:13–19; Judg 1:11–15), and as a Levitical city (Josh 21:15; 1 Chr 6:58). Like Hebron (Kiriath Arba), Debir had an earlier name (Kiriath Sepher), which seems to be corrupted in Josh 15:49 (MT) to Kiriath Sannah. Following a host of earlier suggestions, Galling identified Debir with Khirbet

---

In this stratum, a proto-Canaanite inscription was also found (Fargo, "Hesi, Tell El-," 631). Given the rudimentary methodology of Petrie and Bliss's excavations, the question of whether or not Tell el-Hesi was inhabited during the thirteenth and twelfth centuries BC should remain open. An eleventh century BC layer was uncovered by Doermann and Fargo, "Tell El-Hesi, 1983," 8–9.

For the Amarna letter, see Wayne Horowitz, Takayoshi Oshima, and Seth L. Sanders, *Cuneiform in Canaan: Cuneiform Sources from the Land of Israel in Ancient Times* (Jerusalem: Israel Exploration Society; Hebrew University of Jerusalem, 2006), 91–94.

64. Fargo, "Hesi, Tell El-," 631–32.

65. For the original identification, see Charles Clermont-Ganneau, "Discovery of the Royal Canaanite City of Gezer by M. Clermont-Ganneau," *PEQ* 5.2 (1873): 78–80. For the most recent treatment of the archaeology of the site, see Steven Ortiz and Samuel Wolff, "Guarding the Border to Jerusalem: The Iron Age City of Gezer," *NEA* 75.1 (2012): 4–19; Steven Ortiz and Samuel Wolff, *Tel Gezer Excavations 2006–2015: The Transformation of a Border City*, ed. Oded Lipschitz and Aren M. Maeir (Winona Lake, IN: Eisenbrauns, 2017); Steven Ortiz and Samuel Wolff, "A Reevaluation of Gezer in the Late Bronze Age in Light of Renewed Excavations and Recent Scholarship," in *The Late Bronze and Early Iron Ages of Southern Canaan*, ed. Aren M. Maeir, Itzhaq Shai, and Chris McKinny (Berlin: de Gruyter, 2019), 62–85.

66. Ahituv, *Canaanite Toponyms*, 101–2.

Rabud.[67] Since Kochavi's excavation at Khirbet Rabud, it has been shown that the site matches all the criteria in the biblical text associated with the city of Debir/Kiriath Sepher.[68]

Kochavi's short excavation at the end of the 1960s revealed a mound of sixty dunams (15 acres) with two springs, Bir Alaqa el-Foqani and Bir Alaqa et-Tahta, about two miles (3 km) north of the site.[69] These springs closely match the description of the site in the Caleb traditions (Josh 15:13–19; Judg 1:11–15). Kochavi's expedition and subsequent surveys in the vicinity found remains from the Early Bronze, Middle Bronze, and Late Bronze Ages at the site and in tombs surrounding the site.[70] During the Late Bronze Age, Khirbet Rabud was the only major Canaanite city in the hill country south of Hebron. This fourteenth century BC town was fortified and seems to have had far reaching trade connections as evidenced by a rich assemblage of ceramic imports from Cyprus and Mycenae. The site also shows continuity from the Late Bronze Age into the Iron I, as noted by the occupation of Iron I debris directly on top of the Late Bronze IIB debris.[71]

10. GEDER (JOSH 12:13)

Geder is more commonly spelled as Gedor (Josh 15:58; 1 Chr 4:4, 18), but also as Beth Gader (1 Chr 2:51).[72] Geder/Gedor has been preserved at Khirbet Jedur, which revealed continuous occupation from the Middle Bronze II until the Ottoman period.[73] The tell has never been excavated, but work carried out at a Late Bronze Age tomb revealed a very rich deposit that included imported wares from Cyprus and the Aegean, a sickle sword, and many other interesting finds.[74] Besides confirming the site's occupation during the biblical era (Late Bronze through Persian periods), surveys also noted a fortification wall surrounding the site.[75]

11–12. HORMAH AND ARAD (JOSH 12:14; SEE ALSO JUDG 1:16–17)

It is unclear if Joshua's conquest of Hormah and Arad (Josh 12:14) should be

67. Most notably Albright identified the site with Tell Beit Mirsim in William F. Albright, "The Excavation of Tell Beit Mirsim. Vol. II: The Bronze Age," *AASOR* 17 (1936): 5. Noth preferred an identification with Khirbet Terrama (Noth, *Joshua*, 90–91). For Galling's view, see Kurt Galling, "Studien Aus Dem Deutschen Evangelischen Institut Für Altertumswissenschaft in Jerusalem. 50. Zur Lokalisierung von Debir," *ZDPV* 70.2 (1954): 135–41.

68. Moshe Kochavi, "Khirbet Rabud= Debir," *TA* 1.1 (1974): 2–33; Kochavi, "Rabud, Khirbet," *NEAEHL* 4:1252; Aharoni, *Land of the Bible*, 214–15; Gary A. Herion, Dale W. Manor, and Jeffery K. Lott, "Debir (Place)," *ABD* 2:111–12.

69. Kochavi, "Rabud, Khirbet," 1252.

70. Kochavi, "The Land of Judah," site 215, 223; Ofer, "Highland of Judah," site T6–12, 15–17, 20, 64–65, 78.

71. Kochavi, "Rabud, Khirbet," 1252.

72. Gedor of 1 Chr 4:39 is probably a scribal error for Gerar. Gedor of 1 Chr 8:31; 9:37; 12:7 is probably related to Khirbet Jedireh northeast of Gibeon.

73. Boling, *Joshua*, 390; Aharoni, *Land of the Bible*, 355; Kochavi, "Land of Judah," site 60; Ofer, "Highland of Judah," site 270.

74. Vronwy Hankey, "The Aegean Pottery of Khirbet Judur," *Eretz-Israel* 15 (1981): 33*–38*; S. Ben-Arieh, "Tel Gedor," *NEAEHL* 2:468.

75. Kochavi, "Judah," site 60; Ofer, "Highland of Judah," site 270, T27.

Aerial Showing the Locations of Geder and Adullam

considered distinct from the encounter with the "Canaanite king of Arad" by Moses (Num 21:1–3) or the subsequent Judahite and Simeonite conquest of Hormah (Judg 1:17). While there remains uncertainty, I propose the following reconstruction. First, the Israelites encountered the city of Hormah during their ill-advised and unsuccessful attack on the southern hills (Num 14:45; Deut 1:44). Second, Moses defeated the "Canaanite king of Arad" and chased them until "Hormah" while traveling from Mount Hor on the "way of Atharim" to the border of Moab (Num 21:1–6). Third, the tribes of Judah and Simeon conquered and destroyed the city of Zephath, which they renamed Hormah (Judg 1:17). It seems possible that the latter two events are simply listed in Josh 12:14 to include all the areas related to the conquest, although one cannot completely discount multiple conquests of the same region.

Hormah may plausibly be connected with Tel Masos (Khirbet Meshash).[76] Arad is undoubtedly located at Tell Arad, but the site has an occupational gap from the mid-third millennium BC through the eleventh century BC.[77] The lack of Late Bronze or early Iron I remains at

76. For further discussion on Hormah and Arad, see Mark D. Janzen and Chris McKinny, "An Overview of the Historical Geography of the Exodus and the Wilderness Itinerary," in *Lexham Geographic Commentary on the Pentateuch*, ed. Barry J. Beitzel (Bellingham, WA: Lexham Press, 2023), 705–39.

77. See especially Ze'ev Herzog, "The Date of the Temple at Arad," in *Studies in the Archaeology of the Iron Age in Israel and Jordan*, ed. Amihai Mazar (Sheffield: Sheffield Academic, 2001), 156–78; Herzog, "The Fortress Mound at Tel Arad an Interim Report," *TA* 29.1

Tell Arad has led many scholars to assert that the biblical tradition of Arad's conquest is an etiological tale ascribed to a legendary hero by later writers. This hypothesis is based on the idea that the later writers, perhaps the occupants of the Judahite fortress during the Iron Age, believed that Moses conquered the once great city of Arad, marked by the visible monumental Early Bronze Age architecture on the surface.[78] However, it is possible that the king of Arad was simply a local chieftain patrolling the Negev who sought to defend a section of his territory against a newcomer (i.e., Moses and the Israelites).[79] Recent studies in the Arabah—especially on the Edomite copper industry at Timna and the Feinan region—have demonstrated that scholars have an architectural bias when it comes to reconstructing historical and political power. These excavations have revealed a highly developed polity (i.e., Edom) with residents likely living in tents, which are archaeologically untraceable.[80]

13. Libnah (Josh 12:15; see also Josh 10:29–32, 39)

In the narrative of Josh 10, Libnah occurs between Makkedah and Lachish (Josh 10:29–32), but in the list of slain kings, Libnah appears after several towns that are not mentioned in Josh 10. Following Elliger's suggestion, the best candidate for Libnah is Tell Bornat, as it matches the geographical setting, the chronological background, and the description of Eusebius (*Onom.* 630/120:23).[81] I have demonstrated elsewhere that Tel Burna's oldest known Arabic name was Tell Bulnab, which could preserve a corrupted form of the ancient name of Libnah.[82] Excavations have revealed a significant thirteenth century BC settlement with some fragmentary evidence of fourteenth century BC occupation as well, but no evidence of Late Bronze I.[83] While

(2002): 3–109; compare with Ruth Amiran, *Early Arad: The Chalcolitic Settlement and Early Bronze City*, vol. 2 (Jerusalem: Israel Exploration Society, 1978).

78. E.g., Aharoni, "Nothing," 59; Doron Ben-Ami, "The Iron Age I at Tel Hazor in Light of the Renewed Excavations," *IEJ* 51.2 (2001): 169.

79. E.g., Rainey and Notley, *Sacred Bridge*, 121.

80. Erez Ben-Yosef, "The Architectural Bias in Current Biblical Archaeology," *VT* 69.3 (2019): 361–87; Erez Ben-Yosef et al., "Ancient Technology and Punctuated Change: Detecting the Emergence of the Edomite Kingdom in the Southern Levant," *Public Library of Science ONE* 14.9 (2019): e0221967, https://doi.org/10.1371/journal.pone.0221967.

81. Elliger, "Josua," 58–63; see also Albright, "Researches," 9; Aharoni, *Land of the Bible*, 439; Anson F. Rainey, "The Administrative Division of the Shephelah," *TA* 7.3–4 (1980): 198.

82. Chris McKinny and Aharon Tavger, "From Lebonah to Libnah: Historical Geographical Details from the PEF and Other Early Secondary Sources on the Toponymy of Two Homonymous Sites," in *Exploring the Holy Land: 150 Years of the Palestine Exploration Fund*, ed. David Gurevich and Anat Kidron (London: Equinox, 2018), 107–22; see also Chris McKinny and Amit Dagan, "The Explorations of Tel Burna," *PEQ* 145.4 (2013): 294–305.

83. Itzhaq Shai, Chris McKinny, and Joel Uziel, "Late Bronze Age Cultic Activity in Ancient Canaan: A View from Tel Burna," *BASOR* 374 (2015): 115–33; Chris McKinny, Aharon Tavger, and Itzhaq Shai, "Tel Burna in the Late Bronze: Assessing the 13th Century BCE Landscape of the Shephelah," in *The Late Bronze and Early Iron Ages of Southern Canaan*, ed. Aren M. Maeir, Itzhaq Shai, and Chris McKinny (Berlin: de Gruyter, 2019), 148–70; for a discussion of the Iron Age settlement see Itzhaq Shai, "Tel Burna: A Judahite Fortified Town in the

there is no evidence of a destruction by fire, it seems that the site was abandoned at some point in the thirteenth century BC. The cause of this abandonment may be related to an attack on the site, as a number of vessels were found in situ.

14. Adullam (Josh 12:15) and Azekah (Josh 10:10)

Adullam is not mentioned in the narrative of Josh 10 of the MT, but it does mention Azekah in connection with the Amorite retreat (Josh 10:10–11) that eventually led to Makkedah (Josh 10:10; 16–17).[84] Both Adullam (Khirbet Tell Sheikh Madhkur, preserved in id el-Ma) and Azekah (Khirbet Tell Zakariya) have been identified with certainty within the Elah Valley. Eusebius located Adullam "about ten miles to the east of Eleutheropolis" (*Onom.* 77/24:21; see also 945/172:6), and Azekah between Eleutheropolis and Jerusalem (*Onom.* 47/18:10). While Adullam has only been surveyed, it was clearly occupied during the Late Bronze Age.[85] The ongoing excavations at Azekah have revealed a very significant Middle Bronze and Late Bronze city that was occupied until the mid-twelfth century BC, when a fiery destruction brought an end to the Canaanite city.[86]

15. Makkedah (Josh 12:15; see also Josh 10:10, 16, 21, 28–29)

Makkedah appears in two contexts within the book of Joshua: the southern campaign (Josh 10:10, 16, 21, 28–29; 12:15) and in the Zenan District of the Judahite town list (Josh 15:41). Eusebius stated that the site was "eight miles east of Eleutheropolis" (*Onom.* 666/126:22). On account of this, Makkedah has been sought at Khirbet Beit Maqdum south of Idna in the chalk trough, due to the similarity between the names and the correct mileage from Eleutheropolis.[87] Dorsey's proposal to identify nearby Khirbet el-Qom with Makkedah in connection with its close proximity to Khirbet Beit Maqdum (c. 0.62 mi., 1 km northeast of

---

Shephelah," in *The Shephelah During the Iron Age: Recent Archaeological Studies*, ed. Oded Lipschitz and Aren M. Maeir (Winona Lake, IN: Eisenbrauns, 2017), 45–60.

84. Codex Vaticanus of Josh 10:3, 5, 23, 33 has Adullam instead of Eglon (A. Graeme Auld, *Joshua Jesus, Son of Nauē, in Codex Vaticanus*, Septuagint Commentary Series [Leiden: Brill, 2005], 36).

85. Yehuda Dagan, "The Settlement in the Judean Shephelah in the Second and First Millennium BC: A Test Case of Settlement Processes in a Geographical Region" (PhD diss., Tel Aviv, Tel Aviv University, 2000), site 169.

86. Sabine Kleiman, Yuval Gadot, and Oded Lipschits, "A Snapshot of the Destruction Layer of Tell Zakariye/Azekah Seen against the Backdrop of the Final Days of the Late Bronze Age," *ZDPV* 132.2 (2016): 105–33; Oded Lipschits, Yuval Gadot, and Manfred Oeming, "Four Seasons of Excavations at Tel Azekah: The Expected and (Especially) Unexpected Results," in *The Shephelah During the Iron Age: Recent Archaeological Studies*, ed. Oded Lipschitz and Aren M. Maeir (Winona Lake, IN: Eisenbrauns, 2017), 27–44; Sabine Kleiman et al., "Late Bronze Age Azekah: an Almost Forgotten Story," in *The Late Bronze and Early Iron Ages of Southern Canaan*, ed. Aren M. Maeir, Itzhaq Shai, and Chris McKinny (Berlin: de Gruyter, 2019), 37–61.

87. E.g., Elliger, "Josua"; Martin Noth, *Aufsätze Zur Biblischen Landes-Und Altertumskunde: Archäologische, Exegetische Und Topographische Untersuchungen Zur Geschichte Israels*, 2 vols. (Neukirchener Verlag, 1971); contra Yehuda Dagan, *Map of Amazya*, 2 vols. (Jerusalem: Israel Antiquities Authority, 2006), 26* who suggests that Makkedah should be located at Tell Beit Mirsim.

Khirbet el-Qom) has received widespread acceptance.[88] This identification received additional support on account of several occurrences of "MNQDA" (Mankedah, the biblical form seems to have lost the N) on fourth century BC Aramaic ostraca, which were most likely illicitly excavated from Khirbet el-Qom.[89] Despite this, the absence of any Late Bronze remains is a problem for the identification with Makkedah.

Khirbet el-Qom was excavated in two brief seasons: in 1967 by Dever and again in 1971 by Holladay, Strange, and Geraty. Both Holladay and Dever noted the existence of Iron IIA pottery including "a good collection of ninth century BC pottery, including red slipped, hand-burnished and Cypro-Phoenician ('Ashdod') wares."[90] Holladay's excavations revealed a late tenth/early ninth century strongly fortified site with the foundations of a gate dating to the Iron IIA.[91] These finds, as well as abundant remains from the Iron IIB–C and Hellenistic through Byzantine periods,[92] accord well with an identification for Makkedah. On the other hand, Khirbet el-Qom is not the largest Iron Age site in the vicinity of Khirbet Beit Maqdum. That designation goes to Khirbet er-Ras, which is located 1 mile (2 km) to the north of Khirbet Beit Maqdum on the western edge of the Arab town of Idna.

In the area around Idna, there appears to have been significant settlement activity in the Iron II period. Besides Idna, Khirbet er-Ras is the largest site in the vicinity. It appears to have been a large fortified tell of approximately fifty dunams (12 acres) with remains dating to the Early Bronze II–III, Middle Bronze IIA–B, Late Bronze, Iron I–II, and Persian through Byzantine periods.[93] With regards to Makkedah, since every Shephelah town that is mentioned in the narrative of Josh 10 has Late Bronze remains (i.e., Azekah, Jarmuth, Lachish, Eglon [Tell el-Hesi?], Gezer, Libnah, and Adullam; see also Josh 12:11–15) it seems more suitable to identify Makkedah with a site possessing Late Bronze remains. In any case, all the evidence in favor of identifying Khirbet el-Qom with Makkedah also applies to Khirbet er-Ras since they are near one another.

CONCLUSIONS ON JOSH 12:1–16

To this point, this chapter has examined the archaeological and historical-geographical background of Josh 12:1–16. This section of the slain kings' list includes many towns that are well-known to biblical scholars and archaeologists. The Transjordanian conquest of Heshbon (of Sihon) and Ashtaroth and Edrei (of Og) is consistent with the narrative of

88. David A. Dorsey, "The Location of Biblical Makkedah," *TA* 7.3–4 (1980): 185–93; e.g., Rainey, "Administrative Division," 194–202; Yigal Levin, ed., *A Time of Change: Judah and Its Neighbours in the Persian and Early Hellenistic Periods* (London: T&T Clark, 2007).

89. E.g., Rainey and Notley, *Sacred Bridge*, 127; see various studies in Levin, *Time of Change*; but see Dagan, *Map of Amazya*, 28* who suggests that these did not originate from Khirbet el-Qom; but this seems unlikely because several ostraca dating to the same periods were found in Holladay et al.'s excavations (William G. Dever, "Qom, Khirbet El," *NEAEHL* 4:1233–54).

90. John S. Holladay, "Kom, Khirbet El-," *ABD* 4:98; Dever, "Qom, Khirbet El," 1234.

91. Dever, "Qom, Khirbet El," 1234.

92. Dagan, *Map of Amazya*, site 398.

93. Dagan, *Map of Amazya*, site 210.

Num 21:21–35. Hesban remains problematic as it was only very sparsely settled at the end of the Late Bronze and the beginning of the Iron Age. Thus, two resolutions can be offered to solve the problem of Heshbon of Sihon. First, Heshbon may be understood as a regional term that was later localized at Hesban with the large site of Tell Jalul representing the main settlement of Sihon in the Late Bronze Age. Second, as recently argued by Ben-Yosef in light of the remains of early Edom in the Arabah and Transjordan, it is possible that politically and economically advanced polities in the southern Levant did not leave traces in the archaeological record on account of the fact that they lived in tents.[94] This same logic also could apply to the seemingly semi-nomadic entity known as "the Canaanite king of Arad" encountered by Moses (Num 21:1–4) and the nearby settlement of Hormah (Josh 12:14; see also Judg 1:16–17).

The archaeology of Late Bronze Jericho (Tell es-Sultan) and Ai (probably et-Tell or Deir Dibwan) remain problematic, but there is some evidence that both sites were occupied during the Late Bronze Age, perhaps in the thirteenth century BC. With regards to the southern campaign of Josh 10, almost all of the sites have been identified with a fair degree of certainty, and all of them (including my new suggestions) have remains from Late Bronze IIB (thirteenth century BC). New excavations or new analyses of past excavations at Jerusalem, Hebron, Lachish, Gezer, and Libnah over the last decade have shed light on the Late Bronze settlement at these sites. I support the traditional identification of Eglon with Tell el-Hesi in light of the toponymic connection with Ajlun and the mileage given by Eusebius. Instead of Khirbet el-Qom, I suggest an alternative identification for Canaanite Makkedah at the nearby ruin Khirbet er-Ras, which was a larger site occupied during the Late Bronze and Iron II.

CENTRAL HILL COUNTRY CITIES NOT CONNECTED TO THE CAMPAIGN NARRATIVES (JOSH 12:16–18): BETHEL, TAPPUAH, HEPHER, AND APHEK OF SHARON

16. BETHEL (JOSH 12:16; COMPARE WITH JOSH 8:17;[95] JUDG 1:22–25)

Bethel is located at Beitin.[96] Excavations at Beitin revealed remains from the Chalcolithic through Byzantine periods, including remains from Late Bronze through Iron II.[97] According to the excavators, Beitin was not reoccupied until the fourteenth century BC following the destruction of the Middle Bronze II

94. Ben-Yosef, "Architectural Bias."

95. According to Josh 8:12, Bethel also participated in the battle of Ai.

96. Robinson was the first to suggest identifying Beitin with Bethel due to the similarity of the name and its close association with et-Tell (Edward Robinson and Eli Smith, *Biblical Researches in Palestine, Mount Sinai and Arabia Petraea: A Journal of Travels in the Year 1838* [Boston: Crocker & Brewster; London: John Murray, 1841], 2:126–129). For an alternative theory to the traditional identification see Livingston's arguments to identify Bethel with el-Bireh (David P. Livingston, "The Last Word on Bethel and Ai," *BAR* 15.1 [1989]: 11; David P. Livingston, "Further Considerations on the Location of Bethel at El-Bireh," *PEQ* 126.2 [1994]: 154–59, which has not received wide acceptance [see, e.g., Harold Brodsky, "Bethel," *ABD* 1:710–12]).

97. James L. Kelso and William F. Albright, *The Excavation of Bethel (1934–1960)* (Cambridge, MA: American Schools of Oriental Research, 1968).

city. A thirteenth century BC phase was also noted at the site that was destroyed by fire.[98] There is general agreement among archaeologists that the excavation reports were schematic and overly reliant upon biblical syntheses.[99] Nevertheless, the basic archaeological picture matches that of Bethel in the biblical record, even if excavations did not produce similar results to the high place at Tel Dan (see 1 Kgs 12:29; 2 Kgs 10:29). Most of the settlement is located beneath the modern village, which left only four acres (16,187 m^2) accessible to excavators Albright and Kelso.[100] Significantly, Beitin is one of only a few significant Late Bronze settlements in the central hill country.

17. TAPPUAH (JOSH 12:16)

Tappuah of Ephraim (Josh 16:8) and Manasseh (Josh 17:7–8; compare with *Onom.* 494/98:15) has been identified with Sheikh Abu Zarad, which is located to the northwest of Lebonah and Shiloh.[101] Surveys at the site revealed a large tell with occupation from the Early Bronze through the Byzantine periods, including Late Bronze II and Iron I over an area of twenty dunams (5 acres).[102]

18. HEPHER (JOSH 12:17)

The city of Hepher is mentioned in the slain kings' list (Josh 12:17; compare to *Onom.* 756/140:26) and as the "land of Hepher" in the third Solomonic district (1 Kgs 4:10). The city of Hepher may also be related to the Manassehite clan of Hepher (Num 26:32–33; 27:1; Josh 17:2–3).[103] Zertal has persuasively argued that Hepher should be related to Tell Muhaffar, which preserves the name of the site and has remains from the Chalcolithic through Early Roman periods, including occupation from the Late Bronze–Iron II.[104] Tell Muhaffar is located directly north of Dothan on the northern edge of the Dothan Valley. The topography of the site indicates a maximum occupation of around fifty dunams (12.5 acres).

---

98. Kelso and Albright, *Bethel*, xiv; see also Bekkum, *From Conquest to Coexistence*, 496–97; see Israel Finkelstein and Lily Singer-Avitz, "Reevaluating Bethel," *ZDPV* 125.1 (2009): 37, who date the destruction to the end of the thirteenth or the beginning of the twelfth century BC.

99. William G. Dever, "Archaeology and the Ancient Israelite Cult: How the Kh. El-Qom and Kuntillet 'Ajrud 'Asherah' Texts Have Changed the Picture," *Eretz-Israel* 26 (1999): 9*–15*; Rainey and Notley, *Sacred Bridge*, 118; Finkelstein and Singer-Avitz, "Reevaluating Bethel," 33–35.

100. Kelso and Albright, *Bethel*, 1–3.

101. See discussion in Aharon Tavger, "Some Notes on the Southern Boundary of the Territory of Ephraim," *Moreshet Israel* 12 (2015): 176–95.

102. Zecharia Kallai, "The Land of Benjamin and Ephraim," in *Judaea Samaria and the Golan: Archaeological Survey 1967–1968*, ed. Moshe Kochavi (Jerusalem: Carta, 1972), site 36; Israel Finkelstein, Zvi Lederman, and Shlomo Bunimovitz, eds., *Highland of Many Cultures: The Southern Samaria Survey* (Tel Aviv: Tel Aviv University, 1997), 2:606–10. See also the recent survey of the site, which revealed similar occupational remains, Lorenzo Nigro, Chiara Fiaccavento, Mohammed Jaradat, and Jehad Yasine, "Archaeology from A to Z: Abu Zarad, an Ancient Town of Palestine," *Vicino Oriente* 19 (2015): 139–83.

103. See e.g., discussion in Rainey and Notley, *Sacred Bridge*, 152.

104. Adam Zertal, "Hepher," *ABD* 3:138–39; Zertal, "Arubboth," *ABD* 1:465–67. Zertal, *The Manasseh Hill Country Survey, Vol. 1: The Shechem Syncline*, Har/Map ed. (Leiden: Brill, 2004), site 23.

19. APHEK OF SHARON (JOSH 12:18)

Aphek is the last city in this section before the beginning of the cities connected with the northern campaign. While the Hebrew Masoretic Text (MT) also includes the otherwise unknown town of "Lasharon" (לַשָּׁרוֹן, *lasharon*) (Josh 12:18), this is probably a scribal mistake for Aphek of Sharon (a geographical region) as reflected in the Greek Septuagint (LXX; βασιλεα Αφεκ της Σαρων, *basilea Aphek tēs Sarōn*; compare to both textual traditions in *Onom.* 58/22:1; 631/122:1). Aphek is located at Ras el-Ain at the headwaters of the Yarkon River on the International Coastal Highway. Aphek's position was very strategic, as reflected in the biblical (1 Sam 4:1; 29:1; compare to the incorrect locations in *Onom.* 63/22:19; 151/34:11) and extrabiblical literature (e.g., no. 66 on Thutmose III's topographical list at Karnak).[105]

Excavations at Aphek revealed a major city that was continuously occupied from the Early Bronze through modern times, including all phases of the Late Bronze Age (Strata X14–X12), and a fiery destruction in the thirteenth century BC.[106] The Egyptian Governor's Residence from the Late Bronze Age revealed several important tablets in Akkadian, Hittite, and Ugaritic, as well as fragments of bilingual (Sumerian and Akkadian) and trilingual (Sumerian, Akkadian, and Canaanite) lexicons. The subsequent layers from Iron I at Aphek (X11–X9) were marked by Philistine occupation, which aligns well with the references in 1 Samuel (4:1; 29:1).[107]

THE NORTHERN CAMPAIGN (JOSH 12:19–23A; COMPARE WITH JOSH 11:1–16): HAZOR, SHIMRON, MARON/MADON, AKSHAPH, KEDESH, TAANACH, MEGIDDO, JOKNEAM OF CARMEL, AND DOR OF THE HEIGHTS OF DOR

20. HAZOR: KING JABIN[108] (JOSH 12:19; JOSH 11:1–16)

The MT's "Madon" in this position (Josh 12:19) was probably added later after Shimron Meron was understood as a compound toponym (Josh 12:20), whereas in fact the LXX of Josh 12:20 indicates that Shimron and Maron (or Madon) were separate towns.[109]

Hazor is located at Tell el-Qedah. Hazor's upper and lower city comprise over 810 dunams (200 acres), making it the largest tell in the southern Levant and a fitting Late Bronze city for the description that Hazor was "formerly the head of all those kingdoms" (Josh 11:10).[110] Hazor

---

105. Ahituv, *Canaanite Toponyms*, 61.

106. Yuval Gadot and Esther Yadin, *Aphek-Antipatris II: The Remains on the Acropolis. The Moshe Kochavi and Pirhiya Beck* (Tel Aviv: Tel Aviv University, 2009), 4.

107. Moshe Kochavi, Pirhiya Beck, and Esther Yadin, eds., *Aphek-Antipatris I: Excavation of Areas A and B: The 1972–1976 Seasons* (Tel Aviv: Tel Aviv University, 2001); Gadot and Yadin, *Aphek-Antipatris II*.

108. For a discussion of two cuneiform texts that mention the name Jabin (Ibni) in relation to Hazor, see Chris McKinny, "'March on My Soul with Might!'—The Geographical Setting of Judges 4–5," in this volume.

109. Table 1; Rainey and Notley, *Sacred Bridge*, 129.

110. The vast lower city was only briefly excavation by Yadin, but the new excavations, which began in 2019, led by Garfinkel, Yasur-Landau, and Hasel plan to expose large sections of the lower city. For the Egyptian references to Hazor, see Ahituv, *Canaanite Toponyms*, 116–17.

Aerial View of Hazor from the South with Upper and Lower Cities

(Stratum XIII) was destroyed with a massive conflagration from which it never fully recovered. This destruction dates to the mid-late thirteenth century BC, and the new excavations have demonstrated that there was no preceding destruction in either the transition between the Middle and Late Bronze Ages or in the fifteenth century BC.[111] Significantly, the lack of a fifteenth century BC destruction at Hazor is problematic for the "early date" theory of the exodus and conquest (fifteenth century BC).

According to Hazor's past excavator, Yigal Yadin, and current excavator, Amnon Ben-Tor, this fiery destruction relates to Joshua's destruction of the city as described in Josh 11.[112] Besides the destruction of the entire site, including the so-called ceremonial palace, numerous Canaanite cultic figures were decapitated, possibly by the conquerors of Hazor. Moreover, the area of the palace was left as a ruin for the rest of Hazor's lengthy history, despite the fact that it was located at the summit, near the new tenth century BC gate and the ninth through eighth century BC water system. Ben-Ami and Ben-Tor suggest that the abandonment of the "ceremonial palace,"

111. Amnon Ben-Tor, *Hazor: Canaanite Metropolis, Israelite City* (Jerusalem: Israel Exploration Society and Biblical Archaeology Society, 2016), 20.

112. Amnon Ben-Tor and Sharon Zuckerman, "Hazor at the End of the Late Bronze Age: Back to Basics," *BASOR* 350 (2008): 1–6; Ben-Tor, *Hazor*; Amnon Ben-Tor et al., eds., *The Selz Foundation Hazor Excavations in Memory of Yigael Yadin. Hazor VII: The 1990–2012 Excavations: The Bronze Age* (Jerusalem: Israel Exploration Society, Institute of Archaeology, The Hebrew University, 2017).

Canaanite Deity with Head Purposefully Destroyed
from 13th Century BC Destruction of Hazor

along with the emergence of several eleventh and tenth century BC shrines oriented towards it, memorialized Israel's destruction of the once great city.[113]

Given Hazor's destruction in the thirteenth century BC and its appearance in Judg 4:2 (compare with 1 Sam 12:9), an account entirely related to the Jezreel Valley, might indicate that Hazor was reoccupied during the time of the judges—the period of Deborah and Barak (twelfth century BC?). Some late Iron I remains (eleventh to early tenth century BC) were uncovered at Hazor, but this layer (Strata XII/XI) is usually connected with a meager early Israelite occupation of the site and not a revitalized Canaanite city.[114] Judges 4–5 does not indicate that Hazor was destroyed again following Sisera's defeat at the hands of Deborah and Barak. It is possible that Hazor in Judg 4:2 refers to a regional entity situated in the same vicinity as the collection of city-states referenced in Josh 11:1–5 (Madon/Maron, Shimron, and Akshaph).[115] Perhaps the new excava-

113. Doron Ben-Ami, "Early Iron Age Cult Places—New Evidence from Tel Hazor," *TA* 33.2 (2006): 121–33; Ben-Tor, *Hazor*, 126–31.

114. Doron Ben-Ami, "The Iron Age I at Tel Hazor in Light of the Renewed Excavations," *IEJ* 51.2 (2001): 148–70; Ben-Ami, "Early Iron Age Cult Places."

115. See proposal in Charles R. Krahmalkov, "Exodus Itinerary," 54–62, 79.

tions of the lower city will shed further light on the transition of Canaanite to Israelite Hazor.[116]

21. SHIMRON (JOSH 12:20; COMPARE TO JOSH 11:1, 13)

Shimron appears as one of the towns in league with Jabin king of Hazor (Josh 11:1; 12:20; compare with *Onom.* 827/154:21—confused with Samaria/Sebaste; 855/158:10) and was allotted to the tribe of Zebulun (Josh 19:15). It seems most likely that the actual ancient name was "Simeon," which is reflected in the Amarna correspondence (EA 225:4) and other Egyptian texts, references to the town of Simonias in Josephus, the Mishnah, and Talmud (Josephus, *Life* 115; m. Megillah I.77a; y. Kil'ayim 2:8, 28c; y. Yevamot 12:6, 13a), and the Arabic name of Khirbet Sammuniyeh, identified with biblical Shimron/Simeon.[117] Khirbet Sammuniyeh is a large tell of one hundred sixty dunams (forty acres), located directly north of Megiddo on the northern edge of the Jezreel Valley. While there have been several surveys and salvage excavations at Khirbet Sammuniyeh, large-scale excavations began at the site in 2017 under the direction of Master, Martin, and Aja. Khirbet Sammuniyeh was clearly occupied from the Chalcolithic period through modern times, including the Late Bronze Age, but the new excavations have not yet reached the Late Bronze layers.[118]

It should be noted that Josh 11:13 states that, besides Hazor, "none of the cities that stood on tells did Israel burn." This would clearly include Shimron, Maron, and Akshaph, but could also relate to the other northern towns that do not appear in the narrative of Josh 11.

22. MARON/MADON: KING JOBAB (JOSH 12:19; COMPARE TO JOSH 11:1–7, 13)

As indicated above, the LXX indicates that Maron/Madon should be present following Shimron (Josh 12:20; *Onom.* 667/126:26; 669/128:4—which places Merom near

---

116. Finkelstein has argued that the lower city of Hazor was reoccupied following the late thirteenth century BC destruction of the site (Israel Finkelstein, "Hazor at the End of the Late Bronze Age. A Reassessment," *UF* 37 (2005): 341–50; but see Ben-Tor and Zuckerman, "Hazor at the End of the Late Bronze Age"). Garfinkel, Cline, and Yasur-Landau began a project related to the lower city, but this project was abandoned after a single season.

117. For the ancient name, see Ahituv, *Canaanite Toponyms*, 183. The name may also be reconstructed in a list of defeated cities by Tiglath-Pileser III (Annal Fragments) (see Mordechai Cogan, *The Raging Torrent: Historical Inscriptions from Assyria and Babylonia Relating to Ancient Israel* [Jerusalem: Carta, 2008], 77–78). Simonias was located sixty furlongs (7.5 mi./12 km) from Gaba—apparently Tell Abu Shushah just north of Megiddo—which is located 7.5 mi. (12 km) southwest of Tell Abu Shushah (Rainey and Notley, *Sacred Bridge*, 71). Eusebius misidentified Shimron with Samaria (*Onom.* 827/154:21; 855/158:10). See also the discussion in Benjamin Maisler, "Shimron — Semûnieh / סמוניה — שמרון," *Bulletin of the Jewish Palestine Exploration Society* א, no. ד' (1934): 1–7; Anson F. Rainey, "Toponymic Problems (Cont.)," *TA* 3.2 (1976): 57–69; Rainey, "Toponymic Problems (Cont.)," *TA* 8.2 (1981): 146–51.

118. Avner Raban, *Archeological Survey of Israel, Map 28: Map of Nahalal*, ed. Y. Tsafrir, (Jerusalem: Israel Antiquities Authority, 2012), site 83, https://survey.antiquities.org.il/index_Eng.html#/MapSurvey/26; Nurit Feig, "Tel Shimron," *Hadashot Arkheologiot* 119 (2007): n.p., http://www.hadashot-esi.org.il/report_detail_eng.aspx?id=636&mag_id=112; Feig, "Tel Shimron," *Hadashot Arkheologiot* 121 (2009): n.p., http://www.hadashot-esi.org.il/report_detail_eng.aspx?id=1109&mag_id=115.

Dothan).[119] This confusion is added to the spelling of the toponym, which is likely due to the close resemblance of the letters *dalet* (ד) and *resh* (ר). In all likelihood, the original name was Maron instead of Madon and is probably identical with the "waters of Maron" (Josh 11:5, 7).[120] Maron does not appear in the Bible, but it appears numerous times in Egyptian New Kingdom inscriptions as "Maromim" and as "Marum" in an inscription of Assyrian king, Tiglath-Pileser III, regarding his conquest of Galilee.[121] While some identify Maron with Qarnei Hattin, the toponymic connection between Maron and Marun er-Ras (just north of the Israeli-Lebanese border, five miles [8 km] west of Kedesh) seems more likely.[122] Aharoni identified Maron with Tell el-Khureibeh, a ruin categorized as "a large Canaanite tell in Upper Galilee" following Garstang's earlier explorations of the site that apparently revealed Late Bronze remains.[123] Given the fact that Garstang's investigation took place almost a century ago, a reexamination of Tell el-Khureibeh is certainly warranted. However, the modern security situation makes this unlikely, as Tell el-Khureibeh is located less than a kilometer west of the border.

23. AKSHAPH (JOSH 12:20; COMPARE TO JOSH 11:1, 13)

Akshaph is mentioned as a city in league with Jabin of Hazor that was defeated by Joshua (Josh 11:1; 12:20) and allotted to Asher (Josh 19:25; *Onom.* 118/30:1).[124] Outside of the Bible, the name "Akshaph" first appears in the Egyptian Execration Texts of the nineteenth and eighteenth centuries BC, indicating that the city should have a significant Middle Bronze layer.[125] Akshaph appears numerous times in New Kingdom inscriptions including in a riddle which indicates a location south of Akko (Acre).[126] In the Karnak list of Thutmose III, Akshaph (no. 40) appears following Shunem and Mashal (Nos. 38–39) and before Geba-shemen (Tell el-Amr) and Taanach

---

119. Maron is not mentioned in the Bible outside of these references (e.g., *Onom.* 667/126:26; 669/128:4).

120. Aharoni, *Land of the Bible*, 117–18; Rainey and Notley, *Sacred Bridge*, 129.

121. For Egyptian references, see Ahituv, *Canaanite Toponyms*, 137. For Tiglath-Pileser III references, see Cogan, *Raging Torrent*, 78.

122. For Tell el-Khureibeh suggestions, see Félix-Marie Abel, *Géographie de La Palestine* (Paris: Lecoffre, 1938), 2:372–73; Nadav Na'aman, *Borders and Districts in Biblical Historiography: Seven Studies in Biblical Geographic Lists* (Jerusalem: Simor, 1986), 127–28; Zvi Gal, *Lower Galilee during the Iron Age* (Winona Lake, IN: Eisenbrauns, 1992), 105. For Marun er-Ras suggestions, see Aharoni, *Land of the Bible*, 225–26; Rainey and Notley, *Sacred Bridge*, 129.

123. Yohanan Aharoni, *The Settlement of the Israelite Tribes in Upper Galilee* (Jerusalem: Magnes Press, 1957), 91; Aharoni, *Land of the Bible*, 225; John Garstang, *Joshua, Judges*, 101–2, 191.

124. Eusebius confused the site with Chesulloth (Iksal), which he located eight miles (13 km) from Diocaesarea (Sepphoris) near Mount Tabor (*Onom.* 59/22:2; compare with 118/30:1).

125. *ANET*, 329 n. 8. The Egyptian Execration Texts are bowls or figures with the names of foreign cities and rulers that were ritually smashed by Egyptian priests. Two groups date to the early second millennium BC and include Canaanite settlements and rulers. They are our earliest textual witness into the history of Canaan.

126. See especially Papyrus Anastasi I 21:4–5 (riddle); see inscriptions in Ahituv, *Canaanite Toponyms*, 48–49.

(nos. 41–42).[127] Two main candidates have been suggested for Akshaph: Tell Keisan, (4 mi., 6 km) southeast of Akko in the plain of Asher, and Khirbet el-Harbaj, on the southern part of the plain of Asher near Kfar Hasidim. While both are possible, Tell Keisan is preferable given the probable identifications of several towns in southern Asher. These include the following towns from Josh 19:25–26: Helkath (Tell el-Qassis?), Hali (Ras Ali), Beten (Tell el-Far near Abtun), Akshaph (Tell Keisan?), Allammelech (preserved in Wadi Melek?), Amad (Tell Amr?), and Mishal (Tell Abu Hawam?).

Excavations at Tell Keisan have revealed significant Early Bronze through Iron II occupation over one hundred forty-five dunams (36 acres).[128] While the Late Bronze city is clearly present in pottery sherds, the stratigraphic sequence has yet to be established.

24. KEDESH (JOSH 12:22; COMPARE TO JOSH 11:13)

Kedesh, Megiddo, Taanach, or Jokneam (Josh 12:21–22) do not appear in the narrative of Josh 11:1–6. However, their proximity to Shimron and Hazor likely indicate that their inclusion in the slain kings' list should be related to the campaign against Hazor. Kedesh in Galilee of the tribal allotment of Naphtali (e.g., Josh 19:37; 20:7; 21:32; 2 Kgs 15:29; *Onom*. 586/114:8; 601/116:8) is almost certainly intended in Josh 12:22.[129] The ancient name of Kedesh has been preserved in Tell Qades in Upper Galilee.[130] The site was almost continuously occupied from the Early Bronze Age until the Ottoman era, including significant Late Bronze, Iron I, and Iron II occupation; however, only the later remains at the site, primarily Persian through Roman, have been exposed in excavations.[131]

25. TAANACH (JOSH 12:21; COMPARE TO JOSH 11:13)

Taanach has been identified with Tell Tiinnik, which is a well-known and excavated tell located in the southwestern part of the Jezreel Valley on the edge of Mount Carmel.[132] In the Bible, Taanach was a Canaanite town during the Israelite conquest and settlement (Josh 12:21;

---

127. Rainey and Notley, *Sacred Bridge*, 72.

128. Gunnar Lehmann and Martin Peilstöcker, *Archeological Survey of Israel, Map 20: Map of Ahihud*, ed. Ofer Sion (Jerusalem: Israel Antiquities Authority, 2012), site 24, https://survey.antiquities.org.il/index.html#/MapSurvey/12.

129. See also 1 Macc 11:63, 73; *J.W.* 2.459. Somewhat surprisingly the name does not appear in the various Egyptian itineraries, although Ahituv suggests that "Galilee" in New Kingdom sources may be a substitute for Kedesh (Ahituv, *Canaanite Toponyms*, 94).

130. Robinson and Smith, *Biblical Researches*, 3:355; Rainey and Notley, *Sacred Bridge*, 185.

131. Sharon C. Herbert and Andrea M. Berlin, "A New Administrative Center for Persian and Hellenistic Galilee: Preliminary Report of the University of Michigan/University of Minnesota Excavations at Kedesh," *BASOR* 329 (2003): 13–59; Adi Erlich, "Happily Ever After? A Hellenistic Hoard from Tel Kedesh in Israel," *American Journal of Archaeology* 121.1 (2017): 39–59. A new project (beginning in 2019) led by Uri Davidovich, Ido Wachtel, and R. Sabai, began excavating the massive 350 dunam Early Bronze settlement as well as the impressive Early Roman architecture at the site, https://www.biblicalarchaeology.org/dig/tel-qedesh/#detailsSec.

132. Robinson and Smith, *Biblical Researches*, 3:179. Besides perfectly preserving the name, the site also fits with Eusebius's mileage of either three or four miles (5–6 km) from Legio (*Onom*. 490/98:5; 504/100:7).

Taanach from the West

Onom. 492/98:10), it was allotted to Manasseh, who could not drive out the Canaanites living there (Josh 17:11; Judg 1:27; compare to Judg 5:19; 1 Chr 7:29) and was one of the towns of Baana's district during the reign of Solomon (1 Kgs 4:12). Outside of the Bible, Taanach appears in a number of Egyptian texts, including the conquest lists of Thutmose III (no. 42) and Shishak I (no. 14) from Karnak.[133] The site was inhabited from the Early Bronze Age until modern times, and includes extensive Late Bronze remains and the Taanach letters.[134] The excavators of Taanach concluded that the city was destroyed by Thutmose III in the mid-fifteenth century BC. Taanach was less intensely populated in the fourteenth and thirteenth centuries BC and suffered a destruction in the late twelfth century BC.[135]

26. MEGIDDO (JOSH 12:21; COMPARE WITH JOSH 11:13)

Extensive excavations and numerous references in extrabiblical inscriptions indicate that Megiddo was one of the most important cities in Canaan.[136] Megiddo's significance is made most evident by Thutmose III's boast following his defeat of the city that "capturing Megiddo is the capture of 1,000 cities" (*COS* 2.2.2A). Excavations at Tel Megiddo (Tell Mutesellim) have revealed an enormous

133. Ahituv, *Canaanite Toponyms*, 184–85.

134. The Taanach letters (or tablets) are a group of seventeen cuneiform documents found at Tell Tiinnik that date to Late Bronze I, see Albert E. Glock, "Taanach," *NEAEHL* 4:1428–33; for translation and commentary see Rainey and Notley, *Sacred Bridge*, 75–76.

135. Glock, "Taanach," 1432.

136. See the most recent final publication: Israel Finkelstein, David Ussishkin, and Eric Cline, eds., *Megiddo V: The 2004–2008 Seasons*, 3 vols. (Tel Aviv: Tel Aviv University, 2013). See also Ahituv, *Canaanite Toponyms*, 138–39.

amount of material related to the Late Bronze Age throughout the entire chronological sequence of settlement (Strata IX–VIIA). Late Bronze remains were found both on the main mound and a lower city covering an area of around one hundred twenty dunams (30 acres). Late Bronze I Megiddo (Stratum IX) was destroyed by Thutmose III and is dated to c. 1450 BC. Neither Amarna-era (Stratum VIII) nor Ramesside-era (Stratum VIIB) Megiddo were destroyed. Like Lachish, Megiddo was occupied into the mid-twelfth century BC (Stratum VIIA) when it underwent a fiery destruction c. 1130 BC.[137] These findings accord well with the conquest and settlement details relayed in Joshua and Judges, which indicates that Megiddo remained outside of Israelite control (Josh 17:11; Judg 1:27; 5:19).

27. JOKNEAM OF CARMEL (JOSH 12:22; COMPARE WITH JOSH 11:13)

The identification of Jokneam (Josh 12:22; 19:11; 21:34) is well-established both through the preservation of the toponym (Tell Qeimun) and the archaeological remains present at the large, elevated tell (40 dunams; 10 acres).[138] Ben-Tor's excavations revealed that the site was continuously occupied from the Early Bronze Age through the Ottoman period, including the Late Bronze Age.[139] Jokneam was destroyed by fire in the thirteenth century BC (Stratum XIX) before being reoccupied in the late twelfth or early eleventh century BC (Strata XVII–XVIII).[140]

28. DOR OF THE HEIGHTS OF DOR (JOSH 12:23; COMPARE WITH JOSH 11:13)

Dor is not mentioned in Egyptian inscriptions until the reign of Ramesses II.[141] During the eleventh century BC, the Tale of Wenamun indicates that Dor was under the control of the Sicels, one of the groups of Sea Peoples who settled in Canaan following the collapse of Egyptian control.[142] In the Bible, Dor was allotted to Manasseh, who could not drive out the inhabitants who dwelled there (Josh 17:11;

---

137. E.g., Israel Finkelstein, "Archaeological and Historical Conclusions," in *Megiddo V: The 2004–2008 Seasons*, ed. Israel Finkelstein, David Ussishkin, and Eric Cline (Tel Aviv: Tel Aviv University, 2013), 3:1329–40; Michael B. Toffolo et al., "Absolute Chronology of Megiddo, Israel, in the Late Bronze and Iron Ages: High-Resolution Radiocarbon Dating," *Radiocarbon* 56.1 (2014): 221–44.

138. E.g., Edward Robinson and Eli Smith, *Later Biblical Researches in Palestine and in the Adjacent Regions* (London: Murray, 1856), 115. Jokneam also appears in two versions of Thutmose III's conquest itineraries and as "Camona" in classical literature (e.g., *Onom.* 535/106:17; 555/108:27; 605/116:20—incorrectly connected with Kamon of Judg 8:10 but matches Eusebius's mileage of six milestones from Legio (Ahituv, *Canaanite Toponyms*, 123).

139. E.g., Amnon Ben-Tor, "Jokneam," *NEAEHL* 3:805–11; Ben-Tor, Miriam Avissar, and Yuval Portugali, *Yoqne'am I: The Late Periods* (Jerusalem: Hebrew University, 1996); Ben-Tor et al., *Yoqne'am II: The Iron Age and the Persian Period: Final Report of the Archaeological Excavations (1977–1988)* (Jerusalem: The Institute of Archaeology, The Hebrew University of Jerusalem, 2005); Ben-Tor et al., *Yoqne'am III: The Middle and Late Bronze Ages: Final Report of the Archaeological Excavations (1977–1988)* (Jerusalem: Institute of Archaeology, Hebrew University of Jerusalem in cooperation with the Israel Exploration Society, 2005); Miriam Avissar, *Tel Yoqne'am: Excavations on the Acropolis* (Jerusalem: Israel Antiquities Authority, 2005).

140. Ben-Tor, "Jokneam," 808.

141. Ahituv, *Canaanite Toponyms*, 88–89.

142. E.g., Rainey and Notley, *Sacred Bridge*, 132.

1:27; 1 Chr 7:29; see also Naphoth Dor in 1 Kgs 4:11; compare to *Onom.* 376/78:8; 727/136:16).[143] Eusebius located Dor "nine miles [15 km] from Caesarea" (*Onom.* 376/78:8; 727/136:16), which indicates the site of Khirbet el-Burj.[144] Middle to Late Bronze Dor was much smaller than the later Iron Age city and was situated on the western edge of the hill overlooking the Mediterranean Sea.[145] Excavations have revealed extensive finds from all phases of the Late Bronze but without accompanying architecture, making it difficult to determine the size of Late Bronze Dor. Late Bronze IIB remains were found in the center of the mound in Area G (Phases 12–11).[146] The twelfth and eleventh century Sicel city (Phases 10–9) ended in a fiery destruction dated to the last quarter of the eleventh century BC.[147]

Additional Towns (Josh 12:23b–24)

29. Goyim of Gilgal (MT) or Galilee (LXX) (Josh 12:23b)

Goyim is the most enigmatic toponym in the list, which is comprised mostly of well-known cities in the land of Canaan. Goyim means "nations," which has caused some scholars to relate the place to Harosheth Hagoyim of Sisera (Judg 4:2, 13, 16) and/or "Galilee of the nations" (Isa 9:1; compare with Matt 4:15).[148] The MT has "Goyim of Gilgal" (גּוֹיִם לְגִלְגָּל, *goyim legilgal*), but the LXX reads "Goyim of Galilee" (Γωιμ της Γαλιλαιας, *Gōim tēs Galilaias*; see *Onom.* 320/68:13). Most translations and commentators favor the LXX; however, both readings remain possible.[149]

143. "Naphoth" is translated in various ways (e.g., heights, dunes, etc.).

144. Tabula Peutingeriana placed it eight miles (13 km) from Caesarea.

145. Ephraim Stern, "Dor," *NEAEHL* 5:1695–1703.

146. Ephraim Stern, *Dor, Ruler of the Seas: Nineteen Years of Excavations at the Israelite-Phoenician Harbor Town on the Carmel Coast* (Israel Exploration Society, 2000); Stern, *Excavations at Dor: Figurines, Cult Objects and Amulets, 1980–2000 Seasons* (Jerusalem: Israel Exploration Society, 2010); Ayelet Gilboa et al., eds., *Excavations at Dor Final Report: Volume IIA Area G, The Late Bronze and Iron Ages: Synthesis, Architecture and Stratigraphy* (Jerusalem: Institute of Archaeology of The Hebrew University, 2018); Ayelet Gilboa et al., eds., *Excavations at Dor Final Report: Volume IIA Area G, The Late Bronze and Iron Ages: Pottery, Artifacts, Ecofacts, and Other Studies* (Jerusalem: Institute of Archaeology of The Hebrew University, 2018); Ayelet Gilboa et al., eds., *Excavations at Dor Final Report: Volume IIA Area G, The Late Bronze and Iron Ages: Pottery Plates and Index of Loci* (Jerusalem: Institute of Archaeology of The Hebrew University, 2018).

147. Ayelet Gilboa, Ilan Sharon, and Jeffrey R. Zorn, "The Late Bronze and Iron Ages in Area G: An Architectural, Contextual, Functional and Chronological Synthesis," in *Excavations at Dor Final Report: Volume IIA Area G, The Late Bronze and Iron Ages: Synthesis, Architecture and Stratigraphy*, ed. Ayelet Gilboa et al. (Jerusalem: Institute of Archaeology of The Hebrew University, 2018), 66.

148. Rainey suggests that the LXX of Josh 12:23b should be understood as the "District of the Nations" and Harosheth Hagoyim of Sisera should be understood as "the plantations of the Gentiles" both of which he locates in the vicinity of Jokneam and Taanach (Rainey and Notley, *Sacred Bridge*, 150–51).

149. See, e.g., ESV. See discussion in Dozeman, *Joshua 1–12*, 492.

Assuming the reading "of Galilee," it is possible that Goyim can be related to Harosheth Haggoyim of Sisera and situated in the Jezreel Valley. If so, perhaps Goyim is related to either Tell Salem or Khirbet Yannun.[150] In this case, Goyim would be among the northern towns of Josh 11. However, Goyim along with Tirzah may also go with the list of towns in the central part of the country (Bethel, Tappuah, Hepher, and Aphek of Sharon), as opposed to the towns connected with the northern campaign (table 1). It is possible that the northern towns relating to Josh 11 were inserted into the list and that Goyim and Tirzah (Josh 12:23b) originally followed Aphek of Sharon (Josh 12:18). If so, Goyim could be related to Jaljuliya, which is located three miles (5 km) north of Aphek.[151] Jaljuliya remains heavily populated and has never been excavated, but a survey revealed remains from the Middle Bronze (perhaps hinting at Late Bronze remains), Iron I, Iron II, Hellenistic, and Byzantine periods, as well as extensive remains from later periods.[152] A recent salvage excavation near Jaljuliya revealed a large Late Acheulian site of approximately ten dunams (2.5 acres).[153] Finally, it should be noted that Eusebius identified Gilgal of Josh 12:23 with Jaljuliya as he located the site "about six miles north of Antipatris" (*Onom.* 321/68:18). This is an important detail as it reflects the MT reading, as opposed to the LXX reading which the *Onomasticon* usually reflects.

30. TIRZAH (JOSH 12:24)

Tirzah is usually connected with Tell el-Farah, which is situated on the western end of Wadi Farah.[154] The inclusion of Tirzah at the end of the list does not match the geographical distribution of the preceding cities. One might expect Tirzah to occur in the group of towns in the region of Ephraim and Manasseh (Josh 12:16–18; compare to *Onom.* 497/98:19; 512/102:3; 513/102:4—incorrectly associated with a village in the Golan). Like Hepher above, Tirzah was the name of a Manassehite clan, one of the daughters of Zelophehad (Num 26:33; 27:1; 36:11; Josh 17:3).[155] Probably following the campaign of Shishak in c. 925 BC, Tirzah became the capital of the northern kingdom of Israel from the reign of Jeroboam I (1 Kgs 14:17; 15:21, 33; 16:8–9, 15–17; 16:23–24) until Omri moved the capital to Samaria midway through his reign (1 Kgs 16:24). After

---

150. See discussion in McKinny, "'March on My Soul with Might,'" in this volume.

151. Abel, *Géographie de la Palestine*, 2:324, 28.

152. I. Ayalon E. Beit-Arieh, *Archeological Survey of Israel, Map 77: Map of Kefar Sava*, ed. Ofer Sion and Shalom Yanklevitz (Jerusalem: Israel Antiquities Authority, 2012), site 82, http://survey.antiquities.org.il/index_Eng.html#/MapSurvey/37.

153. See press release https://mfa.gov.il/MFA/IsraelExperience/History/Pages/Important-and-rare-prehistoric-site-uncovered-in-central-Israel-7-January-2017.aspx.

154. William F. Albright, "The Site of Tirzah and the Topography of Western Manasseh," *Journal of Palestine Oriental Society* 11 (1931): 241–51. While Albright rejected Robinson's suggestion of Tulluza for Tirzah (1 mi., 2 km west of Tell el-Farah), it is possible that Tulluza retains the ancient name Tirzah (Robinson and Smith, *Biblical Researches*, 3:302).

155. See Chris McKinny and Steven M. Ortiz, "'The Land that Remains'—Evidence in Favor of the Thirteenth Century BC View of the Israelite Conquest and Settlement," in this volume.

Aerial View of Excavations at Tirzah, Tell el-Farah South

killing and replacing Shallum, Menahem sacked the city of Tirzah (2 Kgs 15:16).[156]

Tell el-Farah is a mound of fifty dunams (12.5 acres) that was excavated by Roland De Vaux between 1946–1960.[157] According to Finkelstein's assessment, Tell el-Farah was occupied throughout the Late Bronze as evidenced through pottery sherds and finds in tombs, but it was unoccupied during the Iron I after being destroyed with fire towards the end of the thirteenth century BC.[158] The impressive Iron II layers align well with the biblical references to Tirzah's status as an Israelite capital.

DISCUSSION AND CONCLUSIONS

In my analysis of Josh 12, I have examined the historical geography and archaeology of the thirty-three towns mentioned in the slain king's list. As I have demonstrated, about half (16) of the thirty towns are directly mentioned in the narrative of Josh 5–11. An additional seven towns are probably related to Josh 8 (perhaps Bethel), Josh 10 (Geder and Adullam), and Josh 11 (Taanach, Kedesh, Megiddo, and Jokneam). Hormah and Arad relate to Moses' defeat of the Canaanite king of Arad (Num 21:1–14) and/or the campaigns of Judah and Simeon against Hormah (Judg 1:16–17).

156. See also Song 6:4; Thebez of Abimelech (Judg 9:50; 2 Sam 11:21) is sometimes considered to be a corruption for Tirzah.

157. Roland de Vaux, "The Excavations at Tell El-Far'ah and the Site of Ancient Tirzah," *PEQ* 88.2 (1956): 125–40; Alain Chambon, *Tell El-Far'ah I: L'âge Du Fer* (Paris: Éditions Recherche sur les civilisations, 1984); Roland De Vaux, Pierre de Miroschedji, and Alain Chambon, "Far'ah, Tell El- (North),"*NEAEHL* 2:433–44; Ze'ev Herzog and Lily Singer-Avitz, "Sub-Dividing the Iron Age IIA in Northern Israel: A Suggested Solution to the Chronological Debate," *TA* 33.2 (2006): 185; Israel Finkelstein, "Tell El-Farah (Tirzah) and the Early Days of the Northern Kingdom," *Revue Biblique* 119.3 (2012): 331–46; Finkelstein, *The Forgotten Kingdom: The Archaeology and History of Northern Israel* (Atlanta: Society of Biblical Literature, 2013), 66–74.

158. Finkelstein, *Forgotten Kingdom*, 69–70. A new excavation of the site began in 2017 under the direction of Fenollós, Caramelo, and Yasin.

The remaining seven or eight towns might be related to a list of towns that belong to the central hill country and Sharon Plain (perhaps Bethel, Tappuah, Hepher, Aphek of Sharon, Goyim of Gilgal, and Tirzah), which has no connected narrative in the Bible. This list includes many of the important sites in the land of Israel, and most of them can be identified with relative certainty. Still, I have either suggested alternate identifications or favored past suggestions against recent consensus for the sites Makkedah (Khirbet er-Ras instead of Khirbet el-Qom), Eglon (Tell el-Hesi instead of Tell Eton), and Goyim of Gilgal (Jaljuliya instead of Harosheth Haggoyim).

While noting the oft-mentioned archaeological problems with Jericho, Ai, Arad, and Heshbon, it is striking that thirty-one or thirty-two of the thirty-three toponyms (94–97 percent) in the list of Josh 12 have Late Bronze remains. By contrast, the Judahite register of towns of Josh 15:21–62, comprising of one hundred twenty-seven towns has only around thirty-seven sites (30 percent) that were occupied during the Late Bronze Age.[159] A comparison between these two town registers demonstrates that the writer of the book of Joshua had a nuanced understanding of Late Bronze Age Canaan. Regardless, if one accepts the historicity of the Israelite conquest as described in Joshua or not, it seems clear that the author(s) and/or redactor(s) of Josh 1–12 were aware of the preexisting Canaanite political dynamics that predominated before the Iron Age.

This is not the venue to discuss the nature of the Israelite "conquest" in an in-depth manner. However, the fact that most of the sites in the list have been excavated to varying degrees (25 out of 33) allows us to determine when the various sites were occupied within the Late Bronze Age and whether they were destroyed. Out of the excavated sites, Debir, Hormah (Tel Masos?), Arad, Libnah, and Bethel were apparently not occupied in Late Bronze I, which argues against the late fifteenth century BC date of the conquest. Besides Arad, which was not occupied during the Late Bronze, all of the other towns mentioned were occupied in Late Bronze IIB.[160] Eight of the excavated sites showed a distinctive fiery destruction dated to the thirteenth century BC while another four sites showed possible signs of a destruction and/or abandonment in the same period. Only Megiddo revealed a destruction that can be related to the Late Bronze I, and this should be associated with Thutmose III. The biblical text claims that only Jericho, Ai, and Hazor were destroyed with fire, and specifically indicates that none of the related "tells" of the northern campaign were burned except Hazor (Josh 11:13). Still, it is possible to understand that the biblical text indicates a destruction or abandonment for the cities of Hebron, Lachish, Eglon, Debir, Geder, Hormah, Arad, Libnah, Adullam, Makkedah, Bethel, Tappuah, Hepher, Aphek of Sharon, Goyim of Gilgal, and Tirzah.[161] Of these sites, nine have been excavated and seven (except Arad and Debir) have shown destruction/aban-

159. McKinny, "A Historical Geography."

160. Kedesh and Shimron have not yet reached the Late Bronze layers in their excavations, but the Egyptian references to the sites would seem to confirm occupation throughout the Late Bronze sequence.

161. See discussion in Kitchen, *On the Reliability of the Old Testament*, 182–90.

donment layers related to the thirteenth century BC.[162] Clearly, these destructions could be related to factors other than the Israelite conquest (e.g., Merenptah, local conflict, etc.). Although, from a textual perspective it is not necessary to conclude that the towns that were "struck with the edge of the sword" in Josh 10 were actually destroyed.

In short, archaeological investigations over the past several decades have revealed that almost all of the towns in Josh 12, which reflects the narrative of Josh 1–11, were occupied in the thirteenth century BC. A significant number of these sites also suffered a destruction during this timeframe that can conceivably be related to the Israelite conquest.

TABLE 1: MT/LXX COMPARISON OF JOSH 12 WITH RECONSTRUCTED ROSTER OF TOWNS

MT List	LXX List	Reconstructed List	Related Narrative
A. Heshbon (חֶשְׁבּוֹן)	A. Heshbon (Εσεβων)	A. Heshbon	Num 21:21–35 - Conquest of Transjordan
B–C. Ashtaroth (עַשְׁתָּרוֹת) and Edrei (אֶדְרֶעִי)	B–C. Ashtaroth (Ασταρωθ) and Edrei (Εδραϊν)	B–C. Ashtaroth and Edrei	Num 21:21–35 - Conquest of Transjordan
1. Jericho (יְרִיחוֹ)	1. Jericho (Ἰερειχὼ)	1. Jericho	Josh 5–6 - Conquest of Jericho
2. Ai, beside Bethel (הָעַי אֲשֶׁר־מִצַּד בֵּית־אֵל)	2. Ai, beside Bethel (τῆς Γαι ἥ ἐστιν πλησίον Βαιθηλ)	2. Ai, beside Bethel	Josh 7–8 - Conquest of Ai
3. Jerusalem (יְרוּשָׁלַםִ)	3. Jerusalem (Ιερουσαλημ)	3. Jerusalem	Josh 10 - Central and Southern Campaigns
4. Hebron (חֶבְרוֹן)	4. Hebron (Χεβρων)	4. Hebron	Josh 10 - Central and Southern Campaigns
5. Jarmuth (יַרְמוּת)	5. Jarmuth (Ιεριμουθ)	5. Jarmuth	Josh 10 - Central and Southern Campaigns
6. Lachish (לָכִישׁ)	6. Lachish (Λαχις)	6. Lachish	Josh 10 - Central and Southern Campaigns
7. Eglon (עֶגְלוֹן)	7. Eglon (Αιλαμ)	7. Eglon	Josh 10 - Central and Southern Campaigns

162. Gezer was destroyed in the late thirteenth century BC, but this destruction likely relates to Pharaoh Merenptah. Moreover, Josh 10:33 indicates that "Horam king of Gezer" was defeated while aiding Lachish, indicating that the city was not attacked.

MT List	LXX List	Reconstructed List	Related Narrative
8. Gezer (גֶּזֶר)	8. Gezer (Γαζερ)	8. Gezer	Josh 10 - Central and Southern Campaigns
9. Debir (דְּבִר)	9. Debir (Δαβιρ)	9. Debir	Josh 10 - Central and Southern Campaigns
10. Geder (גֶּדֶר)	10. Geder (Γαδερ)	10. Geder	Not mentioned; probably related to Josh 10
11. Hormah (חָרְמָה)	11. Hormah (Ερμαθ)	11. Hormah	Num 21:1–4 (Moses); Judg 1:16–17 (Judah and Simeon)
12. Arad (עֲרָד)	12. Arad (Αραθ)	12. Arad	Num 21:1–4 (Moses); Judg 1:16–17 (Judah and Simeon)
13. Libnah (לִבְנָה)	13. Libnah (Λεβνα)	13. Libnah	Josh 10 - Central and Southern Campaigns
14. Adullam (עֲדֻלָּם)	14. Adullam (Οδολλαμ)	14. Adullam	Not mentioned; probably related to Josh 10
15. Makkedah (מַקֵּדָה)	15. Makkedah (Μακηδα)	15. Makkedah	Josh 10 - Central and Southern Campaigns
16. Bethel (בֵּית־אֵל)	*missing; MT superior*	16. Bethel	Mentioned in Josh 7–8 - Conquest of Ai (see Josh 8:17; Judg 1:22–26); perhaps related to a central region list
17. Tappuah (תַּפּוּחַ)	16. Tappuah (Ταφουγ)	17. Tappuah	Not mentioned; perhaps related to a central region list
18. Hepher (חֵפֶר)	17. Hepher (Οφερ)	18. Hepher	Not mentioned; perhaps related to a central region list
19. Aphek (אֲפֵק)	18. Aphek of Sharon (Αφεκ τῆς Σαρων)	19. Aphek	Not mentioned; perhaps related to a central region list
20. Lasharon (לַשָּׁרוֹן; *scribal error*)	-	-	-
21. Madon (מָדוֹן; *duplicate - Maron in Shimron Meron*)	-	-	-

MT List	LXX List	Reconstructed List	Related Narrative
22. Hazor (חָצוֹר)	19. Hazor (Ασωρ)	20. Hazor	Josh 11 - Northern Campaign
23. Shimron Meron (שִׁמְרוֹן מְראוֹן; *LXX superior*)	20. Shimron (Συμοων)	21. Shimron	Josh 11 - Northern Campaign
-	21. Maron (Μαρρων)	22. Maron	Josh 11 - Northern Campaign
24. Akshaph (אַכְשָׁף)	22. Akshaph (Αζιφ)	23. Akshaph	Josh 11 - Northern Campaign
25. Taanach (תַּעְנַךְ; different order)	23. Kedesh (Καδης)	24. Kedesh	Not mentioned; probably related to Josh 11; compare with Josh 17:11; Judg 1:27; 5:19
26. Megiddo (מְגִדּוֹ different order)	24. Taanach (Ταναχ)	25. Taanach	Not mentioned; probably related to Josh 11; compare with Josh 17:11; Judg 1:27; 5:19
27. Kedesh (קֶדֶשׁ; different order)	25. Megiddo (Μαγεδων)	26. Megiddo	Not mentioned; probably related to Josh 11
28. Jokneam of Carmel (יָקְנְעָם לַכַּרְמֶל)	26. Jokneam of Carmel (Ιεκοναμ τοῦ Χερμελ)	27. Jokneam of Carmel	Not mentioned; probably related to Josh 11
29. Dor of the Heights of Dor (דּוֹר לְנָפַת דּוֹר)	27. Dor of the Heights of Dor (Δωρ τοῦ Ναφεδδωρ)	28. Dor of the Heights of Dor	Not mentioned; probably related to Josh 11
30. Goyim of Gilgal (גּוֹיִם לְגִלְגָּל)	28. Goim of Galilee (Γωιμ τῆς Γαλιλαίας)	29. Goim of Gilgal or Galilee	Not mentioned; either related to Josh 11 or a central region list of towns
31. Tirzah (תִּרְצָה)	29. Tirzah (Θαρσα)	30. Tirzah	Not mentioned; perhaps related to a central region list
31 kings (scribal mistake of Lasharon; duplicate of Madon/Maron)	29 kings (missing Bethel)	30 kings (LXX roster plus Bethel)	Summary: 16 towns from Josh 5–11; 7 towns related to Josh 5–11; 2 towns from Num 21:1–4; 5 towns probably related to central region list of towns

TABLE 2: HISTORICAL GEOGRAPHY AND ARCHAEOLOGICAL ASSESSMENT OF THE SLAIN KING'S LIST - JOSH 12[163]

Town	Modern Identification (*excavated)	EB	MB	LB	LB I	LB IIA	LB IIB	LB III/ Iron IA	Iron I	Iron II	Size (dunams)
A. Heshbon	Hesban	-	-	-	-	-	X?	X?	X	X	60 (Iron)
A. Heshbon/ Gilgal?	Tell Jalul?*	-	X	X	X	X	X	X	X	X	65
B. Ashtaroth	Tell Ashtarah	X	X	X	?	?	?	?	X	X	85?
C. Edrei	Dera	X	X	X	?	?	?	?	X	X	?
1. Jericho	Tell es-Sultan*	X	X	X	X?	X	X^^	-	X	X	40 (EB–MB)
2. Ai	et-Tell?*	X	-	X?	?	?	X?	X?	X	-	110 (EB)
3. Jerusalem	City of David*	X	X	X	X?	X	X	?	X	X	40
4. Hebron	Tell er-Rumeide*	X	X	X	X	X	X^	?	X	X	28–33
5. Jarmuth	Khirbet Yarmuk*	X	X	X	-	-	X^^	-	X^	X	24 (acropolis); 160 (EB)
6. Lachish	Tell ed-Duweir*	X	X	X	X	X	X^	X^	-	X	120
7. Eglon	Tell el-Hesi?*	X	X	X	X	X^	X^^	-	X	X	16; 25 (EB)
8. Gezer	Tell Jazar*	X	X	X	X	X^	X^	X	X	X	130
9. Debir	Khirbet Rabud*	-	X	X	-	X	X	?	X	X	60
10. Geder	Khirbet Jedur*	-	X	X	?	X	X	?	X	X	24
11. Hormah	Khirbet Meshash*	-	X	X	-	-	X	X	X	X (IIC)	15
12. Arad	Tell Arad*	X	-	-	-	-	-	-	X	X	100 (EB); 2.5 (Iron II)
13. Libnah	Tell Bornat*	X	X	X	-	X	X^^	-	X	X	20

163. * = excavated; ^ = Late Bronze destruction; ^^ = possible Late Bronze destruction and/or abandonment. The presence of other periods is noted without reference to excavated destructions.

Town	Modern Identification (*excavated)	EB	MB	LB	LB I	LB IIA	LB IIB	LB III/ Iron IA	Iron I	Iron II	Size (dunams)
14. Adullam	Tell esh-Sheikh Madkhur	-	X	X	?	?	?	?	-	X	10
15. Makkedah	Khirbet er-Ras?	-	X	X	?	?	?	?	X	X	50
16. Bethel	Beitin*	X	X	X	-	X	X^	?	X	X	17
17. Tappuah	Sheikh Abu Zarad	X	X	X	?	X	X	?	X	X	20
18. Hepher	Tell Muhaffar	X	X	X	?	?	X	?	X	X	50?
19. Aphek of Sharon	Ras el-Ain*	X	X	X	X	X	X^	X	X	X	120
20. Hazor	Tell el-Qedah*	X	X	X	X	X	X^	-	X (elev-enth)	X	800 (MB–LB)
21. Shimron	Tell Sammuniyeh*	X	X	X	X	?	?	?	X	X	160
22. Maron	Tell el-Khureibeh?	?	X?	X?	?	?	?	?	?	?	?
23. Akshaph	Tell Keisan?*	X	X	X	?	?	?	?	X	X	145
24. Kedesh	Tell Qades*	X	X	X	?	?	?	?	X	X	350 (EB)
25. Taanach	Tell Tiinnik*	X	X	X	X	X	X	X^	X	X	55
26. Megiddo	Tell el-Mutesellim*	X	X	X	X^	X	X	X^	X	X	120
27. Jokneam of Carmel	Tell Qeimun*	X	X	X	X	X	X^	-	X	X	40
28. Dor of the heights of Dor	Khirbet el-Burj*	-	X	X	X	X	X	X	X	X	120 (Iron)
29. Goyim of Galilee (LXX)	Khirbet Yannun?	-	X	X	?	?	?	?	X	X	7
29. Goyim of Gilgal (MT)	Jaljuliya?	-	X	?	?	?	?	?	X	X	?
30. Tirzah	Tell el-Farah (north)*	X	X	X	?	X	X^	?	X?	X	50

BIBLIOGRAPHY

Abel, Félix-Marie. *Géographie de la Palestine*. 2 vols. Paris: Lecoffre, 1938.

Aharoni, Yohanan. *The Land of the Bible: A Historical Geography*. Translated by Anson F. Rainey. Rev. and enl. ed. Philadelphia: Westminster, 1979.

———. "Nothing Early and Nothing Late: Re-Writing Israel's Conquest." *BA* 39.2 (1976): 55–76.

———. *The Settlement of the Israelite Tribes in Upper Galilee*. Jerusalem: Magnes Press, 1957.

Aharoni, Yohanan, and Michael Avi-Yonah. *The Carta Bible Atlas*. Translated by Anson F. Rainey. 3rd ed. Jerusalem: Carta, 2002.

Ahituv, Shmuel. *Canaanite Toponyms in Ancient Egyptian Documents*. Jerusalem: Magnes Press, Hebrew University, 1984.

Albright, William F. "The American Excavations at Tell Beit Mirsim." *ZAW* 47 (1929): 1–17.

———. "Bronze Age Mounds of Northern Palestine and the Hauran: The Spring Trip of the School in Jerusalem." *BASOR* 19 (1925): 5–19.

———. "The Excavation of Tell Beit Mirsim. Vol. II: The Bronze Age." *AASOR* 17 (1936): xi–141.

———. "The Israelite Conquest of Canaan in the Light of Archaeology." *BASOR* 74 (1939): 11–23.

———. "Researches of the School in Western Judaea." *BASOR* 15 (1924): 2–11.

———. "The Site of Tirzah and the Topography of Western Manasseh." *Journal of Palestine Oriental Society* 11 (1931): 241–51.

Amiran, Ruth. *Early Arad: The Chalcolithic Settlement and Early Bronze City*. Vol. 2. Jerusalem: Israel Exploration Society, 1978.

Auld, A. Graeme. *Joshua Jesus, Son of Nauē, in Codex Vaticanus*. Septuagint Commentary Series. Leiden: Brill, 2005.

Avissar, Miriam. *Tel Yoqne'am: Excavations on the Acropolis*. Jerusalem: Israel Antiquities Authority, 2005.

Bartlett, John R. *Jericho*. Guildford, UK: Lutterworth Press, 1982.

Beit-Arieh, I. Ayalon E. *Archeological Survey of Israel, Map 77: Map of Kefar Sava*. Edited by Ofer Sion and Shalom Yanklevitz. Jerusalem: Israel Antiquities Authority, 2012. http://survey.antiquities.org.il/index_Eng.html#/MapSurvey/37.

Bekkum, Koert van. *From Conquest to Coexistence: Ideology and Antiquarian Intent in the Historiography of Israel's Settlement in Canaan*. Leiden: Brill, 2011.

Ben-Ami, Doron. "Early Iron Age Cult Places—New Evidence from Tel Hazor." *TA* 33.2 (2006): 121–133.

———. "The Iron Age I at Tel Hazor in Light of the Renewed Excavations." *IEJ* 51.2 (2001): 148–70.

Ben-Arieh, S. "Tel Gedor." *NEAEHL* 2:468.

Ben-Tor, Amnon. *Hazor: Canaanite Metropolis, Israelite City*. Jerusalem: Israel Exploration Society and Biblical Archaeology Society, 2016.

———. "Jokneam." *NEAEHL* 3:805–11.

Ben-Tor, Amnon, Miriam Avissar, and Yuval Portugali. *Yoqne'am I: The Late Periods*. Jerusalem: Hebrew University, 1996.

Ben-Tor, Amnon, Doron Ben-Ami, Ariella Livneh, and R. Bankirer. *Yoqne'am III: The Middle and Late Bronze Ages : Final Report of the Archaeological Excavations (1977–1988)*. Jerusalem: Institute of Archaeology, Hebrew University of

Jerusalem in cooperation with the Israel Exploration Society, 2005.

Ben-Tor, Amnon, Anabel Zarzecki-Peleg, Shlomit Cohen-Anidjar, and Doron Ben-Ami. *Yoqne'am II: The Iron Age and the Persian Period: Final Report of the Archaeological Excavations (1977–1988)*. Jerusalem: The Institute of Archaeology, Hebrew University of Jerusalem, 2005.

Ben-Tor, Amnon, and Sharon Zuckerman. "Hazor at the End of the Late Bronze Age: Back to Basics." *BASOR* 350 (2008): 1–6.

Ben-Tor, Amnon, Sharon Zuckerman, Shlomit Bechar, and Debora Sandhaus, eds. *The Selz Foundation Hazor Excavations in Memory of Yigael Yadin. Hazor VII: The 1990–2012 Excavations: The Bronze Age*. Jerusalem: Israel Exploration Society. Institute of Archaeology, The Hebrew University, 2017.

Ben-Yosef, Erez. "The Architectural Bias in Current Biblical Archaeology." *VT* 69.3 (2019): 361–87.

Ben-Yosef, Erez, Brady Liss, Omri A. Yagel, Ofir Tirosh, Mohammad Najjar, and Thomas E. Levy. "Ancient Technology and Punctuated Change: Detecting the Emergence of the Edomite Kingdom in the Southern Levant." *Public Library of Science ONE* 14.9 (September 18, 2019): e0221967. https://doi.org/10.1371/journal.pone.0221967.

Bienkowski, Piotr. *Jericho in the Late Bronze Age*. Oxford: Aris & Phillips, 1986.

Blakely, Jeffery A. "Ajlan: Locating the Estate of Amr b. al-As." *NEA* 73.4 (2010): 210–22.

Blakely, Jeffery A., and Fred L. Horton Jr. "On Site Identifications Old and New: The Example of Tell El-Hesi." *NEA* 64.1/2 (2001): 24–36.

Bliss, Frederick J. *A Mound of Many Cities; or Tell El Hesy Excavated*. 2nd ed. London: The Committee of the Palestine Exploration Fund, 1898.

Boling, Robert G. *Joshua: A New Translation with Notes and Commentary*. Introduction by G. Ernest Wright. AB. New York: Doubleday, 1982.

Brodsky, Harold. "Bethel." *ABD* 1:710–12.

Bruins, Hendrik J., and Johannes Van Der Plight. "Tell Es-Sultan (Jericho): Radiocarbon Results of Short-Lived Cereal and Multiyear Charcoal Samples from the End of the Middle Bronze Age." *Radiocarbon* 37.2 (1995): 213–20.

Callaway, Joseph A. "Ai." *ABD* 1:125–30.

———. "Ai." *NEAEHL* 1:39–45.

Chadwick, Jeffrey R. "The Archaeology of Biblical Hebron in the Bronze and Iron Ages: An Examination of the Discoveries of the American Expedition to Hebron." PhD diss., University of Utah, 1992.

———. "Hebron in Early Bronze Age III and Middle Bronze Age II: Fortification Walls in Area I.3 of the American Expedition to Hebron (Tell Er-Rumeide)." Pages 167–86 in *Tell It in Gath: Studies in the History and Archaeology of Israel. Essays in Honor of Aren M. Maeir on the Occasion of His Sixtieth Birthday*. Edited by Itzhaq Shai, Jeffrey R. Chadwick, Louise Hitchcock, Amit Dagan, Chris McKinny, and Joe Uziel. Münster: Zaphon, 2018.

———. "Hebron in the Late Bronze Age: Discoveries of the of the American Expedition to Hebron (Tell Er-Rumeide)." Pages 185–216 in *The Late Bronze and Early Iron Ages of Southern Canaan*. Edited by Aren M. Maeir,

Itzhaq Shai, and Chris McKinny. Berlin: de Gruyter, 2019.
Chambon, Alain. *Tell El-Far'ah I: L'âge Du Fer*. Paris: Éditions Recherche sur les civilisations, 1984.
Clermont-Ganneau, Charles. "Discovery of the Royal Canaanite City of Gezer by M. Clermont-Ganneau." *PEQ* 5.2 (1873): 78–80.
Cogan, Mordechai. *The Raging Torrent: Historical Inscriptions from Assyria and Babylonia Relating to Ancient Israel*. Jerusalem: Carta, 2008.
Dagan, Yehuda. *Map of Amazya*. 2 vols. Jerusalem: Israel Antiquities Authority, 2006.
———. *The Ramat Bet Shemesh Regional Project: Landscapes of Settlement: From the Paleolithic to the Ottoman Periods*. Jerusalem: Israel Antiquities Authority, 2011.
———. *The Ramat Bet Shemesh Regional Project: The Gazetteer*. Jerusalem: Israel Antiquities Authority, 2010.
———. "The Settlement in the Judean Shephelah in the Second and First Millennium BC: A Test Case of Settlement Processes in a Geographical Region." PhD diss., Tel Aviv University, 2000.
Dahlberg, Bruce T., and Kevin G. O'Connell, eds. *Tell El-Hesi: The Site and the Expedition*. Winona Lake, IN: Eisenbrauns, 1989.
Dever, William G. "Archaeology and the Ancient Israelite Cult: How the Kh. El-Qom and Kuntillet 'Ajrud 'Asherah' Texts Have Changed the Picture." *Eretz-Israel* 26 (1999): 9*–15*.
———. "Qom, Khirbet El." *NEAEHL* 4:1233–34.
———. *Who Were the Early Israelites, and Where Did They Come From?* Grand Rapids: Eerdmans, 2003.
Doermann, Ralph W., and Valerie M. Fargo. "Tell El-Hesi, 1983." *PEQ* 117.1 (1985): 1–24.
Dorsey, David A. "The Location of Biblical Makkedah." *TA* 7.3–4 (1980): 185–93.
Dozeman, Thomas B. *Joshua 1–12: A New Translation with Introduction and Commentary*. AB. New Haven, CT: Yale University Press, 2015.
Eisenberg, Emmanuel, and David Ben-Shlomo. *The Tel Ḥevron 2014 Excavations: Final Report*. Ariel: Ariel University Press, 2017.
Elliger, Karl. "Josua in Judäa." *Paliistina-jahrbuch* 30 (1934): 47–71.
Erlich, Adi. "Happily Ever After? A Hellenistic Hoard from Tel Kedesh in Israel." *American Journal of Archaeology* 121.1 (2017): 39–59.
Fargo, Valerie M. "Hesi, Tell El-." *NEAEHL* 2:630–34.
Faust, Avraham. "The Excavations at Tel 'Eton (2006–2009): A Preliminary Report." *PEQ* 143.3 (2011): 198–224.
Feig, Nurit. "Tel Shimron." *Hadashot Arkheologiot* 119 (2007): n.p. http://www.hadashot-esi.org.il/report_detail_eng.aspx?id=636&mag_id=112.
———. "Tel Shimron." *Hadashot Arkheologiot* 121 (2009): n.p. http://www.hadashot-esi.org.il/report_detail_eng.aspx?id=1109&mag_id=115.
Finkelstein, Israel. "Archaeological and Historical Conclusions." Pages 1329–40 in *Megiddo V: The 2004–2008 Seasons*. Edited by Israel Finkelstein, David Ussishkin, and Eric Cline. Tel Aviv: Tel Aviv University, 2013.
———. *The Archaeology of the Israelite Settlement*. Jerusalem: Israel Exploration Society, 1988.

———. *The Forgotten Kingdom: The Archaeology and History of Northern Israel*. Atlanta: Society of Biblical Literature, 2013.

———. "Hazor at the End of the Late Bronze Age. A Reassessment." *UF* 37 (2005): 341–50.

———. "Tell El-Farah (Tirzah) and the Early Days of the Northern Kingdom." *Revue Biblique* 119.3 (2012): 331–46.

———. "What the Biblical Authors Knew about Canaan before and in the Early Days of the Hebrew Kingdoms." *UF* 48 (2017): 173–98.

Finkelstein, Israel, Ido Koch, and Oded Lipschits. "The Mound on the Mount: A Possible Solution to the Problem with Jerusalem." *Journal of Hebrew Scriptures* 11 (2011): art. 12, pp. 1–24. https://doi.org/10.5508/jhs.2011.v11.a12.

Finkelstein, Israel, Zvi Lederman, and Shlomo Bunimovitz, eds. *Highland of Many Cultures: The Southern Samaria Survey*. 2 vols. Tel Aviv: Tel Aviv University, 1997.

Finkelstein, Israel, and Neil Asher Silberman. *The Bible Unearthed: Archaeology's New Vision of Ancient Israel and the Origin of Its Sacred Texts*. New York: Free Press, 2001.

Finkelstein, Israel, and Lily Singer-Avitz. "Reevaluating Bethel." *ZDPV* 125.1 (2009): 33–48.

Finkelstein, Israel, David Ussishkin, and Eric Cline, eds. *Megiddo V: The 2004-2008 Seasons*. 3 vols. Tel Aviv: Tel Aviv University, 2013.

Fritz, Volkmar. "Conquest or Settlement? The Early Iron Age in Palestine." *BA* 50.2 (1987): 84–100.

Gadot, Yuval, and Esther Yadin. *Aphek-Antipatris II: The Remains on the Acropolis. The Moshe Kochavi and Pirhiya Beck*. Tel Aviv: Tel Aviv University, 2009.

Gal, Zvi. *Lower Galilee during the Iron Age*. Winona Lake, IN: Eisenbrauns, 1992.

Galling, Kurt. "Studien Aus Dem Deutschen Evangelischen Institut Für Altertumswissenschaft in Jerusalem. 50. Zur Lokalisierung von Debir." *ZDPV* 70.2 (1954): 135–41.

Garfinkel, Yosef, Igor Kreimerman, Michael G. Hasel, and Martin G. Klingbeil. "First Impression on the Urban Layout of the Last Canaanite City of Lachish: A View from the Northeast Corner of the Site." Pages 122–32 in *The Late Bronze and Early Iron Ages of Southern Canaan*. Edited by Aren M. Maeir, Itzhaq Shai, and Chris McKinny. Berlin: de Gruyter, 2019.

Garstang, J. *Joshua, Judges: Foundations of Bible History*. London: Palestine Exploration Fund, 1931. Repr., Grand Rapids: Kregel, 1978.

———. *The Story of Jericho*. London: Hodder & Stoughton, 1940.

Geraty, Lawrence T. "Heshbon." *NEAEHL* 2:626–30.

Gilboa, Ayelet, Ilan Sharon, and Jeffrey R. Zorn. "The Late Bronze and Iron Ages in Area G: An Architectural, Contextual, Functional and Chronological Synthesis." Pages 27–80 in *Excavations at Dor Final Report: Volume IIA Area G, The Late Bronze and Iron Ages: Synthesis, Architecture and Stratigraphy*. Edited by Ayelet Gilboa, Ilan Sharon, Jeffrey R. Zorn, and Sveta Matskevich. Jerusalem: Institute of Archaeology of The Hebrew University, 2018.

Gilboa, Ayelet, Ilan Sharon, Jeffrey R. Zorn, and Sveta Matskevich, eds. *Excavations at Dor Final Report: Volume IIA Area G, The Late Bronze and Iron Ages: Pottery, Artifacts, Ecofacts, and Other Studies*. Jerusalem: Institute of Archaeology of The Hebrew University, 2018.

———, eds. *Excavations at Dor Final Report: Volume IIA Area G, The Late Bronze and Iron Ages: Pottery Plates and Index of Loci*. Jerusalem: Institute of Archaeology of The Hebrew University, 2018.

———, eds. *Excavations at Dor Final Report: Volume IIA Area G, The Late Bronze and Iron Ages: Synthesis, Architecture and Stratigraphy*. Jerusalem: Institute of Archaeology of The Hebrew University, 2018.

Glock, Albert E. "Taanach." *NEAEHL* 4:1428–33.

Guérin, Victor. *Description Géographique, Historique et Archéologique de la Palestine*. 3 vols. Paris: Impériale, 1869.

Hankey, Vronwy. "The Aegean Pottery of Khirbet Judur." *Eretz-Israel* 15 (1981): 33*–38*.

Hardin, James W., Christopher A. Rollston, and Jeffery A. Blakely. "Biblical Geography in Southwestern Judah." *NEA* 75.1 (2012): 20–35.

Herbert, Sharon C., and Andrea M. Berlin. "A New Administrative Center for Persian and Hellenistic Galilee: Preliminary Report of the University of Michigan/University of Minnesota Excavations at Kedesh." *BASOR* 329 (2003): 13–59.

Herion, Gary A., Dale W. Manor, and Jeffery K. Lott. "Debir (Place)." *ABD* 2:111–12.

Herzog, Ze'ev. "The Date of the Temple at Arad." Pages 156–78 in *Studies in the Archaeology of the Iron Age in Israel and Jordan*. Edited by Amihai Mazar. Sheffield: Sheffield Academic, 2001.

———. "The Fortress Mound at Tel Arad an Interim Report." *TA* 29.1 (2002): 3–109.

Herzog, Ze'ev, and Lily Singer-Avitz. "Sub-Dividing the Iron Age IIA in Northern Israel: A Suggested Solution to the Chronological Debate." *TA* 33.2 (2006): 163–195.

Hess, Richard. "Joshua." *ZIBBCOT* 2:2–93.

Holladay, John S. "Kom, Khirbet El-." *ABD* 4:97–99.

Holland, Thomas A., and Ehud Netzer. "Jericho (Place)." *ABD* 3:723–37.

Horowitz, Wayne, Takayoshi Oshima, and Seth L. Sanders. *Cuneiform in Canaan: Cuneiform Sources from the Land of Israel in Ancient Times*. Jerusalem: Israel Exploration Society; Hebrew University of Jerusalem, 2006.

James, Peter. "The Levantine War-Records of Ramesses III: Changing Attitudes, Past, Present and Future." *Antiguo Oriente* 15 (2017): 57–148.

Janzen, Mark, and Chris McKinny. "An Overview of the Historical Geography of the Exodus and Wilderness Itinerary." Pages 705–39 in *Lexham Geographic Commentary on the Pentateuch*. Edited by Barry J. Beitzel. Bellingham, WA: Lexham, 2023.

Kallai, Zecharia. "The Land of Benjamin and Ephraim." Pages 153–93 in *Judaea Samaria and the Golan: Archaeological Survey 1967–1968*. Edited by Moshe Kochavi. Jerusalem: Carta, 1972.

Kelso, James L., and William F. Albright. *The Excavation of Bethel (1934–1960)*. Cambridge: American Schools of Oriental Research, 1968.

Kenyon, Kathleen M. "Jericho: Tell Es-Sultan." *NEAEHL* 2:674–81.

Kenyon, Kathleen M., and Thomas A. Holland. *Excavations at Jericho: The Architecture and Stratigraphy of the*

Tell. 3 vols. Jerusalem: British School of Archaeology in Jerusalem, 1981.

Kitchen, Kenneth A. *On the Reliability of the Old Testament*. Grand Rapids: Eerdmans, 2003.

Kleiman, Sabine, Yuval Gadot, and Oded Lipschits. "A Snapshot of the Destruction Layer of Tell Zakariye/Azekah Seen against the Backdrop of the Final Days of the Late Bronze Age." *ZDPV* 132.2 (2016): 105–33.

Kleiman, Sabine, Ido Koch, Lyndelle Webster, Karl Berendt, Omer Sergi, Manfred Oeming, Yuval Gadot, and Oded Lipschits. "Late Bronze Age Azekah: An Almost Forgotten Story." Pages 37–61 in *The Late Bronze and Early Iron Ages of Southern Canaan*. Edited by Aren M. Maeir, Itzhaq Shai, and Chris McKinny. Berlin: de Gruyter, 2019.

Kochavi, Moshe. "Khirbet Rabud= Debir." *TA* 1.1 (1974): 2–33.

———. "The Land of Judah." Pages 19–89 in *Judaea, Samaria and the Golan: Archaeological Survey 1967–1968*. Edited by Moshe Kochavi. Jerusalem: Archaeological Survey of Israel and Carta, 1972.

———. "Rabud, Khirbet." *NEAEHL* 4:1252. Jerusalem: Carta, 1993.

Kochavi, Moshe, Pirhiya Beck, and Esther Yadin, eds. *Aphek-Antipatris I: Excavation of Areas A and B: The 1972–1976 Seasons*. Tel Aviv: Tel Aviv University, 2001.

Krahmalkov, Charles R. "Exodus Itinerary Confirmed by Egyptian Evidence." *BAR* 20.5 (1994): 54–62, 79.

Lehmann, Gunnar, and Martin Peilstöcker. *Archeological Survey of Israel, Map 20: Map of Ahihud*. Edited by Ofer Sion. Jerusalem: Israel Antiquities Authority, 2012. https://survey.antiquities.org.il/index.html#/MapSurvey/12.

Le Strange, Guy. *Palestine under the Moslems. A Description of Syria and the Holy Land from A.D. 650 to 1500*. London: Palestine Exploration Fund, 1890.

Levin, Yigal. "Conquered and Unconquered: Reality and Historiography in the Geography of Joshua." Pages 361–70 in *The Book of Joshua*. Edited by Edward Noort. Leuven: Peeters, 2012.

———, ed. *A Time of Change: Judah and Its Neighbours in the Persian and Early Hellenistic Periods*. London: T&T Clark, 2007.

Lipschits, Oded, Yuval Gadot, and Manfred Oeming. "Four Seasons of Excavations at Tel Azekah: The Expected and (Especially) Unexpected Results." Pages 27–44 in *The Shephelah During the Iron Age: Recent Archaeological Studies*. Edited by Oded Lipschitz and Aren M. Maeir. Winona Lake, IN: Eisenbrauns, 2017.

Livingston, David P. "Further Considerations on the Location of Bethel at El-Bireh." *PEQ* 126.2 (1994): 154–59.

———. "The Last Word on Bethel and Ai." *BAR* 15.1 (1989): 11.

Magen, Yitzak, Yoab Peleg, and Ibrahim Sruh. "The Church at 'Anab el-Kebir." *Qadmoniot* 125 (2003): 47–54.

Maisler, Benjamin. "Shimron — Semûnieh / סמוניה — שמרון." *Bulletin of the Jewish Palestine Exploration Society* א, no. ד' (1934): 1–7.

Mazar, Eilat, Wayne Horowitz, Takayoshi Oshima, and Yuval Goren. "A Cuneiform Tablet from the Ophel in Jerusalem." *IEJ* 60.1 (2010): 4–21.

Mazar, Eilat, Yuval Goren, Wayne Horowitz, and Takayoshi Oshima. "Jerusalem 2: A Fragment of a Cuneiform Tablet from the Ophel Excavations." *IEJ* 64.2 (2014): 129–39.

McKinny, Chris. "A Historical Geography of The Administrative Division of Judah: The Town Lists of Judah and Benjamin in Joshua 15:21–62 and 18:21–28." PhD diss, Bar-Ilan University, 2017.

———. "The Historical Geography of the Settlements of the Transjordanian Tribes of Reuben, Gad, and Manasseh (Num 32:2–4, 33–42; Josh 13)." Pages 660–704 in *Lexham Geographic Commentary on the Pentateuch*. Edited by Barry J. Beitzel. Bellingham, WA: Lexham, 2023.

———. "'March on My Soul with Might!'—The Geographical Setting of Judges 4–5." In vol. 1 of *Lexham Geographic Commentary on the Historical Books*. Edited by Barry J. Beitzel. Bellingham, WA: Lexham, 2025.

McKinny, Chris, Steven A. Anderson, Kris Udd, and Todd Bolen. *Photo Companion to the Bible: Joshua*. BiblePlaces, 2019.

McKinny, Chris, and Amit Dagan. "The Explorations of Tel Burna." *PEQ* 145.4 (2013): 294–305.

McKinny, Chris, and Steven M. Ortiz. "'The Land that Remains'—Evidence in Favor of the Thirteenth Century BC View of the Israelite Conquest and Settlement." In vol. 1 of *Lexham Geographic Commentary on the Historical Books*. Edited Barry J. Beitzel. Bellingham, WA: Lexham, 2025.

McKinny, Chris, and Aharon Tavger. "From Lebonah to Libnah: Historical Geographical Details from the PEF and Other Early Secondary Sources on the Toponymy of Two Homonymous Sites." Pages 107–22 in *Exploring the Holy Land: 150 Years of the Palestine Exploration Fund*. Edited by David Gurevich and Anat Kidron. London: Equinox, 2018.

McKinny, Chris, Aharon Tavger, and Itzhaq Shai. "Tel Burna in the Late Bronze—Assessing the 13th Century BCE Landscape of the Shephelah." Pages 148–70 in *The Late Bronze and Early Iron Ages of Southern Canaan*. Edited by Aren M. Maeir, Itzhaq Shai, and Chris McKinny. Berlin: de Gruyter, 2019.

Miroschedji, Pierre de. "Jarmuth, Tel." *NEAEHL* 5:1792–97.

———. "Jarmuth." *ABD* 3:645–46.

———. "Yarmuth: The Dawn of City-States in Southern Canaan." *NEA* 62.1 (1999): 2–19.

Moran, William L. *The Amarna Letters*. Baltimore: Johns Hopkins University Press, 1992.

Mullins, Robert A. "The Emergence of Israel in Retrospect." Pages 449–56 in *Israel's Exodus in Transdisciplinary Perspective: Text, Archaeology, Culture, and Geoscience*. Edited by Thomas E. Levy, Thomas Schneider, and William H. C. Propp. New York: Springer, 2015.

Na'aman, Nadav. *Borders and Districts in Biblical Historiography: Seven Studies in Biblical Geographic Lists*. Jerusalem: Simor, 1986.

———. *Canaan in the Second Millennium B.C.E.* Winona Lake, IN: Eisenbrauns, 2005.

Nigro, Lorenzo. "Tell Es-Sultan 2015: A Pilot Project for Archaeology in Palestine." *NEA* 79.1 (2016): 4–17.

———. "The Italian-Palestinian Expedition to Tell Es-Sultan, Ancient Jericho (1997-2015): Archaeology and Valorisation of Material and Immaterial Heritage." Pages 175–214 in *Digging Up Jericho: Past, Present and Future*. Edited by Rachael

Thyrza Sparks, Bill Finlayson, Bart Wagemakers, and Josef Mario Briffa. Oxford: Archaeopress, 2020.

Nigro, Lorenzo, Chiara Fiaccavento, Mohammed Jaradat, and Jehad Yasine. "Archaeology from A to Z: Abu Zarad, an Ancient Town of Palestine." *Vicino Oriente* 19 (2015): 139–83.

Notley, R. Steven, and Ze'ev Safrai. *Eusebius, Onomasticon: A Triglott Edition with Notes and Commentary*. Leiden: Brill, 2005.

Noth, Martin. *Aufsätze Zur Biblischen Landes-Und Altertumskunde: Archäologische, Exegetische Und Topographische Untersuchungen Zur Geschichte Israels*. 2 vols. Neukirchen-Vluyn: Neukirchener Verlag, 1971.

———. *Das Buch Joshua*. Tubingen: Mohr Siebeck, 1953.

Ofer, Avi. "Hebron." *NEAEHL* 1:606–9.

———. "The Highland of Judah during the Biblical Period." PhD diss., Tel Aviv University, 1993.

Ortiz, Steven, and Samuel Wolff. "Guarding the Border to Jerusalem: The Iron Age City of Gezer." *NEA* 75.1 (2012): 4–19.

———. "A Reevaluation of Gezer in the Late Bronze Age in Light of Renewed Excavations and Recent Scholarship." Pages 62–85 in *The Late Bronze and Early Iron Ages of Southern Canaan*. Edited by Aren M. Maeir, Itzhaq Shai, and Chris McKinny. Berlin: de Gruyter, 2019.

———. *Tel Gezer Excavations 2006–2015: The Transformation of a Border City*. Edited by Oded Lipschitz and Aren M. Maeir. Winona Lake, IN: Eisenbrauns, 2017.

Peleg, Yoab, and Ibrahim Shruch. "Rujum el-Qaṣr." *Hadashot Arkheologiyot: Excavations and Surveys in Israel* / חדשות ארכיאולוגיות: חפירות וסקרים בישראל 112 (2000): 109*.

Petrie, William M. F. *Tell El Hesy (Lachish)*. London: Palestine Exploration Fund, 1891.

Raban, Avner. *Archeological Survey of Israel, Map 28: Map of Nahalal*. Edited by Y. Tsafrir. Jerusalem: Israel Antiquities Authority, 2012. https://survey.antiquities.org.il/index_Eng.html#/MapSurvey/26.

Rainey, Anson F. "The Administrative Division of the Shephelah." *TA* 7.3–4 (1980): 194–202.

———. "The Biblical Shephelah of Judah." *BASOR* 251 (1983): 1–22.

———. "Toponymic Problems (Cont.)." *TA* 3.2 (June 1976): 57–69.

———. "Toponymic Problems (Cont.)." *TA* 8.2 (September 1981): 146–51.

Rainey, Anson F., and R. Steven Notley. *The Sacred Bridge: Carta's Atlas of the Biblical World*. Jerusalem: Carta, 2006.

Ray, Paul J., Jr. *Tell Hesban and Vicinity in the Iron Age*. Berrien Springs, MI: Andrews University Press, 2001.

Regev, Johanna, Joel Uziel, Nahshon Szanton, and Elisabetta Boaretto. "Absolute Dating of the Gihon Spring Fortifications, Jerusalem." *Radiocarbon* 59.4 (2017): 1171–93.

Robinson, Edward, and Eli Smith. *Biblical Researches in Palestine, Mount Sinai and Arabia Petraea: A Journal of Travels in the Year 1838*. 3 vols. Boston: Crocker & Brewster; London: John Murray, 1841.

———. *Later Biblical Researches in Palestine and in the Adjacent Regions: A Journal of Travels in the Year 1852*. Boston: Crocker & Brewster; London: Murray, 1856.

Sass, Benjamin, Yosef Garfinkel, Michael G. Hasel, and Martin G.

Klingbeil. "The Lachish Jar Sherd: An Early Alphabetic Inscription Discovered in 2014." *BASOR* 374 (2015): 233–45.

Sauer, James A., Larry G. Herr, and Paul J. Ray Jr., eds. *Ceramic Finds: Typological and Technological Studies of the Pottery Remains from Tell Hesban and Vicinity*. Berrien Springs, MI: Andrews University Press, 2012.

Sayce, Archibald H. "Excavations in Judaea." *The Contemporary Review* 58 (1890): 427–34.

Shai, Itzhaq. "Tel Burna: A Judahite Fortified Town in the Shephelah." Pages 45–60 in *The Shephelah During the Iron Age: Recent Archaeological Studies*. Edited by Oded Lipschitz and Aren M. Maeir. Winona Lake, IN: Eisenbrauns, 2017.

Shai, Itzhaq, Chris McKinny, and Joe Uziel. "Late Bronze Age Cultic Activity in Ancient Canaan: A View from Tel Burna." *BASOR* 374 (2015): 115–33.

Shalev, Omer, and Amir Golani. "Tel Yarmut." *Hadashot Arkheologiot* 130 (2018). http://www.hadashot-esi.org.il/report_detail_eng.aspx?id=25508&mag_id=126.

Stern, Ephraim. "Dor." 5:1695–1703.

———. *Dor, Ruler of the Seas: Nineteen Years of Excavations at the Israelite-Phoenician Harbor Town on the Carmel Coast*. Israel Exploration Society, 2000.

———. *Excavations at Dor: Figurines, Cult Objects and Amulets, 1980–2000 Seasons*. Jerusalem: Israel Exploration Society, 2010.

Streit, Katharina, Lyndelle Webster, Vanessa Becker, Ann-Kathrin Jeske, Hadas Misgav, and Felix Höflmayer. "Between Destruction and Diplomacy in Canaan: The Austrian-Israeli Expedition to Tel Lachish." *NEA* 81.4 (2018): 259–68.

Tavger, Aharon. "E.P. 914 East of Beitin and the Location of the Ancient Cult Site of Bethel." *In the Highland's Depth: Ephraim Range and Binyamin Research Study* 5 (2015): 49–69 [Hebrew with English Abstract (pgs. 34*–35*)].

———. "Some Notes on the Southern Boundary of the Territory of Ephraim." *Moreshet Israel* 12 (2015): 176–95.

Toffolo, Michael B., Eran Arie, Mario A. S. Martin, Elisabetta Boaretto, and Israel Finkelstein. "Absolute Chronology of Megiddo, Israel, in the Late Bronze and Iron Ages: High-Resolution Radiocarbon Dating." *Radiocarbon* 56.1 (2014): 221–44.

Ussishkin, David. "A Synopsis of the Stratigraphical, Chronological and Historical Issues." Pages 50–119 in vol. 1 of *The Renewed Archaeological Excavations at Lachish (1973–1994)*. Edited by David Ussishkin. Tel Aviv: Tel Aviv University, 2004.

———. "Was Jerusalem a Fortified Stronghold in the Middle Bronze Age? An Alternative View." *Levant* 48.2 (2016): 135–51.

Uziel, Joel, Yuval Baruch, and Nahshon Szanton. "Jerusalem in the Late Bronze Age: The Glass Half Full." Pages 171–84 in *The Late Bronze and Early Iron Ages of Southern Canaan*. Edited by Aren M. Maeir, Itzhaq Shai, and Chris McKinny. Berlin: de Gruyter, 2019.

Vaux, Roland de. "The Excavations at Tell El-Far'ah and the Site of Ancient Tirzah." *PEQ* 88.2 (December 1956): 125–40.

Vaux, Roland de, Pierre de Miroschedji, and Alain Chambon. "Far'ah, Tell El- (North)." *NEAEHL* 2:433–44.

Weippert, Helga, and Manfred Weippert. "Jericho in Der Eisenzeit." *ZDPV* 92.2 (1976): 105–48.

Wood, Bryant G. "Did the Israelites Conquer Jericho? A New Look at the Archaeological Evidence." *BAR* 16.2 (1990): 44–59.

———. "The Rise and Fall of the 13th-Century Exodus-Conquest Theory." *JETS* 48.3 (2005): 475–89.

———. "Excavations at Kh. El-Maqatir 1995–2000, 2009–2013: A Border Fortress in the Highlands of Canaan and a Proposed New Location for the Ai of Joshua 7–8." *Bible and Interpretation* (2014): 1–16.

Younker, Randall W., Constance C. Gane, and Reem Al-Shqour. "The Madaba Plains Project: Excavations at Tall Jalul." Pages 58–67 in *The Madaba Plains Project: Forty Years of Archaeological Research into Jordan's Past*. Edited by Douglas R. Clark, Larry G. Herr, Øystein S. LaBianca, and Randall W. Younker. London: Routledge, 2011.

Zertal, Adam. "Hepher." *ABD* 3:138–39.

———. "Arubboth." *ABD* 1:465–67.

———. *The Manasseh Hill Country Survey, Vol. 1: The Shechem Syncline*. Har/Map ed. Leiden: Brill, 2004.

CHAPTER 9

EARLY ISRAEL'S SETTLEMENT IN SOUTHERN CANAAN AND TRANSJORDAN: A GEOGRAPHIC AND SOCIO-SPATIAL ANALYSIS

Josh 13–21; Judg 1–3, 17–21

Barry J. Beitzel

KEY POINTS

- A clear geographic correlation can be shown between territory said to have been settled by premonarchic Israel in the biblical record, and territory in which hundreds of Iron Age I settlements have recently been discovered.
- While moving from mostly mute archaeological evidence and related material cultural to a conclusive identity of ethnicity represents an extremely tenuous line to trace, in the case of relating Iron I sites in southern Canaan and the Transjordan with part or all of premonarchic Israel, a reasonable case of historical plausibility must be considered.

INTRODUCTION

> You are about to cross the Jordan to enter and take possession of the land the Lord your God is giving you. When you have taken it over and are living there, be sure that you obey all the decrees and laws I am setting before you today. (Deut 11:31)[1]

Ancient history—including biblical history—is in many notable respects inseparably bound by and subject to geographical limitations.[2] Geography is an

1. Unless otherwise noted, all biblical references are from the New International Version (NIV).

2. Portions of this chapter draw upon my earlier work in *The New Moody Atlas of the Bible* [*MAB*] (Chicago: Moody Press, 2009) (used with permission). Professor Alan Millard

impelling force that both initiates and governs the nature and extent of political history, what one might call geopolitics. Geologic formation and rock type have a decisive effect on altitude, manner and extent of erosion, location and quantity of both celestial precipitation and terrestrial water supply, presence and type of natural resources, and physical topography. These, in turn, have a lasting and profound bearing on certain aspects of climate, raw materials, soil formation, and land use—factors that may have alternately repelled or attracted human settlement in antiquity, and certainly will influence the location, density, and socioeconomic makeup of a settlement. Where settlements are founded, roadways are eventually opened and used by travelers, migrants, merchants, or armies, and culture ultimately arrives at a particular location. Stated more succinctly by the noted French historian Jules Michelet, "With every step back in time, history becomes more and more geographic until, in the beginning, it is all geography."[3]

Students of the effects of geography on history have drawn a most helpful distinction between geography's *determining* effect and its *limiting* effect. Thus, for example, where a frigid winter climate necessitates the wearing of heavy clothing, there is nothing in the temperature itself that decrees whether people shall wear animal pelts, cotton, linen, or wool. *But they will surely procure and wear winter attire*. When a region unsuitable for agriculture somehow becomes populated, very little in the environment itself predetermines how land shall be utilized, which domestic animals shall be grazed, or whether food shall be secured with spears, traps, nets, or hooks. *But a largely non-agrarian society will surely emerge*. It is geopolitically significant that the earliest civilizations tended to arise along the banks of rivers and/or at places that received an average annual precipitation and have a mean temperature capable of sustaining the spontaneous generation of wild grains that could support human existence. These represent some expressions of earlier geopolitical history subjected to the limitations and indirect controls of geography.

Many of these same limitations are discernible even in our modern technological world, where deserts can be extensively irrigated or the effects of oppressive heat can be mitigated by air-conditioning; where Landsat photography equipped with infrared capability can discover reservoirs of natural resources buried deep in the cavities of the earth's interior; where cloud-seeding or water reclamation projects can lessen the gravity of a hostile and arid environment, or desalinization efforts can supply a ready abundance of fresh water; where rampaging rivers can be restrained by huge dams and even harnessed for hydroelectric purposes; where formidable mountain barriers can be leveled, penetrated, or easily surmounted; and where air travel can put faraway places within relatively quick and painless reach. From such a privileged vantage

---

has kindly read and critiqued this chapter. Dr. Shay Bar has generously provided site data relating to the still unpublished *The Manasseh Hill Country Survey* materials (see table below titled "Approximate Number and Distribution of Iron I Sites Discovered"). I am profoundly grateful to receive the benefit of their greathearted kindness and expertise. Naturally, any remaining errors or misstatements are my responsibility alone.

3. Jules Michelet, *Histoire de France* (Paris: A. Lacroix, 1833–1867), 1:2 (author's translation).

point, we moderns can only imagine how much more sharply defined and deeply etched these many geographical limitations would have been in a world that existed before such technological innovation—for example, in a world like the world of the Bible.

AN ANALYSIS OF EARLY ISRAEL'S SETTLEMENT

To begin with, in this regard, it is worth noting some of the limiting geographical factors that were operative in positioning biblical sites and thus, as a seminally significant consequence, in situating a vast array of potential historical and archaeological evidence. Populated sites in the biblical world may have been founded based on one or more of five criteria:

1. As a consequence of copious water accessibility. Examples of such sites include Damascus, situated on an immense oasis fed by the effusive Abana/Barada and Pharpar/Awaj rivers (see 2 Kgs 5:12); Tadmor/Palmyra, located on a lush and prolific oasis in the middle of the great Syrian Desert; and Caesarea Philippi, set adjacent to the effluent headwaters of the Jordan River.
2. At locations adjacent to deep water ports, such as Sidon and Beirut along the eastern Mediterranean shoreline; Piraeus/Athens near to the mid-Mediterranean; Carthage next to the southern Mediterranean coastline; Ephesus and Miletus, hugging the east coast of the Aegean Sea; Puteoli on the edge of the Tyrrhenian Sea; Byzantium/Istanbul on the Bosporus Strait; and Aila/Aqaba at the head of the Gulf of Elat/Aqaba.[4]
3. As a result of the nearly contiguous presence of natural resources. For example, the high-quality, industrial-scale deposit of tin, essential for the production of bronze, at the ancient municipality of Kestel/Göltepe, southwest Anatolia, roughly sixty miles (96 km) north of Tarsus, in modern Turkey; the rich deposit of gold at Sardis; the rare and costly murex seashells, valued for purple dyeing of cloth, found prominently around the island of Tyre; and the almost inexhaustible supply of highly-prized bitumen in the Dead Sea, proximate to Jericho.
4. As an effect of regional topography. Examples of this criterion include the strategic topographic locations of Megiddo, Corinth, or Antioch in Syria, or local topography such as the immediate physical surroundings of Jerusalem, Masada, Carchemish, or Rome.
5. As a function of natural lines of arterial transportation and communication routes, as is the case for Gaza, Hazor, Mari, or Babylon along the Great Trunk Road; Rabbah/Amman, Heshbon, or Kir Hareseth/Kerak along the King's Highway; Susa or Ancyra/Ankara along the Persian Royal Road; and Philippi or Thessalonica along the Egnatian Way.[5]

---

4. See *MAB*, 82–83, 259 (maps 26, 111).

5. For the King's Highway, see *MAB*, 78–79 (map 25); for the Persian Royal Road, see *MAB*, 204–5 (map 86); For the Egnatian Way, see *MAB*, 259 (map 111).

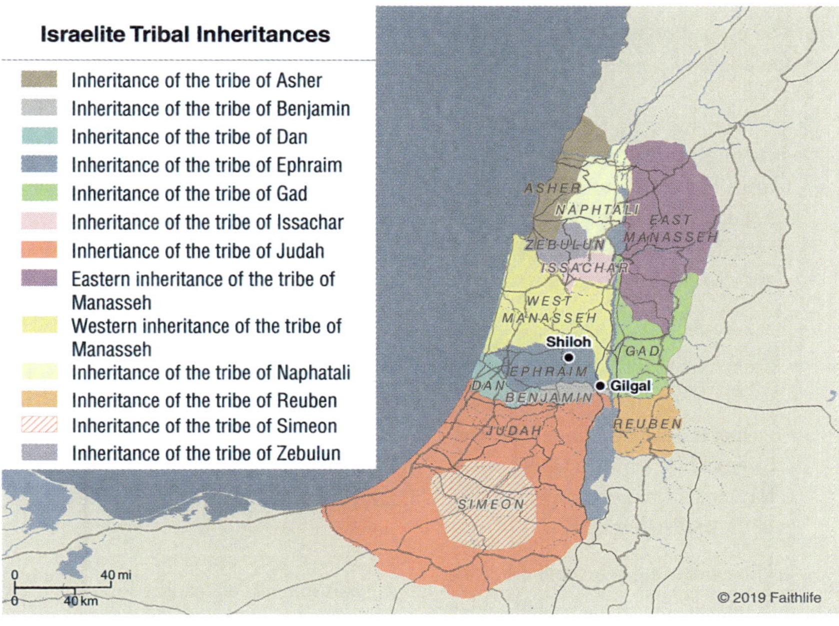

To be sure, there were times when a combination of these limiting locational factors may have blended at a particular site, or where they may not be so evident today. Nevertheless, as with other populated locales in the ancient world, it is axiomatic that biblical sites normally tend to have been situated in accordance with one or another limiting factor of geography, and not in some random or haphazard arrangement.

In similar manner, broader settlement patterns may likewise have been a consequence of geographical limitations. Thus, for example, let us examine the nature and extent of Israel's settlement in its promised land, focusing upon the spatial discordance that existed between the idealized tribal allotments theoretically apportioned to each of the tribes (Josh 13–21; see map—"Israelite Tribal Inheritances"), over against the actual terrain thought to have been settled by early Israel (see map—"Early Israel's Settlement in Southern Canaan and Transjordan," green highlighted areas).

First in this regard, it seems that wherever the Philistines or their Canaanite allies could maneuver iron chariots—on the Philistine plain (e.g., Judg 1:19) or across the Jezreel Valley (e.g., Josh 17:16–19; cf. Judg 4:3, 13; see also Deut 20:1–4; Josh 11:4, 6, 9)—the Israelites were unable to seize surrounding terrain theoretically allotted to them. But in places where the tactical advantage of horses and chariots was neutralized by the rugged mountain highlands of Canaan's interior, or in the lofty Transjordan, from the land of Gilead southwards (Josh 22:9), Israel appears to have been able to fashion for itself a terrestrial mosaic. Second, according to the biblical record (Josh 13:1–13; Judg 1–3), as late as the end of Joshua's life, there still remained huge tracts of allotted territory yet to be possessed by Israel. This territory included:

- the flat and open regions of Philistia (e.g., including the Philistine municipalities of Ekron, Gath, Ashdod, Ashkelon, Gaza; and surrounding villages in the plain; Josh 13:2–7; see also 11:22b)
- the southern Sharon Plain (the plains segment of the Danite inheritance; Judg 1:34a)
- western upper Galilee (e.g., Beth Shemesh [i.e., Beth Shemesh of Naphtali, in western upper Galilee]; Beth Anath; Judg 1:33)
- Phoenicia (e.g., the coastal cities of Akko, Akzib, Rehob, Tyre, Ahlab, Sidon, Gebal/Byblos, as well as Nahalal; Judg 1:31–32), and the contiguous plains
- the sweeping terrain of Geshur and Maakah (i.e., the Transjordanian territory southward from Mount Hermon as far as Gilead; Josh 13:13)
- the major pass from the Mediterranean coastal plain into the Judahite heartland (including the towns of Shaalbim, Aijalon, Beth Shemesh [i.e., Beth Shemesh in the Shephelah, Mount Heres]; Judg 1:34b–36; see also Josh 17:11).

Moreover, the strategic cities and surrounding villages situated adjacent to the Jezreel Valley (e.g., Megiddo, Taanach, Ibleam, Endor, Beth Shan; Judg 1:27–28) and on Canaan's coastal plain (e.g., Dor, Aphek, Gezer; Judg 1:27–29; compare with Josh 16:10; 17:11) still remained outside Israel's territorial domain (see Josh 13:4; 16:10; 17:11–12; Judg 1:27–29; 2:20–21). Finally, the city of Jerusalem continued under the jurisdiction of the Jebusites, not the Israelites (Josh 15:63; Judg 1:21; see also Judg 19:10–12; 2 Sam 5:6–16; note the recurring editorial refrain "to this day" [e.g., Josh 13:13; 15:63; 16:10; Judg 1:21], reflecting a protracted period in which certain areas remained beyond Israelite control). In other words, a rough comparison of the total land area allotted to Israel's tribes vis-à-vis the territory settled by premonarchic Israel suggests that no more than about fifty-five to sixty percent of its allotted land was actually inhabited in the earliest period of settlement.

Accordingly, one appears to find here an example of geographic forces setting the stage for and limiting where and how far ancient Israel succeeded in settling its land. In the heart of highland Galilee, in the rugged and twisted mountains of Samaria and Judah, as well as in the uplifted, remote Transjordanian territory east of the Jordan River and the Dead Sea, nascent Israel may be said to have accomplished a portion of its mission. But, in the immediately adjacent, flat, and open lowlands and plains of Philistia, Sharon, Phoenicia, and Jezreel, the Israelites clearly were unable to stake their claim.[6] Predictably, then, assuming this to be an accurate analysis of the biblical record, albeit a necessarily inexhaustive analysis, it should be in these settled zones that we expect to find some of the earliest archaeological evidence of ancient Israel in southern Canaan and the Transjordan. I should add, much of this evidence will have been created there and can be found

6. Note a residual echo of this even as late as 1 Kgs 20:23–28.

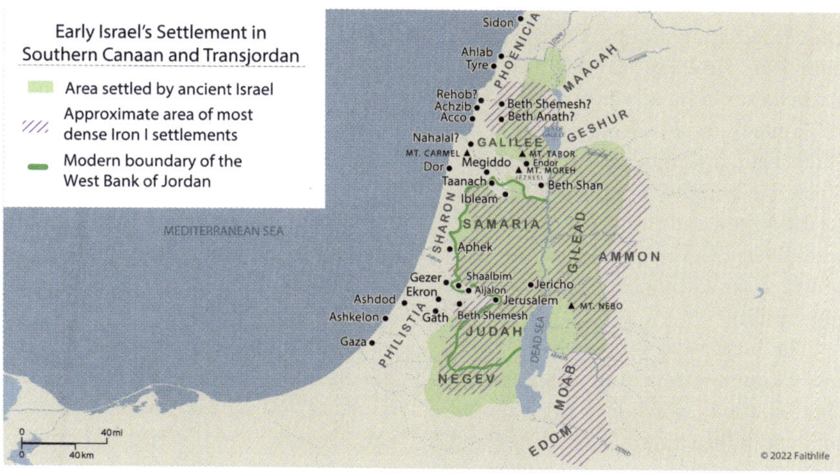

there in large part as a result of seminal geographic limitations.

RECENT INTRIGUING DISCOVERIES

Moreover, one can observe an astonishingly close geographical correlation between the highland territories of Samaria and Judah inhabited by Israel in the process of its ancient settlement (see map— "Early Israel's Settlement in Southern Canaan and Transjordan") and the territory captured by modern Israel in the so-called "Six-Day War" in June 1967.[7] It turns out that modern Israel, during the Six-Day War, crossed the Green Line and captured essentially the same central highland terrain of Samaria and portions of Judah that ancient Israel had come to possess in its original settlement. Here is a poignant illustration of how geographic forces may limit how and where history occurs, notwithstanding the three intermediate millennia and the advances of modern military technology.

In fact, in the immediate aftermath of the June 1967 war, the state of Israel undertook a massive project of comprehensively surveying and mapping its newly acquired territory, east as far as the Jordan River. Though this effort was understandably motivated primarily for modern political, strategic, and military purposes, precisely because this terrain had been a prime settlement area of ancient Israel, Israeli archaeologists were also enlisted into the enterprise. As a result, what in archaeological terms is known as "extensive surveying" or "emergency surveying" was hastily begun in this territory in late 1967. Over

7. Note on the map titled "Early Israel's Settlement in Southern Canaan and Transjordan" that the area circumscribed by the so-called "Green Line" and known today as the "West Bank." The Green Line is a modern demarcation of an armistice boundary, originally set forth by the United Nations Armistice Agreement in 1949 to differentiate land allotted to Israel and other land allotted to its Arab neighbors. For a map depicting various modern boundaries, territories, and designations, see *MAB*, 276 (map 118).

the succeeding years, more than a dozen extensive, systematic surveys have been undertaken within various segments of Samaria and Judah, as well as in the Shephelah, in Galilee, in the territory of Benjamin and the vicinity of Jerusalem, in the Negev, and elsewhere, and subsequently also in the Transjordan—some of which are still ongoing—with remarkable results.[8]

The vestige of hundreds of previously unknown, small circular, or elliptical-shaped, camp-like settlements or small villages have been discovered, archaeologically dating to approximately 1200 BC (known as the "Iron Age I" period in archaeological terms), at what is arguably the time of early Israel's initial premonarchic settlement (see map—"Early Israel's Settlement in Southern Canaan and Transjordan," areas with diagonal linework).[9] The Iron I sites appear suddenly, the majority upon bare bedrock, and without traces of burning or destruction. A site profile generally includes one or more of the following diagnostic features: the new sites are small (i.e., most are about one to three acres [4,047–12,141 m^2] in size, or approximately one hectare), simple (i.e., they are architecturally and aesthetically unsophisticated), open (i.e., the sites are unwalled or not walled beyond terrace walls or what appears in some cases to have been an animal corral), dull (i.e., the residents used simple utilitarian, undecorated pottery wares of a domestic variety—few in type and number—rather than the presence of luxury or imported objects), and many appear to have been abandoned by approximately 900 BC.

These sites—dispersed mostly in the hills of Samaria allotted to the tribes of [West] Manasseh, Ephraim, and Benjamin, and in Transjordan territory allotted to the tribes of [East] Manasseh, Gad, and Reuben, as well as on the highlands of Judah and Galilee, and elsewhere—exhibit no pattern of urbanization or industrialization, with essentially no new city walls, city gates, large public buildings such as a palace or temple, and with no existing network of adjoining roads or pathways. They reveal no sign of central political authority, and the inhabitants appear to have been economically poor (e.g., some sites are attested only with diagnostic Iron I pottery, and/or with unplastered in-ground storage pits for grain, earthen floors, or foundations of huts). The sites reflect a non-agrarian pastoral preoccu-

8. For a fairly comprehensive record of what has been discovered across the West Bank, including a database, see Raphael Greenberg and Adi Keinan, *Israeli Archaeological Activity in the West Bank 1967–2007: A Sourcebook* (Bar-Lev, Israel: Rahas Press, 2009), 23, which identifies some 436 Iron I sites. Naturally, many finds made and/or published over the past decade or findspots beyond the bounds of the Green Line will not appear in this publication.

9. For a standard treatment of archaeological periodization, see Amihai Mazar, *Archaeology and the Land of the Bible 10,000—586 B.C.E.* (New York: Doubleday, 1990), 30; see now with slight modification, Mazar, "The Debate over the Chronology of the Iron Age in the Southern Levant: Its History, the Current Situation, and a Suggested Resolution," in *The Bible and Radiocarbon Dating*, ed. Thomas E. Levy and Thomas Higham (London: Equinox, 2005, 2014), 15–30. See also Robert A. Mullins and Zachary Thomas, "A Geographical Assessment of Tenth Century BC Evidence in Relation to Early Israel, the Jezreel Valley and the Galilee," in vol. 2 of *Lexham Geographic Commentary on the Historical Books*, ed. Barry J. Beitzel (Bellingham, WA: Lexham Press, forthcoming).

Model of Israelite Iron I Highlands Village with Four-Room Houses

pation, with significant faunal remains and with a fair amount of inside living space apparently given over to the care of sheep and goats. A more-or-less uniform house size and shape, with open and easy interior access from room to pillared room, seems to be more indicative of social attitudes favoring equality over hierarchical authority, quite unlike what is known to have been common architecturally in Canaan in the immediately preceding Late Bronze Age period. No shrines have been found at these sites, and practically no weapons or pig bones have been exhumed. All this evidence unmistakably demonstrates that the new sites represent something different, and far more than the mere evolutionary redistribution of Late Bronze Age population groups residing in Canaan, thereby dispelling the notion of prior inhabitants transitioning from a sedentary to a pastoral mode of existence.

To date, approximately seven-hundred Iron I sites have been discovered in the Cisjordan, primarily in the hill country of Samaria and Judah, and in the highlands of Galilee.[10] This can provide a fairly

10. For the distribution and number of sites, see table "Approximate Number and Distribution of Iron I Sites Discovered," entries 1–8, and see map of "Early Israel's Settlement in Southern Canaan and Transjordan." The apolitical term the "Cisjordan" has long been helpfully employed to denote the territory of southern Canaan, west of the Jordan River as far as the Mediterranean coastline. This is in contradistinction to the "Transjordan,"

comprehensive basis for formulating an estimate of the early Iron Age population. Such a demographic analysis indicates that the population of southern Canaan tripled between 1200–1000. Beyond this, an additional five hundred-plus Iron I sites have been discovered in the Transjordan,[11] between Gilead and ancient Edom, again representing what Larry Herr and Douglas Clark describe as a "rapid explosion of Iron I sites."[12] Accordingly, more than twelve hundred Iron I sites have been discovered since late-1967 thus far, and a scattering of additional sites continue to be located.[13]

This number of new sites and rapid increase in population is both rare in ancient history and baffling here.[14] Moreover, one must speculate as to the identity of the new settlers and from where they might have come. The prominent Israeli geographical authority, the late Anson F. Rainey, formerly of Tel Aviv University, declares, "Everyone agrees that there is an amazing multiplication of small village sites in the hill-country areas during this period [i.e., Iron I] and it has even been admitted that there probably weren't enough people from the depleted [Late Bronze Age] Canaanite population to furnish occupants for the new sites."[15] Likewise, Harvard University's highly respected expert in Near Eastern archaeology,

which identifies adjacent territory east of the Jordan River as far as the edge of the Arabian Desert.

11. See Table 1, "Approximate Number and Distribution of Iron I Sites Discovered," entries 9–13 on p. 164; my listing there is admittedly incomplete.

12. Herr and Clark make mention of 517 Iron I sites in Transjordan (as of early 2009; see Larry G. Herr and Douglas R. Clark, "From the Stone Age to the Middle Ages in Jordan: Digging up Tall al-'Umayri," *NEA* 72.2 [2009]: 86). According to Clark (personal communication), this figure derives from the Jordan Antiquities Database and Information Systems (JADIS), established and maintained by the Jordanian Department of Antiquities. While Iron I demographic methodology continues to be a matter of open discussion, and population estimates do vary within certain limits from scholar to scholar, that the Iron I population of southern Canaan and Transjordan *tripled* beyond that of the immediately preceding Late Bronze Age population, by whatever calculation formula, is accepted by nearly all (see Jeffrey R. Zorn, "Estimating the Population Size of Ancient Settlements: Methods, Problems, Solutions, and a Case Study," *BASOR* 295 [1994]: 31–48; William G. Dever, *Who Were the Early Israelites and Where Did They Come From?* [Grand Rapids: Eerdmans, 2003], 97–100; 156–58; Lawrence E. Stager, "Forging an Identity: The Emergence of Ancient Israel," in *The Oxford History of the Biblical World*, ed. Michael D. Coogan [Oxford: Oxford University Press, 1998], 90–131; see also Israel Finkelstein, *The Archaeology of the Israelite Settlement* [Jerusalem: Israel Exploration Society, 1988], 324–35; Magen Broshi, "The Population of Iron Age Palestine," in *Biblical Archaeology Today, 1990*, ed. Avraham Biran and Joseph Aviram [Jerusalem: Israel Exploration Society: 1993], 14–18).

13. For a cartographic placement of Iron Age sites in southern Canaan and Transjordan, see Siegfried Mittmann and Götz Schmitt, eds., *Tübinger Bibelatlas* (Wiesbaden: Deutsche Bibelgesellschaft, 2001), map B/IV/6, northern and southern maps.

14. No substantial evidence exists to suggest that this geopolitical upheaval was the result of climate change, widespread warfare, migration, regional or international politics, or socioeconomics.

15. Anson F. Rainey and R. Steven Notley, *The Sacred Bridge* (Jerusalem: Carta, 2006), 111. See also Volkmar Fritz, *The Emergence of Israel in the Twelfth and Eleventh Centuries B.C.E.* (Atlanta: Society of Biblical Literature, 2011), 82–103.

the late Lawrence E. Stager, comments, "Given the low aggregate of the Late Bronze population throughout Canaan, it appears unlikely that the peasantry, even if they had all 'revolted' [i.e., in an alleged social revolution], could have been large enough to account for the total Iron Age population throughout Canaan."[16] Professor William G. Dever, one of America's most distinguished Near Eastern archaeologists, formerly of the University of Arizona, adds, "This growth of the new settlements resulted in a sharp rise in population in the central hills in early Iron I ... Demographers would hardly attribute this sharp increase [in population] to natural growth alone. Clearly there has been an influx of new settlers; but who *were* they, and where did they *come* from?"[17]

POSSIBLE EVIDENCE OF EARLY ISRAEL'S SETTLEMENT

Could there be any evidentiary connection between these sites and pre-monarchic Israel? Could some, or all, of these new settlers have been "Proto-Israelites," "Pre-Israelites," or even "Israelites," or in some way related to early Israel? As with any historical question of such magnitude and import, especially given that a response must be based on archaeological and demographic evidence only recently adduced, including contemporaneous evidence, a scholarly verdict is still far from unanimous. There are many complex and puzzling details which have yet to be fully processed and explicated. Nevertheless, I believe it is fair to indicate that the pendulum of general scholarship is moving in a more positive direction on this question. In this regard, Avraham Faust, a highly regarded professor in the Martin (Szusz) Department of Land of Israel Studies and Archaeology at Bar-Ilan University, has recently observed, "until a few years ago, it seemed as if a majority of scholars tended to adopt a skeptical approach to the issue, and questioned the attribution of the term 'Israelite' to the Iron I highlands villages. ... it appears, however, that an interesting and important shift is beginning, as most specialists today ... accept this connection."[18]

Preferring to identify the newcomers as "Proto-Israelites," Dever proceeds to answer his own question about their identity, "the [Iron I] peoples of the highlands were not yet citizens of a State of Israel with fixed boundaries, a unified sense of ethnic identity, and passports saying 'Israelite.' But I will argue that these were the *ancestors*—the authentic and direct progenitors—of those who later became the biblical Israelites."[19]

---

16. Lawrence E. Stager, "Respondents," in *Biblical Archaeology Today: Proceedings of the International Congress on Biblical Archaeology, Jerusalem, April 1984*, ed. Janet Amitai (Jerusalem: Israel Exploration Society, 1985), 84.

17. William G. Dever, "Israel, History of: Archaeology and the Israelite 'Conquest,'" *ABD* 3:549 (emphasis original).

18. Avraham Faust, "A Review of *Biblical Peoples and Ethnicity*," *NEA* 72.2 (2009): 108. See, e.g., Faust, "How Did Israel Become a People?," *BAR* 35.6 (2009), 62–69, 92–93; Faust, *Israel's Ethnogenesis: Settlement, Interaction, Expansion and Resistance* (London: Equinox, 2006); Faust, "Between Reality and Ideology: Revisiting the Israelite Ethos of Egalitarianism and Simplicity," in this volume.

19. Dever, *Who Were the Early Israelites*, 153–221 (quote taken from page 194; emphasis original).

Iron Age Israelite Four-Room House at Hazor

Professor Amihai Mazar, one of Israel's most renowned professors of archaeology and professor emeritus at the Hebrew University of Jerusalem, avers:

> The environmental and economic background of the emergence of these [Iron I] settlements, together with their architectural and other material cultural characteristics, reflect the wide-scale settlement of a people with a specific socio-economic life-style, which in my opinion accords with premonarchic Israelite society as described in the biblical narratives ... [the] term 'Proto-Israelites' introduced by Dever and adopted by others to designate the inhabitants of these sites is in my view superfluous.[20]

Finally, Professor Stager adds, "What can be said is that Iron Age I settlements throughout the highlands display a similar material culture, which is best identified with rural communities based on mixed economies of agriculture and sheep-goat herding. That many of these villages belonged to premonarchic Israel (as known from Judg 5 and perhaps from the Merenptah Stela [see below]) is beyond doubt."[21]

What evidence from these sites might be adduced and highlighted in the sup-

20. Amihai Mazar, "Remarks on Biblical Traditions and Archaeological Evidence concerning Early Israel," in *Symbiosis, Symbolism, and the Power of the Past*, ed. William G. Dever and Seymour Gitin (Winona Lake, IN: Eisenbrauns, 2003), 87.

21. Stager, "Forging an Identity," 100.

port of such a proposition? I wish to provide here a brief, general overview of six lines of evidence, which together, in my view, can offer a rational case of plausibility.

(1) GEOGRAPHY

As already addressed above, an arresting geographic correlation exists between the location of the wide majority of the Iron I sites and where, according to the biblical record, the ancient Israelites were able to settle in southern Canaan and the Transjordan. Moreover, there is an inverse correlation between where in southern Canaan and the Transjordan the majority of Iron I sites are not found and where, according to the Bible, ancient Israel was explicitly said to have been unable to gain an early settlement foothold.

(2) MATERIAL CULTURE

In certain respects, the material culture of these new sites is both similar and dissimilar from what immediately preceded in the Late Bronze Age. On the one hand, ceramic assemblages bear certain elements of continuity with their predecessors, and yet some distinctive new trends emerge in the Iron I period, such as the slight movement from wheel-made pottery to handmade pottery; a pronounced reduction in the number of repertoire forms; a lack of imported or luxury wares; and somewhat distinctive forms.[22] On the other hand, Iron I domestic architecture is decidedly distinct; for example, the preponderance of the so-called "four-room house" or "pillared house," in contrast to the "courtyard house" characteristic of the Late Bronze Age. At the same time, the new sites exhibit strong links of cultural continuity with the later Iron II sites (c. 800 BC).[23] The inhabitants of many of the Iron II sites are almost universally recognized as "Israelites," by which scholars are referring to the Israelites of the Bible.[24]

---

22. For the most recent, definitive, presentation of Iron I pottery characteristics and forms, see Amihai Mazar, "Iron Age I: Northern Coastal Plain, Galilee, Samaria, Jezreel Valley, Judah, and Negev," in *The Ancient Pottery of Israel and Its Neighbors from the Iron Age through the Hellenistic Period*, ed. Seymour Gitin (Jerusalem: Israel Exploration Society, 2015), 1:5–70. On Iron I pottery in Transjordan, see Larry G. Herr, "Iron Age I: Transjordan," in Gitin, *Ancient Pottery of Israel*, 1:97–114. See also Finkelstein, *Israelite Settlement*, 270–91; Anne E. Killebrew, *Biblical Peoples and Ethnicity: An Archaeological Study of Egyptians, Canaanites, Philistines, and Early Israel, 1300–1100 B.C.E.* (Atlanta: Society of Biblical Literature, 2005), 177–81; Dever, *Who Were the Early Israelites*, 95, 118–25; Avraham Faust, *Israel's Ethnogenesis: Settlement, Interaction, Expansion and Resistance* (London: Equinox, 2006), 41–70.

23. See Michal Bieniada, "Factors which Effected Changes in Settlement Pattern and the Character of 'Israelite Settlement' during the Transitional Late Bronze and Early Iron Age in Palestine," *The Polish Journal of Biblical Research* 1.2 (2001): 157–97; Shlomo Bunimovitz and Avraham Faust, "Building Identity: The Four-Room House and the Israelite Mind," in Dever and Gitin, *Symbiosis, Symbolism, and the Power of the Past*, 411–23; Douglas R. Clark, "Bricks, Sweat and Tears: The Human Investment in Constructing a 'Four-room' House," *NEA* 66.1–2 (2003): 34–43.

24. See Douglas R. Clark and Monique D. Roddy, "Evidence of Early Israel? A Socio-spatial Analysis of the So-Called 'Four-Room' House in Context," in this volume.

Qeiyafa Ostracon, Tenth Century BC

(3) WRITING PATTERN

While these new sites and their immediate environs have thus far yielded only a scant number of written documents, the few early Iron Age snippets that have been found deserve comment.[25] These

25. Early written materials so far discovered on Iron I sites include the following: [1] the Izbet Sartah alphabetic sherd (Aaron Demsky, "A Proto-Canaanite Abecedary ('Izbet Ṣarṭah)," *TA* 4 [1977]: 14–27); [2] the reused Tell Zayit alphabetic stone (Ron E. Tappy, P. Kyle McCarter, Marilyn J. Lundberg, and Bruce Zuckerman, "An Abecedary of the Mid-Tenth Century B.C.E. from the Judaean Shephelah," *BASOR* 344 [2006]: 5–46); [3] a five-line broken ostracon, containing perhaps as many as eighteen different alphabetic characters, but of uncertain context, found at Tell Qeiyafa (Haggai Misgav, Yosef Garfinkel, and Saar Ganor, "The Ostracon," in *Khirbet Qeiyafa, Vol. 1: Excavation Report 2007–2008*, ed. Yosef Garfinkel and Saar Ganor [Jerusalem: Israel Exploration Society, 2009], 243–57; Alan Millard, "The Ostracon from the Days of David Found at Khirbet Qeiyafa," *TynBul* 62.1 [2011]: 1–13); [4-5-6] three short inscriptions from Tell Batash, Tell 'Amal, and Rosh Zayit (see Amihai Mazar, "The Spade and the Text: The Interaction between Archaeology and Israelite History Relating to the Tenth-Ninth Centuries BCE," in *Understanding the History of Ancient* Israel, ed. H. G. M. Williamson [Oxford: Oxford University Press, 2007], 158, 164–66); [7] a name carved on a game board at Beth Shemesh (Shlomo Bunimovitz and Zvi Lederman, "Beth-Shemesh: Culture Conflict in Judah's Frontier," *BAR* 23.1 [1997]: 42–49, 75–77; see photograph on page 48); [8] a three-line fragmentary jar inscription from Lachish (William M. Schniedewind, "The Alphabetic 'Scribe' of the Lachish Jar Inscription and the Hieratic Tradition in the Early Iron Age," *BASOR* 383 [2020]: 137–40); and [9] a short piece from Tel Rehov (Mazar, "Remarks on Biblical Traditions," 90; see now Omer Sergi, "The Formation of Israelite Identity in the Central Canaanite Highlands in the Iron Age I-IIA," *NEA* 82.1 [2019]: 49; compare William M. Schniedewind, "Problems in the Paleographic Dating of Inscriptions," in Levy and Highman, *The Bible and Radiocarbon Dating*, remove 405–12). For an assortment of Iron I seals, seal impressions,

texts are still in the process of analysis, both linguistically and historically, and more clarity will surely emerge in the coming years, but currently it can be confidently stated that, epigraphically speaking, these documents without exception are written in a simple, archaic alphabetic script, also known from other locations across the ancient Near East and most often identified as "Canaanite/Phoenician/Old Hebrew."[26] It is unmistakably this "mother script" used by Israelites only a few years later.[27]

(4) Faunal Remains

The type of woodlands that dominated the central highlands of the Cisjordan are ideally suited for pig production, and several species of pigs/swine were native to the region.[28] Thus the virtual absence of pig bones is significant.[29] In fact, pig bones are found in these central high lands, sometimes in large quantities, both *before* and *after* the Iron I settlements,[30] whereas they almost disappear in the highlands *during* this period but are concurrently found in areas adjacent to the highlands.[31]

---

and bullae, see Graham I. Davies, "Some Uses of Writing in Ancient Israel in Light of Recently Published Inscriptions," in *Writing and Ancient Near Eastern Society: Papers in Honour of Alan R. Millard*, ed. Piotr Bienkowski, Christopher Mee, and Elizabeth Slater (London: T&T Clark, 2005), 155–74.

26. See Christopher A. Rollston, "What's the Oldest Hebrew Inscription?" *BAR* 38.3 (2012): 32–40, 66–68; Shmuel Ahituv and Amihai Mazar, "The Inscriptions from Tel Reḥov and their Contribution to the Study of Script and Writing During Iron Age IIA," *Maarav* 20.2 (2013): 205–72; Alan Millard, "Ancient Hebrew Inscriptions: Their Distribution and Significance," in *Alphabets, Texts and Artifacts in the Ancient Near East: Studies Presented to Benjamin Sass*, ed. Israel Finkelstein, Christian Robin, and Thomas Römer (Paris: Van Dieren, 2017), 270–78 (I owe this final reference to the kindness of Professor Millard).

27. See Graham I. Davies, *Ancient Hebrew Inscriptions: Corpus and Concordance*, 2 vols. (Cambridge: Cambridge University, 2004).

28. Lawrence E. Stager, "When Canaanites and Philistines Ruled Ashkelon," *BAR* 17.2 (1991), 24–37, 40–43. See also Edwin Formage, "Zoology (Animal Profiles)," *ABD* 6:1119–51, esp. 1130–35, and the bibliography there. Note also Matt 8:28–34//Mark 5:1–20//Luke 8:26–39 and Luke 15:11–32.

29. E.g., Ehrlich stresses the presence/absence of pig bones as an authentic ethnic marker (Carl S. Ehrlich, "'How the Mighty Are Fallen': The Philistines in Their Tenth Century Context," in *The Age of Solomon: Scholarship at the Turn of the Millennium*, ed. Lowell K. Handy [Leiden: Brill, 1997], 179–201). See also Richard S. Hess, "Early Israel in Canaan: A Survey of Recent Evidence and Interpretation," *PEQ* 125.2 (1993): 138–40.

30. Paula Wapnish and Brian Hesse, "Urbanization and the Organization of Animal Production at Tell Jemmeh in the Middle Bronze Age Levant," *JNES* 47 (1988): 81–94; Avraham Faust, *Ethnogenesis* 35–40. The entire skeleton of a small pig has recently been discovered among Iron Age IIB (eighth century) remains, in the vicinity of the Gihon Spring, on the eastern slopes of the City of David, immediately east of OT Zion, in what would appear to be a Judahite context (see Lidar Sapir-Hen, Joe Uziel, and Ortal Chalaf, "Everything but the Oink: On the Discovery of an Articulated Pig in Iron Age Jerusalem and Its Meaning to Judahite Consumption Practices," *NEA* 84.2 [2021]: 110–19, and note the extensive bibliography there).

31. Several scholars in the past have argued that the introduction of pork on the Philistine coastlands at this point in time was a cultural change introduced by Philistine newcomers from abroad. Leaving open the question of identifiable ethnic markers, recent DNA examination of pig bones from the lowland sites reveals a European genetic signature, not a native Canaanite signature, suggesting that these pigs were, in fact, brought along to Canaan around

The Merenptah Stele

Coastal sites in particular show a transition from Late Bronze consumption of sheep/goats to an Iron I consumption of pigs/cattle, but by virtue of the pottery also found at these sites, they are indisputably Philistine settlements.[32] As a specific case study in this regard, the Israelites of this period were said to have settled on the east end of the Sorek Valley, at the site of Beth Shemesh (1 Sam 6:9–18; see on-site archaeological evidence), whereas the Philistines occupied both the interior

1200 BC by the Sea Peoples, and presumably by the Philistines in particular. See Meirav Meiri et al., "Ancient DNA and Population Turnover in Southern Levantine Pigs–Signature of the Sea Peoples Migration?," in *Scientific Reports* 3.3035 (2013): 1–8; Lidar Sapir-Hen et al., "Pig Husbandry in Iron Age Israel and Judah," *ZDPV* 129.1 (2013): 1–20; and especially Lidar Sapir-Hen, Meirav Meiri, and Israel Finkelstein, "Iron Age Pigs: New Evidence on Their Origin and Role in Forming Identity Boundaries," *Radiocarbon* 57.2 (2015): 307–15. See most recently Lidar Sapir-Hen, "Food, Pork Consumption, and Identity in Ancient Israel," *NEA* 82.1 (2019): 52–59.

32. Lawrence E. Stager, "Biblical Philistines: A Hellenistic Literary Creation?" in *"I Will Speak the Riddles of Ancient Times": Archaeological and Historical Studies in Honor of Amihai Mazar*, ed. Aren M. Maeir and Pierre de Miroschedji (Winona Lake, IN: Eisenbrauns, 2006), 1:378–80; see also Elizabeth Bloch-Smith, "Israelite Ethnicity in Iron I: Archaeology Preserves What is Remembered and What is Forgotten in Israel's History," *JBL* 122.3 (2003): 409–11, 423–24.

Inscribed Poem Commemorating Merenptah's Triumph over Israel

of the Sorek, at Timnah, as well as the western end of the valley, at Ekron (see Judg 14:1; 1 Sam 5:10).[33] The presence of pig bones at Ekron (26%) and Timnah (8%), and the near absence of pig bones at nearby Beth Shemesh (0%) is surely eloquent in this regard.

Several sociocultural reasons are postulated for why people migrating out of a desert culture into a more sedentary lifestyle might not consume swine (e.g., cost, ignorance of the option, limited usefulness, cultural prejudice, pigs unsuited for a rural setting), but one must not overlook the taboo expressed in the Old Testament itself as a plausible explanation for this distinction. Israel's dietary laws forbade the consumption of swine or any other unclean animal (Lev 11:26–28; Deut 14:8).[34] Pigs were raised in substantial numbers across Canaan in certain periods, a fact which suggests that their virtual disappearance in the central highlands during the Iron I may have been a function of ethnicity and/or culture, not simply environment or ecology.[35] In the same way, Ann Killebrew argues that the significant introduction of pork consumption in Iron I Philistia is a function of culture by newcomers from abroad, this same consideration offers scholarly traction with reference to an

33. See Brian Hesse, "Animal Use at Tell Miqne-Ekron in the Bronze Age and Iron Age," *BASOR* 264 (1986): 17–27. See also Shlomo Bunimovitz and Zvi Lederman, "Canaanite Resistance: The Philistines and Beth-Shemesh—A Case Study from Iron Age I," *BASOR* 364 (2011): 37–51; Brian Hesse, Emmett Brown, and Timothy Griffin, "Animal Husbandry in the Early Iron Age at Tel Beth-Shemesh," in *Tel Beth-Shemesh: A Border Community in Judah: Renewed Excavations 1990–2000: The Iron Age*, ed. Shlomo Bunimovitz and Zvi Lederman, 2 vols. (Winona Lake, IN: Eisenbrauns, 2016), 1:257–65.

34. No matter the date(s) of this particular piece of legislation, a cultural taboo must certainly have been in place by the time of the appearance of Israel's premonarchic confederation.

35. See Stager, "Canaanites and Philistines," 31. For a somewhat contrastive viewpoint, see Brian Hesse and Paula Wapnish, "Can Pig Remains be Used for Ethnic Diagnosis in the Ancient Near East?," in *The Archaeology of Israel: Constructing the Past, Interpreting the Present*, ed. Neil Asher Silberman and David Small (Sheffield: Sheffield Academic, 1997), 238–70.

inverse reality in the central highlands during this same period.[36]

(5) SOCIAL STRUCTURE

Ancient Israel is often described in an essentially "pastoralist" mode of existence, with flocks and herds, much like the occupants of the newly discovered settlements. The Bible consistently presents the notion of a group of premonarchic Israelite forebears who entered Canaan from abroad, having lived in a desert environment for a considerable time. Such social and socioeconomic reality comports well with settlements that lack cultural sophistication, are small, and are comparatively impoverished. Whatever else we learn from the books of Joshua and Judges about the Israelite settlement, it is clear that premonarchic Israel functioned basically as a tribal social organization that lacked the sort of national identity found, for example, in the office of a king. Few political structures existed, and ties to the clan or tribe were the center of social focus. Early Israelites tend to be depicted as depending on themselves—on their own clan, their own crops, and their own flocks/herds—for material necessities and survival. Early on, an essentially egalitarian or communitarian mentality is clearly reflected in their settlement narratives, thus, for example, the recurring phraseology, "there was no king in Israel in those days, and everyone did what was right in his own eyes" (Judg 17:6; 18:1; 19:1; 21:25; compare with Deut 17:14–20). This same social pattern seems to be reflected in the contemporaneous Iron I settlements.[37]

(6) MERENPTAH STELA

Pharaoh Merenptah (or Merneptah) was the twelfth or thirteenth son and successor of Ramesses II, and he reigned as the Egyptian monarch for a period of ten years (1213–1203 BC).[38] In the fifth year of Merenptah's reign (1209/8), he succeeded in defeating a Libyan invasion of Egypt and, in consequence, he recorded his victory upon a ten-foot slab of black granite and installed the stela in his mortuary temple in Thebes, on display today in the Cairo Museum.

At the very bottom of the slab, seemingly as an afterthought to fill an otherwise unused space, Merenptah's scribes appended a short poem commemorating his triumph over forces in Canaan. Among other themes, the poem mentions that he had vanquished the Canaanite cities of Ashkelon, Gezer, and Yenoam, and that he had laid waste to an *ethnic* entity known

36. On this subject, see Steven M. Ortiz and Chris McKinny, "'The Land that Remains': Evidence in Favor of the Thirteenth Century BC View of the Israelite Conquest and Settlement," in this volume.

37. Killebrew, *Biblical Peoples*, 250–51. Killebrew's conclusion is based on evidence of Aegean-style material culture and decorated pottery, as well as significant pork consumption. See also Yosef Garfinkel, "The Birth & Death of Biblical Minimalism," *BAR* 37.3 (2011): 51; Avraham Faust, "Between Reality and Ideology: Revisiting the Israelite Ethos of Egalitarianism and Simplicity," in this volume.

38. For an Egyptian chronological standard, see Kenneth A. Kitchen, "Egypt, History of (Chronology)," *ABD* 2:321–31; see also William J. Murnane, *The Penguin Guide to Ancient Egypt* (Harrisonburg, VA: R. R. Donnelley & Sons, 1983); William W. Hallo and William Kelly Simpson, *The Ancient Near East, A History* (New York: Harcourt Brace College Publishers, 1998), 297–300.

as "Israel."[39] This is the oldest extrabiblical reference to Israel, and it is the only such reference known before the ninth century. Moreover, the reference fits remarkably well—both chronologically and spatially—with the date and location of the biblical settlement of Canaan and the contemporaneous introduction of the Iron I highland sites.[40]

Parenthetically, Merenptah's presence in Canaan is also attested by distinctive cartouches bearing his name. An ivory chain with two cartouches referencing Merenptah was exhumed from a late-thirteenth-century stratum at Gezer, one of the cities Merenptah claims to have vanquished, and an ivory tusk bearing his cartouche was discovered in a securely-dated late-thirteenth century temple complex at nearby Ekron.[41] Accordingly, it is clear that by Merenptah's fifth regnal year, an ethnic entity known as "Israel" is said to have been present inside Canaan and in some way to have come into contact with the Egyptian pharaoh.

CONCLUSION

Individual lines of evidence admittedly offer us only historical snapshots, not a video, and they cannot account for the whole picture. Nevertheless, their overall congruence in this instance seems, at least at the present moment, to paint a rather well-defined mosaic of historical plausibility. Finally, I would contend that the general locational context of most of this evidence may be said to represent a pristine example of the significance of geography and geographic limitations in biblical, historical, and archaeological studies.

39. Raz Kletter, "Can a Proto-Israelite Please Stand Up? Notes on the Ethnicity of Iron Age Israel and Judah," in *"I Will Speak the Riddles of Ancient Times": Archaeological and Historical Studies in Honor of Amihai Mazar*, ed. Aren M. Maeir and Pierre de Miroschedji (Winona Lake, IN: Eisenbrauns, 2006), 2:581; see also Edward Lipiński, *On the Skirts of Canaan in the Iron Age: Historical and Topographical Researches* (Leuven: Peeters, 2006), 60.

40. On this subject, see Michael G. Hasel, "The Geography of the Campaign of Pharaoh Merenptah and Its Relation to Early Israel," in this volume. In addition, Görg has argued that a small granite stela—unprovenanced and undated but perhaps dating to the fourteenth or early thirteenth century—contains an archaic reference to "Israel" (Manfred Görg, "Neue Erwängungen zur Deutung des Namens, Israel'," *Blätter Abrahams* 11 [2011]: 37–44). If true, this would predate the Merenptah citation. For an evaluation of this proposal, see Wolfgang Zwickel and Pieter van der Veen, "The Earliest Reference to Israel and Its Possible Archaeological and Historical Background," *VT* 67 (2017): 129–40. The possible wider implications of this proposal for southern Canaan in general have also been subjected to historiographical analysis (see Emanuel Pfoh, "The Earliest Reference to Israel: A Historiographical Reflection," *Revue Biblique* 128.3 [2021]: 321–31).

41. See William G. Dever, "Gezer," *NEAEHL* 2:504–5; Seymour Gitin, "Excavating Ekron: Major Philistine City Survived by Absorbing Other Cultures," *BAR* 31.6 (2005): 50–52.

TABLE 1: APPROXIMATE NUMBER AND DISTRIBUTION OF IRON-I SITES DISCOVERED

Region	***Sub-region or Zone***	***Number of Iron Age I Sites***
(1) Galilee	upper and western Galilee[42]	55
	Lower and Eastern Galilee[43]	20–25
(2) (West) Manasseh	zone 1[44]	56
	zone 2[45]	47
	zone 3[46]	50
	zone 4[47]	69
	zone 5[48]	66
	zone 6[49]	44
	zone 7[50]	39

42. Frankel identifies some fifty-five Iron sites (see Rafael Frankel, "Upper Galilee in the Late Bronze-Iron I Transition," in *From Nomadism to Monarchy*, ed. Israel Finkelstein and Nadav Na'aman [Jerusalem: Israel Exploration Society, 1994], 18–34). See also Frankel, *Settlement Dynamics and Regional Diversity in Ancient Upper Galilee: Archaeological Survey of Upper Galilee* (Jerusalem: Israel Exploration Society, 2001); Hayah Katz, "Settlement Processes in the Meron Ridges During the Iron Age I," *BASOR* 383 (2020): 1–18; compare Dever, *Who Were the Early Israelites*, 97, 208–10.

43. Zvi Gal, *Lower Galilee During the Iron Age* (Winona Lake, IN: Eisenbrauns, 1992); Gal, "Iron I in Lower Galilee and the Margins of the Jezreel Valley," in Finkelstein and Na'aman, *From Nomadism to Monarchy*, 35–46.

44. Adam Zertal, *The Manasseh Hill Country Survey, Vol 1: The Shechem Syncline* (Leiden: Brill, 2004); Zertal, "'To the Land of the Perizzites and the Giants': On the Israelite Settlement in the Hill Country of Manasseh," in Finkelstein and Na'aman, *From Nomadism to Monarchy*, 47–69.

45. Adam Zertal, *The Manasseh Hill Country Survey, Vol 2: The Eastern Valleys and the Fringes of the Desert* (Leiden: Brill, 2008).

46. Adam Zertal and N. Mirkam, *The Manasseh Hill Country Survey, Vol 3: From Nahal 'Iron to Nahal Shechem* (Leiden: Brill, 2016).

47. Adam Zertal and Shay Bar, *The Manasseh Hill Country Survey, Vol 4: From Nahal Bezeq to the Sartaba* (Leiden: Brill, 2017).

48. Adam Zertal and Shay Bar, *The Manasseh Hill Country Survey, Vol 5: The Middle Jordan Valley from Wadi Fasael to Wadi 'Aujah* (Leiden: Brill, 2019).

49. Shay Bar and Adam Zertal, *The Manasseh Hill Country Survey, Vol 6: The Eastern Samaria Shoulder* (Leiden: Brill, 2021).

50. Shay Bar and Adam Zertal, *The Manasseh Hill Country Survey, Vol 7: The South-Eastern Samaria Shoulder* (Haifa: Seker, 2019) [Hebrew].

Region	*Sub-region or Zone*	*Number of Iron Age I Sites*
(2) (West) Manasseh (continued)	zone 8[51]	13
	zone 9[52]	40
(3) Ephraim[53]		122
(4) Benjamin and the area around Jerusalem[54]		50
(5) Judah[55]		18
(6) Shephelah (and the Sharon Plain?)[56]		5 (+10)
(7) Negev[57]		6
(8) Jezreel Valley[58]		few?

---

51. Shay Bar and Adam Zertal, *The Manasseh Hill Country Survey, Vol 8: The Slopes of Western Samaria* (Haifa: Seker, 2020) [Hebrew].

52. Shay Bar and Adam Zertal, *The Manasseh Hill Country Survey, Vol 9:* [field still to be named]. Unpublished. (I wish to thank Shay Bar for his generous help on the *The Manasseh Hill Country Survey* materials).

53. Finkelstein, *Israelite Settlement.*

54. Israel Finkelstein and Yitzhak Magen, eds., *Archaeological Survey of the Hill Country of Benjamin* (Jerusalem: Keset, 1993); Israel Finkelstein, Zvi Lederman, and Shlomo Bunimovitz, eds., *Highlands of Many Cultures, The Southern Samaria Survey: The Sites,* 2 vols. (Tel Aviv: Institute of Archaeology, Tel Aviv University, 1997); Amihai Mazar, "Jerusalem and its Vicinity in Iron Age I," in Finkelstein and Na'aman, *From Nomadism to Monarchy,* 70–91; compare with Stager, "Forging an Identity," 90–131; Dever, *Who Were the Early Israelites,* 21A6.

55. Avi Ofer, "'All the Hill Country of Judah': From a Settlement Fringe to a Prosperous Monarchy," in Finkelstein and Na'aman, *From Nomadism to Monarchy*, 92–121; Ofer, "The Monarchic Period in the Judaean Highland: A Spatial Overview," in *Studies in the Archaeology of the Iron Age in Israel and Jordan,* ed. Amihai Mazar (Sheffield: Sheffield Academic, 2001), 14–37. The issue of the presence and extent of Iron I settlements across Judah, and their political implications, has recently been addressed (see Yosef Garfinkel et al., "Lachish Fortifications and State Formation in the Biblical Kingdom of Judah in Light of Radiometric Datings," *Radiocarbon* 61.3 [2019]: 695–712).

56. Yehuda Dagan, "The Shephelah of Judah during the Period of the Monarchy in Light of Archaeological Excavations and Surveys," (MA Thesis; Tel Aviv University, 1992); see also Oded Lipschits and Aren M. Maeir, eds., *The Shephelah during the Iron Age: Recent Archaeological Studies* (Winona Lake, IN: Eisenbrauns, 2017); Finkelstein offers a cautionary note concerning the ten sites in the Sharon Plain (Finklestein, *Israelite Settlement*, 332–33); Avraham Faust, "Between the Highland Polity and Philistia: The United Monarchy and the Resettlement of the Shephelah in the Iron Age IIA, with Special Focus on Tel 'Eton and Khirbet Qeiyafa," *BASOR* 383 (2020): 115–36; compare Dever, *Who Were the Early Israelites,* 97.

57. Ze'ev Herzog, "The Beer-Sheba Valley: From Nomadism to Monarchy," in Finkelstein and Na'aman, *From Nomadism to Monarchy*, 122–49.

58. Drori Inbar, "The Geographical History of Beth-shean Valley and its Adjacent Mountainous Area: From the LB IIB to the End of the Iron IIc Periods," (PhD diss., Bar-Ilan University, 2001); Dever, *Who Were the Early Israelites,* 97, 212.

Region	**Sub-region or Zone**	**Number of Iron Age I Sites**
(9) Gilead[59]		77
(10) Tableland between Amman and Heshbon[60]		31
(11) Moab[61]		120
(12) Edom[62]		35
(13) East Jordan Valley (two separate zones)[63]		19 + 22

BIBLIOGRAPHY

Ahituv, Shmuel, and Amihai Mazar. "The Inscriptions from Tel Reḥov and their Contribution to the Study of Script and Writing During Iron Age IIA." *Maarav* 20.2 (2013): 205–46, and plates IX–XVI.

Bar, Shay, and Adam Zertal. *The Manasseh Hill Country Survey, Volume 6: The Eastern Samaria Shoulder.* Leiden: Brill, 2021.

———. *The Manasseh Hill Country Survey, Volume 7: The South-Eastern*

59. Siegfried Mittmann, *Beiträge zur Siedlungs- und Territorialgeschichte des Nördlichen Ostjordanlandes* (Wiesbaden: Harrassowitz, 1970). Herr and Clark indicate the presence of some 517 Iron I sites across Transjordan, from the Yarmuk River (northern edge of biblical Gilead) as far south as the vicinity of Wadi al-Hasa/Zered River (northern segment of biblical Edom; see Herr and Clark, "Stone Age to the Middle Ages," 86). This figure derives from the database of archaeological sites established and maintained by Jordan's Department of Antiquities.

60. Robert D. Ibach, Jr., *Archaeological Survey of the Hesban Region* (Berrien Springs, MI: Institute of Archaeology, Andrews University Press, 1987).

61. Numbers vary considerably here. Miller identifies seventy-three Iron I sites (J. Maxwell Miller, *Archaeological Survey of the Kerak Plateau* [Atlanta: Scholars Press, 1991], 309). On the other hand, Stager, making an assumption regarding pottery type, identifies some 170 Iron I sites (Stager, "Forging an Identity," 100). More recently, Herr and Clark give indication with a disclaimer of 129 Iron I sites in the territory of Moab, between Wadi Mojib/Arnon River and Wadi al-Hasa/Zered River (Herr and Clark, "Stone Age to the Middle Ages," 86). My figure here is very much of an approximation.

62. MacDonald identifies approximately thirty-five Iron I sites (see Burton MacDonald, *The Wadi el Ḥasā Archaeological Survey 1979–1983, West-Central Jordan* [Waterloo, ON: Wilfrid Laurier University Press, 1988], 171–79; MacDonald, "Evidence from the Wadi el-Hasa and Southern Ghors and North-east Arabah Archaeological Surveys," in *Early Edom and Moab: The Beginning of the Iron Age in Southern Jordan*, ed. Piotr Bienkowski [Sheffield: J. R. Collis, 1992], see esp. 113–15, 119–20).

63. Ibrahim, Sauer, and Yassine indicate they found nineteen Iron I sites in their survey (Moʿawiyah Ibrahim, James Sauer, and Khair Yassine, "The East Jordan Survey, 1975," *BASOR* 222 [1976]: 41–66). Van der Steen locates some twenty-two Iron I sites (Eveline J. van der Steen, "The Central East Jordan Valley in the Late Bronze and Early Iron Ages," *BASOR* 302 [1996]: 51–74; see also van der Steen, *Tribes and Territories in Transition: The Central East Jordan Valley in the Late Bronze and Early Iron Ages. A Study of the Sources* [Leuven: Peeters, 2004]). Stager once again projects a higher number of forty such sites (Stager, "Forging an Identity," 100).

Samaria Shoulder. Haifa: Seker, 2019 [Hebrew].

———. *The Manasseh Hill Country Survey, Volume 8: The Slopes of Western Samaria*. Haifa: Seker, 2020 [Hebrew].

———. *The Manasseh Hill Country Survey, Volume 9:* [the field still to be named]. Unpublished.

Beitzel, Barry J. *The New Moody Atlas of the Bible*. Chicago: Moody Press, 2009.

Bieniada, Michal. "Factors which Effected Changes in Settlement Pattern and the Character of 'Israelite Settlement' during the Transitional Late Bronze and Early Iron Age in Palestine." *The Polish Journal of Biblical Research* 1.2 (2001): 157–97.

Bloch-Smith, Elizabeth. "Israelite Ethnicity in Iron I: Archaeology Preserves What is Remembered and What is Forgotten in Israel's History." *JBL* 122.3 (2003): 401–25.

Broshi, Magen. "The Population of Iron Age Palestine." Pages 14–18 in *Biblical Archaeology Today, 1990*. Edited by Avraham Biran and Joseph Aviram. Jerusalem: Israel Exploration Society, 1993.

Bunimovitz, Shlomo, and Avraham Faust. "Building Identity: The Four-Room House and the Israelite Mind." Pages 411–23 in *Symbiosis, Symbolism, and the Power of the Past*. Edited by William G. Dever and Seymour Gitin. Winona Lake, IN: Eisenbrauns, 2003.

Bunimovitz, Shlomo, and Zvi Lederman. "Beth-Shemesh: Culture Conflict in Judah's Frontier." *BAR* 23.1 (1997): 42–49, 75–77.

———. "Canaanite Resistance: The Philistines and Beth-Shemesh—A Case Study from Iron Age I." *BASOR* 364 (2011): 37–51.

Clark, Douglas R. "Bricks, Sweat and Tears: The Human Investment in Constructing a 'Four-room' House." *NEA* 66.1–2 (2003): 34–43.

———. "Cultural Interaction through the Windows of the Four-Room House at Tall al-'Umayri." *Studies in the History and Archaeology of Jordan* 9 (2007): 103–12.

Clark, Douglas R., and Monique D. Roddy. "Evidence of Early Israel: A Socio-spatial Analysis of the So Called 'Four-Room' House in Context." In vol. 1 of *Lexham Geographic Commentary on the Historical Books*. Edited by Barry J. Beitzel. Bellingham, WA: Lexham Press, 2025.

Dagan, Yehuda. "The Shephelah of Judah during the Period of the Monarchy in Light of Archaeological Excavations and Surveys." MA thesis, Tel Aviv University, 1992.

Davies, Graham I. "Some Uses of Writing in Ancient Israel in Light of Recently Published Inscriptions." Pages 155–74 in *Writing and Ancient Near Eastern Society: Papers in Honour of Alan R. Millard*. Edited by Piotr Bienkowski, Christopher Mee, and Elizabeth Slater. London: T&T Clark, 2005.

———. *Ancient Hebrew Inscriptions: Corpus and Concordance*. 2 vols. Cambridge: Cambridge University Press, 2004.

Demsky, Aaron. "A Proto-Canaanite Abecedary ('Izbet Ṣarṭah)." *TA* 4 (1977): 14–27.

Dever, William G. "Israel, History of: Archaeology and the Israelite 'Conquest.'" *ABD* 3:545–58.

———. "Gezer." *NEAEHL* 2:496–506.

———. *Who Were the Early Israelites and Where Did They Come From?* Grand Rapids: Eerdmans, 2003.

Ehrlich, Carl S. "'How the Mighty Are Fallen': The Philistines in Their Tenth Century Context." Pages 179–201 in *The Age of Solomon: Scholarship at the Turn of the Millennium*. Edited by Lowell K. Handy. Leiden: Brill, 1997.

Faust, Avraham. "Between the Highland Polity and Philistia: The United Monarchy and the Resettlement of the Shephelah in the Iron Age IIA, with a Special Focus on Tel 'Eton and Khirbet Qeiyafa." *BASOR* 383 (2020): 115–36.

———. "Between Reality and Ideology: Revisiting the Israelite Ethos of Egalitarianism and Simplicity." In vol. 1 of *Lexham Geographic Commentary on the Historical Books*. Edited by Barry J. Beitzel. Bellingham, WA: Lexham Press, 2025.

———. *Israel's Ethnogenesis: Settlement, Interaction, Expansion and Resistance*. London: Equinox, 2006.

———. "A Review of *Biblical Peoples and Ethnicity*." *NEA* 72.2 (2009): 107–9.

Finkelstein, Israel. *The Archaeology of the Israelite Settlement*. Jerusalem: Israel Exploration Society, 1988.

Finkelstein, Israel, Zvi Lederman, and Shlomo Bunimovitz, eds. *Highlands of Many Cultures: The Southern Samaria Survey: The Sites*. 2 vols. Tel Aviv: Institute of Archaeology, Tel Aviv University, 1997.

Finkelstein, Israel, and Yitzhak Magen, eds. *Archaeological Survey of the Hill Country of Benjamin*. Jerusalem: Keset, 1993.

Formage, Edwin. "Zoology (Animal Profiles)." *ABD* 6:1119–51.

Frankel, Rafael. "Upper Galilee in the Late Bronze-Iron I Transition." Pages 18–34 in *From Nomadism to Monarchy*. Edited by Israel Finkelstein and Nadav Na'aman. Jerusalem: Israel Exploration Society, 1994.

———. *Settlement Dynamics and Regional Diversity in Ancient Upper Galilee: Archaeological Survey of Upper Galilee*. Jerusalem: Israel Exploration Society, 2001.

Fritz, Volkmar. *The Emergence of Israel in the Twelfth and Eleventh Centuries B.C.E.* Atlanta: Society of Biblical Literature, 2011.

Gal, Zvi. *Lower Galilee During the Iron Age*. Winona Lake, IN: Eisenbrauns, 1992.

———. "Iron I in Lower Galilee and the Margins of the Jezreel Valley." Pages 35–46 in *From Nomadism to Monarchy*. Edited by Israel Finkelstein and Nadav Na'aman. Jerusalem: Israel Exploration Society, 1994.

Garfinkel, Yosef. "The Birth & Death of Biblical Minimalism." *BAR* 37.3 (2011): 46–53, 78.

Garfinkel, Yosef, Michael Hasel, Martin G. Klingbeil, Hoo-Goo Kang, Gwanghyun Choi, Sang-Yeup Chang, Soonhwa Hong, Saar Ganor, Igor Kreimerman, and Christopher Bronk Ramsey. "Lachish Fortifications and State Formation in the Biblical Kingdom of Judah in Light of Radiometric Datings." *Radiocarbon* 61.3 (2010): 695–712.

Gitin, Seymour. "Excavating Ekron: Major Philistine City Survived by Absorbing Other Cultures." *BAR* 31.6 (2005): 50–52.

Görg, Manfred. "Neue Erwägungen zur Deutung des Namens 'Israel'." *Blätter Abrahams* 11 (2011): 37–44.

Greenberg, Raphael, and Adi Keinan. *Israeli Archaeological Activity in the West Bank 1967–2007: A Sourcebook*. Bar-Lev, Israel: Rahas Press, 2009.

Hallo, William W., and William Kelly Simpson. *The Ancient Near East, A History.* New York: Harcourt Brace College Publishers, 1998.

Hasel, Michael G. "The Geography of the Campaign of Pharaoh Merenptah and Its Relation with Early Israel." In vol. 1 of *Lexham Geographic Commentary on the Historical Books.* Edited by Barry J. Beitzel. Bellingham, WA: Lexham Press, 2025.

Herr, Larry G. "Iron Age I: Transjordan." Pages 97–114 in vol. 1 of *The Ancient Pottery of Israel and Its Neighbors from the Iron Age through the Hellenistic Period.* Edited by Seymour Gitin. Jerusalem: Israel Exploration Society, 2015.

Herr, Larry G., and Clark, Douglas R. "From the Stone Age to the Middle Ages in Jordan: Digging up Tall al-ʿUmayri." *NEA* 72.2 (2009): 68–97.

Herzog, Ze'ev. "The Beer-Sheba Valley: From Nomadism to Monarchy." Pages 122–49 in *From Nomadism to Monarchy.* Edited by Israel Finkelstein and Nadav Na'aman. Jerusalem: Israel Exploration Society, 1994.

Hess, Richard S. "Early Israel in Canaan: A Survey of Recent Evidence and Interpretation." *PEQ* 125.2 (1993): 125–42.

Hesse, Brian. "Animal Use at Tell Miqne-Ekron in the Bronze Age and Iron Age." *BASOR* 264 (1986): 17–27.

Hesse, Brian, Emmett Brown, and Timothy Griffith. "Animal Husbandry in the Early Iron Age at Tel Beth-Shemesh." Pages 257–65 in vol. 1 of *Tel Beth-Shemesh: A Border Community in Judah: Renewed Excavations 1990–2000: the Iron Age.* Edited by Shlomo Bunimovitz and Zvi Lederman. 2 vols. Winona Lake, IN: Eisenbrauns, 2016.

Hesse, Brian, and Paula Wapnish. "Can Pig Remains be Used for Ethnic Diagnosis in the Ancient Near East?" Pages 238–70 in *The Archaeology of Israel: Constructing the Past, Interpreting the Present.* Edited by Neil Asher Silberman and David Small. Sheffield: Sheffield Academic, 1997.

Ibach, Robert D., Jr. *Archaeological Survey of the Hesban Region.* Berrien Springs, MI: Institute of Archaeology, Andrews University Press, 1987.

Ibrahim, Moʿawiyah, James Sauer, and Khair Yassine. "The East Jordan Survey, 1975." *BASOR* 222 (1976): 41–66.

Inbar, Drori. "The Geographical History of Beth-shean Valley and its Adjacent Mountainous Area: From the LB IIB to the End of the Iron IIc Periods." PhD diss., Bar-Ilan University, 2001.

Katz, Hayah. "Settlement Processes in the Meron Ridges During the Iron Age I." *BASOR* 383 (2020): 1–18.

Killebrew, Ann E. *Biblical Peoples and Ethnicity: An Archaeological Study of Egyptians, Canaanites, Philistines, and Early Israel, 1300–1100 B.C.E.* Atlanta: Society of Biblical Literature, 2005.

Kitchen, Kenneth A. "Egypt, History of (Chronology)." *ABD* 2:321–31.

Kletter, Raz. "Can a Proto-Israelite Please Stand Up? Notes on the Ethnicity of Iron Age Israel and Judah." Pages 573–86 in vol. 2 of *"I Will Speak the Riddles of Ancient Times": Archaeological and Historical Studies in Honor of Amihai Mazar.* Edited by Aren M. Maeir and Pierre de Miroschedji. Winona Lake, IN: Eisenbrauns, 2006.

Lipiński, Edward. *On the Skirts of Canaan in the Iron Age: Historical and*

Topographical Researches. Leuven: Peeters, 2006.

Lipschits, Oded, and Aren M. Maeir, eds. *The Shephelah During the Iron Age: Recent Archaeological Studies*. Winona Lake, IN: Eisenbrauns, 2017.

MacDonald, Burton. *The Wadi el Ḥasā Archaeological Survey 1979–1983, West Central Jordan*. Waterloo, ON: Wilfrid Laurier University Press, 1988.

MacDonald, Burton. "Evidence from the Wadi el-Hasa and Southern Ghors and North-east Arabah Archaeological Surveys." Pages 113–42 in *Early Edom and Moab: The Beginning of the Iron Age in Southern Jordan*. Edited by Piotr Bienkowski. Sheffield: J. R. Collis, 1992.

Mazar, Amihai. *Archaeology and the Land of the Bible 10,000—586 B.C.E.* New York: Doubleday, 1990.

———. "Jerusalem and its Vicinity in Iron Age I." Pages 70–91 in *From Nomadism to Monarchy*. Edited by Israel Finkelstein and Nadav Na'aman. Jerusalem: Israel Exploration Society, 1994.

———. "Remarks on Biblical Traditions and Archaeological Evidence concerning Early Israel." Pages 85–98 in *Symbiosis, Symbolism, and the Power of the Past*. Edited by William G. Dever and Seymour Gitin. Winona Lake, IN: Eisenbrauns, 2003.

———. "The Spade and the Text: The Interaction between Archaeology and Israelite History Relating to the Tenth-Ninth Centuries BCE." Pages 143–71 in *Understanding the History of Ancient Israel*. Edited by Hugh G. M. Williamson. Oxford: Oxford University Press, 2007.

———. "The Debate over the Chronology of the Iron Age in the Southern Levant: Its History, the Current Situation, and a Suggested Resolution." Pages 15–30 in *The Bible and Radiocarbon Dating*. Edited by Thomas E. Levy and Thomas Higham. London: Equinox, 2005, 2014.

———. "Iron Age I: Northern Coastal Plain, Galilee, Samaria, Jezreel Valley, Judah, and Negev." Pages 5–70 in vol. 1 of *The Ancient Pottery of Israel and Its Neighbors from the Iron Age through the Hellenistic Period*. Edited by Seymour Gitin. Jerusalem: Israel Exploration Society, 2015.

McKinny, Chris, and Steven M. Ortiz. "'The Land that Remains': Evidence in Favor of the Thirteenth Century BC View of the Israelite Conquest and Settlement." In vol. 1 of *Lexham Geographic Commentary on the Historical Books*. Edited by Barry J. Beitzel. Bellingham, WA: Lexham Press, 2025.

Meiri, Meirav, Dorothée Huchon, Guy Bar-Oz, Elisabetta Boaretto, Liora Kolska Horwitz, Aren M. Maeir, Lidar Sapir-Hen, Greger Larson, Steve Weimer, and Israel Finkelstein. "Ancient DNA and Population Turnover in Southern Levantine Pigs–Signature of the Sea Peoples Migration?" *Scientific Reports* 3.3035 (2013): 1–8.

Michelet, Jules. *Histoire de France*. 19 vols. Paris: A. Lacroix, 1833–1867.

Miller, J. Maxwell. *Archaeological Survey of the Kerak Plateau*. Atlanta: Scholars Press, 1991.

Millard, Alan. "The Ostracon from the Days of David Found at Khirbet Qeiyafa." *TynBul* 62.1 (2011): 1–13.

———. "Ancient Hebrew Inscriptions: Their Distribution and Significance." Pages 270–78 in *Alphabets, Texts and Artifacts in the Ancient Near East: Studies Presented to Benjamin*

Sass. Edited by Israel Finkelstein, Christian Robin, and Thomas Römer. Paris: Van Dieren, 2017.

Misgav, Haggai, Yosef Garfinkel, and Saar Ganor. "The Ostracon." Pages 243–57 in *Khirbet Qeiyafa, Vol. 1: Excavation Report 2007–2008*. Edited by Yosef Garfinkel and Saar Ganor. Jerusalem: Israel Exploration Society, 2009.

Mittmann, Siegfried. *Beiträge zur Siedlungs- und Territorialgeschichte des nördlichen Ostjordanlandes*. Wiesbaden: Harrassowitz, 1970.

Mittmann, Siegfried, and Götz Schmitt, eds. *Tübinger Bibelatlas*. Wiesbaden: Deutsche Bibelgesellschaft, 2001.

Murnane, William J. *The Penguin Guide to Ancient Egypt*. Harrisonburg, VA: R. R. Donnelley & Sons, 1983.

Mullins, Robert A., and Zachary Thomas. "A Geographical Assessment of Tenth Century Evidence in Relation to Early Israel, the Jezreel Valley and the Galilee." In vol. 2 of *Lexham Geographic Commentary on the Historical Books*. Edited by Barry J. Beitzel. Bellingham, WA: Lexham Press, forthcoming.

Ofer, Avi. "'All the Hill Country of Judah': From a Settlement Fringe to a Prosperous Monarchy." Pages 92–121 in *From Nomadism to Monarchy*. Edited by Israel Finkelstein and Nadav Na'aman. Jerusalem: Israel Exploration Society, 1994.

———. "The Monarchic Period in the Judaean Highland: A Spatial Overview." Pages 14–37 in *Studies in the Archaeology of the Iron Age in Israel and Jordan*. Edited by Amihai Mazar. Sheffield: Sheffield Academic, 2001.

Pfoh, Emanuel. "The Earliest Reference to Israel: A Historiographical Reflection." *Revue Biblique* 128.3 (2021): 321–31.

Rainey, Anson F., and R. Steven Notley. *The Sacred Bridge: Carta's Atlas of the Biblical World*. Jerusalem: Carta, 2006.

Rollston, Christopher A. "What's the Oldest Hebrew Inscription?" *BAR* 38.3 (2012): 32–40, 66–68.

Sapir-Hen, Lidar. "Food, Pork Consumption, and Identity in Ancient Israel." *NEA* 82.1 (2019): 52–59.

Sapir-Hen, Lidar, Meirav Meiri, and Israel Finkelstein. "Iron Age Pigs: New Evidence on Their Origin and Role in Forming Identity Boundaries." *Radiocarbon* 57.2 (2015): 307–15.

Sapir-Hen, Lidar, Guy Bar-Oz, Yuval Gadot, and Israel Finkelstein. "Pig Husbandry in Iron Age Israel and Judah." *ZDPV* 129.1 (2013): 1–20.

Sapir-Hen, Lidar, Joe Uziel, and Ortal Chalaf. "Everything but the Oink: On the Discovery of an Articulated Pig in Iron Age Jerusalem and Its Meaning to Judahite Consumption Practices." *NEA* 84.2 (2021): 110–19.

Schniedewind, William M. "Problems in the Paleographic Dating of Inscriptions." Pages 405–12 in *The Bible and Radiocarbon Dating*. Edited by Thomas E. Levy and Thomas Higham. London: Equinox, 2005, 2014.

———. "The Alphabetic 'Scribe' of the Lachish Jar Inscription and the Hieratic Tradition in the Early Iron Age." *BASOR* 383 (2020): 137–40.

Sergi, Omer. "The Formation of Israelite Identity in the Central Canaanite Highlands in the Iron Age I–IIA." *NEA* 82.1 (2019): 42–51.

Stager, Lawrence E. "Respondents." Pages 83–87 in *Biblical Archaeology Today: Proceedings of the International*

Congress on Biblical Archaeology, Jerusalem, April 1984. Edited by Janet Amitai. Jerusalem: Israel Exploration Society, 1985.

———. "When Canaanites and Philistines Ruled Ashkelon." *BAR* 17.2 (1991): 24–37, 40–43.

———. "Forging an Identity: The Emergence of Ancient Israel." Pages 90–131 in *The Oxford History of the Biblical World*. Edited by Michael D. Coogan. Oxford: Oxford University Press, 1998.

———. "Biblical Philistines: A Hellenistic Literary Creation?" Pages 375–84 in vol. 1 of *"I Will Speak the Riddles of Ancient Times": Archaeological and Historical Studies in Honor of Amihai Mazar*. Edited by Aren M. Maeir and Pierre de Miroschedji. Winona Lake, IN: Eisenbrauns, 2006.

Steen, Eveline J. van der. "The Central East Jordan Valley in the Late Bronze Age and Early Iron Ages." *BASOR* 302 (1996): 51–74.

———. *Tribes and Territories in Transition: The Central East Jordan Valley in the Late Bronze and Early Iron Ages: A Study of the Sources*. Leuven: Peeters, 2004.

Tappy, Ron E., P. Kyle McCarter, Marilyn J. Lundberg, and Bruce Zuckerman. "An Abecedary of the Mid-Tenth Century B.C.E. from the Judaean Shephelah." *BASOR* 344 (2006): 5–46.

Wapnish, Paula, and Brian Hesse. "Urbanization and the Organization of Animal Production at Tell Jemmeh in the Middle Bronze Age Levant." *JNES* 47 (1988): 81–94.

Zertal, Adam. "'To the Land of the Perizzites and the Giants': On the Israelite Settlement in the Hill Country of Manasseh." Pages 47–69 in *From Nomadism to Monarchy*. Edited by Israel Finkelstein and Nadav Na'aman. Jerusalem: Israel Exploration Society, 1994.

———. *The Manasseh Hill Country Survey, Volume 1: The Shechem Syncline*. Leiden: Brill, 2004.

———. *The Manasseh Hill Country Survey, Volume 2: The Eastern Valleys and the Fringes of the Desert*. Leiden: Brill, 2008.

Zertal, Adam, and Shay Bar. *The Manasseh Hill Country, Volume 4: From Nahal Bezeq to the Sarbata*. Leiden: Brill, 2017.

———. *The Manasseh Hill Country Survey, Volume 5: The Middle Jordan Valley, from Wadi Fasael to Wadi 'Aujah*. Leiden: Brill, 2019.

Zertal, Adam, and N. Mirkam. *The Manasseh Hill Country Survey, Volume 3: From Nahal 'Iron to Nahal Shechem*. Leiden: Brill, 2016.

Zorn, Jeffrey R. "Estimating the Population Size of Ancient Settlements: Methods, Problems, Solutions, and a Case Study." *BASOR* 295 (1994): 31–48.

Zwickel, Wolfgang, and Pieter van der Veen. "The Earliest Reference to Israel and Its Possible Archaeological and Historical Background." *VT* 67 (2017): 129–40.

CHAPTER 10

THE PHILISTINES AND SEA PEOPLES IN LIGHT OF RECENT EXCAVATIONS

Josh 13:2–3; Judg 13:1–16:31; 1 Sam 4:1–7:17; 13:2–14:52; 17:1–58; 18:17–30; 23:1–29; 27:1–12; 29:1–11; 31:1–13

Aren M. Maeir

KEY POINTS

- In light of finds from the excavations at Tell es-Safi/Gath, as well as other research and excavations in recent years, many assumptions about the Philistines have been revised.
- The appearance of the Philistines was not due to one specific migration or conquest event dating to the early twelfth century BC but, rather, was the result of a long series of migration events and other actions spanning decades.
- Philistine culture was not a monolithic culture but an "entangled culture" that reflected the influence of a broad range of cultures, suggesting that its members had origins in a variety of places while also adapting to life among their new neighbors.
- The Philistines and Judeans influenced one another in many ways, including but not limited to pottery styles and cultic practices.

Relief of Battle Between Ramesses III and Sea Peoples at Medinet Habu

INTRODUCTION

The Philistines have been the focus of an extraordinary volume of research in the last century and a half, particularly in the last few decades.[1] Until quite recently, the dominant interpretation relating to the "Philistine Phenomenon," quite unchanged since the beginning of modern archaeological research in the Levant, was largely a reflection of a somewhat traditional understanding of the biblical texts. That is, the Philistines were an organized ethnic group of foreign origin, most likely deriving from somewhere in the region of Bronze Age Greece, who migrated to the southern Levant and conquered the region of Philistia in the southern Coastal Plain of Canaan in the early Iron Age (early twelfth century BC). This was seen as connected to other aspects of the transition between the Late Bronze and Iron Ages, which included historical and archaeological evidence of the appearance of other

1. E.g., Trude Dothan, *The Philistines and Their Material Culture* (Jerusalem: Israel Exploration Society, 1982); Nancy K. Sandars, *The Sea Peoples: Warriors of the Ancient Mediterranean* (London: Thames & Hudson, 1985); Eliezer Oren, ed., *The Sea Peoples and Their World: A Reassessment* (Philadelphia: University Museum, 2000); Ann E. Killebrew and Gunnar Lehmann, eds., *The Philistines and Other "Sea Peoples" in Text and Archaeology* (Atlanta: Society of Biblical Literature, 2013); Assaf Yasur-Landau, *The Philistines and Aegean Migration at the End of the Late Bronze Age* (Cambridge: Cambridge University Press, 2010); Peter M. Fischer and Teresa Bürge, eds., *"Sea Peoples" Up-to-Date: New Research on Transformations in the Eastern Mediterranean in the 13th–11th Centuries BCE* (Vienna: Austrian Academy of Sciences, 2017); Aren M. Maeir, "Iron Age I Philistines: Entangled Identities in a Transformative Period," in *The Social Archaeology of the Levant: From Prehistory to the Present*, ed. Assaf Yasur-Landau, Eric H. Cline, and Yorke Rowan (Cambridge: Cambridge University Press, 2019), 310–23.

Detail View of Medinet Habu Relief Illustrating Sea Battle with Ship

groups at this time (e.g., Israelites or Arameans). In addition, depictions of the so-called "Sea Peoples" in Egyptian sources were integrated into this picture, especially the Medinet Habu reliefs from the Ramesses III mortuary temple that depict a sea and land battle against "Sea Peoples," including the Philistines.

According to this reigning paradigm, the Philistines were one of the groups of the so-called "Sea Peoples" who arrived in the Levant in the early twelfth century.[2] It was believed that they originated from somewhere in the Aegean world and were highly connected to and/or influenced by the Mycenaean culture. When they arrived in the southern Levant as migrants during the Late Bronze/Iron Age transition, they conquered the southern Coastal Plain of Canaan ("Philistia"), taking over the region from the local, indigenous Canaanite population. Accordingly, from the early Iron Age up to approximately the tenth century, they were the dominant polity in the region, but with the rise of the Israelite and Judahite kingdoms in the tenth century onward, the power of the Philistines was curtailed. Nevertheless, throughout the Iron Age, the Philistines were among the primary enemies and adversaries of the Israelites and Judahites. Finally, throughout the Iron Age, the Philistines went through a slow but constant process of assimilation and acculturation in which more and more of the original Aegean components of the Philistine culture were discarded, while local Levantine facets were incorporated into their culture. Thus, by the end of the Iron Age, the Philistines had more or less assimilated into the local cultures.

2. E.g., Dothan, *The Philistines*.

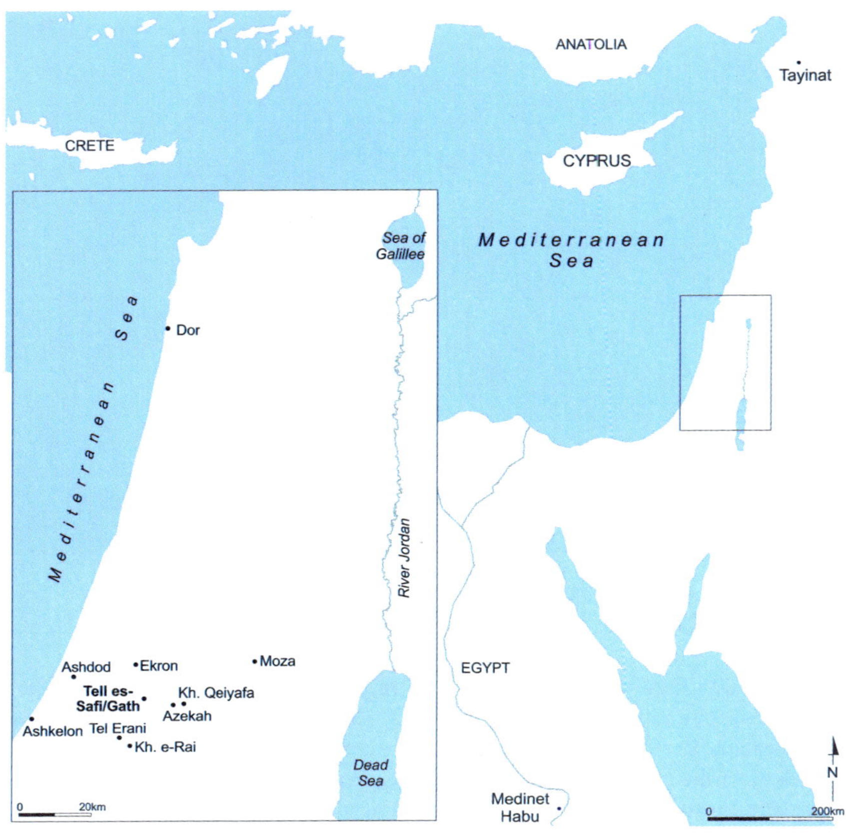

Sites in Iron Age Philistia and Surrounding Regions

If one summarizes these points, one sees that the accepted paradigm about the Philistines was that of a group of monolithic origin who invaded the southern Levant in the early Iron Age. This culture then went through rather simplistic cultural processes and relations with their neighbors during the rest of the Iron Age. As I demonstrate below, in light of the finds from the excavations at Tell es-Safi/Gath, as well as other research and excavations in recent years, many of these assumptions have been revised.[3]

NEW PERSPECTIVES

The Philistine paradigm began to be questioned in the last decade or so, and not only from the excavations at Tell es-Safi/Gath. For example, it was postulated that the processes relating to the appearance of the Philistine culture were not due to one specific migration or conquest event dating

3. For an overview of my views, see, e.g., Aren M. Maeir and Louise A. Hitchcock, "The Appearance, Formation and Transformation of Philistine Culture: New Perspectives and New Finds," in Fischer and Bürge, *"Sea Peoples" Up-to-Date*, 149–62; Maeir, "Iron Age I Philistines."

to the early twelfth century, but rather, were the result of a long, drawn out set of mechanisms and events, possibly beginning in the late thirteenth century, and continuing for quite a few decades. This was not a monolithic "invasion"; it was more likely a series of migration events and other actions spanning decades.[4]

At the same time, there was little if any evidence of destruction levels at the various urban Canaanite sites in Philistia, at sites such as Ashkelon, Ashdod, Miqne-Ekron, and Tell es-Safi/Gath.[5] Instead, along with limited evidence of destruction of some parts of these sites, in most cases, there is a continuity from the Late Bronze Age into the Iron Age. In fact, it seems that while foreign elements undoubtedly did arrive in Philistia in the early Iron Age, they lived side by side with the local Canaanite population. While there may have been limited destructions at some of the Philistine sites, perhaps in elite zones, by and large, the sites continued to exist during the transition between the Late Bronze (LB) and the early Iron Age. This fits with a general lack of (or, at least, much fewer than previously assumed) "catastrophic events" in the eastern Mediterranean before, during, and after the LB/Iron Age transition. In other words, if in the past, massive migrations and conquests were seen as the major motif of this transition, a more complex and multi-faceted set of underlying mechanisms and processes came together at this time.

No less important is the realization that the view of a monolithic origin of the Philistine culture, often associated with the Mycenaeans, was likewise hard to accept. While undoubtedly there were substantial non-local facets in early Philistine culture, this was a mixed bag of foreign elements. Although some things were related to the Mycenaean culture, other things were not. In fact, these non-local facets have parallels in a broad range of cultures in the eastern and even central Mediterranean. So much so, that the early Philistine culture is not similar to any specific culture in the Mediterranean region. In addition to this, side by side with the non-local facets of the early Philistine culture, evidence of local Canaanite elements could be seen as well.[6]

This has led to the realization that early Philistine culture is a much more complex and multi-faceted phenomenon than previously assumed. My colleague, Louise Hitchcock, and I have suggested defining the Philistine culture as an "entangled culture," sort of a "Mediterranean salad," which is comprised of various population groups of different cultural backgrounds who came together in Philistia in the early Iron Age. This included an assortment of groups of different foreign origins, possibly of differing socio-economic backgrounds, along with local components. We further suggested that one must take into account that portions of the populations that comprised the Philistines—and the Sea Peoples in general—might be seen as pirate-like groups who may have flourished during the breakdown of the Late Bronze Age world order. This, based on historical examples of piracy, is quite

4. Noted already by Yasur-Landau, *The Philistines*, 323.

5. Noted already by Yasur-Landau, *The Philistines*, 237.

6. E.g., Maeir and Hitchcock, "Appearance, Formation, and Transformation," 149–62.

Pottery from Tell es-Safi/Gath

common in times of chaos and societal collapse such as the LB/Iron Age transition.[7] All of these influences and people of various origins, foreign and local, came together to form the entangled early Iron Age Philistine culture.[8]

The entangled character of the early Philistine culture is reflected in numerous aspects of the material culture of early Iron Age Philistia, several examples of which are discussed below. The unique decorated pottery of the Philistine culture is perhaps the best-known aspect of their material culture.[9] Three phases of this pottery are known in the Iron I, while more recently, an additional phase has been defined for the late Iron I and Iron IIA. These stages are: Philistine 1 (Mycenaean IIIC; see above image), Philistine 2 (Philistine Bichrome; see image immediately below), Philistine 3 (Philistine degenerated), and Late Philistine Decorated Ware (Ashdod Ware; see image below).

In the past, it was thought that the Philistine 1 pottery was directly influenced from contemporaneous Mycenaean IIIC (Myc IIIC) pottery from the Aegean and should be seen as clear evidence of the transferal of a ceramic tradition from the Aegean to Philistia. This thought has been critiqued.[10] To start with, not all Myc IIIC forms known in the Aegean appear in Philistia. Clearly, only part of the ceramic repertoire of the Aegean was used in early Iron Age Philistia. In addition, it appears that Aegean-style Myc IIIC pottery was appropriated for use

---

7. E.g., Louise A. Hitchcock and Aren M. Maeir, "A Pirate's Life for Me: The Maritime Culture of the Sea People," *PEQ* 148.4 (2016): 245–64.

8. See recently Maeir, "Iron Age I Philistines."

9. E.g., Aren M. Maeir, "Philister-Keramik," in *Reallexikon der Assyriologie und vorderasiatischen Archäologie*, ed. G. Frantz-Szabo and U. Hellwag (Berlin: de Gruyter, 2005), 14:528–36.

10. E.g., Philipp Stockhammer, "How Aegean is Philistine Pottery? The Use of Aegean-Type Pottery in the Early 12th Century BCE Southern Levant," in Fischer and Bürge, *"Sea Peoples" Up-to-Date*, 379–78.

Philistine 2 (Philistine Bichrome) Decorated Vessel from Tell es-Safi/Gath

Late Philistine Decorated Ware (Ashdod Ware) Vessel from Tell es-Safi/Gath

in Philistia in ways that were different from how they were used in the Aegean cultures. Finally, it has been noted that the Myc IIIC pottery in Philistia is stylistically unique and differs from Aegean styles, incorporating local Levantine traditions in form and decoration. In the later phases of the decorated Philistine pottery, more and more influence of local Levantine traditions can be seen. This indicates, as opposed to what was previously thought, that while the earliest Philistine pottery is fully Aegean in character and only subsequently goes through a process of transformation through local influences, the entangled character of the Philistine pottery is apparent from the very earliest stages.

This entangled nature is apparent in a broad range of facets of Philistine culture, far beyond the decorated pottery. Significantly, this is seen in many levels of Philistine traditions and praxis.[11] In the past, focus was placed on a limited repertoire of new aspects seen in the Philistine culture, supposedly indicating an Aegean origin. This included architecture such as the appearance of hearths, megaron-like buildings, pillars, bathtubs and other features, changes in foodways (the preference of pork being a well-known example), cultic objects, and more. Recent studies have shown that this is more complex than previously thought. While there is a broad range of new aspects in early Philistine culture, it is now quite clear that they do not originate from the Aegean region only. Some can be traced to other regions.

Revealing as well is the study of the new technological traditions in early Iron Age Philistia. While attempts to identify groups (e.g., ethnicities, polities) based on archaeological materials is wrought with problems (e.g., the so-called "pots equal people" approach), technological traditions have been shown to be very indicative of groups—and the differentiation between groups. In fact, when analyzing numerous technological traditions in early Iron Age Philistia, a broad

11. E.g., Aren M. Maeir et al., "Technological Insights on Philistine Culture: Perspectives from Tell es-Safi/Gath," *Journal of Eastern Mediterranean Archaeology and Heritage Studies* 7.1 (2019): 76–118.

Philistine Pebbled Hearth from Tell es-Safi/Gath

range of new types of technological practices (*chaîne opératoire*), first appearing in the early Iron Age, can be seen. Most likely, this reflects various "communities of practice" and "communities of belonging," indicating both the complex origins of the Philistines but, no less important, the diverse and multi-faceted groups and communities that existed in the Iron Age Levant as well.

Our attempt to define the Philistine language and writing is intimately connected to this.[12] For many years, the basic assumption was that the language spoken in Philistia in the early Iron Age should be seen as connected to Bronze Age Greek. Based on supposed similarities between certain words and names connected to the Philistines, mainly in the Bible, such as *seren* (סֶרֶן), "Goliath," "Achish," and others, it was assumed that the language of the Philistines, like their material culture, should be related to the languages of the Bronze Age Aegean. Based on this, it was assumed that if there was a strong Bronze Age Greek linguistic influence on the Philistines, then they most likely also used writings systems known from Bronze Age Greece, such as Linear B and Cypro-Minoan. In fact, a few undeciphered inscriptions from early Iron Age Philistia, and in some cases, from other regions, were identified as being Philistine inscriptions in Aegean related scripts.

After more than a century of excavations in Philistia, the lack of inscrip-

12. For a summary, see, e.g., Brent Davis, Aren M. Maeir, and Louise A. Hitchcock, "Disentangling Entangled Objects: Iron Age Inscriptions from Philistia as a Reflection of Cultural Processes," *IEJ* 65.2 (2015): 140–46; Aren M. Maeir, Brent Davis, and Louise A. Hitchcock, "Philistine Names and Terms Once Again: A Recent Perspective," *Journal of Eastern Mediterranean Archaeology and Heritage* 4.4 (2016): 321–40.

Archaic Alphabetic Inscription from Tell es-Safi/Gath

tions that can be clearly related to the early Philistine culture, and, at the same time, related without a doubt to any of the Bronze Age Aegean scripts is of note. Thus, it has been suggested that perhaps the search for such inscriptions is a futile endeavor. Rather, the use of the scripts in the Aegean Bronze Age was limited to very specific contexts, more or less always related to a palace-oriented polity. With the collapse of the Aegean Bronze Age polities, these writing methods, for the most part, went out of use. Similarly, even if some of the population of early Iron Age Philistia derives from these same Aegean Bronze Age cultures, the need and knowledge of these Aegean writing systems no longer existed. Thus, the traditions and technologies related to these writing systems were either barely used or not used at all in early Iron Age Philistia. Only in the early Iron II with the rising need for literacy, as seen in other cultures in the southern Levant, did the Philistines start writing using a variant of the local Levantine alphabetic script.

As to the "Philistine language," this too is a complex issue. It appears that some of the words associated with Mycenaean Greek, such as *seren*, may, in fact, be related to other languages, such as Luwian (an Anatolian language). Names such as "Goliath" find parallels in non-Greek languages.[13] It would appear then, that if one can identify non-Semitic languages in use in early Iron Age Philistia, they were part of complex language communities comprised of both local and foreign languages, which were then molded into the language spoken in Philistia at later stages of the Iron Age—a language which was very much a Semitic

13. Maeir et al., "Philistine Names."

language, quite similar to contemporaneous Northwest Semitic language and dialects spoken in the Iron Age southern Levant, as can be seen from inscriptions from Philistia in the late Iron Age.

Foodways are another topic that have been extensively discussed regarding the definition of early Philistine culture, its development in the Iron Age, and how this reflects relations with neighboring cultures. In particular, attempts to identify differences in the diet of the Philistines in comparison to other cultures were stressed. Famously, attempts to identify preferences or lack thereof in the consumption of specific species, of both fauna and flora, was seen as a crucial aspect of Philistine identity from an archaeological perspective, which supposedly made it easy to identify Philistine and non-Philistine sites.[14] This was particularly the case with the consumption of pork, but also of dog meat and specific types of plants. It was thought that these specific species, or at least the inclination to consume them, were brought by the Philistines from the Aegean.

Recent research has shown that this is a much more complex issue. To start with, the botanical evidence from early Iron Age Philistia does show plants species that first appear at this time. Likewise, there is evidence of the earliest utilization of certain plants and possibly evidence of changes in agricultural practices as well. That said, the new plants and the new traditions of using plants do not derive from the Aegean only, but from other regions of the Mediterranean as well.[15]

Similarly, the issue of the consumption of pig is a complex issue.[16] While there is evidence of pig use at urban sites in Philistia, it is less so in rural ones. Similarly, while pig consumption is curtailed in the Iron II in certain sites in Philistia (e.g., Ekron or Ashkelon), at others (Gath) it is not. To make the issue even more complex, while some "Canaanite" sites, as well as Judahite sites, show an abstention from pig in the early and, in some cases, later Iron Age, this is not the case for sites in the Northern Kingdom where at some sites the inhabitants did consume pig, while others did not! Clearly then, a simplistic connection between pig consumption and identity is problematic, as is any attempt to simplistically connect between material culture and identity. The "pots don't equal people" adage is true here as well!

The diversity of the early Iron Age Philistine population is supported as well by bio-archaeological studies of skeletal materials from burials in Iron Age Philistia. Published aDNA (i.e., ancient

14. E.g., Israel Finkelstein, "Pots and People Revisited: Ethnic Boundaries in the Iron Age I," in *The Archaeology of Israel: Constructing the Past, Interpreting the Present*, ed. Neil. A. Silberman and David Small (Sheffield: Sheffield Academic, 1997), 216–37; Mordechai E. Kislev and Yael Mahler-Slasky, "Lathyrus Consumption in Late Bronze and Iron Age Sites in Israel: An Aegean Affinity," *Journal of Archaeological Science* 37 (2010): 2477–85; Avraham Faust, "Pigs in Space (and Time): Pork Consumption and Identity Negotiations in the Late Bronze and Iron Ages of Ancient Israel," *NEA* 81.4 (2018): 276–99.

15. Suembikya Frumin et al., "Studying Ancient Anthropogenic Impact on Current Floral Biodiversity in the Southern Levant as Reflected by the Philistine Migration," *Scientific Reports* 5.1 (2015): 1–10.

16. E.g., Lidar Sapir-Hen, "Food, Pork Consumption, and Identity in Ancient Israel," *NEA* 82.1 (2019): 52–59.

DNA) evidence from Ashkelon, as well as isotopic studies from Gath and Tel Erani, indicate that both local and non-local populations intermixed in the region during the Iron Age.[17]

Another issue that has been discussed is whether there was a cessation of international trade in early Iron Age Philistia. While in the past it was thought that international trade collapsed completely after the Late Bronze Age, in recent years evidence has mounted that, while the volume of trade diminished in the early Iron Age, it nevertheless continued. This is seen both in Philistia (e.g., Ashkelon and Gath) and in other regions of the coastal southern Levant (e.g., Dor).[18] This being the case, it can possibly be seen as an indication that non-local influences and, perhaps, populations continued to arrive in Philistia throughout the early Iron Age, and one does not have to assume that the foreign influences all derived from the initial non-local migrant populations. The continuity of inter-regional trade in the Iron I, even if at smaller volumes than in the previous and later periods, fits well with current understandings of the long-term processes in the Mediterranean, possibly Peregrine Horden and Nicholas Purcell's processes of fragmentation and connectivity that they see throughout Mediterranean history.[19]

The insights from Tell es-Safi/Gath reflect on issues relating to the Sea Peoples, beyond the region of Philistia itself. Thus, in recent years it has been suggested that there is another Philistine group in the northern Levant. Finds from sites in the Amuq Valley and, in particular, at Tel Tayinat, were understood as representing peoples of Aegean origin, with Aegean-influenced material culture (e.g., pottery, loom weights, and other aspects) that arrived in the region in a similar process as the Philistines in the south. In addition to this, the identification of a group called *Walistin* or *Palistin* in tenth century inscriptions from the region led to the suggestion that these were Aegean originating migrants and could be seen as "northern Philistines" related to the better-known "southern Philistines."[20] This interpretation was accepted by many, and it was even suggested that the land route that the Philistines took on their

17. E.g., Michal Feldman et al., "Ancient DNA Sheds Light on the Genetic Origins of Early Iron Age Philistines," *Science Advances* 5.7 (2019): eaax0061. Additional studies, currently in progress, will add to this as well.

18. For Ashkelon and Gath, see Daniel M. Master, "The Renewal of Trade at Iron Age I Ashkelon," *Eretz-Israel* (2009): 111–22; Aren M. Maeir, "Between Philistia, Phoenicia, and Beyond: A View from Tell es-Safi/Gath," in *Material Method and Meaning: Papers in Eastern Mediterranean Archeology in Honor of Ilan Sharon*, ed. Uri Davidovich, Sveta Matskevich, and Naama Yahalom-Mack (Münster: Zaphon, 2022), 185–94. For Dor, see Paula Waiman-Barak, Ayelet Gilboa, and Yuval Goren, "A Stratified Sequence of Early Iron Age Egyptian Ceramics at Tel Dor, Israel," *Ägypten und Levante* 24 (2014): 317–42.

19. Peregrine Horden and Nicholas Purcell, *The Corrupting Sea: A Study of Mediterranean History* (Oxford: Blackwell, 2000).

20. E.g., Timothy P. Harrison, "Lifting the Veil on a 'Dark Age': Ta'ayinat and the North Orontes Valley During the Early Iron Age," in *Exploring the Longue Durée: Essays in Honor of Lawrence E. Stager*, ed. J. David Schloen (Winona Lake, IN: Eisenbrauns, 2009), 127–36.

way to southern Canaan went through the Amuq Valley.[21] This, though, is hard to accept for various reasons. The reading of the name as *Palistin* is questionable and, even if accepted, is hard to equate it with the *plishtim* (פְּלִשְׁתִּים) of the Bible and other sources.[22] More importantly, the material culture of the early Iron Age and the Aegean-style pottery found in these levels are stylistically later than the Philistine 1 (Myc IIIC) from early Iron Age Tell es-Safi/Gath and other sites in Philistia.[23] Thus, while the finds in the Amuq Valley may represent processes that are similar to the mechanisms that occurred in Philistia in the Iron Age, they are of a later date and not directly connected. If at all, they seem to indicate that the complex and multi-faceted mechanisms and processes that occurred during the LB/Iron Age transition probably continued well into the late twelfth century.

Another common motif in the study of the Philistines was the view that, while the Philistine culture was dominant during the early Iron Age, from the tenth century and later, with the rise of the Judahite and Israelite kingdoms, the role and strength of Philistia declined. Accordingly, it was suggested that from this phase onward, the Aegean character of the Philistine culture was for the most part lost, the Philistine were dominated, both politically and culturally, by the other groups surrounding them.[24]

The finds from Tell es-Safi/Gath do not support this view. To start with, evidence of the continuity of unique and very specific cultural facets in Philistia until the very late Iron Age are known.[25] This includes use of terms and names connecting to the Aegean-related components of early Iron Age Philistia. Secondly, current evidence from Philistia and, in particular, Tell es-Safi/Gath demonstrate that Gath and the larger area of Philistia were not dominated and curtailed in the early Iron Age IIA by an early Judahite kingdom. *Au contraire!* It appears that this was a period of growth and prosperity at Gath. Recent finds from Tell es-Safi/Gath, in the lower city, in several excavation areas, have provided solid evidence that the city of Gath expanded from the upper city to the lower city during the Iron IB (c. eleventh century), and continued to thrive and expand until the destruction of the site by Hazael in c. 830 BC. There is no archaeological evidence of any site-wide destruction from the early Iron Age until the Hazael destruction. The finds in the lower city include massive fortifications, public buildings, a temple, and large metallurgical area, as well as well-planned domestic structures in which large-scale olive oil production

21. E.g., Dan'el Kahn, "Ramesses III and the Northern Levant: A Reassessment of the Sources," in *The Ramesside Period in Egypt: Studies into Cultural and Historical Processes of the 19th and 20th Dynasties. Proceedings of the International Symposium Held in Heidelberg, 5th to 7th June 2015*, ed. Sabine Kubisch and Ute Rummel (Berlin: de Gruyter, 2018), 175–88.

22. K. Lawson Younger Jr., *A Political History of the Arameans: From Their Origins to the End of Their Polities* (Atlanta: Society of Biblical Literature, 2016), 127–35.

23. E.g., Aren M. Maeir, review of *Sea Peoples of the Northern Levant? Aegean-Style Pottery from Early Iron Age Tell Tayinat*, by Brian Janeway, *Review of Biblical Literature* (Feb 2018), n.p.

24. E.g., Faust, "Pigs in Space."

25. See summary in Maeir and Hitchcock, "Appearance, Formation, and Transformation," 149–62.

Area D West at Tell es-Safi/Gath with Remains of Iron IIA Temple on the Left and Metal Production Area on the Right

was carried out. The overall size of the city (c. 111–124 acres; 45–50 hectares) and these impressive remains are strong indications of the geopolitical status of the kingdom of Gath. With all probability, it was the strongest polity in the region until the Hazael destruction, and in fact its status may have been one of the main reasons why Hazael made such an effort to conquer the site and destroy it so totally.[26]

All this indicates that there is no basis for suggestions that Philistia was dominated by the kingdom of Judah from the tenth century and onward. While it is possible that Judah did expand its influence towards the southwestern Shephelah from this time onward, the central Shephelah was still dominated by the kingdom of Gath, most likely the most powerful kingdom in the region at this time. As I have suggested previously, the destruction and abandonment of Khirbet Qeiyafa c. 1000 BC (and perhaps at Khirbet el-Rai as well) may reflect this dominance, as well as lack of substantial settlement after the early Iron I at Tel Azekah.[27]

When one examines the evidence for contacts and influences between Philistia and Judah in the Iron IIA, one does not see unidirectional contacts from

26. E.g., Aren M. Maeir, "Introduction and Overview," in *Tell es-Safi/Gath II: Excavations and Studies*, ed. Aren M. Maeir and Joe Uziel (Münster: Zaphon, 2020), 1–52.

27. Aren M. Maeir, "Khirbet Qeiyafa in Its Regional Context: A View from Philistine Gath," in *Khirbet Qeiyafa in the Shephelah: Papers Presented at a Colloquium of the Swiss Society for Ancient Near Eastern Studies Held at the University of Bern, September 6, 2014*, ed. Sylvia Schroer and Stefan Münger (Fribourg: Academic Press, 2017), 61–71.

Iron IIA Cooking Jug from Tell es-Safi/Gath

Judah to Philistia. Despite claims that the Philistines stopped participating in pork consumption, or that they started circumcising—claims that are very hard to accept—other evidence indicates a much more complex, bidirectional relationship between the two regions.[28] While, without a doubt, Philistine culture was influenced by the surrounding cultures from the Iron IIA and later, strong influences from Philistia to Judah can be seen as well. This is evidenced in the pottery, such as Late Philistine Decorated Ware pottery appearing in Judah, both imported and locally made, the utilization of the iconic Philistine cooking jug in Judah, and most recently, finds indicating Philistine cultic influences in Judah, including figurines and "headcups."[29]

New insights into the interface between cultic traditions in Philistia and other regions during the Iron Age have also been provided by the finds from Tell es-Safi/Gath. A few examples can be noted. Four-horned altars were well known from Iron Age Israel and Judah, so when such altars were found in late Iron Age Ekron, it was thought that this is an Israelite influence reaching Philistia by way of Israelites who escaped the Assyrian destruction of the kingdom of Israel in the late eighth century.[30] A stone two-horned altar situated in a late Iron IIA (mid/late ninth century) temple at Tell es-Safi/Gath with morphological characteristics similar to later Iron Age altars suggests that these altars appear in Philistia earlier than thought and that cultic influences between the regions existed earlier.[31] In addition to this, adjacent to the horned altar from Tell es-Safi/Gath, a jar of Judahite origin with a Judahite name on it was found, indicating that people from

28. For pork and circumcision, see Faust, "Pigs in Space." For the counterpoint, see Maeir, "Introduction," 20–21. On the bidirectional relationship, see Aren M. Maeir, "Jerusalem and the West—Via Philistia: An Early Iron Age Perspective from Tell es-Safi/Gath," in *Jerusalem and the West: Perspectives from Archaeology, Biblical Studies and History*, ed. Felix Hagemeyer (Tübingen: Mohr Siebeck, 2022), 7–22.

29. E.g., Anat Cohen-Weinberger, Nahshon Szanton, and Joe Uziel, "Ethnofabrics: Petrographic Analysis as a Tool for Illuminating Cultural Interactions and Trade Relations Between Judah and Philistia During the Iron II," *BASOR* 377 (2017): 1–20; David Ben-Shlomo, "Petrographic Analysis of the Pottery," in *The Iron Age Pottery of Jerusalem: A Typological and Technological Study* (Ariel: Ariel University Press, 2019), 169–308; Maeir, "Jerusalem and the West."

30. E.g., Seymour Gitin, "New Incense Altars from Ekron: Context, Typology and Function," *Eretz-Israel* 23 (1992): 43–49.

31. Maeir, "Chapter 1," 24.

Monolithic Two-horned Stone Altar from Tell es-Safi/Gath In Situ in a Late Iron IIA Temple in Area D West, Lower City of Tell es-Safi/Gath

Judah participated in cultic activities at this Philistine temple at Gath.[32] In other words, bi-, and perhaps multi-directional influences in cultic traditions and praxis existed in Philistia and adjacent regions. This ties in with the evidence noted above of bidirectional cultural influences seen in Philistia and adjacent regions in aspects such as pottery, cooking traditions, and cultic objects. It can be perhaps suggested that the intense and multidirectional interactions between

32. Aren M. Maeir and Esther Eshel, "Four Short Alphabetic Inscriptions from Iron Age IIA Tell es-Safi/Gath and Their Contribution for Understanding the Process of the Development of Literacy in Iron Age Philistia," in *"See, I Will Bring a Scroll Recounting What Befell Me" (Ps 40:8): Epigraphy and Daily Life—From the Bible to the Talmud Dedicated to the Memory of Professor Hanan Eshel*, ed. Esther Eshel and Yigal Levin (Göttingen: Vandenhoeck & Ruprecht, 2014), 69–88.

A Horned Altar

Sacrificial blood was smeared on the horns

Ropes could be tied to horns

Examples date back to 6000 BC

Judah and Philistia, as depicted in the biblical Samson cycle (Judg 13:1–16:31), might in some way mirror the complex interactions that existed in this region during the Iron Age.[33]

When one views the biblical narratives about the Philistines and, in particular, their relationship with Israel and Judah during the early Iron Age, a repeating motif in the Bible is the Philistine's strength and military dominance, something that has been accentuated in ancient and modern biblical interpretations. Somewhat surprisingly, there is little evidence of this in the archaeological record. After more than a century of excavations in Philistia, there is very little evidence that the Philistines had an overly martial and military dominant culture. Thus, while there were certainly cases where the Philistines were the dominant polities (such as Gath during Iron IB–IIA), it would appear that the biblical image of a mighty and feared enemy was perhaps over accentuated for ideological reasons, both in the Bible and in later interpretations.[34]

Only after Gath's destruction does the geopolitical structure in the region change. On the one hand, Judah has the ability to expand into the Shephelah, while on the other hand, other Philistine cities, such as Ekron and Ashkelon, can expand as well.[35]

CONCLUSION

Following more than a century and a half of research on the Philistine culture, a broad range of important and groundbreaking finds have been revealed. This

33. E.g., Steve Weitzman, "The Samson Story as Border Fiction," *Biblical Interpretation* 10 (2002): 158–74.

34. Aren M. Maeir, "The Philistines Be Upon Thee, Samson (Jud. 16:20): Reassessing the Martial Nature of the Philistines - Archaeological Evidence Vs. Ideological Image?" in *Change, Continuity and Connectivity: North-Eastern Mediterranean at the Turn of the Bronze Age and in the Early Iron Age*, ed. Łukasz Niesiołowski-Spanò and Marek Węcowski (Wiesbaden: Harrassowitz, 2018), 158–68; Aren M. Maeir, "Memories, Myths and Megalithics: Reconsidering the Giants of Gath," *JBL* 139.4 (2020): 675–90.

35. E.g., Aren M. Maeir, "Philistia and the Judean Shephelah After Hazael: The Power Play Between the Philistines, Judeans and Assyrians in the 8th Century BCE in Light of the Excavations at Tell es-Safi/Gath," in *Disaster and Relief Management—Katastrophen und ihre Bewältigung*, ed. Angelika Berlejung (Tübingen: Mohr Siebeck, 2012), 241–62.

research is of a vibrant character, with ongoing realignments of our understanding of various facets regarding the Philistines. As we have seen above, in light of new finds in the last years and in particular at Tell es-Safi/Gath, many of the accepted paradigms are now questioned and seen quite differently. I would hardly assume that the last word has been said on understanding the Philistines, the Sea Peoples, and related issues. I am convinced that continuing research at sites in and around Philistia, in the near and more distant future, will provide exciting and game changing data and analyses on these issues, and perhaps, once again bring about paradigm shifts in how we understand these biblical people.

BIBLIOGRAPHY

Ben-Shlomo, David. "Petrographic Analysis of the Pottery." Pages 169–308 in *The Iron Age Pottery of Jerusalem: A Typological and Technological Study*. Ariel: Ariel University Press, 2019.

Cohen-Weinberger, Anat, Nahshon Szanton, and Joe Uziel. "Ethnofabrics: Petrographic Analysis as a Tool for Illuminating Cultural Interactions and Trade Relations between Judah and Philistia during the Iron II." *BASOR* 377 (2017): 1–20.

Davis, Brent, Aren M. Maeir, and Louise A. Hitchcock. "Disentangling Entangled Objects: Iron Age Inscriptions from Philistia as a Reflection of Cultural Processes." *IEJ* 65.2 (2015): 140–65.

Dothan, Trude. *The Philistines and Their Material Culture*. Jerusalem: Israel Exploration Society, 1982.

Faust, Avraham. "Pigs in Space (and Time): Pork Consumption and Identity Negotiations in the Late Bronze and Iron Ages of Ancient Israel." *NEA* 81 (2018): 276–99.

Feldman, Michal, Daniel M. Master, Raffaela A. Bianco, Marta Burri, Philipp W. Stockhammer, Alissa Mittnik, Adam J. Aja, Choongwon Jeong, and Johannes Krause. "Ancient DNA Sheds Light on the Genetic Origins of Early Iron Age Philistines." *Science Advances* 5.7 (2019): eaax0061.

Finkelstein, Israel. "Pots and People Revisited: Ethnic Boundaries in the Iron Age I." Pages 216–37 in *The Archaeology of Israel: Constructing the Past, Interpreting the Present*. Edited by Neil Asher Silberman and David Small. Sheffield: Sheffield Academic, 1997.

Fischer, Peter M., and Teresa Bürge, eds. *"Sea Peoples" Up-to-Date: New Research on Transformation in the Eastern Mediterranean in the 13th–11th Centuries BCE*. Vienna: Austrian Academy of Sciences, 2017.

Frumin, Suembikya, Aren M. Maeir, Liora Kolska Horwitz, and Ehud Weiss. "Studying Ancient Anthropogenic Impact on Current Floral Biodiversity in the Southern Levant as Reflected by the Philistine Migration." *Scientific Reports* 5.1 (2015): 1–10

Gitin, Seymour. "New Incense Altars from Ekron: Context, Typology and Function." *Eretz-Israel* 23 (1992): 43–49.

Harrison, Timothy P. "Lifting the Veil on a 'Dark Age': Taʿayinat and the North Orontes Valley During the Early Iron Age." Pages 127–36 in *Exploring the Longue Durée: Essays in Honor of Lawrence E. Stager*. Edited by J. David Schloen. Winona Lake, IN: Eisenbrauns, 2009.

Hitchcock, Louise A., and Aren M. Maeir. "A Pirate's Life for Me: The

Maritime Culture of the Sea People." *PEQ* 148.4 (2016): 245–64.

Horden, Peregrine, and Nicholas Purcell. *The Corrupting Sea: A Study of Mediterranean History*. Oxford: Blackwell, 2000.

Kahn, Dan'el. "Ramesses III and the Northern Levant: A Reassessment of the Sources." Pages 175–88 in *The Ramesside Period in Egypt: Studies into Cultural and Historical Processes of the 19th and 20th Dynasties. Proceedings of the International Symposium Held in Heidelberg, 5th to 7th June 2015*. Edited by Sabine Kubisch and Ute Rummel. Berlin: de Gruyter, 2018.

Killebrew, Ann E., and Gunnar Lehmann, eds. *The Philistines and Other "Sea Peoples" in Text and Archaeology*. Atlanta: Society of Biblical Literature, 2013.

Kislev, Mordechai E., and Yael Mahler-Slasky. "Lathyrus Consumption in Late Bronze and Iron Age Sites in Israel: An Aegean Affinity." *Journal of Archaeological Science* 37 (2010): 2477–85.

Maeir, Aren M. "Between Philistia, Phoenicia, and Beyond: A View from Tell es-Safi/Gath." Pages 85–94 in *Material, Method, and Meaning: Papers in Eastern Mediterranean Archeology in Honor of Ilan Sharon*. Edited by U. Davidovich, Sveta Matskevich, and Naama Yahalom-Mack. Münster: Zaphon, 2022.

———. "Introduction and Overview." Pages 1–52 in *Tell es-Safi/Gath II: Excavations and Studies*. Edited by Aren M. Maeir and Joe Uziel. Münster: Zaphon, 2020.

———. "Iron Age I Philistines: Entangled Identities in a Transformative Period." Pages 310–23 in *The Social Archaeology of the Levant: From Prehistory to the Present*. Edited by Assaf Yasur-Landau, Eric H. Cline, and Yorke Rowan. Cambridge: Cambridge University Press, 2019.

———. "Jerusalem and the West—Via Philistia: An Early Iron Age Perspective from Tell es-Safi/Gath." In *Jerusalem and the West: Perspectives from Archaeology, Biblical Studies and History*. Edited by Felix Hagemeyer. Tübingen: Mohr Siebeck, 2022.

———. "Khirbet Qeiyafa in Its Regional Context: A View from Philistine Gath." Pages 61–71 in *Khirbet Qeiyafa in the Shephelah. Papers Presented at a Colloquium of the Swiss Society for Ancient Near Eastern Studies Held at the University of Bern, September 6, 2014*. Edited by Sylvia Schroer and Stefan Münger. Fribourg: Academic Press, 2017.

———. "Memories, Myths and Megalithics: Reconsidering the Giants of Gath." *JBL* 139 (2020): 675–90.

———. "Philister-Keramik." Pages 528–36 in vol. 14 of *Reallexikon der Assyriologie und vorderasiatischen Archäologie*. Edited by G. Frantz-Szabo and U. Hellwag. Berlin: de Gruyter, 2005.

———. "Philistia and the Judean Shephelah After Hazael: The Power Play Between the Philistines, Judeans and Assyrians in the 8th Century BC in Light of the Excavations at Tell es-Safi/Gath." Pages 241–62 in *Disaster and Relief Management—Katastrophen und ihre Bewältigung*. Edited by Angelika Berlejung. Tübingen: Mohr Siebeck, 2012.

———. "The Philistines Be Upon Thee, Samson (Jud. 16:20): Reassessing the Martial Nature of the Philistines—Archaeological Evidence Vs. Ideological Image?" Pages 158–68 in *Change, Continuity and Connectivity: North-Eastern Mediterranean at the Turn of the Bronze Age and in the Early Iron Age*. Edited by Łukasz Niesiołowski-Spanò and Marek Węcowski. Wiesbaden: Harrassowitz, 2018.

———. Review of *Sea Peoples of the Northern Levant? Aegean-Style Pottery from Early Iron Age Tell Tayinat*, by Brian Janeway. *Review of Biblical Literature* (Feb. 2018): n.p.

Maeir, Aren M., and Esther Eshel. "Four Short Alphabetic Inscriptions from Iron Age IIA Tell es-Safi/Gath and Their Contribution for Understanding the Process of the Development of Literacy in Iron Age Philistia." Pages 69–88 in *"See, I Will Bring a Scroll Recounting What Befell Me" (Ps 40:8): Epigraphy and Daily Life—From the Bible to the Talmud Dedicated to the Memory of Professor Hanan Eshel*. Edited by Esther Eshel and Yigal Levin. Göttingen: Vandenhoeck & Ruprecht, 2014.

Maeir, Aren M., and Louise A Hitchcock. "The Appearance, Formation and Transformation of Philistine Culture: New Perspectives and New Finds." Pages 149–62 in Fischer and Bürge *"Sea Peoples" Up-to-Date*.

Maeir, Aren M., Brent Davis, and Louise A. Hitchcock. "Philistine Names and Terms Once Again: A Recent Perspective." *Journal of Eastern Mediterranean Archaeology and Heritage* 4 (2016): 321–40.

Maeir, Aren M., David Ben-Shlomo, Deborah Cassuto, Jeffrey R. Chadwick, Brent Davis, Adi Eliyahu Behar, Suembikya Frumin, Shira Gur-Arieh, Louise A. Hitchcock, Liora K. Horwitz, Francesca Manclossi, Steven A Rosen, Josephine Verduci, Ehud Weiss, Eric L. Welch, Vanessa Workman. "Technological Insights on Philistine Culture: Perspectives from Tell es-Safi/Gath." *Journal of Eastern Mediterranean Archaeology and Heritage Studies* 7 (2019): 76–118.

Master, Daniel M. "The Renewal of Trade at Iron Age I Ashkelon." *Eretz-Israel* 28 (2009): 111–22.

Oren, Eliezer, ed. *The Sea Peoples and Their World: A Reassessment*. Philadelphia: University Museum, 2000.

Sandars, Nancy K. *The Sea Peoples: Warriors of the Ancient Mediterranean*. Ancient Peoples and Places. London: Thames & Hudson, 1985.

Sapir-Hen, Lidar. "Food, Pork Consumption, and Identity in Ancient Israel." *NEA* 82.1 (2019): 52–59.

Stockhammer, Philipp. "How Aegean is Philistine Pottery? The Use of Aegean-Type Pottery in the Early 12th Century BCE Southern Levant." Page 379–87 in Fischer and Bürge, *"Sea Peoples" Up-to-Date*.

Waiman-Barak, Paula, Ayelet Gilboa, and Yuval Goren. "A Stratified Sequence of Early Iron Age Egyptian Ceramics at Tel Dor, Israel." *Ägypten und Levante* 24 (2014): 315–42.

Weitzman, Steve. "The Samson Story as Border Fiction." *Biblical Interpretation* 10 (2002) 158–74.

Yasur-Landau, Assaf. *The Philistines and Aegean Migration at the End of the Late Bronze Age*. Cambridge: Cambridge University Press, 2010.

Younger, K. Lawson, Jr. *A Political History of the Arameans: From Their Origins to the End of Their Polities*. Atlanta: Society of Biblical Literature, 2016.

CHAPTER 11

"THE LAND THAT REMAINS": EVIDENCE IN FAVOR OF THE THIRTEENTH CENTURY BC VIEW OF THE ISRAELITE CONQUEST AND SETTLEMENT

Josh 13:2–3; Josh 16–17; Judg 11:26; 1 Kgs 6:1

Chris McKinny and Steven M. Ortiz

KEY POINTS

- A text-critical examination of 1 Kgs 6:1 and Judg 11:26 demonstrates the various interpretative options (ancient and modern) for dating the conquest and settlement of Israel.
- The synthesis of Josh 13:2–3 with the arrival of the Philistines in the late thirteenth and early twelfth century BC strongly favors the thirteenth-century viewpoint.
- The Iron I settlement in Ephraim and Manasseh favors the thirteenth-century view, particularly in light of Josh 17 and the historical geographical evidence of the Samaria Ostraca.

INTRODUCTION

The historicity of Israel's exodus from Egypt and the conquest and settlement of Canaan is not usually questioned among conservative scholars.[1] However, there remains a considerable debate

1. For the scope of the debate and discussion within varying academic circles, see studies in Thomas E. Levy, Thomas Schneider, and William H. C. Propp, eds., *Israel's Exodus in Transdisciplinary Perspective: Text, Archaeology, Culture, and Geoscience* (New York: Springer, 2015); Alan R. Millard, Gary A. Rendsburg, and James K. Hoffmeier, eds., *"Did I Not Bring Israel Out of Egypt?": Biblical, Archaeological, and Egyptological Perspectives on the Exodus Narratives*

about the dating of these events within biblical studies and archaeology. While some fringe suggestions have been made, most scholars assuming a historical background of the exodus and conquest would date these events to either the fifteenth or the thirteenth century BC.[2] The fifteenth century viewpoint is usually referred to as either the early or high date, and the thirteenth century viewpoint as either the late or low date. In general, the Hyksos period (ending in the mid-sixteenth century BC) provides the earliest possible period for the exodus while Merenptah's campaign (end of the thirteenth century BC), the commemorative stela of which mentions Israel in the context of several toponyms in Canaan, provides a rough end date for the conquest.[3]

Those holding to the fifteenth-century exodus normally cast the argument as a debate between "archaeology" (thirteenth century BC) and "the Bible" (fifteenth century BC).[4] In our estimation, this is a problematic assertion. The archaeological and historical evidence favors a mid-thirteenth-century BC exodus, a late thirteenth century conquest, and a subsequent settlement during the Late Bronze/Iron I transition, but so does the Bible.[5] In this paper, we will not attempt to present an exhaustive argument in

---

(Winona Lake, IN: Eisenbrauns, 2016). References to the exodus in Hosea and Amos indicate that the exodus traditions must be dated at least as early as the eighth century BC. Many scholars date these traditions to at least as early as the tenth century BC. See Stephen C. Russell, *Images of Egypt in Early Biblical Literature: Cisjordan-Israelite, Transjordan-Israelite, and Judahite Portrayals* (Berlin: de Gruyter, 2009); Israel Finkelstein, *The Forgotten Kingdom: The Archaeology and History of Northern Israel* (Atlanta: Society of Biblical Literature, 2013), 145–51.

2. See, e.g., Bryant G. Wood, "The Rise and Fall of the Thirteenth-Century Exodus-Conquest Theory," *JETS* 48.3 (2005): 475–89; James K. Hoffmeier, "What Is the Biblical Date for the Exodus? A Response to Bryant Wood," *JETS* 50.2 (2007): 225–47; Kenneth A. Kitchen, *On the Reliability of the Old Testament* (Grand Rapids: Eerdmans, 2003), 159–312. For a slightly later date in the early twelfth century BC, see Gary A. Rendsburg, "The Date of the Exodus and the Conquest/Settlement: The Case for the 1100s," *VT* 42.4 (1992): 510–27; Larry D. Bruce, "The Merenptah Stele and the Biblical Origins of Israel," *JETS* 62.3 (2019): 246–66. For an example of a fringe dating view, see David M. Rohl, *Pharaohs and Kings: A Biblical Quest* (New York: Crown Publishers, 1995), the so-called "New Chronology," which is popularized in the "Patterns of Evidence: Exodus" film.

3. See, e.g., Michael G. Hasel, "Israel in the Merenptah Stela," *BASOR* 296 (1994): 45–61.

4. See, e.g., Charles H. Dyer, "The Date of the Exodus Reexamined," *Bibliotheca Sacra* 140 (1983): 224–43; Tremper Longman III and Raymond B. Dillard, *An Introduction to the Old Testament*, 2nd ed. (Grand Rapids: Zondervan, 2006), 122–29.

5. For the exodus, see James K. Hoffmeier, *Israel in Egypt: The Evidence for the Authenticity of the Exodus Tradition* (Oxford: Oxford University Press, 1996); Hoffmeier, *Ancient Israel in Sinai: The Evidence for the Authenticity of the Wilderness Tradition* (Oxford: Oxford University Press, 2005); Joshua Berman, "Was There an Exodus?" *Mosaic Magazine* (2015), https://mosaicmagazine.com/essay/2015/03/was-there-an-exodus/. For the conquest, see contra Wood, "Thirteenth-Century Exodus-Conquest Theory." We will not discuss the archaeology of the conquest in this chapter. However, the evidence against Wood's suggestions concerning the destruction at Jericho, the identification of Khirbet el-Maqatir with Ai, and the fifteenth-century BC destruction of the final Late Bronze city of Hazor are addressed in the following chapters in this volume: Chris McKinny, "The Archaeology and Historical Geography of the Slain Kings of Joshua 12" and McKinny, "'March on My Soul with Might!'—The Geographical Setting of Judges 4–5." In this paper, we use the following archaeological periodization (only

support of the thirteenth century viewpoint.[6] Instead, we want to draw attention to several less-discussed elements in the debate that we believe strongly suggest a thirteenth century BC date.

UNSETTLED MATH IN JUDG 11:26 AND 1 KGS 6:1

Judges 11:26 and 1 Kgs 6:1 are the two main chronological proofs given by proponents in favor of the fifteenth century BC date.[7] In the case of 1 Kgs 6:1, 480 years from the exodus to Solomon's fourth year (probably c. 966 BC) would result in the year 1446 BC for the date of the exodus and c. 1400 BC for the date of the conquest and beginning of the Israelite settlement.[8] Likewise, Jephthah's boast that Israel had been in possession of Sihon's former kingdom for "300 years" (Judg 11:26) would seem to fit with a late fifteenth century conquest, although the probable dating of Jephthah's career to the mid-eleventh century BC may actually be too late to match a fifteenth century date (see below).[9]

The textual support for the number of years in 1 Kgs 6:1 is divided between the Hebrew MT's 480 years, the Greek LXX's 440 years, and Josephus's 592 years (*Ant.* 8.61). Dead Sea Scroll fragment 4Q247 (4QPesher on the Apocalypse of Weeks) refers to the 480 years of 1 Kgs 6:1, which supports the MT's reading.[10] In the case of Judg 11:26 (compare *Ant.* 5.262), all three sources agree with the 300 years of Jephthah's boast. However, it is a distinct possibility that the 300 years in Judg 11:26 may be related to a calculated number from the chronological details from Exodus through Judges.[11] If one simply adds together the years from Moses to Jephthah, the MT equals 301 years, the LXX equals 311 years, and *Antiquities* equals 317 years (Tola's 23 years in Judg 10:2 are missing from Josephus, but he has additional years for Joshua and the years following Joshua, see table 1).

---

biblical periods included and all dates are approximate): Middle Bronze (c. 2000–1550 BC), Late Bronze (c. 1550–1200 BC), Iron I (c. 1200–1000 BC), Early Iron IIA (c. 1000–900 BC), Late Iron IIA (c. 900–800 BC), Iron IIB (c. 800–701 BC), Iron IIC (c. 701–586/539 BC), Persian (c. 539–332 BC), Hellenistic (332–63 BC), and Early Roman (63 BC–AD 70).

6. For an overview see, e.g., Lawrence T. Geraty, "Exodus Dates and Theories," in *Israel's Exodus in Transdisciplinary Perspective: Text, Archaeology, Culture, and Geoscience*, ed. Thomas E. Levy, Thomas Schneider, and William H. C. Propp (New York: Springer, 2015), 55–64; John D. Currid and David W. Chapman, eds., *ESV Archaeology Study Bible* (Grand Rapids: Crossway, 2018), 85–86; see also Bruce K. Waltke, "The Date of the Conquest," *WTJ* 52.2 (1990): 181–200.

7. Wood's use of the genealogical details of Kohath from 1 Chr 6:33–37 is problematic and certainly not the only way that the timeframe can be mathematically estimated (see Wood, "Thirteenth-Century Exodus-Conquest Theory," 486).

8. For Solomonic dates, see, e.g., Edwin R. Thiele, *The Mysterious Numbers of the Hebrew Kings*, 3rd ed. (Grand Rapids: Kregel Academic, 1994), 80.

9. Kitchen, *On the Reliability*, 207. Unless otherwise indicated, biblical quotations follow the English Standard Version (ESV).

10. Ariel Feldman, *The Dead Sea Scrolls Rewriting Samuel and Kings: Texts and Commentary* (Berlin: de Gruyter, 2015), 24.

11. The argument that Jephthah's claim was not a "mathematically precise chronological datum" remains possible and a distinct interpretive option (Kitchen, *On the Reliability*, 209, 309, table 28). See also K. Lawson Younger Jr., *Judges, Ruth*, NIVAC (Grand Rapids: Zondervan Academic, 2011), 258 n. 41.

Turning to 1 Kgs 6:1, Josephus's 592 years (*Ant.* 8.61) instead of 480 (MT) or 440 (LXX) years is likely a calculation (see table 1), although it could also be evidence of a textual variant.[12] With regards to this latter possibility, one should also note that Josephus's other chronological details are mostly in agreement with Josh–1 Kgs. Thus, a calculation for his version of 1 Kgs 6:1 seems more probable. Indeed, Josephus provided calculations for a variety of biblical events throughout *Antiquities*. One example of this is the timeframe of 515 years from Joshua's conquest to David's conquest of Jebus (*Ant.* 7.68), a figure which seems to match a calculation of the years given in *Antiquities* from Joshua to David's taking of Jerusalem.[13] It should be noted that we are not arguing for the historicity of Josephus's chronology (or for his consistency in calculating!), but rather that his lengthy year totals (e.g., 592 years in *Ant.* 8.61) are an example of an ancient method of expressing passages of time through calculation of raw numbers.[14]

Likewise, the MT's 480 years could simply be a calculation—from either a biblical author/redactor or copyist—taking the chronological data from the preceding narrative until the construction of the temple.[15] The sum of the years provided in the MT equals 557. One possible way for calculating the MT's 480 would be to subtract the 18 years of the Philistine/Ammonite oppression (Judg 10:8; referred to only as an Ammonite oppression in Josephus, *Ant.* 5.270), the 20 years of Samson's judgeship (Judg 16:31), and the 40 years of Eli's career (1 Sam 4:18) as these all could overlap with the 40 years of the Philistine oppression (Judg 13:1). This would result in the sum of 479 years, which could have been rounded to the 480 years in 1 Kgs 6:1.[16] If this calculation is correct, it is impossible to know if

12. This total probably does not include the twenty-five years that Josephus allotted for Joshua's governance (*Ant.* 5.117).

13. One difficulty in recalculating Josephus's year totals is that it is hard to know if a biblical text has simply dropped from the extant texts of *Antiquities* (e.g., Tola's missing entry; Abdon's missing years; Josephus's additions; etc.). One should not also assume that Josephus always calculated the years accurately or consistently within his own works. In any case, there are a variety of ways to arrive at his 515 (*Ant.* 7.68) and 592 years (*Ant.* 8.61). For the calculation in table 1 for Josephus's 592 years, Saul's reign was counted as 40 years (*Ant.* 6.378) with 18 years subtracted for the overlap between Samuel and Saul, and the 20 years of the ark at Kiriath Jearim were subtracted from the total as an obvious overlap with Samuel's "governance," which results in 594 years. There seems to be an internal consistency between *Ant.* 8.61 (592 years from the exodus to the initial building of the temple by Solomon) and *Ant.* 7.68 (515 years from Joshua's conquest to David's conquest), as both the Bible and Josephus indicate that David reigned in Jerusalem for 33 years and Solomon had reigned for 4 years when he began the construction of the temple (i.e., 37 years versus 77 years).

14. Josephus also gave the number of 612 years from the exodus to Solomon's construction of the temple (*Ant.* 20.230; *Apion* 2.19), but this seems to be inclusive of the 20 years of the building of the temple and his house (*Ant.* 8.141; compare with 1 Kgs 9:10) plus his 592 years (*Ant.* 8.61).

15. First Kings 6:1 (LXX) 440 years from the exodus to Solomon's fourth year does not fit an interpretation for LXX calculated years (see table 1)

16. There are other ways at arriving at a number close to 480 (MT) or 440 (LXX) through calculation. The 12 generations multiplied by 40 years (general time period of life) equals

TABLE 1: CHRONOLOGICAL DATA FROM MOSES TO SOLOMON'S FOURTH YEAR (1 KGS 6:1) FROM THE MT, LXX, AND JOSEPHUS

Leader	**References**	**Oppressor**
Moses	E.g., Exod 16:35; *Ant.* 5.21	-
Joshua	*Ant.* 5.117	-
No leader	*Ant.* 6.84	-
Othniel	Judg 3:8–11; *Ant.* 5.181, 184	Cushan-Rishathaim of Mesopotamia?
Ehud	Judg 3:14, 30; *Ant.* 5.187, 197	Eglon of Moab
Shamgar	Judg 3:31; *Ant.* 5.197	Philistines
Deborah and Barak	Judg 4:3, 5:31; *Ant.* 5.200, 209	Jabin of Canaan/ Hazor
Gideon	Judg 6:1; 8:28; *Ant.* 5.210–211, 232	Midianites and Ishmaelites
Abimelech	Judg 9:22; *Ant.* 5.239	Abimelech/Shechem
Tola	Judg 10:2	-
Jair	Judg 10:3; *Ant.* 5.254	-
"Israel lived in Heshbon... **300 years**..." (Judg 11:26; compare Josephus, *Ant.* 2.26)		
Jephthah	Judg 10:8; 12:7; *Ant.* 5.263, 270	Ammonites (and Philistines)
Ibzan	Judg 12:9; *Ant.* 5.271	-
Elon	Judg 12:11; *Ant.* 5.272	-
Abdon	Judg 12:14; Ant. 5.273	-
Samson	Judg 13:1; 16:31; *Ant.* 5.275; 5.316; compare with 1 Sam 7:2	Philistines
Eli	1 Sam 4:18; *Ant.* 5.359; compare with *Ant.* 5.319	Philistines
-	1 Sam 7:2; *Ant.* 6.18	Philistines
Samuel	*Ant.* 6.294 (12 years after Eli and 18 with Saul)	Philistines
Saul	1 Sam 13:1; *Ant.* 6:378; compare with *Ant.* 10.143 (20 years); Acts 13:21 (40 years)	Philistines
515 years from Joshua's conquest completion to David's conquest of Jebus		
David	E.g., 2 Sam 5:4; 1 Kgs 2:11; *Ant.* 7.389	-
Solomon's fourth	1 Kgs 6:1; *Ant.* 8.61	-
Calculated Exodus–Solomon with total years		
"In the fourth year... 480/440/592 years..." 1 Kings 6:1; *Ant.* 8:61		
Subtract years of overlap with Philistines/Ark		
Total years with possible overlap subtracted		

Description	**MT Years**	**LXX^A Years**	**LXX^B Years**	**Josephus Years**
wilderness	40	40	40	40
conquest	-	-	-	25
"anarchy"	-	-	-	18
oppression	8	8	8	8
rest	40	50	40	40
oppression	18	18	18	18
rest	80	80	80	80
-	-	-	-	-
oppression	20	20	20	20
rest	40	40	40	40
oppression	7	7	7	3
rest	40	40	40	40
rule	3	3	3	3
rest	23	23	23	-
rest	22	22	22	22
	301	**311**	**301**	**317**
oppression	18	18	18	18
rest	6	6	6	6
rest	7	7	7	7
rest	10	10	10	10
rest	8	8	8	-
oppression	40	40	40	40
rest	20	20	20	20
ruled	40	20	20	40
Ark at Kiriath Jearim	20	20	20	20
rule	-	-	-	30
reign	3	-	-	40
(7.5 years reigning in Hebron) (*Ant.* 7.68)				**512.5**
reign	40	40	40	40
reign	4	4	4	4
	557	544	534	632
	480 (MT)	440 (LXXA)	440 (LXXB)	592 (*Ant.*)
	78	58	58	38 (Samuel/ark)
	479	486	476	594

this proposed calculation was original or updated at a later date to reflect a harmonized timeline, as seems to be the case for Josephus's rendering of 1 Kgs 6:1 and could be the case for all three textual witnesses of Judg 11:26.[17] Regardless, there remain several interpretative options for 1 Kgs 6:1 and Judg 11:26 that account for ancient calculation methods and maintain the basic historicity of these passages while at the same time also allowing for the thirteenth century BC date of the exodus and conquest. Moreover, given the textual critical complexities outlined above, it seems problematic to place so much weight on 1 Kgs 6:1 and Judg 11:26 as proof for a fifteenth century BC date. Unlike Assyria, which developed a sophisticated chronological system by which each year had its own distinct name (the Assyrian Eponym Canon), we know of no such chronological system in Judah or Israel. Israel and Judah's regnal reckoning system was similar to Assyria and Babylon, but it apparently did not include a recording system for specific years, which is necessary for calculating long periods time. At least such a system has not been preserved in Kings, other biblical texts, or come to light from archaeological investigation.[18]

In light of this, and besides the example of Josephus for 1 Kgs 6:1, there may be a biblical example of the above-outlined method of calculation. The example comes from Ezek 4, which is around the time of the final redaction of the book of Kings (i.e., the sixth century BC, see 2 Kgs 25:27–30, which concludes the book with Jehoiachin's release from prison, around 562 BC). The book of Ezekiel includes a series of signs that signify Judah's destruction, exile, and return. Ezekiel 4 has the prophet lying before a brick with miniature siege equipment that symbolizes Jerusalem's coming siege and destruction by Babylon. The prophet himself was told to lie down on his left side for "a number of days, 390 days, equal to the number of the years of their punishment" for the house of Israel (Ezek 4:5). After this was completed, he was to lie on his right side for "forty days ... a day for each year" for the house of Judah (Ezek 4:6), which together total four hundred thirty years (see table 2).

Scholars have been greatly divided over how to understand the 430 years. Block suggests adding the 390 years to 586 BC, which results in the year 976 BC.[19] A time period he correlates with the building of Solomon's temple—an event which actually occurred a bit later than this. Solomon's temple would have been completed around 960 BC according to the chronology in 1 Kgs, assuming a correlation with the campaign of Shishak in 926/925 BC (1 Kgs 14:25). While we agree with much of Block's conclu-

480 years also remains a possible interpretive solution as well. See also other similar options in Kitchen, *On the Reliability*, 307–8; Hoffmeier, "Biblical Date for the Exodus?," 235–39.

17. For a similar argument that discusses earlier suggestions for 1 Kgs 6:1, see Gershon Galil, "The Chronological Framework of the Deuteronomistic History," *Biblica* 85.3 (2004): 413–21; see also Galil, *The Chronology of the Kings of Israel and Judah* (Leiden: Brill, 1996), 1–11. Galil's conclusion that the minor judges were not included in this chronology is hard to accept.

18. First Kings 6:1 cannot be cited as an example because it is itself dealing with a timeframe long before the monarchy.

19. Daniel I. Block, *The Book of Ezekiel, Chapters 1–24*, rev. ed.(Grand Rapids: Eerdmans, 1997), 170–80. See Block also for a discussion of the various views.

sions including that the sign should be related to Israel's wilderness punishment (forty years for forty days of the spies' bad report; Num 14:34–35) and that the years should be counted backwards, we disagree with how he was counting the years. Indeed, what does one do with the other forty years in Ezek 4, as this would take you further back into the eleventh century BC without any clear referent?[20]

Assuming that Ezekiel gave this prophetic symbol in or around 593 BC (Ezek 1:2—the "fifth year of Jehoiachin's exile"—instead of 586 BC), one can count backwards to 983 BC—a date of no great significance. However, what if Ezekiel was using the raw regnal years of Judahite kings as recorded in the book of Kings, but certainly also available to Ezekiel? As has long been noted, these regnal years include coregencies between kings (e.g., coregency between Amaziah and Uzziah in 2 Kgs 14:21), which ultimately means that the total number of regnal years for Judahite kings (389) is much more than the actual number of years (338) between the division of the kingdom (931 BC) and the fifth year of Jehoiachin's exile (593 BC).[21] Indeed, this 389 years of Judahite regnal years is very close to the 390 years of Ezek 4:5. The remaining "forty years" could be applied to the reign of Solomon (2 Kgs 11:42), which would mean that the 430 years of Ezekiel's punishment for Israel/Judah match the regnal chronological years from Solomon through the fifth year of Jehoiachin's exile—a period of time that was actually only 378 years.[22] If this tentative conclusion is more than a coincidence, then it seems that Ezek 4 is an example of calculating raw numbers by a biblical author.

Settling Philistine Culture in the "Land that Remains" (Josh 13:2–3)

In our view, the chronological information in Judg 11:26 and 1 Kgs 6:1 does not settle the debate, as there are multiple ways of understanding the numbers given in these passages. On the other hand, those holding to a fifteenth century BC viewpoint run into considerable textual difficulties when it comes to the biblical portrayal of cultural realities in texts connected with the exodus, conquest, and settlement. The following are some general points of correspondence that argue for the thirteenth century BC date against the fifteenth century BC date.

Biblical Textual Evidence in Favor of a Thirteenth Century Exodus and Conquest

The references to "Rameses" in Genesis (47:11) and Exodus (1:11; see also Exod 12:37; and Num 33:3, 5) should most likely be connected with the Egyptian Ramesside period (thirteenth century BC).[23] Moreover, despite the fact that numerous foreign entities are mentioned (see table 1), neither Joshua nor Judges

20. Moshe Greenberg, *Ezekiel 1–20*, AB (New Haven: Yale University Press, 1983), 104–6.

21. On coregency, see Thiele, *Mysterious Numbers*.

22. Of course, there is a clear intertextual link with the forty years of punishment from Num 14:34–35.

23. Proponents of the thirteenth century view connect the city of Rameses (Qantir) with the Ramesside Dynasty, i.e., the nineteenth Egyptian dynasty which came to power around the beginning of the thirteenth century. Some who hold to this view believe that the oppression began under Horemheb (1323–1295 BC) (see, e.g., Kitchen, *On the Reliability*, 309–10).

TABLE 2: THE SYMBOLIC 430 YEARS OF PUNISHMENT IN EZEKIEL 4:1–17

Kings (actual years)	**r.**
Solomon (971–931)	40
Rehoboam (931–914)	17
Abijah (914–911)	3
Asa (911–870)	42
Jehoshaphat (872–848)	25
Jehoram (853–841)	8
Ahaziah (841)	1
Athaliah (841–836)	7
Joash (836–796)	40
Amaziah (796–768)	29
Azariah (792–740)	52
Jotham (751–731)	16
Ahaz (735–715)	16
Hezekiah (729–686)	29
Manasseh (697–642)	55
Amon (642–640)	2
Josiah (640–609)	31
Jehoahaz (609)	0
Jehoiakim (609–598)	11
Jehoiachin (598–597)	0
Zedekiah (597–586)	11

Summary (Rehoboam onward)
Total of regnal years in 1–2 Kgs: Rehoboam through Zedekiah (586 BC): **395 years**
Actual years between 931 and 586 BC: **345 years**
Total of regnal years in 1–2 Kgs: Rehoboam to fifth year of Jehoiachin's exile (593 BC – Ezek 1:1–2): **389 years**
Actual years between 931 and 593 BC: **338 years**
Ezek 4:5, 9 – 390 days for Israel = **390 regnal years between Rehoboam to fifth year of Jehoiachin's exile**

Summary (Solomon onward)
Ezek 4:6 – 40 days for Judah = **40 years of Solomon's reign**; 430 years/days of Ezekiel = **430 regnal years of 1–2 Kgs**
Actual years between 971 and 593 BC: **378 years**

makes reference to the Egyptians despite the fact that the Egyptian New Kingdom was dominating Canaan from the fifteenth to the thirteenth century BC. The lack of reference to the Egyptians is particularly striking given the fact that many important Canaanite cities that were dominated by Egyptians are mentioned in Joshua and Judges (e.g., Beth Shan).[24] In a similar fashion, the Amarna correspondence (mid-fourteenth century BC), which consists of numerous letters written from presumably Israelite regions (e.g., Shechem) to Egyptian suzerains, make no reference to the Israelites.[25]

The Arrival of the Philistines and the "Land that Remains" (Josh 13:2–3)

Besides these usual lines of argumentation, there is another, often overlooked piece of textual data that strongly favors the thirteenth century BC date: the occurrence of the Philistines in the "land that remains" following the conquest of Canaan (Josh 13:2–3). Joshua 13 represents a shift from the narrative of the conquest (Josh 1–12) to the allotment of the land (Josh 13–21). The section begins by indicating Joshua's advanced age (Josh 13:1), which may denote that some time had passed between the conquest and the allotment. The passage then lays out the land that had yet to be conquered by Israel (Josh 13:2–7) before listing the allotment of the Transjordanian tribes (Josh 13:8–33). Joshua 13:2–7 can be broken down into the following foreign groups: Philistines, Geshurites, and the Avvim along the southern coastal plain (Josh 13:2–3; see also Judg 3:3); the Canaanites "in the south" (Josh 12:4a); the Sidonians

24. But see the suggestion to connect Merenptah's campaign to Judg 10:11 in S. Cameron Coyle and Steven M. Ortiz, "Judges 10:11: A Memory of Merenptah's Campaign in Transjordan," in *"An Excellent Fortress for His Armies, A Refuge for The People": Egyptological, Archaeological, and Biblical Studies in Honor of James K. Hoffmeier*, ed. Richard E. Averbeck and K. Lawson Younger Jr. (Winona Lake, IN: Eisenbrauns, 2020), 298–308. Even those who deny the historicity of the exodus note that it is such an influential event they have to associate the tradition with events during the Saite period in the seventh to sixth centuries BC, a period where several scholars place the final redaction of the Pentateuch (e.g., Donald B. Redford, *Egypt, Canaan, and Israel in Ancient Times* [Princeton: Princeton University Press, 1992], 395–429; William G. Dever, *Beyond the Texts: An Archaeological Portrait of Ancient Israel and Judah* [Atlanta: Society of Biblical Literature, 2017], 243).

25. In short, all of the textual arguments made by Hoffmeier in response to Wood remain valid. See Wood, "Thirteenth-Century Exodus-Conquest Theory"; Hoffmeier, "Biblical Date for the Exodus?"; Bryant G. Wood, "The Biblical Date for the Exodus is 1446 BC: A Response to James Hoffmeier," *JETS* 50.2 (2007): 249–58. See also the continuation of the debate between Hawkins and Wood (along with Young): Ralph K. Hawkins, "Propositions for Evangelical Acceptance of a Late-Date Exodus-Conquest: Biblical Data and the Royal Scarabs from Mt. Ebal," *JETS* 50.1 (2007): 31–46; Rodger C. Young and Bryant G. Wood, "A Critical Analysis of the Evidence from Ralph Hawkins for a Late-Date Exodus-Conquest," *JETS* 51.2 (2008): 225–43; Ralph K. Hawkins, "The Date of the Exodus-Conquest Is Still an Open Question: A Response to Rodger Young and Bryant Wood," *JETS* 51.2 (2008): 246–66. For more recent discussions of this, see Mark D. Janzen, ed., *Five Views on the Exodus: Historicity, Chronology, and Theological Implications* (Grand Rapids: Zondervan Academic, 2021); Manfred Bietak and Gary A. Rendsburg, "Egypt and the Exodus," in *Ancient Israel, From Abraham to the Roman Destruction of the Temple*, ed. Hershel Shanks and John Merrill, rev. and exp. ed. (Washington: Biblical Archaeology Society, 2021).

and Gebalites of the Phoenician coast and the hill country occupations of the Lebanon range and (presumably) Upper Galilee (Josh 12:5–6).[26] We will only focus on the first group, as the latter two groups refer to peoples that were long associated with the land of Canaan before and after the arrival of the Israelites.

The southern Geshurites (Josh 13:2) were a sub-people of the Philistines that were apparently similar to the Cherethites and the Pelethites (1 Sam 27:8).[27] This latter passage indicates that the Geshurites should likely be located in the same vicinity as the Amalekites, i.e., the Negev, southwestern coastal plain, and northern Sinai (see also Josh 13:3).

The Avvim also appear in the list of remaining giant clans (Anakim/ Rephaim) in different parts of the land of Canaan (Deut 2:10–12, 20–23). The Avvim (Deut 2:23) were specifically connected to the coastal plain ("as far as Gaza") and the "Caphtorim who came from Caphtor destroyed them and settled in their place" (i.e., the Philistines, compare with Gen 10:14; 1 Chr 1:12; Jer 47:4; Amos 9:7). Likewise, Josh 11:22 connects the giant clans of the Anakim that remained "only in Gaza, in Gath, and in Ashdod." The presence of the Avvim in Philistia also seems to be related to the great height of Goliath (1 Sam 17) and his fellow giants from Gath (2 Sam 21:15–22; 1 Chr 20:4–8). Interestingly, the persistence of giant characteristics in Gath may represent a textual understanding of the acculturation of the Philistines with the previous Canaanite/Avvim populations.[28]

THE ACCULTURATION OF THE PHILISTINES WITH THE LOCAL CANAANITE POPULATION

The end of the thirteenth and beginning of the twelfth century BC saw a major collapse of the burgeoning Late Bronze political and economic system. All the major empires of the Mediterranean either completely collapsed or were severely weakened.[29] It is clear that Egypt controlled and dominated the southern Levant throughout the eighteenth and nineteenth dynasties (c. 1500–1200 BC). However, the nature of Egyptian policy and activity at the end of the New Kingdom (twentieth dynasty; c. 1186–1069 BC) is not as clear. It seems that Egypt maintained control of some of their strategic strongholds, which included some of the major Canaanite city-states (e.g., Jaffa, Megiddo, Beth Shan). Still, the thirteenth century BC collapse created a power vacuum that allowed various secondary states to develop in the southern Levant, including the Philistines and the Israelites.

From an archaeological perspective, several elements of material culture have

---

26. The references to the Canaanites and Amorites seem to be general terms defining the southern and northern ends of the promised land.

27. The Gizrites (1 Sam 27:8) may be another of these peoples, although the name could also be related to either Gezer or a scribal mistake for Gaza.

28. For a discussion of the Rephaim at Gath and its surrounding, see Aren M. Maeir, "The Rephaim in Iron Age Philistia: Evidence of a Multi-Generational Family," in *"Vom Leben Umfangen": Ägypten, Das Alte Testament Und Das Gespräch Der Religionen. Gedenkschrift Für Manfred Görg*, ed. Stefan J. Wimmer and G. Gafus (Münster: Ugarit-Verlag, 2014), 289–97.

29. Eric H. Cline, *1177 B.C.: The Year Civilization Collapsed* (Princeton: Princeton University Press, 2015).

Portion of Pottery Timeline Featuring Iron Age I Philistine Decorated Sherds

been discovered that suggest the acculturation of the Philistines with existing Canaanite culture. These include the following: the gradual adoption of Canaanite ceramic traditions across the twelfth and eleventh centuries (i.e., the transition from Philistine 1/Monochrome to Philistine 2/Bichrome), the contemporary use of Canaanite and Philistine cooking practices (tabuns versus hearths) and utensils (cooking pot versus cooking jug), architecture (representing some characteristics from the Aegean), and cultic-related items (various Aegean and Cypriot influences).[30]

PORK AVOIDANCE/CONSUMPTION: AN ETHNIC IDENTIFIER?

With regards to the appearance of the Philistines and the Israelites in the Late Bronze/Iron I transition, Philistine pork consumption and Israelite pork avoidance (e.g., Lev 11:7–8; Deut 14:7–8) has been a major point of discussion.[31] While there remains debate, the assertion that Philistines consumed pork in high quantities and the Israelites/Judahites always avoided it—and, thus pork consumption was a key ethnic identifier—has been re-examined.[32] As it now stands, it seems that Philistine urban sites, espe-

30. See, especially, Joe Uziel, "The Development Process of Philistine Material Culture: Assimilation, Acculturation and Everything in Between," *Levant* 39.1 (2007): 165–73; Aren M. Maeir, Louise A. Hitchcock, and Liora K. Horwitz, "On the Constitution and Transformation of Philistine Identity," *Oxford Journal of Archaeology* 32.1 (2013): 1–38.

31. See most recently Lidar Sapir-Hen, "Food, Pork Consumption, and Identity in Ancient Israel," *NEA* 82.1 (2019): 52–59.

32. For the debate regarding Philistine versus Israelite pork consumption, see Avraham Faust and Justin Lev-Tov, "The Constitution of Philistine Identity: Ethnic Dynamics in Twelfth to Tenth Century Philistia," *Oxford Journal of Archaeology* 30.1 (2011): 13–31; Maeir, Hitchcock, and Horwitz, "Philistine Identity," 1–38; Avraham Faust and Justin Lev-Tov, "Philistia and the Philistines in the Iron Age I: Interaction, Ethnic Dynamics and Boundary Maintenance,"

cially Gath and Ekron, consumed pork throughout the Iron Age, but pork never was the dominant component of their diet. At rural Philistine sites, there is a general lack of evidence for pork consumption, which matches the avoidance of pork consumption for Judah in both the Iron I and throughout the Iron II. Conversely, for the northern regions the situation is more complicated as it seems that in the Iron I, Canaanite and Israelite populations avoided pork—continuing a Bronze Age practice. However, it seems that in the Iron IIB the northern kingdom of Israel began to consume pork. This reversal may be related to economic improvements in the kingdom of Israel.[33]

On the other hand, a multi-disciplinary study has shown that the modern wild pigs (i.e., hogs or wild boars) in Israel possess the same DNA sequence as European wild boars and domestic pigs that seem to have been introduced to the region in the Iron Age by the Sea Peoples, including the Philistines, who migrated to the southern Levant.[34] Pig bone DNA from Late Bronze Age contexts show clear similarities with other Near Eastern wild boars, which seems to indicate that new pig populations were introduced into the southern Levant during the early part of the Iron Age, when both the Philistines and the Israelites were settling the southern Levant.[35]

PHILISTINE DNA: EUROPEAN, NOT LEVANTINE STOCK

In addition to the distinctive Philistine material elements described above, the extraordinary discovery of a massive Philistine cemetery at Ashkelon has shed light on the origins of the Philistines, which both the biblical text (e.g., Amos 9:7) and Egyptian sources related to the Aegean.[36] The recent publication of the DNA testing of ten (out of 108) skeletons from Ashkelon has confirmed long-held theories about the European origins of the Philistines.[37] Significantly, Feldman et al. were able to demonstrate that the DNA of three individuals from the Middle and Late Bronze Age were of local origin, whereas the skeletal remains of four infants from the twelfth century BC

Hiphil Novum 1.1 (2014): 1–24; Avraham Faust, "Pigs in Space (and Time): Pork Consumption and Identity Negotiations in the Late Bronze and Iron Ages of Ancient Israel," *NEA* 81.4 (December 1, 2018): 276–99. On pork as an ethnic identifier, see Brian Hesse, "Can Pig Remains Be Used for Ethnic Diagnosis in the Ancient Near East?," in *The Archaeology of Israel: Constructing the Past, Interpreting the Present*, ed. Neil A. Silberman and David B. Small (Sheffield: A&C Black, 1997), 238–70. For a re-examination, see especially Lidar Sapir-Hen et al., "Pig Husbandry in Iron Age Israel and Judah: New Insights Regarding the Origin of the Taboo," *ZDPV* 129.1 (2013): 1–20.

33. Summarized from Sapir-Hen, "Consumption, and Identity."

34. Meirav Meiri et al., "Ancient DNA and Population Turnover in Southern Levantine Pigs-Signature of the Sea Peoples Migration?," *Nature* 3 (2013): http://www.nature.com/srep/2013/131028/srep03035/full/srep03035.html.

35. Meiri et al., "Ancient DNA."

36. See Ann E. Killebrew, *Biblical Peoples and Ethnicity: An Archaeological Study of Egyptians, Canaanites, Philistines, and Early Israel, 1300–1100 B.C.E.* (Atlanta: Society of Biblical Literature, 2005), 9.

37. Michal Feldman et al., "Ancient DNA Sheds Light on the Genetic Origins of Early Iron Age Philistines," *Science Advances* 5.7 (July 1, 2019): eaax0061, https://doi.org/10.1126/sciadv.aax0061.

clearly showed genetic connections with the European gene pool.[38] Finally, the last three skeletons—dated to the tenth and ninth centuries BC—reflected similar DNA evidence to the Levantine genetic pool of the Middle and Late Bronze skeletal remains demonstrating the mixing of the Philistine and local gene pools in the Iron II.[39]

The Arrival of the Philistines in the Late Thirteenth Century BC?

The timing of the Philistine arrival to the coast of Canaan seems to coincide with their defeat by Ramesses III as indicated by reliefs and inscriptions from mortuary temple of Ramesses III at Medinet Habu. Papyrus Harris I may indicate that the Philistines and other Sea Peoples were settled in forts, although the location of these forts is not mentioned (Papyrus Harris I, 76:6–9).[40] Ramesses III's war with the Sea Peoples occurred in his eighth year, which can be dated to either 1177 BC, following Kitchen's chronology, or 1186 BC, according to the revised chronology suggested by Schneider.[41] The method, timing, purpose, and causes of the migration of the Sea Peoples remain debated, but for our purposes it seems clear that the Philistines arrived in Canaan by the early twelfth century BC, settling especially in the former Canaanite cities of Ekron, Gath, Ashdod, Ashkelon, and Gaza.[42] Significantly, new radiocarbon dates from Tell es-Safi/Gath and Qubur al-Walaydah, a Philistine site located in the northwestern Negev, seem to indicate that these sites were actually settled by the Philistines as early as the late thirteenth century BC.[43]

In light of this evidence, the reference to the Philistine Pentapolis in the "land that remains" of Josh 13:2–3 closely match the arrival of the Philistines on the coast of Canaan in the late thirteenth and early twelfth centuries BC. There is no evidence of Philistine presence in Canaan during either the fifteenth or the fourteenth centuries BC, which mitigates strongly against the fifteenth century BC viewpoint.[44] In this regard, the

38. Feldman et al., "Ancient DNA."

39. Feldman et al., "Ancient DNA."

40. Anson F. Rainey and Steven Notley, *The Sacred Bridge: Carta's Atlas of the Biblical World* (Jerusalem: Carta, 2006), 109.

41. Compare Kenneth A. Kitchen, "History of Egypt (Chronology)," *ABD* 2.328; Thomas Schneider, "Contributions to the Chronology of the New Kingdom and the Third Intermediate Period," *Ägypten Und Levante/Egypt and the Levant* 20 (2010): 202.

42. The three coastal towns along with the Philistines, Sikel, and Sherden (nos. 262–64, 268–70) also appear in the Onomasticon of Amenope, which dates no later than the reign of Ramesses IX (1126–1108 BC [Kitchen, "Chronology," 328]) (Rainey and Notley, *Sacred Bridge*, 110).

43. Yotam Asscher et al., "Radiocarbon Dating Shows an Early Appearance of Philistine Material Culture in Tell Es-Safi/Gath, Philistia," *Radiocarbon* 57.5 (2015): 825–50; Elisabetta Boaretto et al., "The Chronology of the Late Bronze (LB)–Iron Age (IA) Transition in the Southern Levant: A Response to Finkelstein's Critique," *Radiocarbon* 61.1 (2019): 1–11; for the dissenting view, see Israel Finkelstein, "To Date or Not to Date: Radiocarbon and the Arrival of the Philistines," *Ägypten Und Levante/Egypt and the Levant* 26 (2016): 275–84.

44. References to the Philistines in the Abimelech episodes (Gen 21:32, 34; 26:1, 8, 14–15, 18) are anachronistic for both viewpoints. Merrill's view that these were an earlier migration of Philistines is hard to accept (Eugene H. Merrill, *Kingdom of Priests: A History of Old Testament Israel* [Grand Rapids: Baker Academic, 2008], 57–58). As they could reflect realities of the late

Illustration of Land Battle of Ramesses III and Sea Peoples from Medinet Habu

DNA evidence from Ashkelon is particularly devastating. Thus, we would hold to the primacy of the biblical cultural references to the Philistines in Canaan along with the references to Rameses and the land of Goshen as being primary evidence of cultural memory versus the chronological details (Judg 11:26; 1 Kgs 6:1) that require more interpretive analysis. This Philistine settlement data is absent in discussions related to the dating of the exodus, conquest, and Israelite settlement, but in light of this new data and its correlation with the biblical text (i.e., Josh 13:2–3; Judg 3:3) it should be understood as a key chronological element.

SETTLING ISRAELITE CULTURE: THE CENTRAL HIGHLAND SETTLEMENTS (JOSH 16–17)[45]

We will turn our attention to the archaeology of the highlands of Ephraim and Manasseh and related biblical texts, which seems to show the arrival of a new people—the Israelites—sometime in the late thirteenth into the twelfth centuries BC.

ISRAELITES IN THE HIGHLANDS OF EPHRAIM AND MANASSEH?

Finkelstein's and Bunimovitz's hill country surveys of southern Manasseh, Ephraim, and Benjamin, and Zertal's survey of Manasseh clearly demonstrate

thirteenth century BC, the Genesis references, as well as the "way of the land of the Philistines" and the "Sea of the Philistines" in Exodus (13:17; 23:31) match better with the thirteenth century view.

45. This chapter will not address other arguments related to the question of the Iron I populations in upper Galilee, the Huleh Valley, the Jezreel Valley, and Transjordan.

Relief Illustrating Sea Peoples Engaged in Sea Battle with Ship from Medinet Habu

that a major demographic change took place in the central highlands and elsewhere during the transition between the Late Bronze and Iron I.[46] Gadot and Sergi recently complied the available data during their discussions of this massive settlement shift.[47] All told, it seems that there was a 550 percent increase from the number of Late Bronze sites (61) to the number of Iron I sites (334).[48] In our view, this massive increase may be associated with the settlement of early Israel, which included both the incoming Israelite population as well as a "mixed multitude" of

46. Israel Finkelstein, *The Archaeology of the Israelite Settlement* (Jerusalem: Israel Exploration Society, 1988); Israel Finkelstein, Zvi Lederman, and Shlomo Bunimovitz, eds., *Highland of Many Cultures: The Southern Samaria Survey*, 2 vols. (Tel Aviv: Tel Aviv University, 1997). Adam Zertal, *The Manasseh Hill Country Survey, Volume 1: The Shechem Syncline*, Har/Map ed. (Leiden: Brill, 2004); Adam Zertal, ed., *The Manasseh Hill Country Survey, Volume 2: The Eastern Valleys and the Fringes of the Desert* (Leiden: Brill, 2007); Adam Zertal, Nivi Mirkam, *The Manasseh Hill Country Survey, Volume 3: From Nahal 'Iron to Nahal Shechem*, ed. Shay Bar (Leiden: Brill, 2016); Adam Zertal and Shay Bar, *The Manasseh Hill Country Survey, Volume 4: From Nahal Bezeq to the Sartaba* (Leiden: Brill, 2017); Adam Zertal and Shay Bar, *The Manasseh Hill Country Survey, Volume 5: The Middle Jordan Valley, from Wadi Fasael to Wadi 'Aujah* (Leiden: Brill, 2019).

47. Omer Sergi and Yuval Gadot, "The Rise of Ancient Israel in the Iron I–IIA: The Need for a Closer Look," *NEA* 82.1 (2019): 5–7; Sergi, "The Formation of Israelite Identity in the Central Canaanite Highlands in the Iron Age I–IIA," *NEA* 82.1 (2019): 42–51; Gadot, "The Iron I Settlement Wave in the Samaria Highlands and Its Connection with the Urban Centers," *NEA* 82.1 (2019): 32–41.

48. Gadot, "Iron I Settlement," table 1. Dever presents similar data with a shift from fifty-eight to over three hundred fifty sites (Dever, *Beyond the Texts*).

Model of Iron I Settlement in Ephraim and Manasseh

locals who underwent a process of "ruralization" (e.g., Exod 12:38; "the sojourners" of Josh 8:35; the Hivites in Josh 9).[49]

NATURE OF IRON I CENTRAL HIGHLAND SETTLEMENTS

Most of these sites were newly established small agrarian villages not built on earlier Late Bronze cities.[50] These new sites are in contrast to large urban Canaanite settlements that were not abandoned during the Late Bronze–Iron I transition (e.g., Megiddo) or Philistine sites (e.g., Gath, Ekron). Most of the highland sites were only occupied from the Iron I until the Iron Age II, or between c. 1200 BC to 722 BC when the Assyrians conquered the northern kingdom of Israel. Thus, not only is there a drastic change in settlement patterns, but also in the nature of the settlements themselves. The highland sites were made up of unwalled settlements that lack public buildings (e.g., temples), but possess a new house type—the four-room house.[51] The four-room house seems to have originated in the Iron I and does not continue into the Persian Period. Such houses

49. See, e.g., Gadot, "Iron I Settlement." However, even if part of the patterns we are attributing to Israelite ethnicity are based on ruralization, it is still a new pattern of social transformation discerned in the Iron Age I. This social transformation that we see in the Iron Age I reflects what we see in the biblical tradition of Joshua and Judges.

50. See discussion in Finkelstein, *Israelite Settlement*.

51. Shlomo Bunimovitz and Avraham Faust, "Building Identity: The Four-Room House and the Israelite Mind," in *Symbiosis, Symbolism, and the Power of the Past: Canaan, Ancient Israel, and Their Neighbors from the Late Bronze Age through Roman Palaestina*, ed. William G. Dever and Seymour Gitin (Winona Lake, IN: Eisenbrauns, 2003), 63–74.

are mostly missing in Iron I Philistia, are rarer in the Shephelah, and are not known anywhere north of the Jezreel Valley or in the Jordan Valley before the Iron II.[52] The ceramic assemblage is also distinctly utilitarian, as the Iron I hill country pottery is marked by the absence of imports and lack of decorations.

UNSETTLING PROBLEM FOR THE EARLY DATE VIEW?

While the fifteenth century BC view now lacks any destruction layer for Jericho (sixteenth century BC) and Hazor (only a single LB destruction dated to the thirteenth century BC), the lack of any evidence of Israelite settlement in the fourteenth and thirteenth centuries BC remains the most glaring deficiency of the early date view.[53] It is certainly possible that significant populations lived outside of settlements and, thus, left no archaeological evidence.[54] However, it seems most unlikely that the Israelites would have resided nomadically in the same area for two centuries (c. 1400–1200 BC) before actually beginning the process of sedenterization that is observed in the Iron I highlands sites.[55] Unfortunately, we do not have definitive data about the exact dating of the over three hundred Iron I highland's sites as the only dateable evidence comes from Shiloh (carbon-14 - c. eleventh century BC) and the initial phase at the cultic structure on Mount Ebal (two nineteenth dynasty scarabs).[56] It seems possible—perhaps even likely—that the process of settlement began already in the late thirteenth century BC.[57] While one can understand the wave of settlement in the highlands as only an archaeological argument, it should be noted that the historical geographical details in the Bible and the Samaria Ostraca also fit a thirteenth to twelfth century BC period for the beginning of the Israelite settlement. In what follows, we will discuss the historical geography of the hill country of Ephraim and Manasseh from the biblical text and the Samaria Ostraca.

---

52. But see Manfred Bietak, "An Iron Age Four-Room House in Ramesside Egypt," *Eretz-Israel* 23 (1992): 10*–12*.

53. For a discussion of the problems with Jericho and Hazor, see McKinny, "The Archaeology and Historical Geography of the Slain Kings of Joshua 12:1–16 in this volume. Ai remains a problem for both views. See Gary A. Byers, Scott Stripling, and Bryant G. Wood, "Excavations at Khirbet El-Maqatir: The 2009–2011 Seasons," *Judea and Samaria Research Studies* 25.2 (2016): 69*–109*. In our view, Khirbet el-Maqatir was a small, rural Middle Bronze site that may have continued to be occupied into the sixteenth and fifteenth century BC before it was abandoned. It was then re-occupied in the Iron I and largely abandoned in the Iron II.

54. Erez Ben-Yosef, "The Architectural Bias in Current Biblical Archaeology," *VT* 69.3 (2019): 361–87.

55. See, e.g., Bryant G. Wood, "David Rohl's Revised Egyptian Chronology: A View from Palestine," *Bible and Spade (Second Run)* 14.3 (2001): n.p. See also especially Ralph K. Hawkins, *The Iron Age I: Structure on Mt Ebal* (Winona Lake, IN: Eisenbrauns, 2012).

56. For the Shiloh evidence, see Gadot, "Iron I Settlement," 37. On Mount Ebal, see Hawkins, *Iron Age 1*, 66–71. This structure remains an intriguing candidate for the "altar" of Joshua (Deut 27:1–8; Josh 8:30–35).

57. Hawkins, *Iron Age*, 66–71; Gadot, "Iron I Settlement," 36–37, who notes the difficulty of dating pottery from the late thirteenth, twelfth, and eleventh centuries BCE.

The Settlement of Ephraim and Manasseh (Josh 16–17)

When compared with the other tribal descriptions, the allotment of Ephraim (Josh 16) is somewhat schematic and does not include an accompanying town list. However, other texts aid in filling out Ephraim's territory (table 3). Besides towns associated with conquest narratives (e.g., Gezer), almost all of the towns related to Ephraim's settlement were either abandoned in the Late Bronze or were initially founded in the Iron I. These include the important settlement-era sites of Timnah-serah/heres, Gibeah of Pinehas, and Shiloh. Of the important Canaanite centers in the territory of Ephraim, Gezer remained Canaanite (Josh 16:10; Judg 1:29) while Bethel was conquered by the "sons of Ephraim" (Judg 1:22–26).

The situation for Manasseh is even more important for our discussion, as the majority of the sites connected with Manasseh were established or re-established in the Iron I. As the "heir" of Joseph (Gen 41:51), Manasseh received a double allotment of land (Josh 13:29–31; 17:1–18). Like Ephraim above, a clear division can be seen between sites associated with the conquest and sites connected with the settlement. Joshua 17 indicates that Manasseh was allotted some of the most powerful Late Bronze sites in Canaan: those of the Jezreel (e.g., Megiddo, Ibleam, Taanach) and Beth Shan valleys (Josh 17:11–13). However, Manasseh was not able to "drive out the Canaanites" from these regions (Josh 17:16; Judg 1:27–28), but instead cleared out and settled in the forested hill country (Josh 17:18). In general, this description closely matches the archaeological data of the Iron I settlement wave in the central hill country, as well as perhaps the continued influence of the Egyptian New Kingdom in the northern valleys into the twelfth century BC. This correspondence is also observed in identified towns from the book of Judges (e.g., Shamir, Pirathon, Beer), which provide a similar picture of Iron I established towns that remained occupied during the monarchical period.

The Manassehite Clans (Num 26:30–33; Josh 17:2–3) and the Samaria Ostraca

The Samaria Ostraca provide an extrabiblical connection between the Manassehite clans (Num 26:30–33; Josh 17:2–3) and the central highland sites. The Samaria Ostraca are a group of over a hundred (63 are legible) pen-ink inscriptions on potsherds (ostraca) that record the shipment of wine and fine oil from approximately fourteen villages and cities to Samaria during the early eighth century.[58] Except for Mahlah, Milkah, and Tirzah, all of the Manassehite clans (Num 26:30–33; Josh 17:2–3) appear in the Samaria Ostraca. Since these receipts were written in the early eighth century BC, it is obviously not necessary that the identified towns possess Iron I remains. Almost all of the sites can be identified with certainty (see table 3).[59] Of the fourteen towns, excluding

58. See, e.g., Rainey and Notley, *Sacred Bridge*, 221–24.

59. See, e.g., André Lemaire, *Inscriptions Hebraiques: Tome I* (Paris: Cerf, 1977); Arye Bornstein, "The Economy of the Mannassite Territory in Light of the Samaria Ostraca," *Judea and Samaria Research Studies* 1 (1991): 61–121; Aaron Demsky, "The Daughters of Zelophehad: A Historical-Geographical Approach," *TheTorah.Com* (blog), 2019, https://www.thetorah.com/article/the-daughters-of-zelophehad-a-historical-geographical-approach.

Samaria Ostraca, Early 8th Century BC

Shechem, which was continuously occupied and associated with the conquest and settlement, eight of the sites were either founded or refounded in the Iron I. Thus, there is a basic correspondence between the Iron I settlement wave in the central highlands, the Cisjordan Manassehite clans (Num 26:30–33; Josh 17:2–3), and the continuation of that settlement as reflected in the historical geography of the Samaria Ostraca. In what follows, we will demonstrate the correspondence between the specific Manassehite clans and their related towns with placed mentioned in the Samaria Ostraca and their associated ruins.

1. Abiezer (Num 26:30; Josh 17:2)

The Abiezrite clan (Num 26:30; Josh 17:2; 1 Chr 7:18) was probably situated southwest of Shechem in and around Ophrah of the Abiezrites, as indicated by the narratives of Gideon (Judg 6:11, 24, 8:2, 27, 32) and Abimelek (e.g., Judg 9:5), as well as the Samaria Ostraca (nos. 13 and 28).[60] In the early eighth century BC, the Abiezrites also possessed the nearby towns of *T-W-L* (nos. 13, 21) and El-mathan (no. 28). On account of the name and the close proximity to Ophrah of the Abiezrites, *T-W-L* should probably be connected with the Arab village of Tell, despite the current lack of confirmation of Iron Age

60. Shmuel Ahituv, *Echoes from the Past: Hebrew and Cognate Inscriptions from the Biblical Period* (Jerusalem: Carta, 2008), 273, 286. Apparently Khirbet Sur near Khirbet Awfar, which preserves Ophrah. See Chris McKinny and Aharon Tavger, "'Flames from the Bramble': The Geography of the Abimelech Episode in Judges 9 and the Identification of Beth-Millo," *In the Highland's Depth* 7 (2017): 16*; Hanan Eshel, "The Possible Location of Ophra, Town of Gideon," *Cathedra* 22 (1982): 3–8; Dvir Raviv and Nahshon Szanton, "Identification of Ophrah of the Abiezrites," *In the Highland's Depth* 2 (2012): 13–32.

finds.[61] El-mathan should be connected with Immatin, four miles (6 km) west of Ophrah.[62] Iron II remains were surveyed at the site, but it has not been examined since Kallai's work in the 1960s.[63]

While not explicitly connected to the Abiezrite clan in the Samaria Ostraca, Beeraim (no. 1) should probably be related to Beer of Judg 9:21.[64] Burin seems to preserve the ancient name, but the ancient site was probably located at the nearby ruin of Khirbet en-Nabi.[65] Khirbet en-Nabi seems to have been reoccupied in the Iron I after being abandoned during the Late Bronze Age.[66]

2. Helek (Num 26:30; Josh 17:2)

Helek (Num 26:30; Josh 17:2) was another Cisjordanian Manassehite clan. The Helek clan is mentioned in the Samaria Ostraca (nos. 22–24, 27) in connection with the towns of Hazeroth (see also no. 18) and perhaps Baal Meon (no. 27). Hazeroth was probably located at Asirat el-Hatab/Asireh esh-Shamaliyeh, which is located five miles (8 km) southeast of Samaria and just north of Mount Ebal.[67] Surveys at this site revealed remains from the Iron I and II over sixty dunams (fifteen acres).[68] Instead of a separate town in Manasseh, Baal Meon (no. 27, given in the gentilic) may refer to biblical Baal Meon (e.g., Num 32:38) and the Transjordanian origins of Asa son of Ahimelek.[69]

3. Asriel (Num 26:31; Josh 17:2; 1 Chr 7:14)

The Asrielite clan is only mentioned in the above-cited genealogies (Num 26:31; Josh 17:2; 1 Chr 7:14). However, it also appears in the Samaria Ostraca (nos. 42 and 48) with the towns of Asereth and Yashub.[70] Yashub is usually identified with Yasuf, which is located twelve miles (19 km) south of Samaria.[71] Yashub may also appear in the LXX of Josh 17:7 (Ιασσιβ, *Iassib*) in connection with Tappuah (Sheikh Abu Zarad), a town whose king was slain by Joshua (Josh 12:17).[72] Yasuf remains a settled Arab village, but surveys revealed Iron II and later periods at the site.[73] The close proximity

---

61. Rainey and Notley, *Sacred Bridge*, 221. Ofer Sion, "Settlement History in the Central Samaria Region in the Byzantine Period" (PhD diss., Hebrew University, 2001), site 332.

62. Ahituv, *Echoes from the Past*, 287.

63. Zecharia Kallai, "The Land of Benjamin and Ephraim," in *Judaea Samaria and the Golan: Archaeological Survey 1967–1968*, ed. Moshe Kochavi (Jerusalem: Carta, 1972), site 19.

64. McKinny and Tavger, "'Flames from the Bramble,'" 18*.

65. Lemaire, *Inscriptions Hebraiques*, 57; Arye Bornstein, "Administration and Economics of the Land of Manasseh in the Late Kingdom of Israel, in Light of a New Analysis of the Shomron," *Judah and Samaria Research Studies* 1 (1992): 107.

66. Finkelstein, Lederman, and Bunimovitz, *Southern Samaria Survey*, 694–98.

67. Ahituv, *Echoes from the Past*, 279.

68. Zertal, *Manasseh Hill Country Survey*, site 271. Despite Zertal's hesitation, it is somewhat common for *ayin* (ע) and *het* (ח) to interchange in toponyms.

69. Ahituv, *Echoes from the Past*, 286.

70. Ahituv, *Echoes from the Past*, 295–96, 301–2.

71. Rainey and Notley, *Sacred Bridge*, 222; Ahituv, *Echoes from the Past*, 302.

72. Ahituv also suggests that the town appears in connection with Issacharites living in Ephraim (Num 26:23–24 to Judg 10:1, see also "Yob" in Gen 46:13) (Ahituv, *Echoes from the Past*, 302).

73. Finkelstein, Lederman, and Bunimovitz, *Southern Samaria Survey*, 618.

to Tappuah (0.9 mi. [1.5 km] northeast) might indicate that Yashub was the less important of the two sites, as Sheikh Abu Zarad was a significant Late Bronze, Iron I, and Iron II site of twenty dunams (5 acres).[74] Asereth has not been identified with certainty. Since Yashub is the southernmost town in the Samaria Ostraca and Asereth is also related to Asriel, perhaps the nearby site of Khirbet esh-Shejerah (1 mi. [2 km] west, on the southern outskirts of Ariel) is a good candidate for Asereth.[75] Surveys at Khirbet esh-Shejerah revealed remains from the Iron I and II over ten dunams (2.5 acres).[76]

4. Shechem (Num 26:31; Josh 17:2; 1 Chr 7:19)

Shechem is, of course, the same as the major Bronze and Iron Age city of Tell Balatah, which remained a significant settlement during the conquest (Josh 8:30–35; 24:1, 25, 32), settlement (Judg 9), and monarchy (1 Kgs 12:1, 25). The town also appears in the Samaria Ostraca (no. 44).[77]

5. Hepher (Num 26:32–33; 27:1; Josh 12:17; 17:2–3)

The Manassehite clan of Hepher (Num 26:32–33; 27:1; Josh 17:2–3) is significant as Hepher was the father of the sonless Zelophehad (see below). Hepher is most likely identical with the city of "Hepher" whose king Joshua killed (Josh 12:17) and the "land of Hepher" of Solomon's third district (1 Kgs 4:10). Zertal has persuasively argued that Hepher can be associated with the large site of Tell Muhaffar, which is situated on the northern edge of the Dothan Valley.[78] Tell Muhaffar preserves the name of the site and has remains from Chalcolithic through the Early Roman period including occupation from the Late Bronze–Iron II over one hundred twenty dunams (30 acres).[79]

6. Shemida (Num 26:32; Josh 17:2; 1 Chr 7:19)

Shemida was the last of the sons of Manasseh to receive an allotment (Num 26:32; Josh 17:2; 1 Chr 7:19). The clan appears several times in the Samaria Ostraca (nos. 29–32, 37–38, and 63), but only the town of Sepher is mentioned (no. 29, also referenced in no. 16a).[80] Sepher is normally associated with Safarin, four miles (7 km) west of Samaria.[81] This area was not included in Zertal's regional survey of the central highlands, but Dar's survey revealed early Iron II pottery.[82]

---

74. Kallai, "Benjamin and Ephraim," site 36; Finkelstein, Lederman, and Bunimovitz, *Southern Samaria Survey*, 606–10.

75. There is some correspondence between the names.

76. Finkelstein, Lederman, and Bunimovitz, *Southern Samaria Survey*, 475–78.

77. Ahituv, *Echoes from the Past*, 296–97.

78. Adam Zertal, "Hepher," *ABD* 3:138–139; Zertal, "Arubboth," *ABD* 1:465–467.

79. Zertal, *Manasseh Hill Country Survey*, site 23.

80. Ahituv, *Echoes from the Past*, 277, 288–94, 309–10.

81. Rainey and Notley, *Sacred Bridge*, 222; Ahituv, *Echoes from the Past*, 277.

82. A survey of the nearby ruin of Ras Abu Balat also revealed Iron II remains (Ram Gophna and Yuval Porat, "The Land of Ephraim and Manasseh," in *Judaea, Samaria and the Golan: Archaeological Survey 1967–1968*, ed. Moshe Kochavi [Jerusalem: Carta, 1972], site 132). See also Shim'on Dar and Shimon Applebaum, *Landscape and Pattern: An Archaeological Survey of Samaria 800 B.C.E.-636 C.E.* (Oxford: BAR International Series, 1986), 139.

7–11. The Daughters of Zelophehad the son of Hepher: Mahlah, Noah, Hoglah, Milkah, and Tirzah (Num 26:33; 27:1; 36:11; Josh 17:3)

Noah (no. 50) occurs without a specific town. Mahlah (see also 1 Chr 7:18) is often associated with Abel Meholah (Tell Abu Sus) of the central Jordan Valley (e.g., Judg 7:22; 1 Kgs 4:12; 19:16). Hoglah (no. 45, 47) appears in connection with the town of Yasith. Yasith (nos. 9–10, 19, 45, 47) is preserved at Yasid, which was apparently founded in the Iron I, as well as occupied in the Iron II.[83] The location of Milkah is unknown.[84] The name is probably corrupted to Hammoleketh in 1 Chr 7:18. Tirzah is Tell el-Farah (South), the second capital of the northern kingdom of Israel (e.g., 1 Kgs 15:21). Like Hepher above, Tirzah's "king" was purportedly "slain" by Joshua (12:24).

Other Towns in the Samaria Ostraca

Azzah (nos. 2, 17A) is usually connected with Zawata with the nearby site of Khirbet Qumy marking the location of Azzah.[85] Qosoh (no. 5) has been associated with the Arab village of Khirbet Qusin.[86] Geba (no. 8) is preserved at Jaba north of Samaria, surveys at the Arab village indicate that it was abandoned during the Late Bronze, but occupied in the Iron I and II.[87] Siptan (no. 12) is usually connected with Shufeh, an Arab village with Iron I and Iron II remains located six miles (10 km) to the west of Samaria.[88] Gath Paran (no. 14) should probably be associated with Kuryet Jit, but the village has not been surveyed. Ostracon no. 51 includes the gentilic "Yehudite" (compare with Baal Meon), which may reflect the kingdom of Judah or a similarly named village.[89] If it is the latter, this Yehudah may be connected with Khirbet Yahuda, but the site lacks Iron Age remains.[90] In light of the other positively identified sites in relation to their Manassehite clans, we can assume the following: Azzah was associated with either Abiezer or Helek, Qosoh

83. Ahituv, *Echoes from the Past*, 270; Zertal, *Manasseh Hill Country Survey*, site 261.

84. Perhaps there is a connection between Milcah and Khirbet el-Malih southwest of Tell el-Hamma. The region between Mahlah/Abel Meholah and Tirzah (Num 27:1; 36:11; Josh 17:3) has not been connected with a specific clan and there is a basic correspondence between the biblical and Arabic toponym. In connection with this, the large (18 dunams; 4 acres) Late Bronze III (i.e., early twelfth century BC), Iron I and II site at nearby el-Bird is worth mentioning (Zertal, *Manasseh Hill Country Survey*, site 91).

85. Occupied in the Middle Bronze, Late Bronze I, Iron I, Iron II, and Persian period (Zertal, *Manasseh Hill Country Survey*, site 148). Zertal's suggestion to connect Azzah with Anza is unlikely given the difference in the initial consonant (Zertal, *Manasseh Hill Country Survey*, 262; Ahituv, *Echoes from the Past*, 264, 278).

86. Iron II, Persian, and later remains, but not included in more recent surveys (see Gophna and Porat, "Ephraim and Manasseh," site 157; Ahituv, *Echoes from the Past*, 267).

87. Ahituv, *Echoes from the Past*, 268; Zertal, *Manasseh Hill Country Survey*, site 125.

88. Ahituv, *Echoes from the Past*, 272–73; Dar and Applebaum, *Landscape and Pattern*, 213–14.

89. Ahituv, *Echoes from the Past*, 275–76, 303–4.

90. The locations of the "Vineyard/Kerem of the Tell" (nos. 53–54) and "Vineyard of Yəḥāwʿēlî" (no. 55) are unknown but might represent specific vineyards/orchards at or around Samaria itself (see discussion in Ahituv, *Echoes from the Past*, 304–8; Matthew J. Suriano, "Wine Shipments to Samaria from Royal Vineyards," *TA* 43.1 [2016]: 99–110).

with Abiezer, Geba with either Noah or Hoglah, and Siptan with Shemida.

Summary

The vast increase of Iron I rural settlements in the highlands of Ephraim and Manasseh demonstrates that a major change occurred in the late thirteenth and twelfth centuries BC, that can be generally associated with the arrival of the Israelites in this same time period. This detail has long been noted by proponents of the thirteenth century BC view, as well as more broadly within discussions about the emergence of ancient Israel in Canaan. This remains a vital piece of evidence for establishing the date of the exodus, conquest, and settlement. However, the correspondence between the Manassehite clans and towns in the biblical texts related to Israel's settlement (e.g., Josh 17), the Manassehite clans and towns in the Samaria Ostraca, and the archaeology of the Iron I–II provides specific historical geographical evidence that strongly favors the thirteenth century position (table 3). Simply put, the settlement pattern in Ephraim and Manasseh closely matches the textual information for the Samaria Ostraca and the Bible, and is radically different than the preceding Late Bronze I–IIA settlement pattern.

CONCLUSION

In this chapter, we discussed several aspects connected with the debate about the date of the Israelite exodus, conquest, and settlement. Taking the chronological data from Judg 11:26 and 1 Kgs 6:1 at face value seems to support an early date in the fifteenth century BC. However, we have demonstrated the viability of several interpretations that take both these texts seriously while also permitting for a late date in the thirteenth century BC. In our view, there are several layers of correspondence between the Nineteenth Dynasty and the exodus and conquest that argue strongly in favor of the thirteenth century view. Instead of addressing these much-discussed topics, we focused our attention on the biblical and archaeological information connected with the Philistines and the highland settlements of Ephraim and Manasseh. The arrival of the Philistines as early as the late thirteenth century BC and the emergence of the Israelite highland settlements in the same period strongly favors a late date. This argument is based both on the biblical text and archaeology. Joshua 12:2–3 and other texts indicate that the Philistines were present in the "land that remains." Joshua 17 demonstrates that the Israelites did not settle in the Jezreel and Beth Shan valleys, where Canaanite (and perhaps Egyptian) forces remained strong, but instead established new settlements in the forested hill country. Significantly, this seems to be the same archaeological picture in Philistia and Ephraim/Manasseh during the Late Bronze/Iron I transition. Besides a general archaeological correspondence, Joshua, Judges, and the Samaria Ostraca provide numerous place names, most of which have been identified with a high degree of certainty. Most of these sites share the same chronological sequence as the surveyed highland sites in that they were either newly established or re-established in the Iron I. In light of this evidence, it seems that this archaeological data supports the biblical text. In our view, proponents of the early date examine only mathematical and chronological texts (e.g., 1 Kgs 6:1), but do not consider texts that include direct evidence of material culture (e.g., Josh 12:2–3).

TABLE 3: PLACE NAMES IN EPHRAIM AND MANASSEH FROM THE BIBLICAL TEXT AND THE SAMARIA OSTRACA

Site	Conquest	Settlement	Samaria Ostraca/ 1–2 Kgs
Jericho	Josh 5–6; 12:9	Josh 16:1; 18:21	e.g., 1 Kgs 16:34
Bethel/Luz	Josh 7:2; 8:9, 12, 17; 12:16	Josh 16:1; 18:13, 22; see also Judg 1:22–26; 2:1, 5; 20:18, 26, 31; 21:2, 19	e.g., 1 Kgs 12:32–33
Ai/Ayyah	Josh 7–8; 12:9	Josh 18:23; see also 1 Chr 7:28	-
Altar on Mt. Ebal	Deut 27:1–8; Josh 8:30–35	-	-
Ataroth- of the Archites	-	Josh 16:2	-
L. Beth Horon	Josh 10:10–11	Josh 16:3; 18:13–14; 21:22	1 Kgs 9:15–17
U. Beth Horon	Josh 10:10–11	Josh 16:5; 18:13–14; 21:22	1 Kgs 9:15–17
Gezer	Josh 10:33; 12:12	Josh 16:3, 10; 21:21; Judg 1:29 (not settled)	1 Kgs 9:15–17
Ataroth Addar	-	Josh 16:5	-
Taanath Shiloh	-	Josh 16:6	-
Janoah	-	Josh 16:6–7	-
Ataroth	-	Josh 16:7	-
Naarah	-	Josh 16:7; see also 1 Chr 7:28	-
Hepher	Josh 12:17	Num 26:32–33; 27:1; Josh 17:2–3	1 Kgs 4:10
Tappuah	Josh 12:17	Josh 16:8; 17:8	compare with Yashub (no. 48)
Tirzah	Josh 12:24	Josh 17:3	1 Kgs 14:17; 15:21, 33; 16:6–23; 2 Kgs 15:14, 16
Beth Shan	-	Josh 17:11–12, 16; Judg 1:27 (not settled)	1 Kgs 4:12
Ibleam	-	Josh 17:11; Judg 1:27 (not settled); Josh 21:25	2 Kgs 9:27; 15:10
Dor	Josh 12:23	Josh 17:11–12; Judg 1:27 (not settled)	1 Kgs 4:11

1. Middle Bronze remains at Khirbet el-Maqatir.
2. Iron II remains at Deir Dibwan and Khirbet Haiyan.

Tribe/Clan	Identification (*excavated)	MB	LB	Iron I	Iron II
Ephraim/ Benjamin	Tell es-Sultan*	X	X	X	X
Ephraim	Beitin*	X	X	X	X
Ephraim	Et-Tell?*	X1	X?	X	X2
Manasseh	El-Burnat?	-	X (LBIIB)	X	-
Ephraim	Ain Arik/ Khirbet el-Hafi?	-	-	X	X
Ephraim	Beit Ur et-Tahta	X	X	X	X
Ephraim	Beit Ur el-Foqa	X	X	X	X
Ephraim	Tell Jazar*	X	X	X	X
Ephraim/ Benjamin	Khirbet Raddana?*	-	-	X	-
Ephraim	Khirbet Tana el-Foqa	-	-	X	X
Ephraim	Khirbet Yanun	-	-	X	X
Ephraim	Khirbet el-Auja el-Foqa?*	-	-	X	X
Ephraim	near Tell Jisr? (Byzantine Naarah)	-	-	-	-
Manasseh	Tell Muhaffar	X	X (LBIIB)	X	X
Ephraim/ Manasseh	Sheikh Abu Zarad	X	X	X	X
Manasseh	Tell el-Farah (South)*	X	X	X?	X
Manasseh (in Issachar)	Tell el-Husn*	X	X	X	X
Manasseh	Khirbet Belameh*	X	X	X	X
Manasseh (in Asher?)	Khirbet el-Burj*	X	X	X	X

Site	Conquest	Settlement	Samaria Ostraca/ 1–2 Kgs
En Dor	-	Josh 17:11–12 (not settled)	-
Taanach	Josh 12:21	Josh 17:11–12; Judg 1:27 (not settled); Josh 21:25	1 Kgs 4:12
Megiddo	Josh 12:21	Josh 17:11–12; Judg 1:27 (not settled)	1 Kgs 4:12; 9:15; 2 Kgs 9:27; 23:29–30
Shiloh	-	Josh 18:1, 8–10; 19:51; 21:2; 22:9, 12; Judg 18:31; 21:12, 19, 21	1 Kgs 2:27; 14:2, 4
Timnah Serah/Heres	-	Josh 19:50; 24:30; Judg 2:9	
Gibeah of Phinehas	-	Josh 24:33	-
Ophrah of the Abiezrites	-	Judg 6:11, 24, 8:2, 27, 32 (Gideon)	-
Beth Millo	-	Judg 9:6, 20 (Abimelech)	-
Arumah	-	Judg 9:41 (Abimelech)	-
Shamir	-	Judg 10:1–2 (Tola)	-
Pirathon	-	Judg 12:15 (Abdon)	-
Beer/ Beeraim	-	Judg 9:22 (Gideon/Jotham)	No. 1
Azzah	-	-	Nos. 2, 17A
Qōṣôh	-	-	No. 5
Geba‘	-	Num 26:33; 27:1; 36:11; Josh 17:3	No. 8
Yaṣith	-	Num 26:33; 27:1; 36:11; Josh 17:3	Nos. 9–10, 19, 45, 47
Śiptān	-	Num 26:32; Josh 17:2; 1 Chr 7:19	No. 12
T-W-L	-	-	Nos. 13, 21
Gath-paran	-	-	No. 14
Sepher	-	Num 26:32; Josh 17:2; 1 Chr 7:19	Nos. 16A, 29
Hazeroth	-	-	Nos. 18, 22–24, 27
El-mathan	-	-	No. 28
Asereth	-	-	No. 42
Shechem	Josh 8:30–35; 24:1, 25, 32	Josh 21:21; Judg 9; see also 1 Chr 7:28	e.g., 1 Kgs 12:1, 25; No. 44
Yashub	-	Josh 17:7 (LXX); see also Gen 46:3; Num 26:23–24	No. 48
-	-	Num 27:1; 36:11; Josh 17:3	-

Tribe/Clan	Identification (*excavated)	MB	LB	Iron I	Iron II
Manasseh (in Issachar)	Indur/Khirbet Safsafeh	X	X	X	X
Manasseh (in Issachar)	Tell Tiinnik*	X	X	X	X
Manasseh (in Issachar)	Tell el-Mutesellim*	X	X	X	X
Ephraim	Khirbet Seilun*	X	X (LBI)	X	X
Ephraim	Khirbet Tibne	X	-	X	X
Ephraim	Jibiya/Kaubar	-	-	X	X
Manasseh/ Abiezer	Khirbet Awfar/ Khirbet Sur	X	X	X	X
Manasseh	Ain Beit Ilma/ Tell Sufan*	-	X (LBII)	X	X
Ephraim	Khirbet el-Ormah	X	X	X	X
Ephraim	Khirbet Sammir?	-	-	X	X
Ephraim	Khirbet Tarafein?	-	-	X	X
Manasseh/ Abiezer	Khirbet en-Nabi	X	-	X	X
Manasseh/ Abiezer? Helek?	Zawata/Khirbet Qumy	X	X (LBI)	X	X
Manasseh/ Abiezer?	Khirbet Qusin	-	-	-	X
Manasseh/ Noah? Hoglah?	Jaba	X	-	X	X
Manasseh/ Hoglah	Yasid	-	-	X	X
Manasseh/ Shemida?	Shufeh	-	-	X	X
Manasseh/ Abiezer	Tell	?	?	?	?
Manasseh/ Abiezer?	Kuryet Jit	?	?	?	?
Manasseh/ Shemida	Safarin	-	-	-	X
Manasseh/ Helek	Asirat el-Hatab	-	-	X	X
Manasseh/ Abiezer	Immatin	-	-	-	X
Manasseh/ Asriel	Khirbet esh-Shejerah?	-	-	X	X
Manasseh/ Shechem	Tell Balata*	X	X	X	X
Manasseh/ Asriel (Issachar?)	Yāsûf	-	-	-	X
Manasseh/ Milcah	Khirbet el-Malih?/ el-Bird?	X	X (LBIII)	X	X

BIBLIOGRAPHY

Ahituv, Shmuel. *Echoes from the Past: Hebrew and Cognate Inscriptions from the Biblical Period*. Jerusalem: Carta, 2008.

Asscher, Yotam, Dan Cabanes, Louise A. Hitchcock, Aren M. Maeir, Steve Weiner, and Elisabetta Boaretto. "Radiocarbon Dating Shows an Early Appearance of Philistine Material Culture in Tell Es-Safi/Gath, Philistia." *Radiocarbon* 57.5 (2015): 825–50.

Ben-Yosef, Erez. "The Architectural Bias in Current Biblical Archaeology." *VT* 69.3 (2019): 361–87.

Berman, Joshua. "Was There an Exodus?" *Mosaic Magazine*, 2015. https://mosaicmagazine.com/essay/2015/03/was-there-an-exodus/.

Bietak, Manfred. "An Iron Age Four-Room House in Ramesside Egypt." *Eretz-Israel* 23 (1992): 10*–12*.

Bietak, Manfred, and Gary A. Rendsburg. "Egypt and the Exodus." In *Ancient Israel, From Abraham to the Roman Destruction of the Temple*. Edited by Hershel Shanks and John Merrill. Rev. and exp. ed. Washington: Biblical Archaeology Society, 2021.

Block, Daniel I. *The Book of Ezekiel, Chapters 1–24*. NICOT. Grand Rapids: Eerdmans, 1997.

Boaretto, Elisabetta, Yotam Asscher, Louise A. Hitchcock, Gunnar Lehmann, Aren M. Maeir, and Steve Weiner. "The Chronology of the Late Bronze (LB)–Iron Age (IA) Transition in the Southern Levant: A Response to Finkelstein's Critique." *Radiocarbon* 61.1 (2019): 1–11.

Bornstein, Arye. "Administration and Economics of the Land of Manasseh in the Late Kingdom of Israel, in Light of a New Analysis of the Shomron." *Judea and Samaria Research Studies* 1 (1992): 61–121.

———. "The Economy of the Mannassite Territory in Light of the Samaria Ostraca." *Judea and Samaria Research Studies* 1 (1991): 61–121.

Bruce, Larry D. "The Merenptah Stele and the Biblical Origins of Israel." *JETS* 62.3 (2019): 246–66.

Bunimovitz, Shlomo, and Avraham Faust. "Building Identity: The Four-Room House and the Israelite Mind." Pages 63–74 in *Symbiosis, Symbolism, and the Power of the Past. Canaan, Ancient Israel, and Their Neighbors from the Late Bronze Age through Roman Palaestina*. Edited by William G. Dever and Seymour Gitin. Winona Lake, IN: Eisenbrauns, 2003.

Byers, Gary A., Scott Stripling, and Bryant G. Wood. "Excavations at Khirbet El-Maqatir: The 2009–2011 Seasons." *Judea and Samaria Research Studies* 25.2 (2016): 69*–109*.

Cline, Eric H. *1177 B.C.: The Year Civilization Collapsed*. Princeton: Princeton University Press, 2015.

Coyle, S. Cameron, and Steven M. Ortiz. "Judges 10:11: A Memory of Merneptah's Campaign in Transjordan." Pages 298–308 in *"An Excellent Fortress for His Armies, A Refuge for The People": Egyptological, Archaeological, and Biblical Studies in Honor of James K. Hoffmeier*. Edited by Richard E. Averbeck and K. Lawson Younger Jr. Winona Lake, IN: Eisenbrauns, 2020.

Currid, John D., and David W. Chapman, eds. *ESV Archaeology Study Bible*. Grand Rapids: Crossway, 2018.

Dar, Shim'on, and Shimon Applebaum. *Landscape and Pattern: An Archaeological Survey of Samaria 800 B.C.E.–636 C.E.* Oxford: BAR International Series, 1986.

Demsky, Aaron. "The Daughters of Zelophehad: A Historical-Geographical Approach." *TheTorah.com (blog)*, 2019. https://www.thetorah.com/article/the-daughters-of-zelophehad-a-historical-geographical-approach.

Dever, William G. *Beyond the Texts: An Archaeological Portrait of Ancient Israel and Judah*. Atlanta: Society of Biblical Literature, 2017.

Dyer, Charles H. "The Date of the Exodus Reexamined." *Bibliotheca Sacra* 140 (1983): 224–43.

Eshel, Hanan. "The Possible Location of Ophra, Town of Gideon." *Cathedra* 22 (1982): 3–8.

Faust, Avraham. "Pigs in Space (and Time): Pork Consumption and Identity Negotiations in the Late Bronze and Iron Ages of Ancient Israel." *NEA* 81.4 (2018): 276–99.

Faust, Avraham, and Justin Lev-Tov. "The Constitution of Philistine Identity: Ethnic Dynamics in Twelfth to Tenth Century Philistia." *Oxford Journal of Archaeology* 30.1 (2011): 13–31.

———. "Philistia and the Philistines in the Iron Age I: Interaction, Ethnic Dynamics and Boundary Maintenance." *Hiphil Novum* 1.1 (2014): 1–24.

Feldman, Ariel. *The Dead Sea Scrolls Rewriting Samuel and Kings: Texts and Commentary*. Berlin: de Gruyter, 2015.

Feldman, Michal, Daniel M. Master, Raffaela A. Bianco, Marta Burri, Philipp W. Stockhammer, Alissa Mittnik, Adam J. Aja, Choongwon Jeong, and Johannes Krause. "Ancient DNA Sheds Light on the Genetic Origins of Early Iron Age Philistines." *Science Advances* 5.7 (2019): eaax0061. https://doi.org/10.1126/sciadv.aax0061.

Finkelstein, Israel. *The Archaeology of the Israelite Settlement*. Jerusalem: Israel Exploration Society, 1988.

———. *The Forgotten Kingdom: The Archaeology and History of Northern Israel*. Atlanta: Society of Biblical Literature, 2013.

———. "To Date or Not to Date: Radiocarbon and the Arrival of the Philistines." *Ägypten Und Levante/Egypt and the Levant* 26 (2016): 275–84.

Finkelstein, Israel, Zvi Lederman, and Shlomo Bunimovitz, eds. *Highland of Many Cultures: The Southern Samaria Survey*. 2 vols. Tel Aviv: Tel Aviv University, 1997.

Gadot, Yuval. "The Iron I Settlement Wave in the Samaria Highlands and Its Connection with the Urban Centers." *NEA* 82.1 (2019): 32–41.

Galil, Gershon. "The Chronological Framework of the Deuteronomistic History." *Biblica* 85.3 (2004): 413–21.

———. *The Chronology of the Kings of Israel and Judah*. Leiden: Brill, 1996.

Geraty, Lawrence T. "Exodus Dates and Theories." Pages 55–64 in *Israel's Exodus in Transdisciplinary Perspective: Text, Archaeology, Culture, and Geoscience*. Edited by Thomas E. Levy, Thomas Schneider, and William H. C. Propp. New York: Springer, 2015.

Gophna, Ram, and Yuval Porat. "The Land of Ephraim and Manasseh." Pages 196–241 in *Judaea, Samaria and the Golan: Archaeological Survey 1967–1968*. Edited by Moshe Kochavi. Jerusalem: Carta, 1972.

Greenberg, Moshe. *Ezekiel 1–20*. New Haven: Yale University Press, 1983.

Hasel, Michael G. "Israel in the Merenptah Stela." *BASOR* 296 (1994): 45–61.

Hawkins, Ralph K. "The Date of the Exodus-Conquest Is Still an Open

Question: A Response to Rodger Young and Bryant Wood." *JETS* 51.2 (2008): 246–66.

———. *The Iron Age I: Structure on Mt. Ebal*. Winona Lake, IN: Eisenbrauns, 2012.

———. "Propositions for Evangelical Acceptance of A Late-Date Exodus-Conquest: Biblical Data and the Royal Scarabs from Mt. Ebal." *JETS* 50.1 (2007): 31–46.

Hesse, Brian. "Can Pig Remains Be Used for Ethnic Diagnosis in the Ancient Near East?" Pages 238–70 in *The Archaeology of Israel: Constructing the Past, Interpreting the Present*. Edited by Neil A. Silberman and David B. Small. Sheffield: A&C Black, 1997.

Hoffmeier, James K. *Ancient Israel in Sinai: The Evidence for the Authenticity of the Wilderness Tradition*. Oxford: Oxford University Press, 2005.

———. *Israel in Egypt: The Evidence for the Authenticity of the Exodus Tradition*. Oxford: Oxford University Press, 1996.

———. "What Is the Biblical Date for the Exodus? A Response to Bryant Wood." *JETS* 50.2 (2007): 225–47.

Janzen, Mark D., ed. *Five Views on the Exodus: Historicity, Chronology, and Theological Implications*. Grand Rapids: Zondervan Academic, 2021.

Kallai, Zecharia. "The Land of Benjamin and Ephraim." Page 153–93 in *Judaea Samaria and the Golan: Archaeological Survey 1967–1968*. Edited by Moshe Kochavi. Jerusalem: Carta, 1972.

Killebrew, Ann E. *Biblical Peoples and Ethnicity: An Archaeological Study of Egyptians, Canaanites, Philistines, and Early Israel, 1300–1100 B.C.E.* Atlanta: Society of Biblical Literature, 2005.

Kitchen, Kenneth A. "History of Egypt (Chronology)." *ABD* 2:321–31.

———. *On the Reliability of the Old Testament*. Grand Rapids: Eerdmans, 2003.

Lemaire, André. *Inscriptions Hebraiques: Tome I*. Paris: Cerf, 1977.

Levy, Thomas E., Thomas Schneider, and William H. C. Propp, eds. *Israel's Exodus in Transdisciplinary Perspective: Text, Archaeology, Culture, and Geoscience*. New York: Springer, 2015.

Longman, Tremper, III, and Raymond B. Dillard. *An Introduction to the Old Testament*. 2nd ed. Grand Rapids: Zondervan, 2006.

Maeir, Aren M. "The Rephaim in Iron Age Philistia: Evidence of a Multi-Generational Family." Pages 289–97 in *Vom Leben Umfangen': Ägypten, Das Alte Testament Und Das Gespräch Der Religionen. Gedenkschrift Für Manfred Görg*. Edited by Stefan J. Wimmer and G. Gafus. Münster: Ugarit-Verlag, 2014.

Maeir, Aren M., Louise A. Hitchcock, and Liora K. Horwitz. "On the Constitution and Transformation of Philistine Identity." *Oxford Journal of Archaeology* 32.1 (2013): 1–38.

McKinny, Chris. "The Archaeology and Historical Geography of the Slain Kings of Joshua 12." In vol. 1 of *Lexham Geographic Commentary on the Historical Books*. Edited by Barry J. Beitzel. Bellingham, WA: Lexham Press, 2025.

———. "'March on My Soul with Might!'—The Geographical Setting of Judges 4–5." In vol. 1 of *Lexham Geographic Commentary on the Historical Books*. Edited by Barry J. Beitzel. Bellingham, WA: Lexham Press, 2025.

McKinny, Chris, and Aharon Tavger. "'Flames from the Bramble': The

Geography of the Abimelech Episode in Judges 9 and the Identification of Beth-Millo." *In the Highland's Depth* 7 (2017): 11*–34*.

Meiri, Meirav, Dorothée Huchon, Guy Bar-Oz, Elisabetta Boaretto, Liora Kolska Horwitz, Aren M. Maeir, Lidar Sapir-Hen, Greger Larson, Steve Weiner, and Israel Finkelstein. "Ancient DNA and Population Turnover in Southern Levantine Pigs-Signature of the Sea Peoples Migration?" *Nature* 3 (2013). http://www.nature.com/srep/2013/131028/srep03035/full/srep03035.html.

Merrill, Eugene H. *Kingdom of Priests: A History of Old Testament Israel*. Grand Rapids: Baker Academic, 2008.

Millard, Alan R., Gary A. Rendsburg, and James K. Hoffmeier, eds. *"Did I Not Bring Israel Out of Egypt?": Biblical, Archaeological, and Egyptological Perspectives on the Exodus Narratives*. Winona Lake, IN: Eisenbrauns, 2016.

Rainey, Anson F., and Steven Notley. *The Sacred Bridge: Carta's Atlas of the Biblical World*. Jerusalem: Carta, 2006.

Raviv, Dvir, and Nahshon Szanton. "Identification of Ophrah of the Abiezrites." *In the Highland's Depth* 2 (2012): 13–32.

Redford, Donald B. *Egypt, Canaan, and Israel in Ancient Times*. Princeton: Princeton University Press, 1992.

Rendsburg, Gary A. "The Date of the Exodus and the Conquest/Settlement: The Case for the 1100S." *VT* 42.4 (1992): 510–27.

Rohl, David M. *Pharaohs and Kings: A Biblical Quest*. New York: Crown Publishers, 1995.

Russell, Stephen C. *Images of Egypt in Early Biblical Literature: Cisjordan-Israelite, Transjordan-Israelite, and Judahite Portrayals*. Berlin: de Gruyter, 2009.

Sapir-Hen, Lidar. "Food, Pork Consumption, and Identity in Ancient Israel." *NEA* 82.1 (2019): 52–59.

Sapir-Hen, Lidar, Guy Bar-Oz, Yuval Gadot, and Israel Finkelstein. "Pig Husbandry in Iron Age Israel and Judah: New Insights Regarding the Origin of the Taboo." *ZDPV* 129.1 (2013): 1–20.

Schneider, Thomas. "Contributions to the Chronology of the New Kingdom and the Third Intermediate Period." *Ägypten Und Levante/Egypt and the Levant* 20 (2010): 373–403.

Sergi, Omer. "The Formation of Israelite Identity in the Central Canaanite Highlands in the Iron Age I–IIA." *NEA* 82.1 (2019): 42–51.

Sergi, Omer, and Yuval Gadot. "The Rise of Ancient Israel in the Iron I–IIA: The Need for a Closer Look." *NEA* 82.1 (2019): 5–7.

Sion, Ofer. "Settlement History in the Central Samaria Region in the Byzantine Period." PhD diss., Jerusalem: Hebrew University, 2001.

Suriano, Matthew J. "Wine Shipments to Samaria from Royal Vineyards." *TA* 43.1 (2016): 99–110.

Thiele, Edwin R. *The Mysterious Numbers of the Hebrew Kings*. 3rd ed. Grand Rapids: Kregel Academic, 1994.

Uziel, Joe. "The Development Process of Philistine Material Culture: Assimilation, Acculturation and Everything in Between." *Levant* 39.1 (2007): 165–73.

Waltke, Bruce K. "The Date of the Conquest." *WTJ* 52.2 (1990): 181–200.

Wood, Bryant G. "The Biblical Date for the Exodus is 1446 BC: A Response to James Hoffmeier." *JETS* 50.2 (2007): 249–58.

———. "David Rohl's Revised Egyptian Chronology: A View from Palestine." *Bible and Spade (Second Run)* 14.3 (2001): n.p.

———. "The Rise and Fall of the 13th-Century Exodus-Conquest Theory." *JETS* 48.3 (2005): 475–89.

Young, Rodger C., and Bryant G. Wood. "A Critical Analysis of the Evidence from Ralph Hawkins for a Late-Date Exodus-Conquest." *JETS* 51.2 (2008): 225–43.

Younger, K. Lawson, Jr. *Judges, Ruth*. NIVAC. Grand Rapids: Zondervan, 2011.

Zertal, Adam. "Arubboth." *ABD* 1:465–67.

———. "Hepher." *ABD* 3:138–39.

———. *The Manasseh Hill Country Survey, Volume 1: The Shechem Syncline*. Har/Map ed. Leiden: Brill, 2004.

———. *The Manasseh Hill Country Survey, Volume 2: The Eastern Valleys and the Fringes of the Desert*. Leiden: Brill, 2007.

Zertal, Adam, and Shay Bar. *The Manasseh Hill Country Survey, Volume 4: From Nahal Bezeq to the Sartaba*. Leiden: Brill, 2017.

———. *The Manasseh Hill Country Survey, Volume 5: The Middle Jordan Valley, from Wadi Fasael to Wadi 'Aujah*. Leiden: Brill, 2019.

Zertal, Adam, and Nivi Mirkam. *The Manasseh Hill Country Survey, Volume 3: From Nahal 'Iron to Nahal Shechem*. Edited by Shay Bar. Leiden: Brill, 2016.

CHAPTER 12

APPORTIONMENT OF THE PROMISED LAND TO THE TRANSJORDANIAN TRIBES OF REUBEN, GAD, AND EAST MANASSEH

Josh 13:8–13; 22:1–34; see also Num 21:10–35; 32:1–42; 34:1–12

Aubrey Taylor McClain

KEY POINTS

- In the Hebrew Bible, Israel's territory east of the Jordan River (Transjordan) is sometimes represented as equal in status to the land west of the Jordan (Cisjordan) and accepted as part of Israel's promised land, and sometimes it is stigmatized.
- The physical geography of the region permits both interpretations: the regions east and west of the Jordan are both connected and divided, similar and different.
- This physical ambiguity, in conjunction with people's experiences in the region and their worldview, had the power to evoke a variety of conceptual associations with these spaces.
- Joshua 22 illustrates this variety of conceptual associations. The narrative acknowledges legitimate concerns while creatively utilizing alternative interpretations of the space to address the question of the Transjordan's inclusion within Israelite territory.

INTRODUCTION

The territory east of the Jordan River receives ambiguous treatment in the Hebrew Bible. In some texts, it appears to be fully accepted as Israelite territory (Josh 13:8–13), and in other texts, it seems excluded and even stigmatized.[1] This inconsistency has led scholars to suggest that Israelite views of the region changed over time, perhaps accepting the region as part of the "promised land" early in Israelite history and only later coming to exclude it out of concern for ritual purity during the postexilic era.[2] However, some texts defy this categorization, suggesting that a variety of perspectives may have coexisted throughout Israelite history.[3] This indicates that Israel's ideas about its eastern territory were more complex than a simple inclusion/exclusion evaluation. Rather, it seems likely that a range of associations and evaluations developed, influenced by worldview, experiences living in the region, and the physical characteristics of the land. This variety of meanings was then available to the biblical authors, who creatively used space to communicate on a conceptual level and to shape the real world around them.[4]

Joshua 22 attracts perhaps the most attention for its seemingly harsh evaluation of Israel's eastern territory. However,

---

1. The ideas in this essay are more fully expressed in Aubrey Taylor McClain, "The Transjordan in Biblical Literature: A Critical Spatial Approach" (PhD diss., Bar-Ilan University, 2021).

2. Textual elements that are purportedly critical of the Transjordan settlement within Num 32 and Josh 22 are assigned by most scholars to the P source and dated to the postexilic era, presumably overlying an older, traditional core that did not question the territory's legitimacy. See Lloyd R. Bailey, *Leviticus–Numbers*, Smyth & Helwys Bible Commentary (Macon, GA: Smyth & Helwys, 2005), 587–89, 91; Baruch A. Levine, *Numbers 21–36*, AB (New York: Doubleday, 2000), 478, 99–500, 507; Robert G. Boling, *Joshua*, AB (Garden City, NY: Doubleday, 1984), 517.

3. Texts such as Pss 135; 136; Jer 50:19; Mic 7:14; Neh 9:22 evidence a positive perspective on the Transjordan and can also be dated to the close of the monarchy or postexile. Further, there are texts dating to the early monarchy that already equate separation from YHWH and uncleanness with lands outside of Israel (see Hos 9:3–4; Amos 7:17). Yehezkel Kaufmann, *The Biblical Account of the Conquest of Canaan*, trans. Merton Dagut (Jerusalem: Magnes Press, 1985), 126–30; John S. Kloppenborg, "Joshua 22: The Priestly Editing of an Ancient Tradition," *Biblica* 62.3 (1981): 347–71. Some also question such a definitive assignment of P to the postexilic era. See Jacob Milgrom, "The Case for the Pre-Exilic and Exilic Provenance of the Books of Exodus, Leviticus and Numbers," in *Reading the Law: Studies in Honour of Gordon J. Wenham*, ed. J. Gordon McConville and Karl Möller (New York: T&T Clark, 2007), 48–56; Milgrom, "The Antiquity of the Priestly Source: A Reply to Joseph Blenkinsopp," *ZAW* 111 (1999): 10–22; Avi Hurvitz, "Dating the Priestly Source in Light of the Historical Study of Biblical Hebrew a Century after Wellhausen," *ZAW* 100.s1 (1988): 88–100.

4. This is the basis for a critical spatial approach to textual interpretation. It assumes that people interact not only with the physical space, but with their ideas about that space, and that they often see reality through a conceptual overlay. For a fuller discussion, see Aubrey Taylor McClain, "A Literary Exploration of the Promised Land Boundaries," in *Lexham Geographic Commentary on the Pentateuch*, ed. Barry J. Beitzel (Bellingham, WA: Lexham Press, 2023), 221–33; Jon L. Berquist, "Introduction: Critical Spatiality and the Uses of Theory," in *Constructions of Space I: Theory, Geography, and Narrative*, ed. Jon L. Berquist and Claudia V. Camp (New York: T&T Clark, 2007), 1–12; Thomas B. Dozeman, "Biblical Geography and Critical Spatial Studies," in *Constructions of Space I: Theory, Geography, and Narrative*, ed. Jon L. Berquist and Claudia V. Camp (New York: T&T Clark, 2007), 87–108.

Aerial View of the Jordan River and Surrounding Hills near Nahal Jabbok

a spatially sensitive reading of this story reveals a more nuanced perspective. The unity and division of the land are dramatized in the story of two groups of settlers: those settling east of the Jordan River and those settling west of it. Ultimately a commentary on the spaces in question, the story narrates concerns for unity and division amongst the tribes that stem from the landscape itself. Shaping the perceptions and choices of the people involved, the physical geography is a third character in the drama whose influence is felt and, at a few key moments, directly referenced. By attending to the language and choices of the characters, as well as the physical features of the land and elements of ancient cosmology, we can gain insight into the perceptions of the Transjordan and the active role Israel played in claiming it as part of the promised land.

PHYSICAL GEOGRAPHY

Standing upon the banks of the Jordan River and looking up to the east and then to the west, one might be forgiven for seeing two separate lands. The formidable Rift Valley, through which the Jordan flows, forms the boundary between two geographical regions known as the Cisjordan (west) and the Transjordan (east). The valley itself can be quite wide, especially in the south where it approaches ten miles (16 km) across, with hills towering dramatically on either side.[5] In some places rising over four thousand feet (1,219 m) from the valley floor, these hills present an inhospitable climb to the heartland on either side. The author of Num 34:1–12 seems aware of this physical reality, drawing the border of Canaan along the Jordan River. The modern nations of Israel and Jordan fix their borders similarly.

5. Denis Baly, *The Geography of the Bible* (New York: Harper & Row, 1974), 199.

Cisjordan and Transjordan

The Transjordan itself is a narrow strip of inhabitable land running from the foot of Mt. Hermon to the Red Sea and bounded by the Arabian desert on the east. In the south, the region was historically occupied by the Edomites and Moabites, with the Ammonites maintaining a position east of the Medeba plateau. This plateau, lying north of the Arnon River, begins the territory associated with Israelite holdings in the Transjordan. Further north, one finds the hills of Gilead, which lie both north and south of the Jabbok River, and the Bashan, the northernmost area of the region, completes the picture, lying east of the Sea of Galilee and extending to the foot of Mt. Hermon.[6]

Many biblical references to the Transjordan support the assumption that the lands east and west of the Jordan are indeed separate. Canaan is frequently identified as Israel's intended territory (Gen 17:8; Exod 6:4), defined as lying west of the Jordan (Num 13:17–24; 34:1–12), and the book of Deuteronomy speaks of Israel's Jordan River crossing as the definitive moment in which they would realize the promises made to the patriarchs (Deut 4:21–22; 27:2). These characterizations develop the perception that there is a world of difference between the east and west. However, there are other descriptions of Israelite territory that identify the land intended for Israelite dominion as stretching from the "river of Egypt" to the Euphrates, which is vague and broad enough to suggest a unified land encompassing both sides of the Jordan River (e.g., Gen 15:18; Exod 23:31; Deut 11:24). The

6. For further discussion of these regional divisions, see *MAB*, 35–39; Baly, *Geography of the Bible*, 210–40.

conquest account of the Transjordan in Num 21:10–35 suggests that the region is a valid acquisition. During the reigns of David and Solomon, Israel is described as subjugating its eastern neighbors in terms that communicate a full acceptance of eastward expansion (2 Sam 12:26–31; 1 Kgs 4:21), and those texts which record the extent of the northern kingdom of Israel suggest that the territories on the east side of the Jordan River were accepted as a fully legitimate part of Israelite territory (1 Kgs 4:7–19; 12:25; 22:1–4; 2 Kgs 3:4–19; 10:32–33). Regardless of what intent lies behind these accounts, the way the authors speak of the Transjordan suggests that physically and historically, this valley need not be interpreted as a divisive feature and that the relationship between east and west is perhaps more nuanced than one might initially suppose.

Based on this variety of representations, it is reasonable to suggest that something about the physical space itself allows for diverse interpretations. Indeed, though there are features that communicate division, there are also significant structural reasons for seeing the Cisjordan and the Transjordan as integrated parts of a larger whole. First, the formation of the eastern seaboard of the Mediterranean predates the formation of the Rift Valley. As a result, the Cisjordan and the Transjordan share the same geological and topographical characteristics.[7] Their climate is also shared, resulting in the similar ecology and subsistence strategies. Furthermore, they lie in the same position between continents and empires and share a road network that serves to connect these empires as well as bind the two lands lying east and west of the Jordan.[8] All of this makes for a similar economy and cultural identity.

Additionally, in a land of limited resources, wadis and valleys contain-

7. For a more detailed description of these factors, see Baly, *Geography of the Bible*, 15–27.

8. The road network of the southern Levant is constrained by the topography, and, thus, the predominant pattern is NE-SW. However, there are several places in which E-W traffic is made possible through geological disruptions in the typical pattern. These opportunities

ing water and fertile farmland are more likely to unite people groups than serve as a boundary.[9] From a modern perspective, it is common to view rivers as useful borders. The Jordan River is especially susceptible to this, given its current role in dividing the modern state of Israel from the nation of Jordan. However, this is not how many people experienced the space historically. Rather, it would have been a shared resource to which communities on either side were drawn.[10]

Finally, Denis Baly observes that "traditional societies usually expand, even across the most imposing physical obstacles, to the limit of that area in which their own way of life is possible, and there their expansion normally stops."[11] The possibility of maintaining a similar way of life depends on a similarity of resources, based on the physical characteristics of the land. Since the Transjordan and the Cisjordan hold many physical characteristics in common, we should not be surprised to find the various people groups involved in the biblical account fluidly expanding across what might otherwise be seen as a formidable barrier, comfortably calling both sides of the Jordan home.[12]

However, these two regions also have differences, and it is perhaps these differences that lay behind the ambiguity with which the biblical authors portray the region. First, the Transjordan mirrors the Cisjordan topographically from east to west, with a fertile plain, a central highland region, a steppe land, and finally, a desert region. However, the Transjordan experiences less rainfall than the Cisjordan and as a result, the inhabitable portion of this land is truncated. Accordingly, though the resources are similar, the Transjordan is poorer than the Cisjordan.

Second, the Transjordan rises to a plateau that seamlessly merges with the Syrian desert to the east, exposing the settled land to political and ecological instability. The Cisjordan is protected from this experience. The Transjordan's relationship with the desert plays a significant role in its history.[13] For one, this permeable eastern frontier allowed

---

for E-W travel became significant thoroughfares and served to draw the Cisjordan and the Transjordan into relationship. See Yohanan Aharoni, *The Land of the Bible: A Historical Geography*, trans. Anson F. Rainey, rev. and enl. ed. (Philadelphia: Westminster, 1979), 52–53, 58–63; Carl G. Rasmussen, *Zondervan Atlas of the Bible* (Grand Rapids: Zondervan, 2010), 31–33, 40, 56; Yohanan Aharoni et al., *The Carta Bible Atlas* (Jerusalem: Carta, 2002), 16–17.

9. Paul H. Wright, "The Illustrated Guide to Biblical Geography" (unpublished manuscript, 2012), typescript, 314–15, 32.

10. Perhaps not always peacefully, but drawn together, nonetheless. Charles Cheney Hyde, "Notes on Rivers as Boundaries," *The American Journal of International Law* 6.4 (1912): 901–9; Anders Jägerskog, "Why States Co-Operate over Shared Water: The Water Negotiations in the Jordan River Basin," in *Water Resources in the Middle East: Israel-Palestinian Water Issues—from Conflict to Cooperation*, ed. Hillel Shuval and Hassan Dweik (Berlin: Springer-Verlag, 2007), 195–202.

11. Baly, *Geography of the Bible*, 212.

12. E.g., the story of Ruth, the Moabite incursion westward in Judg 3:12–30, or the position of Manasseh on both sides the Jordan.

13. "On the east the highlands gradually blend into the Syrian-Arabian Desert, and there exists no natural border but the wilderness itself. This is the reason why the fate of

raiders to easily infiltrate settlements and disappear again eastward into the ungovernable expanses.[14] So too, this same accessibility allowed primary road networks to pass through the heartland of the Transjordan, whereas they skirted the hill country of the Cisjordan along the western coastline. As a result, traders could easily access the population centers of the Transjordan, providing economic opportunities and cultural exposure from which the hill country of the Cisjordan was insulated.[15] Additionally, the Transjordan received more tenuous rainfall than the Cisjordan, resulting in greater waxing and waning of agricultural land. Thus, the Transjordan community was especially vulnerable to famine and displacement.

Based on these factors, those in the Transjordan lived with an ever-present awareness of the opportunities and risks posed by their uncontrollable eastern frontier. This, coupled with a cosmological worldview that likely associated the eastern desert with the "ends of the earth" and thus possible separation from God, it is conceivable that the region of the Transjordan developed both positive and negative associations and could be seen as both similar to and quite different from the lands to the west.[16]

NARRATIVE CONTEXT

Typical nation-states expand and contract their territorial compass as their power waxes and wanes. Israel experienced this phenomenon when they conquered territory in the Transjordan. However, within the biblical account, there seems to be more at stake. Here, Israel's national identity is constructed around obedience to YHWH, which results in their possession of a particular land: Canaan. Israel's unwillingness to trust YHWH and take said land in Num 13 results in a generation exiled in the wilderness. Deuteronomy particularly focuses on the new genera-

---

Transjordan is so closely intertwined with the desert" (Aharoni, *Land of the Bible*, 36; e.g., Judg 6:1–6; Ezek 25:1–7; Gen 49:19; Jer 18:17).

14. "The area of East Jordan has been since the start of history the contact line between the desert and the agricultural areas. This line has always been contested by the people on both sides. Population movement generally occurred across it from the east, and this always brought instability and devastation of the settled areas" (Raouf Sa'd Abujaber, "Agriculture and Population Movement in East Jordan during the Nineteenth Century," in *Studies in the History and Archaeology of Jordan II*, ed. Adnan Hadidi [Amman: Department of Antiquities; London: Routledge & Kegan Paul, 1985], 278). The Transjordan remains most vulnerable to this, but Judg 6:1–6 suggests that in extreme times, even the Cisjordan might suffer from eastern raiders.

15. Baly, *Geography of the Bible*, 8–9, 97; Rasmussen, *Zondervan Atlas of the Bible*, 33.

16. Ancient Israel, like most ancient Near Eastern cultures, imagined the earth as a disk of land, surrounded by water, often with the deity residing at the center. The surrounding water, often conceived of as the antithesis of the land of the living, was associated with ideas of chaos, danger, death, and separation from God. It is likely that ancient people associated these concepts with literal geographical features in their experience, at times viewing the landscape through a cosmic lens. In Israel's case, the eastern desert served as a mirror image of the Mediterranean Sea on the west: unlivable and treacherous landscapes that surrounded them and limited their territory. For a fuller discussion of this, see Aubrey L. Taylor, "Ministry in the Wilderness," in *Lexham Geographic Commentary on the Gospels*, ed. Barry J. Beitzel (Bellingham, WA: Lexham Press, 2017), 45; McClain, "Promised Land Boundaries," 221–33; Nicolas Wyatt, "Sea and Desert: Symbolic Geography in West Semitic Religious Thought," *UF* 19 (1987): 375–89.

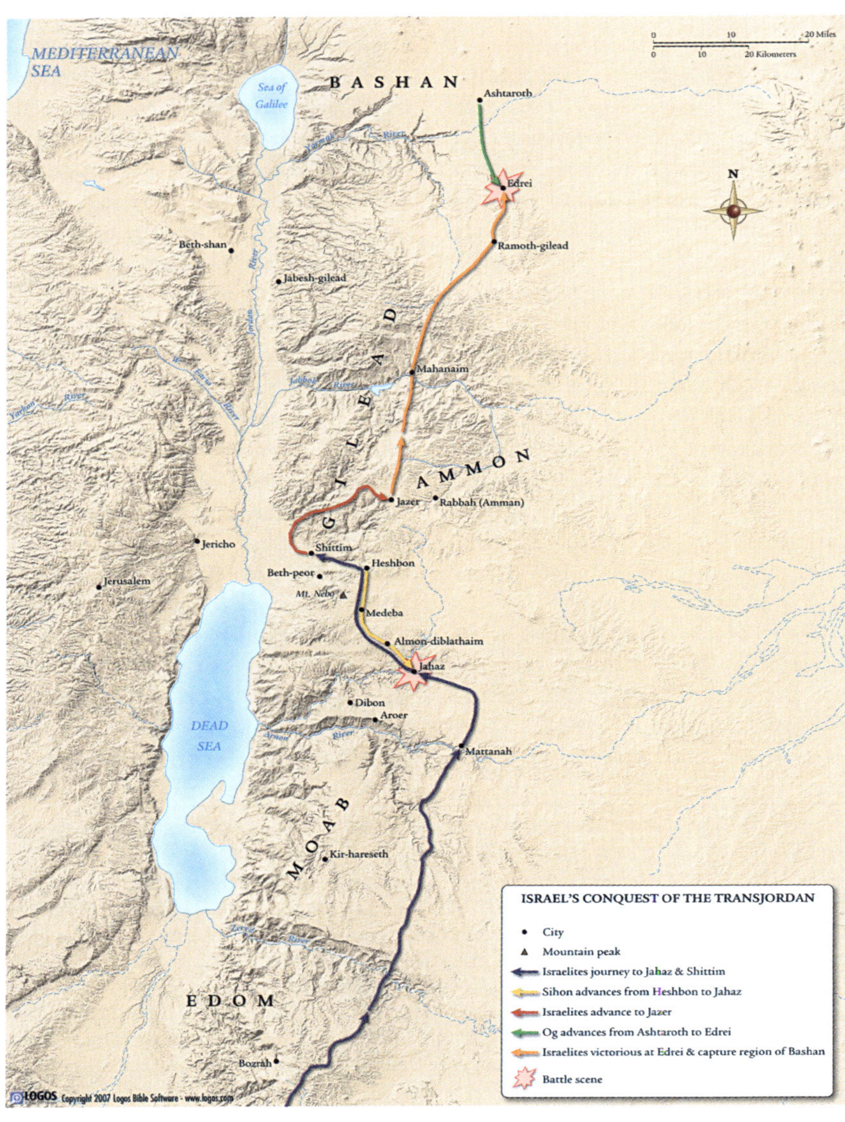

tion's preparation to obey the call to "cross the Jordan" (e.g., Deut 9:1). However, as this new generation begins their transition from wilderness to conquest, an unexpected encounter with the Amorites of the Transjordan leaves them in possession of the entire region north of the Arnon, and a new question emerges: what should Israel's relationship be to this land east of the Jordan?

Numbers 32 recounts the first attempt to answer this question. Here, Gad, Reuben, and the half-tribe of Manasseh ask for special dispensation from Moses to receive their inheritance east of the Jordan River. Initially distrustful of the arrangement, Moses eventually agrees and grants them the territory that will come to be summarized as extending "from Wadi Arnon to Mount Hermon" (Deut 3:8; Josh 12:1).[17] This was, however, given on condition of their performing a particular role in the invasion and conquest of Canaan. They were to serve as a "vanguard," an elite, advanced fighting force (חֻשִׁים, *hushim*), going before the rest of the army.[18] Thus, in the first chapter of Joshua, we have this reminder:

> To the Reubenites, the Gadites, and the half-tribe of Manasseh Joshua said, "Remember the word that Moses the servant of the LORD commanded you, saying, 'The LORD your God is providing you a place of rest, and will give you this land.' Your wives, your little ones, and your livestock shall remain in the land that Moses gave you beyond the Jordan. But all the warriors among you shall cross over armed before your kindred and shall help them, until the LORD gives rest to your kindred as well as to you, and they too take possession of the land that the LORD your God is giving them. Then you shall return to your own land and take possession of it, the land that Moses the servant of the LORD gave you beyond the Jordan to the east." (Josh 1:12–15)[19]

It is not until the conquest project is complete that these tribes may be released to occupy this eastern territory. Thus, in Josh 4:12, we are reassured that "The Reubenites, the Gadites, and the half-tribe of Manasseh crossed over armed before the Israelites, as Moses had ordered them," earning them the right to maintain their hold on the Transjordan territories. Finally, in Josh 22, these tribes are officially released from military duties. Having fulfilled their vow, they are permitted to return to the lands of the Transjordan (Josh 22:1–9). Joshua's speech celebrates the two and a half tribes' exemplary service and identifies them as faithful and obedient (22:2–3). However, in the ensuing account, a tension is revealed that calls into question Israel's satisfaction with this arrangement and their acceptance of the land east of the Jordan.

JOSHUA 22

First, in light of the events that will follow, Joshua's injunction, "Take good care to observe the commandment and instruction that Moses the servant of the LORD commanded you" (Josh 22:5) may communicate a latent concern that the Transjordan tribes require a little extra reminder and assistance in *remaining* obedient. The Transjordan is, as previously noted, vulnerable to outside influences. The proximity of Edom, Moab, and Ammon, as well as other semi-nomadic tribal groups, presented a threat.

17. The original request for this land identifies a selection of cities, but later descriptions expand, eventually referencing the whole region north of the Arnon. See Num 32:3; 33–42; Deut 3:12–17.

18. See Num 32:17. The word *hushim* here is unique. Typically, a verb meaning "to make haste," here it seems to be in participial form and most likely takes on the meaning of an elite or advance fighting force. See Levine, *Numbers 21–36*, 490.

19. Unless otherwise noted, all biblical quotations are taken from the New Revised Standard Version (NRSV).

The prior incident at Baal Peor (Num 25), referenced later in the story (Josh 22:17), is paradigmatic of the dangers of a close relationship with neighboring tribes.[20] Cultural contamination and even apostasy are the potential hazards of such an environment.[21] Thus, Joshua's reminder in 22:5 to remain faithful to the covenant may stem from a well-warranted concern based on the actual physical circumstances into which he was sending the Transjordan tribes.

Following Joshua's speech, we are told that Reuben, Gad, and half-Manasseh return, thus "parting from the Israelites at Shiloh" (22:9). This is the first of several instances in which "the Israelites," "Israel," or "children of Israel" is used to refer, not to the twelve tribes, but to the tribes of the Cisjordan (22:11, 12, 13, 32, 33).[22] The reference to Shiloh additionally communicates their separation from the central cult and thus the life of the community.[23] More specifically, we are told that they are leaving Canaan, the land Israel has been journeying toward for so long, to "go to the land of Gilead" (22:9). This highlights the separation of the two regions and implies a regression from the divine plan.[24]

Parting from their Cisjordan kin, the Transjordan tribes journey eastward until they reach the region of the Jordan. Here, the story takes an unexpected and dramatic turn:

> When they came to the region near the Jordan that lies in the land of Canaan, the Reubenites and the Gadites and the half-tribe of Manasseh built there an altar by the Jordan, an altar of great size. The Israelites heard that the Reubenites and the Gadites and the half-tribe of Manasseh had built an altar at the frontier of the land of Canaan, in the region near the Jordan, on the side that belongs to the Israelites. And when the people of Israel heard of it, the whole assembly of the Israelites gathered at Shiloh, to make war against them. (Josh 22:10–12)

Not fully apparent in translation, the language in these verses is remarkably ambiguous and reveals something of the interpretive nature of the space itself. First, we are told that they stop to build an altar that is unusual in some way.[25] Later, we learn that what makes this altar unusual is its intended use: it was symbolic and not to be used for sacrifice (22:26–27). Furthermore, the location of the altar is difficult to determine, high-

20. At Baal Peor, Moabite or perhaps Midianite women seem to have drawn Israel into participating in the local cult, resulting in YHWH's anger and a plague.

21. E.g., Deut 7:1–6; 20:16–18.

22. Richard D. Nelson, *Joshua: A Commentary*, OTL (Louisville: Westminster John Knox, 1997), 251.

23. Elie Assis, "'For It Shall Be a Witness between Us': A Literary Reading of Josh 22," *SJOT* 18.2 (2004): 215.

24. Characters who choose to move east may be interpreted as symbolically removing themselves from the divine plan. See Gen 4:16; 13:11; 33:16; 36:8.

25. The Hebrew *gadol lemareh* (גָּדוֹל לְמַרְאֶה) could be literally translated "big to see" or "big in appearance"; however, *gadol* can also mean "great" or "significant" and thus might indicate that the altar is notable in some way other than size.

lighting the perspectival nature of the space involved.[26] In 22:10, we are told that the two and a half tribes built the altar *al-hayarden* (עַל־הַיַּרְדֵּן). Translated here "by the Jordan," this could also be translated "over," or "in front of," suggesting a variety of positions for the altar in question. Similarly, though the above translation quite definitively places the altar "on the side that belongs to the Israelites," the Hebrew is less than clear (22:11). In a complex statement that seems anxious to specify the altar's location, three phrases attempt to describe the position of the altar, all beginning with the word *el* (אֶל). A preposition that generally indicates motion or action toward something, the interpretation of this directional term depends upon the perspective of the speaker. The literal translations below demonstrate the interpretive options:

el-mul erets kenaan (אֶל־מוּל אֶרֶץ כְּנַעַן): "toward, opposite" or "against the land of Canaan"

el-gelilot hayarden (אֶל־גְּלִילוֹת הַיַּרְדֵּן): "toward the boundary" or "toward the territory of the Jordan"

el-ever bene yisrael (אֶל־עֵבֶר בְּנֵי יִשְׂרָאֵל): "toward, across" or "across from the sons of Israel"

Depending on the point of view of the author, these descriptors could place the altar on either side of the Jordan River.[27] This lack of clarity regarding the location of the altar underscores the artificiality of the perceived boundary itself. The Jordan is serving as a boundary, but perhaps an uncertain one, and one between people who also seem uncertain of their relation to one another.

The enraged tribes of the Cisjordan assemble for battle against their brethren (22:12), but before going out to war, they send a delegation of elders, headed by the priest Phinehas to confront the eastern tribes (22:13–14). The appearance of Phinehas is one that, canonically, represents concerns for the integrity of the cult at all costs.[28] In the discussion that follows, the building of the altar is identified as an act of rebellion against the Lord and likened to the sin of Peor (22:17; compare with Num 25). What was until now an undercurrent of division between the two groups becomes the primary focal point, with us/you language drawing the boundary lines at the Jordan River. However, there are subtle indications of unity as well.

> Thus says the whole congregation of the Lord, "What is this treachery that you have committed against the God of Israel in turning away today from following the Lord, by building yourselves an altar today in rebellion against the Lord? [17] Have we not had enough of the sin at Peor from which even yet we have not cleansed ourselves, and for which a plague came upon the congregation of the Lord, [18] that you must turn away today from following the Lord! If you rebel against the Lord today, he will be angry with

26. Norman Henry Snaith, "Altar at Gilgal: Joshua 22:23–29," *VT* 28.3 (1978): 330–35; Matren H. Woudstra, *Book of Joshua*, NICOT (Grand Rapids: Eerdmans, 1981), 321–22.

27. For further discussion of the linguistic concerns in Josh 22:11, see Levine, *Numbers 21–36*, 505.

28. Barbara E. Organ, "Pursuing Phinehas: A Synchronic Reading," *CBQ* 63.2 (2001): 212–14.

> the whole congregation of Israel tomorrow. [19] But now, if your land is unclean, cross over into the LORD's land where the LORD's tabernacle now stands, and take for yourselves a possession among us; only do not rebel against the LORD, or rebel against us by building yourselves an altar other than the altar of the LORD our God. [20] Did not Achan son of Zerah break faith in the matter of the devoted things, and wrath fell upon all the congregation of Israel? And he did not perish alone for his iniquity!" (Josh 22:16–20)

First, divisiveness is apparent in the western tribes' interpretation of the altar as a competing Yahwistic altar in defiance of the centralized cult at Shiloh (22:16). The Cisjordan tribes' willingness to go to war is certainly divisive as well. However, their concern to protect themselves from YHWH's anger also acknowledges the inherent unity of Israel. Their argument is based on the concept of corporate guilt, expressing concern for communal punishment from YHWH, and referencing Achan's sin and the resulting consequences for all Israel (22:18, 20; cf. Josh 7). Through this, a shared history is recalled, and they speak of the Transjordan tribes as being in rebellion, both against God and against them (22:19), which is only possible if they are a part of a unified community with a shared past and code of behavior.

In the midst of this speech, the congregation comments on the land itself (22:19). Here, the Cisjordan tribes propose an alternative to the Transjordan tribes' altar building, suggesting: "if your land is unclean, cross over into the LORD's land where the LORD's tabernacle now stands, and take for yourselves a possession among us." Implied here is that the Cisjordan tribes do not believe that the Transjordan is "the Lord's land." Indeed, it questions if the Transjordan might even be "unclean." We have already identified ways in which this eastern territory might have held negative associations. Taken from a western agriculturalist perspective, the east is a "landscape of fear," uncontrollable and undesirable, and so perhaps indeed God-forsaken.[29] Based on the surrounding cultural influences, apostasy is identified as a potential hazard, and concern for separation from the central cult is communicated.

The word "unclean" (טָמֵא, *tame*) that is used here typically refers to ritual impurity, which separates an individual from access to the sacred and is resolved through a prescribed sacrificial ritual (e.g., Lev 5:1–6). Based on the Cisjordan tribes' statement, they perceive that the Transjordan itself is potentially ritually impure, perhaps due to its contact with "unclean" elements, which would suggest that YHWH could not be present. However, though this statement suggests that the Transjordan holds an inferior position to the Cisjordan, its uncleanness is *not* a certainty. It is only expressed as a possibility, reiterating the ambiguity already apparent and further revealing the perceptions of the land that drive the narrative.

In response to these accusations, the Transjordan tribes express apparent horror at the suggestion that they would act "in rebellion or in breach of faith toward the Lord" (22:22). They explain that the altar was made, not for sacrifice, but as a witness. In fear of eventual exclusion from larger Israel, this altar would be a visible sign that the tribes of the Transjordan also "perform the service of the Lord" (22:27). As they make their defense, they express the fear that future generations of Israel west of the Jordan may one day come to perceive the Jordan as a boundary.

> We did it from fear that in time to come your children might say to our children, "What have you to do with the Lord, the God of Israel? For the Lord has made the Jordan a boundary between us and you, you Reubenites and Gadites; you have no portion in the Lord." So your children might make our children cease to worship the Lord. (Josh 22:24–25)

The speakers do not say that the Jordan *is* a border, but rather that it might be viewed as such, clearly pointing toward the conceptual nature of the space. Their awareness of this inherent ambiguity and thus the opportunity for interpretation offers a unique glimmer of hope that among the various latent meanings associated with the Jordan, unity, rather than division, might be chosen. With this awareness, the altar was built between the two people groups as a witness to their commonalities and to defy a divisive interpretation. Yes, there is a tacit acceptance in this representation of two separate people groups, and the fact that they require an external witness to their connectedness is telling. However, this witness between "us and you" (22:27) also communicates unity simply because it was constructed with that intent. In fact, the entire discourse of 22:22–29

29. Denis Baly, "The Nature of Environment, with Special Relation to the Country of Jordan," in Hadidi, *Studies*, 23.

indicates that the tribes of the Transjordan very much desire to be understood as belonging to larger "Israel" and would not want to be seen in rebellion against it. Their altar building is in defiance of one potential interpretation of the Jordan River, choosing unity rather than division. The altar was meant to serve as a visual reminder for future generations that on either side the Jordan lie Israelites and worshipers of YHWH (22:26–29). The elders and Phinehas are satisfied with this answer, who then return word to the nine and a half tribes west of the Jordan (22:30–33). The verdict is accepted, and the site is named "Witness" (22:34).

CONCLUSION

Throughout this narrative, it appears that though the exclusion of the Transjordan and the people who lived there was a *potential* outcome, it was not an inevitable one. Perceiving this, the Transjordan tribes take the initiative to alter the landscape in hopes that their exclusion from the life of Israel might be averted. Built as a symbol of unity, the altar communicates that in fact, nothing changes by crossing this apparent boundary: Israelites and worshipers of YHWH can be found on both sides. More than mere expressions of ideas and hopes, symbols are a way of tangibly re-presenting and *creating* a desired reality. Manipulating our perception of the physical world, they have the power to reify intangible truths and shape the future. Such is the expressed hope of the Transjordan tribes. Thus, according to Josh 22, the Transjordan is indeed a part of the promised land, not because of its intrinsic qualities, but because Israel decided to make it so.

BIBLIOGRAPHY

Abujaber, Raouf Sa'd. "Agriculture and Population Movement in East Jordan during the Nineteenth Century." Pages 273–78 in *Studies in the History and Archaeology of Jordan II*. Edited by Adnan Hadidi. Amman: Department of Antiquities; London: Routledge & Kegan Paul, 1985.

Aharoni, Yohanan. *The Land of the Bible: A Historical Geography*. Rev. and enl. ed. Translated by Anson F. Rainey. Philadelphia: Westminster, 1979.

Aharoni, Yohanan, Anson F. Rainey, Michael Avi-Yonah, and Ze'ev Safrai. *The Carta Bible Atlas*. 4th ed. Jerusalem: Carta, 2002.

Assis, Elie. "'For It Shall Be a Witness between Us': A Literary Reading of Josh 22." *SJOT* 18.2 (2004): 208–31.

Bailey, Lloyd R. *Leviticus-Numbers*. The Smyth & Helwys Bible Commentary. Macon, GA: Smyth & Helwys, 2005.

Baly, Denis. *The Geography of the Bible*. New York: Harper & Row, 1974.

———. "The Nature of Environment, with Special Relation to the Country of Jordan." Pages 19–24 in *Studies in the History and Archaeology of Jordan II*. Edited by Adnan Hadidi. Amman: Department of Antiquities; London: Routledge & Kegan Paul, 1985.

Berquist, Jon L. "Introduction: Critical Spatiality and the Uses of Theory." Pages 1–12 in *Constructions of Space I: Theory, Geography, and Narrative*. Edited by Jon L. Berquist and Claudia V. Camp. New York: T&T Clark, 2007.

Boling, Robert G. *Joshua*. AB. Garden City, NY: Doubleday, 1984.

Dozeman, Thomas B. "Biblical Geography and Critical Spatial Studies."

Pages 87–108 In *Constructions of Space I: Theory, Geography, and Narrative*. Edited by Jon L. Berquist and Claudia V. Camp. New York: T&T Clark, 2007.

Hurvitz, Avi. "Dating the Priestly Source in Light of the Historical Study of Biblical Hebrew a Century after Wellhausen." *ZAW* 100.s1 (1988): 88–100.

Hyde, Charles Cheney. "Notes on Rivers as Boundaries." *The American Journal of International Law* 6.4 (1912): 901–09.

Jägerskog, Anders. "Why States Co-Operate over Shared Water: The Water Negotiations in the Jordan River Basin." Pages 195–202 in *Water Resources in the Middle East: Israel-Palestinian Water Issues—from Conflict to Cooperation*. Edited by Hillel Shuval and Hassan Dweik. Berlin: Springer-Verlag, 2007.

Kaufmann, Yehezkel. *The Biblical Account of the Conquest of Canaan*. Translated by Merton Dagut. Jerusalem: Magnes Press, 1985.

Kloppenborg, John S. "Joshua 22: The Priestly Editing of an Ancient Tradition." *Biblica* 62.3 (1981): 347–71.

Levine, Baruch A. *Numbers 21–36*. AB. New York: Doubleday, 2000.

McClain, Aubrey Taylor. "A Literary Exploration of the Promised Land Boundaries." Pages 221–33 in *Lexham Geographic Commentary on the Pentateuch*. Edited by Barry J. Beitzel. Bellingham, WA: Lexham Press, 2023.

———. "The Transjordan in Biblical Literature: A Critical Spatial Approach." PhD diss., Bar-Ilan University, 2020.

Milgrom, Jacob. "The Antiquity of the Priestly Source: A Reply to Joseph Blenkinsopp." *ZAW* 111 (1999): 10–22.

———. "The Case for the Pre-Exilic and Exilic Provenance of the Books of Exodus, Leviticus and Numbers." Pages 48–56 in *Reading the Law: Studies in Honour of Gordon J. Wenham*. Edited by J. Gordon McConville and Karl Möller. New York: T&T Clark, 2007.

———. *Numbers*. The JPS Torah Commentary. Philadelphia: Jewish Publication Society, 1990.

Nelson, Richard D. *Joshua: A Commentary*. OTL. Louisville: Westminster John Knox, 1997.

Organ, Barbara E. "Pursuing Phinehas: A Synchronic Reading." *CBQ* 63.2 (2001): 203–18.

Rasmussen, Carl G. *Zondervan Atlas of the Bible*. Rev. ed. Grand Rapids: Zondervan, 2010.

Snaith, Norman Henry. "Altar at Gilgal: Joshua 22:23–29." *VT* 28.3 (1978): 330–35.

Taylor, Aubrey L. "Ministry in the Wilderness." Pages 42–52 in *Lexham Geographic Commentary on the Gospels*. Edited by Barry J. Beitzel. Bellingham, WA: Lexham Press, 2017.

Woudstra, Matren H. *Book of Joshua*. NICOT. Grand Rapids: Eerdmans, 1981.

Wright, Paul H. "The Illustrated Guide to Biblical Geography." Unpublished manuscript, 2012, typescript.

Wyatt, Nicolas. "Sea and Desert: Symbolic Geography in West Semitic Religious Thought." *UF* 19 (1987): 375–89.

CHAPTER 13

ALLOTMENTS OF THE PROMISED LAND TO THE TRIBES OF JUDAH, SIMEON, BENJAMIN, EPHRAIM, AND MANASSEH

Josh 14–17

Thomas Middlebrook

KEY POINTS

- Joshua's allotments are modeled upon similar "royal land grants" from the ancient world.
- The central hill country inheritance is grounded in God's covenant to the patriarchs.
- The divisions of the central hill country mirror later and earlier boundaries, such as Canaan during the Egyptian Amarna period.
- Joseph's children Ephraim and Manasseh receive a double portion, but Judah's boundaries are the most developed in Joshua.
- Joseph's lands comprise the heart of the northern kingdom of Israel; Judah's lands comprise the heart of the southern kingdom.
- Confusing and conflicting boundaries are due, in part, to natural social processes.

INTRODUCTION

This article addresses the allotments of land in the book of Joshua to the tribal groups of Judah (with Simeon), Benjamin, Ephraim, and west Manasseh in the central hill country and Negev of ancient Israel. By granting these allotments, God signals his power and authority to clear and distribute the land as he sees fit. Moreover, these allotments signal the faithfulness of God to keep his covenantal promises to Abraham (Gen 12:7) and his children (23:3; 28:13; 35:12). In a sad contrast, the Bible also records Israel's unfaithfulness to the covenant and its ramifications for their possession of the allotted lands.

THE FOUNDATION OF JOSHUA'S ALLOTMENTS

The allotment of land in the book of Joshua is fully dependent upon the storyline of Genesis. Most importantly, these specific lands represent the fulfillment of God's covenant with Abraham in Gen 12:2–3; 15:7, 18–21; and 17:8. It is first described as either the land of Canaan or the land between the Euphrates River and the brook of Egypt commonly identified with Wadi Arish.[1] Considering the beginning of Genesis, this gift of land to Adam's children redeems their experience of displacement from the garden of Eden.[2] Towards the end of Genesis, the patriarch Jacob bestows his final blessing upon his children (Gen 49). Among them, Joseph's two sons receive a double portion of the blessing, which is reflected in the two allotments for Ephraim and Manasseh instead of a single allotment for the house of Joseph (Gen 48; Josh 14:4a).

DIVINE LAND GRANT

The closest parallel for this divine gift of land can be found in the "royal grants" bestowed by kings of the ancient Near East (hereafter ANE). Royal figures could grant many things: land, human and material resources, as well as titles or offices.[3] Abraham and his descendants appear to have been granted each of these through the Abrahamic and Mosaic covenants: the promise of land, children, the blessing of material goods and protection, as well as the office of priests (Gen 17:4–8; Exod 19:5–6). Specific literary parallels between ANE and biblical land grants include (1) the recitation of previous ownership, (2) the assignment of towns "with their pasturelands," (3) the presentation of the grant within a *larger* treaty between the two parties, and (4) the divine sanction and support of the territorial acquisition.[4] For example, the "weapon of the weather god" supported the reconquest of the Middle Bronze Age town of Irridi, while Joshua was supported by the "large hailstones" sent by the Lord against five Amorite kings (Josh 10:11).[5] The historical and literary comparability of royal grants to the allotments in Joshua can affirm the antiquity and authenticity of the biblical record.

MOSES AND JOSHUA'S AUTHORITY

The assumption behind this parallel, presented throughout the Hebrew Bible, is that Yahweh is a *royal* figure.[6] Gideon

---

1. *MAB*, 27.

2. Walter Brueggemann, *The Land: Place as Gift, Promise, and Challenge in Biblical Faith*, 2nd ed. (Minneapolis: Fortress, 2002), 1–14.

3. Moshe Weinfeld, "The Covenant of Grant in the Old Testament and in the Ancient Near East," *Journal of the American Oriental Society* 90.2 (1970): 184–203.

4. Compare Josh 3–4 with "Abbael's Gift of Alalakh (*AT* 1)," trans. Richard S. Hess, *COS* 2.127:329 and "Land Grant *AT* 456*," trans. Richard S. Hess, *COS* 2.137:369–70.

5. See previous footnote, especially *COS* 2.137:370.

6. Thomas R. Schreiner, *The King in His Beauty: A Biblical Theology of the Old and New Testaments* (Grand Rapids: Baker Academic, 2013). One ideological implication of God fulfilling the role of king is how it mitigates the criticism of scholars who restrict the dating of the

states in Judg 8:23, "The LORD himself will rule over you," and in Isa 33:22 the author expands, "The LORD is our judge. The LORD is our lawgiver. The LORD is our king."[7] God's authority entails granting lands of "inheritance" and "fixing the borders" of all nations (Deut 32:8), not just Israel. The authority of Moses and Joshua (sometimes accompanied by the priest Eleazar, e.g., Num 34:17–18) to fix the borders of the tribes of Israel is legitimate only as an *extension* of God's authority, hence the importance of confirming their election as divine spokesmen (Exod 4:1–17; Num 16; Josh 1).

THE SOCIOLOGICAL REALITIES OF THE ALLOTMENTS

The allotments in Joshua represents a constellation of important sociological realities for the Israelites. In the first place, we know from anthropological research that the very notion of "land" was conceptualized differently in ancient and agrarian-based societies, like Israel, than in modern and industrial-based societies.[8] For example, studies show that the self-identity of such groups is constructed by their *participation with the landscape*, so that even "the language of topopoiesis, the figurative language of place naming, is indistinguishable from the conduct of everyday life," as is the case for north Australian Aborigines to this day.[9] Their daily engagement with the local landscape, in other words, is the means by which social memory and identity is maintained in cultures like ancient Israel's.[10]

SOCIAL IDENTITY AND THE LAND

Secondly and relatedly, the Israelites seem to have understood that all the land is a divine product (Gen 1–2), some of which they received as an essential component of their social and theological identity (Gen 15:7).[11] Christopher Wright summarizes, "The theological

---

allotment texts to the monarchial period or later, based in part upon the requirements of a royal administration. E.g., Zecharia Kallai, *Historical Geography of the Bible: The Tribal Territories of Israel* (Jerusalem: Magnes, 1986); Nadav Na'aman, *Borders and Districts in Biblical Historiography: Seven Studies in Biblical Geographic Lists* (Jerusalem: Simor, 1986).

7. Compare with 1 Sam 8:7; Ps 10:16; Isa 6:5. Unless otherwise indicated, biblical translations are the author's own.

8. Don Mitchell, "Landscape," in *Cultural Geography: A Critical Dictionary of Key Concepts*, ed. David Atkinson et al. (New York: I. B. Tauris, 2005), 49–56; John J. Bradley, "'Whitefellas Have to Learn about Country, It Is Not Just Land': How Landscape Becomes Country and Not an 'Imagined' Place," in *The Place of Landscape: Concepts, Contexts, Studies*, ed. Jeff Malpas (Cambridge, MA: MIT Press, 2011), 45–64.

9. Paul Carter, "Lips in Language and Space: Imaginary Places in James Dawson's Australian Aborigines (1881)," in *Spatiality and Symbolic Expression*, ed. Bill Richardson (New York: Palgrave Macmillan, 2015), 114–15.

10. For this topic, see: Maurice Halbwachs, "Space and the Collective Memory," in *The Collective Memory*, trans. Francis J. Ditter Jr. and Vida Yazdi Ditter (New York: Harper & Row, 1980), 128–57; Chris Gosden and Gary Lock, "Prehistoric Histories," *World Archaeology* 30.1 (1998): 2–12; Susanne Küchler, "Landscape as Memory: The Mapping of Process and Its Representation in a Melanesian Society," in *Landscape: Politics and Perspectives*, ed. Barbara Bender (Providence: Berg, 1993), 85–106.

11. Ronald A. Simkins, *Creator and Creation: Nature in the Worldview of Ancient Israel* (Peabody, MA: Hendrickson, 1994), 90–126.

status of Israel was *earthed and rooted* in the socio-economic fabric of their kinship structure and their land tenure."[12] Because the allotments were given "according to their clans" (see, e.g., Josh 15:1, 12, 20; 16:8; 17:2), each clan could pass on a tale of God's gift to "us." Walter Brueggemann adds that the land of the Bible is a *storied place*—a place where sacred "words have been spoken which have established identity, defined vocations, and envisioned destiny."[13] By this reasoning, the allotments in Joshua comprise an essential story about how Israel's land was given by God to specific kin-groups.[14]

Tribal Conflict and the Land

Third, modern readers of Josh 14–17 may scratch their heads at the sheer space dedicated to the allotments (not unlike the reactions of moderns to the genealogies in 1 Chr 1–9). But lest we assume the relationships between the Israelite tribes did not require an explicit and divine designation of borders, recall that the remainder of Israelite history is characterized by violent inter-tribal conflict. A few examples are the culling of Ephraim in Judg 12:1–6, the battle of Gibeah in Judg 20, the battle for Benjamin in 1 Kgs 15:16–22, and the Syro-Ephraimite war in 2 Kgs 16:5–9. For the same reason, strict laws were instituted that prohibited the dishonest (re)moving of boundary stones, e.g., Deut 19:14: "You shall not move your neighbor's boundary marker, which the ancestors have set, in your inheritance."[15] The authority of Joshua's allotments should have afforded a peaceful cohabitation. Sadly, not all boasted with the psalmist: "The lines have fallen for me in pleasant places; indeed, I have a beautiful inheritance" (Ps 16:6).

Redistribution of the Land

A final social reality entailed within the allotments derives from God's assertion, "The land is mine" (Lev 25:23). Based on this, each tribe could maintain their allotment as "inalienable" and in perpetuity.[16] However, the realities of marriage, fluctuations in weather, economic and military fortunes, etc., inevitably created a fractured map of land ownership. The biblical answers to this conundrum include the kin-based redemption of unclaimed lands (i.e., levirate marriage in Deut 25:5–10) and the Jubilee, a fifty-year cycle that resets the tribal boundaries (Lev 25:8–22; Num 36:4).[17] Although there is no direct evidence that the Jubilee was ever enacted in the idealized form presented in the Torah, the practice of communal discernment regarding the long-term (but still tempo-

12. Christopher J. H. Wright, *God's People in God's Land: Family, Land, and Property in the Old Testament* (Grand Rapids: Eerdmans, 1990), 109. Emphasis added.

13. Brueggemann, *Land*, 5.

14. The casting of lots would have introduced an element of "chance" that was considered within the control of God (Prov 16:33) and perhaps less offensive than other methods of divination (Rob Fleener, "Lots," *LBD*, n.p.). Lots in Joshua are said to be "cast" (ירה, *yrh*) or "thrown" (שׁלך, *shlk*) in 18:6, 8, and 10. The Urim and Thummim are not mentioned in the book of Joshua but may represent an analogous process of "sanctioned" divination.

15. Compare with Deut 27:17; Job 24:2; Prov 22:28; and Hos 5:10.

16. Wright, *God's People*, 55–58.

17. Wright, *God's People*, 66–70.

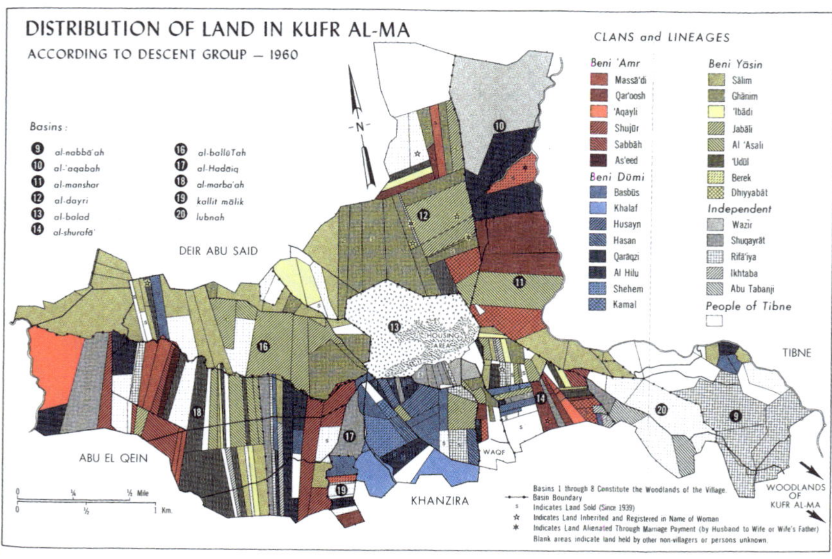

rary) use of land can be studied even in modern times. The necessity of this practice is clearly shown in Richard Antoun's model of descent groups within Kufr al-Ma, Jordan.[18] The checkerboard of ownership does not adhere to an idealized distribution. Instead, it reflects the complex sociological realities that are likely present in other tribal societies, such as ancient Israel.

Eventually, a coordinated decision by the *community* leaders would be needed in order to create a release-valve for the "inefficiencies" resulting from the natural fluctuations in agrarian societies mentioned above. The biblical Jubilee likewise reflects the *community's* priority when resetting the boundaries of agricultural lands (notice the repetition of returning to the "clans" in Lev 25).[19] Historical reconstructions of Joshua's allotments rarely incorporate these complex social realities which might otherwise explain the presence of conflicting tribal allotments (e.g., irregular or overlapping boundaries).

HOW ARE THE ALLOTMENTS DESCRIBED LITERARILY?

The literary description of tribal allotments in Joshua employs two distinct methods, as argued by Albrecht Alt in

18. Richard T. Antoun, *Arab Village: A Social Structural Study of a Trans-Jordanian Peasant Community* (Bloomington, IN: Indiana University Press, 1972).

19. This explanation adds insight into the other title for the Jubilee: a year of "release" (Lev 25:10). This "release meant that all Israelites would have a fresh start, *returning to* their own *property*, surrounded by their closest relatives (*clan*; vv. 10–13)" (Jay Sklar, *Leviticus: An Introduction and Commentary*, TOTC [Downers Grove, IL: InterVarsity, 2014], 301). The legislation resulting from the complaint of the daughters of Zelophehad in Num 36:1–13 is another example that addresses the natural social fluctuations which threatened the ideal process of inheritance.

1925.[20] The first method is *to list a group of towns and villages*.[21] For instance, Simeon "had for their inheritance Beersheba, Shema/Sheba, Moladah, Hazar Shual ..." (Josh 19:2–3). The resulting cluster of dots on a two-dimensional map can be outlined for approximate boundaries of the tribes and clans of Israel. The order of presentation is not critical, although neighboring towns are often grouped together. In Josh 15:33 the text further specifies one of these groupings as "In the lowlands" and another grouping in 15:48 as: "In the hill country." These reveal the basic geographical zones by which the Israelites divided the landscape. Often in the Hebrew text, the listing of town names are given plainly with no intervening words or with a simple conjunction (*waw*). The conclusion of a group of town names often provides a total number of towns and then the designation of an untold number of "villages" (חָצֵר, *hatser*) as part of the allotment. Villages were an important component in taxation, as illustrated by records from the Late Bronze Age kingdom of Ugarit and could also be bestowed through royal land grants.[22] Tabulating the number of villages in Israel may have been prohibitive due to their relative impermanence, variable organization, and high quantity.

The second method used to describe the allotments is *to create a boundary description* that lists a series of towns, rivers, or other geographic features that lie along the outermost perimeter of the tribe. A boundary (גְּבוּל, *gevul*) is typically described in a continuous and roughly counterclockwise fashion and frequently mentions the Jordan River in the east.[23]

The minimum number of features in a biblical boundary description is two, as in the repeated phrase "from Dan to Beersheba" (e.g., 2 Sam 24:2, 15). These are the last towns of significance as one travels north and south through Israel.

---

20. See the history of research in Richard S. Hess, "Asking Historical Questions of Joshua 13–19: Recent Discussion Concerning the Date of the Boundary Lists," in *Faith, Tradition, and History: Old Testament Historiography in Its Near Eastern Context*, ed. Alan R. Millard, James K. Hoffmeier, and David W. Baker (Winona Lake, IN: Eisenbrauns, 1994), 191–92.

21. The earliest recorded lists of this kind come from Sumerian scribes in the middle of the third millennium BC, perhaps based upon works as old as the early third millennium. This knowledge set the stage for the creation of graphic maps, but the earliest examples of them come from the middle of the second millennium. See Alan R. Millard, "Cartography in the Ancient Near East," in *Cartography in Prehistoric, Ancient, and Medieval Europe and the Mediterranean*, ed. John B. Harley and David Woodward (Chicago: University of Chicago Press, 1987), 107–16.

22. "Royal Land Grant," *COS* 3.110:258.

23. East/sunrise was Israel's primary orientation. For the literary and archaeological evidence from Israel, see Nicholas Wyatt, "The Vocabulary and Neurology of Orientation: The Ugaritic and Hebrew Evidence," in *Ugarit, Religion and Culture: Proceedings of the International Colloquium on Ugarit, Religion and Culture, Edinburgh, July 1994. Essays Presented in Honour of Professor John C. L. Gibson*, ed. Nicolas Wyatt, Wilfred G. E. Watson, and Jeffery B. Lloyd (Münster: Ugarit-Verlag, 1996), 351–80; Avraham Faust, "Doorway Orientation, Settlement Planning and Cosmology in Ancient Israel During Iron Age II," *Oxford Journal of Archaeology* 20.2 (2001): 129–54. A preference for an eastward orientation was shared by medieval mapmakers as in the classic T-O maps. In Latin, *oriens* means "east" and gave rise to our modern designations of "the Orient."

This demarcation of Israel's boundaries is idealized but still shy of the utopian boundary presented elsewhere: "from the brook/border of Egypt to the Euphrates River" (Gen 15:18; Exod 23:31; 1 Kgs 4:21; 8:65; 2 Kgs 24:7; 2 Chr 9:26). Neither the phrase "Dan to Beersheba" nor "brook of Egypt to the River" appears in Joshua.[24] The features referenced by Joshua's boundary descriptions include: the Mediterranean Sea and its coastline (Josh 15:12), the Dead Sea (15:2), the Jordan and its "mouth" (15:5), wadis (16:8), springs (15:9), multiple wildernesses (16:1), the Arabah (18:18), the Shephelah (15:33), valleys and ravines (15:7), mountains and their peaks (15:8), cliffs (15:10), the Oak in Zaanannim (אֵלוֹן בְּצַעֲנַנִּים, *elon betsaanannim*) (19:33), travel paths/passes (18:17), towns (19:11), and political districts (19:27).[25]

Most of the tribes are provided with boundary descriptions. The exceptions are Simeon and Levi—whose incorporation into Judah and all Israel, respectively, explains the omission—and the tribe of Dan, who failed to hold their inheritance and migrated north to Laish/Dan (Tel Qadi).[26]

Similarly, most of the tribes are provided with town lists. The only tribes without them are Ephraim and west Manasseh, but the data is complicated by disputes about the precise distinction between certain town lists and boundaries as well as by opinions about the historical development of Josh 16–17.[27] It may be that the lack of town lists for both of these tribes evinces a rhetorical strategy. One may ask: At what point did the house of Joseph lose its town lists? Were they ever incorporated into the text of Joshua or excluded from the outset? Why or why not? Richard Hess argues that the lacuna was original, based upon two evidences from the text itself: (1) the dense forestation of the hill country (Josh 17:18) prevented a more detailed survey of the territory, and (2) the majority of the descendants of Manasseh mentioned in Josh 17:2–6 have names (e.g., Tirzah) identical to or associated with hill country districts/towns in the biblical text (and in the Samaria Ostraca).[28] Because of this, the further inclusion of town names (identical to the personal names) would be redundant. For scholars committed to a late-monarchial or postexilic date of composition (unlike Hess), the omission of the town lists may be explained in other ways. For example, a late Deuteronomistic editor could have

24. But see a related formulation in Josh 1:4.

25. Hoffmeier (citing Caminos and Rendsburg) has noted that "the spring of the waters of Nephtoah" in Josh 15:9 and 18:15 is redundant and is better read as the "Spring of Meneptoaḥ," as in Pharaoh Merenptah. Egyptian pharaohs routinely fortified water resources along their campaign trail in order to secure the supply chain (James K. Hoffmeier, "What Is the Biblical Date for the Exodus? A Response to Bryant Wood," *JETS* 50.2 [2007]: 243). I would suggest that Joshua's mention of springs in the conquest/allotment accounts may reflect the same practice.

26. For the tribal allotments for Simeon, see Josh 19:1–9, 40–48; for Levi, see Josh 21.

27. See comments and bibliography in Hess, "Asking Historical Questions of Joshua 13–19"; John Laughlin, *Reading Joshua: A Historical-Critical, Archaeological Commentary* (Macon, GA: Smyth & Helwys, 2015), 179.

28. Richard S. Hess, *Joshua: An Introduction and Commentary*, TOTC (Downers Grove, IL: InterVarsity Press, 1996), 258. The text of Joshua also points out the obstacle of armed resistance from the local Canaanites (17:12–13), especially in the chariot-friendly lowlands.

redacted the land claims of the exiled and idolatrous Northern Kingdom.[29]

When we consider the literary choices made in the boundary descriptions and town lists, we can conclude that the author of Joshua wants to highlight the characters/tribes of Judah and Joseph (like the book of Genesis), probably because they were the major centers of the later southern and northern kingdoms of Israel. For example, Judah's allotment (*sans* Caleb) in Josh 15 covers sixty-three verses and the house of Joseph covers twenty-eight in Josh 16–17, which stresses their relative importance. The remaining tribes receive a mere nine verses or less in Josh 19, except Benjamin (18 verses in Josh 18) and the special case of the Levites (42 verses in Josh 21).

THE HISTORICAL GEOGRAPHY OF THE ALLOTMENTS

Some scholars have criticized the historical reliability of Joshua's allotments, grounded within a wider argument for a late-monarchial redaction of the Deuteronomistic history. The proposed dating of each tribal allotment may differ widely, from premonarchic to late-monarchic, as well as the dating of each tribe's distinct town list and boundary description.[30] This historical hodgepodge probably reflects a general confusion concerning the textual history of Joshua—unsurprising given the absence of manuscript evidence—and a failure to fully appreciate Joshua's complex literary strategies.[31] These strategies include hyperbole, irony, and idealized descriptions of the conquest *and* the allotment.[32] In any event, it is important to keep in mind that the *reliability* of historical records is not always in direct proportion to their temporal proximity to the events in question. The passing of time, decades even, can provide an important space for mature reflection and the collation of source materials before the most accurate histories are composed.[33]

29. Robert G. Boling, *Joshua: A New Translation with Notes and Commentary*, AB (Garden City, NY: Doubleday, 1982), 405.

30. For example, even Kallai states, "Each of the town-lists of the southern tribes ... reflects a different period" (Kallai, *Historical Geography of the Bible*, 345).

31. For a recent survey of narrative studies on Joshua, see Ovidiu Creangă, "The Conquest of Memory in the Book of Joshua," in *The Oxford Handbook of Biblical Narrative*, ed. Danna Nolan Fewell (Oxford: Oxford University Press, 2016), 168–79.

32. The source critical estrangement of Josh 13–21 from the rest of the book seems to have restricted the application of these literary conclusions drawn from the *conquest* accounts to the *allotment* accounts. Although this essay cannot pursue the question further, the stark separation of literary analysis of early and later Joshua is not a requirement of the text. For a discussion of relevant literary strategies, see K. Lawson Younger Jr., *Ancient Conquest Accounts: A Study in Ancient Near Eastern and Biblical History Writing* (Sheffield: JSOT, 1990), 241–64; Younger, "Rhetorical Structuring in the Joshua Conquest Narratives," in *Critical Issues in Early Israelite History*, ed. Richard S. Hess, Gerald A. Klingbeil, and Paul J. Ray Jr. (Winona Lake, IN: Eisenbrauns, 2008).

33. See discussion in Younger, *Ancient Conquest Accounts*, 241–66. Many scholars assent to the use of prior sources in compilation of boundary lists in the monarchical era, as McKinny writes, "It seems probable that the town lists of Judah and Benjamin in the book of Joshua (15:21–26; 18:21–28) were a later, more detailed edition of the Solomonic district system (1 Kgs 4:7–19) for Benjamin (1 Kgs 7:19) and the unmentioned territory of Judah that followed the

The Amarna Letters

This collection of cuneiform tablets is named after the place they were discovered—modern Amarna, the ancient Egyptian city of Akhetaten. Written in the late 14th century BC, these letters record correspondence between Egypt (under Pharaohs Akhenaten and Tutankhamun) and its vassal states. They provide information about trade and government of the time.

The Amarna letters and the biblical text describe the land of Canaan similarly. Both indicate that Canaan had several territories, various kings, and chariots that served as the means of military control.

The Amarna letters describe the city of Shechem as a dangerous place full of political intrigue; the book of Judges does the same at a later date. The Amarna letters also show that the kingdoms of Canaan were under military pressure from nomadic tribes.

The Amarna letters are a collection of 388 tablets, with the largest measuring about 8 in. by 4 in.

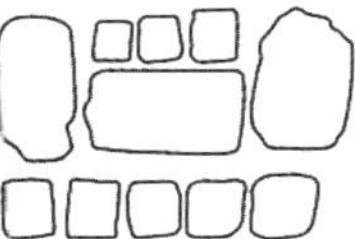

TRADITIONAL TERRITORIES

An important historical comparison regarding Joshua's division of the land has been made by Hess, namely:

> If one were to date Joshua 13–19 solely on the basis of the period in which the known political-geographical divisions most closely correspond to the boundary descriptions, the closest correspondence would be with the Late Bronze Age world of the [Egyptian-Canaanite] Amarna correspondence.[34]

The Amarna letters (c. 1350–1330 BC) reveal the Canaanite political situation which Israel either lived through—in an early date of the exodus—or was later influenced by—in either the late date of the exodus or in the emergence theories

---

division of the kingdom in 931 BCE" (Chris McKinny, "A Historical Geography of the Administrative Division of Judah: The Town Lists of Judah and Benjamin in Joshua 15:21–62 and 18:21–28" [PhD diss., Bar-Ilan University, 2017], 19–20, see also 29–49).

34. Hess, "Asking Historical Questions of Joshua 13–19," 197. He has compiled further comparative materials in Richard S. Hess, "Late Bronze Age and Biblical Boundary Descriptions of the West Semitic World," in *Ugarit and the Bible*, ed. George J. Brooks, Adrian H. W. Curtis, and John F. Healey (Münster: Ugarit-Verlag, 1994), 123–38.

of Israel's ethnogenesis. The author of Numbers seems to accept that the contemporary land of Canaan is coterminous with the promised land (Num 34:2–5; 35:14). Thus, some argue that the general contour of Late Bronze Age Canaan must ground our reading of Joshua. A prime example is how the Amarna letters—which traveled to and from the highland cities of King Labayu of Shechem and King Abdi-heba of Jerusalem requesting the intervention of the Egyptian pharaoh—reveal a web of provincial conflicts and suspicious factions. This mirrors the episode of the Gibeonite defection from the allied kings of the southern highlands, led by Adoni-Zedek, king of Jerusalem (Josh 10). Significantly, then, the story of Joshua and its basic territorial divisions are at home in one of the few Canaanite texts from this general time period.

RITUAL TERRITORIES

Another method of establishing how the allotments were divided in the biblical era has to do with the construction of altars. Because the landscape was not *merely* physical in the eyes of the ancients, due to the authority and presence of spiritual beings, the expression of territorial claims was also a religious act. The construction of altars by the patriarchs in the promised land demonstrates their religious *and* material interest in the central hill country. Altars were built at or around Shechem (Gen 12:7; 33:20), Bethel (12:8; 35:7), Jerusalem (22:9), Hebron (13:18), and Beersheba (26:25). These lie in the respective territories of Cisjordan Manasseh, Ephraim, Benjamin, Judah, and Simeon. Later, the *extension* of Israel's territory into the Transjordan needed to be ritually affirmed through the construction of an altar (Josh 22:10). This structure copied the altar of the Lord (22:28) and witnessed to the Transjordan tribes' rightful inheritance and inclusion as legitimate worshipers before the tabernacle (22:24–29). Ordinarily, the natural physical features of the landscape, i.e., its rivers, bodies of water, valleys, mountains, and arid regions, had a deterministic influence on the sociopolitical separation of its inhabitants. The landscape was a divine creation to be respected (Gen 1:1, 9–10). Therefore, Josh 22's crucial conclusion was that even the physical boundary of the Jordan River should not confuse the incorporation of Israel's Transjordan inheritance. This was achieved *by means of* the construction of yet another altar to God.

JUDAH

Judah's allotment, which included Simeon, is the most explicit of all the tribes in terms of geographic and toponymic details (Josh 15). The map below divides the tribal allotments of Judah and Benjamin into districts.[35] These districts derive from the periodic summaries in the town lists for each tribe, e.g., Josh 15:44: "a total of nine towns with their villages," and are much debated regarding their precise delineation and numeration.[36] McKinny's map reflects a recent

35. The word "district" does not reflect any underlying Hebrew word in Joshua. It is contrived for convenience in order to describe the groups within the town lists. The numbering of those districts is based upon their order of mention in Joshua and is relatively consistent between different scholarly reconstructions.

36. See discussion in McKinny, "Historical Geography," 29–48. Furthermore, the reader may notice a discrepancy regarding the size of Judah with other maps of Judah's allotment,

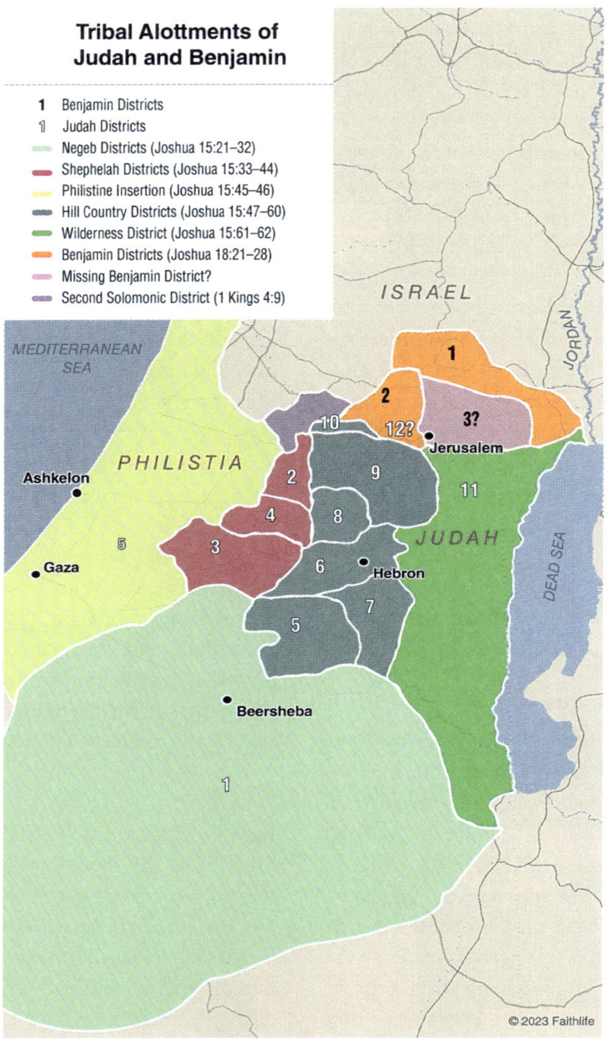

especially regarding the Philistine territory in the west. Most maps in study Bibles extend Judah out to the Mediterranean by following the text of Josh 15:11–12, 45–47. Because the Hebrew Bible never records Judah's complete possession of Philistia, one might label these dimensions of Judah *aspirational* versus *actual*. Many scholars, McKinny included, reconstruct the allotments of Judah with the aid of later biblical narratives and the archaeological evidence of settlements in order to better approximate the actual dimensions of Judah. This often depreciates the potential literary/rhetorical aims of Joshua as it stands, as mentioned above. The same debate regarding boundary delineation pervades the task of specific site identifications, which must proceed on a case-by-case basis according to the extant textual and archaeological data. Conclusions based upon the absence of evidence are often *overturned* by the ever-widening scope of excavations in Israel.

and comprehensive investigation of the sites and districts. The numbers attached to each of the districts and the towns represent their order of appearance within the text of Joshua.

The map clearly shows that the "Negeb district (Josh 15:2–32) is the largest Judahite district in terms of both number of towns and land-size."[37] The size of the Negev comes as little surprise since the aridity of the region requires its sparse population to spread out in order to secure resources. The size of this district also requires naming a higher number of sites in order to define its territory, but we may also speculate that Simeon's absorption into this district of Judah's allotment required increased attention to its sites.

The hill country and Shephelah of Judah, however, surpass all others in terms of the *density* of sites. At the center of these districts lies Hebron, which David chose as the capital of Judah by divine lot (2 Sam 2:1). Before this, Hebron served as a regional capital for the Canaanites (note its "king" in Josh 12:10) and was given to Caleb as an inheritance (Josh 14:13, compare with Judg 1:10, 20). The story of David's early life is intertwined with this region—his hometown in District 9, capital in District 6 (later in District 12), his military exploits in District 2 and 3, his refuge in District 7, and so on (1 Sam 16:1; 2 Sam 5:5; 1 Sam 17; 23–26). The agricultural resources of the Judahite hill country and Shephelah made them an ideal heartland for the Davidic monarchy.

The rarity of named settlements in the Judean wilderness and Philistine districts require different explanations. The wilderness exists within a "rain shadow" which provides less than twelve inches (300 mm) of rain per year, down to two inches (50 mm) in the southern regions.[38] The aridity of this wilderness and the difficulty of its steep terrain make it a land suited only for seasonal pastoral activities and for refuges of last resort (1 Sam 24–26). Philistia, on the other hand, comprises a long-contested area that was never fully controlled nor inherited by the tribes of Israel (Josh 13:2; Jer 25:20; compare with Judg 1:18–19). This may explain the sparse listing of its settlements. The centralized power of these city-states, the so-called Philistine Pentapolis (Josh 13:3), may also be reflected in the limited number of named sites. Allotting this land to Judah would have constituted a continual challenge that was met "only imperfectly."[39] Thus, one might describe these boundaries as "aspirational."

There remain several areas of overlap and/or omission from these tribal allotments. As mentioned above, the complexity of the description of the allotments is due, in part, to the complexity of the socio-political situation at the time of composition (regardless of one's position of when that occurred). The region surrounding Gezer, for instance, sat close to the borders of Ephraim, Dan, Benjamin, Philistia, and later Judah and Israel.[40] Unsurprisingly then, this was disputed territory for much of biblical history. The city of Jerusalem

37. McKinny, "Historical Geography," 79.

38. Burton MacDonald, *"East of the Jordan": Territories and Sites of the Hebrew Scriptures* (Boston: American Schools of Oriental Research, 2000), 31–32.

39. Marten H. Woudstra, *The Book of Joshua*, NICOT (Grand Rapids: Eerdmans, 1981), 250.

40. McKinny writes, "The boundary description (Josh 16:3, 5–6; 18:13–15; [see also] Judg 1:29; 1 Chr 7:24, 28), the Levitical town lists (Josh 21:21–22; 1 Chr 6:67–68) and the book of

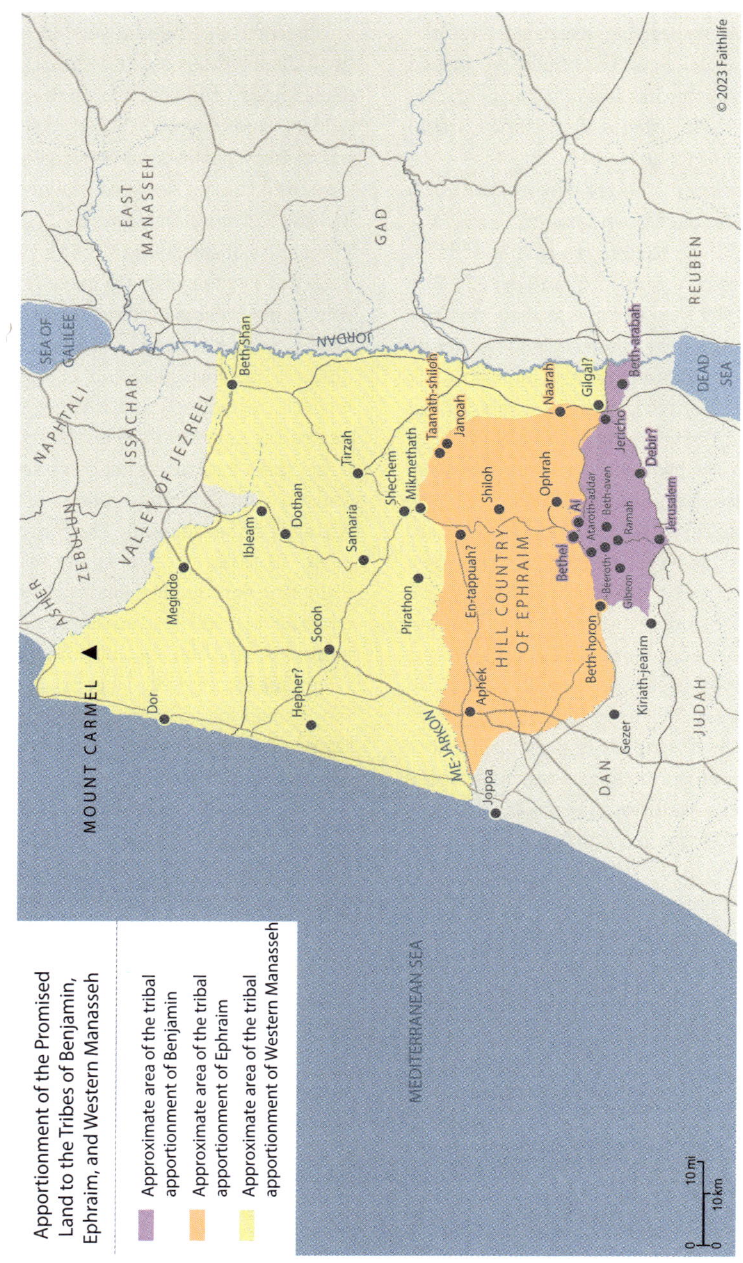

Kings (1 Kgs 15:27; 16:15, 17; [see also] 2 Chr 25:13) make clear that Israel/Ephraim possessed Upper/Lower Beth Horon and Gezer throughout their history, however, the exact delineation of the border in the Shephelah between Israel and Judah following the division of the kingdom in 931 BCE remains unclear" (McKinny, "Historical Geography," 141–42).

likewise sat on the border between Judah and Benjamin, another cause for textual elaboration and modern confusion.[41]

BENJAMIN

The territory of Benjamin is outlined in Josh 18:12–20. This diminutive but influential tribe sits *between* Judah and Joseph (i.e., Ephraim and west Manasseh) (18:11). Benjamin was Joseph's younger brother, the second son of the beloved Rachel, and the last son of Jacob. Significant for later biblical history, the Benjamite town of Jebus sat on the southern border shared with Judah. Neither tribe succeeded in permanently ousting the Jebusite population (Josh 15:63; Judg 1:21). This centralized and unconquered location made Jerusalem a fortuitous choice for the united monarchy's capital. Notice that its first capital also lay in Benjamin, at Gibeah of Saul. After the secession of the northern tribes, however, the proximity of Jerusalem to the southern border of the house of Joseph became a liability. This ultimately resulted in a proxy war for the territory of Benjamin, which likely concluded after Omri consolidated his authority over the northern tribes (1 Kgs 15–16).

JOSEPH

The house of Joseph was allotted the lands of Ephraim and west Manasseh as outlined in Josh 16–17. The title "house of Joseph" is relatively rare (ten times) but occurs throughout the biblical text (e.g., Gen 50:8; Josh 17:17; Judg 1:22; 1 Kgs 11:28; Zech 10:6). The town lists for these tribes are absent from Joshua. Notwithstanding, the house of Joseph contained numerous towns that were influential in the history of the Israelites.

For instance, by the time of the settlement period, Israel already had a close relationship with the city of Shechem (Gen 12:6; 34; 37:12). Joshua's covenant renewal ceremonies at Shechem reaffirmed this close connection (Josh 8:30–35; 24). Abimelek was also made king at Shechem (Judg 9:6). Moreover, Manasseh contained all three capitals of the Northern Kingdom: Shechem (1 Kgs 12:25), Tirzah (1 Kgs 15:33), and Samaria (1 Kgs 16:23–24).[42] Shiloh in Ephraim was also the location of the tabernacle during the period of the judges (Josh 18:1–1 Sam 14:3).

The hill country of Joseph begins in the mountainous (cenomanian limestone) terrain of Ephraim and fades into the gentler slopes of Manasseh (primarily eocene chalks and limestone).[43] Manasseh's shallow valleys retain pockets of rich, alluvial soil from the eroded limestone. The map below illustrates these changes in elevation. One important feature to notice is Wadi Farah (Nahal Tirza) which is the narrow intrusion in blue on the eastern side of Manasseh. This provided easy access from Joseph's

41. See, e.g., Josh 15:8//18:16 and Josh 15:63; Judg 1:8, 21. McKinny, "Historical Geography," 56–68.

42. The half-tribe of Manasseh also contained the capital of Saul's son Ish-Bosheth/-Baal: Mahanaim (2 Sam 2:8–9). The MT differentiates the Cisjordan tribe of Manasseh from its eastern counterpart by the designation "half-tribe" for the Manassites living in the Transjordan (Josh 1:12, *passim*).

43. Aharoni notes, "Mount Ephraim is a geographical expression nearly always associated with all of the central mountain region (Josh. 17.15; 20.7; 21.21; Judg. 7.24; 1 Sam. 1.1; 1 Kings 4.8)" (Yohanan Aharoni, *The Land of the Bible: A Historical Geography*, trans. Anson F. Rainey, rev. and enl. ed. [Philadelphia: Westminster, 1979], 210).

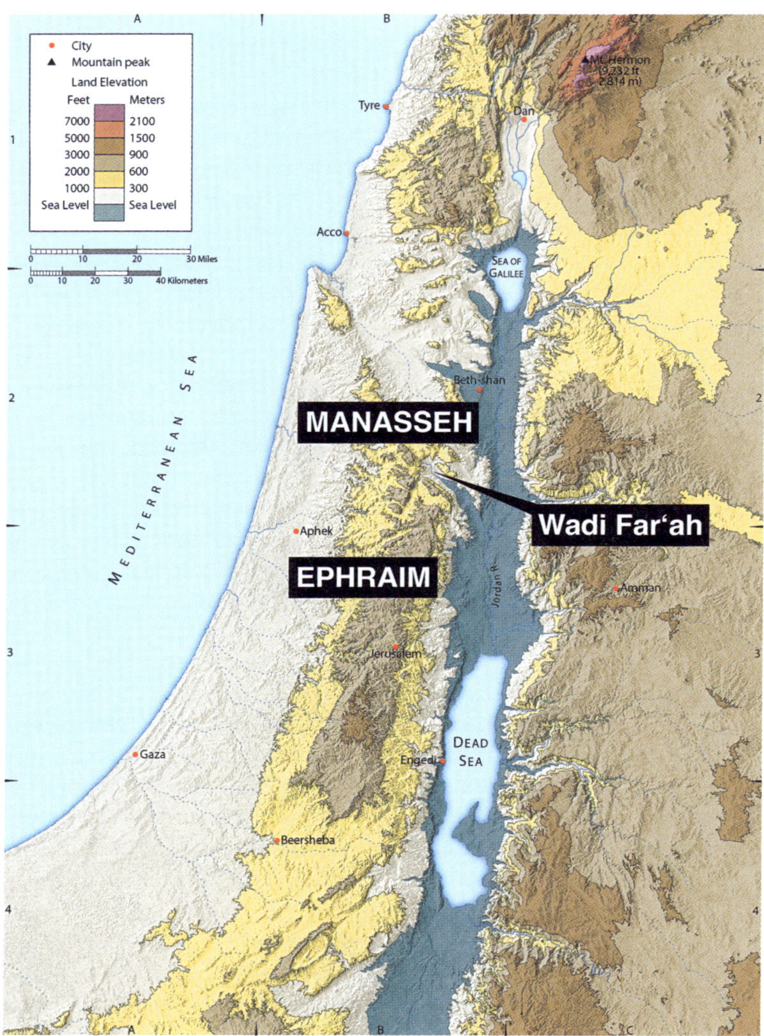

The Elevation of Palestine with Annotations

heartland to the Jordan River at the exact point where the fords of Adam assisted those crossing over to the Transjordan.[44]

The house of Joseph had a unique combination of fertile lands and a long tradition of socio-religious connection to its territory by the time of Israel's settlement period. It is hard not to associate these biblical texts and geographic realities with the modern archaeological evidence for a population explosion during the Iron Age I (see Josh 17:14). Surveys

44. Aharoni, *Land of the Bible*, 34.

suggest the settlements of the hill country of Joseph increase from approximately twelve thousand to thirty or forty thousand during this time period.[45] This increase does not correlate with exotic cultural artifacts but does display a distinctive pattern of new settlement features.[46] Joseph's conquest and allotment narratives from Joshua, again, are hard not to associate with this evidence.

ALLOTMENTS IN THE CANON

Looking beyond the book of Joshua, the allotments of Josh 14–17 play a pivotal role in the legitimation of later Judah and Israel. The bulk of the inheritance was claimed as promised through the military prowess of various Spirit-filled leaders such as Othniel, Deborah, Saul, and David (Judg 3–5; 1 Sam 11; 2 Sam 5; 8). Considering Israel's idolatry, God's provision of the land became more of an act of grace than a requirement of the covenant stipulations (Deut 9:5–6; 2 Kgs 17:7–23). Biblical authors offer little evidence of Israel's covenant faithfulness, and this is precisely the condition of Israel's possession of their allotments (Deut 4:1–31; 30:15–20). The alternative would be expulsion (Lev 26:33; Deut 28:36). Eventually, the allotments dissolved in the chaotic and fatal events of multiple exiles (Assyrian: 2 Kgs 15:29; 17:6; 18:11; Babylonian: 2 Kgs 24:12–16; 25:7). This concludes the primary story of Joshua's allotments. The Jewish exiles returned to a mere token of their inheritances. But hope springs eternal, as demonstrated by later messianic movements and the concept of a "heavenly" inheritance (1 Pet 1:4).

ALLOTMENTS TODAY

The biblical dimensions of the promised land have been expectantly applied numerous times in modern-day Israel, according to a number of studies by Rachel Havrelock. Israel's first prime minister, David Ben-Gurion, and his colleagues envisioned themselves quite explicitly as a new "Joshua generation" reacquiring their allotted territory.[47] Today, the entire central hill country is governed by modern Israel, with almost 900,000 inhabitants in Jerusalem and 3,250,000 inhabitants in the Palestinian West Bank, including approximately 750,000 Israeli settlers. Havrelock shows how the modern state of Israel viewed the Jordan River as their destiny from the outset, in contrast to the biblical dimensions of ancient Israel, which included lands on *both* sides of

45. See sources in next footnote and *MAB*, 127. Mittman's survey, cited in *MAB*, also finds a comparable increase for the Transjordan LBA–IAI transition.

46. See discussions in Israel Finkelstein, *The Archaeology of the Israelite Settlement* (Jerusalem: Israel Exploration Society, 1988); Finkelstein, "The Great Transformation: The 'Conquest' of the Highlands Frontiers and the Rise of the Territorial States," in *The Archaeology of Society in the Holy Land*, ed. Thomas E. Levy (New York: Facts on File, 1995), 349–65; Finkelstein and Nadav Na'aman, eds., *From Nomadism to Monarchy* (Jerusalem: Yad Izhak Ben-Zvi, 1994); Adam Zertal, "'To the Land of the Perizzites and the Giants': On the Israelite Settlement in the Hill Country of Manasseh," in *From Nomadism to Monarchy*, ed. Israel Finkelstein and Nadav Na'aman (Jerusalem: Yad Izhak Ben-Zvi, 1994), 47–69; Lawrence E. Stager, "Forging an Identity: The Emergence of Israel," in *The Oxford History of the Biblical World*, ed. Michael D. Coogan (Oxford: Oxford University Press, 1998), 123–75.

47. Rachel S. Havrelock, "The Joshua Generation: Conquest and the Promised Land," *Critical Research on Religion* 1.3 (2013): 308–26.

the Jordan—the vital lesson of Josh 22.[48] Havrelock notes that "the modern political configurations that rely on the Jordan as a border are discontinuous with prior geographic conceptions in which the Jordan River plays a connective rather than a divisive role."[49]

The history of Israel, the Jewish people, and even the Crusades demonstrate how later "canonical communities" were eager to apply the divine allotments of the book of Joshua to contemporary situations. Modern scholars and preachers of Joshua should take caution given its mixed history of interpretation and pay close attention to the stipulations of the biblical covenants that undergird the allotments (Josh 24:25–27).[50]

CONCLUSION

This overview of the biblical allotments of land to the tribal groups of Judah (with Simeon), Benjamin, Ephraim, and west Manasseh highlights the importance of biblical history and geography. These allotment lines winded their way around the physical and political realities of Canaan. Yet, the foundation for Israel's right to possess the land was grounded in the grace and faithfulness of God. In a tragic reversal, Israel's subsequent exile from the land would stem from her unfaithfulness to that same God. In the end, a hopeful theological picture is created of a God who desires every Israelite to know stability, provision, and even abundance for their families.

BIBLIOGRAPHY

Aharoni, Yohanan. *The Land of the Bible: A Historical Geography*. Translated by Anson F. Rainey. Rev. and enl. ed. Philadelphia: Westminster, 1979.

Antoun, Richard T. *Arab Village: A Social Structural Study of a Trans-Jordanian Peasant Community*. Bloomington, IN: Indiana University Press, 1972.

Boling, Robert G. *Joshua: A New Translation with Notes and Commentary*. AB. Garden City, NY: Doubleday, 1982.

Bradley, John J. "'Whitefellas Have to Learn about Country, It Is Not Just Land': How Landscape Becomes Country and Not an 'Imagined' Place." Pages 45–64 in *The Place of Landscape: Concepts, Contexts, Studies*. Edited by Jeff Malpas. Cambridge: MIT Press, 2011.

Brueggemann, Walter. *The Land: Place as Gift, Promise, and Challenge in Biblical Faith*. 2nd ed. Minneapolis: Fortress, 2002.

Carter, Paul. "Lips in Language and Space: Imaginary Places in James Dawson's Australian Aborigines (1881)." Pages 105–28 in *Spatiality and Symbolic Expression*. Edited by Bill Richardson. New York: Palgrave Macmillan, 2015.

Creangă, Ovidiu. "The Conquest of Memory in the Book of Joshua." Pages 168–79 in *The Oxford Handbook of Biblical Narrative*. Edited by Danna Nolan Fewell. Oxford: Oxford University Press, 2016.

---

48. Rachel S. Havrelock, *River Jordan: The Mythology of a Dividing Line* (Chicago: University of Chicago Press, 2011).

49. Rachel S. Havrelock, "The Jordan River in Ancient and Modern Maps," in *Art and Identity at the Water's Edge*, ed. Tricia Cusack (Burlington, VT: Ashgate, 2012), 108.

50. Consult reception history and other works listed in Thomas B. Dozeman, "The Book of Joshua in Recent Research," *Currents in Biblical Research* 15.3 (2017): 270–88.

Dozeman, Thomas B. "The Book of Joshua in Recent Research." *Currents in Biblical Research* 15.3 (2017): 270–88.

Faust, Avraham. "Doorway Orientation, Settlement Planning and Cosmology in Ancient Israel During Iron Age II." *Oxford Journal of Archaeology* 20.2 (2001): 129–54.

Finkelstein, Israel. *The Archaeology of the Israelite Settlement*. Jerusalem: Israel Exploration Society, 1988.

———. "The Great Transformation: The 'Conquest' of the Highlands Frontiers and the Rise of the Territorial States." Pages 349–65 in *The Archaeology of Society in the Holy Land*. Edited by Thomas Evan Levy. New York: Facts on File, 1995.

Finkelstein, Israel, and Nadav Na'aman, eds. *From Nomadism to Monarchy*. Jerusalem: Yad Izhak Ben-Zvi, 1994.

Fleener, Rob. "Lots." *LBD*. n.p.

Gosden, Chris, and Gary Lock. "Prehistoric Histories." *World Archaeology* 30.1 (1998): 2–12.

Halbwachs, Maurice. "Space and the Collective Memory." Pages 128–57 in *The Collective Memory*. Translated by Francis J. Ditter Jr. and Vida Yazdi Ditter. New York: Harper & Row, 1980.

Havrelock, Rachel S. "The Jordan River in Ancient and Modern Maps." Pages 107–22 in *Art and Identity at the Water's Edge*. Edited by Tricia Cusack. Burlington, VT: Ashgate, 2012.

———. "The Joshua Generation: Conquest and the Promised Land." *Critical Research on Religion* 1.3 (2013): 308–326.

———. *River Jordan: The Mythology of a Dividing Line*. Chicago: University of Chicago Press, 2011.

Hess, Richard S. "Asking Historical Questions of Joshua 13–19: Recent Discussion Concerning the Date of the Boundary Lists." Pages 191-206 in *Faith, Tradition, and History: Old Testament Historiography in Its Near Eastern Context*. Edited by Alan R. Millard, James K. Hoffmeier, and David W. Baker. Winona Lake, IN: Eisenbrauns, 1994.

———. *Joshua: An Introduction and Commentary*. TOTC. Downers Grove, IL: InterVarsity Press, 1996.

———. "Late Bronze Age and Biblical Boundary Descriptions of the West Semitic World." Pages 123–38 in *Ugarit and the Bible*. Edited by George J. Brooks, Adrian H. W. Curtis, and John F. Healey. Münster: Ugarit-Verlag, 1994.

Hess, Richard S., trans. "Abbael's Gift of Alalakh (*AT* 1)." *COS* 2.127:329.

———, trans. "Land Grant (*AT* 456)." *COS* 2.137:369–70.

Hoffmeier, James K. "What Is the Biblical Date for the Exodus? A Response to Bryant Wood." *JETS* 50.2 (2007): 225–47.

Kallai, Zecharia. *Historical Geography of the Bible: The Tribal Territories of Israel*. Jerusalem: Magnes, 1986.

Küchler, Susanne. "Landscape as Memory: The Mapping of Process and Its Representation in a Melanesian Society." Pages 85-106 in *Landscape: Politics and Perspectives*. Edited by Barbara Bender. Providence: Berg, 1993.

Laughlin, John. *Reading Joshua: A Historical-Critical, Archaeological Commentary*. Macon, GA: Smyth & Helwys, 2015.

McKinny, Chris. "A Historical Geography of the Administrative Division of Judah: The Town Lists of Judah and Benjamin in Joshua 15:21–62 and 18:21–28." PhD diss., Bar-Ilan University, 2017.

Millard, Alan R. "Cartography in the Ancient Near East." Pages 107–16 in *Cartography in Prehistoric, Ancient, and Medieval Europe and the Mediterranean*. Edited by John B. Harley and David Woodward. Chicago: University of Chicago Press, 1987.

Mitchell, Don. "Landscape." Pages 49–56 in *Cultural Geography: A Critical Dictionary of Key Concepts*. Edited by David Atkinson, Peter Jackson, David Sibley, and Neil Washbourne. New York: I. B. Tauris, 2005.

Na'aman, Nadav. *Borders and Districts in Biblical Historiography: Seven Studies in Biblical Geographic Lists*. Jerusalem: Simor, 1986.

Schreiner, Thomas R. *The King in His Beauty: A Biblical Theology of the Old and New Testaments*. Grand Rapids: Baker Academic, 2013.

Simkins, Ronald A. *Creator and Creation: Nature in the Worldview of Ancient Israel*. Peabody, MA: Hendrickson, 1994.

Sklar, Jay. *Leviticus: An Introduction and Commentary*. TOTC. Downers Grove, IL: InterVarsity, 2014.

Stager, Lawrence E. "Forging an Identity: The Emergence of Israel." Pages 123–75 in *The Oxford History of the Biblical World*. Edited by Michael D. Coogan. Oxford: Oxford University Press, 1998.

Weinfeld, Moshe. "The Covenant of Grant in the Old Testament and in the Ancient Near East." *Journal of the American Oriental Society* 90.2 (1970): 184–203.

Woudstra, Marten H. *The Book of Joshua*. NICOT. Grand Rapids: Eerdmans, 1981.

Wright, Christopher J. H. *God's People in God's Land: Family, Land, and Property in the Old Testament*. Grand Rapids: Eerdmans, 1990.

Wyatt, Nicholas. "The Vocabulary and Neurology of Orientation: The Ugaritic and Hebrew Evidence." Pages 351–80 in *Ugarit, Religion and Culture: Proceedings of the International Colloquium on Ugarit, Religion and Culture, Edinburgh, July 1994. Essays Presented in Honour of Professor John C. L. Gibson*. Edited by Nicolas Wyatt, Wilfred G. E. Watson, and Jeffery B. Lloyd. Münster: Ugarit-Verlag, 1996.

Younger, K. Lawson Jr. *Ancient Conquest Accounts: A Study in Ancient Near Eastern and Biblical History Writing*. Sheffield: JSOT, 1990.

———. "Rhetorical Structuring in the Joshua Conquest Narratives." Pages 3–32 in *Critical Issues in Early Israelite History*. Edited by Richard S. Hess, Gerald A. Klingbeil, and Paul J. Ray Jr. Winona Lake, IN: Eisenbrauns, 2008.

Zertal, Adam. "'To the Land of the Perizzites and the Giants': On the Israelite Settlement in the Hill Country of Manasseh." Pages 47–69 in *From Nomadism to Monarchy*. Edited by Israel Finkelstein and Nadav Na'aman. Jerusalem: Yad Izhak Ben-Zvi, 1994.

CHAPTER 14

APPORTIONMENT OF THE PROMISED LAND TO THE TRIBES OF JUDAH, BENJAMIN, EPHRAIM, WEST MANASSEH, AND SIMEON

Josh 15:1–19:9

Brian Donnelly-Lewis

KEY POINTS

- Each apportionment has a distinct geographic and social-spatial character which informs its unique history.
- Geographically, the southern apportionments span the length of the central hill country, a region of rugged mountains and narrow valley passes that provided protection from foreign incursions in the early period of Israelite history.

INTRODUCTION

The book of Joshua tells the story of the conquest and settlement of the people of Israel in the promised land. Between the miraculous victories and stirring religious speeches recorded in the book lay a large portion dedicated to more mundane matters, describing the apportionment of the regions of the promised land to each of the twelve tribes of Israel. These descriptions span several chapters, beginning in Josh 13 with two and a half tribes who chose to remain east of the Jordan: the half tribe of Manasseh, the Reubenites, and the Gadites. The apportionment continues through the end of Josh 19 with a description of the boundaries of the nine and a half tribes that settled to the west of the Jordan. The first five tribes apportioned land west of the Jordan are the southern tribes: Judah, Benjamin, Ephraim, west Manasseh, and Simeon. Each of these tribal apportionments is described slightly differently. On occasion the text gives some specific geographic boundaries in detail (see below on Judah, for example); in many other cases, however, the text gives us only a list of cities, which when located on a map give us the general region considered to be the apportionment of that tribe. Therefore, site identification is central to an accurate appraisal of the boundaries of each tribal apportionment.[1]

Each apportionment is given a distinct geographic region situated in between the other tribal apportionments. These characteristics inform their distinct history in unique ways. Factors like whether the geography hinders or encourages travel is important for the economic possibilities, political connections, and religious character of a tribe. Likewise, geography and topography influence climate, a force which can powerfully influence subsistence patterns that have a broad effect on the socio-cultural character of a tribal group. These, at times, subtle influences impact the stories of the Bible in different ways and provide a context for the history of biblical Israel, from initial settlement to exile and back again.

JUDAH (JOSH 15:1–63)

BORDER DESCRIPTION

The tribe of Judah is the first to receive an apportioned land west of the Jordan. The territory is described for the majority of Josh 15. The chapter is divided into three sections with only the first and third sections being of interest here. The first section (15:1–12) gives a detailed account of the boundaries of the allotment while an excursus, the second section (15:13–19), recounts the history of the region of Hebron, given to Caleb earlier in the narrative (14:6–15). The third section (15:20–63) consists of forty-three verses naming 132 cities and villages within the borders of the tribe of Judah. The length and specificity of the description of the borders of Judah far outstrips any other apportionment. The large city list is quite detailed, with cities divided into eleven districts, a fact which has led many to suggest that the list preserved here is augmented from an original administrative document that may have been updated over time.[2] This city list allows scholars to reconstruct the interior cities of Judah at an unprecedented scale, making this allotment extremely important for periods beyond the initial settlement of Israel.

The borders of Judah as described are expansive, stretching across the south of Israel from the Dead Sea in the east to the Mediterranean Sea in the west. Hence, only the northern and southern borders are in need of elucidation. The text's description proceeds in a counterclockwise fashion, beginning with the southern border. The description of the southern border presents several difficulties from the outset. For instance, the origin point, the "bay that faces southward" (15:2), lacks a clear identification and likely denotes some point at the southernmost edge of the Dead Sea.[3] As the border extends south, it is said to go by way of "Scorpion Pass" (NIV),

---

1. Site identifications are given only once. Questionable identifications are included when deemed appropriate and noted as such with a question mark. All identifications rely on Aharoni unless otherwise noted (Yohanan Aharoni, *The Land of the Bible: A Historical Geography*, trans. Anson F. Rainey [London: Burns & Oates, 1967]).

2. Aharoni, *Historical Geography*, 297–304.

3. All biblical quotations are from the Revised Standard Version (RSV) unless otherwise noted.

sometimes referred to as "the ascent of Akrabbim," a route sometimes associated with Naqb es-Sfar, though again difficult to identify.[4] Further south it arrives at Zin, which may be a city from which the wilderness of Zin derives its name or a short name for the wilderness itself.[5] While the trajectory is clear enough, only tentative boundaries can be set for this southeastern border because of the lack of certain identifications.

Moving from the ambiguous Zin, the border points become easier to identify. It goes south of Kadesh Barnea (Tell el-Qudeirat) by Hezron to Addar, where the identification requires some investigation.[6] In the book of Numbers, the account of the borders of Canaan refers to a "Hazar Addar," which may be a joint spelling of Hezron and Addar (Num 34:4). If this is the case, then we may accept Aharoni's suggestion that Hazar Addar, Karka, and Azmon represent a triplet that corresponds to three wells in the region of Kadesh Barnea, which may have marked ancient waystations through the desert. He argues that the border moves between these ancient wells, from Hazar Addar (Ain Qedeis), turning to Karka (Ain Qeseimeh), toward Azmon (Ain Muweilich). The border then follows along the "Brook of Egypt" (Wadi el-Arish) finally ending at the Mediterranean Sea.[7]

The text returns east where the eastern border is formed by the Dead Sea. North of the Dead Sea, at the mouth of the Jordan, the eastern border connects with the northern border, which is described in quite specific geographic detail (Josh 15:5–11). In six verses, the northern boundary weaves through cities, towns, hills, and valleys, giving texture to the complexity of tribal and cultural associations, and describing the sort of detailed boundaries that are seldom provided for the tribal apportionments. The description is sometimes presented from an almost intuitive perspective, making a few key identifications difficult. One example of such a reference is the "stone of Bohan the son of Reuben" (15:6), obviously referring to some well-known landmark in the region.[8] References like this should not take us by surprise. In the following sketch, it is important to remember that these boundaries were established from the perspective of tribal and cultural affiliation, recalling well-known routes through familiar ter-

4. Aharoni, *Historical Geography*, 63–65.

5. See Aharoni, *Historical Geography*, 63–65; Manfred Görg, "Akrabbim (Place)," *ABD* 1:141.

6. When available, I prefer to use the Arabic names for many sites instead of the modern Hebrew names, as the modern Hebrew names have, in many cases, been assigned after historical geographers have conjectured an identification with a biblical site. For instance, Tell el-Ifshar is modern Hebrew "Tel Hepher," despite its unlikely association with biblical Hepher (Josh 12:17, 1 Kgs 4:17). Nevertheless, some famous sites with a secure identification, such as Gezer (Tel Gezer), Dan (Tel Dan), Megiddo (Tel Megiddo), and Hazor (Tel Hazor), will be marked according to their modern Hebrew name.

7. Aharoni, *Historical Geography*, 65.

8. There has been some suggestion that the Hebrew name is preserved in the Arabic Hajar al-Usba. Though it may be a stretch, Charles Clermont-Ganneau argued long ago that a stone in the region strongly resembles a thumb and that the ridge upon which it rests rises out of the Rift Valley as a natural horizon after descending from the Wadi ed-Dabr (Clermont-Ganneau, *Archaeological Researches in Palestine* [London: Palestinian Exploration Fund, 1896], 2:10–14).

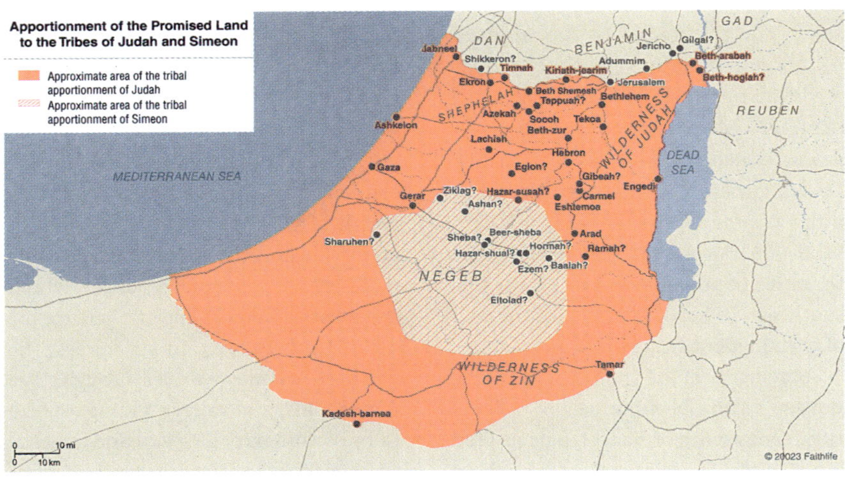

rain. As such, the boundaries of mental geography often assume familiarity with the landscape and an association between places, routes, and people, perspectives we must consider in order to fully appreciate these boundaries.

The border begins in the Rift Valley with two reasonably identifiable sites, Beth Hoglah (Ain Hajla) and Beth Arabah (Ain el-Gharabeh). Yet, as it approaches the ascent from the Rift Valley floor, we encounter some difficulties. Beyond the "stone of Bohan," the text states that the border goes up to Debir from the Valley of Achor. The Valley of Achor seems to refer to the el-Buqeia Valley, yet scholars have noted that this valley is too far south to be the northern boundary.[9] Debir is to be identified as the Wadi ed-Dabr at the northern edge of the el-Buqeia Valley.[10] The phrase "Debir from the Valley of Achor" could perhaps be resolved by an emendation, removing the preposition and reading "Debir of the Valley of Achor," where the valley specifies the Debir (Wadi ed-Dabr) in contrast to Debir (Khirbet Rabud) in the hill country (15:15). Whatever the case may be, the border extends northward looking toward Gilgal, which is in view of the pass of Adummim south of the gorge (Wadi Qilt). Following a familiar and well-traveled route from Jericho (Tel Jericho) to Jerusalem, the boundary passes En Shemesh (Ain el-Hod) coming out at En Rogel (Bir Ayyub) just south of Jerusalem. The border traces around Jerusalem, straddling the hills west of the Hinnom Valley and extends to Baalah, specified as Kiriath Jearim (Tell Deir el-Azir), weaving through various mountains out to the edge of the hill country at Beth Shemesh (Tell er-Rumeileh). From this point the border follows the Sorek Valley toward the coast, past Timnah (Tell Batashi), Shikkeron (Tell el-Ful), and Jabneel (Yebna), meeting the Mediterranean Sea, which is the whole of the western boundary.

9. Carolyn J. Pressler, "Achor (Place)," *ABD* 1:56.

10. Menashe Har-el, "The Route of Salt, Sugar and Balsam Caravans in the Judean Desert," *GeoJournal* 2.6 (1978): 554.

Shephelah and the Hill Country of Judah East of Lachish

GEOGRAPHICAL ANALYSIS

The apportionment to Judah is geographically diverse, extending from the Dead Sea in the east, across the barren Judean wilderness, through the Judean hill country, over the Shephelah, and, at least from the perspective of Joshua, controlling the coastal plain all the way to the Mediterranean. This wide apportionment is appropriately understood as having the ideal boundaries. The Israelites were never able to capture much of the lowlands, especially the coastal plain as recounted in the book of Judges: "they took possession of the hill country, but they were unable to drive the people from the plains, because they had chariots fitted with iron" (Judg 1:19 NIV). For much of early biblical history, the Judeans were pressured by the Philistines on the coastal plain, with the Shephelah being conceptualized as a boundary area by some of the earliest settlement traditions (e.g., 13:1–16:31). In contrast to this ideal, the reality of Israelite settlement and the later history of the united and divided monarchies is reflected in the city list, which is largely restricted to the central hill country and the Shephelah. A large portion of cities named in this chapter, including the three capitals of the united monarchy—Gibeah, Hebron, and Jerusalem—are identified by the text as being "in the hill country," the heartland of biblical history.

Outside of the hill country, Judah's unconquered regions and towns enjoyed incredible access to international trade. In the western area of the apportionment, the coastal plain, the major north-south international highway serviced merchants and armies marching to and from the major empires of the day. Home to major port cities like Ashkelon that provided access to trade opportunities, the coastal plain drew trade from the hinterlands of Judah, but major empires also had a vested interest in controlling and protecting the exchange. In a similar fashion, the inclusion of sites far south in the allotment of Judah should have provided the tribe access to the spice route from the Arabian Peninsula, but any influence or control was likely sporadic and tenuous due to foreign influence. Unable to extend west or south because of conflict with foreign peoples and powers, the Israelite settlement in the highlands became a haven. The geography of Judah provided protection from hostile powers both on the east, with the Judean wilderness and the Dead Sea, and on the west, with the only corridors of entry being through the Shephelah into the rugged hinterland. This protective aspect was important for ancient Israelite settlers and mirrored the protection they received from God; a psalmist states, "as the mountains surround Jerusalem, so the LORD surrounds his people both now and forevermore" (Ps 125:2 NIV). While east-west travel was restricted by the topography, the central ridge route running on the central hill country watershed connected Judah, Benjamin, Ephraim, and Manasseh, allowing for some intertribal connectivity.

EPHRAIM (JOSH 16:1–10)

BORDER DESCRIPTION

The second apportionment was given to the tribe of Ephraim as a subset of the apportionment of the people of Joseph. The southern boundary of the people of Joseph is given in Josh 16:1–3, before the boundaries of Ephraim alone is described in 16:5–10. The boundaries are not described in as much detail as those of Judah previously, but identifiable border sites taken in conjunction with the other apportionments—Benjamin, Manasseh, and Dan—allow firm boundaries to be drawn.

The boundary's description begins with medial border towns in the north and the south, tracing outward from each. The southern border point must be taken in conjunction with the broad border information provided in the beginning of the chapter (16:1–3), which defines the border at the southeastern edge. Taken together we may trace the border from the southeast. The border ascends north from Jericho along a familiar ridge route into the interior of Ephraim toward the town of Bethel (EP 914?).[11] From Bethel, it runs to Ataroth Addar, an unknown site somewhere in the region of Bethel; moving westward on the ridge route to Upper Beth Horon (Beit Ur el-Foqa) and Lower Beth-Horon (Beit Ur et-Tahta); turning south through the Aijalon Valley around Gezer, which remained unconquered; and continuing out to the Mediterranean.[12] Narratively, this description excludes the later apportionment to Dan that will hem in the western border of Ephraim

11. EP 914 is the designation of a survey site that has recently been argued as the location of Bethel. For a new analysis and description of the boundary, see Aharon Tavger, "Some Notes On the Southern Boundary of the Territory of Ephraim," *Moreshet Israel* 12 (2015): 176–95 [Hebrew]; for the location of Bethel, see both Aharon Tavger, "E.P. 914 East of Beitin and the Location of the Ancient Cult Site of Bethel," *In the Highland's Depth: Ephraim Range and Binyamin Research Study* 5 (2015): 49–69 [Hebrew with English abstract (pgs. 34*-35*)], and an evaluation of the options in Oded Lipschits, "Bethel Revisited," in *Rethinking Israel: Studies in the History and Archaeological of Ancient Israel in Honor of Israel Finkelstein*, ed. Oded Lipschits, Yuval Gadot, and Matthew J. Adams (University Park, PA: Eisenbrauns, 2017), 233–46.

12. See discussion of the possible locations of Ataroth Addar in Zecharia Kallai, *Historical Geography of the Bible: The Tribal Territories of Israel* (Leiden: Brill, 1986), 131–32.

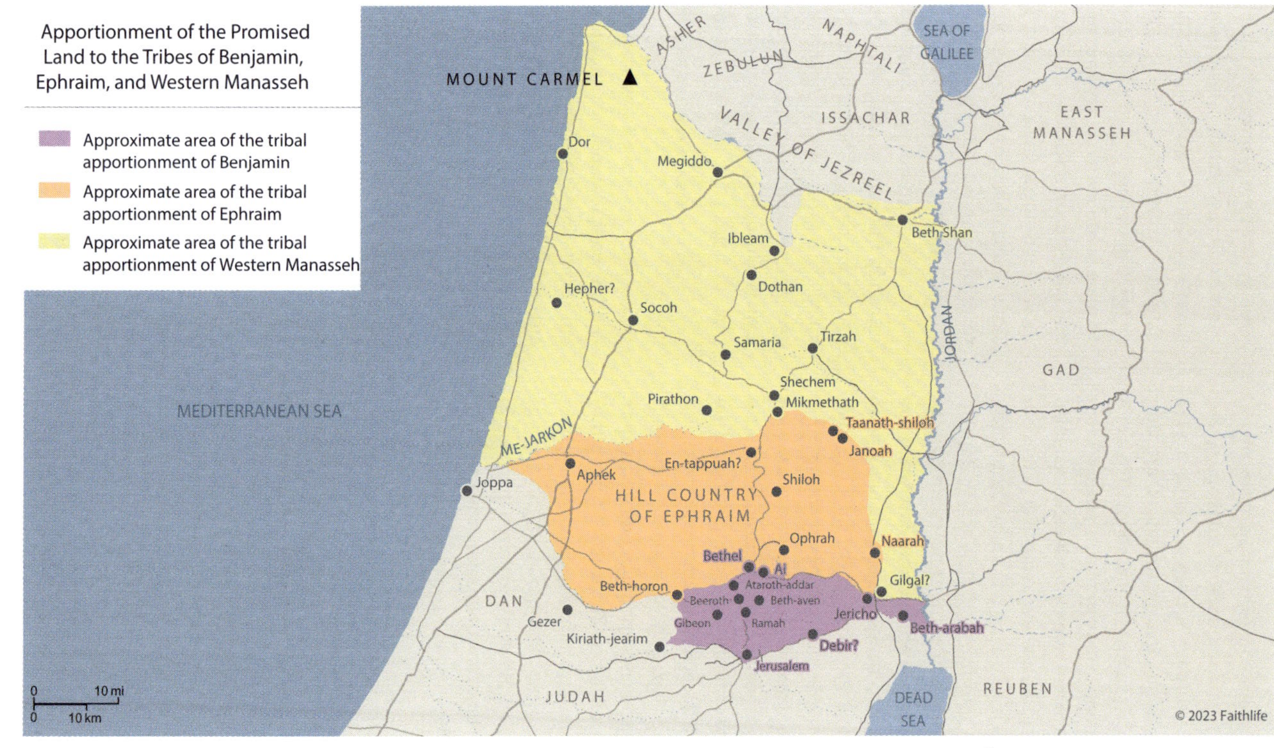

Apportionment of the Promised Land to the Tribes of Benjamin, Ephraim, and Western Manasseh

on the coastal plain, blocking access to the Mediterranean coast. In the north, the border site of Mikmethath (Khirbet Makhneh el-Foqa?) is identified as a key site, from which point the northeastern border is described. The border moves from Mikmethath to the northeast edge around Taanath Shiloh (Khirbet Tana el-Foqa), passing several sites, meeting Naarah (Tell el-Jisr) before touching Jericho and ending in the Jordan Valley. The description returns north, this time identifying another border site exclusively in the apportionment to Ephraim (17:8), Tappuah (Sheikh Abu Zarad). From this site, the border traces westward along the Kanah Valley and out to the sea via the Yarkon River, which will later mark the division between west Manasseh and the tribe of Dan on the coast. Unlike Judah, the Ephraimite apportionment is not supplemented with a city list.

GEOGRAPHICAL ANALYSIS

Like Judah before it, Ephraim was restricted to the central hill country. The mountainous terrain restricted east-west travel while the central ridge route which passed through Judah continued its march northward through Ephraim. The Ephraimite hill country is even more secluded than that of Judah. Rugged terrain to the east and west of the central ridge provides even fewer traversable routes than other apportionments, with a few routes emanating from Aphek and Joppa in the east and only one true highway rising out of the Jordan Rift Valley leading to Shiloh.[13] Because of its restrictive nature, the book of Judges calls the Ephraimite hill country the "remote" interior of Ephraim (Judg 19:1). In addition, the location of Shiloh (where a yearly feast of the Lord was held) is given in detail from the perspective of a traveler, stating, "Shiloh, which lies north of Bethel, east of the road that goes from Bethel to Shechem [the central ridge route], and south of Lebonah" (21:19 NIV). These passages give an inside perspective as to how ancient Israelites perceived life in and travel through the mountainous, insular hills of the tribal apportionment of Ephraim.

WEST MANASSEH (JOSH 17:1–18)

BORDER DESCRIPTION

The third apportionment is given to one of the half-tribes of Manasseh, west of the Jordan. The text begins with the historical context of the apportionment to Manasseh, recounting the negotiation with Moses for lands both east and west of the Jordan (Josh 17:1–6). In 17:7–13, the text proceeds to describe the territory, though only the southwestern border is given a detailed account. The description provides only broad points of reference. It begins with the north-south boundary areas, the tribe of Asher in the north and the town of Mikmethath in the south. The southern boundary extends toward Tappuah in the apportionment of Ephraim, but, unlike Mikmethath, Tappuah is an Ephraimite town and only its surrounding region is given to Manasseh. The only detailed border is the southwestern border, though even this detailed border does little more than follow the northern border of Ephraim along the Kanah Valley by the Yarkon River and to the Mediterranean Sea. While some geographic detail is given for the southwestern border, the text dis-

13. David A. Dorsey, *The Roads and Highways of Ancient Israel* (Eugene, OR: Wipf & Stock, 1991), 136–38.

Aerial View of Tel Megiddo

tinguishes the northern border only on the basis of tribe, abutting the tribes of Asher and Issachar in the Jezreel Valley. What this means geographically is that the border must have reached just north of the Carmel ridge in the west and continued, moving eastward, into the Jezreel Valley. Here the border passes along the southern edge of the Jezreel, touching Asher, Zebulun, and Isaachar, and continuing down the Harod Valley, encompassing Beth Shan (Tel Bet Shean) at the far eastern end until it reaches the Jordan River that forms a natural eastern boundary.

GEOGRAPHICAL ANALYSIS

The apportionment to west Manasseh intersects with the Jezreel Valley in the north, touches the Jordan Rift Valley in the east, and the Mediterranean Sea in the west. This extensive apportionment encompasses the northmost reaches of the rugged mountainous region of the central hill country. In this region, the central ridge route (the northern stretch of the regional highway) weaves its way past major connection points like Shechem, eventually opening into the Jezreel Valley, getting greater access to regional and international exchange than its southerly neighbors. The expanse of the Jezreel Valley gave ease of travel to the coast, connecting with Phoenician and eastern Mediterranean trade, as well as the international highway running past Galilee to Damascus. Interaction with these great powers in the north would significantly impact the history of the northern kingdom of Israel, as the apportionment of west Manasseh would become home to the Northern Kingdom's capital cities: Shechem, Tirzah, and Samaria. These sites were strategically located in the central hill country, each being a node through which routes east-

Aerial View of Gibeon and the Central Benjaminite Plateau

west and north-south would travel.[14] The location of Manasseh allowed the later Northern Kingdom to take advantage of the safety and security of the hill country while not being as secluded as the other southern apportionments. This led to both greater interconnectivity with foreign powers, as well as greater threat of invasion or influence.

In addition, the apportionment to west Manasseh included the Carmel ridge, home to several paths on the major international coastal highway, most notably the route cutting through the ridge next to the ancient and powerful city of Megiddo. This site, like many other ancient sites in this region, is mentioned as a city-state in the Late Bronze Age Amarna letters.[15] Though their power waned in the absence of overt Egyptian control in the Levant, the Bible explains that many of these cities remained unconquered by the early Israelites (Josh 17: 11–13; Judg 1:27–28). Early on, the low-lying regions would prove elusive because of the strength of Canaanite control of these fortified cities; the northern Israelite kings would later be able to seize control of the lowland cities and thus, the routes running through them, which in turn was a powerful asset in asserting economic, political, and military control.

14. Dorsey, *Roads and Highways*, 179–80.

15. The Amarna letters are a collection of diplomatic correspondences written in cuneiform and discovered at the site of Tell el-Amarna in Egypt, the ancient capital of Akhenaten during the fourteenth century BC. These letters preserve the correspondences of the Egyptian Pharaoh with various kingdoms and city-states around the Near East, including several ancient cities from modern day Israel-Palestine. See Anson F. Rainey and R. Steven Notley, *The Sacred Bridge: Carta's Atlas of the Biblical World* (Jerusalem: Carta, 2006), particularly "The Amarna Age," 71–90. For a translation of these letters, see Anson F. Rainey, *The El-Amarna Correspondence*, ed. William M. Schniedewind, vol. 1 (Leiden: Brill, 2015).

BENJAMIN (JOSH 18:11–28)

BORDER DESCRIPTION

After the first three apportionments had been distributed by lots, the people of Israel came to Shiloh and cast lots again, this time to apportion the remainder of the land. The first lot fell to Benjamin. The tribe of Benjamin took the land between Judah in the south and Ephraim in the north. Consequently, Benjamin's boundaries can be traced along the same lines, but on occasion the text gives greater specificity. The northern border begins at the Jordan River, travelling a familiar line from the rift valley into the hill country ending at the wilderness of Beth Aven.[16] It continues to Bethel and Ataroth Addar before turning southward toward Kiriath Jearim in the territory of Judah. Like the boundary of Judah before it, though in reverse order, it passes through the hill country near Jerusalem, coming out in the Jordan Valley and returning to the mouth of the Jordan River at the Dead Sea.

GEOGRAPHICAL ANALYSIS

Surrounded by Israelite tribes on the north and south, the apportionment to Benjamin covered a relatively small portion of land which was, nevertheless, strategically valuable. Several major inland routes pass into hill country here, coming from both east and west.[17] The border itself traces by major routes to the east, coming up into the hill country from Jericho, which was a node for several important routes. On the west, the apportionment of Benjamin contains an important portion of the route from Gezer into the hill country. During the reign of Solomon, it would seem

16. The site of Beth Aven is uncertain, furthermore the range of the "wilderness of Beth Aven" makes the association more ambiguous. A recent evaluation of the location suggests Khirbet Nisieh (see Chris McKinny, "Dividing the Spoil: A Discussion of the Identification of Beth-Aven, Emek-Keziz, and Zemaraim in the Territory of Benjamin," *In the Highland's Depth* 5 [2015]: *10–*32).

17. See Dorsey, *Roads and Highways*, 181–207.

Aerial View of the Negev East of Beersheba

that he understood the strategic importance of the Benjaminite territory, as he fortified cities along the western route from the coastal plain to the central hill country (1 Kgs 9:17). After the end of his reign, this route would be exploited by Pharaoh Shishak (c. 924 BC).[18] His devastating campaign is a roadmap for foreign incursions into the central hill country. Shishak first destroyed Gezer at the very edge of the hill country. This site protected the two major routes from the coast to the central Benjamin plateau. The southern route moved past Aijalon through the Aijalon Valley to Kiriath Jearim. The northern route again moved through the Aijalon Valley, only this time, northward to Beth Horon. From here, the Beth Horon ridge route opened access to Gibeon in the central Benjamin plateau. Pharaoh Shishak destroyed all of these cities before moving up the central ridge route to wreak even more havoc and subject the northern kingdom of Israel to Egyptian imperial power.

SIMEON (JOSH 19:1–9)

BORDER DESCRIPTION

The second lot at Shiloh fell to Simeon. The apportionment of Simeon is defined only by a city list (Josh 19:2–8) and the comment that the inheritance lay "within the territory of Judah" (19:1 NIV). Almost all of the cities in Simeon's city list were previously mentioned in the extensive city list of Judah. These sites encompass the region of the biblical Negev, penetrat-

18. For what follows, see Aharoni, *Historical Geography*, 283–90.

ing the southern foothills of Judah, and parts of the Shephelah. Since it lacks a border description, its borders must be discerned on the basis of the identification of these sites, making these borders tentative at best. In the west, the apportionment must have stretched out of the Negev into the coastal plain, as is suggested by the inclusion of the sites of Ziklag (Tell esh-Shariah?) and Sharuhen (Tell el-Farah South?). No sites in either Judah or Simeon are mentioned between these coastal sites and the core of Simeon was in the biblical Negev. Therefore, we only have the broadest sense of the demarcations here. The northern extent is a little more complex. It seems that Beth Markaboth in the city list should be equated with Madmannah (Khirbet Tatrit?) due to the association between the Joshua account and the later account of Chronicles (1 Chr 4:24–33, especially 31).[19] Meanwhile, the sites of Debir (Khirbet Rabud) and Jattir (Khirbet Attir) lay in Judean territory, perhaps making Madmannah the furthest point north in the Judean foothills. If Aharoni's suggestion that Ramah of the Negev should be identified with Horvat Uza, then the border of Simeon in the east extended to the edge of the eastern Negev.[20] The southern extent is unfortunately unknown. As described above, the border of Judah pushes far into the south, to Kadesh Barnea, therefore Simeon's territory was completely subsumed by the Judean apportionment, centered around the Beersheba Valley and the Negev (see the map of the tribal allotment of Judah and Simeon).

GEOGRAPHICAL ANALYSIS

During the early settlement period, the tribe of Simeon was likely the southernmost tribe as the Judean apportionment was ideal and difficult to control outside of the central hill country. Being the southernmost tribe, the apportionment of Simeon was located in the arid Beersheba Valley and was home to a culturally unique tribe that maintained its tribal affiliation throughout the history of Israel. The cultural continuity is evidenced during the time of Hezekiah (1 Chr 4:24–43), where it is mentioned that the Simeonites are a shepherding people know for their flocks. The cultural and ecological realities inform one another, as the arid desert of the Beersheba Valley receives only ten inches (25 cm) of rain each year.[21] The conservative nature of agro-pastoralist life in the biblical Negev likely also helped Simeon retain their unique cultural identity until late in the history of the Judean monarchy.

CONCLUSION

The southern apportionments enjoy a primary place in Israelite history. Being the central homeland for the united monarchy and later the kingdoms of Israel and Judah, many of the Bible's most memorable stories play out on the stage set in these chapters of Joshua. Though from a glance at a map, the hill country appears uniform, this region of the land of ancient Israel, from north to south, is complex and unique, giving a beauty of depth and character to the tribes of ancient Israel that can only be under-

19. Nadav Na'aman "The Inheritance of the Sons of Simeon," *ZDPV* 96 (1980): 136–52.

20. Kallai disputes this suggestion (Kallai, *Historical Geography*, 359–60). See also Na'aman, "Inheritance."

21. Carl G. Rassmussen, *Zondervan Atlas of the Bible* (Grand Rapids: Zondervan, 2010), 114.

stood through an intimate knowledge of the physical landscape.

BIBLIOGRAPHY

Aharoni, Yohanan. *The Land of the Bible: A Historical Geography*. Translated by Anson F. Rainey. London: Burns & Oates, 1967.

Clermont-Ganneau, Charles. *Archaeological Researches in Palestine*. Vol. 2. London: Palestinian Exploration Fund, 1896.

Dorsey, David A. *The Roads and Highways of Ancient Israel*. Eugene, OR: Wipf & Stock, 1991.

Görg, Manfred. "Akrabbim (Place)." *ABD* 1:141.

Har-el, Menashe. "The Route of Salt, Sugar and Balsam Caravans in the Judean Desert," *GeoJournal* 2.6 (1978): 549–56.

Kallai, Zecharia. *Historical Geography of the Bible: The Tribal Territories of Israel*. Leiden: Brill, 1986.

Lipschits, Oded. "Bethel Revisited." Pages 233–46 in *Rethinking Israel: Studies in the History and Archaeological of Ancient Israel in Honor of Israel Finkelstein*. Edited by Oded Lipschits, Yuval Gadot, and Matthew J. Adams. University Park, PA: Eisenbrauns, 2017.

McKinny, Chris. "Dividing the Spoil: A Discussion of the Identification of Beth-Aven, Emek-Keziz, and Zemaraim in the Territory of Benjamin." *In the Highland's Depth* 5 (2015): *10–*32.

Na'aman, Nadav. "The Inheritance of the Sons of Simeon." *ZDPV* 96 (1980): 136–52.

Pressler, Carolyn J. "Achor (Place)." *ABD* 1:56.

Rainey, Anson F. *The El-Amarna Correspondence*. Edited William M. Schniedewind. Vol 1. Leiden: Brill, 2015.

Rainey, Anson F., and R. Steven Notley. *The Sacred Bridge: Carta's Atlas of the Biblical World*. Jerusalem: Carta, 2006.

Rassmussen, Carl G. *Zondervan Atlas of the Bible*. Grand Rapids: Zondervan, 2010.

Tavger, Aharon. "E.P. 914 East of Beitin and the Location of the Ancient Cult Site of Bethel." *In the Highland's Depth: Ephraim Range and Binyamin Research Study* 5 (2015): 49–69. [Hebrew with English abstract (pgs. 34*–35*)]

———. "Some Notes on the Southern Boundary of the Territory of Ephraim." *Moreshet Israel* 12 (2015): 176–95. [Hebrew]

CHAPTER 15

THE GEOGRAPHY OF THE CAMPAIGN OF PHARAOH MERENPTAH AND ITS RELATION TO EARLY ISRAEL

Josh 15:9; 18:15

Michael G. Hasel

KEY POINTS

- Merenptah's reference to Israel is central to all major studies on the origin of early Israel.
- The geographical designations are largely agreed upon with some debate and discussion about Pa-Canaan and Yenoam. The location of these sites has influenced the suggested location of Israel.
- The entities and their position in the final hymnic-poetic unit are the key to Israel's location within the territory of Canaan/Kharu, and Merenptah's Israel is to be located by following standard conventions of Egyptian campaign accounts.

INTRODUCTION

Pharaoh Merenptah's campaign continues to be central to recent studies on the origin of Israel, because it is the first reference to Israel outside the Bible.[1] Although the Egyptian campaign is not mentioned specifically in the Bible, some suggest a vague reference to Merenptah

1. Mer-en-ptah, "beloved of Ptah" is the birth name of Ramesses II's thirteenth son who succeeded him to the throne in 1213 BC and reigned for nearly ten years. On his throne name and titulary, see Jürgen von Beckerath, *Handbuch der ägyptischen Königsnamen* (München: Deutscher Kunstverlag, 1984), 239; *RITANC* 4:1. His name is also spelled "Merneptah" in the literature.

Statue of Pharaoh Merenptah at the Egyptian Museum in Cairo

(r. 1213–1203 BC) may be contained in the geographical designation "waters of Nephtoah" in Josh 15:9; 18:15. The date of the campaign implies that Israel was already located in the land of Canaan by Merenptah's Year 5, or 1209/08 BC, and so the exodus would have occurred sometime before this event. Every account of Israel's history must, therefore, relate this historical event chronologically to the exodus, conquest, and period of the judges. The campaign is documented in four Egyptian monuments: (1) the famous Merenptah or "Israel" stela in the Egyptian Museum, dated to Year 5 of Merenptah's reign (Cairo stela); (2) the duplicate, more fragmentary stela inscribed at Karnak on the inner face of the east wall of the "Cour de la Cachette" (Karnak stela); (3) the reliefs on the west wall of the "Cour de la Cachette" in Karnak[2]; and (4) and the Amada stela referring to Merenptah as "the plunderer of Gezer."[3] This essay

2. Peter J. Brand definitively demonstrated these reliefs to be that of Merenptah, later usurped by Seti II. Brand, "Usurped Cartouches of Merenptah at Karnak and Luxor," in *Causing His Name to Live: Studies in Egyptian Epigraphy and History in Memory of William J. Murnane*, ed. Peter J. Brand and Louise Cooper (Leiden: Brill, 2009), 29–48; Brand, "The Date of the War Scenes at Karnak and the History of the Late Nineteenth Dynasty," in *Ramesside Studies in Honour of K. A. Kitchen*, ed. Mark Collier and Steven Snape (Bolton: Rutherford, 2011), 51–84.

3. Michael G. Hasel, "*Israel* in the Merneptah Stela." *BASOR* 296 (1994): 45–61; Hasel, *Domination and Resistance: Egyptian Military Activity in the Southern Levant, 1300–1185 B.C.* (Leiden: Brill, 1998), 260–71; Hasel, "Merenptah's Reference to Israel: Critical Issues for the

Detail of the Merenptah Stela Discovered in 1896 by Sir William Flinders Petrie

will examine the geography of the campaign in order to ascertain the location of Merenptah's Israel. The approach will be to focus on the immediate context of the sources themselves beginning with the structure of the final hymnic-poetic unit in the Merenptah Stela, then moving to the identification of the specific entities mentioned and/or depicted from both historical and archaeological sources, and finally concluding with a proposal for identifying the geographical route of Merenptah's campaign.

THE DEFINITION OF PLACE AND PEOPLE NAMES IN MERENPTAH'S CAMPAIGN

The geography of Merenptah's campaign is dependent on a careful analysis and definition of the names found in the final hymnic-poetic unit. Six toponyms are provided in Merenptah's records concerning his Asiatic campaign: Pa-Canaan, Ashkelon, Gezer, Yenoam, Israel, and Kharu. The designation of each impacts the conclusions of the whole and so we must begin with the individual entities in their order before moving to the larger context. The text with its proposed structure is presented below.

PA-CANAAN

The campaign against Israel begins with the place name Pa-Canaan. The name Canaan or ethnic designation Canaanite is found a total of sixteen times in Egyptian texts, thirteen of which are preserved from the New Kingdom.[4] The most frequent translation of the place name Pa-Canaan is simply "the territory Canaan," or "the Canaan." Others have interpreted this toponym specifically as

Origin of Israel," in *Critical Issues in Early Israelite History*, ed. Richard S. Hess, Gerald A. Klingbeil, and Paul J. Ray, Jr. (Winona Lake, IN: Eisenbrauns, 2008), 47–59.

4. Manfred Görg, "Der Name 'Kanaan' in ägyptische Wiedergabe," *Biblische Notizen* 18 (1982): 26–27. Shmuel Ahituv, *Canaanite Toponyms in Ancient Egyptian Documents* (Jerusalem: Magnes, 1984), 83–85.

the city of Gaza and not a region or territory.[5] So which is it—the city of Gaza or the land of Canaan? The implications are wide-ranging. It would mean that all occurrences of the name Pa-Canaan in narrative contexts of the Nineteenth and Twentieth Dynasties would need to be read "Gaza," for they all are written the same way. A careful analysis of all other texts and reliefs from the reigns of Seti I (1290–1279 BC) and Ramesses II (1279–1213 BC) indicate that Pa-Canaan should be understood as a reference to "the land of Canaan," as these few examples indicate.[6]

In Papyrus Anastasi I, dated to the Ramesside period (1290–1152 BC), this exact extended reading is found after a long discussion of place names within the same territory during the early reign of Ramesses II, son of Seti I: "I have described to you the hill countries of the northern reaches of the land of the Canaan."[7] The scribe is chastising his apprentice for his lack of knowledge of these lands and their many cities, including Hazor, Akko, Shechem, Rehob, Beth Shan, and Joppa. In this passage, Pa-Canaan is clearly defined as "the land of the Canaan," a slight rephrasing of what Seti I's scribe may have meant at Karnak. It is highly significant that only a few lines later the writer asks: "How many miles march is it in going to Gaza?"[8] Here Gaza is written out syllabically and not as Pa-Canaan. Gaza is a city not a land or territory. Thus, Papyrus Anastasi I indicates that there is a distinct differentiation between the land of Pa-Canaan (27:1) and the city of Gaza at the end of the Ways of Horus (the military road leading from Egypt to Canaan, referred to as the "Way of the Philistines" in the Pentateuch) (27:8), which is written syllabically as it has been since the reign of Thutmose III.[9] Indeed, Pa-Canaan followed by a list of place names is also the contextual usage

5. Gardiner insisted that there is "sufficient evidence to show that the region designated by the Egyptians as 'Canaan,' 'the Canaan,' was the maritime plain" that is a territory not a city (Alan H. Gardiner, "The Ancient Military Road Between Egypt and Palestine," *Journal of Egyptian Archaeology* 6 [1920]: 100).

6. For full references, see Michael G. Hasel, "Pa-Canaan in the Egyptian New Kingdom: Canaan or Gaza?," *Journal of Ancient Egyptian Connections* 1 (2009): 8–17.

7. Papyrus Anastasi I:27,1; Text: Alan H. Gardiner, *Egyptian Hieratic Texts*. Series 1: *Literary Texts of the New Kingdom*. Part 1. *The Papyrus Anastasi I and the Papyrus Loller together with the Parallel Texts* (Leipzig: Hinrichs, 1911); Hans-Werner Fischer–Elfert, *Die Satirische Streitschrift des Papyrus Anastasi I: Textzusammenstellung* (Wiesbaden: Harrassowitz, 1983), 150. The widely cited article in favor of the reading Gaza for Pa-Canaan by Katzenstein, did not properly reproduce the full reading of this passage of Papyrus Anastasi I. H. Jacob Katzenstein, "Gaza in Egyptian Texts of the New Kingdom," *Journal of the American Oriental Society* 102 (1982): 111–13.

8. Papyrus Anastasi I:27,8; Fischer-Elfert, *Die Satirische Streitschrift*, 153; Edward F. Wente, trans., *Letters from Ancient Egypt*, ed. Edmund S. Meltzer (Atlanta: Scholars, 1990), 109.

9. Wolfgang Helck, *Urkunden der 18. Dynastie*, vol. 4 (Leipzig: Hinrichs, 1958), 648:10–11. References to Gaza occur once in the annals of Thutmose III; once in Papyrus Anastasi I (written defectively with a "q" instead of a "g"; Papyrus Anastasi I:27,8); twice in Papyrus Anastasi III *verso* (Papyrus Anastasi III:6, 1; 6,6; Alan H. Gardiner, *Late-Egyptian Miscellanies* [Brussels: Édition de la Fondation égyptologique Reine Élisabeth, 1937], 31). In all cases Gaza is consistently accompanied by the hill-country determinative, see Ahituv, *Toponyms*, 97–98; Frank J. Yurco, "Merenptah's Canaànite Campaign," *Journal of the American Research Center in Egypt* 23 (1986): 200.

Merenptah's Reliefs at the Cour de la Cachette, Karnak

found in the Merenptah Stela. Pierre Grandet and Kenneth A. Kitchen are also correct in seeing Djahy, Pa-Canaan, and Retenu as synonymous terms for a general region in Papyrus Harris I (1182–1153 BC) and not as the city of Gaza.[10]

From the surveyed Egyptian texts, it can be established that Canaan/Pa-Canaan was the Egyptian territory in Asia that encompassed a wide geographical region. Pa-Canaan is to be understood as a distinct territory not to be confused or equated with Gaza. This is clarified by the distinct use of both terms, Gaza and Pa-Canaan, separately in the same texts.

Ashkelon

Ashkelon is written eleven times in Egyptian records: twice in the Execration Texts (eighteenth century BC), once in the reign of Amenhotep II, twice(?) in the topographical lists of Amenhotep III, three times by Merenptah (Cairo, Karnak, and reliefs), twice on the Megiddo ivories, and once on the stela of Hori from the reign of Ramesses III.[11] Merenptah's Karnak reliefs depict the city as heavily fortified, evidence of its role prior to the Sea People invasion.[12] The Karnak reliefs show the army attacking from both sides of the city trapping the defenders

10. Pierre Grandet, "Deux établissements de Ramsès III en Nubie et en Palestine," *Journal of Egyptian Archaeology* 69 (1983): 111 n. 24; Grandet, *Le Papyrus Harris I, BM9999* (Le Caire: Institut français d'archéologique orientale du Caire, 1999), 2:50 n. 194; Kenneth A. Kitchen, "Review of Nibbi, 1975," *Journal of Egyptian Archaeology* 64 (1978): 170, see discussion in Hasel, "Pa-Canaan," 12–13.

11. Ahituv, *Toponyms*, 69–70.

12. Lawrence E. Stager, "Merneptah, Israel and the Sea Peoples: New Light on an Old Relief," *Eretz-Israel* 18 (1985), 56*–64*.

between Merenptah's chariot and the foot infantry. The inhabitants within the city raise their hands in subservience to the king. One is burning incense. Others are lowering children over the inner walls. Egyptian soldiers are climbing over the walls on scaling ladders and approaching the gate with axes. Since the battle is in progress, the outcome is not known, except for the inscription which says, "the wretched city which His Majesty carried off when it was wicked: Ashkelon."[13] It has been unanimously translated by Egyptologists as Ashkelon, the Canaanite site located on the Mediterranean coast north of Gaza and south of Ashdod that was extensively excavated by Harvard University from 1985–2016. Excavations revealed an extensive Canaanite city in the Late Bronze Age (c. 1550–1185 BC).[14]

GEZER

Gezer appears eight times in Egyptian records: three times on the topographical lists of Thutmose III (1504–1450 BC), once on the Soleb list of Amenhotep III, once by Thutmose IV, twice during the reign of Merenptah (on the Amada and Merenptah Stela), and finally on the list of Shoshenq I at Karnak.[15] It has been largely identified with the site of Tel Jezer (Tell el-Jazari), guarding the Valley of Aijalon and the route up to the hill country. Three large scale excavations were conducted by R. A. S. Macalister (1902–1909) followed by modern excavations by the Hebrew Union College and Harvard Semitic Museum (1964–74), by the University of Arizona (1986) and Andrews University (1990); and by Southwestern Baptist Theological Seminary and the Israel Antiquities Authority (2006–2017).[16] Earlier excavations had attributed the destruction of Stratum XV with Merenptah, and the modern excavations have now confirmed this association and destruction.[17]

YENOAM

Yenoam appears eighteen times in Egyptian records: the topographical lists of both Thutmose III and Amenhotep III (1390–1352 BC), seven times in the inscriptions of Seti I, five times by Ramesses II, once in the Merenptah Stela, and once by Ramesses III (1183–1152 BC) at Medinet

---

13. Hasel, *Domination and Resistance*, 50–51, fig. 6.

14. On the Ashkelon excavations, see Lawrence E. Stager, J. David Schloen, and Daniel M. Master, *Ashkelon 1: Introduction and Overview (1985–2006)* (Winona Lake, IN: Eisenbrauns, 2008).

15. Ahituv, *Toponyms*, 101–02.

16. Steven M. Ortiz and Samuel R. Wolff, "Tel Gezer Excavations 2006–2015: The Transformation of a Border City," in *The Shephelah During the Iron Age: Recent Archaeological Studies*, ed. Oded Lipschits and Aren M. Maeir (Winona Lake, IN: Eisenbrauns, 2017), 61–102.

17. William G. Dever et al., "Further Excavations at Gezer 1967–71," *BA* 34 (1971): 128; Dever et al., *Gezer II: Report of the 1967–71 Seasons in Fields I and II* (Jerusalem: Hebrew Union College; Nelson Glueck School of Biblical Archaeology, 1974), 50; Dever and Lance, *Gezer IV: Report of the 1967–71 Seasons in Field VI, the "Acropolis"* (Jerusalem: Hebrew Union College; Nelson Glueck School of Biblical Archaeology, 1986), 50; Ortiz and Wolff, "Tel Gezer Excavations," 72; Steven M. Ortiz and Samuel R. Wolff, "Pharaoh's Fury: Merneptah's Destruction of Gezer," *BAR* 48.2 (2022): 48–54.

Habu, as well as Amarna letter EA 197 (fourteenth century BC).[18] The location of the site has been disputed. Possible identifications have ranged from Tell en-Naameh in the Huleh Valley, Tell el-Abeidiyeh in the Jordan Valley south of the Sea of Galilee, Tel Yinam (Arabic Tell en-Naam) also south of the Sea of Galilee, and Tell esh-Shihab in the southern Bashan region of Transjordan.[19] Each of these sites remain possibilities due to their Late Bronze Age occupation, although the depiction on Seti's reliefs accord well with Tell el-Abeidiyeh in a loop of the Jordan River, a tall mound to this day.[20] The Transjordanian location for Israel assumes that Merenptah continued on his campaign past Tell esh-Shihab into that region. Although it is a possibility, some caution is also due. Seti I's Beth Shan stela records that his liberation of Beth Shan from a coalition of cities that revolted against it was completed in a single day. If Seti's armies had traveled to each of the rebel coalition cities in order to subdue them (Rehob, Pella, Hammath, and Yenoam), and if Tell esh-Shihab is Yenoam, it would seem more difficult to have been accomplished in a single day, even with sending out the three branches of his armies. From Seti's reliefs it would seem that a location closer to Beth Shan would be warranted by the geographical nature of the account.

ISRAEL

The name Israel appears only once in the Egyptian New Kingdom, although recent studies have suggested it may already be attested on a small pedestal from the reign of Amenhotep II (1452–1417 BC).[21] Merenptah states, "Israel is laid waste, its seed is not."[22] The determinative of a seated man and woman over three strokes

---

18. Ahituv, *Toponyms*, 198–99; see more recently Muhamed Rafaat Abbas, "The Town of Yenoam in the Ramesside War Scenes and Texts of Karnak," *Cahiers de Karnak* 16 (2017): 329–41.

19. For Tell en-Naameh, see H. Clauss, "Die Städte der El-Amarnabriefe und die Bibel," *ZDPV* 30 (1907): 1–79; William F. Albright, "Bronze Age Mounds of Northern Palestine and Hauran," *BASOR* 19 (1925): 12–13; Albright, "The Jordan Valley in the Bronze Age," *Annual of the American Schools of Oriental Research* 6 (1926): 18–24. For Tell el-Abeidiyeh, see John Garstang, *The Foundations of Biblical History: Joshua, Judges* (London: Constable, 1931), 73; Yohanan Aharoni, *The Settlement of the Israelite Tribes in Upper Galilee* (Jerusalem: Magnes, 1957), 125–29 [Hebrew]; Aharoni, *The Land of the Bible: A Historical Geography*, trans. Anson F. Rainey, rev. and enl. ed. (Philadelphia: Westminster, 1979), 165; William G. Dever, *Who Were the Early Israelites and Where Did They Come From?* (Grand Rapids: Eerdmans, 2003), 202. For Tel Yinam, see Aapeli Saarisalo, *The Boundary Between Issachar and Naphtali: An Archaeological and Literary Study of Israel's Settlement in Canaan* (Helsinki: Suomalaisen Kirjallisuuden Seuran Kirjapainon, 1927), 112–18; see Hasel, *Domination and Resistance*, 147. For Tell esh-Shihab, see Nadav Na'aman, "Yeno'am," *TA* 4 (1977): 168–77.

20. Abbas, "Town of Yenoam," 332.

21. Wolfgang Zwickel and Peter van der Veen, "The Earliest Reference to Israel and Its Possible Archaeological and Historical Background," *VT* 67 (2017): 129–40; Peter van der Veen, Christoffer Theis, and Manfred Görg, "Israel in Canaan (long) before Pharaoh Merenptah? A Fresh Look at Berlin Statue Pedestal-Relief 21687," *Journal of Ancient Egyptian Interconnections* 2–4 (2010): 15–21.

22. On the discussion of the meaning of Israel, see Hasel, "*Israel* in the Merneptah Stela," 46–7; "Merenptah's Reference to Israel," 47–51; and for the early support for translating *prt*, "seed" as grain, see Hasel, "Merenptah's Inscriptions and Reliefs and the Origin of Israel," in *The*

Detail of the Name "Israel" on the Merenptah Stela

for the plural indicates that the term Israel was a socio-ethnic entity or people that was distinguished by Merenptah's scribes from all the other entities in the final hymnic-poetic unit.[23] Most scholars have understood that Israel's unique designation in the stela may reflect the fact that it is not recognized as a territory, region, or city-state. This has important implications for issues of geography and location, but only in the wider comparative usage of these names within the context of the Merenptah Stela.

KHARU

The name Kharu appears at the very end of the section dealing with Pa-Canaan and the entities found within its territory. As the Merenptah Stela states, "Kharu has become a widow because of Egypt," in that the entities within its territory have been dealt with. As will be seen below, Kharu here is to be understood as a synonym for Pa-Canaan. Kharu then closes the section dealing with Pa-Canaan forming an inclusion of the hymnic-poetic structure. It is this structure that provides indications of the historical geography of the campaign.

THE STRUCTURE OF THE MERENPTAH STELA AND HISTORICAL GEOGRAPHY

It has been recognized by a number of scholars that Merenptah's campaign is structured in the sequence of conquered

Near East in the Southwest: Essays in Honor of William G. Dever, ed. Beth Alpert Nakhai (Boston: American Schools of Oriental Research, 2003), 19–44.

23. A determinative in the Egyptian language is one or more hieroglyphic signs that determine the category of a word. In this case, the determinatives used for the name "Israel" indicated that it is a foreign people and not a city or place.

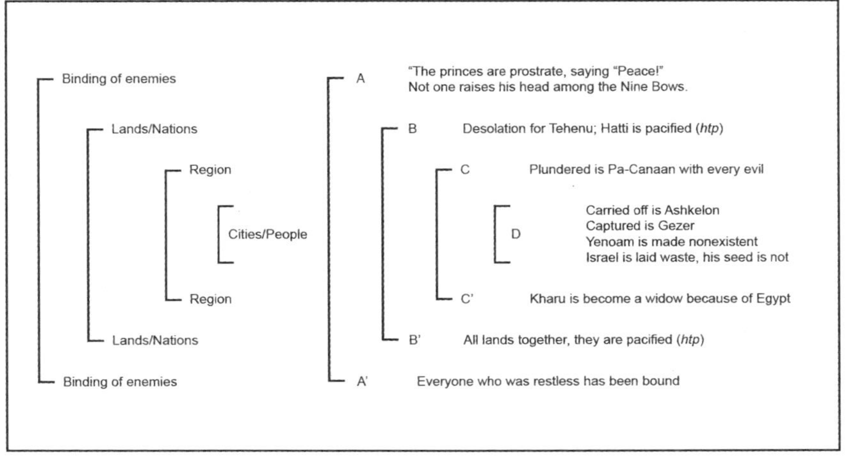

The Hymnic Poetic Unit of the Merenptah Stela Pertaining to Canaan

entities—geographical regions, cities, and the socio-ethnic entity Israel—written in a metered hymnic-poetic unit at the conclusion of the stela.[24] In 1994 the various proposed structures for this final hymnic-poetic unit were reviewed and evaluated for the first time.[25] These include the "ring structure" of Gösta Ahlström and Diana Edelman, the "modified ring structure" by Ahlström, Lawrence Stager's and Frank Yurco's proposed structures, and the "chiastic structure" of John J. Bimson.[26] Following an extensive critique of these proposals, I suggested a new, independently developed structure based on the "parallelism of political and geographical sequences and terms which most accurately maintains the integrity of the text."[27]

(1) The phrases in A and A' parallel each other, providing a general description that encloses all the entities mentioned by name in the hymn. Furthermore, it is an *inclusio* which expresses the major goals of Merenptah's campaign, namely, the "binding" of all enemies (the "Nine Bows").

(2) The internal structure of B–C–D–C'–B' depicts the details of how the "binding" of enemies has taken place and was accomplished. It was accomplished by subduing the various enemy entities which are depicted in the chiasm from larger to smaller entities in the form of B–B', the

24. It has been recognized that this section of stela is written as a hymn in a format referred to as a hymnic-poetic structure which is characterized by a certain rhythmic meter using poetic parallelisms in a structured way that indicates a pattern of entities located within other entities.

25. Hasel, "*Israel* in the Merneptah Stela," 45–61; *Domination and Resistance*, 260–71; "Merenptah's Reference to Israel," 47–59.

26. Gösta Ahlström and Diana Edelman, "Merneptah's Israel," *JNES* 44 (1985): 59–61; Ahlström, "The Origin of Israel in Palestine," *SJOT* 2 (1991): 19–34; Stager, "Merneptah," 56*; Yurco, "Merenptah's Canaanite Campaign," 189; John J. Bimson, "Merenptah's Israel and Recent Theories of Israelite Origins," *JSOT* 49 (1991): 3–29.

27. Hasel, "*Israel* in the Merneptah Stela," 48, fig. 1; *Domination and Resistance*, 267, fig. 15.

lands/nations of Tehenu and Hatti, C–C' the region of Pa-Canaan/Kharu, and D the city-state and people entities.

(3) The sequence indicates a progression from those on the edges of Egyptian control with a movement toward those in closer proximity. The nations/lands Tehenu (Libya) and Hatti (Hittite Empire) were located in the western and northeastern extremes of Egyptian domination at that time, while the region Pa-Canaan/Kharu together with its city-state and people entities appears to be its closest enemy to the (north)east.

(4) The structure of the hymn communicates that the movement of "binding the enemies" is from the more powerful sociopolitical polities to the less powerful ones that are in the center, such as the city-state and people entities.

(5) The reason that D, with the less powerful sociopolitical and socio-ethnic entities, is in the center of the chiasm seems to rest on the fact that it details military activities within the region of C, that is Pa-Canaan/Kharu. In other words, the entities of D are located within the region depicted in C–C'. Therefore, D is in the center.

The central section of the structure D within the region Pa-Canaan/Kharu is presented in the sequence of major city-states (Ashkelon, Gezer, and Yenoam) and a socio-ethnic people (Israel). Thus, the hymnic-poetic unit is structured in the sequence of the general description or binding of the enemies (A), the "pacifying" of lands/nations (B), the plundering of a major region (C), and the subduing of city-state and people entities (D). As I have suggested elsewhere, Pa-Canaan and Kharu (C') correspond to each other in the hymnic-poetic structure as a major geographical region that encompasses much of the Egyptian territory of Asia. The clause "Kharu has become a widow because of Egypt" neatly provides a closure for the segment concerning this geographical region. Pa-Canaan/Kharu has become a widow because the listed entities within its area no longer have their previously known existence (D).

(6) This is followed by the phrase, "All lands together are pacified" (B'). The reference to "all lands together" indicates a correlation with the two lands of Tehenu and Hatti (B). It is significant that both B and B' end with the word *ḥtp*, "pacified." It is now possible to point out a terminological (*ḥtp* = "pacified") as well as geographical correspondence (Pa-Canaan/Kharu).

(7) This hymnic-poetic unit at the end of the Merenptah Stela functions as a historical summary of the accomplishments of Merenptah during his reign.[28]

The welcome publication of James K. Hoffmeier's *Israel in Egypt* proposes a new grammatical structure that adds addi-

28. Others in support of this structure include, Yurco, "Merneptah's Canaanite Campaign," 189; Yurco, "3,200-Year-Old Picture of Israelites Found in Egypt" *BAR* 16.5 (1990): 27; Anson F. Rainey, "Israel in Merenptah's Inscription and Reliefs." *IEJ* 51 (2001): 63; Rainey, "Amarna and Later: Aspects of Social History" in *Symbiosis, Symbolism, and the Power of the Past: Canaan, Ancient Israel, and Their Neighbors from the Late Bronze Age through Roman Palestina. Proceedings of the Centennial Symposium W. F. Albright Institute of Archaeological Research and American Schools of Oriental Research, Jerusalem, May 29–May 31, 2000*, ed. William G. Dever and Seymour Gitin (Winona Lake, IN: Eisenbrauns, 2003), 179.

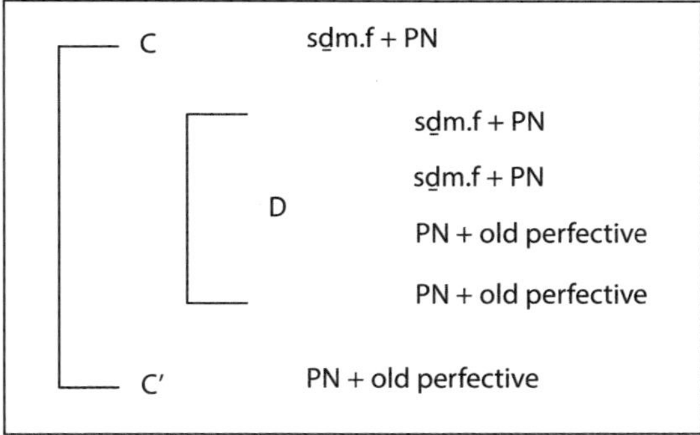

The Grammatical Structure in the Hymnic-Poetic Unit

tional support to the proposed structure above.[29] Hoffmeier has correctly observed that the specific activities concerning the synonymous designations Canaan/Kharu (C–C′) are also syntactically parallel. Notice that Canaan is written with the pattern *sḏm.f* + PN (proper name)—a pattern occurring with the next two city-states, Ashkelon and Gezer. Yenoam and Israel, however, appear with the PN + old perfective, as does Kharu, the region closing the inclusio C–C′. Thus, there is a distinct syntactical change in the very center of this final hymnic-poetic unit dealing with Canaan/Kharu so that the entities within its territory poetically match with the synonymous names used for the region (D).

As Kitchen has recently stated, Kharu "is a synonym for Canaan" for "between Canaan and Khurru is sandwiched their content—the four specific entities claimed by Merenptah as captured or destroyed: Ascalon, Gezer, Yenoam, and Israel."[30] Its stance as a synonymous term with Kharu indicates that Pa-Canaan extended to the north and encompassed those territories designated in other texts as Kharu.[31] This means that the campaign of Merenptah places Israel firmly within the territory of Canaan/Kharu and not in Egypt as some have recently suggested.[32]

29. Hoffmeier, *Israel in Egypt* (New York: Oxford University Press, 1997), 28–31; but see his translation in *COS* 2.6:41; see discussion in Michael G. Hasel, "The Structure of the Final Hymnic-Poetic Unit on the Merenptah Stela," *ZAW* 116 (2004): 75–81.

30. Kenneth A. Kitchen, "The Physical Text of Merenptah's Victory Hymn (The 'Israel' Stela)," *Journal of the Society for the Study of Egyptian Antiquities* 24 (1994/97): 74.

31. The terms Canaanite and Kharu are employed synonymously in Papyrus Anastasi IIIA and IV where "Canaanite slaves from Kharu" indicate that inhabitants of this territory received ethnic names reflecting their home territory, see Gardiner, *Late-Egyptian Miscellanies*, 33, 52; Papyrus Anastasi IIIA, 5–6; Papyrus Anastasi IV:16,4.

32. On the suggestion that Israel was in Egypt during Merenptah's campaign and a critique of this hypothesis, see Hasel, "*Israel* in the Merneptah Stela," 46; 56 n. 11. Recently the idea has been revived by Larry Bruce, "The Merenptah Stele and the Origins of Ancient Israel," *JETS* 62 (2019): 463. His conclusions cannot stand on the textual and contextual evidence of the Merenptah Stela and Karnak reliefs. Unless all the surrounding entities (Canaan, Ashkelon, Gezer, Yenoam, and Kharu) are reinterpreted as being within Egypt, the

RECONSTRUCTING THE GEOGRAPHY OF THE CAMPAIGN

Merenptah would have followed the traditional route of his predecessors as he travelled from Egypt, leaving Sile/*Tjaru*, as his grandfather Seti I had done, and traveling along on the northern Sinai coast on the Ways of Horus, before entering the region of the land of Pa-Canaan. Gaza need not have been mentioned since it was still under Egypt's control during the New Kingdom, having been firmly established as one of the residencies for Egyptian governance over Canaan. It could possibly have been a stop for resupplying his armies before heading up the coastal plain toward Ashkelon. Ashkelon was another matter, and Merenptah ensured that this city would remain firmly under his dominion as indicated in both the Karnak reliefs and stela.

The city tentatively identified as Gezer on Merenptah's Karnak reliefs, together with the mention of Gezer in both the Amada stela and the Merenptah Stela as being subdued is significant and in contrast to the biblical account where Israel does not take the city during their conquest/settlement (Josh 16:10; Judg 1:29).[33] It remains an important Canaanite city until an unnamed Egyptian king of the tenth century conquers it and delivers it

context of the final hymnic-poetic unit on the stela simply does not support a location for Israel in Egypt. Moreover, both determinatives—the hill-country and throwstick signs—indicate foreign entities *outside* the boundaries of Egypt. The throwstick accompanying Israel together with Israel's context within Pa-Canaan/Kharu confirms Israel as a foreign designation as is consistent in Egyptian military campaigns. For the consistency of Egyptian scribal use of determinatives, see Michael G. Hasel, "The Battle of Kadesh: Identifying New Kingdom Polities, Places, and Peoples in Canaan and Syria," in *Egypt, Canaan, and Israel: History, Imperialism, and Ideology. Proceedings of a Conference at the University of Haifa, 3–7 May 2009*, ed. Shay Bar, Dan'el Kahn, and JJ Shirley (Leiden: Brill, 2011), 65–85; see also Kitchen, "Physical Text," on scribal consistency within the Merenptah Stela itself.

33. On the identity of Gezer on the Karnak reliefs, see Yurco, "Merenptah's Canaanite Campaign"; Hasel, "Merenptah's Inscriptions and Reliefs," 19–44.

to Solomon as a dowry (1 Kgs 9:15–16). The next phase of Merenptah's campaign is less clear. Ashkelon and Gezer are a logical progression in a northeastern direction. But Yenoam is much further afield with all possible locations either just south or north of Galilee or even across the Jordan in the Bashan region. We will consider three possibilities for the next two phases of the campaign.

Route 1

One possibility is that the locations and entities on the Merenptah Stela, after Ashkelon and Gezer, do not follow a precise sequential and chronological order. In this scenario, Israel is last on the list of conquered entities not because it is last encountered but because of its importance as a major socio-ethnic people and not a mere city. In this case, Merenptah proceeds up past Gezer, heads east along the Valley of Aijalon up into the hill country where he claims to lay waste Israel as he heads north. Or he might have continued up the coast further and attacked Israel in the central hillcountry as he continued his northern campaign. In either case, Merenptah would have attacked Israel *before* he reached Yenoam in the north. Although this does not specifically follow the sequence of the stela and Karnak reliefs, it remains a possibility to consider, although less likely given the recording techniques and sequences often found in other Egyptian military records.

Route 2

A second possibility is to follow a precise chronological and sequential route that takes Merenptah past Gezer up the coastal plain, crossing over the Afula pass into the Jezreel. Before possibly resupplying his troops in the Egyptian-held garrison of Beth Shan, Merenptah then heads to Yenoam in the north. After he subjugates Yenoam, either in the Galilee region or the Bashan, he moves even further north in his trajectory from south to north to attack Israel. This would mean that Merenptah's Israel would be located *beyond* Yenoam in Upper Galilee, the Bashan of Transjordan, or even both.[34] But even though this is a possibility, it is not a required sequence by the textual or iconographic evidence for Merenptah's campaign. The chronological and sequential order of the campaign would remain firmly in place if Merenptah did not head north, but instead, turned immediately south after his conquest of Yenoam.

Route 3

This brings us to the third possibility. Merenptah, instead of continuing north from Yenoam, turned south, encountering Israel on his return to Egypt. This would place Merenptah's Israel anywhere south of the Galilee or Bashan region. Israel could be located in the area of the central hillcountry yet would not necessarily preclude locations further east in the Transjordan or even areas further south. Both route 1 and route 3

34. This is the view of Na'aman, "Yeno'am," and Anson F. Rainey, "Whence Came the Israelites and Their Language?," *IEJ* 57 (2007): 56; Rainey and R. Steven Notley, *The Sacred Bridge: Carta's Atlas of the Biblical World* (Jerusalem: Carta, 2006), 82.

could explain the toponym "the waters of Nephtoah" near Kiriath Jearim (Josh 15:9; 18:15), which some have seen as etymologically related to the name Merenptah.[35] This location would also provide a closer connection to the hill country sites of the Iron I period that are later identified as early Israel.[36]

CONCLUSION

The corroborating evidence from the four Egyptian sources commemorating Merenptah's campaign to Canaan, etched in stone, continue to provide the necessary data to unequivocally assert Israel's existence in the thirteenth century BC.[37] The Merenptah Stela, now 125 years after its discovery, still cuts through current scholarly reconstructions and rhetoric with a simple declaration: Israel exists along with other well recognized geographical entities as a socio-ethnic people already located in the land of Canaan by 1209 BC.

BIBLIOGRAPHY

Abbas, Muhamed Raafat. "The Town of Yenoam in the Ramesside War Scenes and Texts of Karnak." *Cahiers de Karnak* 16 (2017): 329–41.

Aharoni, Yohanan. *The Land of the Bible: A Historical Geography*. Translated by Anson F. Rainey. Rev. and enl. ed. Philadelphia: Westminster, 1979.

———. *The Settlement of the Israelite Tribes in Upper Galilee*. Jerusalem: Magnes, 1957 [Hebrew].

Ahituv, Shmuel. *Canaanite Toponyms in Ancient Egyptian Documents*. Jerusalem: Magnes, 1984.

Ahlström, Gösta. "The Origin of Israel in Palestine." *SJOT* 2 (1991): 19–34.

Ahlström, Gösta and Edelman, Diana V. "Merneptah's Israel." *JNES* 44 (1985): 59–61.

Albright, William F. "Bronze Age Mounds of Northern Palestine and Hauran." *BASOR* 19 (1925): 5–19.

———. "The Jordan Valley in the Bronze Age." *Annual of the American Schools of Oriental Research* 6 (1926): 18–24.

Bimson, John J. "Merenptah's Israel and Recent Theories of Israelite Origins." *JSOT* 49 (1991): 3–29.

Brand, Peter J. "The Date of the War Scenes at Karnak and the History of the Late Nineteenth Dynasty." Pages 51–84 in *Ramesside Studies in Honour of K. A. Kitchen*. Edited by Mark Collier and Steven Snape. Bolton: Rutherford, 2011.

35. Aharoni, *The Land of the Bible*,184; Hans Y. Priebatsch, "Jerusalem und die Brunnenstrasse Merneptahs," *ZDPV* 91 (1975): 21–22.

36. This is the view supported by the majority of scholars, including Kenneth A. Kitchen, *On the Reliability of the Old Testament* (Grand Rapids: Eerdmans, 2003), 460; Hoffmeier, *Israel in Egypt*, 29; Avraham Faust, *Israel's Ethnogenesis: Interaction, Expansion and Resistance* (London: Routledge, 2006), 164–66; William G. Dever, "Merenptah's 'Israel,' the Bible's and Ours," in *Exploring the* Longue Durée: *Essays in Honor of Lawrence E. Stager*, ed. J. David Schloen (Winona Lake, IN: Eisenbrauns, 2009), 89–96.

37. For two more recent postmodern exercises in theoretical nihilism, see Ingrid Hjelm and Thomas L. Thompson, "The Victory Song of Merneptah, Israel and the People of Palestine," *JSOT* 27 (2002): 3–18 (and the response by Kenneth A. Kitchen, "The Victories of Merenptah and the Nature of His Record," *JSOT* 28 [2004]: 259–72); Dermot Nestor, "Merneptah's 'Israel' and the Absence of Origins in Biblical Scholarship," *Currents in Biblical Research* 13 (2015): 293–329.

———. "Usurped Cartouches of Merenptah at Karnak and Luxor." Pages 29–48 in *Causing His Name to Live: Studies in Egyptian Epigraphy and History in Memory of William J. Murnane.* Edited by Peter J. Brand and Louise Cooper. Leiden: Brill, 2009.

Bruce, Larry. "The Merenptah Stele and the Origins of Ancient Israel." *JETS* 62 (2019): 463–93.

Clauss, H. "Die Städte der El-Amarnabriefe und die Bibel." *ZDPV* 30 (1907): 1–79.

Dever, William G. "Merenptah's 'Israel,' the Bible's and Ours." Pages 89–96 in *Exploring the Longue Durée: Essays in Honor of Lawrence E. Stager*. Edited by J. David Schloen. Winona Lake, IN: Eisenbrauns, 2009.

———. *Who Were the Israelites and Where Did They Come From?* Grand Rapids: Eerdmans, 2003.

Dever, William G., H. Darrell Lance, Reuben G. Bullard, Dan P. Cole, Anita M. Furshpan, John S. Holladay Jr., Joe D. Seger, and Robert B. Wright. "Further Excavations at Gezer 1967–71." *BA* 34 (1971): 94–132.

Dever, William G., H. Darrell Lance, Reuben G. Bullard, Dan P. Cole, Joe D. Seger, A. Eran, John S. Holladay Jr., Thomas A. Holland, A. Wilkinson, R. B. Wright. *Gezer II: Report of the 1967–70 Seasons in Fields 1 and 2*. Jerusalem: Hebrew Union College; Nelson Glueck School of Biblical Archaeology, 1974.

Dever, William G., and H. Darrell Lance. *Gezer IV: The 1969–71 Seasons in Field VI, the "Acropolis."* Jerusalem: Hebrew Union College; Nelson Glueck School of Biblical Archaeology, 1986.

Faust, Avraham. *Israel's Ethnogenesis: Interaction, Expansion and Resistance.* London: Routledge, 2006.

Fischer-Elfert, Hans-Werner. *Die Satirische Streitschrift des Papyrus Anastasi I: Textzusammenstellung*. Wiesbaden: Harrassowitz, 1983.

Gardiner, Alan H. "The Ancient Military Road Between Egypt and Palestine." *Journal of Egyptian Archaeology* 6 (1920): 99–116.

———. *Egyptian Hieratic Texts*. Series 1: *Literary Texts of the New Kingdom*. Part 1. *Papyrus Anastisi I and the Papyrus Loller together with the Parallel Texts*. Leipzig: Hinrichs, 1911.

———. *Late-Egyptian Miscellanies*. Brussels: Édition de la Fondation eégyptologique Reine Élisabeth, 1937.

Garstang, John. *The Foundations of Biblical History: Joshua, Judges*. London: Constable, 1931.

Görg, Manfred. "Der Name Kanaan in ägyptische Wiedergabe." *Biblische Notizen* 18 (1982): 26–7.

Grandet, Pierre. "Deux établissements de Ramsès III en Nubie et en Palestine." *Journal of Egyptian Archaeology* 69 (1983): 108–14.

———. *Le Papyrus Harris I, BM9999* Le Caire: Institut français d'archéologique orientale du Caire, 1999.

Hasel, Michael G. "The Battle of Kadesh: Identifying New Kingdom Polities, Places, and Peoples in Canaan and Syria." Pages 65–86 in *Egypt, Canaan, and Israel: History, Imperialism, and Ideology. Proceedings of a Conference at the University of Haifa, 3–7 May 2009*. Edited by Shay Bar, Dan'el Kahn, and JJ Shirley. Leiden: Brill, 2011.

———. *Domination and Resistance: Egyptian Military Activity in the Southern Levant, 1300–1185 B.C.* Leiden: Brill, 1998.

———. "*Israel* in the Merneptah Stela." *BASOR* 296 (1994): 45–61.

———. "Merenptah's Inscriptions and Reliefs and the Origin of Israel." Pages 19–44 in *The Near East in the Southwest: Essays in Honor of William G. Dever*. Edited by Beth Alpert Nakhai. Boston: American Schools of Oriental Research, 2003.

———. "Merenptah's Reference to Israel: Critical Issues for the Origin of Israel." Pages 47–59 in *Critical Issues in Early Israelite History*. Edited by Richard S. Hess, Gerald A. Klingbeil, and Paul J. Ray, Jr. Winona Lake, IN: Eisenbrauns, 2008.

———. "Pa-Canaan in the Egyptian New Kingdom: Canaan or Gaza?" *Journal of Ancient Egyptian Interconnections* 1/1 (2009): 8–17.

———. "The Structure of the Final Hymnic-Poetic Unit on the Merenptah Stela." *ZAW* 116 (2004): 75–81.

Hjelm, Ingrid, and Thomas L. Thompson. "The Victory Song of Merneptah, Israel and the People of Palestine." *JSOT* 27 (2002): 3–18.

Hoffmeier, James K. *Israel in Egypt*. New York: Oxford University Press, 1997.

Katzenstein, H. Jacob. "Gaza in Egyptian Texts of the New Kingdom." *Journal of the American Oriental Society* 102 (1982): 111–13.

Kitchen, Kenneth A. *On the Reliability of the Old Testament*. Grand Rapids: Eerdmans, 2003.

———. "The Physical Text of Merenptah's Victory Hymn (The 'Israel' Stela)." *Journal of the Society for the Study of Egyptian Antiquities* 24 (1994/97): 71–76.

———. "Review of Nibbi, 1975." *Journal of Egyptian Archaeology* 64 (1978): 170.

———. "The Victories of Merenptah and the Nature of His Record." *JSOT* 28 (2004): 259–72.

Na'aman, Nadav. "Yenoʿam." *TA* 4 (1977): 168–77.

Nestor, Dermot. "Merneptah's 'Israel' and the Absence of Origins in Biblical Scholarship." *Currents in Biblical Research* 13 (2015): 293–329.

Ortiz, Steven M., and Samuel R. Wolff. "Pharaoh's Fury: Merneptah's Destruction of Gezer." *BAR* 48.2 (2022): 48–54.

———. "Tel Gezer Excavations 2006–2015: The Transformation of a Border City." Pages 61–102 in *The Shephelah During the Iron Age: Recent Archaeological Studies*. Edited by Oded Lipschits and Aren M. Maeir. Winona Lake, IN: Eisenbrauns, 2017.

Priebatsch, Hans Y. "Jerusalem und die Brunnenstrasse Merneptahs." *ZDPV* 91 (1975): 18–29.

Rainey, Anson F. "Amarna and Later: Aspects of Social History." Pages 169–88 in *Symbiosis, Symbolism, and the Power of the Past: Canaan, Ancient Israel, and Their Neighbors from the Late Bronze Age through Roman Palestina. Proceedings of the Centennial Symposium W. F. Albright Institute of Archaeological Research and American Schools of Oriental Research, Jerusalem, May 29–May 31, 2000*. Edited by William G. Dever and Seymour Gitin. Winona Lake, IN: Eisenbrauns, 2003.

———. "Israel in Merenptah's Inscription and Reliefs." *IEJ* 51 (2001): 57–75.

———. "Whence Came the Israelites and Their Language?" *IEJ* 57 (2007): 41–64.

Rainey, Anson F., and R. Steven Notley. *The Sacred Bridge: Carta's Atlas of the Biblical World*. Jerusalem: Carta, 2006.

Saarisalo, Aapeli. *The Boundary Between Issachar and Naphtali: An Archaeological and Literary Study of Israel's Settlement in Canaan*. Helsinki: Suomalaisen Kirjallisuuden Seuran Kirjapainon, 1927.

Sethe, Kurt, and Wolfgang Helck, ed. *Urkunden der 18. Dynastie, IV*. Leipzig: Hinrichs, 1906–1921.

Stager, Lawrence E. "Merneptah, Israel and the Sea Peoples: New Light on an Old Relief." *Eretz-Israel* 18 (1985): 56–64.

Stager, Lawrence E., J. David Schloen, and Daniel M. Master. *Ashkelon 1: Introduction and Overview (1985–2006)*. Winona Lake, IN: Eisenbrauns, 2008.

Veen, Peter van der, Christoffer Theis, and Manfred Görg. "Israel in Canaan (long) before Pharaoh Merenptah? A Fresh Look at Berlin Statue Pedestal-Relief 21687." *Journal of Ancient Egyptian Interconnections* 2–4 (2010): 15–21.

Von Beckerath, Jürgen. *Handbuch der ägyptischen Königsnamen*. München: Deutscher Kunstverlag, 1984.

Wente, Edward F, trans. *Letters from Ancient Egypt*. Edited by Edmund S. Meltzer. Atlanta: Scholars, 1990.

Yurco, Frank J. "3,200-Year-Old Picture of Israelites Found in Egypt." *BAR* 16.5 (1990): 20–38.

———. "Merenptah's Canaanite Campaign." *Journal of the American Research Center in Egypt* 23 (1986): 189–215.

Zwickel, Wolfgang, and Peter van der Veen. "The Earliest Reference to Israel and Its Possible Archaeological and Historical Background." *VT* 67 (2017): 129–40.

CHAPTER 16

THE PROMINENCE OF THE LAND OF EPHRAIM AND MANASSEH IN THE CONQUEST AND EARLY SETTLEMENT NARRATIVES

Josh 17:14–18; 24:29–33; Deut 33:13–17

Paul Wright

KEY POINTS

- Persons and places connected with the tribes of Ephraim and Manasseh play a prominent role in the narrative flow of the books of Joshua and Judges.
- The lands given to the tribes of Ephraim and Manasseh had distinct geographical advantages for settlement.
- Archaeological data suggests that Israel first settled down in the area given to the tribes of Ephraim and Manasseh.
- The question of why there is no conquest account for this region remains puzzling but likely stems from the ideology of the biblical author.

INTRODUCTION

The rise of Jerusalem as "the place in which the Lord your God will choose for His name to dwell" (Deut 12:11, NASB; *et passim*), its presence as the seat of political and religious authority during the monarchy, and its reestablishment under Jewish control following the return from the Babylonian exile, all overshadow the narrative structure of the Old Testament.[1] Geographically, historically, and spiritually, the Old Testament focuses on Jerusalem and the redemptive events that happened within its walls. Given this auspicious treatment, it seems odd that Jerusalem is never

1. All biblical quotations are from the New American Standard Bible (NASB), unless otherwise noted.

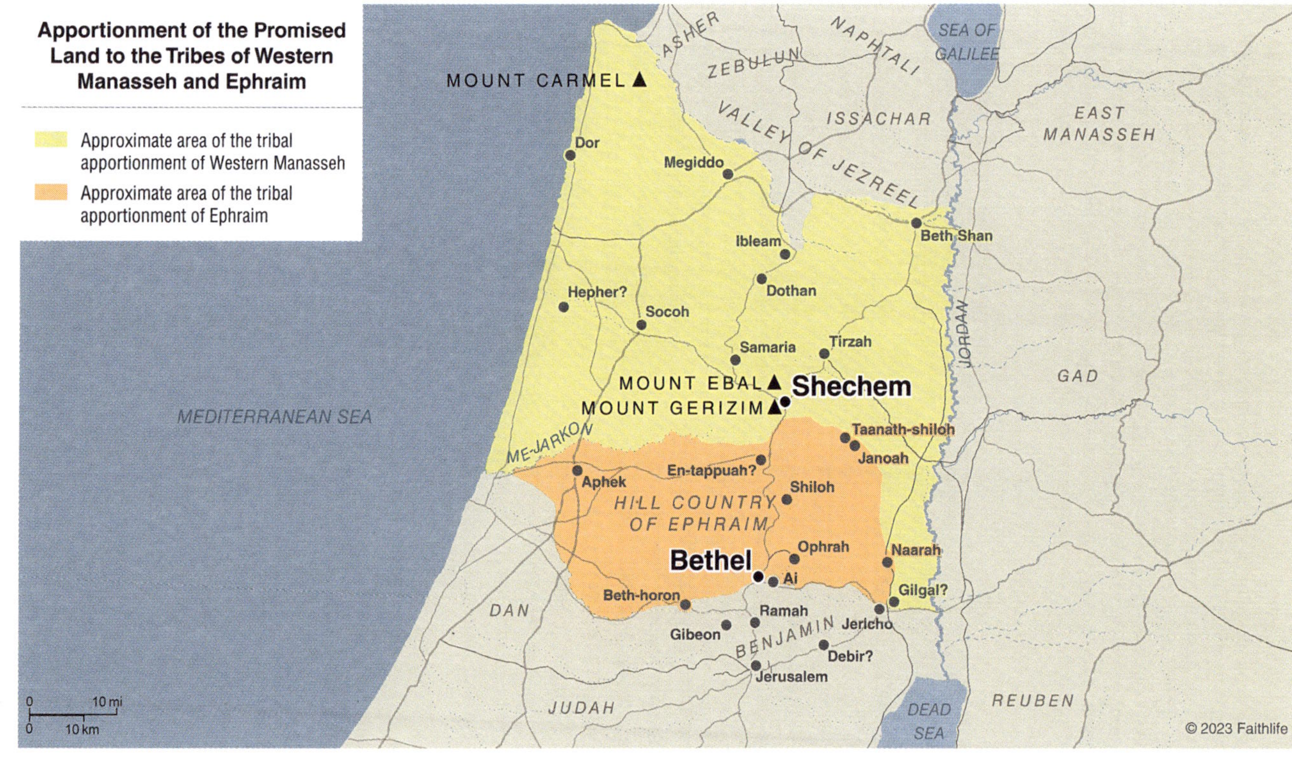

Apportionment of the Promised Land to the Tribes of Western Manasseh and Ephraim
Approximate area of the tribal apportionment of Western Manasseh
Approximate area of the tribal apportionment of Ephraim
MOUNT CARMEL
ASHER
ZEBULUN
NAPHTALI
SEA OF GALILEE
ISSACHAR
VALLEY OF JEZREEL
EAST MANASSEH
Dor
Megiddo
Beth Shan
Ibleam
Dothan
Hepher?
Socoh
Samaria
Tirzah
JORDAN
MOUNT EBAL
Shechem
MOUNT GERIZIM
GAD
MEDITERRANEAN SEA
ME-JARKON
Taanath-shiloh
Janoah
Aphek
En-tappuah?
Shiloh
HILL COUNTRY OF EPHRAIM
Ophrah
Naarah
Bethel
Ai
Beth-horon
Gilgal?
DAN
Ramah
Gibeon
BENJAMIN
Jericho
Debir?
Jerusalem
JUDAH
DEAD SEA
REUBEN
0 10 mi
0 10 km
© 2023 Faithlife

mentioned by name in the Pentateuch.[2] Moreover, Moses commanded that once Israel enters Canaan, the tribes should renew their covenant obligations with the Lord not in Jerusalem but on Mount Gerizim and Mount Ebal (Deut 11:29–32; 27:11–13). Some of Israel's most significant founding stories—not the battles of conquest but the actual living in the land—took place in the central hills between Bethel and the Jezreel Valley rather than on territory that was to become the southern kingdom of Judah (e.g., Gen 12:4–7; 33:18–20; Josh 18:1; 24:1–28; 1 Sam 1:3). Despite the dominance of Judah and Jerusalem during and after the monarchy, these founding stories were preserved in a way that favored the prominence of these central hills in the memory of Israel's earliest formation. This essay will itemize elements of the biblical narrative that indicate the prominence of Ephraim and Manasseh, suggest geographical and archaeological correspondences, then ask a persistent, yet unanswerable, question, "but why is there no conquest narrative for these hills?"[3]

KEY PEOPLE AND KEY PLACES IN THE BIBLICAL NARRATIVE

The Genesis narrative sets the stage, with key people establishing rights at key places in the portion of Canaan that would become the tribal inheritance of Ephraim and Manasseh. While the storyline of Genesis includes significant activity in and around Hebron and Beersheba, places that are associated with Judah, it is sites in the central hills that carry pride of place as the location of significant "firsts." For example:

- Upon entering Canaan, Abraham's first stopping point was the oak of Moreh outside of Shechem, where for the first time God promised that Abraham's descendants would receive the land (Gen 12:5–7).
- Shechem was the first place in Canaan (i.e., west of the Jordan River) where Jacob settled after being renamed Israel (Gen 33:18–20; compare 32:28). There he bought a plot of ground, the first purchase of land for the purpose of living in the land (compare Gen 23:17–20).
- It was at Bethel that Abraham first divided his family resources and hence the line of inheritance, with the result that God's land promise would focus on an individual line of descent (Gen 13:2–17; compare 12:8).

---

2. Melchizedek's Salem may well have been Jerusalem (Gen 14:17–18; compare Ps 76:1–2), as the majority of Jewish and Christian exegetes have maintained since at least the testimony of Josephus (*Ant* 1.180), but if so, why did the biblical author not use the name Jerusalem since it was already known in texts as early as the Middle Bronze Age? For Execration Text e27 (*ru-u-sh-l-m-m*) and EA 287: 25, 46, 61, 63 (*u-ru-sa-lim*), see Anson F. Rainey and R. Steven Notley, *The Sacred Bridge: Carta's Atlas of the Biblical World*, 2nd ed. (Jerusalem: Carta, 2014), 58; Anson F. Rainey, *The El-Amarna Correspondence: An New Edition of the Cuneiform Letters from the Site of El-Amarna based on Collations of all Extant Tablets*, ed. William M. Schniedewind (Leiden: Brill, 2015), 1:1110–12.

3. This prominence was noted by Albrecht Alt and has been recognized by a host of scholars since. See Alt, "The Settlement of the Israelites in Palestine," in *Essays on Old Testament History and Religion*, trans. Richard A. Wilson (Sheffield: JSOT Press, 1989), 165–69.

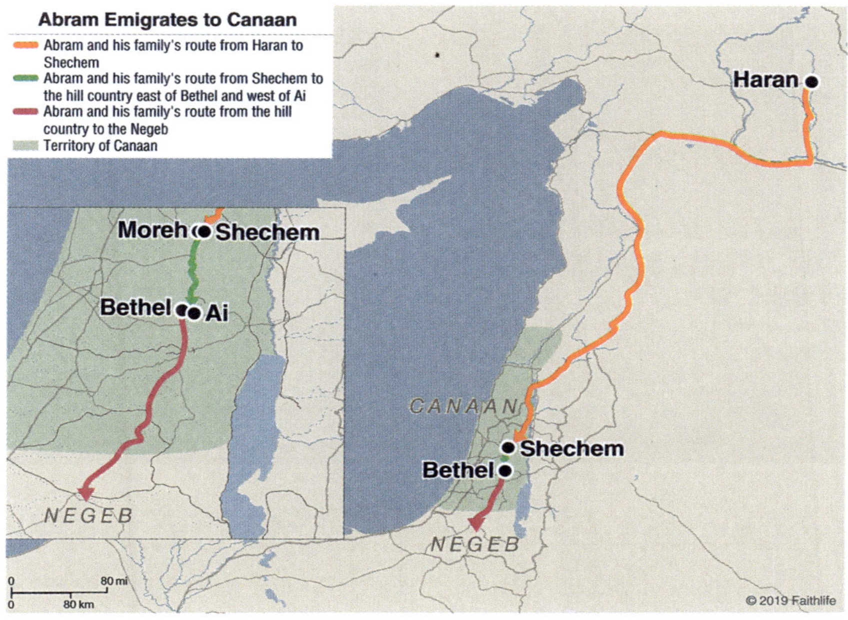

- Joseph was the oldest son of Jacob's favorite wife, making him the heir-apparent of the patriarch and supposed recipient of the favored portion of the inheritance. (Gen 30:22–24). The land that Joseph and his sons, Ephraim and Manasseh, inherited encompassed the territory between Bethel and the Jezreel Valley.
- In terms of raw beauty and abundance of landed resources, Jacob's deathbed blessing to Joseph, which describes him in terms that reflect the fruitful land that his descendants would eventually call home, surpassed that of his brothers (Gen 49:22–26).

All of this sets the expectation that the narrative flow would continue to favor these central hills once Israel returned to Canaan from Egypt. Indeed, Moses' only directive as to exactly where Israel was to return was the area first entered by Abraham, "beside the oaks of Moreh" (Deut 11:29–30). Like Jacob, Moses' deathbed blessing favored the landed fortunes of Joseph, "with the choice things of the everlasting hills, and with the choice things of the earth and its fullness" (Deut 33:15).[4] And indeed, persons from the line of Joseph and places within this favored

4. Moses' blessings to the twelve tribes (Deut 33:6–25) are a mixed bag geographically. While a good case can be made that each relates to the specific landed inheritance that its tribe received once they settled in Canaan, some of the geographical information in the text is more "up front" than others. The blessing to Joseph (33:13–17) is not only the longest but the one with the most vivid language about the bounty of the land. The intent seems to be that Joseph, "the one most distinguished among his brothers" (Deut 33:16), received land

Aerial View of Shiloh Excavations

tribal inheritance of the sons of Joseph appear at critical junctures in the subsequent conquest and settlement narratives. Again, to summarize:

- Following his conquest of Jericho, the gateway into Canaan from the east, Joshua followed the most direct natural route into the hill country that would take him to mounts Gerizim and Ebal (Ai lay on that route). He then built an altar on Mount Ebal and renewed the covenant. Half of Israel stood on Gerizim, half of Ebal, flanking the valley of Shechem near where Abraham had first encountered God in Canaan (Josh 8:30–35).
- Joshua's final address to Israel was also at Shechem, which by now had a "sanctuary of the Lord" and a large permanent memorial stone (Josh 24:1, 26).
- The first, albeit failed, attempt at kingship was by Abimelek, son of Gideon, at Shechem (Judg 9), the main center of the tribal inheritance of Manasseh.
- The tent of meeting, or tabernacle, was in Shiloh, the heartland of the tribe of Ephraim. Its central role in the development of Israel's early tribal identity is illustrated by the account of the distribution of the land among the "lesser" tribes (Josh 18:1; 21:1–2).
- Shiloh continued as the main tribal center into the days of Samuel (1 Sam 1:3).
- Only the Joseph tribes, Ephraim and Manasseh, took initiative to expand their tribal holdings (Josh 17:14–18; but note Caleb, below). The narrative pictures the tribe of Joseph as a numerous people,

similarly distinguished. See Paul H. Wright, *Holman Illustrated Guide to Biblical Geography: Reading the Land* (Nashville: B&H, 2020), 133, 149, 152–53, 158, 193, 205–6, 212–13, 229, 250, 265, 279.

blessed by the Lord and destined to clear the forest and possess their land to the farthest borders. In doing so, it established a template of which the other tribes fell short. The episode fits the rubric of "gradual settlement" rather than "conquest" as the primary method by which ancient Israel became established in Canaan.

- The key leadership was all associated with the Joseph tribal region. Joshua was an Ephraimite (Num 13:8; 1 Chr 7:20–27), buried in Timnath Serah (Khirbet Tibnah) in southern Ephraim (Josh 24:29–30). The high priest, Eleazer son of Aaron, was buried at Gibeah of Pinchas, an unknown location somewhere "in the hill country of Ephraim" (Josh 24:33). Of all the sons of Jacob, it was only the bones of Joseph that Israel brought out of Egypt for burial back in Canaan, specifically on the plot of ground that Jacob had purchased in Shechem (Josh 24:32).
- Twice in the narrative of Israel's early deliverers, the men of Ephraim were offended because they were not asked to participate in battle (Judg 8:1; 12:1).
- Japhet submits that David was an ethnic Ephramite (from the gentillic "Ephrathite"; אֶפְרָתִי, *ephrathi*), though living in Bethlehem and socially and politically Judean.[5]

Wazana and Assis both note that the narrative of the book of Joshua fronts Judah as an equal player to Ephraim and Manasseh (e.g., the city list and border descriptions, and the initiative of Caleb to settle land around Debir; Josh 14–15), in comparison to the "slacker" tribes that had to receive their land by special dispensation from Shiloh.[6] However, we must remember that Caleb, Judah's early hero, was not Judean but a Kenizzite (Num 13:6; Josh 14:14). He was a member of an outlier clan that, while an early ally of Judah, was not descended from Jacob, and this in a time and place when blood was the strongest marker of identity. Moreover, the only native Judean mentioned in the conquest narrative of the book of Joshua was Achan (Josh 7:16–26), the consummate anti-hero who single-handedly very nearly undermined the entire endeavor.

All this needs to be set against the reality that the Bible contains no proper conquest narrative of the portion of the hill country lying between Bethel and the Jezreel Valley.

THE GEOGRAPHICAL SETTING

The geographical setting of Ephraim and Manasseh compliments the prominence of these two tribes in the early

5. Sara Japhet, "Was David a Judahite or an Ephraimite? Light from the Genealogies," in *Let Us Go Up to Zion: Essays in Honour of H. G. M. Williamson on the Occasion of His Sixty-Fifth Birthday*, ed. Iain Provan and Mark J. Boda (Leiden, Brill, 2012), 299–306. Samuel of Ramah (1 Sam 1:1), Elimelech of Bethlehem (Ruth 1:2) and Jesse of Bethlehem (1 Sam 17:12) are all labelled *ephrathi*.

6. Nili Wazana, *All the Boundaries of the Land: The Promised Land in Biblical Thought in Light of the Ancient Near East* (Winona Lake, IN: Eisenbrauns, 2013), 244–51; Elie Assis, "'How Long are You Slack to Go to Possess the Land' (Jos. XVIII 3): Ideal and Reality in the Distribution Descriptions in Joshua XIII–XIX," *VT* 53.1 (2003): 1–25.

Shiloh and the Surrounding Hill Country

settlement narratives. In short, the favorable poetic description of Joseph's inheritance recorded in Gen 49:22–26 and Deut 33:13–17 is an accurate portrayal of the landscape, including the "things of heaven [above] ... and the deep lying beneath" (Deut 33:13), i.e., ample rainfall and spring water, on which Ephraim and Manasseh settled.

A comparative view of the geography of the heartland hills of ancient Israel, from Beersheba to the Jezreel Valley, shows that the balance of available resources conducive to settlement is tipped in favor of the north, i.e., Ephraim and Manasseh, over Judah. "Halves of the same range, how opposite in disposition and history," intoned George Adam Smith with an eye toward functionality.[7] The differences between the Ephraim/Manasseh hills and Judah hills are more of degree than kind, yet significant enough to favor the former over the latter for Israel's initial settlement and, eventually, kingdom building processes.

The hills of Ephraim are composed of a rise of hard limestone angled north-northeastward, with heavily eroded terrain cut by twisted wadis sloping toward the coast and a narrow, steep drop into the Jordan Valley. Lacking an open Shephelah with longitudinal valleys that draw coastal people into the hills, the relatively closed terrain of Ephraim runs right down to the coastal plain, creating a larger contiguous settlement zone for its own inhabitants than is present in Judah. The rainfall here is more favorable than that of the Judean hills further south, eroding the watershed ridge eastward and creating a larger area of potentially arable land facing the prevailing rains. In the biblical periods, these westward slopes were covered by a tangled mass of dense brush, low trees, and high bushes (Mediterranean

7. George Adam Smith, *The Historical Geography of the Holy Land* (London: Hodder and Stoughton, 1894), 323.

Fields near Shechem

maquis), filling its hoots and hollows. As a result, "the remote part of the hill country of Ephraim" (Judg 19:1) was difficult to penetrate, providing a setting that nicely fits the account of the Joseph tribes' westward move into a land that had to be cleared of forests (Josh 17:14–18). Because of the north-northeast angle of the watershed ridge in relationship to the north-south cut of the rift, the eastern Ephraim hills are closer to, and hence drop more steeply into, the Jordan Valley than do those of Judah. This provides a more secure barrier from penetration from the east. At the same time, due to their underlying bedrock—hard limestone rather than the chalk of the Judean wilderness—the Ephraim hills have a greater potential to sustain settled life due to its various uses in construction. Shiloh, Ephraim's center of settlement, possesses every geographical advantage for a natural sanctuary setting: it is nestled in a secluded spot high in the Ephraim hills, off the ancient north-south route (Judg 21:19), near a large, pleasant agricultural valley (Emeq Shiloh/Wadi Musa) and a large spring. All in all, the geographical shape of the Ephraim hill country fosters self-sufficient, conservative lifestyles, making it a favorable place for an emerging people to settle down and stay put.[8]

The Manasseh hills differ from those of Ephraim from the ground up. Here, a series of geological folds on the same north-northeast line have pulled the mass of hills into blocks separated by wide valleys. Side faults angling off the rift have created additional broad valleys that intersect this main line perpendicularly. All are filled with wide swaths of arable soil and are dotted with springs. These valleys also function as open, natural routes connecting the heartland of Manasseh with: (1) the coast via the

8. Wright, *Illustrated Guide to Biblical Geography*, 146–53.

Shechem wadi, (2) with the Jezreel Valley via the Vale of Dothan, and (3) with the Jordan Valley via the Bezek trough and Wadi Farah/Nahal Tirzah. These geographic features angle toward Shechem, a natural capital surrounded by broad, fertile, well-watered, and naturally linked landscapes. Prior and even subsequent to Israel's establishment in the Manasseh hills, the indigenous Canaanites lived in cities adjacent to these open, intermountain valleys (i.e., Shechem, Dothan, and Tirzah/Tell el-Farah North) where they forged productive lives from rich soils. In time, these cities, with the city of Samaria, became the main control centers of the northern kingdom of Israel, while the more difficult terrain of Ephraim to the south remained a habitat of smaller, rural settlements.[9] Perhaps there was something more "original" or "authentic" about the ongoing patterns of life in the hill country of Ephraim that allowed Ephraim to become the nostalgic nickname for all Israel by the late monarchy (e.g., Hos 5:3; Jer 31:9).[10]

AN ARCHAEOLOGICAL PROFILE

For decades, scholars have wrestled with the contentious issue of what archaeology can or cannot contribute to our understanding of the origins of ancient Israel, and if, or how, Israel can be identified as a distinguishable ethnic group(s) in the archaeological record.[11] For the territory inhabited by the Joseph tribes, the baseline has been established by archaeological surveys, primarily those of Finkelstein in Ephraim and Zertal in Manassseh.[12] The survey data, which indicates that the main thrust of settlement took place in the areas of Ephraim and Manasseh, falls in a similar pattern for both regions.[13] To summarize, there was a veritable explosion of small, unfortified sites in the central hills beginning in the late thirteenth century BC, which accelerated through the twelfth and extended into the eleventh century (Iron Age I). The material culture associated with these sites includes a preponderance of simple domestic ware, such as collared rim jars and cooking pots, and near total absence of imported or prestige

9. Adam Zertal, "The Heart of the Monarchy: Patterns of Settlement and Historical Considerations of the Israelite Kingdom of Samaria," in *Studies in the Archaeology of the Iron Age in Israel and Jordan*, ed. Amihai Mazar (Sheffield: Sheffield Academic, 2001), 38–64.

10. Wright, *Illustrated Guide to Biblical Geography*, 154–62.

11. For details and summary of the discussion see Richard S. Hess, "Early Israel in Canaan: A Survey of Recent Evidence and Interpretations," *PEQ* 125 (1993), 125–42; Ralph K. Hawkins, *How Israel Became a People* (Nashville: Abingdon, 2013), 30–48.

12. Israel Finkelstein, *The Archaeology of the Israelite Settlement* (Jerusalem: Israel Exploration Society, 1998); Israel Finkelstein, Zvi Lederman, and Shlomo Bunimovitz, *Highland of Many Cultures: The Southern Samaria Survey, The Sites*, 2 vols. (Tel Aviv: Tel Aviv University, 1997); see also Moshe Kochavi, ed., *Judaea, Samaria and the Golan: Archaeological Survey 1967–1968* (Jerusalem: Carta; The Archaeological Survey of Israel, 1972); Adam Zertal, *The Manasseh Hill Country Survey: Volume 1, The Shechem Syncline* (Leiden: Brill, 2004); Zertal, *The Manasseh Hill Country Survey: Volume 2, The Eastern Valleys and the Fringes of the Desert* (London: Brill, 2008).

13. The initial summary of the data was by Finkelstein, *Israelite Settlement*, 65–91, 324–35, 352–56; Adam Zertal, "'To the Land of the Perizzites and the Giants': On the Israelite Settlement in the Hill Country of Manasseh," in *From Nomadism to Monarchy: Archaeological & Historical Aspects of Early Israel*, ed. Israel Finkelstein and Nadav Na'aman (Jerusalem: Israel Exploration Society, 1994), 47–69.

Model of Iron I Settlement in Ephraim and Manasseh

items. The site architecture is characterized by four-room houses, small stone-lined silos, and ring-shaped settlements in which the houses form a perimeter enclosure.[14] These sites are typically small or very small, with a sedentary farming or herding character. While these traits are unique to neither this region nor this timeframe, on the whole, they suggest the emergence of a people group distinct from the preexisting urban Canaanites of the Late Bronze Age in lifestyle and ecological adaptation.[15] Whether or not they also indicate a distinct ethnicity is much more difficult to show from the archaeological record.[16]

The vast majority of these sites were built at new locations in the central hills, places that did not have prior settlement. Finkelstein identified over one

14. Zertal offers a list of eleven variables that he identified in the archaeological and cultural record which together, he maintains, distinguish the inhabitants of these sites from earlier (Late Bronze) sites in the same region, and from their neighbors in Iron I (Zertal, "Iron Age I Culture in the Hill-Country of Canaan: A Manassite Perspective," in *Mediterranean Peoples in Transition: Thirteenth to Early Tenth Centuries BCE*, ed. Seymour Gitin, Amihai Mazar, and Ephraim Stern [Jerusalem: Israel Exploration Society, 1998], 238).

15. Aren M. Maeir, "The Archaeology of Iron Age I," in *Behind the Scenes of the Old Testament*, ed. Jonathan S. Greer, John W. Hilber, and John H. Walton (Grand Rapids: Baker Academic, 2018), 57.

16. Avraham Faust, *Israel's Ethnogenesis: Settlement, Interaction, Expansion, and Resistance* (London: Equinox, 2006), 111–34; Israel Finkelstein, "The Emergence of Israel: A Phase in the Cyclic History of Canaan in the Third and Second Millennium BCE," in Finkelstein and Na'aman, *From Nomadism to Monarchy*, 169.

hundred twenty such sites in Ephraim, and Zertal over two hundred forty in Manasseh. By comparison, the same region had only around forty sites in the prior Late Bronze Age, several of which were larger and exhibited an urban (i.e., classic Canaanite) character. Perhaps most significantly, an estimated ninety percent of all Iron I sites in the twelfth century BC lay between ancient Bethel and the Jezreel Valley, precisely the area of the biblical tribal inheritances of Ephraim and Manasseh. According to Finkelstein and Zertal (though strongly countered by Faust[17]), the survey data also suggests a strong continuity of settlement into the Iron Age II, with the settled area and number of sites expanding in the Iron Age II from the eastern slopes and watershed ridge to contiguous areas to the west, south, and north, with the exception of the Jezreel Valley. More specifically, Zertal and Rainey interpret the survey data as indicating an overall east to west settlement movement by a semi-nomadic population that originated in Transjordan.[18] All of this is consistent with the broad outline of the biblical settlement narrative, especially the movement of Jacob from Gilead to Shechem, and the house of Joseph into forested areas.

A HISTORIC QUESTION

We have seen that data from the biblical narrative, geography, and archaeology correlate at important juncture points to favor the priority of Ephraim and Manasseh in the early settlement narratives, despite the Jerusalem-orientation that dominates the final shape of the biblical text. Overall, the data suggests that Israel's settlement started (i.e., can first be traced in the textual and archaeological record) in the hills of Ephraim and Manasseh. Yet even this statement is fraught with questions both unanswered and unanswerable. I will conjecture about only one. Given that the battle accounts figure prominently in the narrative structure of the book of Joshua, why is there no conquest narrative for the hill country of Ephraim and Manasseh, a place that otherwise was so prominent in the actual settlement of the land? The details of Israel's penetration into the land—how many can be put under the categories of conquest, gradual adaptation, skirmish, assimilation, or any combination thereof—will never be known. That there was conquest activity in the Ephraim/Manasseh hills, the nature of which was likely symptomatic of any people's movement in to any new land, can be inferred from Jacob's vengeance at Shechem (Gen 34:26–29), Joshua's directive that the house of Joseph "clear the land to its farthest borders" and "drive out the Canaanites" (Josh 17:18), and the inclusion of Tappuah and Tirzah in the list of conquered cities (Josh 12:17, 24). But these are not part of the main narrative line. Perhaps—and this is a majority

17. Faust argues that the data from these surveys needs to be reinterpreted based on the actual excavation of sites that indicate a settlement gap in the rural villages in the tenth century BC, with a reestablishment of the villages only in the ninth through seventh centuries BC concurrent with the rise of the Israelite monarchy (Faust, *Israel's Ethnogenesis*, 33, 111–134; Faust, "Chronological and Spatial Changes in the Rural Settlement Sector of Ancient Israel during the Iron Age: An Overview," *Revue Biblique* 122 [2015]: 247–67).

18. Zertal, "Iron Age I Culture," 242–43, 247–48; Rainey and Notley, *Sacred Bridge*, 111.

view—the source material was lacking, gapped, or inconsistent.[19] If so, there is little substantive reason to pursue the question any further.

Still, some scholars have attempted tentative historic reconstructions. Bright, for instance, in a classic solution, posited that the *Apiru* of the Amarna texts, together with certain allied elements of an indigenous Canaanite population that was already established in the central·hills during the weakened Amarna Period (fourteenth century BC), "made common cause" with Israel over time, thus negating the need for a formal conquest by an outside population.[20] Aharoni and others, noting that the house of Joseph had become a (the?) dominant factor in the central hills by the beginning of the Iron Age, essentially concur, citing the natural development of symbiotic relationships between settled, urban populations and emergent semi-nomadic ones that sometimes tip the balance of power in favor of the latter.[21] This could explain, for instance, the genealogy of Manasseh including Shechem and Tirzah as the name of two of his descendants (Num 26:28–34).

There remains another possibility. Irrespective of these historic uncertainties, it seems that the absence of a conquest *narrative* should be explained first within the confines of the literary strategy of the book itself. The people of Israel had just come out of a long sojourn in Egypt, where they dwelt in a place of mixed memories but one that was never "home;" *that* concept was reserved for the land where Abraham, Isaac, and Jacob had lived. The last thing that the writer of the Joshua narrative could admit is that, having left Egypt behind, Israel found another people—not just Canaanites but even remnants of an Egyptian economic and imperial presence—still well entrenched in the old, new homeland to which they were returning. Here ideology shapes the tale: one should not have to admit the need to conquer what should already be yours. What Israel *had* to conquer and secure was the doorway in, hence the battle accounts of Jericho and Ai (Josh 6:1–8:29), and the perimeter, that is, the southern border of Ephraim (i.e., the conquest of Gibeon and the coalition of kings in the southern hills; Josh 9:1–10:43) and the northern border of Manasseh (represented by the coalition of kings allied with Hazor; Josh 11:1–15). In this way, the conquest accounts within the narrative of Joshua strengthen the idea of the prominence of Ephraim and Manasseh within the book *precisely because* they take place elsewhere, with the periphery embracing the center.

---

19. See, for instance, Rainey and Notley, *Sacred Bridge*, 129.

20. The majority of the Amarna texts are letters written by the Canaanite kings to either Pharaoh Amenhotep III or his son Amenhotep IV (Akhenaten) in the mid-fourteenth century BC. In them, the kings inform the pharaoh about relations between various Canaanite cities, often asking for Egyptian help on their behalf. A frequent term mentioned in these texts is *Apiru*. The meaning of the term is highly debated. Some scholars have equated it with the Hebrews (*ibrim*). Others find the *Apiru* to have been freelancers, persons of various ethnicities or social backgrounds who allied themselves either for, or against, a variety of causes or political movements as opportunities arose. See John Bright, *A History of Israel*, 3rd ed. (Philadelphia: Westminster, 1981), 136; Rainey and Notley, *Sacred Bridge*, 62, 88–89.

21. Yohanan Aharoni, *The Land of the Bible: A Historical Geography*, trans. Anson F. Rainey, rev. and enl. ed. (Philadelphia: Westminster, 1979), 192.

CONCLUSION

A close reading of the biblical texts related to the period of ancient Israel's conquest and settlement of Canaan, coupled with archaeological data from the Late Bronze and Iron I Ages, suggests that the Joseph tribes (Ephraim and Manasseh) played the prominent role in the establishment of early Israel in Canaan. If so, it is natural that the biblical record would highlight the territory in which Ephraim and Manasseh settled as being a particularly suitable homeland, as we see, for instance, in the blessings of Jacob and Moses to Joseph (Gen 49; Deut 33). We might also expect that by including formal conquest narratives only for portions of Canaan that bordered the tribal inheritances of Ephraim and Manasseh, the biblical writers signaled that this was Israel's proper heartland, now secured, from which Israel could grow.

BIBLIOGRAPHY

Aharoni, Yohanan. *The Land of the Bible: A Historical Geography*. Translated by Anson F. Rainey. Rev. and enl. ed. Philadelphia: Westminster, 1979.

Alt, Albrecht. *Essays on Old Testament History and Religion*. Translated by Richard A. Wilson. Sheffield: JSOT Press, 1989.

Assis, Elie. "'How Long are You Slack to Go to Possess the Land' (Jos. XVIII 3): Ideal and Reality in the Distribution Descriptions in Joshua XIII–XIX." *VT* 53.1 (2003): 1–25.

Bright, John. *A History of Israel*. 3rd ed. Philadelphia: Westminster, 1981.

Faust, Avraham. "Chronological and Spatial Changes in the Rural Settlement Sector of Ancient Israel during the Iron Age: An Overview." *Revue Biblique* 122 (2015): 247–67.

———. *Israel's Ethnogenesis: Settlement, Interaction, Expansion and Resistance*. London: Equinox, 2006.

Finkelstein, Israel. *The Archaeology of the Israelite Settlement*. Jerusalem: Israel Exploration Society, 1988.

———. "The Emergence of Israel: A Phase in the Cyclic History of Canaan in the Third and Second Millennium BCE." Pages 150–78 in *From Nomadism to Monarchy: Archaeological & Historical Aspects of Early Israel*. Edited by Israel Finkelstein and Nadav Na'aman. Jerusalem: Israel Exploration Society, 1994.

Finkelstein, Israel, Zvi Lederman, and Shlomo Bunimovitz. *Highland of Many Cultures: The Southern Samaria Survey, The Sites*. 2 vols. Tel Aviv: Tel Aviv University, 1997.

Hawkins, Ralph K. *How Israel Became a People*. Nashville: Abingdon, 2013.

Hess, Richard S. "Early Israel in Canaan: A Survey of Recent Evidence and Interpretations." *PEQ* 125 (1993): 125–42.

Japhet, Sara. "Was David a Judahite or an Ephraimite? Light from the Genealogies." Pages 297–306 in *Let Us Go Up to Zion: Essays in Honour of H.G.M. Williamson on the Occasion of His Sixty-Fifth Birthday*. Edited by Iain Provan and Mark J. Boda. Leiden: Brill, 2012.

Kochavi, Moshe, ed. *Judaea, Samaria and the Golan: Archaeological Survey 1967–1968*. Jerusalem: Carta; The Archaeological Survey of Israel, 1972.

Maeir, Aren M. "Archaeology of the Iron Age I." Pages 54–61 in *Behind the Scenes of the Old Testament: Cultural, Social, and Historical Contexts*. Edited by Jonathan S. Greer, John W. Hilber, and John H. Walton. Grand Rapids: Baker Academic, 2018.

Rainey, Anson F. *The El-Amarna Correspondence: An New Edition of the Cuneiform Letters from the Site of El-Amarna based on Collations of all Extant Tablets*. Edited by William M. Schniedewind. Vol. 1. Leiden: Brill, 2015.

Rainey, Anson F., and R. Steven Notley. *The Sacred Bridge: Carta's Atlas of the Biblical World*. 2nd ed. Jerusalem: Carta, 2014.

Smith, George Adam. *The Historical Geography of the Holy Land*. London: Hodder and Stoughton, 1894.

Wazana, Nili. *All the Boundaries of the Land: The Promised Land in Biblical Thought in Light of the Ancient Near East*. Winona Lake, IN: Eisenbrauns, 2013.

Wright, Paul H. *Holman Illustrated Guide to Biblical Geography: Reading the Land*. Nashville: B&H, 2020.

Zertal, Adam. "The Heart of the Monarchy: Pattern of Settlement and Historical Considerations of the Israelite Kingdom of Samaria." Pages 38–64 in *Studies in the Archaeology of the Iron Age in Israel and Jordan*." Edited by Amihai Mazar. Sheffield: Sheffield Academic, 2001.

———. "The Iron Age I Culture in the Hill-Country of Canaan: A Manassite Perspective." Pages 238–50 in *Mediterranean Peoples in Transition: Thirteenth to Early Tenth Centuries BCE*. Edited by Seymour Gitin, Amihai Mazar, and Ephraim Stern. Jerusalem: Israel Exploration Society, 1998.

———. "'To the Land of the Perizzites and the Giants': On the Israelite Settlement in the Hill Country of Manasseh." Pages 47–69 in *From Nomadism to Monarchy: Archaeological & Historical Aspects of Early Israel*. Edited by Israel Finkelstein and Nadav Na'aman. Jerusalem: Israel Exploration Society, 1994.

———. *The Manasseh Hill Country Survey: Volume 1, The Shechem Syncline*. Leiden: Brill, 2004.

———. *The Manasseh Hill Country Survey: Volume 2, The Eastern Valleys and the Fringes of the Desert*. Leiden: Brill, 2008.

CHAPTER 17

THE REITERATIVE MENTION OF THE TOWN OF BETHEL

Josh 16:1; 18:13; Judg 1:22–26; 20:18, 26–28; 21:2; 1 Sam 7:16; 10:3–4; 1 Kgs 12:29–33; 13:1–34; 2 Kgs 2:1–24; 10:29; 17:28; 23:15–19; Gen 28:10–22; 35:1–15; Hos 4:15; 5:8; 10:5, 8; 12:1–6; Amos 4:4; 5:5–6; 7:10–13

Victor H. Matthews

KEY POINTS

- Bethel is second only to Jerusalem in the number of citations in the biblical text and makes a perfect example of geographic reiteration.
- Bethel's authority begins with its association with the ancestral narratives.
- During the divided monarchy, Bethel functions as a major cultic center.
- Josiah's reform includes the desacralization of Bethel's shrine, ending its cultic role.

INTRODUCTION

When the biblical writers include a place name or a distinctive geographic feature in the narrative, they rely on their audience's familiarity with the reference. Their shared experience as geographic "insiders" allows them to evoke memories in the minds of their listeners that bring the story to life. However, modern readers who do not share these collective memories can be put off by strange-sounding place names and wonder why particular places so frequently appear in the text. This means that special attention to geographic information and to scribal strategy in mentioning them is necessary to draw fuller meaning from a story.

GEOGRAPHIC REITERATION

Because Syro-Palestine is a small geographic region with a limited number of cities and towns of any size, it is not surprising to find that the same places appear repeatedly in the biblical narrative.[1] Major cities are generally located at strategic points. Megiddo, for instance, guarded the western end of the Jezreel Valley, a major trade route that bisects east-west the region just south of the Galilee. Similarly, Jericho benefited from a perennial spring (Ain es-Sultan) and sat at the point north of the Dead Sea that provides an entry way from the highlands down to the fords of the Jordan River.

Given the topographical, political, and economic realities of this region, it is statistically more likely that major events will occur at the same few places throughout the history of ancient Israel. Because of their placement, it is to be expected that major battles (Megiddo, Lachish), political conferences (Shechem), prophetic pronouncements (Jerusalem, Samaria), or annual festivals (Jerusalem, Bethel, Dan) take place in or near towns that stand at a crossroads or contain significant temples or shrines. For that reason, the memory of major historical events at these significant sites plays into a literary strategy employed by Israelite scribes in which they place events in settings that will give the characters or the events greater authority. In that way, and with the help of the writers, these sites not only have a history of their own but naturally become the setting for future significant events. It is the repetition of geographic citation, sometimes based on physical characteristics and sometimes on the desire of the authors of the narrative to give greater importance to the events of the story, that signal this scribal strategy.

Over time, this strategy of geographic reiteration contributes to the development of a city's or a site's physical and traditional reputation. These cities become a part of a scribal "database" that can then be drawn upon to enhance a story. Recognizing the value of tying the nation's or a king's successes to those of earlier leaders or victorious generals (e.g., compare Saul's use of Gilgal in 1 Sam 11:14–15 to Joshua's association with that site in Josh 4:9–20; 5:8–12), scenes such as coronations, battles, or meetings of heads of state are staged at the site of previous triumphs or turning points for the nation or dynasty.

SIGNIFICANCE OF BETHEL

As a way of demonstrating the use of geographic reiteration by ancient scribes, priests, and rulers, attention is now turned to the city of Bethel (modern Beitin), and how it has been used and reused in biblical narratives and prophetic literature. Mentioned seventy-one times—second only to Jerusalem—Bethel is located ten miles (16 km) north of Jerusalem on the Ephraim-Benjamin border (Josh 16:2). It is situated on a hill top with nearby perennial springs and is strategically placed at a crossroads between the Judean Plateau and the Ephraimite hill country, on a road leading to the Jordan Valley.[2] Its archaeo-

1. For a fuller treatment of this scribal strategy, see Victor H. Matthews, "Back to Bethel: Geographical Reiteration in Biblical Narrative," *JBL* 128 (2009): 149–65.

2. Anson Rainey, "Looking for Bethel: An Exercise in Historical Geography," in *Confronting the Past: Archaeological and Historical Essays on Ancient Israel in Honor of William G. Dever*, ed. Seymour Gitin, J. Edward Wright, and J. P. Dessel (Winona Lake, IN: Eisenbrauns, 2006), 269–73.

Bethel, Modern-Day Beitin

logical history contains evidence of almost continual settlement from the Middle Bronze to the Byzantine Period (2200 BC to AD 600), with four phases during the Iron Age, and a brief period of destruction and ruin as part of the sixth century BC Babylonian campaign that also resulted in the destruction of Jerusalem. The site was rebuilt during the Persian era (Zech 7:1–2; Neh 11:31).

The chart below outlines the major appearances of Bethel in the biblical narrative and forms a pattern that suggests that the city not only served a cultic role but became increasing important during the monarchy period. In prophetic texts, the city becomes synonymous with the northern kingdom of Israel's failure to obey the covenant and to maintain allegiance to the house of David and the temple in Jerusalem.

Bethel is one of several cultic sites in the hill country, including Shechem, Shiloh, and Gilgal. It is also included as one of the cities in Samuel's judicial circuit (1 Sam 7:16). When Shiloh loses much of its prominence after the loss of the ark of the covenant to the Philistines (1 Sam 4:10–11), the more centrally located Bethel rises in importance as the monarchy is established. Throughout its history, Bethel is linked to a fluctuating political and cultic situation. Focus on the city's cultic activity occurs when Jeroboam chooses Bethel and Dan to serve as shrines at either end of his kingdom (1 Kgs 12:28–30). When the Assyrians conquered the Northern Kingdom in 722/1 BC, Bethel retained some measure of authority as the seat for priests to instruct newly resettled peoples in the "law of the god of the land" (2 Kgs 17:28).[3] The shrine's final

3. All Bible translations are from the New Revised Standard Version (NRSV) unless otherwise indicated.

demise occurs when Josiah desacralizes the site and destroys its cultic precincts.[4]

USE AND REUSE OF BETHEL

Given the long history and significance of the city of Bethel, the scribal practice of geographic reiteration ties foundation events from the ancestral narratives and settlement period to specific, significant sites that then play a part in the rise of the Davidic dynasty to power and to the rivalry with the kings of the Northern Kingdom. In this section, these appearances of Bethel will be examined.

In the ancestral narratives, Bethel first appears when Abraham constructs one of his altars in the vicinity between Bethel and Ai (Gen 12:8). While they remained intact, these altars and other monuments set up by the ancestors (e.g., Jacob's pillar in Gen 35:14) functioned as "topographies of memory" that reinforced social memories of the group (i.e., the nation of Israel).[5] By marking his journey through the promise land, Abraham "staked out" the dimensions of the divine bequest, from Shechem south to Beersheba. Bethel next appears in the Jacob cycle of stories. After deceiving Isaac and Esau to obtain blessing, Jacob quickly departs for Harran to find a bride. He leaves his encampment at Beersheba (28:10) and stops at a "certain place" (28:11), Luz. Here he experiences a dream theophany and receives the covenant promise (28:13–15). Jacob then applies an "incident name" or "bestowed name" on the place, calling it Bethel, "the house of God," in acknowledgement of his theophanic experience.[6] Then, like Abraham, he formalizes this event by erecting a pillar, pouring out an oil libation, and voicing the terms of a vow to God (28:18–22). After spending over twenty years in Harran, Jacob is once again visited by the "God of Bethel," who instructs him to leave Harran and Laban's household and return to the land of his family (31:13). The cycle of stories is then completed when Jacob is commanded to go to Bethel after the massacre at Shechem. A geo-cultic *inclusio* is formed when he erects a pillar and once again renames the spot Bethel (35:1–15).

During the settlement period, Bethel is assigned to the territory of the Josephites (Josh 16:1) and is said to be captured by the tribe of Benjamin (Josh 18:13). Both events tie Bethel firmly to the Northern Kingdom and set up later political rivalries. Also, during this period, Bethel can claim direct association with the ark of the covenant in the story of the civil war between the tribes in Judg 20–21. Three times the allied tribes went to Bethel to consult God, "for the ark of the covenant of God was there in those days" (Judg 20:18, 26; 21:2). While the Judges account does provide a "verbal map" of the northern cultic sites (Shechem, Shiloh, and Bethel; 21:19), only Bethel

4. W. Boyd Barrick, *The King and the Cemeteries: Toward a New Understanding of Josiah's Reform* (Leiden: Brill, 2002), 59–61.

5. Patricia Murrieta-Flores and Howard Williams, "Placed the Pillar of Eliseg: Movement, Visibility and Memory in the Early Medieval Landscape," *Medieval Archaeology* 61 (2017): 75.

6. George R. Stewart, *Names on the Globe* (New York: Oxford, 1975), 5–6, 105–6. Jacob combines bestowing a new name on a place with basing his action on the incident being commemorated. There is also an associative aspect to the naming since persons seeking the presence of a god would be attracted to a place known as the "House of God."

MAJOR APPEARANCES OF BETHEL

Gen 12:8	Abraham builds an altar at Bethel, one of several (Shechem, Hebron, Beersheba)
Gen 13:3–16	After sojourn in Egypt, Abraham comes again to Bethel, receives covenant promise of land after Lot separates with him and goes to Sodom
Gen 28:19	Following a theophany at Luz, Jacob renames the city Bethel
Gen 31:13	Jacob is told by the "God of Bethel" to leave Laban's household in Harran and return to "land of your birth"
Gen 35:1–15	After hurriedly leaving Shechem (Gen 34), Jacob is told by God to go to Bethel. He builds an altar, names the place El-Bethel, buries Rachel's nurse, has a theophany providing him with a name change to Israel, has the covenant reiterated, sets up a pillar and pours out a drink offering and oil, and names Luz Bethel again (35:6, 15)
Josh 16:1	Bethel is included in the allotment of land designated for the Josephites
Josh 18:13	The equation of Luz = Bethel found again in Benjaminite allot-ment of land
Judg 1:22–26	Joseph's tribe captures Bethel (formerly Luz)
Judg 20:18, 26–28; 21:2	During civil war Israelite tribes go to Bethel to inquire of God "Which of us shall go up first?" and return there after initial defeat. They return again after the war to consult God about wives for the tribe of Benjamin
1 Sam 7:16	Bethel is included in Samuel's judicial circuit, as well as Gilgal and Mizpah
1 Sam 10:3–4	Three men "going up to God at Bethel" with offerings give Saul two loaves of bread indicating that he is the divinely chosen king
1 Kgs 12:29–33	Jeroboam designates Dan and Bethel as his royal shrines, places golden calf images in each, and appoints a festival there on the fifteenth day of the eighth month
1 Kgs 13:1–34	Unnamed prophet from Judah goes to Bethel and "cried out against the altar at Bethel" (13:4)
2 Kgs 2:1–24	Elijah and Elisha follow a reverse conquest itinerary, going from Bethel to Jericho to the Jordan River, in preparation for Elijah's being taken away; there is a company of prophets in Bethel (2:3)
2 Kgs 10:29	Jehu fails to remove the golden calves from Dan and Bethel

2 Kgs 17:28	After Samaria falls to Assyria, the king orders a priest to teach the new peoples brought to Samaria "the law of the god of the land" and he goes to Bethel and "taught them how they should worship the Lord"
2 Kgs 23:15–19	Josiah desacralizes the altar and high place at Bethel
Jer 48:13	Moab's shame in serving Chemosh compared to Israel's worship at Bethel
Hos 10:5–13	Among the cites condemned as sources of Israel's sin is Bethel
Hos 12:4	Jacob's supplication when he "met [God] at Bethel" is a warning to Israel to take a similar path rather than continue foreign alliances (12:1)
Amos 3:14	Indicting "Jacob," God will "punish the altars of Bethel" and cut off its horns
Amos 4:4	Amos sarcastically urges the Israelites to "come to Bethel and transgress"
Amos 5:5	Amos urges people not to "seek Bethel" since "Bethel shall come to nothing"
Amos 5:6	God's fire will break out against Bethel with no one to quench it
Amos 7:10–13	Amos's confrontation with Amaziah, "the priest of Bethel"—the priest calls it "the king's sanctuary and it is a temple of the kingdom"

emerges in this story as a place where Yahweh can be reliably consulted.[7]

Bethel continues to serve as a cultic site in the period leading up to the establishment of the monarchy. For example, Saul encounters three men, who are "going up to God at Bethel" with offerings (kids, loaves, and wine), and they give Saul two loaves of bread as an acknowledgement that he is God's chosen king (1 Sam 10:3–4). This event adds a political association to Bethel's story that will continue throughout the remainder of its history. For example, the fact that the signs forecast by Samuel for Saul's kingship occur in Benjaminite territory and Saul's tribal ties are to Benjamin associate this location with kingship. Furthermore, as the geographic link in these stories, Bethel's importance as a regional cultic and political center, located strategically between the northern and southern areas of Israelite territory, is reiterated for the story's audience.[8]

For a time, Bethel's cultic importance seems to have been overshadowed by the shift in political authority from the house of Saul to the house of David, with its association with Hebron and Jerusalem. The emergence of a new ruling family,

7. Susan Niditch, *Judges*, OTL (Louisville: Westminster John Knox, 2008), 47.

8. See Jules F. Gomes, *The Sanctuary of Bethel and the Configuration of Israelite Identity* (Berlin: de Gruyter, 2006), 135–36.

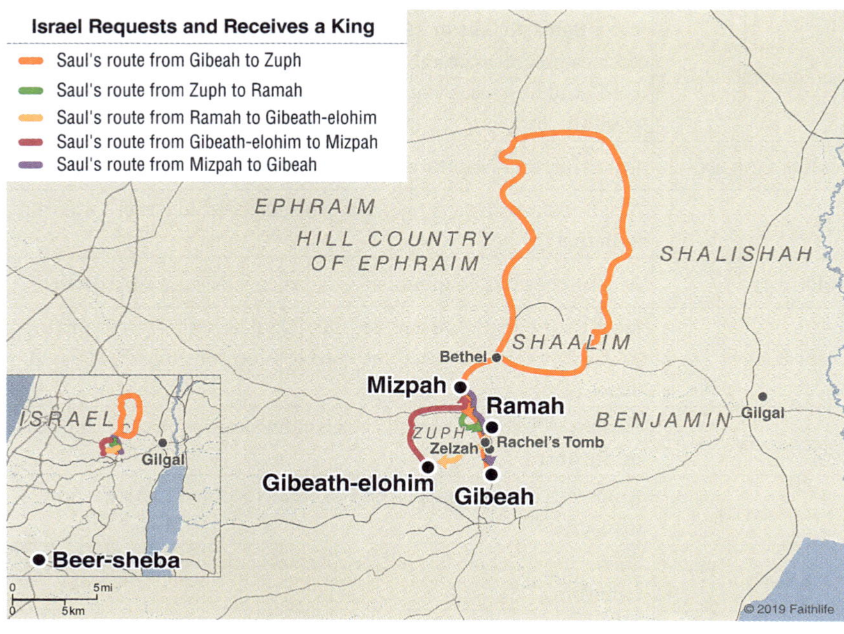

the transference of the ark of the covenant and the construction of the temple in Jerusalem by Solomon eclipsed the importance of other cultic centers like Bethel. However, the division of the kingdom during Rehoboam's reign allowed Bethel's significance to reemerge as one of Jeroboam's two royal sanctuaries.

Determining why Jeroboam chose Bethel and Dan as his sanctuary sites hinges on both geography and traditional association as a cultic facility.[9] These two cities represent the north-south geographic poles of the new kingdom, with Bethel sitting right on the border with Judah, providing an attractive, nearby cultic option for the people in the central portion of both kingdoms instead of going to Jerusalem. Plus, both sites have a history as cultic centers that played into the scheme of geographic reiteration, which has the dual advantages of placing political pressure on the Southern Kingdom and satisfying the need for well-known religious centers.

Despite being identified as the antithesis of David in the Deuteronomistic History, Jeroboam is an astute politician, who understands the importance of both physical and authoritative space. He asserts his political independence while rallying the support of his subjects to reject Jerusalem, its temple, and the ark, and substitutes these two cult centers, a hand-picked priestly staff not tied to the Zadokites, and golden

9. Baruch Halpern, "Levitic Participation in the Reform Cult of Jeroboam I," *JBL* 95 (1976): 32. Dan is associated with the idol and shrine erected by the migrating tribe of Dan (Judg 18:27–31).

calves as visual representations of God's presence.[10]

In its enhanced capacity, Bethel and its newly formed priesthood become firmly associated with the political fortunes of the rulers of the Northern Kingdom. Undoubtedly, this meant great prosperity for its priesthood as Israel emerged as an independent kingdom under the Omrides. However, it is the Deuteronomistic Historian that ultimately will tell the story found in the biblical narrative. Whatever fame Bethel may have obtained, is transformed by these scribal editors into condemnation and ridicule. Bethel for them functioned as the seat of invalid worship and from the beginning is defamed, starting with the prediction of its destruction by the unnamed prophet of Judah (1 Kgs 13:1–10).[11]

The final recounting for Bethel occurs when Josiah's reform movement expands north into the former Northern Kingdom. In his effort to reclaim at least a portion of that territory and to end any further cultic threat to Jerusalem's supremacy, he orders the desecration of both the sacred precinct and of the bodies of the priests who had served there.[12] This account functions as another example of geographic reiteration in the form of a fulfillment of the prophetic statement of the unnamed prophet in 1 Kgs 13:2–3. In the course of this extended reiteration process, the audience, as well as King Josiah, has to be convinced of the sacred associations that had made Bethel a place closely

10. See Mark Leuchter, "Jeroboam the Ephratite," *JBL* 125 (2006): 51–72.

11. See Erik Eynikel, "Prophecy and Fulfillment in the Deuteronomistic History (1 Kgs 13; 2 Kgs 23, 16–18)," in *Pentateuchal and Deuteronomistic Studies*, ed. Christianus Brekelmans (Louvain: Leuven University Press, 1990), 227–37.

12. Lauren A. S. Monroe, *Josiah's Reform and the Dynamics of Defilement: Israelite Rites of Violence and the Making of a Biblical Text* (New York: Oxford, 2011), 107.

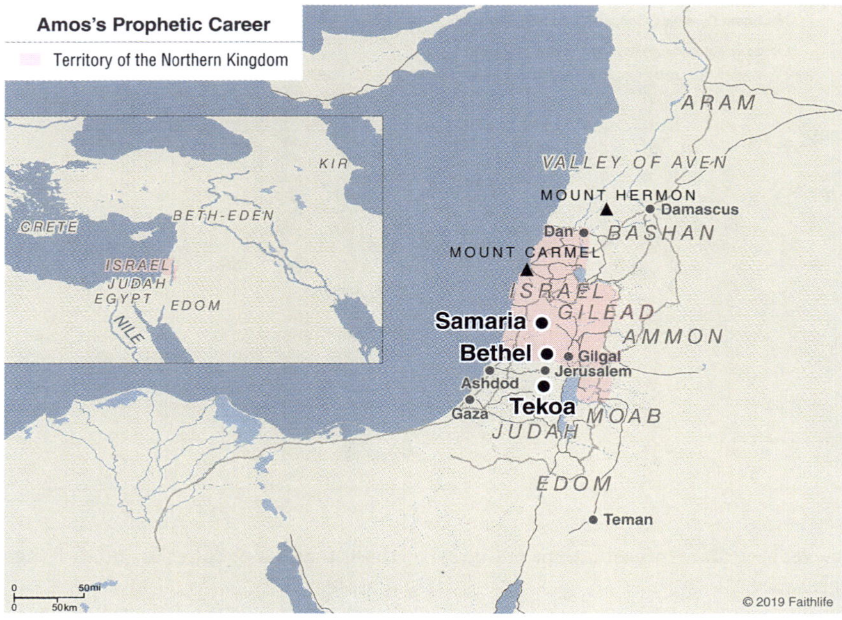

tied to God's covenantal promise.[13] Then, just as Jeremiah reminds the people of Jerusalem about Shiloh's fate (Jer 7:13–15), the case is made that no place is so sacred that it is immune to destruction when its sacred function and character come into question. Thus, the royal expedition, representing the true sanctuary of Yahweh at Jerusalem, completes the process by eliminating this rival shrine.

It is quite possible, however, that despite Josiah's efforts, this sacred precinct, even in a ruined condition, continued to have some religious function into the period of Neo-Babylonian and Persian administration down through the fifth century BC (see Zech 7:1–7). Like other sites in Benjaminite territory, Bethel was not destroyed when Jerusalem met its fate in 587/6 BC.[14] Indications in the census lists contained in Ezra and Nehemiah (Ezra 2:28; Neh 7:32) also suggest that the city of Bethel was either rebuilt or restored, but it is unlikely that it served as a major cultic center at that time.

BETHEL IN THE PROPHETS

Prophetic voices also play a part in the demonization of Bethel, although these references are primarily in Amos and

13. See D. W. Van Winkle, "1 Kings XII 25–XIII 34: Jeroboam's Cultic Innovations and the Man of God from Judah," *VT* 46 (1996): 101–14. Gary Knoppers extends the theme of "surprise" to Josiah, at least for the editor's purposes, to add more authority to the centuries' old connection (Knoppers, *Two Nations Under God* [Atlanta: Scholars Press, 1994], 2:209).

14. Joseph Blenkinsopp, "Bethel in the Neo-Babylonian Period," in *Judah and the Judeans in the Neo-Babylonian Period*, ed. Oded Lipschits and Joseph Blenkinsopp (Winona Lake, IN: Eisenbrauns, 2003), 95–96.

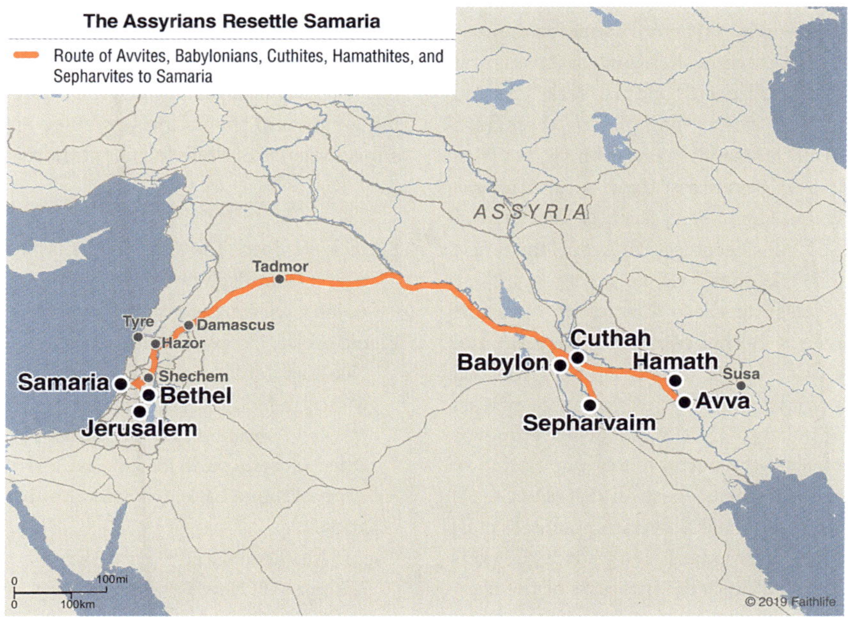

Hosea. The Judahite prophet Amos journeys from his village, Tekoa, north to Bethel to pronounce his message condemning the many social injustices in Israel and the "king's sanctuary" (Amos 7:13). In a speech filled with irony, he calls on the people to "come to Bethel"—something that Jeroboam and his successors certainly would deem appropriate (Amos 4:4). However, in this instance, Amos is launching a sarcastic attack on the shrine and its false practices, not granting it a measure of legitimacy.[15] Reversing his rhetoric, Amos then provides the more standard warning, urging the people to seek Yahweh rather than Bethel, for that place "shall come to nothing" (Amos 5:5–6).

The verbal confrontation with Amaziah, "the priest of Bethel," brings Amos's anti-Bethel message into sharper focus. Amaziah ridicules the untrained country prophet for presuming to speak in the "king's sanctuary" and instructs him to return home and never again dare to "prophesy at Bethel" (7:12–13). Amos refuses to be silenced or to accept Amaziah's assertion of sole authority to speak for God. His retort serves as a badge of honor that he is not to be identified with royal prophets (חֹזֶה, *hozeh*; 7:12) or the illegitimate priesthood at Bethel.

Hosea uses the association of Jacob with Bethel (Gen 28:10–22) as the basis for his condemnation of Israel. He indicates that, just as Jacob had been a contentious man, even willing to wrestle with God (Gen 32:22–32), the people of Israel repeatedly have contended with

15. For an examination of the rhetorical usage of irony and sarcasm, see John S. Leggitt and Raymond W. Gibbs, "Emotional Reactions to Verbal Irony," *Discourse Processes* 29 (2000): 3–4.

God as well.[16] The only way for them to truly return to their proper covenantal relationship with God is to seek "love and justice" rather than placing their faith in alliances with Assyria and Egypt (Hos 12:1–6). Because of their unfaithfulness, Bethel, renamed by Jacob as "the house of God," has become Beth Aven, "the house of Wickedness" (Hos 4:15; 5:8; 10:5, 8).

Despite these dire prophetic statements, Bethel remains a cultural and cultic center during the eighth and seventh centuries BC in which priests appointed by the Assyrian emperor educate the newly mixed population in the worship of Yahweh (2 Kgs 17:24–29). However, these Assyrian appointees most likely were expected to provide religious instruction in the interests of the occupying government, and the new settlers undoubtedly continued to combine worship of Yahweh with that of their own foreign gods.[17]

CONCLUSION

Making careful use of Bethel's history and cultic significance, the scribal strategy of geographic reiteration as it appears in the biblical narrative effectively redefined the story of the site to serve the theological purposes of the editors and the kings of Judah that they served. The political and priestly forces employed in this process drew on the traditional authority associated with the site since the time of the ancestors, and then when political expediency demanded, they undermined that authority to eliminate Bethel's influence. The ultimate purpose and result were to ensure that Bethel never again shadowed Jerusalem as a major cultic center. While a lingering memory existed of Bethel's former cultic role, the events of history and the changing fortunes of the nation prevented an effort to revive Bethel's former authority.

BIBLIOGRAPHY

Barrick, W. Boyd. *The King and the Cemeteries: Toward a New Understanding of Josiah's Reform*. Leiden: Brill, 2002.

Blenkinsopp, Joseph. "Bethel in the Neo-Babylonian Period." Pages 93–107 in *Judah and the Judeans in the Neo-Babylonian Period*. Edited by Oded Lipschits and Joseph Blenkinsopp. Winona Lake, IN: Eisenbrauns, 2003.

Cogan, Mordechai and Hayim Tadmor. *II Kings*. AB. New York: Doubleday, 1988.

Eynikel, Eric. "Prophecy and Fulfillment in the Deuteronomistic History (1 Kgs 13; 2 Kgs 23, 16–18)." Pages 227–37 in *Pentateuchal and Deuteronomistic Studies*. Edited by Christianus Brekelmans. Louvain: Leuven University Press, 1990.

Gomes, Jules F. *The Sanctuary of Bethel and the Configuration of Israelite Identity*. Berlin: de Gruyter, 2006.

Halpern, Baruch. "Levitic Participation in the Reform Cult of Jeroboam I." *JBL* 95 (1976): 31–42.

Knoppers, Gary. *Two Nations Under God.* Vol. 2. Atlanta: Scholars Press, 1994.

Leggitt, John S., and Raymond W. Gibbs. "Emotional Reactions to Verbal Irony." *Discourse Processes* 29 (2000): 1–24.

Leuchter, Mark. "Jeroboam the Ephratite." *JBL* 125 (2006): 51–72.

16. Steven L. McKenzie, "The Jacob Tradition in Hosea 12:4–5," *VT* 36 (1986): 317–18.

17. Marvin A. Sweeney, *I & II Kings*, OTL (Louisville: Westminster John Knox, 2007), 390–91. Mordechai Cogan and Hayim Tadmor, *II Kings*, AB (New York: Doubleday, 1988), 213.

Matthews, Victor H. “Back to Bethel: Geographical Reiteration in Biblical Narrative.” *JBL* 128 (2009): 149–65.

McKenzie, Steven L. “The Jacob Tradition in Hosea 12:4–5.” *VT* 36 (1986): 311–22.

Monroe, Lauren A. S. *Josiah's Reform and the Dynamics of Defilement: Israelite Rites of Violence and the Making of a Biblical Text*. New York: Oxford, 2011.

Murrieta-Flores, Patricia and Howard Williams. “Placed the Pillar of Eliseg: Movement, Visibility and Memory in the Early Medieval Landscape.” *Medieval Archaeology* 61 (2017): 69–103.

Niditch, Susan. *Judges*. OTL. Louisville: Westminster John Knox, 2008.

Rainey, Anson. “Looking for Bethel: An Exercise in Historical Geography.” Pages 269–73 in *Confronting the Past: Archaeological and Historical Essays on Ancient Israel in Honor of William G. Dever*. Edited by Seymour Gitin, J. Edward Wright, and J. P. Dessel. Winona Lake, IN: Eisenbrauns, 2006.

Stewart, George R. *Names on the Globe*. New York: Oxford, 1975.

Sweeney, Marvin A. *I & II Kings*. OTL. Louisville: Westminster John Knox, 2007.

Van Winkle, D. W. “1 Kings XII 25–XIII 34: Jeroboam's Cultic Innovations and the Man of God from Judah.” *VT* 46 (1996): 101–14.

CHAPTER 18

APPORTIONMENT OF THE PROMISED LAND TO THE TRIBES OF ZEBULUN, ISSACHAR, ASHER, NAPHTALI, AND DAN

Josh 19:10–48

Brian Donnelly-Lewis

KEY POINTS

- Defining the tribal boundaries of Zebulun, Issachar, Asher, Naphtali, and Dan requires an intimate knowledge of the geography of the land of Israel coupled with the identification of key sites within each apportionment.
- The complex landscape of the Galilee gives context to various aspects of the history of the northern tribes, including their size, distribution, and ultimate failure to drive out the Canaanites.
- The migration of the tribe of Dan is motivated by the geographical realities of the coastal plain, a region which eluded Israelite control for much of its history.

INTRODUCTION

Much of the latter half of the book of Joshua is devoted to the apportioning of the promised land to the various tribes of Israel. The most detailed descriptions of the apportionments concern the tribes of the central hill country: Judah, Ephraim and Manasseh, and Benjamin. The book of Joshua describes that these tribes took precedence, and the remainder of the land was apportioned by casting lots at Shiloh (Josh 18:9–10). The first two lots came out for Benjamin and Simeon (Josh 18:11; 19:1), while the remainder, three through seven, were assigned to Zebulun, Issachar, Asher, Naphtali, and Dan. The descriptions of these latter apportionments in Josh 19:10–48 is a very limited account. Many of these descriptions are terse, containing little more than a few

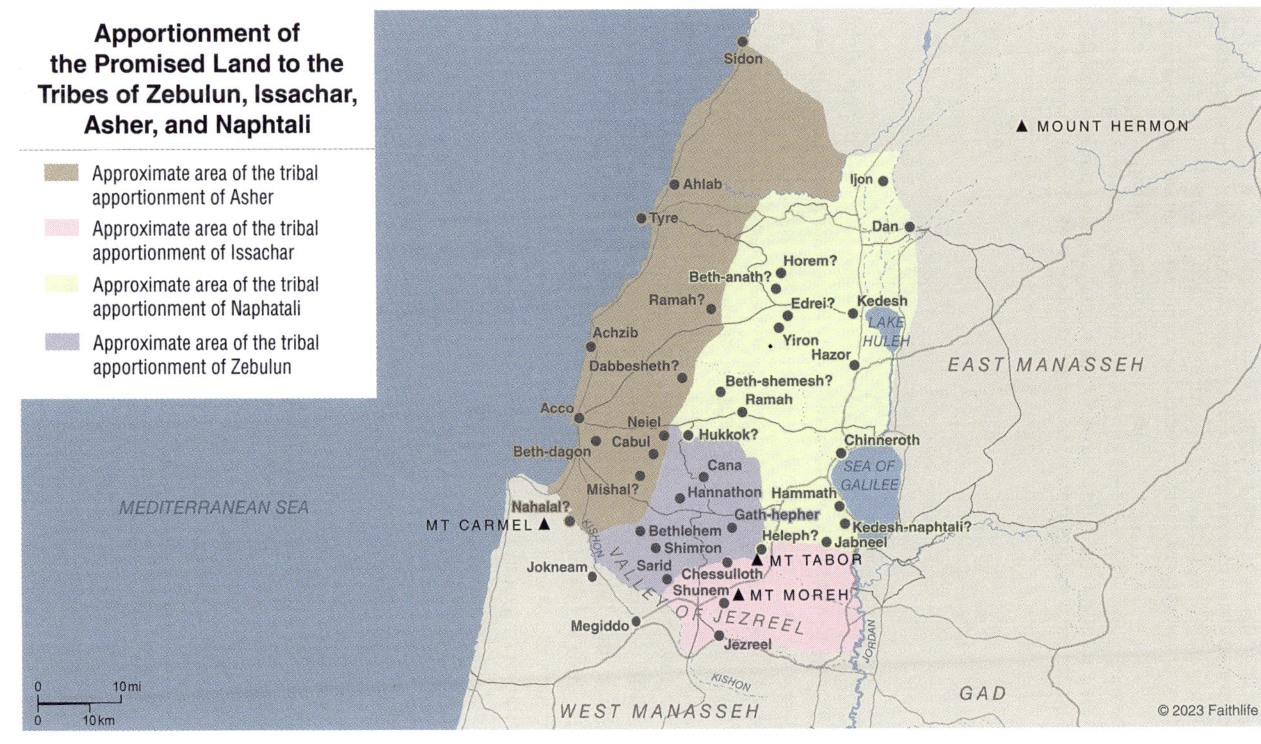
Apportionment of the Promised Land to the Tribes of Zebulun, Issachar, Asher, and Naphtali
Approximate area of the tribal apportionment of Asher
Approximate area of the tribal apportionment of Issachar
Approximate area of the tribal apportionment of Naphatali
Approximate area of the tribal apportionment of Zebulun
Sidon
▲ MOUNT HERMON
Ahlab
Ijon
Tyre
Dan
Horem?
Beth-anath?
Ramah?
Edrei?
Kedesh
LAKE HULEH
Achzib
Yiron
Hazor
Dabbesheth?
EAST MANASSEH
Beth-shemesh?
Ramah
Acco
Neiel
Cabul
Hukkok?
Chinneroth
Beth-dagon
Cana
SEA OF GALILEE
Mishal?
Hannathon
Hammath
MEDITERRANEAN SEA
Nahalal?
Gath-hepher
MT CARMEL ▲
KISHON
Bethlehem
Kedesh-naphtali?
Heleph?
Jabneel
Shimron
MT TABOR
Jokneam
Sarid
Chessulloth
VALLEY OF JEZREEL
Shunem
MT MOREH
Megiddo
Jezreel
JORDAN
KISHON
GAD
WEST MANASSEH
0 10mi
0 10km
© 2023 Faithlife

boundary marking routes with an accompanying city list. Consequently, these apportionments are difficult to trace without a thorough knowledge of the geographical landscape of each region and a knowledge of the location of the cities apportioned to each tribe. Fortunately for the modern reader, the geography has not changed significantly since the time of Joshua, and, with the help of historical geography, many of the ancient sites can be identified, providing ample evidence with which to confidently reconstruct each tribe's boundaries.[1]

Delineating each apportionment's boundaries and locating it geographically also elucidates some aspects of the history of each tribe, including their distribution of settlement, relative size, and ultimate failure to drive out the Canaanites. The complex geographic realities of the land, both in the north, in the region of Galilee, and on the coast, pertaining to the apportionment of Dan, give texture to the description of each apportionment and provide the reader with a greater appreciation for the complexities of the initial Israelite settlement in the promised land.

ZEBULUN (JOSH 19:10–16)

BORDER DESCRIPTION

In the book of Joshua, the people of Israel gather at Shiloh to cast lots to apportion the land and distribute these apportionments to the remaining tribes. The first two lots came out for the southern tribes of Benjamin and Simeon, but with the third lot begins a series of apportionments of northern tribes, the first of which is Zebulun. The tribal apportionment of Zebulun is important for understanding the borders between the other northern tribes, as it borders Issachar on the east, Asher on the west, and Naphtali on the north. The territory is defined in Josh 19:10–14 with an accompanying city list in verse 15. The boundary begins in the south at Sarid (Tell Shadud), from which point the southern border extends westward to Dabbesheth (Tell esh-Shammam?) and "the ravine near Jokneam," which is the Kishon River at the western end of the Jezreel Valley.[2] From here, the description returns to Sarid and extends eastward to the boundary of Kisloth Tabor (Iksal) and Daberath (Khirbet Dabbura)

1. Site identifications are given only once. Questionable identifications are included when deemed appropriate and noted as such with a question mark. All identifications rely on Aharoni unless otherwise noted (Yohanan Aharoni, *The Land of the Bible: A Historical Geography*, trans. Anson F. Rainey [London: Burns & Oates, 1967]).

2. When available, I prefer to use the Arabic names for many sites instead of the modern Hebrew names, as the modern Hebrew names have, in many cases, been assigned after historical geographers have conjectured an identification with a biblical site. For instance, Tell el-Ifshar is modern Hebrew "Tel Hepher," despite its unlikely association with biblical Hepher (Josh 12:17, 1 Kgs 4:17). Nevertheless, some famous sites with a secure identification, such as Gezer (Tel Gezer), Dan (Tel Dan), Megiddo (Tel Megiddo) and Hazor (Tel Hazor), will be marked according to their modern Hebrew name. All biblical quotations are from the New International Version (NIV) unless otherwise noted.

Mount Tabor (Left) and Hill of Moreh (Right) in the Jezreel Valley, View from the West

up to Japhia (Yafa?).[3] It is from here that the eastern border begins to be formed, as the border bends northward to Gath Hepher (Khirbet el-Zurra) and circles toward Rimmon (Rummanah), beginning the northern boundary. From Rimmon the boundary turns through the Beth-Netofah Valley, through Hannathon (Tell Badawiya), ending at the Valley of Iphtah El (Wadi el-Malik). The whole of the apportionment encompasses the Nazareth ridge and part of the northern Jezreel Valley. Its eastern boundary runs just west of Mount Tabor, and its western boundary excludes the Shephelah of the Galilee. On all sides, the apportionment to Zebulun represents a natural centerpiece around which the following distributions are situated.[4]

GEOGRAPHICAL ANALYSIS

Zebulun's apportionment in the northern Jezreel Valley, encompassing the Nazareth ridge, was positioned to dominate the major north-south and east-west trade routes. The main route of the international highway would have passed to the east of Mount Tabor and northwest of Mount Moreh, going through the Carmel ridge near Megiddo (Tel Megiddo). Just outside of the apportionment of Zebulun, a secondary route passed north of Mount Tabor, south of the Nazareth ridge, through

3. The Arab village of Yafa has often been identified with Yaphia (see Aharoni, *Land of the Bible*, 237), but Kallai notes the linguistic and archaeological difficulties with this identification (Zecharia Kallai, *Historical Geography of the Bible: The Tribal Territories of Israel* [Leiden: Brill, 1986], 185–86). For Daberath, see John L. Peterson, "Daberath," *ABD* 2:1.

4. Kallai, *Historical Geography*, 179.

Harod Valley and Mount Moreh from Mount Gilboa

Kisloth Tabor, turning south at Sarid and intersecting with the main international route at the pass next to Megiddo. Overall, Zebulun had ease of access to this great and important international highway.[5] Likewise, an important east-west route, from the Jezreel Valley to the port of Akko (Tell el-Fukhar) would have passed through the sites of Hannathon and Rimmon.[6] These international routes are but two major connection points which would have traversed the tribal apportionment of Zebulun, connecting the powerful Canaanite cities on the coast to the inland city kingdoms like Shimron (Khirbet Sammuniyeh) in the apportionment of Zebulun. These factors certainly played a role in the outcome described in Judg 1:30: the Canaanites lived among the tribe of Zebulun and subjected them to forced labor.

ISSACHAR (JOSH 19:17–23)

BORDER DESCRIPTION

The fourth lot came out for Issachar. The description of the tribal apportionment of Issachar is laconic, consisting of a city list (19:18–21) and only a brief mention of boundary points (19:22). Much of the boundary can be generalized on the basis of its location: north of the eastern edge of Manasseh, enclosed on the east by the Jordan River, south of Naphtali, and east

5. David A. Dorsey, *The Roads and Highways of Ancient Israel* (Eugene, OR: Wipf & Stock, 1991), 97–98.

6. Dorsey, *Roads and Highways*, 104–6 (route T 1c on Map 5).

of Zebulun. The particularities, however, must primarily be inferred from the location of sites in the city list (19:18–21). The first city mentioned, Jezreel (Tel Yizraal), is the furthest city south and marks the southwester boundary point. This southern boundary continued eastward from Jezreel, through the Harod Valley to the edge of the Jordan River, which marks the whole of its eastern boundary up to the place where it meets the border of Naphtali. From here the northern boundary runs westward toward Beth Shemesh (Khirbet Sheikh esh-Shamsawi?). The city of Jabneel (Tell en-Naam) is noted as a southern border site for the tribal apportionment of Naphtali. Therefore, the northern border of Issachar must have run just south of the Jabneel Valley. If En Gannim is to be identified with Khirbet Beit Jinn, then the boundary would have continued northwest of Beth Shemesh before cutting west past Mount Tabor to Kesulloth (Iksal).[7] This Kesulloth is apparently the same site as Kisloth Tabor, which marks the eastern boundary of Zebulun. From Kesullloth, the western boundary of Issachar runs through Shunem (Solem) and meets Jezreel at the very southwestern corner.

Geographical Analysis

The apportionment to Issachar, like Zebulun before it, includes a combination of elevated landscape, the basalt uplift of the eastern lower Galilee and Mount Moreh, with intervening valleys. Issachar's apportionment includes a significant portion of the northeastern Jezreel Valley as well, and most importantly, the Harod Valley, which provides passage east-west from the Transjordan to the Mediterranean. The major trade route that extended from the Canaanite center of Beth Shan (Tell el-Husn) would have run through Jezreel, another Canaanite center, and continuing to Megiddo, where it would split either southward, through the Megiddo pass toward Egypt, or westward to the plain of Akko.[8] Perhaps, this is why Deut 33:18–19 identifies Issachar and Zebulun as benefitting from the "abundance of the seas."[9] This east-west trade route would have run through the southernmost portion of the apportionment to Issachar, while the north-south international trade route would have intersected with its very western portion, east of Tabor and north of Mount Moreh, running through Kishion (Khirbet Qasyun).[10] The low-lying outer terrain and multitude of entryways would have made defending the periphery difficult, but somehow, Issachar is not mentioned in the list of failed conquests in Judg 1:27–36. The basalt uplift of eastern lower Galilee was perhaps more favorable to Israelite settlement, much like the hinterland settlements of Israel in the central hill country to the south. Compounded by the fact that major trade routes would only peripherally intersect with this apportionment, perhaps in the initial settlement, the Israelites encountered less Canaanite resistance here than in other areas.

---

7. As with many sites, scholars debate the exact location of En Gannim. The location of En Gannim at Khirbet Beit Jinn is generally accepted (John L. Peterson, "En-Gannim," *ABD* 2:501–2).

8. Dorsey, *Roads and Highways*, 63–64, 110–12.

9. Carl G. Rassmussen, *Zondervan Atlas of the Bible* (Grand Rapids: Zondervan, 2010), 116.

10. Dorsey, *Roads and Highways*, 95–97.

Tel Akko

ASHER (JOSH 19:24–31)

BORDER DESCRIPTION

The fifth lot came out for the tribe of Asher. The boundaries of Asher's tribal apportionment are circumscribed on the south by Manasseh; on the east by Zebulun and Naphtali; and on the west by the Mediterranean Sea and Carmel mountain range. The northern extent is described by the phrase, "as far as Greater Sidon" (19:28). That the northern border seems to have encompassed Sidon, rather than just reach its borders can be inferred from Judg 1:31, which explains that the Asherites were unable to dispossess the people of Sidon in accordance with their inheritance. Many of the cities in the apportionment to Asher are unknown, but as with the other apportionments, the contours of the boundaries can be defined based on what we know of the landscape, and those sites which we can identify throughout.

The southern boundary begins at Helkat (Tell el-Qassis) on the southern bank of the Kishon River. From here, the border follows the edge of the Carmel ridge northwest past Akshaph (Tell el-Harbaj?) and Beten (Ibtin).[11] This boundary is described in Josh 19:26 as "On the west the boundary touched Carmel and Shihor Libnath." The latter name, Shihor Libnath, includes the Hebrew word *shihor* (שִׁיחוֹר),which is used of the eastern branch of the Nile (Josh 13:3; 1 Chr 13:5) and thus, likely refers here to the swampy outlet of the Kishon into the

11. Aharoni tentatively identifies Tell el-Harbaj as biblical Akshaph (Aharoni, *Land of the Bible*, 371). Scholars have identified Tell el-Harbaj with at least three biblical cities: Akshaph, Helkath, and Harosheth. See Paul Benjamin "Achsaph," *ABD* 1:57; John L. Peterson, "Helkath," *ABD* 3:125–26.

Mediterranean near Libnath (Tell Abu Huwam).[12] Reaching the Mediterranean Sea, the description returns to Helkath, from which point the border's eastward extent is described. Moving toward Beth Dagon, touching Zebulun and the Valley of Iphtael, encompassing all of the area known as the Shephelah of the Galilee, before turning northward to Neiel (Khirbet Yanin?) and Kabul. The eastern border continues northward to Kanah (Qana, Lebanon), ultimately incorporating the region of Sidon.

Geographical Analysis

The Mediterranean Sea constituted most of the western boundary of Asher, including several important port cities, such as Ahlab (Khirbet el-Mahalib), Akzib (ez-Zib), Tel Akko (Tell el-Fukhar), Sidon, and Tyre. Judges 1:31–32 tells us that it was these coastal strongholds that impeded the successful conquest. Furthermore, the port of Tel Akko, the only natural port on Israel's coast, was an important and strategic center for economic activity. All the sites further north, Aczib, Hosah (Tell Rashidiyeh), Tyre, and Sidon were similarly important sites at which major east-west trade routes terminated. Many of the inland sites apportioned to Asher, such as Akshaph, Mishal (Tell Kisan?), and others, would have also been incredibly important sites connecting these east-west and north-south land trade routes to the maritime trade with the west. The wealth of the well-known Phoenician polities sprung from this geographic position on the Mediterranean, importing and exporting goods across the sea and collecting profit from the exchange. Protected on the east by the elevated landscape of the upper Galilee and the soaring Lebanese mountain ranges, the wealth and status of the coastal ports would very early on pose problems for the Israelite settlement, but ultimately become a boon for the kings of the united monarchy.

Naphtali (Josh 19:32–39)

Border Description

The sixth lot came out for the last of the northern tribes, Naphtali. Only the southern border of Naphtali is described in any detail (Josh 19:33–34). This is because much of the border territory is established by the previous three border descriptions, as well as the unchanging geographical features of the land. To this point Josh 19:34b states, "It touched Zebulun on the south, Asher on the west, and the Jordan on the east." The description of the southern boundary begins at Heleph (Khirbet Irbadah?), north of Mount Tabor, at the intersection of the borders of Zebulun, Issachar, and Naphtali. It extends eastward, passing through Adami-nekeb (Khirbet Damiyeh), Jabneel in the Jabneel Valley, to Lakkum (Khirbet el-Mansurah?), ultimately ending at the Jordan River. As we have seen in previous boundary descriptions, the border returns to the origin point and describes the western section of the southern border, running through Aznoth Tabor (Khirbet el-Jebeil?) and coming out at Hukkok (Khirbet el-Jemeija?). At Hukkok, the border would have turned north, forming the western edge of Naphtali.

The list of the fortified cities of Naphtali in Josh 19:35–38 proceeds from

12. Raphael Frankel, "Shihor-Libnath," *ABD* 5:1212–13; Aharoni, *Land of the Bible*, 238.

Tel Dan

south to north, beginning with the unidentified sites of Zer and Ziddim and ending with northern Beth Shemesh (Khirbet T. Ruweisi) and Beth Anath (Safad el-Battikh). This list gives us a good indication of the extent of Naphtali's borders. From Josh 19:35–38, we know that the eastern border continued from the Jordan River south of the Sea of Galilee, along the western coast of the Sea of Galilee, including the sites of Hammath (Hammam Tabariyeh), Rakkath (Tell Raqqat), and Kinnereth (Tell el-Oreimeh). The apportionment likely included all the land west of the Jordan, north of the Sea of Galilee, including the Rosh Pinah basalt sill and the Huleh basin. The northern extent of the territory is not recorded, but if 1 Kgs 15:20 is to be understood as including Ijon (Tell ed-Dibbin) in "all the land of Naphtali," then it is likely that the northern border of Naphtali extended into the Beqa Valley of Lebanon and was, at least, coextensive with the northernmost reaches of Asher at Sidon.

Geographical Analysis

Like the previous three northern apportionments, at the time of Israelite settlement, Naphtali was dotted with strong Canaanite city centers connecting international trade routes. The main international north-south highway ran the length of Naphtali, entering in the south around Mount Tabor, traveling through Adamah (Qarn Hattin) and Kinnereth, continuing north toward Hazor (Tel Hazor), either into the Lebanese Beqa Valley or branching around Mount Hermon toward Damascus. While the last northern tribe apportioned, Naphtali is given the largest region, a territory that includes a significant portion of upper and lower Galilee. Aside from the main international highway, the apportionment of Naphtali would have been intersected by several east-west

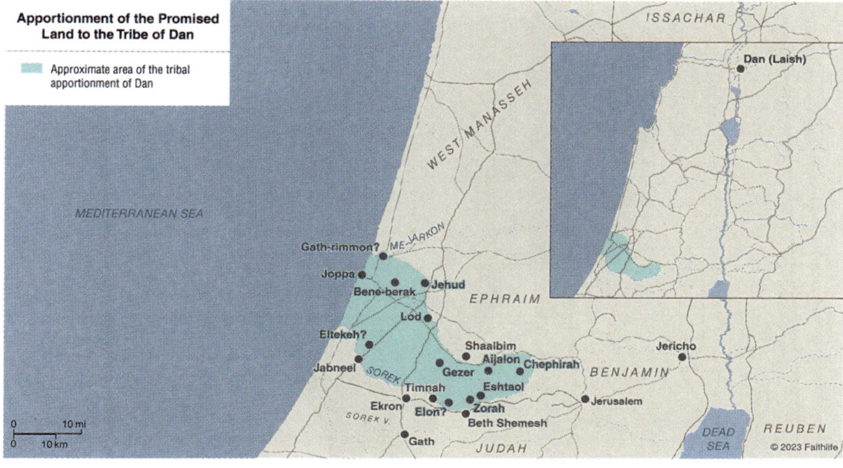

routes heading to the powerful Levantine port cities in the apportionment to Asher. Just like the main international highway, large Canaanite cites such as Beth Shemesh and Beth Anath would have controlled travel on these main routes in the upper Galilee, preventing Israelite access early in the settlement period. Away from the main thoroughfares, relatively scarce Canaanite occupation of the hinterland prior to the Israelite's arrival would have made settlement in this region easier for the arriving Israelites.[13] In spite of this, the tribe of Naphtali is explicitly among those indicted by Judg 1:33–34 for their failure to drive out the inhabitants of the few Canaanite city centers that did exist in the region.

DAN (JOSH 19:40–48)

BORDER DESCRIPTION

The seventh and final lot came out for the tribe of Dan. The borders of Dan are not described at all; only a city list is given in Josh 19:41. Therefore, identification of the sites is paramount for any attempt at describing the boundaries of this apportionment. The city list includes the coastal city of Joppa, displaying that the boundary of Dan reached as far as the Mediterranean Sea on the west. Likewise, Me Yarkon (19:46) refers to the Yarkon River delineating the northernmost boundary. Based on the apportionment of sites here and those previously given to Judah (Josh 15:11), the southern boundary must have followed the Sorek River from the Mediterranean to its valley inlet in the hill country near Zorah (Sarah) and Ir-Shemesh (Tell er-Reumeileh), where the eastern boundary abuts Judah and Benjamin. Because of the location of the cities apportioned here, in conjunction with those apportioned to prior southern territories, the northern boundary of Dan takes a rather irregular shape. The text mentions Shaalabbin (Selbit) in the apportionment of Dan (Josh 19:42), but Gezer (Tel Gezer), just south and west of

13. Rasmussen, *Zondervan Atlas*, 116.

Tel Dan Stele

Shaalabbin, is mentioned in the apportionment of Ephraim (16:10). For this reason, the northern border must have swung around Gezer and proceeded alongside the western border of Ephraim up to Jehud (el-Yehudiyeh), meeting in the north at the Yarkon River with the border of Manasseh. In addition to this southern apportionment, the text tells us that some of the Danites, under pressure from enemies (Josh 19:47; Judg 1:35), migrated from their coastal apportionment to the site of Laish (Tel Dan), also called Leshem, conquering it and renaming it Dan.

GEOGRAPHICAL ANALYSIS

The apportionment to Dan extended from the very edge of the central hill country, across the coastal plain, to the Mediterranean between the Yarkon and Sorek Rivers. This territory protected two important routes from the Shephelah and Philistine plain toward both Saul's capital in Gibeah and David's capital in Jerusalem.[14] In particular, Dan was allotted two sites overlooking critical valley passes: (1) Aijalon (Yalo) protecting the Aijalon Valley, which Judg 1:35 tells us was not captured during the earliest period of settlement, and (2) Beth Shemesh in the Sorek Valley.

On the coast, the low and open plain allotted to the Danites proved difficult to control (Josh 19:47; Judg 1:35). The Israelites would not wrest control of the region until the reigns of David and Solomon, and, even then, the conquest was short lived (1 Kgs 4:9; 2 Chr 2:16).[15] Pressured on the south by the Philistines and Amorites and open to foreign attack via the international coastal highway, the territory in and around Dan would be the stage for many biblical and historical conflicts. In the same

14. Rasmussen, *Zondervan Atlas*, 118; Dorsey, *Roads and Highways*, 185–88.

15. Rasmussen, *Zondervan Atlas*, 118.

way, their second territory in the north was situated in a precarious international location. Though it would later signal the furthest extent north in the land under Israelite control ("from Dan to Beersheba," e.g., Judg 20:1; 2 Sam 24:2; 1 Kgs 4:25), the close proximity to the international trade route running north to Damascus put Dan dangerously close to the kingdoms of Syria. During the period of the divided monarchy, it was conquered by the Aramean king Hazael, a feat commemorated in the famous Tel Dan Stele.[16] It would become many conquers' first point of attack in their campaigns into the land of Israel and on their quest to control the lucrative trade routes to which Dan claimed prime access.

CONCLUSION

Each one of these latter apportionments is geographically unique and this geography informs each tribes' individual and unique history. The history of the lone southern apportionment described here, Dan, is one of conflict and failure. This is partially because the apportionment on the coastal plain, as well as site of Dan in the north, both sat astride the north-south international highway, susceptible to foreign invaders and foreign influence. This geographical and historical reality is confirmed by the biblical account of the loss of Danite territory on the coast, because of Amorite pressure (Judg 1:35) and the subsequent migration north (Josh 19:47).

In much the same way, the northern apportionments were threatened on all sides. Ancient and powerful Canaanite city centers dotted the tribal apportionments of Zebulun, Issachar, Asher, and Naphtali. These city centers were cosmopolitan and well connected to international partners, as evidenced by the Amarna letters and other ancient Near Eastern texts.[17] This deep, interconnected history in the region is motivated by the geographical realities of the upper and lower Galilee. The fractured topography of the lower Galilee, with low lying valleys between elevated mountain ridges, made an easy entryway for conquest by foreign powers, on the one hand, and opened the region to incredible economic and trade potential, on the other. This geographical complexity, however, made it difficult to unite the region, which may explain why apportionments like Zebulun and Issachar are smaller, restricted to a few ridges and

16. See *KAI* 310 for text (Herbert Donner and Wolfgang Rollig, *Kanaanaische und aramaische Inschriften* [Wiesbaden: Harrassowitz Verlag 2002], 76); for translation, see William M. Schniedewind, "Tel Dan Stela: New Light on Aramaic and Jehu's Revolt," *BASOR* 302 (1996): 75–76.

17. The Amarna letters are a collection of diplomatic correspondences written in cuneiform and discovered at the site of Tell el-Amarna in Egypt, the ancient capital of Akhenaten during the fourteenth century BC. These letters preserve the correspondences of the Egyptian pharaoh with various kingdoms and city-states around the Near East, including several ancient cities from modern day Israel-Palestine. See Anson F. Rainey and R. Steven Notley, *The Sacred Bridge: Carta's Atlas of the Biblical World* (Jerusalem: Carta, 2006), particularly "The Amarna Age," 71–90. For a translation of these letters see Anson F. Rainey, *The El-Amarna Correspondence*, ed. William M. Schniedewind, vol. 1 (Leiden: Brill, 2015). The city of Hazor in the far north is also mentioned in the letters of the Middle Bronze Age Syrian kingdom of Mari (Marco Bonechi, "Relationes amicales syro-palestiniennes: Mari et Hasor au XVIIIe siècle av. J.C.," in *Florilegium marianum: Recueil d'études en l'honneur de Michel Fleury*, ed. J.-M. Durand, Mémories de NABU 1 [Paris: Société pour l'Étude du Proche-Orient Ancien, 1992], 9–22).

edges of valleys, as well as explain why the northern apportionments are less defined relative to their southern partners. These facts taken together make it unsurprising that many of these tribes failed to drive the Canaanites out of the region (Judg 1:30–36). While Israelite settlement seems to have been mostly restricted to the inner hill country of the Galilee, Canaanite centers like Megiddo, Shimron, Hazor, Tyre, Sidon, and Beth Shan undoubtedly dominated the low-lands, protecting the lucrative trade routes westward toward the Mediterranean, northward toward Damascus and Mesopotamia, and southward toward Egypt, giving them a strategic and economic advantage over the newly arrived Israelite settlers.

Intersected on every side by these international trade routes, the northern and southern apportionments held incredible economic and strategic potential. Yet, this same interconnectivity also proved a potent threat to the goal of complete conquest, and throughout the history of Israel, provided access for challenges to fidelity and exclusivity in the worship of the God of Israel.

BIBLIOGRAPHY

Aharoni, Yohanan. *The Land of the Bible: A Historical Geography*. Translated by Anson F. Rainey. London: Burns & Oates, 1967.

Bonechi, Marco. "Relationes amicales syro-palestiniennes: Mari et Hasor au XVIIIe siècle av. J.C." Pages 9–22 in *Florilegium marianum: Recueil d'études en l'honneur de Michel Fleury*. Edited by J.-M. Durand. Mémories de NABU 1. Paris: Société pour l'Étude du Proche-Orient Ancien, 1992.

Donner, Herbert, and Wolfgang Rollig. *Kanaanaische und aramaische Inschriften*. Wiesbaden: Harrassowitz Verlag, 2002.

Dorsey, David A. *The Roads and Highways of Ancient Israel*. Eugene, OR: Wipf & Stock, 1991.

Frankel, Raphael. "Shihor-Libnath." *ABD* 5:1212–13.

Kallai, Zecharia. *Historical Geography of the Bible: The Tribal Territories of Israel*. Leiden: Brill, 1986.

Peterson, John L. "Daberath." *ABD* 2:1.

———. "En Gannim." *ABD* 2:501–2.

———. "Helkath." *ABD* 3:125–26.

Benjamin, Paul. "Achsaph." *ABD* 1:57.

Rassmussen, Carl G. *Zondervan Atlas of the Bible*. Grand Rapids: Zondervan, 2010.

Rainey, Anson F. *The El-Amarna Correspondence*. Edited by William M. Schniedewind. Vol. 1. Leiden: Brill, 2015.

Rainey, Anson F., and R. Steven Notley. *The Sacred Bridge: Carta's Atlas of the Biblical World*. Jerusalem: Carta, 2006.

Schniedewind, William M. "Tel Dan Stela: New Light on Aramaic and Jehu's Revolt." *BASOR* 302 (1996): 75–90.

CHAPTER 19

THE HISTORICAL GEOGRAPHY OF THE LEVITICAL TOWNS IN JOSHUA 21 AND 1 CHRONICLES 6:54–81

Josh 21; 1 Chr 6:54–81

Chris McKinny

KEY POINTS

- This chapter offers a detailed identification of all forty-eight Levitical towns, complete with up-to-date archaeological data.
- The chapter provides a geographical assessment of the overall distribution of the Levitical towns.
- A summary of the data appears at the end of the chapter in a table comparing the Masoretic Text (MT) and Septuagint (LXX) versions of the two Levitical town lists, Josh 21 and 1 Chr 6:54–81.

INTRODUCTION

The Bible contains two nearly identical lists of towns set aside for the Levites: Josh 21 and 1 Chr 6:54–81.[1] The rationale for providing towns for the Levites appears in a command from Moses in Num 35:1–8 but, from a literary perspective, goes back to the actions of Simeon and Levi against Shechem that resulted in Jacob predicting their scattered allotment (Gen 34:25–31; 49:5–7). Numbers 35 takes place while Israel is in the plains of Moab, before crossing the Jordan and the conquest of Jericho (Josh 1–6). Moses commands the Israelites to give the Levites towns and their accompanying pasturage for their livestock. Besides the towns, Levi is to be given the fields and pastur-

1. In this chapter, I use the English versification (1 Chr 6:54–81) rather than the Hebrew versification (1 Chr 6:39–66).

age around the city to include either one or two thousand cubits on every side (Num 35:4–5). Finally, Israel is required to set aside forty-eight towns for Levi with six of those representing "cities of refuge" (Num 35:6–8; Deut 4:41–43; Josh 20).

Like most of the geographical sections of Joshua (i.e., Josh 13–21), the Levitical towns list has received considerable scholarly attention. The purpose here is not to rehash the dating, setting, purpose, or function of the Levitical towns in the broader context of ancient Israel, although, the recent attempt to date the Levitical town system to the Hasmonean period seems woefully inadequate.[2] It should be noted that every town that appears in the two versions of this list also appear in the tribal allotments in Josh 13–21. Thus, the dating of the Levitical towns list is directly dependent upon the date of the larger allotment system, which itself seems to have undergone a complex process of editing and redaction.[3] In light of this, due to limited space and the larger purposes of this volume, I will limit my discussion to locating all forty-eight towns while not attempting to provide a date for the Levitical towns or the list.[4]

Thus, the purpose of this chapter is to identify each Levitical town men-

---

2. See William F. Albright, "The List of Levitic Cities," in *Louis Ginzberg Jubilee Volume*, ed. Saul Lieberman et al. (New York: American Academy for Jewish Research, 1945), 49–73; Benjamin Mazar, "The Cities of the Priests and the Levites," *Vetus Testamentum Supplements* 7 (1957): 193–205; Menahem Haran, "Studies in the Account of the Levitical Cities: I. Preliminary Considerations," *JBL* 80.1 (1961): 45–54; J. P. Ross, "The 'Cities of the Levites' in Joshua XXI and I Chron VI" (PhD diss., University of Edinburgh, 1973); John L. Peterson, "A Topographical Surface Survey of the Levitical Cities of Joshua 21 and I Chronicles 6: Studies on the Levites in Israelite Life and Religion" (PhD diss., Seabury-Western Theological Seminary, 1977); A. Graeme Auld, "The Levitical Cities: Texts and History," *ZAW* 91.2 (1979): 194–206; Yohanan Aharoni, *The Land of the Bible: A Historical Geography*, trans. Anson F. Rainey, rev. and enl. ed. (Philadelphia: Westminster, 1979), 301–5; Nadav Na'aman, "A New Look at the List of Levitic Cities," *Zion* 47 (1982): 237–52; John R. Spencer, "The Levitical Cities: A Study of the Role and Function of the Levites in the History of Israel" (PhD diss., University of Chicago, 1980); Spencer, "Levitical Cities," *ABD* 4:310–11; Gary N. Knoppers, "Projected Age Comparisons of the Levitical Townlists: Divergent Theories and Their Significance," *Textus* 22.1 (2005): 21–63; Anson F. Rainey and Steven Notley, *The Sacred Bridge: Carta's Atlas of the Biblical World* (Jerusalem: Carta, 2006), 162; Mark Leuchter and Jeremy M. Hutton, eds., *Levites and Priests in Biblical History and Tradition* (Leiden: Brill, 2012); Jeremy M. Hutton, "The Levitical Diaspora (II): Modern Perspectives on the Levitical Cities List (A Review of Opinions)," in *Levites and Priests in Biblical History and Tradition*, ed. Mark Leuchter and Jeremy M. Hutton (Leiden: Brill, 2012), 45–81; Mark Leuchter, *The Levites and the Boundaries of Israelite Identity* (Oxford: Oxford University Press, 2017). For an attempt to date the town list to the Hasmonean period, see Yitzhak Lee-Sak, "The Lists of Levitical Cities (Joshua 21, 1 Chronicles 6) and the Propagandistic Map for the Hasmonean Territorial Expansion," *JBL* 136.4 (2017): 783–800.

3. See discussion in Chris McKinny, "A Historical Geography of The Administrative Division of Judah: The Town Lists of Judah and Benjamin in Joshua 15:21–62 and 18:21–28" (PhD diss., Bar-Ilan University, 2017), chapter 1.

4. In this chapter, I use the following archaeological periodization (only biblical periods included and all dates are approximate): Middle Bronze (c. 2000–1550 BC), Late Bronze (c. 1550–1200 BC), Iron I (c. 1200–1000 BC), Early Iron IIA (c. 1000–900 BC), Late Iron IIA (c. 900–800 BC), Iron IIB (c. 800–701 BC), Iron IIC (c. 701–586/539 BC), Persian (c. 539–332 BC), Hellenistic (332–63 BC), and Early Roman (63 BC–AD 70).

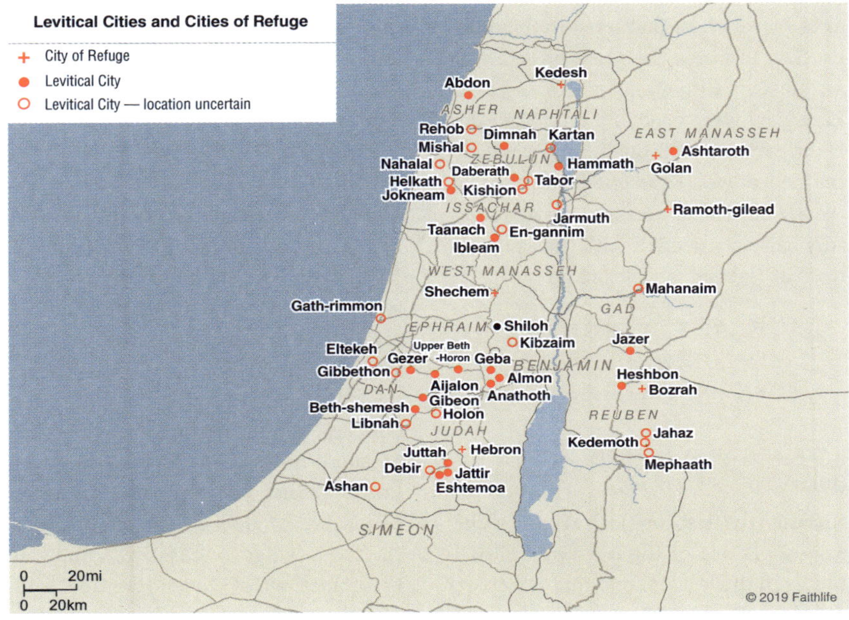

tioned in Josh 21 and 1 Chr 6:54–81 and discuss the archaeological background of each site. The purpose of the Levitical list within the book of Joshua is fairly straightforward as it is explicitly stated that the tribe of Levi—with its various families—was to receive towns within the other tribal allotments (e.g., Josh 18:7; 21:1–8). Unfortunately, there are very few examples that refer to Levitical towns in the context of a narrative. Levites were present at Beth Shemesh when the ark was brought from Philistine Ekron (1 Sam 6:14–15). Anathoth was connected with the priests Abiathar (1 Kgs 2:26) and Jeremiah (Jer 1:1), but the nearby priestly town of Nob was not included as a Levitical town in the list (1 Sam 21:1; 22:9, 11, 19; Isa 10:32). Bethel (e.g., Judg 20:18, 26), Gilgal (Josh 4:19–20; 14:6; Judg 2:1), and Shiloh (e.g., Josh 18:1; Judg 18:31) clearly were important Yahwistic centers where the tabernacle and its priesthood resided, and, yet these towns do not appear in the list. One gets the impression from these examples that the Levitical land holdings/rights may have shifted over time due to political changes. Indeed, Ezekiel's prophetic vision of the tribal allotments has Levi and the priests possessing a centralized area near the renewed sanctuary around Jerusalem (Ezek 45:1–8; 48).

Additionally, some of the regions mentioned in the list were never or very rarely occupied by Israel, such as the tribal territories of Asher (1 Kgs 9:11–13; Judg 1:31–32). It is unclear if the Levitical towns of Asher were actually possessed by Levites (Josh 21:29–31), or if the list reflects the same utopian ideal that the allotted territory should belong to a particular tribe (see e.g., the territory of the Philistines: Josh 13:3; 15:11, 45–46; Judg 1:18–19). On the other hand, it seems that some of the Levitical towns were related to Levitical clans that lived in its vicinity. The Libnites (Exod 6:17; Num 3:18, 21; 26:58; 1 Chr 6:17, 20, 29; see also Ezra 2:45) were probably related to the Levitical town of Libnah (Josh 21:13), as the Hebronites (Exod 6:18; Num 3:19, 27; 26:58; 1 Chr 6:2, 18; 26:23, 30–31) undoubtedly had a connection with the Levitical town of Hebron (e.g., Josh 21:11, 13).

LEVITICAL TOWNS OF JUDAH/ SIMEON: NINE TOWNS (JOSH 21:9–16; 1 CHR 6:54–59)

1. KIRIATH ARBA/HEBRON (JOSH 21:9–13; 1 CHR 6:57)

Kiriath Arba/Hebron (Josh 21:11–13; 1 Chr 6:56–57) is one of the most mentioned towns in the biblical text and is universally identified with Rumeida. Regarding its allotment, Hebron was given to Caleb (Josh 14:13–15; 15:13; Judg 1:20), Judah (Josh 15:54), and Levi (specifically the descendants of Aaron [Josh 21:11–13; 1 Chr 6:56–57]). It was also a city of refuge (Josh 20:7). Recent excavations by Ben-Shlomo and reassessments of Hammond's 1960s excavation by Chadwick have added considerably to our knowledge of ancient Hebron. Hebron was extensively occupied and heavily fortified during the Early, Middle, and Late Bronze Ages, and remained a large Iron Age site from the Iron I through the late Iron II periods.[5]

2. LIBNAH (JOSH 21:13; 1 CHR 6:57)

Libnah appears in the southern campaign of the conquest between Makkedah and Lachish (Josh 10:29–31, 39; 12:15; compare with *Onom.* 630/120:23). It was allotted to the tribe of Judah (Josh 15:12) and was also a Levitical city of the Kohathite clan (Josh 21:13; 1 Chr 6:57). During the kingdom era, Libnah revolted from Jehoram of Judah in the mid-ninth century BC (2 Kgs 8:22; 2 Chr 21:10), was the city Sennacherib fought against after Lachish in 701 BC (2 Kgs 19:8; Isa 37:8), and was the hometown of Queen Hamutal, wife of Josiah and mother of kings Jehoahaz and Zedekiah, during the last days of the kingdom of Judah (2 Kgs 23:31; 24:18; Jer 52:1). These biblical references suggest that Libnah is in the southwestern Judean Shephelah and has remains from the Late Bronze, late Iron IIA, Iron IIB, and Iron IIC periods. These details fit very well with Tel Burna (i.e., Tell Bornat), where recent excavations have confirmed the presence of each of these periods.[6]

---

5. Jeffrey R. Chadwick, "The Archaeology of Biblical Hebron in the Bronze and Iron Ages: An Examination of the Discoveries of the American Expedition to Hebron" (PhD diss., University of Utah, 1992); Emanuel Eisenberg and David Ben-Shlomo, *The Tel Ḥevron 2014 Excavations: Final Report* (Ariel: Ariel University Press, 2017); Jeffrey R. Chadwick, "Hebron in Early Bronze Age III and Middle Bronze Age II: Fortification Walls in Area I.3 of the American Expedition to Hebron (Tell Er-Rumeide)," in *Tell It in Gath: Studies in the History and Archaeology of Israel. Essays in Honor of Aren M. Maeir on the Occasion of His Sixtieth Birthday*, ed. Itzhaq Shai et al. (Münster: Zaphon, 2018), 167–86; Yosef Garfinkel et al., "First Impression on the Urban Layout of the Last Canaanite City of Lachish: A View from the Northeast Corner of the Site," in *The Late Bronze and Early Iron Ages of Southern Canaan*, ed. Aren M. Maeir, Itzhaq Shai, and Chris McKinny (Berlin: de Gruyter, 2019), 122–35.

6. E.g., Itzhaq Shai, Chris McKinny, and Joe Uziel, "Late Bronze Age Cultic Activity in Ancient Canaan: A View from Tel Burna," *BASOR* 374 (2015): 115–33; Itzhaq Shai, "Tel Burna: A Judahite Fortified Town in the Shephelah," in *The Shephelah During the Iron Age: Recent Archaeological Studies*, ed. Oded Lipschits and Aren M. Maeir (Winona Lake, IN: Eisenbrauns, 2017), 45–60; Chris McKinny, Aharon Tavger, and Itzhaq Shai, "Tel Burna in the Late Bronze:

Possible Libnah, Tel Burna, from the Northwest

Moreover, Tel Burna's oldest known Arabic name is Tell Bulnab, which could preserve a corrupted form of the ancient name of Libnah.[7] Finally, it seems possible that the name Libnah derives from the family of Libni, the son of Gershon (i.e., the Libnites, Exod 6:17; Num 3:18, 21; 26:58; 1 Chr 6:17, 20, 29), which may be identical with the sons of Lebana (Neh 7:48; Ezra 2:45; and 1 Esd 5:29).

3. Jattir (Josh 21:14; 1 Chr 6:57)

Besides its appearance as a Levitical town (Josh 21:14; 1 Chr 6:57), Jattir also appears in the Judahite town list (Josh 15:48), and is listed as one of the towns to which David sent spoil (1 Sam 30:27–31).[8] Additionally, the site is mentioned several times by Eusebius, who also confused it with Ether of the Simeonite list (Josh 19:7) and described it as a very

Assessing the 13th Century BCE Landscape of the Shephelah," in Maeir, Shai, and McKinny, *Late Bronze*, 148–70.

7. Chris McKinny and Aharon Tavger, "From Lebonah to Libnah: Historical Geographical Details from the PEF and Other Early Secondary Sources on the Toponymy of Two Homonymous Sites," in *Exploring the Holy Land: 150 Years of the Palestine Exploration Fund*, ed. David Gurevich and Anat Kidron (London: Equinox, 2018), 107–22; see also Chris McKinny and Amit Dagan, "The Explorations of Tel Burna," *PEQ* 145.4 (2013): 294–305.

8. Despite the fact that the LXX represents a different *Vorlage* than the MT (see discussion above), Jattir is present in both texts.

Section of the Medeba Map Showing "Jethor, also Jethera"

large Christian village in the interior of Daroma, lying beside Mallatha "about twenty miles from Eleutheropolis" (*Onom.* 433/88:3; 543/108:1; 569/110:17).[9] The site, along with the confusion of Jattir and Ether, is depicted on the Medeba Map.[10] Since Robinson's original suggestion, Jattir has been associated with Khirbet Attir in the southeastern Judean hill country.[11] One wonders if the name Jattir (יַתִּיר, *yattir*) may be derived from Jethro (יִתְרוֹ, *yitro*), the Midianite priest and father-in-law of Moses (Exod 3:1; 4:18; 18:1–2, 5–6, 9–10, 12). This may be hinted at in Judg 1:16, which records the movements of the Kenites (i.e., relatives of "Moses' father-in-law") into the Negev near Arad.

9. Unless otherwise noted, quotations of *Onom.* are from R. Steven Notley and Ze'ev Safrai, *Eusebius, Onomasticon: A Triglott Edition with Notes and Commentary* (Leiden: Brill, 2005). A Roman mile is slightly shorter (4,860 ft.) than a modern mile (5,280 ft.) or 0.92 of an English mile.

10. The Medeba Map is a sixth century BC mosaic floor of a church in Medeba, Jordan, that has a detailed, although fragmentary, map of the Holy Land as understood by Byzantine Christian authorities (e.g., Eusebius) and pilgrims. See Michael Avi-Yonah, *The Madaba Mosaic Map: With Introduction and Commentary* (Jerusalem: Israel Exploration Society, 1954), 72–73; Herbert Donner, *The Mosaic Map of Madaba: An Introductory Guide* (Leuven: Peeters, 1992), 72.

11. Edward Robinson and Eli Smith, *Biblical Researches in Palestine, Mount Sinai and Arabia Petraea: A Journal of Travels in the Year 1838* (Boston: Crocker & Brewster; London: John Murray, 1841), 2:194. This identification has received general acceptance. See Victor Guérin, *Description Géographique, Historique et Archéologique de la Palestine* (Paris: Impériale, 1869), 199; Claude R. Conder and H. H. Kitchener, *The Survey of Western Palestine* (London: Palestine Exploration Fund, 1880–83), 3:408; Albrecht Alt, "Das Institut Im Jahre 1931," *Palästina-Jahrbuch* 28 (1932): 15; Martin Noth, *Das Buch Joshua* (Tübingen: Mohr Siebeck, 1953), 97; Aharoni, *Land of the Bible*, 437; Robert G. Boling, *Joshua: A New Translation with Notes and Commentary*, AB (New York: Doubleday, 1982), 493; John L. Peterson, "Jattir (Place)," *ABD* 3:649.

Khirbet Attir was surveyed by Peterson, who noted remains from the Iron IIB, Iron IIC, Persian, Roman, Islamic, and Arabic periods. Excavations were carried out at Khirbet Attir from 1995–1999 by Hanan Eshel, Jodi Magness, and Eli Shenhav.[12] The focus of the excavation was on the southern spur of the site where a Byzantine church was excavated.[13] Iron Age IIC and Persian remains were found in Area B on the eastern slope of the hill, and some Chalcolithic and Early Bronze pottery sherds were uncovered in caves filled in during the Byzantine period.[14] Significantly, Ofer's survey of the site revealed remains from the Iron IIA–C over an area of fifteen dunams (4 acres), in addition to the remains that were excavated at the site.[15]

4. Eshtemoa (Josh 21:14; 1 Chr 6:57)

The town of Eshtemoa is mentioned four times in the Bible in the same contexts as Jattir. Eshtemoa was a Levitical town (Josh 21:42; 1 Chr 6:57), a town in the Shamir district (Josh 15:50), and a site that received spoils from David (1 Sam 30:28). Despite Peterson's statement otherwise, the town is also mentioned the *Onomasticon* in several places.[16] Eusebius's first reference indicates that Eshtemoa [spelled Eshtemoh] was "a village in Daroma north of Anaea [i.e., Anim]" (*Onom.* 85/26:11). Jerome added to this entry that it is a village of Jews. The second reference to Eshtemoa confirms these geographic and ethnic details (*Onom.* 429/86:20; see also 448/90:2).

Eshtemoa has been universally identified with es-Semu since Robinson's initial suggestion.[17] The site has been examined several times, revealing remains from the Chalcolithic, Early Bronze I, Iron Age I, early Iron IIA (10 dunams; 2.5 acres), late Iron IIA (25 dunams; 6 acres), Iron IIB (20 dunams; 5 acres), Iron IIC (10 dunams; 2.5 acres), and Roman through Byzantine periods.[18] Es-Semu has also undergone several excavations, most of which were related to the Byzantine synagogue that was later turned into a mosque.[19]

---

12. Hanan Eshel, Jodi Magness, and Eli Shenhav, "Khirbet Yattir, 1995–1999: Preliminary Report," *IEJ* 50.3/4 (2000): 153–68; Eshel, Magness, and Shenhav, "Yattir, Khirbet," *NEAEHL* 5:2069–70.

13. Eshel, Magness, and Shenhav, "Yattir, Khirbet," 2070.

14. Eshel, Magness, and Shenhav, "Yattir, Khirbet," 2070.

15. Avi Ofer, "The Highland of Judah during the Biblical Period" (PhD diss., Tel Aviv University, 1993), site 1. A dunam is equivalent to about a quarter acre (1,000 m^2). Thus, a ten dunam site would be about two and a half acres (10,000 m^2) or about one hectare. For reference, the City of David is roughly ten acres in size, which equals four hectares or forty dunams.

16. John L. Peterson, "Eshtemoa," *ABD* 2:617.

17. Robinson and Smith, *Biblical Researches in Palestine*, 2:626–27; Félix-Marie Abel, *Géographie de la Palestine* (Paris: Lecoffre, 1938), 321; Aharoni, *Land of the Bible*, 434.

18. Moshe Kochavi, "The Land of Judah," in *Judaea, Samaria and the Golan: Archaeological Survey 1967–1968*, ed. Moshe Kochavi (Jerusalem: Archaeological Survey of Israel by Carta, 1972), site 233; Ofer, "Highland of Judah," site 25.

19. Of special note is an Iron II silver hoard of five jugs and weighing twenty-six kg that was found beneath the floors of the synagogue (Shmuel Yeivin, "The Silver Hoard from Eshtemo'a," *'Atiqot* 10 [1990]: 15*; Ze'ev Yeivin, "The Synagogue at Eshtemoa' in Light of the 1969 Excavations," *'Atiqot* 48 [2004]: 59*–98*; 155–58).

5. HOLON/HILEN (JOSH 21:15; 1 CHR 6:58)

Of all the Judahite/Simeonite Levitical towns, Holon (Josh 15:51; 21:15; Hilen in 1 Chr 6:58; compare with *Onom.* 955/172:24; 982/176:20) remains the most difficult to identify. Albright and Abel identified Holon with Khirbet Alin of the Elah Valley due to the similarity of the Arabic and Hebrew names.[20] This suggestion has been cited by several others, but it cannot be sustained since the site is in the Shephelah, far removed from the towns of the Shamir district (Josh 15:48–51).[21] Ofer's suggestion of Khirbet Bism is a possibility; however, Bism may also be related to Zanoah of the Maon district.[22] Khirbet umm el-Amad, which is close to Debir, is another option for Holon. Sheikh Allan's tomb near Khirbet Rabud would presumably be a good candidate for the preservation of the toponym "Holon" for the same reason that Albright argued for a positive identification with Khirbet Alin; however, no Iron Age remains were found at or in immediate proximity to the sheikh's tomb.[23] Khirbet umm el-Amad (5 mi. [8 km] to the east of Sheikh Allan's tomb) appears to be the only unidentified, somewhat significant Iron Age ruin (5–9 dunams; 1–2 acres) in the region associated with the Shamir district (Josh 15:48–51). Surveys at Khirbet umm el-Amad revealed remains from the late Iron IIA (5 dunams; 1 acre), Iron IIB (9 dunams; 2 acres), Iron IIC (6 dunams; 1.5 acres), and Persian through Byzantine periods.[24] This identification would also allow for a close geographical grouping of the Judahite Levitical towns of Jattir, Eshtemoa, Holon/Hilen, Debir, and Juttah.

6. DEBIR (JOSH 21:15; 1 CHR 6:58)

Debir/Kiriath Sepher is one of the most prominent towns in the southern hills (e.g., Josh 10:3, 38–39; 11:21; 12:13; 21:15; 1 Chr 6:58; compare with *Onom.* 378/78:15). Following a host of earlier suggestions,[25] Galling identified Debir with Khirbet Rabud.[26] Since Kochavi's excavation at Khirbet Rabud, which revealed a significant Middle Bronze to Persian period mound (60 dunams; 15 acres), it has been shown that the site matches all

20. William F. Albright, "Researches of the School in Western Judaea," *BASOR* 15 (1924): 10–11; Albright, "Topographical Researches in Judæa," *BASOR* 18 (1925): 9; Abel, *Géographie de la Palestine*, 349.

21. Boling, *Joshua*, 493; Theodore Lewis, "Holon," *ISBE* 2:729.

22. Opfer, "Highland of Judah," 33*. Compare with McKinny, "Historical Geography," 274–75.

23. Holon is linguistically similar to both Alin and Allan as the variation in spelling is only related to different initial gutturals. The phenomenon of Arabic place names retaining earlier place names is an important tool for site identification. On the sheikh's tomb, see Conder and Kitchener, *Survey of Western Palestine*, 3:407.

24. Kochavi, "Land of Judah," site 205; Ofer, "Highland of Judah," site 89.

25. Most notably Albright identified the site with Tell Beit Mirsim (William F. Albright, "The Excavation of Tell Beit Mirsim, Vol. II: The Bronze Age," *The Annual of the American Schools of Oriental Research* 17 [1936]: 5).

26. Kurt Galling, "Studien Aus Dem Deutschen Evangelischen Institut Für Altertumswissenschaft in Jerusalem. 50. Zur Lokalisierung von Debir," *ZDPV* 70.2 (1954): 135–41.

the criteria in the biblical text associated with the city of Debir.[27] The ancient site sits on a prominent ridge about six miles (10 km) south of Hebron along the watershed ridge. It is located equidistantly twelve to fifteen miles (20–25 km) distance from the surrounding sites of Lachish, Beersheba, and Arad. The central location of this site among important Judahite regional and administrative centers suggests that the site may have been of some importance in the heartland of the Judahite kingdom.[28]

7. AIN AND/OR ASHAN (JOSH 21:16; 1 CHR 6:59)

The seventh town in the Levitical list is difficult to determine with certainty. The Hebrew Masoretic Text (MT) of Josh 21:16 would seem to favor Ain (see *Onom.* 74/24:15; 109/28:15), but the Greek Septuagint (LXX) might favor the Chronicler's Ashan (1 Chr 6:59; compare with *Onom.* 81/26:4; 110/28:16).[29] In either case, it appears that these are the only towns in the Levitical list that can be related to Simeon (Josh 19:7; 1 Chr 4:32; see also Josh 15:32; Neh 11:29). Ain is identical with En Rimmon, which has been conclusively identified with Khirbet Khuweilfeh (Tel Halif) on the basis of the nearby Khirbet umm er-Rumamin, which preserves "Rimmon."[30] Identifying Simeonite Ashan is a bit more complicated, but it may be plausibly identified with the Bronze-Iron Age site of Tell Judeideh (i.e., Tel Goded near Mareshah).[31] It is possible that both Ain and Ashan were both Levitical towns with either being removed from the list to arrive at a desired number of forty-eight towns.

8. JUTTAH (JOSH 21:16; 1 CHR 6:59)

Besides its occurrence in both Levitical lists (Josh 21:16; 1 Chr 6:59 LXX only), Juttah also appears in the Maon district (Josh 15:55–57). Eusebius describes *Iettan* (Ιετταν; Juttah) as a large Jewish village in Daroma "eighteen miles south of Eleutheropolis" (*Onom.* 545/108:8). The site of Yatta (2.5 mi. [4 km] south of Hebron) preserves the biblical name and fits the geography. This identification has received widespread support

27. Moshe Kochavi, "Khirbet Rabud= Debir," *TA* 1.1 (1974): 2–33; Kochavi, "Rabud, Khirbet," *NEAEHL* 4:1252; Aharoni, *Land of the Bible*, 214–15; Gary A. Herion, Dale W. Manor, and Jeffery K. Lott, "Debir (Place)," *ABD* 2:111–12.

28. For further discussion, see McKinny, "Historical Geography," 249–50.

29. For Ain, see Eusebius's reference is to the similarly named "Beth-Anin" north of Hebron (*Onom.* 74/24:15), which itself likely represents "Beth-anoth" of the Halhul District (Josh 15:58–59). For Ashan, see Eusebius's reference to a village "fifteen [Roman] miles [13.8 mi., 22 km] west of Jerusalem" (*Onom.* 81/26:4) which cannot be the biblical Ashan (Josh 15:42; 19:7; 1 Chr 4:32; 6:59).

30. Apparently, a single town according to the spelling of Neh 11:29 (Oded Borowski, "The Biblical Identity of Tel Halif," *BA* 51.1 [1988]: 21–27, see earlier literature therein). For the archaeology of the Middle Bronze-Iron II site, see Joel D. Seger and Oded Borowski, "Halif, Tel," *NEAEHL* 2:553–60; Paul F. Jacobs, "Halif, Tel," *NEAEHL* 5:1761–62; James W. Hardin, *Lahav II Households and the Use of Domestic Space at Iron II Tell Halif: An Archaeology of Destruction* (Winona Lake, IN: Eisenbrauns, 2010).

31. McKinny, "Historical Geography," 229–32; for the archaeology of the site, see Shimon Gibson, "The Tell El-Judeideh (Tel Goded) Excavations: A Re-Appraisal Based on Archival Records in the Palestine Exploration Fund," *TA* 21 (1994): 194–234.

Aerial View of 2018 Excavations at Beth Shemesh

starting with Robinson's initial identification.[32] In addition, Yatta is located eighteen Roman milestones (16.5 mi., 27 km) from Eleutheropolis, if one assumes a route on the ridge of Adoraim.

The village is heavily populated and therefore difficult to survey.[33] A few surveys and a small-scale salvage excavation revealed remains from the Chalcolithic, Early Bronze I–III, Intermediate Bronze, Middle Bronze IIB–C, late Iron IIA (16 dunams; 4 acres), Iron IIB (25 dunams; 6 acres), Iron IIC (21 dunams; 5 acres) and Persian through Byzantine periods.[34] The excavators of the site did not distinguish between phases in the Iron II.[35]

9. Beth Shemesh (Josh 21:16; 1 Chr 6:59)

Beth Shemesh was a Judahite (Josh 15:10; 1 Kgs 14:11; *Onom.* 258/54:11), Danite (Ir-shemesh, Josh 19:41; *Onom.* 862/158:20), and Levitical town (Josh 21:16; 1 Chr 6:59). Excavations at Tell Rumeileh have been extensive from the early twentieth century until the ongoing excavations by Bunimovitz and Lederman, making Beth Shemesh one of the most well-known archaeological sites in the Shephelah.[36]

32. Robinson and Smith, *Biblical Researches in Palestine*, 2:190; John L. Peterson, "Juttah," *ABD* 3:1135.

33. Peterson, "Juttah," 1135.

34. Peterson, "Topographical Surface Survey," 551–56; Uri Dinur, "Yatta," *Excavations and Surveys in Israel* 5 (1987): 111–12; Ofer, "Highland of Judah," site 93.

35. Listed as Iron II-III (Yitzhak Magen and Yuval Baruch, "Yaṭṭa," *Hadashot Arkheologiyot* 114 [2002]: 117–19, 95*–96*).

36. Edward Robinson and Eli Smith, *Later Biblical Researches in Palestine and in the Adjacent Regions: A Journal of Travels in the Year 1852* (Boston: Crocker and Brewster; London: John Murray, 1856), 153–54; Duncan MacKenzie, "The Ancient Site of ʿAin Shems, with a Memorandum on the Prospects of Excavation," *PEQ* 43.2 (1911): 69–79; MacKenzie, *Palestine Exploration Fund, 1912–1913 Excavations at Ain Shems (Beth Shemesh)*, vol. 2 (London: Palestine

The massive 2018–2019 salvage project to the east of the tell's summit has revealed a large and previously unknown eighth to seventh century BC town. All told, Beth Shemesh was an important town throughout the Middle Bronze and until the Iron IIC (i.e., the destruction of the Judahite kingdom).[37]

LEVITICAL TOWNS OF BENJAMIN: FOUR TOWNS (JOSH 21:17–18; 1 CHR 6:60)

10. GIBEON (JOSH 21:17; 1 CHR 6:60)

Gibeon (Josh 18:25; 21:27; see also 1 Chr 8:29–30; 9:35; compare with *Onom.* 313/66:11) is the well-known Benjaminite and Hivite town (e.g., Josh 9–10; Shishak List no. 23) preserved at el-Jib.[38] Pritchard's excavations were never fully published, but they revealed a tell of one hundred twenty dunams (30 acres) that was inhabited from the Early Bronze until modern times, including the Late Bronze, Iron I, Iron IIA–C, and Persian periods.[39] Significantly, the Hivites of Gibeon seem to have served a cultic function, as there was a sacred "high place" that, according to the Chronicler, included the tabernacle and Mosaic bronze altar (Josh 9:27; 1 Kgs 3:4–5; 9:1; 1 Chr 16:38–40; 21:28–40; 2 Chr 1:3–4, 12–13).[40]

Gibeon is a Levitical town, but there may be more to its affiliation. As we have noted, both the Deuteronomistic Historian and the Chronicler indicate that Gibeon was also a cultic center. Given its Hivite affiliation and the near proximity of Kiriath Jearim, Chephirah, and Beeroth, it is possible that each of these towns functioned in a Levitical and/or priestly role. This is certainly the case for Kiriath Jearim (e.g., 1 Sam 7:1–2), and one should also remember the cultic/priestly role of Nob (1 Sam 21:1; 22:11, 19), which likewise does not appear in the list.[41]

11. GEBA (JOSH 21:17; 1 CHR 6:60)

Given the high quantity of sites in Benjamin with the linguistic component

Exploration Fund, 1912); Elihu Grant, "Beth Shemesh, 1928," *The Annual of the American Schools of Oriental Research* 9 (1927): 1–15; Grant, "Progress at Beth Shemesh," *BASOR* (1928): 15; Grant, "Beth Shemesh in 1933," *BASOR* 52 (1933): 3–5; Shlomo Bunimovitz and Zvi Lederman, "Beth Shemesh," *NEAEHL* 5:1644–48; Bunimovitz and Lederman, eds., *Tel Beth Shemesh: A Border Community in Judah: Renewed Excavations 1990–2000: The Iron Age* (Winona Lake, IN: Eisenbrauns, 2016).

37. See Chris McKinny, "Pressing On: Identifying the 'Other' Gath and Its Implications for Understanding the Border between the Kingdoms of Israel and Judah," in *Tell It in Gath: Studies in Honor of Aren Maeir on the Occasion of His Sixtieth Birthday*, ed. Itzhaq Shai et al. (Weisbaden: Ugarit-Verlag, 2018), 577–94.

38. Robinson and Smith, *Biblical Researches in Palestine*, 1:60–61.

39. See James B. Pritchard, "Gibeon," *NEAEHL* 2:511–14. The excavations are currently being analyzed by Shimon Gibson (personal communication).

40. Some scholars identify Nebi Samwil with the "high place of Gibeon" (1 Chr 16:39, 21:29; 2 Chr 1:3, 13) (e.g., J. Maxwell Miller and John H. Hayes, *A History of Ancient Israel and Judah*, 2nd ed. [Louisville: Westminster John Knox, 2006], 202). Nebi Samwil sits about a kilometer from Gibeon (el-Jib), showing the close connection between Gibeon and Nebi Samwil. While this remains a possibility, there does not appear to be sufficient textual or archaeological evidence for looking for a "high place" outside of the town Gibeon (el-Jib).

41. Chris McKinny et al., "Kiriath-Jearim (Deir El-ʿÂzar): Archaeological Investigations of a Biblical Town in the Judean Hill Country," *IEJ* 68.1 (2018): 30–49.

Aerial View of Gibeon

geb (גֶּבַע) (i.e., "hill"), it is possible that this Levitical town is related to Gibeah of Saul/Benjamin (Tell el-Ful), Geba of Benjamin (Jeba), or one of the Gebas or Gibeahs of southern Ephraim.[42] However, since the other three towns are in a relatively close geographical area, and both versions support "Geba" over "Gibeah," it would seem likely that Levitical Geba should be related to Geba of Benjamin (Jeba). Surveys at Jeba, which remains inhabited until this day, have revealed remains from the Iron I, Iron II, and Hellenistic through Byzantine periods.[43]

12. ANATHOTH (JOSH 21:18; 1 CHR 6:60)

Because of Anathoth's close proximity to Jerusalem, the town is mentioned numerous times in the biblical account.[44] Anathoth is one of the few Levitical towns that have narratives associated with priestly characters, namely Abiathar and Jeremiah.[45] Anathoth is preserved at Anata, but the pre-Roman site is usually under-

42. See discussion in McKinny, "Historical Geography," chapter 6.

43. Israel Finkelstein et al., *Archeological Survey of Israel, Map 83/2: Map of El Bira: Benjamin Survey*, ed. Yitzhak Magen and Israel Finkelstein (Jerusalem: Israel Antiquities Authority, 2013), site 64, https://survey.antiquities.org.il/index_Eng.html#/MapSurvey.

44. Josh 21:18; 2 Sam 23:27; 1 Kgs 2:26; 1 Chr 6:60; 7:8; 11:28; 12:3; 27:12; Ezra 2:23; Neh 7:27; 10:19; 11:32; Isa 10:30; Jer 1:1; 11:21, 23; 29:27; 32:7–9; compare with *Onom.* 95/26:27 ("a city ... three miles from the vicinity of Jerusalem").

45. Solomon replaced Abiathar with Zadok and exiled him to Anathoth in 1 Kgs 2:26. Jeremiah references his hometown at the beginning of his book (Jer 1:1).

stood to be localized at the nearby hill of Ras el-Kharrubeh. Surveys at Ras el-Kharrubeh revealed remains from the Iron II, Hellenistic, Roman, and Byzantine periods over ten dunams (2.5 acres).[46] While this reconstruction is possible, it should be noted that surveys within the old core of the village of Anata revealed remains from the Intermediate Bronze, Middle Bronze, Iron I, Iron II, Hellenistic, Roman, and Byzantine periods, which would seem to indicate that Anata itself may be the site of ancient Anathoth.[47] If so, then Ras el-Kharrubeh could theoretically be related to another "daughter of Jerusalem" mentioned in the itinerary of towns north of Jerusalem in Isa 10:30–32 (Gebim, Laishah, etc.).

13. Almon/Alemeth (Josh 21:18; 1 Chr 6:60)

Almon/Alemeth (Josh 21:18; 1 Chr 6:60; 7:8; 8:36; 9:42; compare with *Onom.* 97/28:1) is always mentioned in connection with Anathoth and usually with Azmaveth (Hizmeh). It has been identified with Khirbet Almit, which is situated between Geba and Anathoth. Surveys at the ruin and several salvage excavations showed remains from the Middle Bronze, Iron I, Iron II, Persian, and Hellenistic through Byzantine periods over seventy dunams (17 acres).[48]

Levitical Towns of Ephraim: Four Towns (Josh 21:21; 1 Chr 6:67–68)

14–15. Shechem and Gezer (Josh 21:21; 1 Chr 6:67)

Shechem (Tell Balatah) and Gezer (Tell Jazar) are two of the most well-known biblical cities due to the fact that they are mentioned in numerous biblical and extrabiblical texts. Both have been thoroughly excavated. Accordingly, there is no need to spend much time discussing their well-established locations, histories, or archaeological backgrounds.[49] Simply put, both towns were major Middle and Late Bronze city-states that became associated with the kingdom over the course of the monarchy.

16. Kibzaim/Jokmeam (Josh 21:22/1 Chr 6:68)

Kibzaim is mentioned only in Josh 21:22 (compare with *Onom.* 594/114:21). However, in the parallel list in Chronicles, the town of Jokmeam is located between Gezer and

46. Amos Kloner, *Survey of Jerusalem: The Northeastern Sector* (Jerusalem: Israel Antiquities Authority, 2001), site 533 [450], site 136.

47. Uri Dinur, "Khirbat 'Almit," *Excavations and Surveys in Israel* 5 (1986): 1; Kloner, *Survey of Jerusalem*, site 535 [452]; Benjamin Har-Even, "Khirbat 'Almit," *Hadashot Arkheologiyot: Excavations and Surveys in Israel* 115 (2003): 48*–49*.

48. Kloner, *Survey of Jerusalem*, site 579 [496].

49. For Shechem, see Edward F. Campbell and G. Ernest Wright, eds., *Shechem III: The Stratigraphy and Architecture of Shechem/Tell Balâṭah*, 2 vols. (Boston: American Schools of Oriental Research, 2002); Hamdan Taha and Gerrit van der Kooij, *Tell Balata Changing Landscape* (Ramallah: Ministry of Tourism and Antiquities, 2014). For Gezer, see recently Steven Ortiz and Saul Wolff, "Guarding the Border to Jerusalem: The Iron Age City of Gezer," *NEA* 75.1 (2012): 4–19; Ortiz and Wolff, "A Reevaluation of Gezer in the Late Bronze Age in Light of Renewed Excavations and Recent Scholarship," in Maeir, Shai, and McKinny, *The Late Bronze*, 62–85.

Aerial View of Beth Horon

Beth Horon (1 Chr 6:68). Jokmeam is also included in the Solomonic district that corresponds to the tribal area of Manasseh (1 Kgs 4:12; compare with *Onom.* 570/110:19). The Levitical family of Jekameam from Hebron (1 Chr 23:19; 24:23) may also be related to the town of Jokmeam. Thus, it seems possible that Jokmeam and Kibzaim are alternate names for the same town or that Kibzaim is a corrupted form of the name Jokmeam.[50] In light of the geographical indicators from 1 Kgs 4:12 (e.g., Beth Shan, Abel Meholah), Benjamin Mazar suggested identifying Jokmeam/Kibzaim with Tell el-Mazar on the south side of Wadi Farah.[51] Recent surveys of Tell el-Mazar and Tell es-Simadi (c. 0.3 mi. [0.5 km] apart) indicate that the latter is the more prominent tell (15 dunams; 4 acres) in the vicinity with remains from the Early Bronze, Middle Bronze, Late Bronze, Iron I–II, and Persian through Byzantine, which might make it a better identification for Jokmeam/Kibzaim.[52]

50. Albright held that they were distinct towns (Albright, "List of Levitic Cities," 67–68).

51. Mazar, "Cities of the Priests," 193–205; Aharoni, *Land of the Bible*, 437.

52. Adam Zertal and Shay Bar, *The Manasseh Hill Country Survey, Vol. 4: From Nahal Bezeq to the Sartaba* (Leiden: Brill, 2017), site 84; 100–101. Alternately, Kallai suggested Tell esh-Sheikh Dhiab (6 mi., 10 km to the south) near Fatseal on the edge of the Jordan Valley (Zecharia Kallai, *Historical Geography of the Bible: The Tribal Territories of Israel* [Jerusalem: Magnes Press, 1986]). Compare to Tell el-Mazar, which is smaller site (5 dunams; 1 acre) and only has remains from the Early Bronze, Iron IIC, Persian, and Roman through Byzantine (Zertal and Shay, *From Nahal Bezeq to the Sartaba*, site 82; 275).

17. Beth Horon (Josh 21:22/1 Chr 6:68)

Beth Horon is actually two towns that were known as Upper and Lower Beth Horon.[53] Since Robinson, Upper Beth Horon and Lower Beth Horon have been identified with Beit Ur el-Foqa and Beit Ur et-Tahta respectively, which matches Eusebius description that "there are two villages about twelve miles from Jerusalem on the way to Nicopolis" (*Onom.* 212/46:21; Jerome has *Aelia* instead of Jerusalem).[54] Surveys at these sites, which remain inhabited Arabic villages, revealed remains from the Middle Bronze, Late Bronze, Iron I, Iron II, and Persian through Byzantine periods.[55]

Levitical Towns of Dan: Four Towns (Josh 21:23–24; 1 Chr 6:69)

18. Eltekeh (Josh 21:23)

Eltekeh was a Levitical town belonging to Dan (Josh 21:23; *Onom.* 438/88:11). It is included as a Danite city in Josh 19:44, where it is mentioned in close association with Gibbethon (see below). Neither Eltekeh nor Gibbethon appear in the Chronicler's version of the list, which does not include a separate designation for Dan and seems to correlate Aijalon and Gath Rimmon (see below) with Ephraim. Outside of the Bible, Eltekeh is included alongside Timnah in Sennacherib's account of the attack of the Philistine coastal plain following the destruction of several other Danite towns, which were then under the control of Ashkelon (i.e., Jaffa, Bene Berak, Azor and Beth Dagon).[56] The proposed identification with Tell esh-Shallaf remains a strong possibility.[57] Tell esh-Shallaf has remains from the Middle Bronze II, Late Bronze, Iron I, Iron II, Persian, and Hellenistic periods.[58] Since I agree with those who locate Gath Rimmon/Gittaim at Ras Abu Humeid (see below) this means that Tell esh-Shallaf should remain a tentative candidate for Eltekeh.

19. Gibbethon (Josh 21:23)

The city of Gibbethon is mentioned in Josh 19:44; 21:23; 1 Kgs 15:27; 16:15, 17, and no. 103 on Thutmose III's city list, and depicted in a relief of Sargon II's campaign against

---

53. Josh 10:10-11; 16:3, 5; 18:13-14; 1 Sam 13:18; 1 Kgs 9:15–17; 1 Chr 7:24; 2 Chr 8:5–6; 25:13; see also 1 Macc 3:16, 24; 7:39; 9:50; Judith 4:4; Jub. 34:4; *Onom.* 212/46:21 ("twelve miles from Jerusalem on the way to Nicopolis").

54. Robinson and Smith, *Biblical Researches in Palestine*, 2:62.

55. Israel Finkelstein, Zvi Lederman, and Shlomo Bunimovitz, eds., *Highland of Many Cultures: The Southern Samaria Survey* (Tel Aviv: Tel Aviv University, 1997), 161–64, 303–5; Feldstein et al., *Archeological Survey of Israel, Map 83/2: Map of El Bira: Benjamin Survey*, site 143.

56. "Sennacherib's Siege of Jerusalem," trans. Mordechai Cogan (*COS* 2.119B).

57. Mazar, "Cities of the Priests," 201; Aharoni, *Land of the Bible*, 301–5; Rainey and Notley, *Sacred Bridge*, 242; see also John L. Peterson, "Eltekeh (Place)," *ABD* 2:483–84. Although, Tell Melat (Gibbethon?) would theoretically be a better fit for the context of Sennacherib's campaign since it is much closer to Timnah (Tell Batash) and Ekron (Khirbet el-Muqqana) than Tell esh-Shallaf (located c. 14 km from Ekron and 18 km from Timnah).

58. Benjamin Mazar, "The Cities of the Territory of Dan," *IEJ* 10.2 (1960): 73; Peterson, "Topographical Surface Survey," 296–316; Alon Shavit, "Settlement Patterns in Israel's Southern Coastal Plain during the Iron Age II" (PhD diss., Tel Aviv University, 2003), site 112.

Azuri and Yamani.[59] Gibbethon is usually identified with either Ras Abu Humeid or Tell Melat.[60] Both sites match the criteria for Gibbethon, but since it seems plausible to identify Ras Abu Humeid with Gath Rimmon/Gittaim (see below), it is best to locate Gibbethon at Tell Melat. Tell Melat (Tel Malot) has remains from the Neolithic, Chalcolithic, Early Bronze, Late Bronze I–II, Iron I, Iron II, and Persian through Byzantine periods.[61] Like Ras Abu Humeid, Tell Melat is close to Gezer and in Israelite territory, which matches the Nadab/Elah campaigns against Philistia (1 Kgs 15:29; 16:15–17).

20. AIJALON (JOSH 21:24; 1 CHR 6:69)

Aijalon is mentioned ten times in the Hebrew Bible (Josh 10:12; 19:42; 21:24; Judg 1:35; 12:12; 1 Sam 14:31; 1 Chr 6:69; 8:13; 2 Chr 11:10; 28:18). Outside of the Bible, Aijalon is mentioned in the El Amarna correspondence (EA 273.16–24).[62] Additionally, the name may occur in Solomon's second district in the compound toponym Elon Bethhanan, which is perhaps the two towns of Aijalon and Bethhanan (1 Kgs 4:9). The geographical context of this passage is very similar to Judg 1:35, which also includes several Danite towns. Eusebius misidentified Aijalon with a place near Bethel, but Jerome adds the detail that Aijalon "is a village near Nicopolis two miles away as they go to Aelia" (*Onom.* 48/18:13), which corresponds with Yalo.[63]

Yalo preserves the name of the ancient site and provides the name for the valley that sits to the west of the tell (Josh 10:12). The twin tells of Yalo and Tell el-Kokah

---

59. Rainey and Notley, *Sacred Bridge*, 72–74, 236. Eusebius's reference to Gibbethon (*Onom.* 335/70:7) lists several towns with the *geb* ("hill") toponym component, but none of them fit the location of Gibbethon in the Shephelah/coastal plain. See also various toponyms including the *Geb* ("hill") element in Eusebius's statement (*Onom.* 335/70:5), none of which seem that they can be related to Bronze-Iron Age Gibbethon.

60. On Ras Abu Humeid, see Götz Schmitt, "Gat, Gittaim und Gitta," in *Drei Studien zur Archäologie und Topographie Altisraels*, ed. Rudolph Cohen and Götz Schmitt (Wiesbaden: Verlag, 1980), 107–9; Nadav Na'aman, *Ancient Israel and Its Neighbors: Interaction and Counteraction* (Winona Lake, IN: Eisenbrauns, 2005); Saul Wolff and Alon Shavit, "Hamid, Tel," *NEAEHL* 5:1762–63. For Tell Melat, see Gerhard Von Rad, "Das Reich Israel Und Die Philister," *Palästinajahrbuch* 29 (1933): 30–42; Mazar, "Dan"; Aharoni, *Land of the Bible*; Kallai, *Historical Geography*, 369; John L. Peterson, "Gibbethon (Place)," *ABD* 2:1007; Rainey and Notley, *Sacred Bridge*, 195.

61. Alon Shavit, "Tel Malot," *Excavations and Surveys in Israel* 12 (1992): 49–50; Giora Parnos, Ianir Milevski, and Hamoudi Khalaily, "Remains from the Late Prehistoric to Early Islamic Periods at the Foot of Tel Maloṭ (East)," *'Atiqot* 64 (2010): 25–77; Ron Kehati, "Faunal Remains from Tel Maloṭ (East)," *'Atiqot* 64 (2010): 83–84; Sigal Golan and Othmar Keel, "Tombs from the Middle Bronze Age I until the Iron Age at Tel Maloṭ," *'Atiqot* 65 (2011): 64*; Oren Shmueli, "Iron Age Tombs North of Tel Maloṭ," *'Atiqot* 65 (January 1, 2011): 65*.

62. The El Amarna correspondence is a collection of diplomatic letters sent (primarily) to Pharaoh Akhenaten in the mid-fourteenth century BC, by foreign entities—primarily Canaanite city states. See Anson F. Rainey, *The El-Amarna Correspondence: A New Edition of the Cuneiform Letters from the Site of El-Amarna Based on Collations of All Extant Tablets*, ed. William M. Schniedewind and Zipora Cochavi-Rainey, 2 vols. (Leiden: Brill, 2014).

63. Jerome quoted from G. S. P. Freeman-Grenville, trans., *The Onomasticon by Eusebius of Caesarea* (Jerusalem: Carta, 2003), 19. Eusebius does identify the similarly named "Elon" (Josh 19:43; compare to 1 Kgs 4:9) with Yalo in another reference (*Onom.* 135/30:26).

mark the location of ancient Aijalon. The fortified ruins with remains dating from the Early Bronze Age through Roman periods, including Late Bronze–Iron II, and the clear toponymic connection with Yalo make this identification certain.[64]

21. Gath Rimmon (Josh 21:24; 1 Chr 6:69)

Gath Rimmon was a Levitical town (Josh 21:24; 1 Chr 6:69) belonging to Dan. Rainey has persuasively argued that Gath Rimmon and Gittaim were identical sites (Josh 19:45; Neh 11:35; Thutmose III itinerary nos. 63–65) in the general vicinity of Lod and Ramle, which he located at Ras Abu Humeid.[65] Surveys and excavations at Ras Abu Humeid point to the viability of an identification with Gath Rimmon/Gittaim. In particular, Wolff's excavations revealed Early Bronze, Middle Bronze, Late Bronze, Iron I, Iron II, and Persian through Byzantine period activity.[66] Of special note is the discovery of a ninth century BC destruction (Stratum VII).[67] Wolff and Shavit have suggested that this destruction may be related to Hazael's campaign (2 Kgs 10:32; 12:17; 13:22), which parallels the destruction of the nearby sites of Gezer, Aphek, and Gath. Following this destruction, a large casemate fortification was built at the site in the late ninth to early eighth century BC (Stratum VI). Several walls were dated to the second half of the eighth century BC (Stratum V) but may have been destroyed by the Neo-Assyrian campaigns of the late eighth century

64. Ram Gophna and Yuval Porat, "The Land of Ephraim and Manasseh," in *Judaea, Samaria and the Golan: Archaeological Survey 1967–1968*, ed. Moshe Kochavi (Jerusalem: Archaeological Survey of Israel by Carta, 1972), site 241–42; John L. Peterson, "Aijalon," *ABD* 1:131; Raphael Greenberg and Adi Keinan, *Israeli Archaeological Activity in the West Bank 1967-2007: A Sourcebook* (Jerusalem: Ostracon, 2009), site 2635–36. On the toponymic connection, see Robinson and Smith, *Biblical Researches in Palestine*, 1:63; Jan J. Simons, *The Geographical and Topographical Texts of the Old Testament* (Leiden: Brill, 1959), 200; Shmuel Ahituv, *Canaanite Toponyms in Ancient Egyptian Documents* (Jerusalem: Magnes Press, Hebrew University, 1984), 80, 191; Peterson, "Aijalon," 131.

65. For the general location of Gath Rimmon/Gittaim, see Anson F. Rainey, "Tel Gerisa and the Danite Inheritance," *Eretz Israel Museum Yearbook* 5–6 (1990): 59–72; Rainey and Notley, *Sacred Bridge*, 144. For an alternate view that identifies Gittaim with el-Burj (Horbat Tittora), see Schmitt, "Gat, Gittaim und Gitta," 80–92; Nadav Na'aman, *Canaan in the Second Millenium BCE* (Winona Lake, IN: Eisenbrauns, 2005), 375. Na'aman also suggested that Gittaim occurs in the Shishak list (*qdtm* no. 25); however, many other scholars identify this town with Kiriath Jearim (e.g., Ahituv, *Canaanite Toponyms*, 126; Kenneth A. Kitchen, *The Third Intermediate Period in Egypt, 1100-650 B.C.*, 2nd ed. [Warminster, England: Aris & Phillips, 1986], 435; Rainey and Notley, *Sacred Bridge*, 186). For the specific location of Gath Rimmon/Gittaim at Ras Abu Humeid, see Rainey and Notley, *Sacred Bridge*, 144; Michael Avi-Yonah, *Gazetteer of Roman Palestine* (Jerusalem: Hebrew University, 1976), 136; Aharoni, *Land of the Bible*, 435; Yoram Tsafrir, Leah Di Segni, and Judith Green, *Tabula Imperii Romani Iudaea-Palestina: Eretz Israel in the Hellenistic, Roman and Byzantine Periods; Maps and Gazetteer* (Jerusalem: The Israel Academy of Sciences and Humanities, 1994), 136.

66. Oren Tal, "Tel Hamid," *IEJ* 47.3/4 (1997): 273–75; Oren Tal and Noga Blockman, "A Salvage Excavation at Tel Hamid (The Lower Terrace)," *TA* 25.2 (1998): 142–73; Saul Wolff, "Tel Ḥamid," *Hadashot Arkheologiyot: Excavations and Surveys in Israel* 110 (1999): 55*–56*; Wolff and Shavit, "Tel Ḥamid," *Hadashot Arkheologiyot: Excavations and Surveys in Israel* 109 (1999): 68*–70*; Wolff and Shavit, "Hamid, Tel"; Shavit, "Settlement Patterns," site 75.

67. Shavit, "Settlement Patterns"; Wolff and Shavit, "Hamid, Tel."

BC.[68] The evidence of occupation from the Early Bronze through Byzantine periods and substantial remains from the ninth century BC (Iron IIA) and eighth century BC (Iron IIB) fit the biblical and extrabiblical corpus for an identification with Gittaim/Gath Rimmon.[69]

LEVITICAL TOWNS OF MANASSEH: FOUR TOWNS (JOSH 21:25–27; 1 CHR 6:70–71)

22. TAANACH/ANER (JOSH 21:25; 1 CHR 6:70)

Taanach appears in the Joshua version of the Levitical list (Josh 21:25). The Chronicler's "Aner" (1 Chr 6:70) is probably a corrupted form of Taanach with the final *kaph* (ך) accidentally changed to a *resh* (ר) and the initial *tav* (ת) combined with the preceding word (אֶת־עָנֵר, *et-aner*).[70] Thus, both versions of the list originally had Taanach. Taanach has been identified with Tell Ti'innik, which is a well-known and excavated tell located in the southwestern part of the Jezreel Valley on the edge of Mount Carmel.[71] In the Bible, Taanach is a Canaanite town during the Israelite conquest and settlement (Josh 12:21), it is allotted to Manasseh who could not drive out the Canaanites living there (Josh 17:11; Judg 1:27; see also Judg 5:19; 1 Chr 7:29), and it is one of the towns mentioned in Baana's district during the reign of Solomon (1 Kgs 4:12). Outside of the Bible, Taanach appears in a number of Egyptian texts, including the conquest lists of Thutmose III (no. 42) and Shishak I (no. 14) from Karnak. The site was inhabited from the Early Bronze Age until modern times, including extensive Late Bronze and Iron I and II remains.[72]

23. IBLEAM/BILEAM (JOSH 21:25; 1 CHR 6:70)

Ibleam (יִבְלְעָם, *yivleam*) appears as Bileam (בִּלְעָם, *bilam*) in the Chronicler's version (1 Chr 6:70). Instead of Bileam, Joshua's version has an additional Gath Rimmon (Josh 21:25), which may be a doublet from the preceding verse.[73] Like Taanach, Ibleam belonged to Manasseh, who

---

68. Wolff, "Tel Ḥamid," 56*–57*; Wolff and Shavit, "Tel Ḥamid," 66*–68*; "Hamid, Tel," 1763.

69. Wolff and Shavit, "Hamid, Tel," 1762–63. Eusebius's entry on Gath Rimmon (*Onom.* 336/70:14)—"twelve miles from Diospolis on the way to Eleutheropolis"—probably refers to an additional Gath (not Philistine Gath or Gath Rimmon) near Emmaus in the Aijalon Valley. An additional entry (*Onom.* 341/72:2) refers to a "very large village that is called Gittham between Antipatris [i.e., Aphek] and Jamnia [i.e., Yavneh]." In my opinion, Eusebius is referring to the vicinity of Ramle (also known as "Gath" by Ishtori HaParhi in the thirteenth century) and Gath Rimmon/Gittaim should be connected with the nearby site of Ras Abu Humeid. For more information on Gath Rimmon and the "other" Gath (besides Philistine Gath), see McKinny, "Pressing On."

70. Melvin Hunt, "Aner (Place)," *ABD* 1:248. The Chronicler's version characteristically includes the direct object marker.

71. Robinson and Smith, *Biblical Researches in Palestine*, 3:179. Besides perfectly preserving the name, the site also fits with Eusebius's mileage of either three or four miles (5–6 km) from Legio (*Onom.* 504/100:7; 492/98:10 respectively).

72. Albert E. Glock, "Taanach," *NEAEHL* 4:1428–33.

73. On the other hand, the existence of Rummaneh near Taanach would seem to allow for an additional Gath Rimmon in the vicinity. While surveys in the village of Rummaneh did not reveal Iron Age remains, the nearby site of Tell Salim and other sites in the vicinity did reveal Iron Age remains, which would allow for the possibility of identifying another Levitical town

could not drive out the Canaanites who lived there (Josh 17:11; Judg 1:27; compare with *Onom.* 553/108:24). Ibleam was the site of two regicides separated by about a century. In 841 BC, Jehu shot Ahaziah of Judah "at the ascent of Gur, which is by Ibleam" (2 Kgs 9:27) and Zechariah was assassinated by Shallum at Ibleam in 753 BC (2 Kgs 15:10). Ibleam also appears in the Thutmose III conquest list (no. 43). Ibleam has been identified with Khirbet Belameh, which preserves the name and appears to have been inhabited from the Early Bronze, Middle Bronze, Late Bronze, Iron I, Iron II, and Persian through Byzantine periods.[74]

24–25. GOLAN IN BASHAN AND ASHTAROTH (JOSH 21:26; 1 CHR 6:71)

Golan in Bashan (Deut 4:43; Josh 20:8; 21:27; 1 Chr 6:71; *Onom.* 306/64:6) is generally located at Sahm ej-Jolan, but the archaeology of the site is unknown. Joshua's Beeshterah (Josh 21:26; *Onom.* 234/50:22) is usually understood as a misspelling for Ashtaroth, which is supported by the Chronicler's version. Ashtaroth has been located at the important Bronze and Iron Age site of Tell Ashtarah.[75]

LEVITICAL TOWNS OF ISSACHAR (JOSH 21:28–29; 1 CHR 6:72–73)

26. KISHION (JOSH 21:28; 1 CHR 6:76)

In both references to Kishion (Josh 19:20; 21:28; *Onom.* 597/114:28), the town appears in connection with Daberath (Daburieh) and Jarmuth (see discussion below). The Chronicler's Kedesh seems to be an error for Kishion, perhaps influenced by Kedesh in the Naphtalite allotment (1 Chr 6:76). Kishion is typically identified with Tell Qasyun situated just south of Wadi esh-Sherrar, one mile (2 km) south of Mount Tabor, and one mile (2 km) north of Endor (Khirbet Safsafeh).[76] Zori (Zimbalist) argued that Kishion should be identified with Kishon (Tell Qasyun) and that the Kishon River should be related to Wadi el-Bireh, which drains the plain of Issachar to the east, instead of the traditional identification of the Kishon River with Nahr el-Muqatta.[77] Peterson

in this vicinity (Adam Zertal, Nivi Mirkam, *The Manasseh Hill Country Survey, Vol. 3: From Nahal 'Iron to Nahal Shechem*, ed. Shay Bar [Leiden: Brill, 2016], 67–68).

74. Adam Zertal, *The Manasseh Hill Country Survey, Vol. 1: The Shechem Syncline* (Tel Aviv: Tel Aviv University, 1992), site 26; Hamdan Taha and Gerrit van der Kooij, eds., *Khirbet Bal'ama Archaeological Project Report of the 1996-2000 Excavations and Surveys*, 2 vols. (Ramallah: Ministry of Tourism and Antiquities, 2007). The later authors excavated the site from 1996–2000 and revealed a water tunnel system that was apparently constructed in the Iron Age.

75. Eusebius recorded that Ashtaroth was "six miles" from Edrei (*Onom.* 24/12:11; compare with *Onom.* 4/6:4), but the distance is actually more like fourteen Roman miles (13 regular miles, 21 km), but his distance of "twenty-five miles" from Edrei to Bozrah (in this same entry) is very accurate.

76. E.g., Nehemia Zimbalist, "Kishon and Kishyon," *Bulletin of the Jewish Palestine Exploration Society* 13.1/2 (1946): 28–51; Simons, *Geographical and Topographical Texts*, 77; Aharoni, *Land of the Bible*, 438.

77. This town is mentioned in the Thutmose Karnak list (no. 37) in the following sequence of Hazor, Pehel, Chinnereth, Shimeon (i.e., Shimron), Adami(-nekeb?), Qishon (i.e., Kishion), Shunem, Mishal, and Achshah (nos. 32–40) (see Rainey and Notley, *Sacred Bridge*, 72). It may also occur in an itinerary list of Ramesses II. For further discussion, see Chris McKinny, "'March on My Soul with Might!'—The Geographical Setting of Judges 4–5" in this volume;

has pointed out that Tell Qasyun does not appear in the older maps of the region (e.g., *Survey of Western Palestine*) but was instead known as el-Khirba, which caused Peterson to be skeptical about the connection with Kishion.[78] However, Abel recorded the name of a spring and ruin named Qasyun near the base of Mount Tabor, which he suggested retained the name of Kishion.[79] Survey and excavation work at Tell Qasyun revealed remains of a fifty dunams (12 acres) tell with occupation from the Paleolithic until the Early Arab period, including continuous occupation from the Middle Bronze through Iron II periods.[80]

27. Daberath (Josh 21:28; 1 Chr 6:72)

Daberath (Josh 19:12; 21:28; 1 Chr 6:72; *Onom.* 386/78:25) or Rabbith (Josh 19:20; *Onom.* 778/144:19) is preserved in the Arab village of Daburieh on the western side of the base of Mount Tabor (see also *Onom.* 375/78:5).[81] Surveys and salvage work at Daburieh have revealed Bronze, Iron I, Iron II, Persian, Hellenistic, Roman, Byzantine, and later periods.[82] It should be noted that the close proximity between Daberath and Kishion, on the west and south sides of Mount Tabor respectively, represents a geographical unit.

28. Jarmuth/Ramoth (Josh 21:29; 1 Chr 6:73)

Jarmuth or Ramoth (Josh 19:21; 1 Chr 6:73; compare with *Onom.* 559/110:3; 779/144:21) was a Levitical town in the tribal territory of Issachar (as "Ramoth" in Josh 21:29). In 1921, C. S. Fisher found a stele belonging to Seti I at Beth Shan that mentions "Mount Yarmuta."[83] In light of this, Aharoni suggested that Jarmuth should

---

see also Zimbalist, "Kishon and Kishyon"; Charles R. Krahmalkov, "Exodus Itinerary Confirmed by Egyptian Evidence," *BAR* 20 (1994): 54–62.

78. John L. Peterson, "Kishion (Place)," *ABD* 4:89.

79. Although he identified biblical and Egyptian Kishion with Tell el Ajjul, he also believed that Tell Qasyun was the location of the Crusade village of *Casal de Cressum* (see Felix-Marie Abel, *Géographie de la Palestine: Géographie Physique et Historique*, 3rd ed. [Paris: Gabalda, 1967], 2:422–23; see also Simons, *Geographical and Topographical Texts*, 185; Rainey and Notley, *Sacred Bridge*, 67).

80. C. Cohen-Arnon and Ruth Amiran, "Excavations at Tel Qishon: Preliminary Report on the 1977–1978 Seasons," *Eretz-Israel* 15 (1981): 205–12; Zvi Gal, *Archeological Survey of Israel, Map 45: Map of 'En Dor*, ed. Ayala Sussmann (Jerusalem: Israel Antiquities Authority, 2013), site 1, https://survey.antiquities.org.il/index_Eng.html#/MapSurvey/49.

81. Significantly, Daberath is mentioned in the boundary description of Zebulun (Josh 19:12) but was a town of Issachar (Josh 19:20), see William F. Albright, "The Topography of the Tribe of Issachar," *ZAW* 44.1 (1926): 230; John L. Peterson, "Daberath (Place)," *ABD* 2:1. See also Robinson and Smith, *Biblical Researches in Palestine*, 3:210.

82. Peterson, "Topographical Surface Survey," 168–76; Peterson, "Daberath," 1. For various salvage projects in the village, see Zvi Gal, *Archeological Survey of Israel, Map 41: Map of Har Tavor*, ed. Ayala Sussmann (Jerusalem: Israel Antiquities Authority, 2013), site 41, https://survey.antiquities.org.il/index_Eng.html#/MapSurvey/45.

83. Lines 10–12: "On this day, lo [one came to tell] his [majesty]: The ʿApiru of Mount Yarmuta, with Teyer ..., [have ari]sen in attack upon the Asiatics of Rehem. Then [his majesty] said: How can these wretched Asiatics think [of taking] their [arms] for further disorder?" (*ANET*, 255). See also Alan Rowe, *The Topography and History of Beth-Shan, with Details of the Egyptian and Other Inscriptions Found on the Site* (Philadelphia: University of Pennsylvania

be located at Belvoir, the most dramatic height in the vicinity.[84] While no pre-Crusader remains were found at Belvoir, Gal's survey of the nearby site known as En ha-Yadid (less than 0.33 of a mile [0.5 km] to the south) revealed a small tell of only five dunams (1 acre) but with occupation from the Early Bronze, Middle Bronze, Late Bronze II, Iron I, Iron II, Hellenistic, Roman, Byzantine, and later periods.[85] In light of the toponymic connection between Judahite Jarmuth/Amarna Yaramu and Khirbet el-Yarmuk, it would seem possible that Jarmuth/Mount Yarmuta is preserved in Nahr Yarmuk, which flows into the Jordan River below the rise of the basalt mountains of Issachar.[86]

29. EN GANNIM/ANEM (JOSH 21:29; 1 CHR 6:73)

En Gannim of Issachar (Josh 19:21; 21:29; *Onom.* 476/94:25) has the alternate form of Anem in 1 Chr 6:73.[87] There are several candidates that have suitable remains that theoretically preserve the ancient name. Beit Jann has remains from the Late Bronze through Iron II periods. On the other hand, Gal suggests that nearby Khirbet ed-Dir was ancient En Gannim, as it appears to have been a more significant site than Beit Jann.[88] For geographical reasons, modern Jenin cannot be identified with En Gannim.[89] Another possibility would be to connect En Gannim with Umm Junieh, which is the Arab town preceding Kibbutz Degania Alef. Like Beit Jann, Umm Junieh could theoretically preserve the name, and might have a better correspondence on account of the similar toponymic preservation with the southern En Gannim.[90] In any case, there do not appear to be any pre-classical remains at Umm Junieh/Degania Alef. However, the nearby ruin of el-Abeidiyeh (0.6 mi. [1 km] south) has

---

Museum, 1930), 29–30; William F. Albright, "The Smaller Beth-Shan Stele of Sethos I (1309–1290 B. C.)," *BASOR* 125 (1952): 24–32.

84. Aharoni, *Land of the Bible*, 28; Dale W. Manor, "Jarmuth (Place)," *ABD* 3:644.

85. For Belvoir, see Zvi Gal, *Archeological Survey of Israel, Map 46: Map of Gazit*, ed. Ayala Sussmann (Jerusalem: Israel Antiquities Authority, 2012), site 60, https://survey.antiquities.org.il/index_Eng.html#/MapSurvey/34; Meir Ben-Dor, "The Excavations at the Crusader Fortress of Kokhav-Hayarden (Belvoir)," *Qadmoniot* 2.1 (5) (1969): 22–27. For En ha-Yadid, see Gal, *Archeological Survey of Israel, Map 46: Map of Gazit*, site 61.

86. Rainey and Notley, *Sacred Bridge*, 86. It is tempting to suggest a connection between Issacharite Jarmuth and one of the tells near the Jordan River (e.g., Nehemia Tzori and Noy Shemesh [foreward], *Archeological Survey of Jerusalem, Map 47: Map of Gesher*, ed. Ofer Sion [Jerusalem: Israel Antiquities Authority, 2015], sites 15, 18, and 19, https://survey.antiquities.org.il/index_Eng.html#/MapSurvey/2136). It is also worth noting that the segment north of the Gesher Map (i.e., between the Sea of Galilee and Gesher) has not yet been surveyed. Still, the boundary description of Issachar does not seem to point to a place name directly on the Jordan River, as the Jordan itself is referred to as the boundary (Josh 19:22).

87. John L. Peterson, "En-Gannim (Place)," *ABD* 2:501; see also Albright, "Issachar," 232. Albright's suggestion to identify En Gannim with Olam (on the edge of the Jordan Rift, see *Onom.* 752/140:17) has not received widespread acceptance.

88. Zvi Gal, "The Settlement of Issachar: Some New Observations," *TA* 9.1 (1982): 84; Gal, *Lower Galilee during the Iron Age* (Winona Lake, IN: Eisenbrauns, 1992), 32–33.

89. Contra Robinson and Smith, *Later Biblical Researches*, 2:315; see Aharoni, *Land of the Bible*, 430, who suggests that it is identical with Beth Haggan (2 Kgs 9:27).

90. See discussion in McKinny, "Historical Geography," 186–87.

significant Early Bronze, Late Bronze, and Iron Age remains, which makes it a more likely candidate for En Gannim (of Issachar) than Beit Jann.[91]

LEVITICAL TOWNS OF ASHER: FOUR TOWNS (JOSH 21:30–31; 1 CHR 6:74–75)

30. MISHAL/MASHAL (JOSH 21:30; 1 CHR 6:74)

Mishal/Mashal appears only in the Levitical town lists (Josh 19:26; 1 Chr 6:74) and in the allotment of Asher (Josh 21:30). Eusebius and Jerome connected the site with "Carmel-on-the-Sea" indicating close proximity with Mount Carmel (*Onom.* 689/130:18).[92] Mishal appears in several Egyptian texts, including the Execration Texts and the campaign of Thutmose III.[93] There are two main candidates for Mishal: Tell Keisan, located in the central part of the plain of Asher, and Tell en-Nahl situated on the Kishon River in the industrial area of modern-day Haifa.[94] Surveys at Tell en-Nahl revealed remains from the Middle Bronze, Late Bronze, and Iron Age over ten dunams (2.5 acres).[95] Excavations at Tell Keisan have revealed significant Early Bronze through Iron II occupation over one hundred forty-five dunams (36 acres).[96]

While these suggestions fit the general geography and occupational sequence for Mishal (and/or Achshaph), I would like to offer a different proposal for Mishal: Tell Abu Hawam. Tell Abu Hawam was an ancient port that was situated directly below and to the north of the Mount Carmel between the Kishon River (Nahr el-Muqatta) and Wadi Seliman (which could preserve the name Mashal), both of which run into Haifa Bay. Now almost completely lost due to modern construction, Tell Abu Hawam was inhabited from the Middle Bronze II through the early Hellenistic period.[97] Tell Abu Hawam is normally identified with Shihor Libnath from Josh 19:26.[98] In that context, Shihor

91. Abdalla Mokary, "'Ubeidiya," *Hadashot Arkheologiyot* 126 (2014): n.p., http://www.hadashot-esi.org.il/report_detail_eng.aspx?id=13703&mag_id=121; trial excavation of Aharoni, *Land of the Bible*; see also Nadav Na'aman, "Yeno'am," *TA* 4.3–4 (1977): 168–77. Na'aman demonstrates the difficulties with identifying el-Abeidiyeh with Yenoam.

92. Their unique spelling of "Masan" is not reflected in the LXX or MT.

93. Ahituv, *Canaanite Toponyms*, 143.

94. For Tell Keisan, see Rainey and Notley, *Sacred Bridge*, 183, who suggest Tell Keisan, but many would connect Keisan with Achshaph. For Tell en-Nahl, see Benjamin Mazar, *Canaan and Israel: Historical Essays*, 2nd ed. (Jerusalem: Bialik, 1972), 27, 116; Ahituv, *Canaanite Toponyms*, 143.

95. Avraham Ronen and Yaácov Olamy, *Archeological Survey of Israel, Map 23: Map of Haifa-East*, ed. Moshe Kochavi (Jerusalem: Israel Antiquities Authority, 2013), site 33, http://survey.antiquities.org.il/index_Eng.html#/MapSurvey/56. See also nearby site 19 [Tell el-Idham] which revealed Iron II and Persian remains over twenty-five dunams (six acres).

96. Gunnar Lehmann and Martin Peilstöcker, *Archeological Survey of Israel, Map 20: Map of Ahihud*, ed. Ofer Sion (Jerusalem: Israel Antiquities Authority, 2012), site 24, https://survey.antiquities.org.il/index_Eng.html#/MapSurvey/12.

97. See Jacqueline Balensi, "Revising Tell Abu Hawam," *BASOR* 257 (1985): 65–74; Michal Artzy, "Abu Hawam, Tell," *NEAEHL* 5:1553–54.

98. Rafael Frankel, "Shihor-Libnath," *ABD* 5:1212.

Libnath is normally understood to be the southwestern border of the tribe of Asher in connection with Mount Carmel. However, this passage may instead be read as a wider western boundary for the tribe of Asher, which includes specific topographic boundary markers. Shihor Libnath may be identified with Khirbet Lebbuna, which is located above the stream of Wadi Kutayeh (see Guérin's map) just east of Rosh HaNiqra (i.e., Ras en Nakurah) on the border between the modern countries of Israel and Lebanon.[99]

31. ABDON/EBRON (JOSH 21:30; 1 CHR 6:74)

Besides its reference in the Levitical lists (Josh 21:30; 1 Chr 6:74; compare with *Onom.* 121/30:4), Abdon appears as "Ebron" in the tribal list of Asher (Josh 19:28; compare with *Onom.* 123/30:8; 440/88:15).[100] Of the two variant spellings, Abdon is likely correct as the biblical name is preserved in Khirbet Abda, located four miles (6 km) inland from Achzib (ez-Zib; see Josh 19:29; Judg 1:31).[101] Khirbet Abda (Tel Avdon) is a tell of thirty dunams (7 acres) with remains from the Middle Bronze II, Iron I, Iron II, Persian, Hellenistic, Roman Byzantine, Crusader, and Mamluk periods.[102]

32. HELKATH (JOSH 21:31; 1 CHR 6:75)

Helkath appears in the Joshua Levitical list (Josh 21:31) and in Asher's tribal allotment (Josh 19:25; compare with *Onom.* 435/88:6), which probably mitigates against the Chronicler's "Hukok" spelling (1 Chr 6:75). In the Asher allotment, Helkath is the first Asherite town listed and is followed by the known sites of Hali (Ras Ali), Beten (Tell el-Far near Abtun), Achshaph (Tell Keisan?), and Mishal (Tell Abu Hawam? see above) (Josh 19:25–36), all of which can be plausibly identified with ruins in the southern portion of the plain of Asher.[103] Outside the Bible, Helkath appears in a campaign

99. The archaeology of Khirbet Lebbuna is unknown but may preserve the ancient name for Shihor Libnath. It is also a very distinct geographical feature that could have been used to delineate territory. See also Guérin, *Description Géographique*.

100. Eusebius's "Elba" is a corrupted form that is unique from the MT/LXX for Josh 19:28.

101. Ebron is a corrupt form of Abdon with the similar shaped *dalet* (ד) becoming *resh* (ר). For toponymic connections, see Guérin, *Description Géographique*, 2:35–37; Aharoni, *Land of the Bible*, 37; Rainey and Notley, *Sacred Bridge*, 129.

102. Rafael Frankel and Nimrod Gerzov, *Archeological Survey of Israel, Map 2: Map of Hanita*, ed. Ayala Sussmann (Jerusalem: Israel Antiquities Authority, 2013), site 142, http://survey.antiquities.org.il/index_Eng.html#/MapSurvey/86; see also Moshe Prausnitz, "Akhziv and Avdon: On the Planning of a Port and a Fortress City in the Plain of Acre," *Eretz-Israel* 11 (1973): 219–23.

103. Hali (Ras Ali) does not appear on nineteenth and early twentieth century maps. It is located along Wadi el-Melek that empties into the Plain of Asher. Aharoni was the first to suggest that Hali should be identified with Ras Ali. Olam and Gal demonstrated Ras Ali was only inhabited during the Early Bronze, Late Bronze II, Iron I, and Persian period (over 50 dunams), and suggested that it be identified with Hali (Ya'aqov Olami and Zvi Gal, *Archaeological Survey of Israel, Map 24: Map of Shefar'am*, ed. Zvi Gal [Jerusalem: Israel Antiquties Authority, 2011], site 115, https://survey.antiquities.org.il/index_Eng.html#/MapSurvey/9; Aharoni, *Land of the Bible*, 435).

The Beten (Tell el-Far near Abtun) identification is relatively secure due to the description of Eusebius, which connects Beten/Batnai with a site "at the eighth mile [13 km] east

of Thutmose III (no. 112) following Beth Shan (no. 110) and before Jokneam (no. 113) and Geba (no. 114).[104] There are two main suggestions for Helkath: Tell el-Qassis (north of Jokneam) and Tell el-Harbaj (Tel Regev).[105] While both remain possibilities, Tell el-Qassis might be the preferred choice, but it is difficult to be certain given the numerous suitable tells in the vicinity.

33. REHOB (JOSH 21:31; 1 CHR 6:75)

The name Rehob is listed twice in the Asher allotment (Josh 19:28; 30; *Onom.* 780/144:22) and again as a Levitical town within Asher (Josh 21:31; compare with *Onom.* 764/142:18—this refers to the Tel Rehov of the Jordan Valley). The first reference is part of Asher's northeastern boundary that included the towns of Cabul (Kabul), Ebron/Abdon (Khirbet Abde), Rehob, Hammon (Khirbet Umm el-Awamid?), Kanah (Qana), and Sidon (Saida). This northern Rehob may possibly be identified with Tell Rahib or Khirbet el-Belat, but nothing is known concerning the archaeology of either of these sites as the former has not yet been surveyed, and the latter is just inside the Lebanese border.[106] The second reference to Rehob is within a group of towns that are not part of a boundary line. These include the following: Mahalab (Khirbet el-Mahalib), Achzib (Tell Achzib), Akko (el-Fukhkhar), Aphek (Khirbet Kurdaneh), and Rehob. The context of this latter group would seem to indicate that the second Rehob was in the central section of the plain of Asher near Akko. It is unclear which Rehob should be related to the Levitical Rehob of Asher, but in light of the southern location of Abdon, Helkath, and Mishal (Josh 21:30–31), it seems plausible that the second Rehob is the latter Rehob in the Asher allotment (Josh 19:30). This Rehob is usually identified with Tell el-Bir el-Gharbi (Tel Bira), located east of Akko

---

of Ptolemais" (*Onom.* 250/52:19) and the existence of Abtun (eighteen miles [29 km] south of Akko/Ptolemais), which preserves the ancient name of the biblical and Byzantine town (see Rafael Frankel, "Beten," *ABD* 1:680). Frankel argues that the discrepancy between Eusebius's eight miles (13 km) and the actual twelve miles (19 km) to Abtun may be explained by a reference to the eighth Roman mile turnoff from the more significant Ptolemais-Sepphoris Road (Frankel, "Beten," 680). Tell el-Far was briefly examined by Olami and Gal, who found remains from the Middle Bronze, Late Bonze, Iron II, Persian, and Byzantine periods (Olami and Gal, *Archaeological Survey of Israel, Map 24: Map of Shefar'am*, site 111, see also site 112).

104. Ahituv, *Canaanite Toponyms*, 117–18; Rainey and Notley, *Sacred Bridge*, 74.

105. Tell el-Qassis consists of a ten-dunam (2.5 acre) tell that was occupied continuously from the Early Bronze I through the Hellenistic period (Avner Raban, *Archeological Survey of Israel, Map 28: Map of Nahalal*, ed. Y. Tsafrir, (Jerusalem: Israel Antiquities Authority, 2012), site 11, https://survey.antiquities.org.il/index_Eng.html#/MapSurvey/26; Amnon Ben-Tor, Ruhama Bonfil, and Sharon Zuckerman, *Tel Qashish: A Village in the Jezreel Valley: Final Report of the Archaeological Excavations (1978–1987)*, [Jerusalem: Hebrew University, 2003]). It should be noted that the excavators prefer an identification with Dabbesheth (Josh 19:11). Tell el-Harbaj is a low-lying site that was inhabited during the Early Bronze, Middle Bronze, Late Bronze, Iron I, Iron II, Hellenistic, and later periods (Ronen and Olamy, *Archeological Survey of Israel, Map 23: Map of Haifa-East*, site 113). For bibliography, see John L. Peterson, "Helkath (Place)," *ABD* 3:126.

106. See also the recent suggestion to identify this Rehob with Tel Rosh in Upper Galilee (Hayah Katz and Yigal Levin, "Tel Rosh: The Forgotten Rehob in the Upper Galilee," *PEQ* 153.1 [2021]: 24–41).

on the eastern edge of the plain of Asher.[107] Archaeological work at the site has shown that the site was large (c. 17 dunams; 4 acres) and continuously occupied from the Early Bronze through Iron Age II periods.[108]

LEVITICAL TOWNS OF NAPHTALI: THREE TOWNS (JOSH 21:32; 1 CHR 6:76)

34. KEDESH (JOSH 21:32; 1 CHR 6:76)

Kedesh in Galilee (Josh 19:37; 21:34; 1 Chr 6:76; *Onom.* 601/116:8—"twenty miles [32 km] from Tyre near Paneas"; compare with *Onom.* 586/114:8) is one of the most well-known sites in the Levitical list occurring in a number of biblical and extrabiblical texts.[109] The ancient name has been preserved in Tell Qades in Upper Galilee.[110] The site was almost continuously occupied from the Early Bronze until the Ottoman era, including significant Late Bronze, Iron I, and Iron II occupations.[111] However, only the later remains at the site, primarily Persian through Roman, have been exposed in excavations.[112]

35–36. HAMMOTH DOR/HAMMON AND KARTAN/KIRIATHAIM (JOSH 21:32; 1 CHR 6:76)

The Levitical town of Hammoth Dor or Hammon (Josh 21:32; 1 Chr 6:76; *Onom.* 134/30:9; 441/88:19) seems to be the same town as Hammath in the allotment of Naphtali (Josh 19:35). Hammath may also occur in Papyrus Antastasi I from the reign of Ramesses II. Hammath is often identified with Hamman Tabariyeh (Hamat Tiberias).[113] However, there does not appear to be a Bronze or Iron Age tell in the vicinity. Peterson suggests identifying Hammath with Khirbet el-Qanitriyeh (Tel Raqqat), a site that Aharoni identified with Kartan/Rakkath (Josh 19:35; 21:32; 1 Chr 6:76; *Onom.* 602/116:12; 783/144:26), which appears to be more likely.[114] Peterson follows an earlier suggestion to identify Kartan/Kiriathaim with

107. John L. Peterson and Rami Arav, "Rehob," *ABD* 5:661. For the Egyptian references to this Rehob, see Ahituv, *Canaanite Toponyms*, 163–64.

108. Lehmann and Peilstöcker, *Map of Ahihud*, site 70.

109. Josh 12:22 (slain king by Joshua); 19:37 (city of Naphtali); 20:7 (city of refuge); 21:32 (Levitical city, 1 Chr 6:76—note 1 Chr 6:72 is an error for Kishion); and 2 Kgs 15:29 (captured by Tiglath-Pileser III). Despite being in the tribal allotment of Naphtali, Kedesh in Galilee is not the same town as Kadesh of Naphtali (Judg 4:6) of the Deborah/Barak narrative. See also 1 Macc 11:63, 73; *J.W.* 2.459. Somewhat surprisingly the name does not appear in the various Egyptian itineraries.

110. Robinson and Smith, *Biblical Researches in Palestine*, 3:355; Rainey and Notley, *Sacred Bridge*, 185.

111. A new project (beginning in 2019) led by U. Davidovich, I. Wachtel, and R. Sabai plans to excavate the 350 dunam Early Bronze settlement as well as the Roman architecture at the site (https://www.biblicalarchaeology.org/dig/tel-qedesh/#detailsSec).

112. Sharon C. Herbert and Andrea M. Berlin, "A New Administrative Center for Persian and Hellenistic Galilee: Preliminary Report of the University of Michigan/University of Minnesota Excavations at Kedesh," *BASOR* 329 (2003): 13–59; Adi Erlich, "Happily Ever After? A Hellenistic Hoard from Tel Kedesh in Israel," *American Journal of Archaeology* 121.1 (2017): 39–59.

113. Talmudic tradition connects both Hammath and Rakkath with the area of Tiberias.

114. This Kiriathaim seems to be a corruption for either Kartan or Raqqat (see Aharoni, *Land of the Bible*, 438). The small site has remains from the Early Bronze, Middle Bronze, Late

Khirbet el-Qureiyeh. Qureiyeh is located near the Israel-Lebanese border beside Aytarun, but the nature of the archaeological remains at the site are unknown.[115]

Regarding Hammath/Hammon/Hammoth Dor, another possibility is that the ancient name could be related to Wadi Hamam (i.e., the Arbel Pass). While there do not appear to be any significant Bronze or Iron Age sites in the immediate vicinity of Wadi Hamam, Khirbet Abu Shusheh has remains from the Early Bronze through Iron Age and is located reasonably close to Wadi Hamam. Leibner makes a compelling case for identifying Khirbet Abu Shusheh (just west of Kibbutz Nof Ginosar) with Hellenistic and Roman Gennesar.[116] In light of the significant early occupation at Shusheh from the Early Bronze, Middle Bronze, Late Bronze, and throughout the Iron Age over an area of fifty-two dunams (13 acres), it seems plausible that the site had an earlier name that can be related to one of the towns (Hammath?) in Naphtali's allotment.[117]

LEVITICAL TOWNS OF ZEBULUN: FOUR TOWNS (JOSH 21:34–38; 1 CHR 6:77)

37. JOKNEAM (JOSH 21:34)

The identification of Jokneam (Josh 12:22; 19:11; 21:34) is well-established both through the preservation of the toponym (Tell Qeimun) and the fact that it was occupied continuously from the Early Bronze through Ottoman periods.[118] Jokneam was situated on the border of Zebulun, Asher, and eastern Manasseh (Josh 19:10), and also guarded a major route connecting the Sharon Plain and Jezreel Valleys via a pass through Mount Carmel.[119]

38. KARTAH/KISLOTH TABOR (JOSH 21:34; 1 CHR 6:77)

Many scholars understand Kartah of Josh 21:34 (*Onom.* 598/116:1) to be a doublet of Kartan of Naphtali from Josh 21:32 (see above). Most would reconstruct the name as Kisloth Tabor using the parallel list in 1 Chr 6:75, which has Tabor instead of

---

Bronze, Iron I, Iron II, and Persian periods (John L. Peterson, "Kartan (Place)," *ABD* 4:7, which also references Aharoni's brief salvage project there).

115. Peterson, "Kartan," 7.

116. Uzi Leibner, *Settlement and History in Hellenistic, Roman, and Byzantine Galilee: An Archaeological Survey of the Eastern Galilee* (Tübingen: Mohr Siebeck, 2009), 395.

117. Leibner, *Settlement*, 180–82.

118. Jokneam also appears in two versions of Thutmose III's conquest itineraries and as "Camona" in classical literature (e.g., *Onom.* 535/106:17; 555/108:27; 605/116:20; incorrectly connected with Kamon of Judg 8:10 but matches the mileage of "six miles north of Legio") (Ahituv, *Canaanite Toponyms*, 123). For the toponymic identification with Tell Qeimun, see Robinson and Smith, *Later Biblical Researches*, 3:115. For history of occupation and excavation, see Amnon Ben-Tor, "Jokneam," *NEAEHL* 3:805–11; Amnon Ben-Tor, Miriam Avissar, and Yuval Portugali, *Yoqne'am I: The Late Periods* (Jerusalem: Hebrew University, 1996); Amnon Ben-Tor et al., *Yoqne'am II: The Iron Age and the Persian Period: Final Report of the Archaeological Excavations (1977–1988)* (Jerusalem: The Institute of Archaeology, The Hebrew University of Jerusalem, 2005); Amnon Ben-Tor et al., *Yoqne'am III: The Middle and Late Bronze Ages: Final Report of the Archaeological Excavations (1977–1988)* (Jerusalem: Institute of Archaeology, Hebrew University of Jerusalem in cooperation with the Israel Exploration Society, 2005); Miriam Avissar, *Tel Yoqne'am: Excavations on the Acropolis* (Jerusalem: Israel Antiquities Authority, 2005).

119. Kallai, *Historical Geography*, 182; Gal, *Lower Galilee*, 99.

Aerial View of Jokneam Excavations

Kartah. Kisloth Tabor (Josh 19:12; *Onom.* 957/174:2; compare with *Onom.* 59/22:3, which was incorrectly associated with Akshaph) or Chesulloth (Josh 19:18; *Onom.* 114/28:22—beside Mount Tabor and 8 miles from Sepphoris) is located at Iksal, which preserves the name of the site.[120] Surveys within the Arab town of Iksal did not produce pre-Byzantine remains.[121] No suitable alternate site in the vicinity has been published, yet Gal suggests that the actual ancient town was probably located 0.62 miles (1 km) to the west of Iksal.[122] Despite the fact that suitable remains have yet to be found in the Arabic village of Iksal, it seems likely that the ancient town is within the modern settlement given the suitable geographic location and toponymic preservation. Perhaps future excavations in the village will reveal suitable remains for biblical Kisloth Tabor.

39. Dimnah/Rimmon (Josh 21:35; 1 Chr 6:77)

Dimnah (Josh 21:35; *Onom.* 384/78:23) is probably a scribal mistake for Rimmon/Rimmono (Josh 19:13; 1 Chr 6:77).[123] Rimmon has been preserved until modern times at Rummaneh in the Bet Netofa Valley six miles (9 km) north of Nazareth, and already in the mid-ninteenth century Robinson suggested that the nearby Khirbet Rumeh represents the ancient

120. Robinson and Smith, *Biblical Researches in Palestine*, 1:182–83.

121. Gal, *Har Tavor*, site 67.

122. Gal, "The Settlement of Issachar," 82–83.

123. There is no connection between Zeubulunite Rimmon and Hadad Rimmon (Zech 12:11) (*contra* Simons, *Geographical and Topographical Texts*, map IIa). Likewise, in my opinion, there is no connection between this Rimmon and Rumah the hometown of Pedaiah, Josiah's wife and Jehoiakim's mother (2 Kgs 23:36) (see Yoel Elitzur, "Rumah in Judah," *IEJ* 44.1/2 [1994]: 123–28; McKinny, "Historical Geography," 261–63).

site.[124] However, surveys at Khirbet Rumeh showed occupation only from the Persian, Roman-Byzantine, and Ottoman periods, whereas surveys within the Arabic village of Rummaneh revealed remains from the Iron I and II.[125] An additional possibility is that Israelite Rimmon/Rimmono was located at nearby Tell el-Wawiyat (Tel Vavit). Tell el-Wawiyat is an excavated site less than a kilometer north of Rummaneh that has remains from the Middle Bronze IIB, Late Bronze I–II, Iron I, Iron II, and Ottoman periods over five dunams (1 acre).[126] In light of this, it should be noted that the identification of Rimmon should also be related to the boundary description of Zebulun in Josh 19:10–15. Since most of the Zebulunite towns can be identified with a fair degree of confidence, I include the text of Josh 19:10–15 with the identifications in parenthesis.

> The third lot came up for the people of Zebulun, according to their clans. And the territory of their inheritance reached as far as Sarid/Shadud (LXX "Sedoud" = Tell Shadud).[127] Then their boundary goes up westward and on to Mareal (Tell Thorah?)[128] and touches Dabbesheth (Tell esh-Shammam?),[129] then the brook that is east (i.e., the Kishon River/Nahr el-Muqatta) of Jokneam (Tell Qeimuun). From Sarid/Shadud (Tell Shadud) it goes in the other direction eastward toward the sunrise to the boundary of Chisloth-tabor (Iksal). From there it goes to Daberath (Daburieh), then up to Japhia (Yafa). From there it passes along on the east toward the sunrise to Gath-hepher (Khirbet ez-Zurra), to Eth-kazin (LXX Ir-kazin, location unknown),[130] and going on to **Rimmon** (Rummaneh) it bends toward Neah (Tell el-Wawiyat?), then on the north the boundary turns about to Hannathon

124. Robinson and Smith, *Later Biblical Researches*, 1:108–10.

125. Gal, *Lower Galilee*, 24–25; Aapeli Saarisalo, "Topographical Researches in Galilee I," *Journal of the Palestine Oriental Society* 9 (1929): 39–40; David A. Dorsey, *The Roads and Highways of Ancient Israel* (Baltimore: Johns Hopkins University, 1991), 105. Khirbet Rumeh is apparently the same town mentioned by Josephus (*J.W.* 3.233) in connection with the Galilean campaign within the First Jewish Revolt.

126. Gal, *Lower Galilee*, 25. Unfortunately the Survey of Israel has not yet been completed in the Bet Netofa and Turan Valleys; for the excavations of the site, see Beth A. Nakhai, "Wawiyat, Tell El-," *OEANE* 5:333–34; J. P. Dessel, "Tell 'Ein Zippori and the Lower Galilee in the Late Bronze and Iron Ages: A Village Perspective," in *Galilee Through the Centuries: Confluence of Cultures*, ed. Eric M. Meyers (Winona Lake, IN: Eisenbrauns, 1999), 12–23. Khirbet Rujma (i.e., Hurbat Rigma) is yet another site in the vicinity (just south of Khirbet Qana, biblical Cana). Surveys at Khirbet Rujma revealed a site of ten dunams (2.5 acres) with Early Bronze, Middle Bronze, Iron I, Iron II, Persian, and Byzantine remains (Gal, *Lower Galilee*, 27).

127. Rainey and Notley, *Sacred Bridge*, 183.

128. Aharoni, *Land of the Bible*, 257.

129. Aharoni, *Land of the Bible*, 257.

130. Perhaps located at Khirbet Kibshany, east of Gath Hepher and Kefr Kenna. The location is suitable and may contain a corrupted version of Kezin. The site is situated next to a spring and includes remains from the Early Bronze I through the Ottoman period including remains from the Iron I, Iron II, and Persian periods over fifteen dunams (Gal, *Har Tavor*, site 9).

> (Tell el-Bedeiwiyeh), and it ends at the Valley of Iphtahel (either Wadi Abbelin or Wadi el-Malik); and Kattath (possibly the same as Kitron in Judg 1:30, location unknown), Nahalal (Malul, see below), Shimron (Tell Seimunia/Tel Shimron), Idalah (location unknown), and Bethlehem (preserved in Beit Lahhm, but probably located at nearby Khirbet el-Mushreifeh)—twelve cities with their villages. (Josh 19:10–15, based on ESV).

This text shows a clear geographical logic that can be traced from the northern Jezreel Valley into the Bet Netofa Valley, which helps identify specific towns in the boundary description. Since there is a town (Neah) between Rimmon and Hannathon, and Iron Age remains at Rummaneh, it is preferable to locate Rimmon at Rummaneh and Neah at Tell el-Wawiyat.[131]

40. Nahalal (Josh 21:35; Missing from 1 Chr 6:77)

According to the Jerusalem Talmud, Nahalal/Nahalol (Josh 19:15; 21:35; Judg 1:30) was known as Mahalol (y. Megillah I.77a). Some scholars connect Nahalal with Tell en-Nahl near the southeastern edge of modern Haifa (see above), but this identification is unlikely since Tell en-Nahl is firmly within the territory of Asher.[132] Eusebius spoke of a village called Neeila in Batanea (*Onom.* 734/138:2; 735/138:6), but the Golan does not fit the geographical region of Asher. Tsafrir, Di Segni, and Green suggest that Nahalal/Nahalol/Mahalol should be located at Malul just east of Shimron.[133] Surveys and salvage excavations at Malul have revealed remains from the Middle Bronze, Late Bronze, Iron I, Iron II, Persian, Hellenistic, Roman, and Byzantine periods, which seems to support its identification with Nahalal/Nahalol.[134]

Levitical Towns of Reuben: Four Towns (Josh 21:36–37; 1 Chr 6:78–79)

41. Bezer (Josh 21:36; 1 Chr 6:78)

Bezer was a city of refuge (Deut 4:43; Josh 20:8) and Levitical city (Josh 21:36; 1 Chr 6:78; compare with *Onom.* 209/46:8) within the territory of Reuben. It is also spelled "Bozrah" in Jer 48:24, a passage which also includes Jahzah (i.e., Jahaz) and Mephaath (Jer 48:21) along with other Moabite towns of the Medeba Plateau. Bezer was rebuilt by King Mesha of Moab in the mid-to-late ninth century BC (Mesha Stele, line 27). Bezer is mentioned in this context alongside Aroer, Arnon, and Beth-bamoth.[135] Eusebius's description (*Onom.* 209/46:8) misidentified Bezer with Bostra "the metropolis

131. Abel, *Géographie de la Palestine*, 2:396.

132. E.g., Abel, *Géographie de la Palestine*, 2:394.

133. Tsafrir, Di Segni, and Green, *Tabula Imperii Romani*, 174.

134. Avner Raban and Noy Shemesh (intro), *Archeological Survey of Israel, Map 29: Map of Nazareth*, ed. Ofer Sion (Jerusalem: Israel Antiquities Authority, 2016), sites 56 and 71, http://survey.antiquities.org.il/index_Eng.html#/MapSurvey/2154.

135. "The Inscription of King Mesha," trans. Klaas A. D. Smelik, *COS* 2.23.

of Arabia [i.e., Nova Trajana Bostra in Syria]."[136] Summarizing the various views on Bezer's identification, MacDonald suggests identifying Bezer with either Tell Jalul or Umm el-Amud.[137] The presence of the nearby site of Barazen would seem to point to a connection with the nearby Umm el-Amad, a significant Iron I and II site.[138]

42–44. JAHAZ, KEDEMOTH, MEPHAATH (JOSH 21:36–37; 1 CHR 6:78–79)

Jahaz (Num 21:23; Deut 2:32; Josh 13:18; 21:36; Judg 11:20; 1 Chr 6:78; Isa 15:4; Jer 48:21, 34; *Onom.* 525/104:9) is probably located among the closely situated sites of Khirbet Aleiyan, Khirbet Remeil, and Khirbet Medeiniyeh on Wadi Themed. Kedemoth (Deut 2:26; Josh 13:18; 21:37; 1 Chr 6:79; compare with *Onom.* 584/114:5; 587/114:10; 588/114:11) is usually connected with es-Saliyeh. Mephaath (Josh 13:18; 21:37; 1 Chr 6:79; Jer 48:21; *Onom.* 676/128:21; 717/134:14) has been established at Umm er-Rasas.

LEVITICAL TOWNS OF GAD: FOUR TOWNS (JOSH 21:38–39; 1 CHR 6:80–81)

45. RAMOTH IN GILEAD (JOSH 21:38; 1 CHR 6:80)

Ramoth in Gilead (Deut 4:43; Josh 21:38; 1 Chr 6:80; compare with *Onom.* 770/144:4; 787/146:4) is more commonly known as Ramoth Gilead.[139] Ramoth Gilead was the regional capital of one of the Solomonic districts led by Ben-Geber (1 Kgs 4:13). The city was also fought over by the Israelite kings of Ahab and Joram against the Aramean kings Ben-Hadad (II) and Hazael (1 Kgs 22; 2 Kgs 8:28; 9:1–14; 2 Chr 18; 22:5; compare with Tel Dan Stele). Three options have been suggested for Ramoth Gilead: Tell Rumeith, er-Ramtha, and Tell el-Husn.[140]

---

136. Eusebius also referred to Edomite Bozrah (i.e., Buseirah) and another Bozrah south of Petra (Busra eski Sham) (Avi-Yonah, *Gazetteer of Roman Palestine*, 43). Josephus's reference to Bezer "on the border of Arabia," Ramoth Gilead, and Golan (*Ant.* 4.173) simply repeats the biblical details concerning the cities of refuge without providing new details.

137. For Tell Jalul, see Robert D. Ibach, *Archaeological Survey of the Hesban Region: Catalogue of Sites and Characterizations of Periods* (Berrien Springs, MI: Andrews University Press, 1988), site 26; 13–14. For Umm el-Amud, see Burton MacDonald, *"East of the Jordan": Territories and Sites of the Hebrew Scriptures* (Boston: American Schools of Oriental Research, 2000), 177–78.

138. Barazen is not mentioned in the various surveys. Apparently, it was not a significant ancient town. Musil was the first to suggest a connection with Bezer (Alois Musil, *Arabia Petraea* [Vienna: A. Hölder, 1908], 1:218, 232). On Umm el-Amad, see Abel, *Géographie de la Palestine*, 2:264; Aharoni, *Land of the Bible*, 433; Nelson Glueck, "Explorations in Eastern Palestine, II," *The Annual of the American Schools of Oriental Research* 15 (1934): 33; Ibach, *Hesban Region*, site 102; 23–24, 160–7.

139. Eusebius referred to a different town that he located "about fifteen miles [24 km] west of Philadelphia" and near the Jabbok River (El Rumemin) (*Onom.* 467/94:3).

140. A small fortress of 121 by 105 feet (37 x 32 m) at Tel Rumeith was constructed in either the tenth or ninth century BC and was eventually abandoned following the campaign of Tiglath-Pileser III in 733 BC (see Nancy Lapp, "Rumeith, Tell El-," *NEAEHL* 4:1291–93; Israel Finkelstein, Oded Lipschits, and Omer Sergi, "Tell Er-Rumeith in Northern Jordan: Some Archaeological and Historical Observations," *Semitica* 55 [2013]: 7–23). For Tell el-Husn, see Albright, "New Israelite and Pre-Israelite Sites: The Spring Trip of 1929," *BASOR* 35 (1929): 11; Nelson Glueck, "Explorations in Eastern Palestine, IV, Part I: Text," *The Annual of the American Schools of Oriental Research* 25/28 (1945): 96; Albert Leonard, "The Jarash-Tell El-Husn

Er-Ramtha is the most likely location for Ramoth Gilead on account of its location, its name, and the fact that it seems to be a much larger settlement from the Iron I and Iron II than Tell Rumeith.[141] Tell el-Husn was undoubtedly an important Iron Age city, but the connection of the Arabic name with er-Ramtha would seem to argue against Tell el-Husn's identification with Ramoth Gilead.

46. Mahanaim (Josh 21:38; 1 Chr 6:80)

Mahanaim[142] has often been identified with the ruin of Tulul edh-Dhahab in the Jabbok River.[143] Gordon and Villiers' survey at Tell edh-Dhahab esh-Sharqiyya revealed ceramic remains from the Iron Age.[144] A team led by Pola excavated Tell edh-Dhahab al-Garbiyya (the western hill of Tulul edh-Dhahab) from 2005–2011. On the western slope of Tell edh-Dhahab al-Garbiyya, Pola revealed a fortification wall that was dated, on the basis of carbon-14 dating, to between 1305–978 BC.[145] On the summit of the site (Terrace I), the excavators found two layers that they termed an "Earlier and Later Phase."[146] The "Earlier Phase" dates to the Iron Age, although it is unclear why the excavators dated the layer to the ninth and eighth century BC primarily on the basis of quarried stones with carved iconographic imagery (interpreted as orthostats) when their carbon-14 dates provide the range of 1212–988 BC.[147] The excavators interpret the building as an Iron II sanctuary dating to the ninth and eighth century BC. They assume that the site was inhabited during the tenth century BC, which leaves open the possibility for an identification with Penuel.[148] Tell edh-Dhahab esh-Sharqiyya (the eastern hill of Tulul edh-Dhahab) is a smaller site (197 by 98 ft. [60 x 30 m] at the summit) that was primarily inhabited during the Iron Age and Hellenistic period.[149] The excavators also noted remains from the Middle Paleolithic, Neolithic, Early

---

Highway Survey," *Annual of the Department of Antiquities of Jordan* 40 (1987): 388–89; see bibliography in MacDonald, *"East of the Jordan,"* 201–2.

141. Nelson Glueck, "Ramoth-Gilead," *BASOR* 92 (1943): 11; Glueck, "Eastern Palestine, IV," 97; Edward Lipiński, *On the Skirts of Canaan in the Iron Age: Historical and Topographical Perspectives* (Leuven: Peeters, 2006), 277; Finkelstein, Lipschits, and Sergi, "Tell Er-Rumeith," 23.

142. Gen 32:3; Josh 13:26, 30; 21:38; 2:8, 12, 29; 17:24, 27; 19:32; 1 Kgs 2:8; 4:14; 1 Chr 6:60; Shishak Karnak List No. 22; *Onom.* 678/130:4.

143. E.g., MacDonald, *"East of the Jordan,"* 139–42; Jeremy M. Hutton, "Mahanaim, Penuel, and Transhumance Routes: Observations on Genesis 32–33 and Judges 8," *JNES* 65.3 (2006): 161–78.

144. Robert E. Gordon and Linda E. Villiers, "Telul Edh Dhahab and Its Environs Surveys of 1980 and 1982: A Preliminary Report," *Annual of the Department of Antiquities of Jordan* 27 (1983): 275–83.

145. Thomas Pola et al., "A Preliminary Report of the Tulul Adh-Dhahab (Wadi Az-Zarqa) Survey and Excavation Seasons 2005-2011," *Annual of the Department of Antiquities of Jordan* 57 (2013): 88.

146. Which dates to the Hellenistic-Early Roman period (Pola et al., "Tulu Adh-Dhahab," 92–94).

147. Pola et al., "Tulu Adh-Dhahab," 90–91.

148. Pola et al. find the identification of the site with Mahanaim unconvincing but offer no alternative for Mahanaim (Pola et al., "Tulu Adh-Dhahab," 91–92).

149. Gordon and Villiers, "Telul Edh Dhahab," 287; Pola et al., "Tulul Adh-Dhahab," 83–84.

TABLE 1 - THE LEVITICAL TOWNS

Levitical Group	**Tribe**	**Tribe #**	**Town #**	**Josh 21 (refuge)**	**Josh 21 MT**	**Josh 21 LXX**
1. Kohathites (Josh 21:4, 9–19; 1 Chr 6:54–60)	Judah/ Simeon	1	1	Kiriath Arba/ Hebron (3)	קִרְיַת אַרְבַּע/ חֶבְרוֹן	Καριαθαρβοκ/ Χεβρων
		2	2	Libnah	לִבְנָה	Λεμνα
		3	3	Jattir	יַתִּר	Αιλωμ
		4	4	Eshtemoa	אֶשְׁתְּמֹעַ	Τεμα
		5	5	Holon	חֹלֹן	Γελλα
		6	6	Debir	דְּבִר	Δαβιρ
		7	7	Ain	עַיִן	Ασα
		8	8	Juttah	יֻטָּה	Τανυ
		9	9	Beth Shemesh	בֵּית שָׁמֶשׁ	Βαιθσαμυς
	Benjamin	1	10	Gibeon	גִּבְעוֹן	Γαβαων
		2	11	Geba	גֶּבַע	Γαθεθ
		3	12	Anathoth	עֲנָתוֹת	Αναθωθ
		4	13	Almon	עַלְמוֹן	Γαμαλα
2. Kohathites (Josh 21:5, 20–26; 1 Chon 6:66–70)	Ephraim	1	14	Shechem (2)	שְׁכֶם	Συχεμ
		2	15	Gezer	גֶּזֶר	Γαζαρα
		3	16	Kibzaim	קִבְצַיִם	Καβσαϊμ
		4	17	Beth Horon	בֵּית חוֹרֹן	Βαιθωρων
	Dan	1	18	Eltekeh	אֶלְתְּקֵא	Ελκωθαιμ
		2	19	Gibbethon	גִּבְּתוֹן	Γεθεδαν
		3	20	Aijalon	אַיָּלוֹן	Αιλων
		4	21	Gath Rimmon	גַּת־רִמּוֹן	Γεθερεμμων
	1/2 Manasseh	1	22	Taanach	תַּעְנַךְ	Ταναχ
		2	23	Gath Rimmon	גַּת־רִמּוֹן	Ιεβαθα

1 Chr 6 (refuge)	1 Chr 6 MT	1 Chr 6 LXX	Identification	Alternate Identification
Hebron (3)	חֶבְרוֹן	Χεβρων	Rumeida	-
Libnah	לִבְנָה	Λοβνα	Tell Bornat	-
Jattir	יַתִּר	Σελνα	Khirbet Attir	-
Eshtemoa	אֶשְׁתְּמֹעַ	Εσθαμω	es-Semu	-
Hilen	חִילֵז	-	Khirbet umm el-Amad?	
Debir	דְּבִיר	Δαβιρ	Khirbet Rabud	-
Ashan	עָשָׁן	Ασαν	En-rimmon = Khirbet Khuweilfeh	Ashan? = Tell Judeideh?
-	-	Ατταν	Yatta	-
Beth Shemesh	בֵּית שֶׁמֶשׁ	Βασαμυς	Tell Rumeilah	-
Gibeon	-	-	el-Jib	-
Geba	גֶּבַע	Γαβεε	Jeba	-
Alemeth	עָלֶמֶת	Γαλεμεθ	Anata	-
Anathoth	עֲנָתוֹת	Αγχωχ	Khirbet Almit	-
Shechem (2)	שְׁכֶם	Συχεμ	Tell Balatah	-
Gezer	גֶּזֶר	Γαζερ	Tell Jazar	-
Jokmeam	יָקְמְעָם	Ιεκμααμ	Tell es-Simadi?	Tell esh-Sheikh Dhiab?
Beth Horon	בֵּית חוֹרוֹן	Βαιθωρων	Beit Ir el-Foqa (upper) and Beit Ir et-Tahta (lower)	-
-	-	-	Tell esh-Shallaf?	-
-	-	-	Tell Melat	-
Aijalon	אַיָּלוֹן	Εγλαμ	Yalo	-
Gath Rimmon	גַּת־רִמּוֹן	Γεθρεμμων	Ras Abu Hamid	-
Aner	עָנֵר	Αναρ	Tell Tiinnik	-
Bileam/Ibleam	בִּלְעָם	Ιεβλααμ	Khirbet Belameh	-

Levitical Group	Tribe	Tribe #	Town #	Josh 21 (refuge)	Josh 21 MT	Josh 21 LXX
3. Gershonites (Josh 21:6, 27–33; 1 Chr 6:71–76)	1/2 Manasseh	1	24	Golan in Bashan (6)	גַּלוֹן [גּוֹלָן] בַּבָּשָׁן	Γαυλων ἐν τῇ Βασανίτιδι
		2	25	Beeshterah	בְּעֶשְׁתְּרָה	Βοσοραν
	Issachar	1	26	Kishion	קִשְׁיוֹן	Κισων
		2	27	Daberath	דָּבְרַת	Δεββα
		3	28	Jarmuth	יַרְמוּת	Ρεμμαθ
		4	29	En Gannim	עֵין גַּנִּים	Πηγὴν
	Asher	1	30	Mishal	מִשְׁאָל	Βασελλαν
		2	31	Abdon	עַבְדּוֹן	Δαββων
		3	32	Helkath	חֶלְקָת	Χελκατ
		4	33	Rehob	רְחֹב	Ρααβ
	Naphtali	1	34	Kedesh in Galilee (1)	קֶדֶשׁ בַּגָּלִיל	Καδες ἐν τῇ Γαλιλαίᾳ
		2	35	Hammoth Dor	חַמֹּת דֹּאר	Εμμαθ
		3	36	Kartan/ Rakkath	קַרְתָּן	Θεμμων
4. Merarites (Josh 21:7, 34–40; 1 Chr 6:77–81)	Zebulun	1	37	Jokneam	יָקְנְעָם	Μααν
		2	38	Kartah	קַרְתָּה	Καδης
		3	39	Dimnah	דִּמְנָה	Δεμνα
		4	40	Nahalal	נַהֲלָל	Σελλα
	Reuben	1	41	Bezer (4)	בֶּצֶר	Βοσορ
		2	42	Jahaz	יַהְצָה	Ιαζηρ
		3	43	Kedemoth	קְדֵמוֹת	Δεκμων
		4	44	Mephaath	מֵיפָעַת	Μαφα
	Gad	1	45	Ramoth in Gilead (5)	רָמֹת בַּגִּלְעָד	Ραμωθ ἐν τῇ Γαλααδ
		2	46	Mahanaim	מַחֲנַיִם	Καμιν
		3	47	Heshbon	חֶשְׁבּוֹן	Εσεβων
		4	48	Jazer	יַעְזֵר	Ιαζηρ

1 Chr 6 (refuge)	1 Chr 6 MT	1 Chr 6 LXX	Identification	Alternate Identification
Golan in Bashan (6)	גּוֹלָן בַּבָּשָׁן	Γωλαν ἐκ τῆς Βασαν	Saḥem el-Jolan?	-
Ashtaroth	עַשְׁתָּרוֹת	Ασηρωθ	Tell Ashtarah	Tell Ashari
Kedesh	קֶדֶשׁ	Κεδες	Tell Qasyun	-
Daberath	דָּבְרַת	Δεβερι	Daburiyeh	-
Ramoth	רָאמוֹת	Δαβωρ	En ha-Yadid	-
Anem	עָנֵם	Αναμ	Khirbet Beit Jann	
Mashal	מָשָׁל	Μασαλ	Tell Abu Hawam	Tell en-Nahl?
Abdon	עַבְדּוֹן	Αβαραν	Khirbet Abdeh	-
Hukok	חוּקֹק	Ικακ	Tell el-Qassis?	Tell el-Harbaj?
Rehob	רְחֹב	Ροωβ	Tell el-Bir el-Gharbi?	-
Kedesh in Galilee (1)	קֶדֶשׁ בַּגָּלִיל	Κεδες ἐν τῇ Γαλιλαίᾳ	Tell Qades	-
Hammon	חַמּוֹן	Χαμωθ	Khirbet Abu Shusheh?	-
Kiriathaim	קִרְיָתַיִם	Καριαθαιμ	Khirbet el-Quneitireh?	Khirbet el-Qureiyeh?
-	-	-	Tell Qeimun	-
Tabor	תָּבוֹר	Θαχχια	Kisloth Tabor? = Iksal	-
Rimmono	רִמּוֹנוֹ	Ρεμμων	Rummaneneh?	Tell el-Wawiyat?
-	-	-	Malul	-
Bezer (4)	בֶּצֶר	Βοσορ	Umm el-Amad?	Tell Jalul?
Jahzah	יַהְצָה	Ιασα	Khirbet Medeiniyeh?	-
Kedemoth	קְדֵמוֹת	Καδημωθ	es-Saliyeh?	-
Mephaath	מֵיפַעַת	Μωφααθ	Umm er-Rasas	-
Ramoth in Gilead (5)	רָאמוֹת בַּגִּלְעָד	Ραμωθ Γαλααδ	er-Ramtha?	Tell Rumeith?
Mahanaim	מַחֲנַיִם	Μααναιμ	Tell edh-Dhahab el-Gharbi	-
Heshbon	חֶשְׁבּוֹן	Εσεβων	Hesban	Tell Jalul?
Jazer	יַעְזֵיר	Ιαζηρ	Khirbet es-Sir	-

Bronze, and Middle Bronze ages in their survey and excavations of the sites.[150]

The recently exposed archaeological evidence seems to further confirm the hypothesis that Mahanaim should be related to Tulul edh-Dhahab. On the other hand, it remains unclear if both ruins should be related to Mahanaim. Many scholars suggest that Penuel should be related to either Tell edh-Dhahab esh-Sharqiyya or Tell edh-Dhahab al-Garbiyya, while others maintain that Mahanaim should be associated with both ruins and that Penuel should be in the Jordan Valley at Deir Alla.[151] It is most likely that Mahanaim should be identified with Tell edh-Dhahab al-Garbiyya and Penuel with Tell edh-Dhahab esh-Sharqiyya.

47. HESHBON (JOSH 21:39; 1 CHR 6:81)

During the Iron II and later, Heshbon was located at Tell Hisban, which perfectly preserves the name.[152] However, during Middle Bronze through Iron I the main ruin in the vicinity was Tell Jalul, which may relate to Sihon's "city" (e.g., Num 21:26).

48. JAZER (JOSH 21:39; 1 CHR 6:81)

Despite the current consensus identifying Jazer with Khirbet Jazzir, this identification cannot be sustained in light of a new archaeological survey of the site.[153]

CONCLUSION

In this chapter, I have closely examined the site identifications of the Levitical towns as recorded in Josh 21 and 1 Chr 6:54–81. The towns are relatively evenly distributed throughout the tribal allotments of Israel. As noted in the introduction, it was not my goal to provide a date or discuss the function of the list. Rather, my goal is to provide a historical geographical and archaeological assessment for every town in the list. If one looks at the list as a whole, it is clear that the Levitical towns were scattered throughout the land of Israel and that the list was derived from the tribal allotments. Indeed, there is a clear relationship between the tribal allotments (Josh 13–19) to the Levitical towns, which has allowed for us to determine the viability of a town's spelling and/or its presence in the lists. It seems that that the list was constructed to have four towns from each of the twelve tribes. Benjamin, Ephraim, Dan, Manasseh, Issachar, Asher, Zebulun, Reuben, and Gad, each have four towns while Judah/Simeon have nine and Naphtali has only three. This numerical scheme might explain why some Levitical towns are not in the list (e.g., Nob), as well as shedding light on variant names in the list (see e.g., Gath Rimmon of Manasseh—Josh 21:25).

---

150. Pola et al., "Tulul Adh-Dhahab."

151. For those in favor of associating Penuel with Tell edh-Dhahab esh-Sharqiyya or Tell edh-Dhahab al-Garbiyya, see Aharoni, *Land of the Bible*, 34; Robert A. Coughenour, "A Search for Maḥanaim," *BASOR* 273 (1989): 57–66; Hutton, "Mahanaim, Penuel"; Rainey and Notley, *Sacred Bridge*, 115. For the Deir Alla camp, see MacDonald, *"East of the Jordan,"* 139–42; Lipiński, *Skirts of Canaan*, 282–83.

152. Num 21:25–28, 30, 34; 32:3, 37; Deut 1:4; 2:24, 26, 30; 3:2, 6; 4:46; 29:7; Josh 9:10; 12:2, 5; 13:10, 17, 21, 26–27; 21:39; Judg 11:19, 26; 1 Chr 6:81; Neh 9:22; Song 7:4; Isa 15:4; 16:8–9; Jer 48:2, 34, 45; 49:3; Jdt 5:15; *Onom*. 408/84:1.

153. Num 21:32; 32:1, 3, 35; Josh 13:25; 21:39; 2 Sam 24:5; 1 Chr 6:81; 26:31; Isa 16:8–9; Jer 48:32; 1 Macc 5:8; *Onom*. 526/104:13.

I conclude with a few brief notes on the geographical distribution of the towns:

1. Judah and Simeon: the towns are mostly in the southernmost part of the Judahite hill country (Hebron, Juttah, Eshtemoa, Jattir, and Hilen), the Shephelah (Beth Shemesh, Libnah, and perhaps Ashan), and the northernmost Negev (Ain).
2. Benjamin: the towns are situated in a close pattern in the central Benjamin plateau along and just west of the watershed (Gibeon, Geba, Alemeth, and Anathoth).
3. Ephraim: there is no distinct geographical pattern as the towns are literally at the northern (Shechem), western (Beth Horon and Gezer), and eastern (Jokmeam) edges of the tribal allotment.
4. Dan: the towns are situated along Nahal Aijalon, like all of the Danite allotment, with one town on the eastern end (Aijalon) and three in the center of Nahal Aijalon near the transition from the Shephelah to the coastal plain (Eltekeh, Gath Rimmon, and Gibbethon).
5. Manasseh: the two Cisjordan towns of Manasseh are in a geographical group with the nearby towns of Taanach and Ibleam. Likewise, the two Transjordan towns of Manasseh are the nearby towns of Golan in Bashan and Ashtaroth.
6. Issachar: two towns were located beside Mount Tabor (Kishion and Daberath) and two towns were located on the eastern edge of the allotment overlooking the Jordan Valley (Ramoth/Jarmuth and En Gannim/Enam).
7. Asher: the four towns are relatively evenly distributed north-to-south throughout the plain of Asher (Mishal, Abdon, Helkath, and Rehob).
8. Naphtali: the well-known Kedesh in Galilee is situated in Upper Galilee, and the other two towns appear to be situated on the western shores of the Sea of Galilee (Hammoth Dor and Kartan).
9. Zebulun: the towns are spread out from the southwestern (Jokneam) to the northwestern (Kisloth Tabor and Nahalal) Jezreel Valley and into the Beth Netophah Valley (Dimnah/Rimmon).
10. Reuben: the towns are located in a north-south line along the eastern Medeba Plateau near the edge of the wilderness (Bezer, Jahaz, Kedemoth, and Mephaath).
11. Gad: the towns form a north-south line through the heart of Gadite territory (Josh 13:26) from the northern end of the Medeba Plateau (Heshbon) through southern Gilead (Jazer) and the Jabbok River (Mahanaim) until northern Gilead (Ramoth Gilead).

BIBLIOGRAPHY

Abel, Félix-Marie. *Géographie de la Palestine*. 2 vols. Paris: Lecoffre, 1938.

———. *Géographie de la Palestine: Géographie Physique et Historique*. 3rd ed. 2 vols. Paris: Gabalda, 1967.

Aharoni, Yohanan. *The Land of the Bible: A Historical Geography*. Translated by Anson F. Rainey. Rev. and enl. ed. Philadelphia: Westminster, 1979.

Ahituv, Shmuel. *Canaanite Toponyms in Ancient Egyptian Documents*. Jerusalem: Magnes Press, Hebrew University, 1984.

Albright, William F. "The Excavation of Tell Beit Mirsim, Vol. II: The Bronze Age." *The Annual of the American Schools of Oriental Research* 17 (1936): xi–141.

———. "The List of Levitic Cities." Pages 49–73 in *Louis Ginzberg Jubilee Volume*. Edited by Saul Lieberman, Solomon Zeitlin, Shalom Spiegel, and Alexander Marx. New York: American Academy for Jewish Research, 1945.

———. "New Israelite and Pre-Israelite Sites: The Spring Trip of 1929." *BASOR* 35 (1929): 1–14.

———. "Researches of the School in Western Judaea." *BASOR* 15 (1924): 2–11.

———. "The Smaller Beth-Shan Stele of Sethos I (1309–1290 B. C.)." *BASOR* 125 (1952): 24–32.

———. "The Topography of the Tribe of Issachar." *ZAW* 44.1 (1926): 225–36.

———. "Topographical Researches in Judæa." *BASOR* 18 (1925): 6–11.

Alt, Albrecht. "Das Institut Im Jahre 1931." *Palästina-Jahrbuch* 28 (1932): 5–47.

Artzy, Michal. "Abu Hawam, Tell." *NEAEHL* 5:1553–54.

Auld, A. Graeme. "The Levitical Cities: Texts and History." *ZAW* 91.2 (1979): 194–206.

Avissar, Miriam. *Tel Yoqne'am: Excavations on the Acropolis*. Jerusalem: Israel Antiquities Authority, 2005.

Avi-Yonah, Michael. *Gazetteer of Roman Palestine*. Jerusalem: Hebrew University, 1976.

———. *The Madaba Mosaic Map: With Introduction and Commentary*. Jerusalem: Israel Exploration Society, 1954.

Balensi, Jacqueline. "Revising Tell Abu Hawam." *BASOR* 257 (1985): 65–74.

Ben-Dor, Meir. "The Excavations at the Crusader Fortress of Kokhav-Hayarden (Belvoir)." *Qadmoniot* 2.1 (5) (1969): 22–27.

Ben-Tor, Amnon. "Jokneam." *NEAEHL* 3:805–11.

Ben-Tor, Amnon, Michal Avissar, and Yuval Portugali. *Yoqne'am I: The Late Periods*. Jerusalem: Hebrew University, 1996.

Ben-Tor, Amnon, Ruhama Bonfil, and Sharon Zuckerman. *Tel Qashish: A Village in the Jezreel Valley: Final Report of the Archaeological Excavations (1978–1987)*. Jerusalem: Hebrew University, 2003.

Ben-Tor, Amnon, Doron Ben-Ami, Ariella Livneh, and Rina Bankirer. *Yoqne'am III: The Middle and Late Bronze Ages: Final Report of the Archaeological Excavations (1977–1988)*. Jerusalem: Institute of Archaeology, Hebrew University of Jerusalem in cooperation with the Israel Exploration Society, 2005.

Ben-Tor, Amnon, Anabel Zarzecki-Peleg, Shlomit Cohen-Anidjar, and Doron Ben-Ami. *Yoqne'am II: The Iron Age and the Persian Period: Final Report of the Archaeological Excavations (1977–1988)*. Jerusalem: The Institute of Archaeology, The Hebrew University of Jerusalem, 2005.

Boling, Robert G. *Joshua:A New Translation with Notes and Commentary*. Introduction by G. Ernest Wright. AB. New York: Doubleday, 1982.

Borowski, Oded. "The Biblical Identity of Tel Halif." *BA* 51.1 (1988): 21–27.

Bunimovitz, Shlomo, and Zvi Lederman. "Beth Shemesh." *NEAEHL* 5:1644–48.

———, eds. *Tel Beth Shemesh: A Border Community in Judah: Renewed Excavations 1990–2000: The Iron Age*. Vol. 1. Winona Lake, IN: Eisenbrauns, 2016.

Campbell, Edward F., and G. Ernest Wright, eds. *Shechem III: The Stratigraphy and Architecture of Shechem/Tell Balâṭah*. 2 vols. Boston: American Schools of Oriental Research, 2002.

Chadwick, Jeffrey R. "Hebron in Early Bronze Age III and Middle Bronze Age II: Fortification Walls in Area I.3 of the American Expedition to Hebron (Tell Er-Rumeide)." Pages 167–86 in *Tell It in Gath: Studies in the History and Archaeology of Israel. Essays in Honor of Aren M. Maeir on the Occasion of His Sixtieth Birthday*. Edited by Itzhaq Shai, Jeffrey R. Chadwick, Louise Hitchcock, Amit Dagan, Chris McKinny, and Joe Uziel. Münster: Zaphon, 2018.

———. "The Archaeology of Biblical Hebron in the Bronze and Iron Ages: An Examination of the Discoveries of the American Expedition to Hebron." PhD diss., University of Utah, 1992.

Cohen-Arnon, C., and Ruth Amiran. "Excavations at Tel Qishon: Preliminary Report on the 1977–1978 Seasons." *Eretz-Israel* 15 (1981): 205–12.

Conder, Claude R., and H. H. Kitchener. *The Survey of Western Palestine*. 3 vols. London: The Committee of the Palestine Exploration Fund, 1881–83.

Coughenour, Robert A. "A Search for Maḥanaim." *BASOR* 273 (1989): 57–66.

Dessel, J. P. "Tell 'Ein Zippori and the Lower Galilee in the Late Bronze and Iron Ages: A Village Perspective." Pages 1–32 in *Galilee Through the Centuries: Confluence of Cultures*. Edited by Eric M. Meyers. Winona Lake, IN: Eisenbrauns, 1999.

Dinur, Uri. "Khirbat 'Almit." *Excavations and Surveys in Israel* 5 (1986): 1.

———. "Yatta." *Excavations and Surveys in Israel* 5 (1987): 111–12.

Donner, Herbert. *The Mosaic Map of Madaba: An Introductory Guide*. Leuven: Peeters, 1992.

Dorsey, David A. *The Roads and Highways of Ancient Israel*. Baltimore: Johns Hopkins University, 1991.

Eisenberg, Emanuel, and David Ben-Shlomo. *The Tel Ḥevron 2014 Excavations: Final Report*. Ariel: Ariel University Press, 2017.

Elitzur, Yoel. "Rumah in Judah." *IEJ* 44.1/2 (1994): 123–28.

Erlich, Adi. "Happily Ever After? A Hellenistic Hoard from Tel Kedesh in Israel." *American Journal of Archaeology* 121.1 (2017): 39–59.

Eshel, Hanan, Jodi Magness, and Eli Shenhav. "Khirbet Yattir, 1995–1999: Preliminary Report." *IEJ* 50.3/4 (2000): 153–68.

———. "Yattir, Khirbet." *NEAEHL* 5:2069–70.

Finkelstein, Israel (north), Amir Feldstein, Giora Kidron, Nizan Hanin, Yair Kamaisky, and David Eitam (south). *Archeological Survey of Israel, Map 83/2: Map of El Bira: Benjamin Survey*. Edited by Yitzhak Magen and Israel Finkelstein. Jerusalem: Israel Antiquities Authority, 2013. https://survey.antiquities.org.il/index_Eng.html#/MapSurvey/70.

Finkelstein, Israel, Zvi Lederman, and Shlomo Bunimovitz, eds. *Highland of Many Cultures: The Southern Samaria Survey*. 2 vols. Tel Aviv: Tel Aviv University, 1997.

Finkelstein, Israel, Oded Liphshits, and Omer Sergi. "Tell Er-Rumeith in Northern Jordan: Some Archaeological and Historical Observations." *Semitica* 55 (2013): 7–23.

Frankel, Rafael. "Beten (Place)." *ABD* 1:680.

———. "Shihor-Libnath." *ABD* 5:1212.

Frankel, Rafael, and Nimrod Gerzov. *Archeological Survey of Israel, Map 2: Map of Hanita*. Edited by Ayala Sussman. Jerusalem: Israel Antiquities Authority, 2013. http://survey.antiquities.org.il/index_Eng.html#/MapSurvey/86.

Freeman-Grenville, G. S. P., trans. *The Onomasticon by Eusebius of Caesarea*. Jerusalem: Carta, 2003.

Gal, Zvi. *Archeological Survey of Israel, Map 45: Map of 'En Dor*. Edited by Ayala Sussmann. Jerusalem: Israel Antiquities Authority, 2013. https://survey.antiquities.org.il/#/MapSurvey/49.

———. *Archeological Survey of Israel, Map 46: Map of Gazit*. Edited by Ayala Sussmann. Jerusalem: Israel Antiquities Authority, 2012. https://survey.antiquities.org.il/#/MapSurvey/34.

———. *Archeological Survey of Israel, Map 41: Map of Har Tavor*. Edited by Ayala Sussmann. Jerusalem: Israel Antiquities Authority, 2013. https://survey.antiquities.org.il/#/MapSurvey/45.

———. *Lower Galilee during the Iron Age*. Winona Lake, IN: Eisenbrauns, 1992.

———. "The Settlement of Issachar: Some New Observations." *TA* 9.1 (1982): 79–86.

Galling, Kurt. "Studien Aus Dem Deutschen Evangelischen Institut Für Altertumswissenschaft in Jerusalem. 50. Zur Lokalisierung von Debir." *ZDPV* 702 (1954): 135–41.

Garfinkel, Yosef, Igor Kreimerman, Michael G. Hasel, and Martin G. Klingbeil. "First Impression on the Urban Layout of the Last Canaanite City of Lachish: A View from the Northeast Corner of the Site." Pages 122–35 in *The Late Bronze and Early Iron Ages of Southern Canaan*. Edited by Aren M. Maeir, Itzhaq Shai, and Chris McKinny. Berlin: de Gruyter, 2019.

Gibson, Shimon. "The Tell El-Judeideh (Tel Goded) Excavations: A Re-Appraisal Based on Archival Records in the Palestine Exploration Fund." *TA* 21 (1994): 194–234.

Glock, Albert E. "Taanach." *NEAEHL* 4:1428–33.

Glueck, Nelson. "Ramoth-Gilead." *BASOR* 92 (1943): 10–16.

———. "Explorations in Eastern Palestine, II." *The Annual of the American Schools of Oriental Research* 15 (1934): ix–202.

———. "Explorations in Eastern Palestine, IV, Part I: Text." *The Annual of the American Schools of Oriental Research* 25/28 (1945): iii–423.

Golan, Sigal, and Othmar Keel. "Tombs from the Middle Bronze Age I until the Iron Age at Tel Maloṭ." *'Atiqot* 65 (2011): 64*.

Gophna, Ram, and Yuval Porat. "The Land of Ephraim and Manasseh." Pages 153–93 in *Judaea, Samaria and the Golan: Archaeological Survey 1967–1968*. Edited by Moshe Kochavi. Jerusalem: Archaeological Survey of Israel by Carta, 1972.

Gordon, Robert E., and Linda E. Villiers. "Telul Edh Dhahab and Its Environs Surveys of 1980 and 1982: A Preliminary Report." *Annual of the Department of Antiquities of Jordan* 27 (1983): 275–83.

Grant, Elihu. "Beth Shemesh, 1928." *The Annual of the American Schools of Oriental Research* 9 (1927): 1–15.

———. "Beth Shemesh in 1933." *BASOR* (1933): 3–5.

———. "Progress at Beth Shemesh." *BASOR* 31 (1928): 15.

Greenberg, Raphael, and Adi Keinan. *Israeli Archaeological Activity in the West Bank 1967–2007: A Sourcebook.* Jerusalem: Ostracon, 2009.

Guérin, Victor. *Description Géographique, Historique et Archéologique de la Palestine.* 7 vols. Paris: Impériale, 1869–1880.

Haran, Menahem. "Studies in the Account of the Levitical Cities: I. Preliminary Considerations." *JBL* 80.1 (1961): 45–54.

Hardin, James W. *Lahav II Households and the Use of Domestic Space at Iron II Tell Halif: An Archaeology of Destruction.* Winona Lake, IN: Eisenbrauns, 2010.

Har-Even, Benjamin. "Khirbat 'Almit." *Hadashot Arkheologiyot* 115 (2003): 48*–49*.

Herbert, Sharon C., and Andrea M. Berlin. "A New Administrative Center for Persian and Hellenistic Galilee: Preliminary Report of the University of Michigan/University of Minnesota Excavations at Kedesh." *BASOR* 329 (2003): 13–59.

Herion, Gary A., Dale W. Manor, and Jeffery K. Lott. "Debir (Place)." *ABD* 2:111–12.

Hunt, Melvin. "Aner (Place)." *ABD* 1:248.

Hutton, Jeremy M. "The Levitical Diaspora (II): Modern Perspectives on the Levitical Cities List (A Review of Opinions)." Pages 45–81 in *Levites and Priests in Biblical History and Tradition.* Edited by Mark Leuchter and Jeremy M. Hutton. Leiden: Brill, 2012.

———. "Mahanaim, Penuel, and Transhumance Routes: Observations on Genesis 32–33 and Judges 8." *JNES* 65.3 (2006): 161–78.

Ibach, Robert D. *Archaeological Survey of the Hesban Region: Catalogue of Sites and Characterizations of Periods.* Berrien Springs, MI: Andrews University Press, 1988.

Jacobs, Paul F. "Halif, Tel." *NEAEHL* 5:1761–62.

Kallai, Zecharia. *Historical Geography of the Bible: The Tribal Territories of Israel.* Jerusalem: Magnes Press, 1986.

Katz, Hayah, and Yigal Levin. "Tel Rosh: The Forgotten Rehob in the Upper Galilee." *PEQ* 153.1 (2021): 24–41.

Kehati, Ron. "Faunal Remains from Tel Maloṭ (East)." *'Atiqot* 64 (2010): 83–84.

Kitchen, Kenneth A. *The Third Intermediate Period in Egypt, 1100–650 B.C.* 2nd ed. Warminster, England: Aris & Phillips, 1986.

Kloner, Amos. *Survey of Jerusalem: The Northeastern Sector.* Jerusalem: Israel Antiquities Authority, 2001.

Knoppers, Gary N. "Projected Age Comparisons of the Levitical Townlists: Divergent Theories and Their Significance." *Textus* 22.1 (2005): 21–63.

Kochavi, Moshe. "Khirbet Rabud=Debir." *TA* 1.1 (1974): 2–33.

———. "Rabud, Khirbet." *NEAEHL* 4:1252.

———. "The Land of Judah." Pages 19–89 in *Judaea, Samaria and the Golan: Archaeological Survey 1967–1968.* Edited by Moshe Kochavi. Jerusalem: Archaeological Survey of Israel by Carta, 1972.

Krahmalkov, Charles R. "Exodus Itinerary Confirmed by Egyptian Evidence." *BAR* 20 (1994): 54–62, 79.

Lapp, Nancy. "Rumeith, Tell El-." *NEAEHL* 4:1291–93.

Lee-Sak, Yitzhak. "The Lists of Levitical Cities (Joshua 21, 1 Chronicles 6) and the Propagandistic Map for the Hasmonean Territorial Expansion." *JBL* 136.4 (2017): 783–800.

Lehmann, Gunnar, and Martin Peilstöcker. *Archeological Survey of Israel, Map 20: Map of Ahihud*. Edited by Ofer Sion. Jerusalem: Israel Antiquities Authority, 2012. https://survey.antiquities.org.il/index.html#/MapSurvey/12.

Leibner, Uzi. *Settlement and History in Hellenistic, Roman, and Byzantine Galilee: An Archaeological Survey of the Eastern Galilee*. Tübingen: Mohr Siebeck, 2009.

Leonard, Albert. "The Jarash-Tell El-Husn Highway Survey." *Annual of the Department of Antiquities of Jordan* 31 (1987): 343–90.

Leuchter, Mark. *The Levites and the Boundaries of Israelite Identity*. Oxford: Oxford University Press, 2017.

Leuchter, Mark, and Jeremy M. Hutton, eds. *Levites and Priests in Biblical History and Tradition*. Leiden: Brill, 2012.

Lewis, Theodore. "Holon." *ISBE* 2:729.

Lipiński, Edward. *On the Skirts of Canaan in the Iron Age: Historical and Topographical Perspectives*. Leuven: Peeters, 2006.

MacDonald, Burton. *"East of the Jordan": Territories and Sites of the Hebrew Scriptures*. Boston: American Schools of Oriental Research, 2000.

MacKenzie, Duncan. "The Ancient Site of 'Ain Shems, with a Memorandum on the Prospects of Excavation." *PEQ* 43.2 (1911): 69–79.

———. *Palestine Exploration Fund, 1912–1913 Excavations at Ain Shems (Beth-Shemesh)*. Vol. 2. Palestine Exploration Fund. London: Palestine Exploration Fund, 1912.

Maeir, Aren M. "The Tell Es-Safi/Gath Archaeological Project 1996–2010: Introduction, Overview and Synopsis of Results." Pages 1–88 in *Tell Es-Safi/Gath I: Report on the 1996–2005 Seasons*. Edited by Aren M. Maeir. Wiesbaden: Harrassowitz, 2012.

Magen, Yitzhak, and Yuval Baruch. "Yaṭṭa." *Hadashot Arkheologiyot* 114 (2002): 95*–96*.

Manor, Dale W. "Jarmuth (Place)." *ABD* 3:645.

Mazar, Benjamin. *Canaan and Israel: Historical Essays*. 2nd ed. Jerusalem: Bialik, 1972.

———. "The Cities of the Priests and the Levites." *Vetus Testamentum Supplements* 7 (1960): 193–205.

———. "The Cities of the Territory of Dan." *IEJ* 10.2 (1960): 65–77.

McKinny, Chris. "A Historical Geography of the Administrative Division of Judah: The Town Lists of Judah and Benjamin in Joshua 15:21–62 and 18:21–28." PhD diss., Bar-Ilan University, 2017.

———. "'March on My Soul with Might!'—The Geographical Setting of Judges 4–5." In vol. 1 of *Lexham Geographic Commentary on the Historical Books*. Edited by Barry J. Beitzel. Bellingham, WA: Lexham Press, 2025.

———. "Pressing On: Identifying the 'Other' Gath and Its Implications for Understanding the Border between the Kingdoms of Israel and Judah." Pages 577–94 in *Tell It in Gath: Studies in Honor of Aren Maeir on the Occasion of His Sixtieth Birthday*. Edited by Itzhaq Shai, Louise A. Hitchcock,

Jeremy R. Chadwick, Amit Dagan, Chris McKinny, and Joel Uziel. Weisbaden: Ugarit-Verlag, 2018.

McKinny, Chris, and Aharon Tavger. "From Lebonah to Libnah: Historical Geographical Details from the PEF and Other Early Secondary Sources on the Toponymy of Two Homonymous Sites." Pages 107–22 in *Exploring the Holy Land: 150 Years of the Palestine Exploration Fund*. Edited by David Gurevich and Anat Kidron. London: Equinox, 2018.

McKinny, Chris, Aharon Tavger, and Itzhaq Shai. "Tel Burna in the Late Bronze: Assessing the 13th Century BCE Landscape of the Shephelah." Pages 148–70 in *The Late Bronze and Early Iron Ages of Southern Canaan*. Edited by Aren M. Maeir, Itzhaq Shai, and Chris McKinny. Berlin: de Gruyter, 2019.

McKinny, Chris, and Amit Dagan. "The Explorations of Tel Burna." *PEQ* 145.4 (2013): 294–305.

McKinny, Chris, Oron Schwartz, Gabriel Barkay, Alexander Fantalkin, and Boaz Zissu. "Kiriath-Jearim (Deir El-ʿÂzar): Archaeological Investigations of a Biblical Town in the Judean Hill Country." *IEJ* 68.1 (2018): 30–49.

Miller, J. Maxwell, and John H. Hayes. *A History of Ancient Israel and Judah*. 2nd ed. Louisville: Westminster John Knox, 2006.

Mokary, Abdalla. "'Ubeidiya." *Hadashot Arkheologiyot* 126 (2014): n.p. http://www.hadashot-esi.org.il/report_detail_eng.aspx?id=13703&mag_id=121.

Musil, Alois. *Arabia Petraea*. 2 vols. Vienna: A. Hölder, 1908.

Na'aman, Nadav. *Ancient Israel and Its Neighbors: Interaction and Counteraction*. Winona Lake, IN: Eisenbrauns, 2005.

———. "A New Look at the List of Levitic Cities." *Zion* 47 (1982): 237–52.

———. *Canaan in the Second Millenium BCE*. Winona Lake, IN: Eisenbrauns, 2005.

———. "Israel, Edom and Egypt in the 10th Century BCE." *TA* 19.1 (1992): 71–93.

———. "Yenoʿam." *TA* 4.3/4 (1977): 168–77.

Nakhai, Beth A. "Wawiyat, Tell El-." *OEANE* 5:333–34.

Noth, Martin. *Das Buch Joshua*. Tübingen: Mohr Siebeck, 1953.

Notley, R. Steven, and Ze'ev Safrai. *Eusebius, Onomasticon: A Triglott Edition with Notes and Commentary.* Leiden: Brill, 2005.

Ofer, Avi. "The Highland of Judah during the Biblical Period." PhD diss., Tel Aviv University, 1993.

Olami, Ya'aqov, and Zvi Gal. *Archaeological Survey of Israel, Map 24: Map of Shefarʿam*. Edited by Zvi Gal. Jerusalem: Israel Antiquities Authority, 2011. https://survey.antiquities.org.il/index_Eng.html#/MapSurvey/9.

Ortiz, Steven, and Saul Wolff. "A Reevaluation of Gezer in the Late Bronze Age in Light of Renewed Excavations and Recent Scholarship." Pages 62–85 in *The Late Bronze and Early Iron Ages of Southern Canaan*. Edited by Aren M. Maeir, Itzhaq Shai, and Chris McKinny. Berlin: de Gruyter, 2019.

———. "Guarding the Border to Jerusalem: The Iron Age City of Gezer." *NEA* 75.1 (2012): 4–19.

Parnos, Giora, Ianir Milevski, and Hamoudi Khalaily. "Remains from the Late Prehistoric to Early Islamic Periods at the Foot of Tel Maloṭ (East)." *ʿAtiqot* 64 (2010): 25–77.

Peterson, John L. "A Topographical Surface Survey of the Levitical 'Cities' of Joshua 21 and I Chronicles 6." PhD diss., Seabury-Western Theological Seminary, 1977.

———. "Aijalon (Place)." *ABD* 1:131.

———. "Daberath (Place)." *ABD* 2:1.

———. "Eltekeh (Place)." *ABD* 2:483–84.

———. "En-Gannim (Place)." *ABD* 2:501.

———. "Eshtemoa (Place)." *ABD* 2:617–18.

———. "Gibbethon (Place)." *ABD* 2:1007.

———. "Helkath (Place)." *ABD* 3:126.

———. "Jattir (Place)." *ABD* 3:649–50.

———. "Juttah (Place)." *ABD* 3:1135.

———. "Kartan (Place)." *ABD* 4:7.

———. "Kishion (Place)." *ABD* 4:89.

Peterson, John L., and Rami Arav. "Rehob (Place)." *ABD* 5:661.

Pola, Thomas, Hannelore Kröger, Bernd Rasink, Jochen Reinhard, Mohammad al-Balawnah, and Mohammad Abu Abila. "A Preliminary Report of the Tulul Adh-Dhahab (Wadi Az-Zarqa) Survey and Excavation Seasons 2005–2011." *Annual of the Department of Antiquities of Jordan* 57 (2013): 81–96.

Prausnitz, Moshe. "Akhziv and Avdon: On the Planning of a Port and a Fortress City in the Plain of Acre." *Eretz-Israel* 11 (1973): 219–23.

Pritchard, James B. "Gibeon." *NEAEHL* 2:511–14.

Raban, Avner. *Archeological Survey of Israel, Map 28: Map of Nahalal*. Edited by Y. Tsafrir. Jerusalem: Israel Antiquities Authority, 2012. https://survey.antiquities.org.il/index_Eng.html#/MapSurvey/26.

Raban, Avner, and Noy Shemesh (intro). *Archeological Survey of Israel, Map 29: Map of Nazareth*. Edited by Ofer Sion. Jerusalem: Israel Antiquities Authority, 2016. http://survey.antiquities.org.il/index_Eng.html#/MapSurvey/2154.

Rainey, Anson F. *The El-Amarna Correspondence: A New Edition of the Cuneiform Letters from the Site of El-Amarna Based on Collations of All Extant Tablets*. Edited by William M. Schniedewind and Zipora Cochavi-Rainey. 2 vols. Leiden: Brill, 2014.

———. "Tel Gerisa and the Danite Inheritance." *Eretz-Israel Museum Yearbook* 5–6 (1990): 59–72.

Rainey, Anson F., and Steven Notley. *The Sacred Bridge: Carta's Atlas of the Biblical World*. Jerusalem: Carta, 2006.

Robinson, Edward, and Eli Smith. *Biblical Researches in Palestine, Mount Sinai and Arabia Petraea: A Journal of Travels in the Year 1838*. 3 vols. Boston: Crocker & Brewster; London: John Murray, 1841.

———. *Later Biblical Researches in Palestine and in the Adjacent Regions: A Journal of Travels in the Year 1852*. Boston: Crocker & Brewster; London: John Murray, 1856.

Ronen, Avraham, and Yaácov Olamy. *Archeological Survey of Israel, Map 23: Map of Haifa-East*. Edited by Moshe Kochavi. Jerusalem: Israel Antiquities Authority, 2013. http://survey.antiquities.org.il/index_Eng.html#/MapSurvey/56.

Ross, J. P. "The 'Cities of the Levites' in Joshua XXI and I Chron VI." PhD diss., University of Edinburgh, 1973.

Rowe, Alan. *The Topography and History of Beth-Shan, with Details of the Egyptian and Other Inscriptions Found on the Site*. Philadelphia: University of Pennsylvania Museum, 1930.

Saarisalo, Aapeli. "Topographical Researches in Galilee I." *Journal of the Palestine Oriental Society* 9 (1929): 27–40.

Schmitt, Götz. "Gat, Gittaim und Gitta." Pages 77–138 in *Drei Studien zur Archäologie und Topographie Altisraels*. Edited by Rudolph Cohen and Götz Schmitt. Wiesbaden: Verlag, 1980.

Seger, Joe D., and Oded Borowski. "Halif, Tel." *NEAEHL* 2:553–60.

Shai, Itzhaq. "Tel Burna: A Judahite Fortified Town in the Shephelah." Pages 45–60 in *The Shephelah During the Iron Age: Recent Archaeological Studies*. Edited by Oded Lipschitz and Aren M. Maeir. Winona Lake, IN: Eisenbrauns, 2017.

Shai, Itzhaq, and Aren M. Maeir. "The Iron Age IIA Pottery Assemblage from Stratum A3." Pages 313–63 in *Tell Es-Safi/Gath I: Report on the 1996–2005 Seasons*. Edited by Aren M. Maeir. Wiesbaden: Harrassowitz, 2012.

Shai, Itzhaq, Chris McKinny, and Joe Uziel. "Late Bronze Age Cultic Activity in Ancient Canaan: A View from Tel Burna." *BASOR* 374 (2015): 115–33.

Shavit, Alon. "Settlement Patterns in Israel's Southern Coastal Plain during the Iron Age II." PhD diss., Tel Aviv University, 2003.

———. "Tel Malot." *Excavations and Surveys in Israel* 12 (1992): 49–50.

Shmueli, Oren. "Iron Age Tombs North of Tel Maloṭ." *ʿAtiqot* 65 (2011): 65*.

Simons, Jan J. *The Geographical and Topographical Texts of the Old Testament*. 2 vols. Leiden: Brill, 1959.

Spencer, John R. "Levitical Cities." *ABD* 4:310–11.

———. "The Levitical Cities: A Study of the Role and Function of the Levites in the History of Israel." PhD diss., University of Chicago, 1980.

Taha, Hamdan, and Gerrit van der Kooij, eds. *Khirbet Balʿama Archaeological Project Report of the 1996–2000 Excavations and Surveys*. 2 vols. Ramallah: Ministry of Tourism and Antiquities, 2007.

———. *Tell Balata Changing Landscape*. Ramallah: Ministry of Tourism and Antiquities, 2014.

Tal, Oren. "Tel Hamid." *IEJ* 47. 3/4 (1997): 273–75.

Tal, Oren, and Noga Blockman. "A Salvage Excavation at Tel Hamid (The Lower Terrace)." *TA* 25.2 (1998): 142–73.

Tsafrir, Yoram, Leah Di Segni, and Judith Green. *Tabula Imperii Romani Iudaea-Palestina: Eretz Israel in the Hellenistic, Roman and Byzantine Periods; Maps and Gazetteer*. Jerusalem: The Israel Academy of Sciences and Humanities, 1994.

Tzori, Nehemia, and Noy Shemesh (foreward). *Archeological Survey of Israel, Map 47: Map of Gesher*. Edited by Ofer Sion. Jerusalem: Israel Antiquities Authority, 2015. https://survey.antiquities.org.il/index.html#/MapSurvey/2136.

Uziel, Joe. "The Tell Es-Safi Archaeological Survey." Master's Thesis, Bar-Ilan University, 2003.

Uziel, Joe, and Aren Maeir. "Scratching the Surface at Gath: Implications of the Tell Es-Safi/Gath Surface Survey." *TA* 32.1 (2005): 50–75.

Von Rad, Gerhard. "Das Reich Israel Und Die Philister." *Palästinajahrbuch* 29 (1933): 30–42.

Wolff, Saul. "Tel Ḥamid." *Hadashot Arkheologiyot* 110 (1999): 55*–56*.

Wolff, Saul, and Alon Shavit. "Hamid, Tel." *NEAEHL* 5:1762–63.

———. "Tel Ḥamid." *Hadashot Arkheologiyot: Excavations and Surveys in Israel* 109 (1999): 68*–70*.

Yeivin, Shmuel. "The Silver Hoard from Eshtemoʿa." *ʿAtiqot* 10 (1990): 15*.

Yeivin, Ze'ev. "The Synagogue at Eshtemoa' in Light of the 1969 Excavations." *'Atiqot* 48 (2004): 59*–98*; 155–58.

Zertal, Adam. *The Manasseh Hill Country Survey, Vol. 1: The Shechem Syncline.* Tel Aviv: Tel Aviv University, 1992.

Zertal, Adam, and Shay Bar. *The Manasseh Hill Country Survey, Vol 4: From Nahal Bezeq to the Sartaba.* Leiden: Brill, 2017.

Zertal, Adam, Nivi Mirkam. *The Manasseh Hill Country Survey, Vol. 3: From Nahal 'Iron to Nahal Shechem.* Edited by Shay Bar. Leiden: Brill, 2016.

Zimbalist, Nehemia. "Kishon and Kishyon." *Bulletin of the Jewish Palestine Exploration Society* 13.1/2 (1946): 28–51.

CHAPTER 20

A GEOGRAPHICAL ANALYSIS OF THE JUDGESHIPS OF OTHNIEL AND EHUD

Judg 3:7–30

Michelle Knight

KEY POINTS

- Through Othniel, God brought Israel victory over an especially menacing king whose political reach stretched from upper Mesopotamia at least as far as Canaan.
- After Othniel's death, God addressed the sin of his people by strengthening their enemies against them, both through political alliances and economic tribute.
- The Moab-Amalekite-Ammonite confederation established control over Israel by capturing Jericho, a strategic gateway to the heart of Canaan.
- Ehud and the people of Israel prevented Eglon's army from fleeing the battle by taking control of the Jordan River and cutting off their only escape route.

INTRODUCTION

The narratives recounting the deeds of Israel's army under the leadership of Othniel and Ehud are some of the most impressive battle reports in the book of Judges. Significantly shorter than those stories describing other Israelite leaders, the narratives of Judg 3 require close reading and attention to detail—especially those details of geography—to appreciate fully the magnitude of the two victories that God graciously brought to his wayward people.

OTHNIEL JUDGES ISRAEL (3:7–11)

The story of Othniel's exploits against the first oppressor of Israel is one of the book's more enigmatic accounts, yet the narrative is striking in its brevity. In contrast to the episodes that follow, Judg 3:7–11 is a straightforward description, lacking the detail and color of the later stories about Gideon (Judg 6–8), Jephthah (11–12), and Samson (13–16). Instead of highlighting the heroic actions of the judge or the daring feats of Israel's soldiers, the text focuses on the sequence of events: Israel sinned, God responded with an invading army, the people cried out to him, he raised up a judge and delivered them, and the land experienced peace through the rest of Othniel's lifetime. This becomes a pattern in the book of Judges known as "the judges cycle."

CUSHAN-RISHATHAIM FROM ARAM NAHARAIM

The oppressor from whom God would liberate the Israelites is "Cushan-Rishathaim, king of Aram Naharaim" (Judg 3:8).[1] Known only from this text, the exact identity of the man is debated. His full name is mentioned four times in only five verses. The rhythmic quality of that name—evident even in English—suggests to most scholars that his designation has symbolic value. Meaning something like "dark, doubly wicked," the title assigned to the king by the book of Judges is "clearly a pejorative."[2]

While the king's exact identity is unknown, his provenance is not; Cushan-Rishathaim hails from Aram Naharaim. The Hebrew term Aram Naharaim refers to an area in upper Mesopotamia, near the western bend of the Euphrates, under the control of tribal groups that would come to be known as the Arameans.[3] In the books of Kings, Chronicles, and Isaiah, "Aram" refers to a different set of tribes from the areas surrounding Damascus, which becomes an Aramean state that rises to prominence in 1000 BC. However, the designation Aram Naharaim distinguishes this foreign king as one from the area near Nahor and Harran, the home of Abraham's people (Gen 11:31; 24:10). In Gen 24:10, Abraham sends his servant to Aram Naharaim to secure a wife for Isaac. Presumably Paddan Aram—the other designation for Abraham's homeland (e.g., Gen 25:20; 28:2)—is a more specific locale within upper Mesopotamia near Harran.[4] The seer Balaam, hired by the Moabite king to curse Israel (Num 22:5), is also from Aram Naharaim (Deut 23:4 [MT 23:5]).

To imagine that a king from distant Mesopotamia would bother with a tribal leader in Canaan at this period in Israelite history has caused some to question whether the original Hebrew text actually reads "Aram" or "Edom"

---

1. All translations are from the New International Version (NIV) unless otherwise noted.

2. K. Lawson Younger Jr., *Judges, Ruth*, NIVAC (Grand Rapids: Zondervan, 2002), 104. Younger goes on to suggest "[t]he obvious implication is that he is evil, really bad—hence, the worst of the oppressors. The very name of this oppressor is used to invoke fear in the original readers' minds." Abraham Malamat notes that the Babylonian Talmud ascribes to him "two evils" (Malamat, "Cushan Rishathaim and the Decline of the Near East around 1200 BC," *JNES* 13 [1954]: 232).

3. K. Lawson Younger Jr., *A Political History of the Arameans: From Their Origins to the End of their Polities* (Atlanta: SBL Press, 2016), 96. For this reason, many English versions simply translate "Mesopotamia" (e.g., NIV, NASB, NKJV). Some argue that the term "Aramean" is anachronistic, since the term does not come to be used until much later in Israel's history. However, Younger demonstrates that this proleptic usage is a "functional anachronistic usage," not unlike a modern-day reference to "Native Americans" or "the precolonial United States" (105).

4. Younger, *Arameans*, 99.

or "fortress (אַרְמוֹן, *armon*) of the mountains" (i.e., Edom), words that are relatively easy to confuse when written in Hebrew script.[5] By the period of the judges, tensions between Israel and Edom were well established (Gen 36:1–2; Num 20:14–21; 24:18), and a leader from the southernmost tribe would have been especially suited to addressing that threat. Edom seems fitting because "Cushan"—the first part of the oppressor's name—appears in Hab 3:7 as a toponym near Midian. Despite how nicely Edom might fit for all of these reasons, there is simply not sufficient reason to doubt the wording as it has been preserved. Ancient translations of the Hebrew text unilaterally support the reading Aram Naharaim.[6] Moreover, several Egyptian pharaohs reported interactions with a people group in upper Mesopotamia (i.e., Mittani or Hanigalbat) that they referred to as *Naharin(a)* in the same time period.[7] Any kind of political relationship between Egypt and Mesopotamia, hostile or otherwise, sheds light on a context in which a Mesopotamian monarch had good reason to lead a campaign as far south as the Levant.[8]

Othniel of Judah

Just as the inhabitants of Judah were the first to fight against the Canaanites in the introduction (Judg 1:1–2), a representative of Judah is the first to be raised up by God to deal with Israel's oppressor.[9] Othniel is introduced as a "son of Kenaz, Caleb's younger brother," (Judg 1:13) who attacked and defeated Kiriath Sepher in Judg 1:11–13. Caleb's land allotment is in the Judean hill country (Josh 14:6–15), so it is likely that his nephew and son-in-law was living in Hebron or in the recently conquered Kiriath Sepher when he was raised up by God to address the threat from the north. While much of the drama that unfolds in the book of Judges does so in what would eventually be Israel's northern kingdom, the backdrop for the story of Othniel is the Judean hill country just west of the Dead Sea. What transpired there provides the model against which the rest of the stories of the judges are measured: will other judges participate in such decisive battles and overcome such powerful enemies? Will God continue to raise up effective leaders to bring victory to his people, despite their tendency toward apostasy?

---

5. For example, such confusion is evident in 2 Kgs 16:6 and 2 Chr 20:2. For the argument that "fortress of the mountains" makes the best sense of the biblical text and is referring to Edom, see Robert G. Boling, *Judges*, AB (New York: Doubleday, 1975), 81, and *MAB*, 137.

6. The Old Greek explicitly translates "Mesopotamia," and the Targum of Onkelos reads Aram "near the Euphrates" (J. J. Finkelstein, "Mesopotamia," *JNES* 21 [1962]: 85).

7. Inscriptions of Thutmose I (1493–1481) through Ramesses III (1184–1153) refer to this political entity. See Younger, *Arameans*, 96.

8. Malamat hypothesizes this oppressor of Israel was the same foreign ruler that seized the Egyptian throne at the end of the Nineteenth Dynasty (i.e., Irsu). In his view, "[h]is military campaign [against Othniel] is more readily explained if its ultimate goal was Egypt and if the war with Israel was only of secondary importance" (Malamat, "Cushan Rishathaim," 235).

9. It is worth noting that even though Caleb acted as a leader of Judah and is functionally integrated into the tribe (Num 13:6, 30; Josh 15:13), according to Gen 36:11, 15, and 42, he and his forebears were Edomites. See also Daniel I. Block, *Judges, Ruth*, NAC (Nashville: Broadman & Holman, 2001), 97.

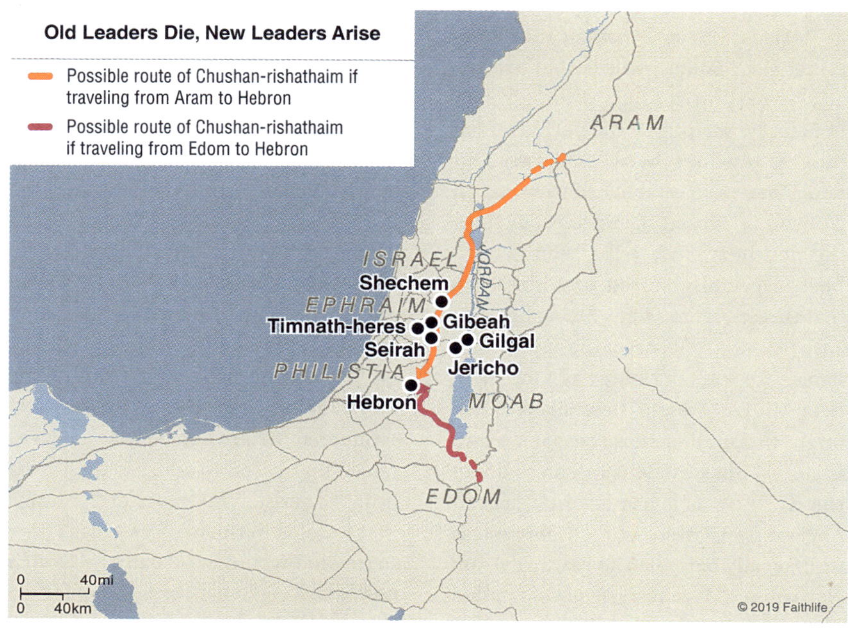

EHUD DELIVERS ISRAEL (3:12–30)

Through Othniel, God brought victory over the cruel and intimidating oppressors; however, the peace Israel experienced following this initial victory was short lived. After the death of Othniel, the people lost sight of God's recent deliverance and fell prey again to the temptations of their cultural context (Judg 3:12). At the sovereign empowerment of Israel's God, a new confederation of foreign peoples exerted their formidable influence over the Israelites (3:13). Rather than being characterized as especially cruel, as was the previous oppressor, the new enemy of Israel was especially strong, both in terms of physical stature and political alliances.

MOAB, AMMON, AND AMALEK (3:12–13)

In response to the religious infidelity of his people, God turned them over to the political control of Eglon the king of Moab. Moab was a territory located on the east side of the Dead Sea, which was populated mainly on the plateau that stretched from the Arnon River in the north to the Zered River in the south.[10] Reuben's tribal allotment therefore shared its southern border with Moab. The tensions between Israel and Moab, however, extended much further into their shared history, when Balak the king of Moab hired Balaam to curse Israel (Num 22:1–6). Because of their hostility, Moabites would be forever excluded from the assembly of Israel (Deut 23:3–6).

10. J. Maxwell Miller, "Moab," *ABD* 4:882–83. As Miller observes, according to Num 21:21–26 (compare with Josh 12:1–6; 13:8–12), the Israelites had conquered the area north of the Arnon, despite this region being designated the "Plains of Moab" in the Pentateuch (e.g., Num 22:1).

Dead Sea and Mountains of Moab

According to Judg 3:13, Eglon secured his hold on Israelite territory with the help of the Ammonites and the Amalekites. Like Moab, the Ammonites were infamous for their lack of hospitality to the Israelites as they attempted to gain entrance into the land (Deut 23:3–4). Ammon was located to the north of Moab and east of the Transjordanian Israelite tribes (Deut 2:19; Josh 13:8–10). By allying himself with another of Israel's hostile neighbors, Eglon effectively put pressure on Israelite lands from the south and the east.

The Amalekite people are the third and most accursed of the long-standing enemies of God's people. Since their first skirmish with Israel after the exodus, this seminomadic group was a consistent obstacle to the people on their journey from Egypt toward the land of promise.[11] The first Amalekite challenge to Israel was on the heels of the exodus, an event for which YHWH condemned them and vowed to "utterly blot out the name of Amalek under heaven" (Exod 17:8–16). Moses would later clarify that the severity of their censure had to do with the vulnerability of God's people in that moment: Amalek had preyed upon the weakness of a group recently liberated from generations of slavery (Deut 25:17–19). When Moses sent twelve men from Kadesh Barnea to spy out Canaan, the spies identified Amalek as one of five groups occupying the land who would prevent their military success (Num 13:29). It was at the hand of the same Amalekites that the initially battle-wary

11. The Amalekites were either nomadic or seminomadic. Gerald L. Mattingly aptly describes them as a "highly-mobile" people who generally "occupied the less desirable fringe areas adjacent to land capable of supporting more sedentary populations" (Mattingly, "Amalek [Person]," *ABD* 1:170).

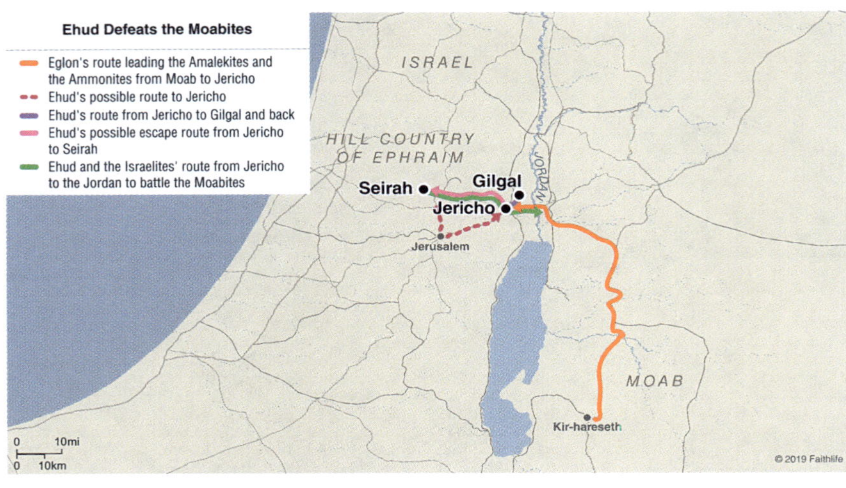

Israelite people suffered defeat in the days that followed, when they attempted to enter the land against the express prohibition of God (Num 14:39–45). In each of these episodes, Israel encountered Amalek in the Sinai Peninsula and the Negev, a slim area south of the Judean hill country near Beersheba,[12] but in the time of the judges, their influence extended much further north. By the time of Jephthah, the Amalekites were settled in the territory of Ephraim (12:15), which highlights the "wide geographical range" of Amalek's activity in the region.[13]

In Judg 3, then, Israel finds itself surrounded by kingdoms united as a highly motivated military confederation strategically situated to lead an incursion into the very heartland of Canaan and in their enmity toward the people of God.

"THE CITY OF PALMS" (3:13–14)

With the help of Ammon and Amalek, Eglon took possession of the "City of Palms" (Judg 3:13). At least twice the Old Testament associates a "City of Palms" with Jericho (Deut 34:3; 2 Chr 28:15), leading the NLT to translate here that "[Eglon] went out and defeated Israel, taking possession of Jericho, the city of palms" (3:13). Jericho, however, is not explicitly named in the text, leaving open the possibility that a different city is being referenced. At least once in the Old Testament, a "City of Palms" seems to exist in a locale other than that of the Benjamite homeland (Judg 1:16). In Judg 1:16, for example, Daniel Block suggests that the reference to "City of Palms" there "functions as a generic designation for a fortified oasis settlement."[14] He suggests that the desig-

12. This area is distinct from the modern Negev, which is a more expansive, triangular-shaped region that extends from the Gulf of Aqaba, north to the Dead Sea, and west to Raphiah; see Avraham Negev, "Negeb," *ABD* 4:1061–68.

13. Mattingly, "Amalek (Person)," 170. As Block highlights, Amalekite presence in Ephraim during the judges period might help to explain the odd statement in the MT of Judg 5:14 that Ephraim's root was "in Amalek" (Block, *Judges, Ruth*, 232).

14. Block, *Judges, Ruth*, 98.

nation refers to Tamar, the Hebrew word for "palm tree" (תָּמָר, *tamar*), which is a city located on the southernmost edge of the Dead Sea, more proximate to the other sites mentioned in the text—the Judean wilderness and the Negev.[15]

Despite such textual ambiguity, the geography of the Ehud narrative makes it very clear that the "City of Palms" captured by Eglon in Judg 3 is, in fact, best interpreted as Jericho. Before the monarchy, judges were often raised up to govern Israel in a region proximate to their homeland.[16] Ehud is from the tribe of Benjamin (Judg 3:15), within whose territory Jericho is located (Josh 18:12). More importantly, Gilgal features prominently in the story of Ehud and, according to Josh 4:19, Gilgal is located on the eastern outskirts of Jericho. Finally, the decisive victory of Ehud's army against the Moabites at the fords of the Jordan requires that the "City of Palms" be to the north of the Dead Sea and along the Jordan River.[17]

Therefore, it is the strategic location of Jericho that the Moabite, Ammonite, and Amalekite armies came together to conquer. The city of Jericho is positioned at the northern edge of the Dead Sea, at the junction of several major roads that connected the Judean desert and the settlement of Benjamin.[18] Jericho functioned as a pivotal entrée into the promised land, not only for the Israelites, but for anyone attempting to gain control of Canaan. As Lawson Stone aptly notes, "by holding Jericho, Eglon cut off Benjamin from any contact to the east and gained three invasion routes."[19]

For eighteen years, the Moabite forces occupied Jericho and held sway over the people of Israel.

An Under-Estimated Warrior and an Imposing Monarch (3:15–17)

It is Ehud from the tribe of Benjamin that YHWH raises up to save his people. The text highlights that he is left-handed, which gives him a strategic advantage on the battlefield because his blade is strapped discretely to his right thigh, where guards were less likely notice and remove it (3:16).[20] "Against the southpaw, the right-hander's whole tactical reper-

15. Block, *Judges, Ruth*, 98. Barry Beitzel associates the reference in Judg 1:16 to 1 Kgs 9:18, which describes Tamar "in the wilderness, in the land of Judah," which fits poorly with the descriptions of Benjamite Jericho elsewhere (*MAB*, 138). Even here, however, the association is questionable as the MT itself suggests that the name should be read Tadmor (2 Chr 8:3) instead; see Jeffrey K. Lott, "Tamar (Place)," *ABD* 6:315.

16. Consider, e.g., Barak, who led the Israelite army to victory in the vicinity of his tribe's allotment, Naphtali (Judg 4:6), or Gideon, from the tribe of Manasseh (Judg 6:15), who went out against the Midianites and the Amalekites in the Jezreel Valley, near his ancestral home.

17. *MAB*, 128.

18. Lawson G. Stone, "Judges," *Cornerstone Biblical Commentary: Joshua, Judges, Ruth*, ed. Philip W. Comfort (Carol Stream, IL: Tyndale, 2012), 238.

19. Stone, "Judges," 238.

20. I am inclined to follow Yairah Amit who observes that the same Hebrew description appears in Judg 20:16 and 1 Chr 12:6, where it seems to function as an idiom "that referred to fearless warriors" from Benjamin (Amit, "The Story of Ehud [Judges 3:12–30]: The Form and the Message," in *Signs and Wonders: Biblical Texts in Literary Focus*, ed. J. Cheryl Exum [Atlanta: Society of Biblical Literature, 1989], 106). As Hans Ausloos explains, the warriors (naturally left-handed or otherwise) are likely to have been trained to fight with their left hand to

toire, and most of his martial experience, is irrelevant."[21] Leading an entourage to offer tribute to the king of Moab, Ehud heads to Jericho, which seems to have been Eglon's temporary "Palestinian base of operations."[22] The opponent Ehud meets at Jericho is imposing, one who is able-bodied and strong, well-nourished from years of comfortable living at the expense of the Israelite people.[23]

TO AND FROM GILGAL (3:18–26)

After presenting the foreign monarch with the requisite economic tribute, Ehud dismisses those who had accompanied him to make the official presentation.[24] The next line suggests that Ehud had recently found himself at Gilgal, whether at an unspecified time preceding this narrative, or as Baruch Halpern has suggested, accompanying his tribute-bearers on their return trip as far as Gilgal, a "central military post"[25] just outside of Jericho, then turning around to approach Eglon alone in Jericho.[26]

The narrator notes that the "carved images" (פְּסִילִים, *pesilim*) were at Gilgal, the identity of which are debated. Two options seem the most plausible: (1) The pillars are the same stones that Joshua erected at Gilgal to commemorate the crossing of the Jordan and the beginning of the inheritance of the promised land (Josh 4:20); or (2) the pillars are examples of the idols worshiped by the people indigenous to the land of Canaan. In reference to the former, Jack Sasson observes the potential "irony" of the nearby commemorative stones, which would "trigger recall of Israel (and not Moab) crossing the Jordan," a people group over whom he was attempting to maintain political control.[27] However, the Hebrew word *pasil* (פָּסִיל) is unlikely to refer to boundary or commemorative stones such as these; everywhere else in the Old Testament, the word refers to Canaanite religious practice.

Most importantly, Deut 7:5 underscores that the Israelites must engage in battle with those inhabiting Canaan, with the express purpose of avoiding their religious practices; in so doing, they were to "break down their altars and dash in

---

function ambidextrously in war (Ausloos, "The Story of Ehud and Eglon in Judges 3:12–30: A Literary Pearl as a Theological Stumbling Block," *Old Testament Essays* 30 [2017]: 228).

21. Baruch Halpern, *The First Historians: The Hebrew Bible and History* (San Francisco: Harper & Row, 1988), 35.

22. Block, *Judges, Ruth*, 158.

23. The Hebrew text does not say that Eglon is obese but rather "healthy" or "well-nourished," much like the cattle in Joseph's dream (Gen 41:2) or Daniel, who appeared healthy and well-fed after ten days of little food (Dan 1:15). For a more extensive argument against Eglon's obesity, see Lawson G. Stone, "Eglon's Belly and Ehud's Blade: A Reconsideration," *JBL* 128 (2009): 649–63.

24. Presumably the subject of the verb is Ehud, though the Hebrew text is ambiguous; Ehud is the grammatical subject of the Hebrew clause that precedes this one, though the grammatical subject of the next clause is similarly ambiguous.

25. Trent C. Butler, *Judges*, WBC (Nashville: Thomas Nelson, 2009), 70.

26. Baruch Halpern, "The Assassination of Eglon: The First Locked-Room Murder Mystery," *Bible Review* 4 (1988): 40.

27. Jack M. Sasson, *Judges 1–12: A New Translation with Introduction and Commentary*, AB (New Haven: Yale University, 2014), 231.

pieces their pillars and chop down their Asherim and burn their carved images [*pesilim*] with fire." Given the theological context of the book of Judges in which syncretism and apostasy are the backdrop against which the narratives unfold, it is best to assume that Canaanite graven images were erected at Gilgal, possibly alongside the stones commemorating the entrance of YHWH's people into the land of Canaan. K. Lawson Younger Jr. is right to accentuate that, whatever their role in indicating the theological state of the people of Israel, within the narrative "these objects mark the limits of Eglon's effective control."[28] By turning back at Gilgal, Ehud refuses to leave Moabite-controlled country until the conflict between Eglon and Israel had been decisively resolved.

Once more in the Jericho palace, Ehud's report that he has a "divine message" to deliver to the king (perhaps made plausible given his proximity to cultic images at Gilgal) allows him private audience with Eglon. With his concealed blade, Ehud slays the Moabite leader and stealthily exits the palace.[29]

From the palace, Ehud escapes to Seirah, an unidentified toponym located in the hill country of Ephraim, whose name might suggest a forested locale of some kind (Judg 3:27).[30] From this spot Ehud musters the nearby Israelites, urging them to follow him out of the hill country (i.e., "down") toward the Jordan River, where they would cut off the Moabite army, leaving their oppressors with no chance of escape.

CONCLUSION

In Judg 3:7–30, the Israelites found themselves under the control of two formidable foes, the strength of whom the narrative highlights using a variety of carefully chosen details. In both accounts, geographical descriptions underscore the threat and strategic advantage of Israel's opponent. The conflict involving Othniel features a far-off foe whose intimidating name is matched only by the extent of his political reach. Similarly, the report of battle between Israel and Eglon's army highlights how the combined forces of Moab, Ammon, and Amalek posed a serious threat to Israel. Eglon's occupation of a strategic stronghold in Israelite territory left God's people politically and geographically isolated, forced to turn over the best of their resources through political tribute. Both accounts: (1) frame isolated Israelite victories as unexpected, and (2) it is the might of YHWH, the God of Israel, that empowers the meager troops of Israel to subdue even the most intimidating or best-positioned foe.

BIBLIOGRAPHY

Amit, Yairah. "The Story of Ehud (Judges 3:12–30): The Form and the Message." Pages 97–123 in *Signs and Wonders: Biblical Texts in Literary Focus*. Edited by J. Cheryl Exum. Atlanta: Society of Biblical Literature, 1989.

28. Younger, *Judges, Ruth*, 117, based on the reference in v. 26, in which he is said to have "escaped" once he passed by these same stones.

29. The text includes several architectural terms that are difficult to define, leading to a variety of creative reconstructions (informed by archeological data) as to the likely floorplan of the palace. See, e.g., Halpern, "Assassination of Eglon," 33–41, 44.

30. Stone, "Judges," 243.

Ausloos, Hans. "The Story of Ehud and Eglon in Judges 3:12–30: A Literary Pearl as a Theological Stumbling Block." *Old Testament Essays* 30 (2017): 225–39.

Block, Daniel I. *Judges, Ruth*. NAC. Nashville: Broadman & Holman, 2001.

Boling, Robert G. *Judges*. AB. New York: Doubleday, 1975.

Butler, Trent C. *Judges*. WBC. Nashville: Thomas Nelson, 2009.

Finkelstein, J. J. "Mesopotamia." *JNES* 21 (1962): 73–92.

Halpern, Baruch. "The Assassination of Eglon: The First Locked-Room Murder Mystery." *Bible Review* 4 (1988): 33–41, 44.

———. *The First Historians: The Hebrew Bible and History*. San Francisco: Harper & Row, 1988.

Lott, Jeffrey K. "Tamar (Place)." *ABD* 6:315–16.

Malamat, Abraham. "Cushan Rishathaim and the Decline of the Near East around 1200 BC." *JNES* 13 (1954): 231–42.

Mattingly, Gerald L. "Amalek (Person)." *ABD* 1:169–71.

Miller, J. Maxwell. "Moab." *ABD* 4:882–93.

Negev, Avraham. "Negeb." *ABD* 4:1061–68.

Sasson, Jack M. *Judges 1–12: A New Translation with Introduction and Commentary*. AB. New Haven: Yale University, 2014.

Stone, Lawson G. "Eglon's Belly and Ehud's Blade: A Reconsideration." *JBL* 128 (2009): 649–63.

———. "Judges." Pages 185–494 In *Cornerstone Biblical Commentary: Joshua, Judges, Ruth*. Edited by Philip W. Comfort. Carol Stream, IL: Tyndale, 2012.

Younger, K. Lawson, Jr. *Judges, Ruth*. NIVAC. Grand Rapids: Zondervan, 2002.

———. *A Political History of the Arameans: From Their Origins to the End of their Polities*. Atlanta: SBL Press, 2016.

CHAPTER 21

A GEOGRAPHICAL ANALYSIS OF THE JUDGESHIP OF DEBORAH AND BARAK

Judg 4–5

Aubrey Taylor McClain

KEY POINTS

- The geography of northern Israel forced international traffic inland, through the heart of Lower Galilee.
- This international traffic influenced political, economic, and cultural conflicts throughout Israel's history.
- The narrative of Deborah and Barak demonstrates the opportunities and risks associated with this region.

INTRODUCTION

The story of Deborah and Barak in Judg 4–5 offers a valuable look at the geographical significance of the northern region of the land of Israel. Set in the Jezreel Valley, the story's larger geographical compass extends north to the city of Hazor and even farther; it might be said to comprehend the whole road network between Egypt and Mesopotamia. Offering insight into the dynamics of the region, the story itself will also become clearer through an understanding of the context in which it is set. Though primarily focused on the narrative in Judg 4, this approach will note several details in the poetic version of the story found in Judg 5 that offer information where the narrative version is silent.[1]

1. A thorough comparison of the prose and poetic versions of this story is beyond the scope of this essay, as is a discussion of the merits of reading them together or apart and the related redactional theories. Though there are many similarities between the two versions of the story, there are differences, some of which may be used to fill out our understanding and some of which complicate it by introducing potentially contradictory elements. Despite

The book of Judges tells the story of Israel in the period leading up to the monarchy. It is a chaotic time, in which individual tribes and small, temporary coalitions attempt to strengthen their foothold in the land of Canaan and resist the local cultures, both religiously and militarily. Observing time and again their failure to remain faithful to YHWH, the author frequently notes that after a period of cooperation and fidelity: "The Israelites again did what was evil in the sight of the LORD" (Judg 3:12, 4:1, 10:6, 13:1), initiating a period of subjugation by their neighbors.

Judges 4 begins with such a note, followed by several geographical references that provide context for the narrative. First, we are told that "the LORD sold [Israel] into the hand of King Jabin of Canaan, who reigned in Hazor; the commander of his army was Sisera, who lived in Harosheth Haggoyim" (Judg 4:2). Later, when Deborah commissions Barak, he is told to gather an army at Mount Tabor. There, Sisera will be drawn out to do battle at the Wadi Kishon. All these sites are in the north of Israel, in strategic locations along the main artery for trade traffic flowing between the Jezreel Valley and the region of Hazor, which lies north of the Sea of Galilee. A portion of what is sometimes referenced as the international highway, the path of this route is critical to our understanding of the narrative.

INTERNATIONAL HIGHWAY

The road network upon which this narrative depends is significant not just to the land of Canaan but to the larger international world of the day. Given the obstacles of the Syrian desert to the east and the Mediterranean Sea to the west, traffic passing between Egypt and Mesopotamia had to travel along the eastern seaboard of the Mediterranean, in the narrow stretch of land that receives enough rainfall to support settled life. Canaan lies within the southern part of this region, carrying the road along its western coastal plain where the terrain is reasonably flat. However, as one reaches the Sharon Plain traveling south to north, the Mount Carmel Range rises along a northwest-southeast axis, projecting out into the Mediterranean and cutting off the coastal plain. This forces traffic to leave the coast and choose an inland route through one of a few mountain passes. Of these mountain passes, the Megiddo (Aruna) Pass is the most direct and convenient option, depositing one at the floor of the Jezreel Valley on its southwest side, opposite Mount Tabor on the northeast side.

The convenience of the Megiddo Pass is recognized on two accounts. One, its position across from Mount Tabor is fortuitous. From there, the road continues further north along the shore of the Sea of Galilee, arriving soon thereafter at Hazor. Past Hazor, traffic could continue northeast toward Damascus and Mesopotamia

---

these concerns, the underlying geographical logic, which is our focus, is plausible and demonstrates an awareness of the strategic function of the region. See Mark E. Biddle, *Reading Judges: A Literary and Theological Commentary* (Macon, GA: Smyth & Helwys, 2012), 54–56; Marc Zvi Brettler, *The Book of Judges* (London: Routledge, 2002), 61–79; Tyler Mayfield, "The Accounts of Deborah in Recent Research (Judges 4–5)," *Community Bible Reading* 7.3 (2009): 306–35; Nadav Na'aman, "Literary and Topographical Notes on the Battle of Kishon (Judges IV–V)," *VT* 40.4 (1990): 423–36; Israel Finkelstein, "Compositional Phases, Geography and Historical Setting Behind Judges 4–5 and the Location of Harosheth-ha-goiim," *SJOT* 31.1 (2017): 26–43.

Aerial View of Jezreel Valley with Megiddo Pass, Mounts Tabor and Moreh in Background

beyond. As a result, this Megiddo to Tabor connection became one of the primary paths for international travel between Egypt and Mesopotamia.[2] Two, the Jezreel Valley could at times present an obstacle to travel, but the Megiddo to Tabor corridor provided the best opportunity to cross the valley with ease.

The Jezreel Valley drains westward toward the Bay of Akko (Acre), dropping only seventy feet (21 m) in elevation over approximately fifteen miles (24 km). Almost completely level and surrounded by hills, the valley floor has collected alluvial soil up to three hundred and thirty feet (100 m) deep. The tiny Kishon River meanders through the valley, collecting runoff and directing it toward the Mediterranean. Sluggish at best, the Kishon is easily overwhelmed in times of heavy rain and overflows its banks. This, coupled with the abundant alluvial soil of the valley floor, means that the valley can become an impassable quagmire when the winter rains come.[3] An often-cited example, in February of 1905, Gertrude Bell records attempting to cross the Jezreel, noting "We waded sometimes for an hour at a time knee-deep in clinging mud, the mules fell down, the donkeys almost disappeared ('By God!' said one of the muleteers, 'you could see nothing but his ears!')."[4] However, the path across the valley between Megiddo and Mount Tabor lay a bit higher in elevation than the surrounding valley floor, draining the runoff more efficiently and offering a direct, less muddy path across the valley. As a result, the Megiddo Pass became the

2. Yohanan Aharoni, *The Land of the Bible: A Historical Geography*, trans. and ed. Anson F. Rainey, rev. and enl. ed. (Philadelphia: Westminster, 1979), 50–54.

3. Denis Baly, *The Geography of the Bible* (New York: Harper & Row, 1974), 146. Israel experiences a rainy winter and a drought-like summer weather pattern. Baly, *The Geography of the Bible*, 43–53. This means that during the summer, the valley is dry and easy to cross.

4. Gertrude Bell, *The Letters of Gertrude Bell: Volume I*, ed. Lady Bell, D. B. E. (New York: Boni and Liveright, 1927), 176.

Hazor Lower City

most attractive access point for those traversing the Jezreel.[5]

HAZOR

Hazor, identified as the seat of King Jabin in Judg 4:2, is located about eight and a half miles (14 km) north of the Sea of Galilee, at Tell el-Qedah.[6] It holds a unique and valuable position along the international highway. Here, traffic is funneled toward the city to avoid the rugged hills of Upper Galilee to the west and the swampy marshes of the Huleh Basin to the east. The Rosh Pinah Sill, forming the northern rim of the Sea of Galilee, lies to the southeast of the city and is also an obstacle to travel, covered in basalt boulder fields that are difficult to traverse. As a result of these dynamics, several roads converge at Hazor, making it the primary northern hub in Canaan for international traffic and trade.

At two hundred acres in its prime, Hazor was the largest city in Canaan in the Late Bronze Age.[7] Hazor would have gained prodigious wealth through the trade traffic that flowed through its gates and seems to have established itself as a powerful city-state, as indicated by references to its commercial role found

5. This is also the background for the famed capture of Megiddo, associated with Thutmose III in 1468 BC. See *ANET*, 235.

6. Yigal Yadin and Amnon Ben-Tor, "Hazor," *NEAEHL* 2:594.

7. Yadin and Ben-Tor, "Hazor," *NEAEHL* 2:595, 603. Hazor's lower city was founded in the mid-eighteenth-century BC and persisted through the thirteenth century. Its peak was the fourteenth century. This narrative is set in the era of Hazor's decline. The biblical text recounts a significant Israelite victory against this stronghold under Joshua, stating that "before that time Hazor was the head of all those kingdoms" (Josh 11:10).

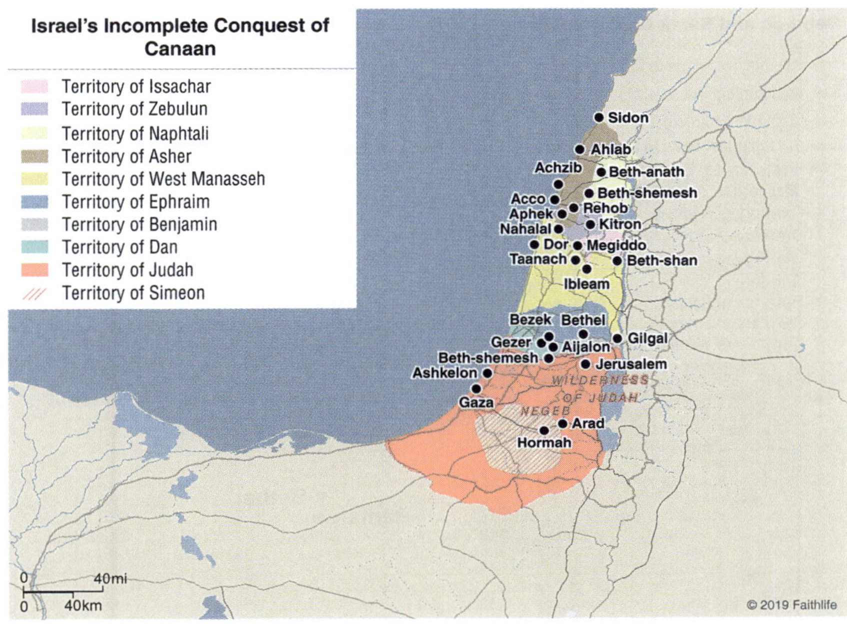

in the Mari archives.[8] The present story, set in the era of the judges, comes toward the end of Hazor's strength; however, the reference to the position of King Jabin's commander suggests something of the city's ongoing influence.

THE SETTING FOR THE BATTLE

King Jabin, we are told, has a commander named Sisera living in Harosheth Haggoyim. An unusual place name, it may reference a region, rather than a specific site.[9] Rainey has offered the plausible translation, "plantations of the nations," suggesting it should be read as a synonym to the poetic "At Taanach, on the waters of Megiddo" (Judg 5:19). He and others have related it to Isaiah's "Galilee of the nations" (Isa 9:1), derived from the internationalism of the area.[10] The specific location has been debated, as no modern site carries the name. However, there is a history of military staging in the region between Taanach and Megiddo, along the southwest rim of the Jezreel valley floor, near the base of the hills. This general

8. Yadin and Ben-Tor, "Hazor," *NEAEHL* 2:594. The Mari archives reveal that Hammurabi of Babylon had ambassadors placed in Hazor. The city was also associated with the tin trade, a valuable commodity in the Bronze Age. Daniel I. Block, "Judges," *ZIBBCOT* 2:134.

9. Anson Rainey, "The Military Campground at Taanach by the Waters of Megiddo," *Eretz-Israel* 15 (1981): *64; Jack M. Sasson, *Judges 1–12*, AB (New Haven: Yale University Press, 2014), 253–54.

10. Rainey and Notley, *Sacred Bridge*, 150–51; Daniel I. Block, *Judges, Ruth*, NAC (Nashville: Boardman & Holman, 1999), 189–90; Anson Rainey, "Toponymic Problems (Cont.)," *TA* 10.1 (1983): 46–48. The alternative, "forested," is difficult to reconcile with the purported use of the site as a staging ground for chariots.

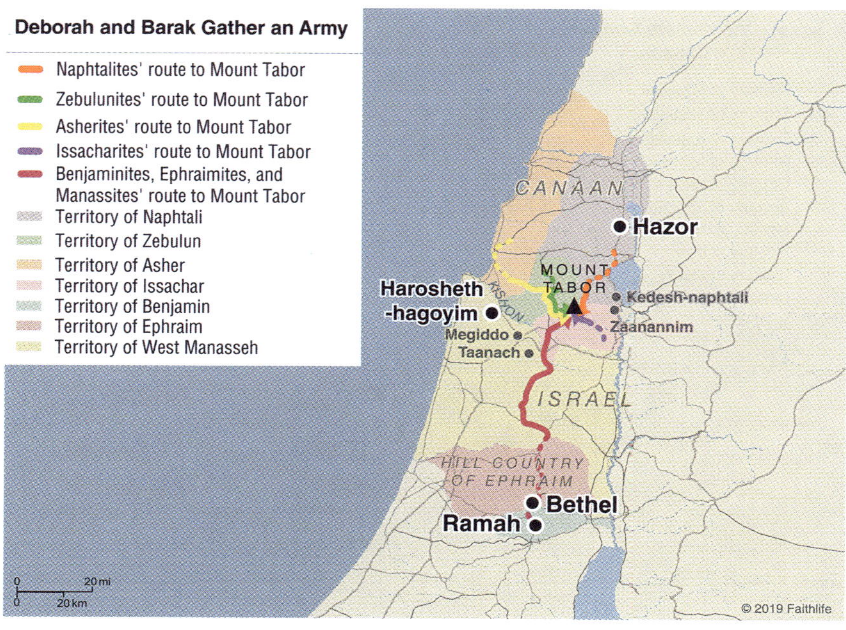

area seems to be the location intended in our text.[11] Here, the Canaanite coalition that opposed Thutmose III prepared for battle, and similarly, Amenhotep II used the location to regroup following his campaign in the region.[12] An ideal staging ground for chariots that operate best on the flat plain of the valley floor, it also places them near the critical Megiddo Pass. It is this position that offers insight into the larger dynamics of the story.

Earlier in the book of Judges, the author lists several cities and territories that Israel was unable to conquer during the conquest of Joshua (Judg 1:27–36, compare with Josh 13:1–7). The result was that though Israel's territory was assigned by tribe in such a way as to create a contiguous map that divided up the whole of Canaan, this was an idealistic representation (Josh 14–19). In many places, the local population was not dispelled, and the Israelite population lived scattered between Canaanite and Philistine strongholds. This was particularly so in the region of the Jezreel Valley, which contained many large and well-fortified cities. In Judg 1:27 we are told particularly that Beth Shan, Taanach, Dor, Ibleam, and Megiddo, as well as the surrounding vil-

11. This site makes sense strategically and within the larger description of the battle in both its prose and poetic version. Having addressed his redactional concerns, Na'aman also arrives at this basic reconstruction. See Na'aman, "Battle of Kishon," 432; Barry G. Webb, *The Book of Judges*, NICOT (Grand Rapids: Eerdmans, 2012), 181.

12. See Rainey, " Military Campground," 61*–66*.

Mount Tabor

lages, all remained in Canaanite hands.[13] These cities are all associated with significant positions in the Jezreel Valley, governing traffic not only on the Egypt-Mesopotamia route but also the east-west connection between the Mediterranean ports and the Arabian trade networks. Creating a block of territory in this strategic center for trade, their continued hold managed to keep Israelite communities separated from one another and maintained control of critical resources in Canaanite hands.

Sisera's position near Megiddo and Taanach is significant considering this information. Jabin, ruling far north in Hazor, has apparently extended his reach all this way south through the arteries of the road network and as a result, gained control of all the major trade traffic from Mount Carmel, north.[14] This has, in essence, divided the northern tribes of Israel from one another, making it difficult for them to prosper or even collaborate. Sisera's role is to keep this artery open, making money for his sovereign. Thus, Deborah's instructions to Barak to take position at Mount Tabor (Judg 4:14) is an instruction to cut off the international highway, an effective means of

13. These cities are associated with Manasseh in Judg 1; however, other tribes in the region have similar lists. See Judg 1:30–33. This may explain the list of tribes involved in Judg 5, which includes several not mentioned in chapter 4. See Judg 5:14–18.

14. Na'aman, "Battle of Kishon," 430. Nadav Na'aman suggests that a later redactor who was unfamiliar with the geography of the region mistakenly located Harosheth Haggoyim in the district of Galilee, thus confusing the original geographical scope of the narrative. This stems from his assumption that such a location would indicate that Jabin ruled a "vast territory," which seems unlikely given what we know of Hazor's diminishing strength in this period. However, this assumption is unnecessary. There are several territorial models that allow for non-contiguous and network type control. Based on the spatial information in the text, it seems most likely that Jabin's oppression is economic in nature. Joe Painter, "Territory-Network" (paper presented at the Association of American Geographers Annual Meeting, Chicago, 7–11 March 2006), 1–29; Monica L. Smith, "Networks, Territories, and the Cartography of Ancient States," *Annals of the Association of American Geographers* 95.4 (2005): 832–49.

drawing Sisera out for battle. The tribes called to participate in this offensive, Zebulun and Naphtali (Barak's tribe), hold significant territory along the road in question and as a result, are those most likely affected by Jabin's rule.[15] A threatening move that Sisera cannot ignore, it is an attempt to unify the northern tribes and dispel the Canaanite control that has kept them divided and subjugated. Thus, "when Sisera was told that Barak son of Abinoam had gone up to Mount Tabor, Sisera called out all his chariots, nine hundred chariots of iron, and all the troops who were with him, from Harosheth Haggoyim to the Wadi Kishon" (Judg 4:12–13).

THE BATTLE

As the battle unfolds, Sisera is dramatically routed in a way that is not fully explained in the narrative. We are told that "the LORD threw Sisera and all his chariots and all his army into a panic before Barak" and that "Sisera got down from his chariot and fled away on foot" (Judg 4:15). Reminiscent of other stories in the Old Testament in which YHWH throws the enemy into a panic before Israel (e.g., Exod 14:24; Deut 7:23; Josh 10:10), it suggests a miraculous intervention. A chariot army would have had a distinct advantage under normal circumstances and Sisera's choice to abandon his chariot and flee on foot would only make sense if his chariot was disabled. It is from Deborah's victory song in chapter 5 that we infer the likely cause of the Israelite victory.

> The kings came, they fought;
> then fought the kings of Canaan,
> at Taanach, by the waters of Megiddo;
> they got no spoils of silver.
> The stars fought from heaven,
> from their courses they fought against Sisera.
> The torrent Kishon swept them away,
> the onrushing torrent, the torrent Kishon.
> March on, my soul, with might!
> (Judg 5:19–20)

Based on this poetic celebration, the Wadi Kishon swept away Sisera's forces in a dramatic torrent.[16] However, this too seems strange as the Kishon is not a torrent, but, as previously mentioned, a small and sluggish stream. The only exception would be in the case of a remarkable downpour, perhaps suggested by the poetic reference to the stars fighting from their courses. Such a weather phenomenon would suddenly swell the stream and flood the valley floor. Once flooded, it would quickly turn to mud, of all things most treacherous to a chariot. Thus, though an ideal chariot ground in the dry season, the Jezreel Valley presented a dangerous obstacle during the rainy season. Either through a miraculous summertime rain-

15. Yohanan Aharoni, Anson F. Rainey, Michael Avi-Yonah, and Ze'ev Safrai, *The Carta Bible Atlas*, 4th ed. (Jerusalem: Carta, 2002), 58. In comparing the narrative of Judg 4 with the poem in Judg 5, a different list of participating tribes is recorded. For a discussion of the potential implications for textual dating and the reconstruction of early Israelite history, see Biddle, *Reading Judges*, 53–56.

16. Biddle, *Reading Judges*, 71–72; Susan Niditch, *Judges: A Commentary*, OTL (Louisville: Westminster John Knox, 2008), 80–81.

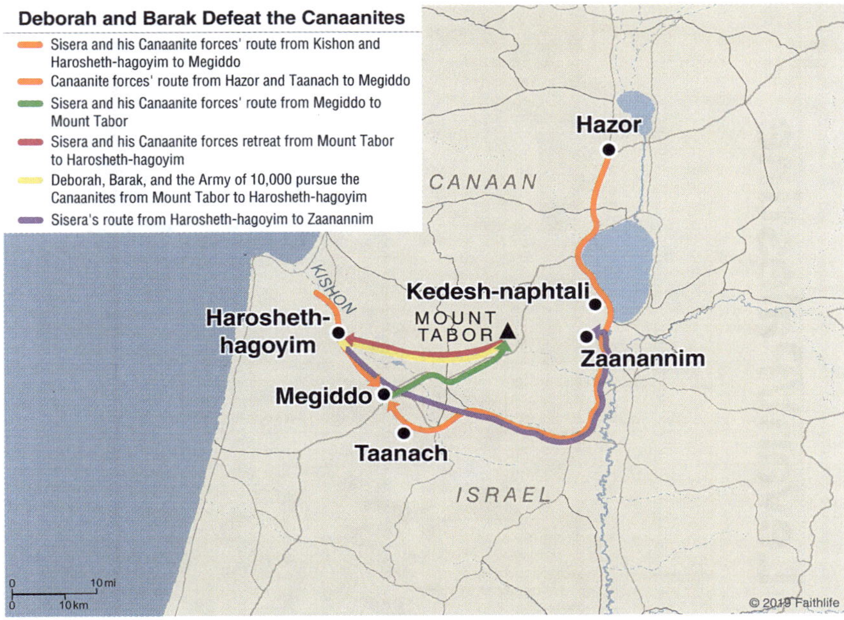

fall or a well-timed winter one, it seems as though Israel was able to lure Sisera's forces out into the low flat ground of the valley floor where they were taken by surprise by muddy conditions.[17] The Israelite army, already on foot, would have had the advantage of agility and mobility. Once the wheels were mired in mud, Sisera's forces were vulnerable and easily overwhelmed by Israel's foot soldiers. Those still alive, like Sisera, would have been forced to get out of their chariots and flee on foot.

JAEL

The rest of this story is centered on the surprise hero of the narrative—Jael. In the opening scene, Deborah is identified as a prophet who is serving as judge over Israel. Presiding in the southern hill country of Ephraim, she is positioned somewhere along the central road that runs north-south between Ramah and Bethel.[18] A strategically central location for the southern tribes, it is far removed from Barak's home of Kedesh in Naphtali.[19] From here, Deborah sends

17. Robert G. Boling, *Judges*, AB (Garden City, NY: Doubleday, 1975), 116–17; Block, "Judges," 148.

18. This is the same general location in which we will later find Samuel (1 Sam 7:15–17). The text records that Deborah sat or, perhaps, dwelt under a palm tree. Palm trees are not typical at this elevation, so the palm may have served as a clear visual for those seeking her. Sasson, *Judges 1–12*, 256.

19. The location of Kedesh has been debated. One possibility is in the hills of Upper Galilee, north of Hazor (Tel Qadas [Tel Kedesh], associated with Josh 20:7, 21:32). The other, east of the Jabneel Valley, on the southwest slope of the Sea of Galilee (Khirbet Qadish), seems more likely given the association between Kedesh and Heber's camp, and its necessary proximity to the battle. See Judg. 4:17. Sasson, *Judges 1–12*, 257–58; Rainey, "Military Campground,"

Agricultural Cycle of the Levant/Palestine

SOLAR MONTHS	SEPT	OCT	NOV	DEC	JAN	FEB	MARCH	APRIL	MAY	JUNE	JULY	AUG	SEPT
HEBREW LUNAR MONTHS	TISHRI	MARCH-ESHVAN	CHISLEV	TEBETH	SHEBAT	ADAR	NISAN	IYYAR	SIVAN	TAMMUZ	AB	ELUL	
FEASTS AND FESTIVALS	TRUMPETS DAY OF ATONEMENT TABERNACLES			DEDICATION			PURIM	PASSOVER UNLEAVENED BREAD		PENTECOST & FIRSTFRUITS			
SEASON	RAINY SEASON								DRY SEASON				
RAINFALL	EARLY RAINS		WINTER RAINS				LATE RAINS		DROUGHT				
AGRICULTURAL ACTIVITIES	PLOW		PLANT			HARVEST							
HARVEST							BARLEY		WHEAT	FIRST FIGS	GRAPES	DATES, SUMMER FIGS	

Jael Smote Sisera, and Slew Him

for Barak, the warrior that YHWH has chosen to rescue Israel from Sisera's oppression. Barak accepts his role on the condition that Deborah accompanies him to battle. Deborah agrees but chastises him saying, "the road on which you are going will not lead to your glory, for the Lord will sell Sisera into the hand of a woman" (Judg 4:9). Thus, throughout the narrative, one suspects that somehow, Deborah will be revealed as the true hero of the battle. It is not until the end that we learn of another woman in the vicinity to whom the victory will belong.

Jael is the wife of Heber, a Kenite. In the Hebrew Bible, the Kenites are a nomadic people associated with the Sinai and who join Israel in settling Canaan, in the vicinity of Arad (Judg 1:16).[20] We are also reminded that Moses' father-in-law, Jethro, was a Kenite, suggesting a friendly relationship between them and the Israelites (4:11). However, we are told that Heber's clan has separated themselves from the other Kenites and is living in the north, in a treaty relationship with Jabin of Hazor (4:17). We are told that Heber has camped at *elon batsannim* (אֵלוֹן בַּצְעַנִּים), or the Oak of Zaanannim, near Kedesh. Another unidentified site, it is in proximity to the Jezreel Valley, perhaps chosen to similarly profit from the

63*–64*; Yohanan Aharoni, "Kedesh (in Upper Galilee)," *NEAEHL* 3:855. A common name, an alternative solution is that these reference two different Kedesh, one in the north and one near the battle.

20. The etymology of the designation "Kenite" suggests the metalworking trade, and some have proposed that they worked as itinerant metalsmiths. Baruch Halpern, "Kenites," *ABD* 4:17.

trade route.[21] Thus, when Israel routes Sisera's forces and Sisera is forced to flee, Heber's camp is conveniently close by and knowing their treaty relationship, he seeks refuge in Heber's camp. However, rather than going to Heber, he enters Jael's tent and asks for water and protection. A breach of etiquette, Jael still responds with compliance, all the while planning treachery. Whether in defense of her honor or out of loyalty to Israel in defiance of her husband, Jael covers Sisera and gives him a drink with soporific effects.[22] While he is asleep, she takes up a hammer and tent peg, the tools of a tent-dwelling woman, and gruesomely drives a peg through Sisera's temple. At this moment, the surprise of the narrative is also brought home—Jael is the woman of whom Deborah prophesied.

RESULTS

With Sisera, his captain, dead, we are told that Jabin's hold on the north of Canaan begins to weaken, perhaps allowing the Israelite tribes in the region to work in greater cooperation or economic independence. The text records that "God subdued King Jabin of Canaan before the Israelites. Then the hand of the Israelites bore harder and harder on King Jabin of Canaan, until they destroyed King Jabin of Canaan" (Judg 4:23–24). Archaeologically, the city of Hazor does begin to decline in the Late Bronze Age, eventually becoming an Israelite stronghold in the days of Solomon (1 Kgs 9:15).[23] If Israel was truly able to disrupt the trade network so eagerly defended by Jabin, Hazor would indeed have suffered, and Jabin's ability to oppress the surrounding people would have diminished.[24]

CONCLUSION

The story of Deborah and Barak is a well-constructed narrative, with ironic twists and compelling characters. It glorifies cunning and courage and celebrates unlikely heroes and heroines. However, when placed within its geographical context, the significance of the victory is more keenly felt. Not a simple skirmish, this military endeavor was a bold disruption of the profit-making networks that supported Israel's oppressors. So too, this story offers a window into the dynamics of the north of Canaan. As the Canaanite strongholds were slowly undermined,

21. If he is indeed a metal smith, this would be a prime location to ply his trade. The site name also occurs in Josh 13:33 in the description of Naphtali's boundary, in proximity to Jabneel, which is near the southwest slopes of the Sea of Galilee. Sasson wisely concludes that this site is unlikely to be identified, indicating as it does an impermanent camp. We can only suggest a general location. For further discussion, see Sasson, *Judges 1–12*, 262.

22. There is a good deal of ambiguity in the language and behavior in Jael and Sisera's encounter. See Niditch, *Judges*, 66–67, 81. Sisera's choice to enter Jael's tent is highly inappropriate based on known cultural norms, as are his demands. Jael may indeed have been acting out of loyalty to Israel throughout. However, she may just as well have been acting out of self-defense. See Victor H. Matthews and Don C. Benjamin, *Social World of Ancient Israel: 1250–587 BCE* (Peabody, MA: Hendrickson, 1993), 87–95; Biddle, *Reading Judges*, 59–61. Sasson offers an interesting suggestion, that as a treaty partner, Heber may have been expected to participate in the battle. If so, his absence from the narrative may indicate that he was one of those defeated or fleeing, or that to avoid military service, he may have absented himself, leaving his camp in the care of his wife (Sasson, *Judges 1–12*, 265).

23. Yadin and Ben-Tor, "Hazor," *NEAEHL* 2:603. See also Webb, *Judges*, 179 n. 2.

24. Webb, *Judges*, 179.

the tribes struggled toward what would become the unified nation of Israel. Yet, as a thoroughfare for trade, the region remained associated with international influences. As a result, Israelites living in this region struggle to maintain their identity and religious fidelity, living as they do, in the "Galilee of the Gentiles."

BIBLIOGRAPHY

Aharoni, Yohanan. "Kedesh (in Upper Galilee)." *NEAEHL* 5:855–66.

———. *The Land of the Bible: A Historical Geography*. Translated and edited by Anson F. Rainey. Rev. and enl. ed. Philadelphia: Westminster, 1979.

Aharoni, Yohanan, Anson F. Rainey, Michael Avi-Yonah, and Ze'ev Safrai. *The Carta Bible Atlas*. 4th ed. Jerusalem: Carta, 2002.

Baly, Denis. *The Geography of the Bible*. New York: Harper & Row, 1974.

Beitzel, Barry J. "The *Via Maris* in Literary and Cartographic Sources." *BA* 54.2 (1991): 64–75.

Bell, Gertrude. *The Letters of Gertrude Bell: Volume I*. Edited by Lady Bell, D. B. E. New York: Boni and Liveright, 1927.

Biddle, Mark E. *Reading Judges: A Literary and Theological Commentary*. Macon, GA: Smyth & Helwys, 2012.

Block, Daniel I. "Judges." *ZIBBCOT* 2: 94–241.

———. *Judges, Ruth*. NAC. Nashville: Broadman & Holman, 1999.

Boling, Robert G. *Judges*. AB. Garden City: Doubleday, 1975.

Brettler, Marc Zvi. *The Book of Judges*. London: Routledge, 2002.

Finkelstein, Israel. "Compositional Phases, Geography and Historical Setting Behind Judges 4–5 and the Location of Harosheth-ha-goiim." *SJOT* 31.1 (2017): 26–43.

Halpern, Baruch. "Kenites." *ABD* 4:17–22.

Kitchen, Kenneth A. *On the Reliability of the Old Testament*. Grand Rapids: Eerdmans, 2003.

Matthews, Victor H., and Don C. Benjamin. *Social World of Ancient Israel: 1250–587 BCE*. Peabody, MA: Hendrickson, 1993.

Mayfield, Tyler. "The Accounts of Deborah in Recent Research (Judges 4–5)." *Community Bible Reading* 7.3 (2009): 306–35.

Na'aman, Nadav. "Literary and Topographical Notes on the Battle of Kishon (Judges IV–V)." *VT* 40.4 (1990): 423–36.

Niditch, Susan. *Judges: A Commentary*. OTL. Louisville: Westminster John Knox, 2008.

Painter, Joe. "Territory-Network." Paper presented at Association of American Geographers Annual Meeting. Chicago, 7–11 March 2006.

Rainey, Anson. "The Military Campground at Taanach by the Waters of Megiddo." *Eretz-Israel* 15 (1981): 61*–66*.

———. "Toponymic Problems (Cont.)." *TA* 10.1 (1983): 46–48.

Rainey, Anson F., and R. Steven Notley. *The Sacred Bridge: Carta's Atlas of the Biblical World*. Jerusalem: Carta, 2006.

Sasson, Jack M. *Judges 1–12*. AB. New Haven: Yale University Press, 2014.

Smith, Monica L. "Networks, Territories, and the Cartography of Ancient States." *Annals of the Association of American Geographers* 95.4 (2005): 832–49.

Webb, Barry G. *The Book of Judges*. NICOT. Grand Rapids: Eerdmans, 2012.

Yadin, Yigal, and Amnon Ben-Tor. "Hazor." *NEAEHL* 2:594–605.

CHAPTER 22

'MARCH ON MY SOUL WITH MIGHT!'—THE GEOGRAPHICAL SETTING OF JUDGES 4–5

Judg 4–5

Chris McKinny

KEY POINTS

- A discussion of the historical geography of Judg 4–5 with an up-to-date analysis of the archaeology of the various locales.
- An alternative viewpoint on the location of the Kishon River (Judg 4:7, 13; 5:21; Ps 83:9).
- New suggestions for the identifications of Harosheth Haggoyim (Judg 4:2, 13, 16) and Meroz (Judg 5:23).

INTRODUCTION

The purpose of this chapter is to examine the geographical setting of the narrative of Deborah and Barak in Judg 4 and 5.[1] A number of the place names, such as Hazor (Judg 4:2); Ramah and Bethel (Judg 4:5);[2] Mount Tabor (Judg 4:6, 12, 14); Seir and the region of Edom and Sinai

1. Sections of this paper have been adapted from Chris McKinny et al., *Photo Companion to the Bible: Judges* (BiblePlaces, 2019).

2. The "hill country of Ephraim" (e.g., Judg 4:5) can probably refer to a wider area than the tribal territory of Ephraim (Josh 16). It seems to have been a regional term for an expansive area that, besides areas within Ephraim (Judg 17:8; 18:2, 13; 19:1, 16, 18; 1 Sam 9:4; 14:22; 1 Kgs 4:8; 2 Kgs 5:22; 2 Chr 15:8; 19:4; 30:10; Jer 31:6), also included parts of Benjamin (Judg 4:5; between Bethel and Ramah [probably er-Ram]; 1 Sam 1:1, Ramathaim of the Zuphites [probably er-Ram]; 2 Sam 20:21, Sheba the son of Bichri, a Benjaminite; 2 Chr 13:4, Mount Zemaraim compare Zemaraim in Benjamin in Josh 18:22), and western Manasseh (Josh 17:15, Manasseh and Ephraim addressed together; Josh 20:7; 21:21; 1 Kgs 12:25; 1 Chr 6:67, Shechem which is on the border of Manasseh and Ephraim; Judg 3:27, Ehud of Benjamin; Judg 7:24, Beth

Cuneiform Letter to Ibni-Addu, King of Hazor

(Judg 5:4); Gilead (Judg 5:17); and Taanach and Megiddo (Judg 5:19), are well-known and discussed elsewhere.[3] This chapter will focus on the following place names: Harosheth Haggoyim (Judg 4:2, 13, 16), Kedesh in Naphtali and the *elon batsannim* (אֵלוֹן בְּצַעֲנַנִּים) or the Oak in Zaanannim (Judg 4:6, 9–11), the Kishon River (Judg 4:7, 13; 5:21), and Meroz (Judg 5:23), as each of these places are vital to understanding the geographical background of Judg 4–5. Before addressing these locales, I will begin with a brief discussion of the references to Jabin king of Hazor in Judges, as it is important to understand the geographical and chronological relationship of Judg 4–5 to Josh 11. There are also some suggested extrabiblical references to "Jabin" that we should briefly examine.

JABIN II?—KING OF HAZOR (JUDG 4:2, 23–24)

In the Bible, Jabin (I) is mentioned as the king of Hazor and leader of "all those kingdoms" at the time of Joshua's conquest (Josh 11:1, 10). In Judg 4, another Jabin (II) is named king of Hazor who had influence in the Jezreel Valley where Sisera was stationed (Judg 5:19). Outside of the Bible, the name "Jabin" (or close

Barah near the Adam fords of the Jordan; Judg 10:1, Shamir [Khirbet Tana el-Tahta/Khirbet Sammir?]). The usage of Ephraim in Hosea (e.g., Hos. 4:17; 5:3) as a synonym for the late eighth century BC Kingdom of Israel (i.e., without the Transjordan and Galilee) also supports the idea that Ephraim could be used much as a regional term that encompassed a broader area than its tribal allotments.

3. For Edom and Egypt, see discussion in Mark Janzen and Chris McKinny, "An Overview of the Historical Geography of the Exodus and Wilderness Itinerary," in *Lexham Geographic Commentary on the Pentateuch*, ed. Barry J. Beitzel (Bellingham, WA: Lexham Press, 2023). For Taanach and Megiddo, see especially Erasmus Gaß, "The Deborah-Barak Composition (Jdg 4–5): Some Topographical Reflections," *PEQ* 149.4 (2017): 326–35.

equivalents) occurs in two texts associated with Hazor. First, the name Ibni-Addu, along with his identification as king of Hazor, is included in a cuneiform letter that was discovered at Hazor dating to the Middle Bronze Age.[4] This name also appears in connection with Hazor in the Mari Archive of the same period.[5] The first element of the name "Ibni" seems to be the Babylonian form for the Semitic name of "Jabin," which could perhaps indicate that "Jabin/Ibni" was popular among the rulers of Hazor or that it was used dynastically in light of its occurrence in both Josh 11 and Judg 4–5.[6]

Krahmalkov argues that the name "Jabin" also appears in the topographic list of Ramesses II at Karnak.[7] From this text, Krahmalkov reconstructs the following toponym: Qerumin-Qishon of Jabin (Ybn)-Shimshon-Hadasht.[8] He then connects Qerumin-Qishon with the Kishon River (Judg 4:7; 5:22) and the Levitical and Issacharite town of Kishon (Josh 19:20; 21:28) that he claims was ruled by Jabin. He also suggests that Hadasht should be related to Harosheth Haggoyim, which he identifies with the nearby spring of Ain el-Hadatha.[9] In the case of the latter, this seems most improbable.[10] With regards to Jabin, Krahmalkov argues that the editor of Judges incorrectly connects Jabin to Hazor due to the influence of Josh 11, and that the Jabin of Ramesses II's list and Judg 4 should be connected with Kishon.[11] While not agreeing with this reading, Kitchen similarly concludes that "Jabin II" retained the title of "king of Hazor" after the site had been destroyed in the thirteenth century BC[12] but resided and ruled elsewhere, which may be hinted at in Ps 83:9.

The new excavations of the lower city of Hazor led by Garfinkel, Hasel, Cline,

4. Wayne Horowitz, Takayoshi Oshima, and Seth L. Sanders, *Cuneiform in Canaan: Cuneiform Sources from the Land of Israel in Ancient Times* (Jerusalem: Israel Exploration Society, 2006), 77–78, see also 69–71.

5. Marco Bonechi, "Relations Amicales Syro-Palestiniennes: Mari et Hasor Au XVIII e Siècle Av. JC," in *Recueil d'études En l'honneur de Michel Fleury*, ed. J.-M. Durand (Paris: Société pour l'Étude du Proche-Orient Ancien, 1992), 9–22.

6. Although this is problematic from a chronological standpoint, as the Ibni references date to the eighteenth century BC, whereas the biblical references reflect the end of the Late Bronze Age and early Iron Age. See also Kenneth A. Kitchen, *On the Reliability of the Old Testament* (Grand Rapids: Eerdmans, 2003), 184, 213.

7. Charles R. Krahmalkov, "Exodus Itinerary Confirmed by Egyptian Evidence," *BAR* 20 (1994): 54–62, 79; see also Jan J. Simons, *Handbook for the Study of Egyptian Topographical Lists Relating to Western Asia* (Leiden: Brill, 1937), 157–59.

8. Nos. 21–23 see Simons, *Egyptian Topographical*, 158–59.

9. Krahmalkov, "Exodus Itinerary," 62.

10. Another or perhaps the same Hadasht, which may be located at Hadeth near Baalbek, is mentioned in other Egyptian inscriptions (Shmuel Ahituv, *Canaanite Toponyms in Ancient Egyptian Documents* [Jerusalem: Magnes Press, 1984], 108).

11. Krahmalkov, "Exodus Itinerary," 56. See also James's similar, albeit hesitant conclusion in Peter James, "The Levantine War-Records of Ramesses III: Changing Attitudes, Past, Present and Future," *Antiguo Oriente* 15 (2017): 115–16.

12. See discussion in Israel Finkelstein, "Hazor at the End of the Late Bronze Age. A Reassessment," *UF* 37 (2005): 341–50; Amnon Ben-Tor and Sharon Zuckerman, "Hazor at the End of the Late Bronze Age: Back to Basics," *BASOR* 350 (2008): 1–6.

and Yasur-Landau beginning in 2019 may reveal a different stratigraphic picture than the upper city. The upper city was destroyed and abandoned in the thirteenth century BC (Josh 11) and unoccupied until the eleventh century BC.[13] The lack of twelfth century BC remains at Hazor is a potential historical problem considering the references to Hazor in Judg 4–5. However, it is possible that the main settlement shifted to a different location within the vicinity as Kitchen has argued.[14] For example, an extensive Iron I settlement was established at Rosh Pinna (seven miles [11 km] south of Hazor) that was destroyed by fire in the tenth century BC.[15] The important sites of Tell Qasab (Tel Yaaf)[16] and Tell Sanjaq (Tel Nes)[17] are also in the same vicinity.

HAROSHETH HAGGOYIM (JUDG 4:2, 13, 16)

The site of Harosheth Haggoyim—the seat of Sisera, the commander of Jabin—is mentioned several times in the narrative (Judg 4:2, 13, 16).[18] The name only appears in the Deborah and Barak account, but it may be identical to Goyim of Galilee (Γωιμ της Γαλιλαιας, *Gōim tēs Galilaias*) in Josh 12:23 (LXX). Many scholars have understood Harosheth Haggoyim as a regional name for the western Jezreel Valley near Megiddo. Those who follow this viewpoint equate Harosheth Haggoyim—the location of the defeat of Sisera's armies (Judg 4:16)—with the location "Taanach, by the waters of Megiddo" (Judg 5:19).[19] The meaning of the toponym has been debated by many scholars.[20] The Hebrew may

13. Doron Ben-Ami, "Hazor at the Beginning of the Iron Age," *NEA* 76.2 (2013): 101–4. In addition, Iron I remains were also seen east of Hazor within Kibbutz Ayelet Ha-Shahar and Tell es-Safa (Hazor's main cemetery) (Yosef Stepansky, *Archeological Survey of Israel, Map 18: Map of Rosh Pina*, ed. Ofer Sion, Liat Weinblum, and Ronnie Avidov [Jerusalem: Israel Antiquities Authority, 2012], sites 21 and 24, http://survey.antiquities.org.il/index_Eng.html#/MapSurvey/2).

14. Kitchen, *On the Reliability*, 213.

15. Yosef Stepansky, "Rosh Pinna," *Hadashot Arkheologiot* 120 (2008): n.p., http://www.hadashot-esi.org.il/report_detail_eng.aspx?id=876&mag_id=114; Moshe Hartal, "Rosh Pinna," *Hadashot Arkheologiot* 121 (2009): n.p., http://www.hadashot-esi.org.il/report_detail_eng.aspx?id=1099&mag_id=115.

16. Remains from the Early Bronze, Middle Bronze, Late Bronze, Iron I, and (mainly) Iron II over thirty dunams (7 acres) (Stepansky, "Rosh Pinna," site 189).

17. Remains from the Early Bronze and Iron Age, including Iron I (Stepansky, *Archeological Survey of Israel, Map 18: Map of Rosh Pina*, site 241). Also, a large Iron II fortress (Stepansky, "Rosh Pinna," site 189).

18. Eusebius confused Jabin with the site of Jabesh Gilead in Transjordan (*Onom*. 138/32:5).

19. Yohanan Aharoni, *The Land of the Bible: A Historical Geography*, trans. Anson F. Rainey, rev. and enl. ed. (Philadelphia: Westminster, 1979), 221–23; Anson F. Rainey and Steven Notley, *The Sacred Bridge: Carta's Atlas of the Biblical World* (Jerusalem: Carta, 2006), 12, 150.

20. The suggestions to connect the site with Khirbet el-Harițiyeh in the Kishon Pass (with the ancient site of Harosheth Haggoyim possibly located at nearby Tell Amr) is toponymically possible (see, e.g., William F. Albright, "Some Additional Notes on the Song of Deborah," *Journal of the Palestine Oriental Society* 2 [1922]: 284–85). However, this identification does not seem to fit the geographical evidence of Judg 4–5. For a summary of past suggestions, see Erasmus Gaß, *Die Ortsnamen Des Richterbuchs in Historischer Und Redaktioneller Perspektive*, (Wiesbaden: Verlag, 2005), 236–40.

mean "plantations" or "plowed place" of the Gentiles.[21] The Greek versions usually transliterate the Hebrew for Harosheth (Αρισωθ των εθνων, *Arisōth tōn ethnōn*), but LXX^A of Judg 4:16 provides the translation "forest of the nations" (δρυμοῦ των εθνων, *drymou tōn ethnōn*), which some scholars believe underlies the Hebrew text as well.[22]

Zertal's suggestion to identify Harosheth Haggoyim with el-Ahwat is an interesting, if problematic one. El-Ahwat fits the general vicinity, and it was a significant and fortified site (30 dunams; 7.5 acres) from the correct period (1220–1150 BC).[23] There are also suggested connections with the Shardana culture, which may possibly be related to Sisera and the "Goyim" (Gentiles).[24] El-Ahwat is located about sixteen miles (25 km) southwest of Megiddo, just off the Arunah/Megiddo Pass (Wadi Arah), and about two and a half miles (4 km) southeast of the Arunah (Ara) of Thutmose III.[25] If Zertal's proposal is correct, it is possible that Arunah, together with el-Ahwat, can be connected with both Goyim in Galilee (Josh 12:22) and Harosheth Haggoyim (Judg 4:2, 13, 16). Conversely, neither El-Ahwat or Arunah are close to Taanach or Megiddo, which mitigates against a connection with the narrative in Judges. In sum, Harosheth Haggoyim was likely a regional term for the western Jezreel Valley, but a particular settlement might have also been located at Tell el-Amr on the northwestern end of the Jezreel Valley.

The regional interpretation for Harosheth Haggoyim remains plausible. However, since Harosheth Haggoyim may be related to Goyim of Galilee (Josh 12:22), it seems possible that there was also a particular settlement in the vicinity. On a related point, the suggestions to connect Harosheth with Khirbet el-Haritiyeh

21. For "plantation," see discussion in Rainey and Notley, *Sacred Bridge*, 160. For "plowed place," see Gaß, "Deborah-Barak," 328.

22. Benjamin Mazar, "Beth She'arim, Gaba, and Harosheth of the Peoples," *Hebrew Union College Annual* 24 (1952): 75–84.

23. A dunam is equivalent to about a quarter acre (1000 m^2). Thus, a ten dunam site would be about two and a half acres (10,000 m^2) or about one hectare. For reference, the City of David is roughly ten acres in size, which equals four hectares or forty dunams.

24. Adam Zertal and Nivi Mirkam, *The Manasseh Hill Country Survey, Vol. 3: From Nahal 'Iron to Nahal Shechem*, ed. Shay Bar (Leiden: Brill, 2016), 2, 70–71, 144–52; for the final excavation report, see Adam Zertal, ed., *El-Ahwat: A Fortified Site from the Early Iron Age Near Nahal 'Iron, Israel: Excavations 1993–2000* (Leiden: Brill, 2012). Zertal claimed that the material evidence of the site should be related to one of the Sea Peoples (Shardana), as there is some textual (e.g., Onomasticon of Amenope and Tale of Wenamun) and archaeological evidence (from Tel Dor) that Sea Peoples settled along the northern coast. A number of scholars dispute Zertal's suggestion in connection with el-Ahwat (e.g., Israel Finkelstein, "El-Aḥwat: A Fortified Sea People City?," *IEJ* 52.2 [2002]: 187–99).

25. Settled in the Middle Bronze, Late Bronze, Iron I, Iron II, and later periods over forty dunams, see Yuval Gadot and Yotam Tepper, *Archeological Survey of Israel , Map 49: Map of Regavim*, ed. Liat Weinblum and Leticia Barda, (Jerusalem: Israel Antiquities Authority, 2009), site 227, http://survey.antiquities.org.il/index_Eng.html#/MapSurvey/1. See also Adam Zertal, "The Arunah Pass," in *Egypt, Canaan and Israel: History, Imperialism, Ideology and Literature: Proceedings of a Conference at the University of Haifa, 3–7 May 2009*, ed. Shay Bar, Dan'el Kahn, and JJ Shirley (Leiden: Brill, 2011), 342–56.

or Silet el-Khartiyeh (*Survey of Western Palestine*: "Sîly") remain toponymically possible. The classical era site of Khirbet el-Haritiyeh (second century BC) and the adjacent tells (Tell el-Amr and Tell Habaj) are located over fifteen and a half miles (25 km) northwest of Megiddo, which is likely too far to be connected with the geography of the prose (Mount Tabor, Judg 4:6, 12, 14) or poetic (waters of Megiddo, Judg 5:19) versions of the events. On the other hand, Silet el-Khartiyeh is situated just to the southeast of Taanach, which fits the details of Judg 5:19, except it does not have remains that predate the Roman period. However, the nearby site of Khirbet Yannun has remains from the Middle Bronze, Late Bronze, and Iron I over an area of seven dunams (2 acres).[26] According to the surveyors, who identify the site with Gath Rimmon/Gitirimmunima (EA 250),[27] Khirbet Yannun was a site of "considerable importance."[28] In addition, the very large site of Tell Salem (100–120 dunams; 25–30 acres) sits just north of Rummaneh. Tell Salem was primarily occupied during the Iron I, Iron II, and Persian periods.[29] In short, Silet el-Khartiyeh possibly preserves the ancient name of "Harosheth" as it fits closely with the geographical setting of Judg 5:19. If so, either Khirbet Yannun and/or Tell Salem may represent Harosheth Haggoyim/Goyim of Galilee.

THE RIVER KISHON (JUDG 4:7, 13; 5:21; PS 83:9)

Outside of Judg 4–5, the Kishon River is mentioned in 1 Kgs 18 as the location of the execution of the prophets of Baal by Elijah (1 Kgs 18:40).[30] In light of the close proximity of this event to Mount Carmel (1 Kgs 18:20, 41–42), most scholars have connected the Kishon River of both 1 Kgs 18 and Judg 4–5 with Nahr el-Muqatta (Nahal Kishon). In antiquity until modern times, Nahr el-Muqatta was a perennial stream that ran below

26. Zertal and Mirkam, *From Nahal 'Iron to Nahal Shechem*, site 42.

27. The Gath Rimmon referenced in EA 250 is possibly identical to the Levitical and Manassehite town of Gath Rimmon in Josh 21:25, if the Joshua reference is not a scribal error for Ibleam (1 Chr 6:70). This suggestion is possible. Yet, since Rummaneh (which preserves Gath Rimmon) has not been surveyed and is located just over four miles (7 km) north of Khirbet Yannun, Rummaneh seems like a better option for Gath Rimmon/Gitirimmunima and perhaps also Hadad Rimmon (Zech 12:11) (Zertal and Mirkam, *From Nahal 'Iron to Nahal Shechem*, 67–68, site 12).

28. Zertal and Mirkam, *From Nahal 'Iron to Nahal Shechem*, site 42.

29. Zertal and Mirkam, *From Nahal 'Iron to Nahal Shechem*, site 8. The surveyors connect the site with the "Valley of Salem," which is mentioned in the Book of Judith (4:4). However, Jdt 4:4 refers to a valley not a specific town, and the Jezreel Valley/Esdraelon is referenced elsewhere in the same passage (Jdt 4:4) (Lawrence M. Wills, *Judith*, Hermeneia [Minneapolis: Fortress, 2019], 206–7).

30. Krahmalkov suggested that the Egyptian "Qerumin-Qishon" (Ramesses II version) is also reflected in the MT (קְדוּמִים נַחַל קִישׁוֹן, *qedumim nahal qishon*) and LXX^{B} (*καδημιμ χειμαρρους* Κισων, *kadēmim cheimarrous Kisōn*) of Judg 5:21, which he argued was a scribal mistake for *qedumim* as reflected in the Egyptian text of Ramesses II (Ramesses III's version has *q-t-m-n*) (Krahmalkov, "Exodus Itinerary," 62). This seems like an unlikely scenario (James, "Levantine War-Records," 115–16). *Qedumim* is a hapax legomenon that is usually translated as "ancient," which seems like the preferable option. See also the discussion in Nadav Na'aman, "Literary and Topographical Notes on the Battle of Kishon (Judges IV–V)," *VT* 40.4 (1990): 423–36.

Kishon River near Mount Carmel

Mount Carmel on the east and drained the Jezreel Valley to the northwest.[31]

Despite widespread agreement that the Kishon River should be related to Nahr el-Muqatta, Ps 83 indicates that the battle with Sisera took place near Endor (Ps 83:9–10; compare to Josh 17:11; 1 Sam 28:7). The name Endor is preserved as Indur, located at the northern base of the hill of Moreh (Judg 7:1), but the ancient site is likely located at Khirbet Safsafeh to the north of Indur.[32] Khirbet Safsafeh is a small tell (5 dunams; 1 acre) located near a spring that has remains from the Paleolithic through Ottoman periods, including remains from the Late Bronze and Iron II.[33] Classical Endor was probably located at Indur, which Eusebius called

31. E.g., Jan J. Simons, *The Geographical and Topographical Texts of the Old Testament* (Leiden: Brill, 1959), 2:77; Aharoni, *Land of the Bible*, 152; Rafael Frankel, "Kishon (Place)," *ABD* 4:89.

32. Nehemia Zori, *The Land of Issachar: Archaeological Survey* (Jerusalem: Israel Exploration Society, 1977), 113–14. Although Tell el Ajjull (located just south of Indur) also has remains from the Bronze and Iron Age (Zori, *Land of Issachar*, 62–63); Zvi Gal, *Archeological Survey of Israel, Map 45: Map of 'En Dor*, ed. Ayala Sussmann (Jerusalem: Israel Antiquities Authority, 2013), site 14, https://survey.antiquities.org.il/index_Eng.html#/MapSurvey/49.

33. Gal, *Archeological Survey of Israel, Map 45: Map of 'En Dor*, Site 7; compare to Rafael Frankel, "An Oil Press at Tel Safsafot," *TA* 15.1 (1988): 77–91. It is also possible that Endor was located at Tell el Ajjul (Tel Agol) near the summit of the hill of Moreh, a survey and recent excavation have shown that Tel Agol was occupied during the Middle Bronze, Iron I, Iron II, and Persian Period, and fortified site from Iron IIA through Iron IIB, when the site was destroyed by Tiglath-Pileser III (Gal, *Archeological Survey of Israel, Map 45: Map of 'En Dor*, site 14). See also Nurit Feig, "Tel 'Agol," *Hadashot Arkheologiyot* 133 (2021): n.p., http://www.hadashot-esi.org.il/report_detail_eng.aspx?id=26054&mag_id=133. Kallai's suggestion to connect it with Endor is possible, but uncertain (Z. Kallai, "En-Dor / עין דור," *Eretz-Israel* 16 [1982]: 168–70). In this case, there are two suitable ancient sites next to Indur, which preserves the name.

"a very large village near Mount Tabor to the south about four miles" and also "nearby is Scythopolis and Nain" (*Onom.* 150/34:8; 475/94:22).[34] The occurrence of Endor alongside the Kishon River in Ps 83 would seem to indicate that the two places should be near one another.

Psalm 83 and Judg 4:6–16 point to the plain between Mount Tabor and the hill of Moreh as the location of the battle, which seems to contradict the evidence from 1 Kgs 18:40 that points to the Kishon River being located below Mount Carmel.[35] On a related point, the town of Kishion (קִשְׁיוֹן, *qishyon*) occurs in the Issachar town list of Josh 19:20 after the sites of Anaharath (Tell el-Mukharkhash/Tel Rekhesh) and Rabbith/Daberath (Daburiyeh), and again in the Levitical towns of Issachar in Josh 21:28–29, which includes Kishion, Daberath, Jarmuth and En Gannim.[36] Kishion also appears in the Thutmose III list and in the topographic list from Ramesses II at Karnak.[37] Kishion is typically identified with Tell Qasyun, which preserves the name.[38] Survey and excavation work at Tell Qasyun revealed remains of a fifty dunam (12.5 acre) tell with occupation from the Paleolithic through Early Arab periods, including continuous occupation from the Middle Bronze through Iron II.[39] Tell Qasyun is situated just south of Wadi esh-Sherrar, one mile (2 km) south of Mount Tabor, and one mile (2 km) north of Endor (Khirbet Safsafeh). Zori (Zimbalist) argued that Kishion should be identified with Kishon (Tell Qasyun) and that the Kishon River should be related to Wadi el-Bireh, which drains towards the plain of Issachar to the east, instead of the traditional identification of the Kishon River with Nahr el-Muqatta.[40] Peterson has pointed out that Tell Qasyun does not appear in the older maps of the region (e.g., *Survey of Western Palestine*; Van de Velde's map), but is instead known as el-Khirba, which causes Peterson

34. Gal, *Archeological Survey of Israel, Map 45: Map of 'En Dor*, site 6; Zori, *Land of Issachar*, 113. See also *Onom.* 469/94:10 where Endor is said to have been close to Nain (Luke 7:11). Eusebius in *Onom.* 748/140:3 indicates that Nain was "twelve miles south of Tabor near En-dor," but Jerome emends this (correctly) to "*secundo miliario*" ("two miles") (all quotations of *Onom.* are from R. Steven Notley and Ze'ev Safrai, *Eusebius, Onomasticon: A Triglott Edition with Notes and Commentary* [Leiden: Brill, 2005]). Indur is located about four miles (6 km; nearly 4 Roman milestones) from Mount Tabor, but Nain is located about one mile (2 km) further south of Mount Tabor than Indur. Eusebius also mistakenly placed Aphek "next to En-dor in the Jezreel" in connection with the battle between the Philistines and Saul (*Onom.* 151/34:11; compare to 1 Sam 29). A Roman mile was about 0.92 of an English mile.

35. Gaß, "Deborah-Barak."

36. See discussion in Chris McKinny, "The Historical Geography of the Levitical Towns in Joshua 21 and 1 Chronicles 6:54–81," in this volume.

37. For Thutmose III, see No. 37 in Simons, *Egyptian Topographical*, 116; Rainey and Notley, *Sacred Bridge*, 73. For Ramesses II, see Krahmalkov, "Exodus Itinerary"; no. 22 in Simons, *Egyptian Topographical*, 158.

38. E.g., N. Zimbalist, "Kishon and Kishyon," *Bulletin of the Jewish Palestine Exploration Society* 13.1/2 (1946): 28–51; Simons, *Geographical and Topographical Texts*, 2:77; Aharoni, *Land of the Bible*, 438.

39. C. Cohen-Arnon and Ruth Amiran, "Excavations at Tel Qishon: Preliminary Report on the 1977–1978 Seasons," *Eretz-Israel* 15 (1981): 205–12; Gal, *'En Dor*, site 1.

40. Zimbalist, "Kishon and Kishyon."

to be skeptical about the connection.[41] However, Abel recorded the name of a spring and ruin named Qasyun near the base of Mount Tabor, which he suggested retained the name Kishion and was the location of the Crusader-era village of *Casal de Cressum*.[42]

Despite Peterson's skepticism, there are later sources that indicate the preservation of the name Kishion/Kishon in the vicinity of el-Khirba/Tell Qasyun.[43] Within early Christian tradition, Eusebius stated that the (brook) Kishon was "near Mount Tabor where Sisera was attacked" (*Onom.* 606/116:34; see also 597/114:28.). In the *Epitaph on Saint Paula*, Jerome recorded the following:

> She (St. Paula) climbed Mount Tabor, where the Lord was transfigured. She beheld in the distance Mounts Hermon and Moreh (*Hermonim*) and the expansive plains of Galilee, where Sisera and his entire army were decimated by Barak. The torrent stream of Kishon divided the plain in half, and the town next to Nain, where the widow's son was raised from the dead, were pointed out to her.[44]

With regard to the medieval literature, Pringle notes several sources which indicate that the Kishon River was related to both the area south of Mount Tabor, as well as below Mount Carmel.[45] Most notably, Marino Sanudo stated the following: "The Kishon Brook (*torrens ist Cyson*) is collected from the rainwaters of Mounts Tabor, Hermon, and Moreh (*Hermonim*): one part descends almost to the end of the Sea of Galilee; the other parts into the Mediterranean Sea a mile from Haifa."[46] In addition, as shown by Pringle, Sanudo's accompanying map of the Holy Land depicts a continuous stream extending from the Mediterranean to the southern end of the Sea of Galilee.[47] While not identifying it with the Kishon River, the Letter to Aristeas (second or first century BC) seems to express a similar understanding of a continuous river that drained westwards from the Jezreel

41. Charles W. M. van de Velde, *Memoir to Accompany the Map of the Holy Land* (Gotha: Justus Perthes, 1858); Claude R. Conder and H. H. Kitchener, *The Survey of Western Palestine*, 3 vols. (London: Palestine Exploration Fund, 1881). Wadi 'Ein al-Qasim appears on British Mandate maps beside el-Khirba; John L. Peterson, "Kishion (Place)," *ABD* 4:89.

42. Abel identified biblical and Egyptian Kishion with Tell el-Ajjull (see above) (Félix-Marie Abel, *Géographie de la Palestine: Géographie Physique et Historique*, 3rd ed. [Paris: Gabalda, 1967], 2:422–23).

43. For a survey of the literature and similar conclusions, see Gaß, "Deborah-Barak," 332–33. Tell Qasyun should not be confused with Khirbet Qeisun that is located north of Safed.

44. Jerome, *Jerome's Epitaph on Paula: A Commentary on the Epitaphium Sanctae Paulae with an Introduction, Text, and Translation*, trans. Andrew Caine (Oxford: Oxford University Press, 2013), 62–63.

45. Denys Pringle, "The Spring of the Cresson in Crusading History," in *Dei Gesta per Francos: Etudes Sur Les Croisades Dédiées à Jean Richard: Crusade Studies in Honour of Jean Richard*, ed. Michel Balard, Benjamin Z. Kedar, and Jonathan S. C. Riley-Smith (New York: Routledge, 2001), 231–40; as well as the location of the "Battle of the Spring of Cresson" (May 1187) which occurred two months before the Battle of the Horns of Hattin.

46. Pringle, "Spring," 238.

47. Pringle, "Spring," 238.

Valley to Akko (Ptolemais). The relevant text from Aristeas reads as follows:

> The river Jordan flows around it and never dries up. The land originally measured not less than sixty million acres; subsequently, neighboring peoples overran it. Six hundred thousand settlers were established upon it, each having one hundred acres. As the river rises, like the Nile, in the days approaching harvest, it waters much of the land, discharging its waters into another river in the region of Ptolemais, which in turn flows into the sea. (Aristeas 1:116–117; *OTP* 2:20)

While there is no direct hydrological relationship between the Jordan and the Kishon River, it seems that this view was widespread from the Hellenistic period down through the medieval period. Taking all of the evidence together, the Hebrew Bible and various Christian traditions indicate that the Kishon River was not only localized in the area below and east of Mount Carmel (i.e., Nahr el-Muqatta), but included Wadi esh-Sherrar and perhaps Wadi el-Bireh. Thus, the main western and one of the main eastern streams, along with Nahal Harod, both received their name from the town of Kishon/Kishion and, accordingly, Kishon was the name of streams in the western and northeastern Jezreel Valley.[48]

Kedesh in Naphtali (Judg 4:6, 9–11) and *Elon Batsannim*/ Oak in Zaanannim (Judg 4:11)

Kedesh in Naphtali (also as Kedesh) appears several times in the narrative (Judg 4:6, 9–11) where it is related specifically to the Oak in Zaanannim (Judg 4:11; compare to *Onom.* 860/158:17). Thus, if one can establish the general location of the Oak in Zaanannim, then Kedesh in Naphtali should be situated in the same vicinity. The Oak in Zaanannim also delineates the border between Issachar and Naphtali (Josh 19:33–34). This section of the border, which runs from the vicinity of Mount Tabor (Aznoth Tabor) to the Jordan River, has several sites that have been identified with some certainty (Adaminekeb [Khirbet Damiyeh] and Jabneel [Tell en-Naam]).[49] Therefore, whatever the exact location of the Oak in Zaanannim, it should be located between the southern shore of the Sea of Galilee and Mount Tabor (Josh 19:33). Thus, Kedesh in Naphtali cannot be identical with Kedesh of Galilee in eastern Upper

48. A watershed divides the main drainage of the Jezreel Valley near Kishon running west of Mount Tabor, the hill of Moreh towards Jezreel (Gaß, "Deborah-Barak," Fig. 2).

49. Aznoth Tabor (Josh 19:34) has been connected with Khirbet umm Jebeil located north of Mount Tabor, which has remains from the Iron II and possibly the Late Bronze (according to Saarisalo) over five dunams (about 1 acre) (Zvi Gal, *The Lower Galilee during the Iron Age*, [Winona Lake, IN: Eisenbrauns, 1992], 17, 105); Aapeli Saarisalo, *The Boundary between Issachar and Naphtali: An Archaeological and Literary Study of Israel's Settlement in Canaan* (Helsinki: Suomalaisen Tiedeakatemian Toimituksia, 1927), 127. Eusebius indicated that "Azanoth-tabor" was "a village in the territory of Diocaesarea [Sepphoris] in the plain" (*Onom.* 134/30:24). However, Aznoth Tabor could also be related to a topographical feature (literally the "ears of Tabor") near Mount Tabor.

Gaß recently suggested that the Oak in Zaanannim may be located near Khirbet Arbita to the northeast of Mount Tabor while allowing that this site may also be Heleph (Josh 19:33), as has been suggested previously (Gaß, "Deborah-Barak," 328); see also, Saarisalo, *Issachar and Naphtali*, 27–28.

Galilee (Tell Qades, see Josh 12:22). The Oak in Zaanannim was probably a well-known forest or, perhaps, even a large well-known oak tree that defined the border of Naphtali and Issachar between Mount Carmel and Adami Nekeb (Josh 19:33).

Using similar logic, locating the Oak in Zaanannim to the northeast of Mount Tabor also rules out the proposal to identify Kedesh in Naphtali with Tell Abu Qudeis near Megiddo and Taanach (Judg 5:19).[50] Many scholars conclude that Khirbet Qadish near the Sea of Galilee preserves the name of Kedesh and is best equated with the site identified as Kedesh in Naphtali, the hometown of Barak (Judg 4:6) and the mustering point of the forces of Zebulun and Naphtali (Judg 4:9–11).[51] Khirbet Qadish is located south of Tiberias above the western shoreline of the Sea of Galilee roughly nine miles (15 km) east of the approximate location for the Oak in Zaanannim (Judg 4:11). The site has never been excavated, but surveys revealed remains from the Middle Bronze, Late Bronze, Iron I–II, and Roman-Byzantine periods over an area of twenty dunams (5 acres).[52]

MEROZ (JUDG 5:23)

Before I discuss the location of Meroz, I should mention the political arrangement between Heber the Kenite and Jabin of Hazor. From a geopolitical perspective, it is worth nothing that the "tent-dwelling" Heber the Kenite was "at peace" with Jabin king of Hazor (Judg 4:11; 17). This suggests that Heber the Kenite was a powerful entity in the region, despite the fact that the Kenites did not possess a sedentary town in the region (Judg 1:16). The geopolitical significance of Heber the Kenite (a nomad) may be understood as an example against the "Bedouin model" and the "architectural bias in biblical archaeology" that Ben-Yosef has criticized.[53]

---

50. Tell Abu Qudeis is located in the Jezreel Valley two and a half miles (4 km) southeast of Megiddo. The site was excavated in 1968 by Stern who found remains from the Late Bronze, Iron, Persian, Late Roman, and Early Arab periods over an area of ten dunams (2.5 acres). The remains from the twelfth century BC, approximately the time of Deborah and Barak has led some to identify this site with the Kedesh in Naphtali of Judg 4:6, 9–11. For this view, see Ephraim Stern and Itzhaq Beit Arieh, "Excavations at Tel Kedesh (Tell Abu Qudeis)," *TA* 6.1–2 (1979): 1–25; see rationale against this view in Rainey and Notley, *Sacred Bridge*, 138; Gaß, "Deborah-Barak," 327–28. Gaß also suggests that Tell Abu Qudeis may be connected with another Kedesh that belonged to Issachar that is recorded in the Chronicler's version of the Levitical towns (1 Chr 6:76) and also Kedesh of Josh 12:22, which appears together with Megiddo, Jokneam, and Taanach (Gaß, "Deborah-Barak," 327–28). This is possible, but not proven, as Kedesh in 1 Chr 6:76 may be an error for Kishion, which appears in the version in Joshua (21:28), and Kedesh in Josh 12:22 may refer to Kedesh in Galilee (Tell Qades). In any case, it seems likely that Tell Abu Qudeis's ancient name was "Kedesh," but it is unclear if it was actually ever mentioned in historical sources.

51. As originally suggested by Claude R. Conder, *Tent Work in Palestine: A Record of Discovery and Adventure* (London: Richard Bentley and Son, 1878), 69.

52. Saarisalo, *Issachar and Naphtali*, 83–84; Moshe Kochavi, "Khirbet Kadesh: Kadesh Naftali," *Yediot Bahaqirat Eretz-Israel Weatiqoteha* 27.3 (1963): 169–71; Aren M. Maeir, *"In the Midst of the Jordan": The Jordan Valley During the Middle Bronze Age (circa 2000–1500 BCE): Archaeological and Historical Correlates* (Verlag der Österreichischen Akademie der Wissenschaften, 2010), site 68.

53. Erez Ben-Yosef, "The Architectural Bias in Current Biblical Archaeology," *VT* 69.3 (2019): 361–87.

Archaeologists and biblical scholars usually equate architectural remains and their level of building sophistication with societal and political sophistication during a given historical period.[54] However, ancient semi-nomadic and nomadic populations, which undoubtedly existed throughout the history of the southern Levant, do not usually show up in the archaeological record. By comparing these ancient populations to relatively unsophisticated and decentralized modern Bedouins, scholars have often concluded that the early Iron Age polities were politically and historically insignificant. However, Levy and Ben-Yosef's work in the Arabah demonstrates that sophisticated, developed nomadic polities existed in the early Iron Age, even though they did not reveal substantial architecture.[55]

Significantly, the actions of Heber (via Jael) against Jabin (via Sisera) were a betrayal of relations with Hazor that resulted in the victory of the Israelites. This interpretation has several important trajectories. First, the political significance of the nomadic Heber would seem to allow for the possibility that Sisera and Jabin, as well as the settlement of Meroz, were also nomadic or seminomadic entities. Second, Heber/Jael and Meroz appear alongside one another in Judg 5:22–23, which might indicate a similar political arrangement between Meroz and Jabin of Hazor to what existed between the clan of Heber the Kenite and Jabin of Hazor. If so, Judg 5:22–23 might be contrasting Heber, an ally of Jabin who acted in favor of Israel thanks to the heroics of Jael, with Meroz, an ally of Israel who failed to come to the aid of Deborah and Barak. This would also fit with the preceding discussion of the various tribes and their action or inaction in the conflict (e.g., "Dan, why did he stay with the ships?" [Judg 5:14–18]).[56]

Meroz is mentioned only in Judg 5:23, where it appears to be a town connected

54. For example, the debate regarding the historicity of the united monarchy is based on the idea that physical archaeological remains are a necessary piece of evidence for complex societies, and since there are only meager tenth century BC remains in Judah it follows that the biblical portrayal of the Davidic kingdom lacks historicity. See the following works for discussion of the Large Stone Structure in relation to Solomon's kingdom: Eilat Mazar, *Discovering the Solomonic Wall in Jerusalem: A Remarkable Archaeological Adventure* (Jerusalem: Shoham Academic Research and Publication, 2011); Avraham Faust, "The Large Stone Structure in the City of David: A Reexamination," *ZDPV* 126.2 (2010): 116–30; Israel Finkelstein, "The Large Stone Structure in Jerusalem: Reality versus Yearning," *ZDPV* 127.1 (2011): 1–10; Amihai Mazar, "Jerusalem in the 10th Cent. B.C.E.: A Response," *ZDPV* 136.2 (2020): 139–51. See also the debate over the interpretation of the architectural remains at Khirbet Qeiyafa in Alexander Fantalkin and Israel Finkelstein, "The Date of Abandonment and Territorial Affiliation of Khirbet Qeiyafa: An Update," *TA* 44.1 (2017): 53–60; Yosef Garfinkel, "The 10th Century BCE in Judah: Archaeology and the Biblical Tradition," *Jerusalem Journal of Archaeology* 1 (2021): 126–54.

55. See Thomas E. Levy, Mohammad Najjar, and Erez Ben-Yosef, eds., *New Insights into the Iron Age Archaeology of Edom, Southern Jordan*, 2 vols. (Los Angeles: Cotsen Institute of Archaeology at UCLA, 2014); Erez Ben-Yosef and Aaron Greener, "Edom's Copper Mines in Timna: Their Significance in the 10th Century," *TheTorah.Com*, 2018, https://thetorah.com/edoms-copper-mines-in-timna-their-significance-in-the-10th-century/.

56. Compare Meroz to the praise (Ephraim, Benjamin, Machir, Zebulun, Issachar, and Naphtali) and criticisms (Reuben, Gilead, Dan, and Asher) of the various tribal elements in the preceding narrative (Judg 5:14–18).

with Israel.[57] Towards the end of the song, Meroz is cursed while Jael the Kenite is blessed (Judg 5:24). Some suggest that Meroz is either a mistaken reading for Maron (Josh 11:5; 12:19) or Shimron Meron (Josh 12:20).[58] Regarding the identification of Meroz, Gass reviews a wide variety of suggested alternatives and concludes that the site cannot be identified with certainty and that the spelling of the toponym itself might have been altered for poetic reasons.[59] This may well be the case, but if so, it remains possible that Meroz is a corrupted form of the name Maron, whether the corruption is accidental or deliberate. Maron is preserved at Marun er-Ras and perhaps located at Tell el-Khureibeh.[60]

Many suggestions have been offered regarding the identity of Meroz. Of these, the site of Mazar is the most compelling. Mazar is located near the events (on the western side of Mount Gilboa), inhabited during the correct timeframe (Middle Bronze through Iron II periods), and may possibly preserve the name Meroz through metathesis of the final two consonants.[61] However, there may be a better alternative.

Abel suggested that Meroz should be identified with Khirbet Marus to the northwest of Hazor on account of the similarity of the name.[62] This identification is usually rejected as Khirbet Marus (Meroth of Josephus, *J.W.* 2.573; 3.40 [Meloth]; *Life* 188), which was only occupied from the second century BC.[63] Around one mile (2 km) to the southeast of Khirbet Marus sits the ruin of Tell er-Rih or Tel Mashav. Tel Mashav has never been excavated, but it appears to have been founded in the Middle Bronze Age and fortified in the Iron II, and perhaps settled during both the Late Bronze and Iron I.[64] During the periods of Hazor's strength (Middle–Late Bronze and Iron IIA–B), Tel Mashav likely functioned as a fortress connected with Hazor, as the site is strategically situated above a main road connecting Hazor to Upper Galilee with views over much of the Huleh Valley and the roads leading to Hazor.[65] If this rationale is correct and Meroz can be identified with Tel Mashav, then it is possible to understand that Meroz in Judg 5:23 is a reference to a particular town connected to the Israelites that was

57. Alt suggested that Meroz should be understood as a Canaanite entity who had failed to enter the fight against Sisera's force (Albrecht Alt, "Meros," *ZAW* 58 [1941]: 244–47).

58. See discussion in Gaß, *Ortsnamen*, 259–63.

59. Gaß, *Ortsnamen*, 259–63.

60. See discussion in Chris McKinny, "The Archaeology and Historical Geography of the Slain Kings of Joshua 12," in this volume.

61. "Mazar" is a common Arabic name that refers to a shrine or Islamic religious structure. For a summary of the different options, see Gaß, *Ortsnamen*, 259–63. For the archaeology of the site, see Nehemia Tzori and Noy Shemesh (foreword), *Archeological Survey of Israel, Map 62: Map of Ein Harod*, ed. Ofer Sion (Jerusalem: Israel Antiquities Authority, 2015), site 34, http://survey.antiquities.org.il/index_Eng.html#/MapSurvey/2141.

62. Félix-Marie Abel, *Géographie de la Palestine* (Paris: Librairie Lecoffre, 1938), 2:305.

63. Zvi Ilan, "The Location of Meroth: A Fortified Settlement on the Galilee Border," *Qadmoniot* 16.2–3 (62–63) (1983): 83–85 [טו]; Ilan, "Meroth," *NEAEHL* 3:1028–31.

64. Stepansky, *Archeological Survey of Israel, Map 18: Map of Rosh Pina*, sites 5 and 7; Shlomit Bechar and Uri Berger, "Tel Mashav: The Eyes of Tel Hazor," *West & East* 3 (2018): 9–23.

65. Bechar and Berger, "Tel Mashav."

in immediate proximity to Hazor (Judg 4:2, 23–34).[66]

SUMMARY

The prose and poetic versions of Deborah and Barak's battle against Sisera and Jabin present several historical and geographical problems. In this chapter, I have offered several solutions to these problems. First, because archaeological surveys reveal a number of Iron I sites around Hazor, it is possible to conclude that Jabin II of Hazor ruled from Hazor or in its general vicinity, despite the lack of significant Iron I remains in the upper city of Hazor. Second, Harosheth Haggoyim may be a regional term for the western portion of the Jezreel Valley, as has been suggested by many scholars. On the other hand, the presence of Silet el-Khartiyeh to the southeast of Taanach would seem to allow for a specific site in this same region. The nearby site of Khirbet Yannun fits these details, particularly if Harosheth Haggoyim (Judg 4:2, 13, 16) is to be related to Goyim of Galilee (Josh 12:22). Also, Tell Salem is situated between Megiddo and Taanach (Judg 5:19) and was a major site in the Iron I, making it an excellent candidate for the seat of Sisera within the region of "Goyim of Galilee."[67] Third, I have argued that the Kishon River was localized with both the Nahr el-Muqatta below Mount Carmel (1 Kgs 18:40) and the plain between Mount Tabor and the hill of Moreh (Judg 4:7, 13; 5:21; Ps 83:9), which was also where the town Kishion (Tell Qasyun) was located (Josh 19:20; 21:28; 1 Chr 6:72). In my view, the Kishon River was understood as the main drainage system of the Jezreel Valley in both the Bible and later sources (e.g., Jerome in the *Epitaph of St. Paula*, Letter of Aristeas, etc.) Fourth, I agree with past suggestions that locate Kedesh in Naphtali (Judg 4:6, 9, 11; Khirbet Qadish) and the Tree/Oak in Zaanannim to the northeast of Mount Tabor, while indicating the geopolitical significance of nomadic Heber of the Kenites (Judg 4:11). Fifth, while not being definitive, I offer the new suggestion that Meroz (Judg 5:23) may be related to Tel Mashav, a Bronze and Iron Age fortress between Khirbet Marus and Hazor. These observations allow us to better understand the geographical and archaeological background of the story of Deborah, Barak, and Jael—a story that took place over a large swath of the Jezreel Valley and Lower Galilee.

BIBLIOGRAPHY

Abel, Félix-Marie. *Géographie de la Palestine*. 2 vols. Paris: Librairie Lecoffre, 1938.

———. *Géographie de la Palestine: Géographie Physique et Historique*. 3rd ed. 2 vols. Paris: Gabalda, 1967.

Aharoni, Yohanan. *The Land of the Bible: A Historical Geography*. Translated by Anson F. Rainey. Rev. and enl. ed. Philadelphia: Westminster, 1979.

Ahituv, Shmuel. *Canaanite Toponyms in Ancient Egyptian Documents*. Jerusalem: Magnes Press, 1984.

Albright, William F. "Some Additional Notes on the Song of Deborah." *Jour-*

66. Stepansky identifies the site with Ramah of Naphtali (Josh 19:36), but this seems unlikely given the fact that Ramah should probably be identified near Rameh in Upper Galilee (Stepansky, *Archeological Survey of Israel, Map 18: Map of Rosh Pina*, site 7); see Aharoni, *Land of the Bible*, 283.

67. Tell Salem is also possibly Gath Rimmon of Manasseh that is mentioned in Josh 21:25. See discussion in McKinny, "Historical Geography of the Levitical Towns" in this volume.

nal of the Palestine Oriental Society 2 (1922): 284–85.

Alt, Albrecht. "Meros." *ZAW* 58 (1941): 244–47.

Bechar, Shlomit, and Uri Berger. "Tel Mashav: The Eyes of Tel Hazor." *West & East* 3 (2018): 9–23.

Ben-Ami, Doron. "Hazor at the Beginning of the Iron Age." *NEA* 76.2 (2013): 101–4.

Ben-Tor, Amnon, and Sharon Zuckerman. "Hazor at the End of the Late Bronze Age: Back to Basics." *BASOR* 350 (2008): 1–6.

Ben-Yosef, Erez. "The Architectural Bias in Current Biblical Archaeology." *VT* 69.3 (2019): 361–87.

Ben-Yosef, Erez, and Aaron Greener. "Edom's Copper Mines in Timna: Their Significance in the 10th Century." *TheTorah.Com*, 2018. https://thetorah.com/edoms-copper-mines-in-timna-their-significance-in-the-10th-century/.

Bonechi, Marco. "Relations Amicales Syro-Palestiniennes: Mari et Hasor Au XVIII e Siècle Av. JC." Pages 9–22 in *Recueil d'études En l'honneur de Michel Fleury*. Edited by J.-M. Durand. Paris: Société pour l'Étude du Proche-Orient Ancien, 1992.

Cohen-Arnon, C., and Ruth Amiran. "Excavations at Tel Qishon: Preliminary Report on the 1977–1978 Seasons." *Eretz-Israel* 15 (1981): 205–12.

Conder, Claude R. *Tent Work in Palestine: A Record of Discovery and Adventure*. London: Richard Bentley and Son, 1878.

Conder, Claude R., and H. H. Kitchener. *The Survey of Western Palestine*. 3 vols. London: The Committee of the Palestine Exploration Fund, 1881–83.

Fantalkin, Alexander, and Israel Finkelstein. "The Date of Abandonment and Territorial Affiliation of Khirbet Qeiyafa: An Update." *TA* 44.1 (2017): 53–60.

Faust, Avraham. "The Large Stone Structure in the City of David: A Reexamination." *ZDPV* 126.2 (2010): 116–30.

Feig, Nurit. "Tel 'Agol." *Hadashot Arkheologiyot* 133 (2021): n.p. http://www.hadashot-esi.org.il/report_detail_eng.aspx?id=26054&mag_id=133.

Finkelstein, Israel. "El-Aḥwat: A Fortified Sea People City?" *IEJ* 52.2 (2002): 187–99.

———. "Hazor at the End of the Late Bronze Age. A Reassessment." *UF* 37 (2005): 341–50.

———. "The Large Stone Structure in Jerusalem: Reality versus Yearning." *ZDPV* 127.1 (2011): 1–10.

Frankel, Rafael. "Kishon (Place)." *ABD* 4:89.

———. "An Oil Press at Tel Safsafot." *TA* 15.1 (1988): 77–91.

Gadot, Yuval, and Yotam Tepper. *Archeological Survey of Israel, Map 49: Map of Regavim*. Edited by Liat Weinblum and Leticia Barda. Jerusalem: Israel Antiquities Authority, 2009. http://survey.antiquities.org.il/index_Eng.html#/MapSurvey/1.

Gal, Zvi. *Archeological Survey of Israel, Map 45: Map of 'En Dor*. Edited by Ayala Sussmann. Jerusalem: Israel Antiquities Authority, 2013. https://survey.antiquities.org.il/index_Eng.html#/MapSurvey/49.

———. *The Lower Galilee during the Iron Age*. Winona Lake, IN: Eisenbrauns, 1992.

Garfinkel, Yosef. "The 10th Century BCE in Judah: Archaeology and the Biblical Tradition." *Jerusalem Journal of Archaeology* 1 (2021): 126–54.

Gaß, Erasmus. "The Deborah-Barak Composition (Jdg 4–5): Some Topographical Reflections." *PEQ* 149.4 (2017): 326–35.

———. *Die Ortsnamen Des Richterbuchs in Historischer Und Redaktioneller Perspektive*. Wiesbaden: Verlag, 2005.

Hartal, Moshe. "Rosh Pinna." *Hadashot Arkheologiot* 121 (2009): n.p. http://www.hadashot-esi.org.il/report_detail_eng.aspx?id=1099&mag_id=115.

Horowitz, Wayne, Takayoshi Oshima, and Seth L. Sanders. *Cuneiform in Canaan: Cuneiform Sources from the Land of Israel in Ancient Times*. Jerusalem: Israel Exploration Society, 2006.

Ilan, Zvi. "The Location of Meroth: A Fortified Settlement on the Galilee Border." *Qadmoniot* 16.2–3 (62–63) (1983): 83–85 [טז].

James, Peter. "The Levantine War-Records of Ramesses III: Changing Attitudes, Past, Present and Future." *Antiguo Oriente* 15 (2017): 57–148.

Janzen, Mark, and Chris McKinny. "An Overview of the Historical Geography of the Exodus and Wilderness Itinerary." Pages 705–739 in *Lexham Geographic Commentary on the Pentateuch*. Edited by Barry J. Beitzel. Bellingham, WA: Lexham Press, 2023.

Jerome. *Jerome's Epitaph on Paula: A Commentary on the Epitaphium Sanctae Paulae with an Introduction, Text, and Translation*. Translated by Andrew Caine. Oxford: Oxford University Press, 2013.

Kallai, Z. "En-Dor / עין דור." *Eretz-Israel* 16 (1982): 168–70.

Kitchen, Kenneth A. *On the Reliability of the Old Testament*. Grand Rapids: Eerdmans, 2003.

Kochavi, Moshe. "Khirbet Kadesh: Kadesh Naftali." *Yediot Bahaqirat Eretz-Israel Weatiqoteha* 27.3 (1963): 165–72.

Krahmalkov, Charles R. "Exodus Itinerary Confirmed by Egyptian Evidence." *BAR* 20 (1994): 54–62, 79.

Levy, Thomas E., Mohammad Najjar, and Erez Ben-Yosef, eds. *New Insights Into the Iron Age Archaeology of Edom, Southern Jordan*. 2 vols. Los Angeles: Cotsen Institute of Archaeology at UCLA, 2014.

Maeir, Aren M. *"In the Midst of the Jordan": The Jordan Valley During the Middle Bronze Age (circa 2000–1500 BCE): Archaeological and Historical Correlates*. Vienna: Verlag der Österreichischen Akademie der Wissenschaften, 2010.

Mazar, Amihai. "Jerusalem in the 10th Cent. B.C.E.: A Response." *ZDPV* 136.2 (2020): 139–51.

Mazar, Benjamin. "Beth She'arim, Gaba, and Harosheth of the Peoples." *Hebrew Union College Annual* 24 (1952): 75–84.

Mazar, Eilat. *Discovering the Solomonic Wall in Jerusalem: A Remarkable Archaeological Adventure*. Jerusalem: Shoham Academic Research and Publication, 2011.

McKinny, Chris, Steven D. Anderson, Kris Udd, and Todd Bolen. *Photo Companion to the Bible: Judges*. BiblePlaces, 2019.

McKinny, Chris. "The Archaeology and Historical Geography of the Slain Kings of Joshua 12." In vol. 1 of *Lexham Geographic Commentary on the Historical Books*. Edited by Barry J. Beitzel. Bellingham, WA: Lexham Press, 2025.

———. "The Historical Geography of the Levitical Towns in Joshua 21 and

1 Chronicles 6:54–81).” In vol. 1 of *Lexham Geographic Commentary on the Historical Books*. Edited by Barry J. Beitzel. Bellingham, WA: Lexham Press, 2025.

Na'aman, Nadav. “Literary and Topographical Notes on the Battle of Kishon (Judges IV-V).” *VT* 40.4 (1990): 423–36.

Notley, R. Steven, and Ze'ev Safrai. *Eusebius, Onomasticon: A Triglott Edition with Notes and Commentary*. Leiden: Brill, 2005.

Peterson, John L. “Kishion (Place).” *ABD* 4:89.

Pringle, Denys. “The Spring of the Cresson in Crusading History.” Pages 231–40 in *Dei Gesta per Francos: Etudes Sur Les Croisades Dédiées à Jean Richard: Crusade Studies in Honour of Jean Richard*. Edited by Michel Balard, Benjamin Z. Kedar, and Jonathan S. C. Riley-Smith. New York: Routledge, 2001.

Rainey, Anson F., and Steven Notley. *The Sacred Bridge: Carta's Atlas of the Biblical World*. Jerusalem: Carta, 2006.

Saarisalo, Aapeli. *The Boundary between Issachar and Naphtali: An Archaeological and Literary Study of Israel's Settlement in Canaan*. Helsinki: Suomalaisen Tiedeakatemian Toimituksia, 1927.

Simons, Jan J. *The Geographical and Topographical Texts of the Old Testament*. 2 vols. Leiden: Brill, 1959.

———. *Handbook for the Study of Egyptian Topographical Lists Relating to Western Asia*. Leiden: Brill, 1937.

Stepansky, Yosef. *Archeological Survey of Israel, Map 18: Map of Rosh Pina*. Edited by Ofer Sion, Liat Weinblum, and Ronnie Avidov. Jerusalem: Israel Antiquities Authority, 2012. http://survey.antiquities.org.il/index_Eng.html#/MapSurvey/2.

———. “Rosh Pinna.” *Hadashot Arkheologiot* 120 (2008): n.p. http://www.hadashot-esi.org.il/report_detail_eng.aspx?id=876&mag_id=114.

Stern, Ephraim, and Itzhaq Beit Arieh. “Excavations at Tel Kedesh (Tell Abu Qudeis).” *TA* 6.1–2 (1979): 1–25.

Tzori, Nehemia, and Noy Shemesh (foreward). *Archeological Survey of Israel, Map 62: Map of Ein Harod*. Edited by Ofer Sion. Jerusalem: Israel Antiquities Authority, 2015. http://survey.antiquities.org.il/index_Eng.html#/MapSurvey/2141.

Velde, Charles W. M. van de. *Memoir to Accompany the Map of the Holy Land*. Gotha: Justus Perthes, 1858.

Wills, Lawrence M. *Judith*. Hermeneia. Minneapolis: Fortress, 2019.

Zertal, Adam. “The Arunah Pass.” Pages 342–56 in *Egypt, Canaan and Israel: History, Imperialism, Ideology and Literature: Proceedings of a Conference at the University of Haifa, 3–7 May 2009*. Edited by Shay Bar, Dan'el Kahn, and JJ Shirley. Leiden: Brill, 2011.

———, ed. *El-Ahwat: A Fortified Site from the Early Iron Age Near Nahal 'Iron, Israel: Excavations 1993–2000*. Leiden: Brill, 2012.

Zertal, Adam, and Nivi Mirkam. *The Manasseh Hill Country Survey, Vol. 3: From Nahal 'Iron to Nahal Shechem*. Edited by Shay Bar. Leiden: Brill, 2016.

Zimbalist, N. “Kishon and Kishyon.” *Bulletin of the Jewish Palestine Exploration Society* 13.1/2 (1946): 28–51.

Zori, Nehemia. *The Land of Issachar: Archaeological Survey*. Jerusalem: Israel Exploration Society, 1977.

CHAPTER 23

GEOGRAPHIC METAPHORS AND SIMILES USED FOR GOD IN THE HISTORICAL BOOKS OF THE HEBREW BIBLE

Judg 5:5, 1 Sam 2:3, 2 Sam 22:2; Gen 49:24, Deut 32:4, 32:30–31

J. Carl Laney

KEY POINTS

- Biblical writers describe God by way of analogy.
- Metaphors and similes enable us to know God better.
- Israel's God is "rock like" in character.

INTRODUCTION

If someone asked you to describe God, how would you begin? If you asked a theologian or perhaps a seminary student, you would probably hear God described in traditional, theological categories. One might say, "God is omniscient, omnipotent, omnipresent, immortal, eternal, sovereign, and holy." While there is absolutely nothing wrong with these descriptions of God, they tend to be derived from Greek theological and philosophical categories. Barry Beitzel comments, "One might call these logical or empirical divine attributes, perceived essentially by way of our mind or our intellect."[1] Even the more familiar abstractions used to describe God, such as "awesome," "majestic," "perfect," or "wonderful," seem to align with the logical and empirical categories.

As we read and explore the Hebrew Bible, we discover that the biblical writers tend to describe God by way of anal-

1. Barry Beitzel, personal correspondence (9/20/2018).

ogy. God is "a rock," "a shelter," "a high tower," "a fortress," "a shepherd," "a warrior," or "a king." Describing God by way of analogy, using metaphor and simile, appeals to a person's senses, experiences, and emotions. These literary devices move the heart, not merely the intellect. When the Bible says, "God is my rock," it leads readers to ponder what a rock is like, what a rock does, and what a rock provides. We are led to reflect on how God has been rock-like in our own lives and spiritual experiences.

Similarly, because God is a spirit without a physical body, it is difficult to think of him as a real person. Therefore, the Hebrew Bible makes use of anthropomorphic language to help us understand who God is and what he is like. While God does not have hands or feet, referring to God's "hands" provides something tangible and familiar with which we can relate. When the Bible says, "Behold, I have inscribed you on the palms of my hands" (Isa 49:16), God is telling his people that they are before him always, and that it is impossible for them to be forgotten.[2]

It should not be surprising that many of the metaphors used to describe God are geographic. From the time of God's great promise to Abraham (Gen 12:2–3), the land of Israel has had an important place in God's dealings with his people. It would not be too much to say that God has used the land (אֶרֶץ, *erets*) of Israel to reveal something about his character and attributes. While much is revealed about God using the traditional theological and systematic categories, this article will explore the metaphors and similes used of God which are *geographic* in nature.[3] This chapter explores these metaphors as found in the Pentateuch and the historical books of the Old Testament.

EXAMPLES OF METAPHOR

The Bible contains a variety of images that the authors of Scripture used to communicate their ideas. A "simile" is a figure of speech which makes a comparison using *like* or *as*. "God is *like* a mountain." A "metaphor," on the other hand, is a literary figure which requires the transfer of an idea from the image or symbol to the reality being described, as in "The Lord is my Shepherd."

Lauren Winner observes that the Bible's inclusion of so many figures for God is "both an invitation and a caution."[4] The invitation is to discover a deeper understanding of who God is and what our relationship with him might become. The caution, she adds, is "assuming that any one image of God, whatever truth it holds, adequately describes God."[5] This may be why the Bible sometimes stacks a series of metaphors, as in Ps 18:2, "The

2. All Scripture quotations are from New American Standard Bible (NASB) unless otherwise noted.

3. For an introduction to the geography of the land of Israel, see Carl G. Rasmussen, *Zondervan Essential Atlas of the Bible* (Grand Rapids: Zondervan, 2013), 10–17; John A. Beck, *Discovery House Bible Atlas* (Grand Rapids: Our Daily Bread Publishing, 2015), 19–41.

4. Lauren Winner, "Why God Uses Metaphors to Describe Himself: Guest Post by Lauren Winner," *Bible Gateway Blog*, ed. Jonathan Petersen, 8 February 2016, https://www.biblegateway.com/blog/2016/02/why-god-uses-metaphors-to-describe-himself-guest-post-by-lauren-winner/.

5. Winner, "Why God Uses Metaphors."

Mount Hermon

Lord is my rock and my fortress and my deliverer, my God, my rock in whom I take refuge; my shield and the horn of my salvation, my stronghold." This text sends a clear message that God's character is multifaceted and cannot be limited to just *one* image.

Acknowledging the literary convention of simile and metaphor, we must be careful to void rigid literalism when interpreting the images used to describe God. Moses charged the Israelites in Deut 32:18, "You neglected the Rock who begot you." This powerful image could be confusing if we fail to appreciate the *poetic* genre of Moses' song in Deut 32. In this example of synonymous parallelism, the second line of a verse provides clarification for the first line, repeating the same thought, but with different words. The "Rock" is identified in the second line of Deut 32:18 as "the God who gave you birth." God is rock-like in character and the source of Israel's national life.

While God's greatness and majesty are ultimately beyond comparison (Exod 15:11), the authors of Scripture use metaphors and similes to provide readers with better visualization and appreciation of his divine attributes.

The Pentateuch

God is presented in Genesis as the Creator of the land, sea, plants, animals, and gardens, but in no way is he identified *with* his creation in the early chapters of Genesis. While he created all things, God is clearly distinct *from* his creation. There are, however, geographical place names associated with God's attributes. Abraham called Mount Moriah *Yahweh Yeraeh* (יְהוָה יִרְאֶה), "the Lord Will Provide," commemorating God's provision of a substitute for Isaac (Gen 22:14). Jacob called Luz *Bethel* (בֵּית־אֵל), "House of God," commemorating the encounter he had with God there (Gen 28:19; 35:7). God's sovereignty over physical geogra-

Aerial View of Masada

phy is evidenced by sending Joseph from one geographical region to another—from Canaan to Egypt (Gen 45:8). The journeys of the patriarchs through the land may have been part of the divine plan to help them understand what they had been given and the importance of embracing God's promise (Gen 12:2; 17:8). Probably the strongest metaphor used for God in Genesis is when he is called "the Stone (אֶבֶן, *even*) of Israel" (Gen 49:24). While God is more often referred to as the "Rock of Israel," in this poetic chapter of Genesis, Jacob is highlighting God's strength and steadfastness. Like a hard basalt or granite stone, the God of Israel will not be easily shattered or worn down with time.

Three times in Exodus, God associates himself with a mountain. When Moses was grazing sheep in the wilderness of Sinai, he "came to Horeb, the mountain (הַר, *har*) of God" (Exod 3:1). Later, Jethro brought Moses' wife, Zipporah, and their two sons, to "the mountain of God" (Exod 18:5). In Exod 24:13, Moses and Joshua ascended the "mountain of God" (Exod 24:13). While none of these texts use the word *har* as a metaphor for God, there is a clear association between God and this geographical location. Why would God associate himself with a mountain? Mountains display the greatness and grandeur of the Creator. Who cannot gaze on 9,200-foot (2,804 m) snowcapped Mount Hermon without thinking of the greatness of the one who made the mountain? Who could not peer into the wilderness of Sinai from 7,498 feet (2,285 m), Jebel Musa (the traditional Mount Sinai), and not be in awe of the Creator God who revealed himself to Moses and the people of Israel in this place?

Since Leviticus is focused on the holiness of God and the holiness of those who share with him in covenant relationship, geographic metaphors are absent from the covenant stipulations presented in

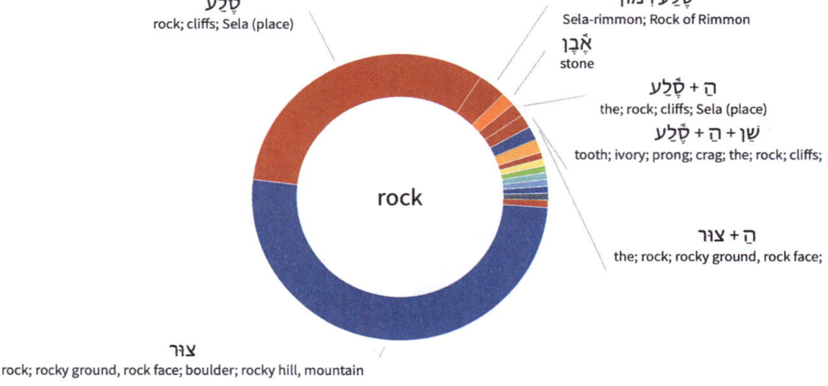

this book. While God is likened to the "horns of a wild ox" (Num 23:22, 24:8) and a crouching lion that none "dares arouse" (Num 24:9), there are no geographical metaphors in Numbers used to describe him.

Although Deuteronomy makes minimal use of geographical metaphors to describe God, Yahweh's association with the land of Israel is prominently featured. He "set the land" before his people Israel to take as their possession (Deut 1:21; 3:18). God's instructions to be generous to the poor are linked to the reminder of God's generosity in giving the land to his people (Deut 15:7). Repeatedly, it is emphasized that the land of Israel is God's gift (Deut 25:19; 26:1). Because the Song of Moses (Deut 32:1–43) is poetic, it is not surprising to find metaphors for God there. Early in the song, Moses proclaims the greatness of God by calling him "the Rock" (Deut 32:4). While the stone (*even*) imagery was used in Gen 49:24, here Moses uses the Hebrew word *tsur* (צוּר). The particular emphasis of this word is that of a *large* rock or boulder. God is not just any old rock or pebble but "the" Rock! Although the kind of rock used in the metaphor cannot be identified by the Hebrew word, Moses would have been most familiar with the granite mountains of southern Sinai, which feature giant monoliths and massive boulders.

Later in the song, Moses uses the "rock" metaphor to remind the people of how Israel "scorned the Rock of his salvation" when they provoked God by their idolatry (Deut 32:15). The metaphor is repeated in 32:18 but with a bold twist. While God is presented as Father in the Hebrew Bible (e.g., Isa 63:16; 64:8; Jer 3:4, 19; 31:9; Mal 1:6; 2:10), "to whom Israel owed its existence as a people," here God is presented as a mother who travails in labor and lovingly cares for the child for whom she has given birth.[6] The God of Israel is set in stark contrast with rock-made idols, which can neither give life nor protect humans (Deut 32:37–39).

The Historical Books

The book of Joshua is focused on the conquest of Canaan and distribution of the

6. Joseph H. Hertz, ed., *The Pentateuch and Haftorahs* (London: Soncino Press, 1981), 899.

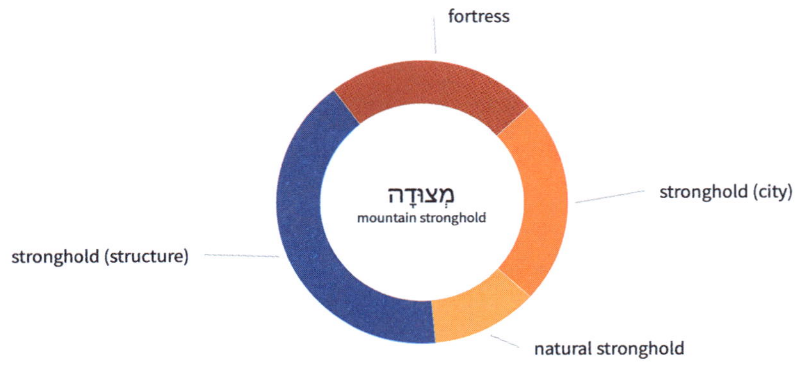

land. There is an understandable absence of geographical metaphors for God here. What is true for the book of Joshua is nearly true for Judges, except for the Song of Deborah that features a poetic description of the heroics of Deborah and Jael in the defeat of the Canaanites. Here, the poet tells of how "the mountains quaked at the presence of the LORD" (Judg 5:5) as God "marched" from Seir and Edom (Judg 5:4). Although the mountains and place names are not metaphors for the deity, they certainly allude to God's sovereignty over and association with the physical geography.

The most powerful imagery for God in the book of Ruth is not geographical, but anatomical. Boaz prays that Ruth would find full provision under the protective "wings" of the God of Israel (Ruth 2:12). The contrast between Israel and Moab should not lead readers to conclude that Yahweh and his sovereignty are geographically limited. He is everywhere present (Ps 139:7–12).

One of the most poetic, as well as theological, passages in the historical books is the prayer of Hannah after she has fulfilled her vow by giving Samuel to the house of the Lord for lifelong Nazirite service. After declaring God's holiness and uniqueness, she proclaims, "Nor is there any rock (*tsur*) like our God" (1 Sam 2:2). This is the same word used by Jacob in Gen 49:24 and describes God as a massive rock or boulder. After giving birth to little Samuel in answer to her prayers, Hannah must have wondered if giving her child to the Lord was the right thing to do. There must have been some sleepless nights as she wrestled with her decision, but her confidence in God as her solid and steadfast "rock" appears to have put her mind at rest, and she was able to fulfill her vow. Hannah's prayer (1 Sam 2:1–10) reflects her personal knowledge of God and her rock-solid faith in his salvation and sovereignty.

The grand finale of the books of Samuel is David's psalm, in which he praises God for delivering him from his enemies. Here, David piles metaphor on top of metaphor to praise the divine attributes and benevolent actions of God. "The LORD is my rock (סֶלַע, *sela*) and my fortress (מְצוּדָה, *metsudah*) and my deliverer" (2 Sam 22:2). David uses the term "rock" (*sela*) again in Pss 18:3 and 34:4 (see also Pss 42:10; 71:3). The Hebrew *sela* is used for solitary rock, as in a rocky spur, cliff, or peak. Once again, the metaphor communicates stability, reliability, and

Granite Casing on Menkaure's Pyramid at Giza

security. The second word for rock, *metsudah*, refers to a "mountain stronghold," like "the stronghold of Zion" (2 Sam 5:7, Ps 31:3). The word *metsudah* bears a phonetic resemblance to a well-known mountain stronghold known today as Masada. It is possible that David was familiar with this place (1 Sam 22:4), which was later fortified by King Herod and served as the last stand of the Zealots during the Jewish Revolt (AD 70–73).[7] In 2 Sam 22:3, David uses the Hebrew word *tsur* to describe the steadfast character of God who is his "refuge," "shield," and "horn of salvation." Each of these metaphors highlight the protection and security found in one's relationship with God. The rock-like character of God is repeatedly featured by David (2 Sam 22:32, 47).

In 1 Kgs 19:8, Elijah is found at the "mountain of God," which was featured in Exod 3:1; 18:5; and 24:13. But it would

7. Josephus, *J.W.* 7.280–303.

Aerial View of the Judean Wilderness

be wrong to associate God with the mountains and not also the valleys (1 Kgs 20:28), for his sovereignty is not limited by physical terrain. Not only is God sometimes associated with a geographic feature of the land, but on occasion a place is given a name which reflects what God has done. The Valley of Berakah, "Valley of Blessing," was so named as the place where the people assembled to *bless* the Lord for giving them victory over their enemies (2 Chr 20:26). The absence of any metaphors for the deity in Ezra, Nehemiah, and Esther is due to the nature of the literature, particularly the absence of poetry. In Esther, God is not mentioned at all but presumed to be working in the background.

GOD AS ISRAEL'S ROCK

The most frequent geographic metaphor for God in the Torah and historical books is "rock." In the ancient world, where dynamite and power drills were unknown, "rock ... was a ready image of impervious solidarity."[8] The word appears in the NASB translation forty-two times. But what kind of rock do the biblical writers have in mind? As there are several different Hebrew words which are translated "rock" (including *tsur, sela,* and *even*), so there are several varieties of rock with which the original readers would have been familiar.[9]

When Moses used the word "rock" in the Torah, he would most likely have in mind the granite rock which makes up the mountains of southern Sinai. Granite is an igneous rock that is hard, tough, and massive when found it its original, mountainous context. These properties have made granite the stone of choice for buildings and monuments since ancient times. Moses would have been very familiar

8. Leland Ryken, James C. Wilhoit, and Tremper Longman III, eds., *Dictionary of Biblical Imagery* (Downers Grove, IL: InterVarsity, 1998), 732.

9. James M. Monson and Steven P. Lancaster, *Geobasics in the Land of Israel* (Rockford, IL: Biblical Backgrounds, 2008), 25.

TABLE 1: GOD AS ISRAEL'S ROCK

Rock	*Quality*	*Metaphorical Meaning*
Granite	Hard, massive, beautiful	God is strong, powerful
Senonian	Soft, chalky, easily eroded	Unlike Israel's God
Cenomanian	Hard, enduring. Useful for building, source of springs	God is dependable; a protector of his people
Eocene	Soft, inaccessible	Unlike Israel's God
Basalt	Hard, rugged, and durable. Useful for building and making tools	God is strong, faithful

with the varicolored granite temples of Egypt, as well as the granite mountains in the Sinai.

When the Israelites arrived in Canaan, they would have been introduced to several varieties of limestone rock. After the conquest of Jericho and Ai, they would have ascended into the mountains of Canaan through senonian limestone, which is a soft, chalky, and easily eroded. Hills made from senonian chalk weather under the elements and collapse. The barren, rounded hills of the Judean wilderness were probably not what David had in mind when he likened God to a rock.

Upon reaching the central hill country, the Israelites would have encountered an uplifted bed of cenomanian limestone which is hard and enduring. With the right tools and skills, cenomanian limestone can be easily quarried and shaped. These qualities made it the building material of choice for the ancient Israelites. Herod remodeled Israel's temple using cenomanian limestone, some of which endures to this day at Jerusalem's Western Wall. While being the strongest of Israel's limestone, cenomanian is water permeable and serves as a massive underground reservoir. The clear, cold water stored in Israel's cenomanian limestone breaks out in abundant springs of "living water" (Jer 2:13) and can be tapped by deep wells (John 4:10). Over time, cenomanian limestone dissolves forming caves which offer refuge and protection (1 Sam 24:3). These features of cenomanian limestone enrich the metaphor of God as Israel's strong, dependable "rock" and protector.

Expanding westward into the foothills of Israel, the Shephelah, the Israelites would have discovered a third kind of limestone known today as eocene. Like senonian, this variety of limestone is a soft chalk that could be accessed only by breaking through the hard nari crust which forms on the surface of the eocene. It is unlikely that this variety of rock would be in the mind of biblical authors when describing God as Israel's "rock."

The three Israelite tribes assigned to region of Galilee, Issachar, Zebulun, and Naphtali, would have discovered a hard, black, basalt rock which came as a result of volcanic activity in the Golan region northeast of the Sea of Galilee. The basalt rock of the Bashan (Golan) region makes for some rugged, boulder-strewn terrain. But in time, this rock weathers into a rich soil suitable for agriculture and grazing (Amos 4:1). Basalt is a durable building material and can be shaped into a variety of stone implements, including grind-

Cenomanian Limestone

Eocene Chalk in the Shephelah, Capped with Nari Limestone

Grain Mill Made of Basalt

ing stones, millstones, and bowls. Basalt rock is featured in the massive defensive gate at Bethsaida and the beautifully decorated synagogue at Chorazin. The features of basalt rock commend it as a powerful image for Israel's strong, creative, and faithful God.

While God is visualized "like" a rock in the imagery of the Hebrew Bible, Moses makes it clear that he *is* a rock (Deut 32:30–31). He is our immovable foundation in the face of insecurity and doubt. He is our refuge and stronghold in the face of threats from evildoers. "In an interplay of these symbols," Earle Ellis observes, "it is not surprising to find God spoken of as a rock who gives security and safety to his people" (see 2 Sam 22:32).[10]

CONCLUSION

While Westerners are much more inclined to describe God with traditional, theological terms, the biblical writers made use of simile and metaphor to provide a more visual and experiential understanding of God. Although appearing with greater frequency in the poetic books, these figures make a significant contribution to the theology of the historical books, especially the metaphor describing God as Israel's steadfast and enduring "rock."

BIBLIOGRAPHY

Beck, John A. *Discovery House Bible Atlas*. Grand Rapids: Our Daily Bread Publishing, 2015.

Ellis, E. Earle. "Rock." Page 1343 in vol. 3 of *The Illustrated Bible Dictionary*. Edited by James D. Douglas. Downers Grove, IL: InterVarsity, 1980.

Hertz, Joseph H. ed. *The Pentateuch and Haftorahs*. London: Soncino Press, 1981.

Monson, James M., and Steven P. Lancaster. *Geobasics in the Land of the Bible*. Rockford, IL: Biblical Backgrounds, 2008.

Rasmussen, Carl G. *Zondervan Essential Atlas of the Bible*. Grand Rapids: Zondervan, 2013.

Ryken, Leland, James C. Wilhoit, and Tremper Longman III, eds. *Dictionary of Biblical Theology*. Downers Grove, IL: InterVarsity, 1998.

Winner, Lauren. "Why God Uses Metaphors to Describe Himself: Guest Post by Lauren Winner." *BibleGateway Blog*, 8 February 2016. https://www.biblegateway.com/blog/2016/02/why-god-uses-metaphors-to-describe-himself-guest-post-by-lauren-winner/.

10. Earle E. Ellis, "Rock," in *The Illustrated Bible Dictionary*, ed. James D. Douglas (Downers Grove, IL: InterVarsity, 1980), 3:1343.

CHAPTER 24

A GEOGRAPHICAL ANALYSIS OF THE JUDGESHIP OF GIDEON

Judg 6–8

John A. Beck

KEY POINTS

- These chapters contain no less than forty-three place names that participate in shaping the story of Gideon and its message.
- The story is told to confirm that one god is enough if your God is the Lord.
- The story highlights Israel's cyclic apostasy by starting and ending in Ophrah.

INTRODUCTION

The story of Gideon is unique. It is the longest story in Judges, and it is built around geographical references—some forty-three place names. Like other stories in Judges, it addresses Israel's unwillingness to trust the Lord and their struggle with the question: is one god enough?[1] Of course, this question was settled by the Lord's declaration (Deut 6:4). But uncertainty endured because Israel adopted the thinking of the polytheistic world around them. For the Canaanites, one god was never enough since they used a pantheon of deities to explain the mysteries of the natural world. Here we see how the Lord used a combination of events and places to passionately seek Israel's return to a correct understanding of who he is.

We will not discuss all forty-three locations but rather those mentioned most frequently and those which make the most vital contribution to the narrative's rhetorical goals. We will see that places are used to highlight Israel's theological confusion and raise our hopes for clearer thinking. They become places that challenge faith, demonstrate the Lord's sufficiency, and confirm absolute

1. Tammi J. Schneider, *Judges*, Berit Olam (Collegeville, MN: The Liturgical Press, 2000), 110.

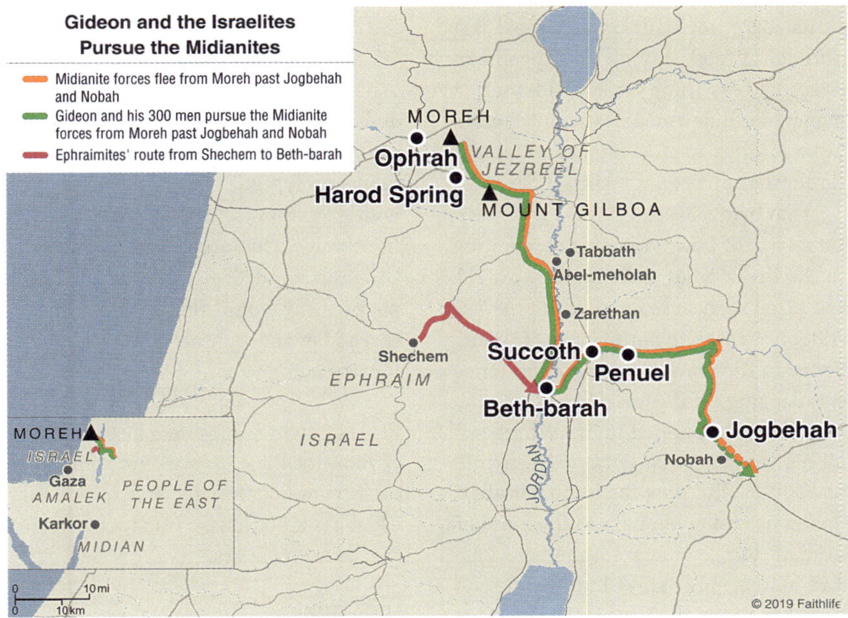

victory over the invaders. But they also illustrate the ongoing problem of tribal cohesion that sends Israel looking for another political solution: monarchy.

OPHRAH

The story begins in Ophrah (Judg 6:11, 24), a community pressured by the invasion of Midianites, Amalekites, and other eastern peoples. But they had a bigger problem. They were struggling with the question of God's identity and sufficiency.

LOCATION

Gideon lived here along with other members of the Abiezrite clan (6:11). This means that our search of Ophrah will take us into the tribal inheritance of Manasseh (Josh 17:2). However, the town's location within Manasseh is unknown. Ophrah of Gideon has been linked to Khirbet Taiyibeh located five miles (8 km) south of Megiddo, or el-Affuleh located within modern Afula at the base of Mount Moreh.[2]

ROLES IN THE STORY

As the story opens, Israel had been hard pressed for seven years because desert-dwelling people, including Midianites and Amalekites, have been invading seasonally during the harvest.[3] Their inva-

2. For Khirbet Taiyibeh, see Carl G. Rasmussen, *Zondervan Atlas of the Bible* (Grand Rapids: Zondervan, 2010), 295. For el-Affuleh, see Yohanan Aharoni, *The Land of the Bible: A Historical Geography*, trans. Anson F. Rainey, rev. and enl. ed. (Philadelphia: Westminster, 1979), 263.

3. The Midianites were a seminomadic people descended from Abraham and Keturah (Gen 25:2) who played a key role in the spice and incense trade from the interior of Arabia (*MAB*, 141). The Amalekites invaded from the area south of Gaza (Anson F. Rainey and R. Steven Notley, *The Sacred Bridge: Carta's Atlas of the Biblical World* [Jerusalem: Carta, 2006], 139).

sions were not bent on conquest but plunder of food, leaving God's people in deep distress (Judg 6:1–6). Gideon had managed to hide a modest amount of grain but was forced to process it in a winepress rather than an open threshing floor (6:11).

That brings us to Ophrah, where we get a taste of how Israel was responding to the invasion of their land by outsiders. What we hear is shocking. Some like Gideon wanted to maintain their confidence in the Lord, but their confidence was flagging. "If the Lord is with us, why has all this happened to us? Where are all his wonders that our ancestors told us about. ... But now the Lord has abandoned us and given us into the hand of Midian" (6:13).[4] It was not the Lord who had abandoned Israel but Israel who had abandoned the Lord (6:1, 7–10). This brings us to the even more shocking response of Gideon's family in Ophrah: they abandoned the Lord in favor of the god Baal, building a worship complex in their town dedicated to Baal and the goddess Asherah (6:25–26).

On the other hand, Ophrah is a place that gives us hope. The "angel of the Lord" appeared to Gideon and demonstrated the authenticity and adequacy of the Lord (6:12–24).[5] Despite his reservations, the Lord turned Gideon into a "mighty warrior" (6:12). His first act of war was theological. He destroyed the sanctuary to Baal and Asherah in Ophrah and built an altar for the Lord (6:27–28). At first, a village mob formed and called for Gideon's death (6:28–32) but then Gideon's father challenged the mob. What kind of a god is Baal if he cannot defend his own sanctuary, even enduring the loss of the altar integral to his food supply![6] Baal worship had become widespread in Israel (6:1). As we watch the changes that occurred in Ophrah by Gideon's hand, we feel hope for God's people. But would this new beginning spread beyond Ophrah?

BASE OF MOUNT GILBOA

The next two scenes take us to the base of Mount Gilboa, to open locations that can accommodate a growing militia that Gideon intends to take into battle against the desert invaders.

LOCATIONS

Gideon camped with his men at the spring of Harod (7:1) below the north face of Mount Gilboa (7:3).[7] This placed them a little over seven miles (11 km) from the invaders camp which was established in the northeastern bay of the Jezreel Valley (6:33; 8:18). Here the Israelite militia could safely hydrate and prepare for battle.

ROLES IN THE STORY

The first scene takes us to a threshing floor (6:37). This would have been a much more efficient place to thresh wheat than the winepress Gideon used earlier. But Gideon traded efficiency for secrecy, hiding his food processing from the invaders. The shift in setting signals the story is headed

4. All biblical quotations are from the New International Version (NIV) unless otherwise noted.

5. For a discussion of the identity of the angel of the Lord, see David M. Howard, *An Introduction to the Old Testament Historical Books* (Chicago: Moody, 1993), 113–16.

6. Daniel I. Block," Judges," *ZIBBCOT* 2:155.

7. Mount Gilead (NIV) appears to be an alternate label for Mount Gilboa. For more on this topic, see Trent C. Butler, *Judges*, WBC (Nashville: Thomas Nelson, 2009), 211–12.

Ein Harod, Spring of Gideon, at the Foot of Mount Gilboa

in the right direction but we don't find Gideon using this facility for threshing as expected; rather the Lord uses it as a stage to affirm for Gideon and for the gathering militia that one God is enough. The message is sent by the manipulation of dewfall. The Lord declared that he controlled both the rain and dew (Deut 11:14–15; 33:13). Baal, the Canaanite god of the storm, also claimed this right. Consequently, by the miraculous manipulation of dew on the fleece, the Lord demonstrated his authenticity and sufficiency at the expense of Baal (Judg 6:39–40).[8] Thus, the threshing floor provided the larger stage that allowed for Gideon and the gathered militia to benefit from this miracle.

But even as the Lord builds faith, he challenges it. We move from the threshing floor to a nearby spring where the Lord proposed a plan that seems outrageous (7:1). In battles like Israel was about to engage, numbers were everything. Given that the tribal militias and the invaders were similarly equipped, it was the army with the most fighters that could absorb the most causalities that would be victorious. We know that the Midianites, Amalekites, and other neighboring peoples already enjoyed the numeric advantage. They are variously described as "swarms of locusts" (6:5), like "sand on the seashore" (7:12) with some 135,000 fighters armed and ready for battle (8:10). Israel's militia totaled 32,000 (7:3), leaving them outnumbered more than four to one. Then the Lord set about reducing Israel's fighting force, first by removing those who were fearful and second by how they drank at the

8. For more see John A. Beck, "Gideon, Dew, and the Narrative-Geographical Shaping of Judges 6:33–40," *Bibliotheca Sacra* 165 (2008): 28–32.

A Winepress in Ancient Israel

spring (7:3–8) until those left totaled only three hundred.[9] His rationale for this unexpected action? "You have too many men. I cannot deliver Midian into their hands, or Israel would boast against me, 'My own strength has saved me.'" (7:2)

Israel had come to the spring to prepare for battle by getting water. The Lord also used this setting to prepare Israel for battle, but not in the way they expected. Here, the Lord used a threshing floor to confirm his identity as the only true God and to reduce Israel's fighting force so he could show his sufficiency.

JEZREEL VALLEY NORTH OF MOUNT MOREH

The next two scenes move us closer to the enemy camp, where the Lord assured Gideon of victory, and then into the enemy camp, where the Lord demonstrated that one God is enough even when outnumbered.

LOCATIONS

From the Harod spring, we move approximately seven miles (11 km) northeast to the enemy camp established north of Mount Moreh in the northeast bay of Jezreel Valley (6:33; 8:1). Mount Moreh is not mentioned in the story but presumed by the directions which the Lord gives Gideon. He is to "go up" (קוּם, *qum*) so that he can "descend" (רֵד, *red*) to the enemy camp. The Hebrew verb for descend is repeated five times (7:8–11), marking the descent into the camp which was "below him in the valley" (7:8). The only way these instructions make sense is if Gideon and his servant, Purah, climb up the southern side of Mount Moreh and descend on the north so that they are near the enemy camp. In similar fashion, Gideon later brought the three hundred soldiers he had divided into three companies over Mount Moreh and placed them in strategic fashion around the enemy camp (7:15–19).

ROLES IN THE STORY

The tension of the story increases as we leave the relative safety of the spring at the base of Mount Gilboa and move closer to the enemy camp. First, the Lord

9. These soldiers do not seem to be sent home but restricted to the camp near the spring until called to engage the fleeing enemy. See Schneider, *Judges*, 112.

Jezreel Valley with the Hill of Moreh in Background

took Gideon and his aide to the southern side of the enemy camp so that they could overhear a conversation between two lookouts (7:13–14). These men were discussing a dream one of them had about a round loaf of barley bread that rolled into their camp and wiped it out. They concluded this could be none other than Gideon, a man who had earlier dismissed his own ability to lead in battle (6:15). The Lord moved Gideon close to the enemy camp and there assured him with the very words of the enemy that he was the mighty warrior who would bring Israel relief.

The tension rises further as Gideon hurried back to camp to rouse the three hundred soldiers so that he could bring them closer to the enemy camp (7:15). He divided the soldiers into three groups of one hundred each, then placed them around the enemy camp in the Jezreel Valley. Each carried a shofar, a torch, and a medium-sized jar (7:16–19). As long as they remained quiet, they could avoid detection. Then Gideon gave the signal. The soldiers smashed the jars, raised their torches, and shouted, "A sword for the Lord and for Gideon!" (7:20–21) The early morning ruckus roused the enemy soldiers. At just the moment we expect the eastern soldiers to turn on the Israelites, the Lord caused the disoriented soldiers to fight with one another (7:22). In the end, the place that characterized the threat in the story became the scene of an amazing victory, won not by Israelite numbers, but by the only God Israel needed.

INVADER'S FLIGHT PATH

The alarmed and confused enemy soldiers now ran headlong for the wilderness areas they called home. But as they fled, they separated into a faster and slower group, each described using a set of geographical references.

LOCATIONS

Now place names go flashing by in rapid succession (7:22). The invaders fled to Beth Shittah (Shatta), which is two and a half miles (4 km) east of the Harod spring

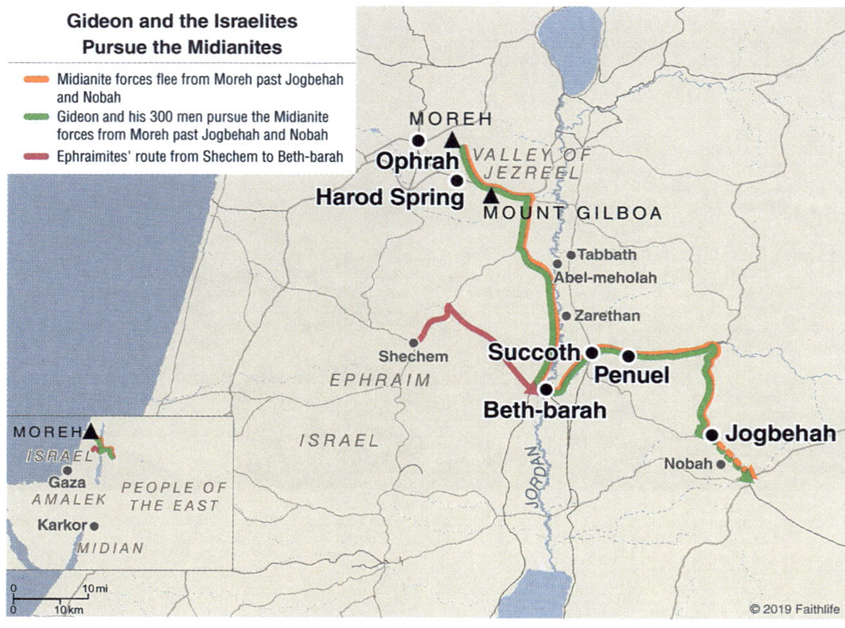

toward Zererah (Tell es-Saidiyah) in the Jordan Valley, as far as Abel Meholah near Tabbath (Ras abu Tabat).[10] Generally, the flight path is east, heading towards the fords of the Jordan River where the second slower group is intercepted by the men of Ephraim. This is the first we hear of their involvement. Their homeland offered ready access to the Jordan River fords along their eastern border. There, they quickly seized the ford at Beth Barah (7:24). This location is uncertain but is either the ford east of Beth Shan or the ford at Adam.

While the Ephraimite soldiers dealt with this slower group, Gideon crossed the Jordan in hot pursuit of the faster group. They were fleeing by the route of the nomads east of Nobah and Jogbehah to arrive at Karkor (8:11–12). Jogbehah is likely Jubeihat fifteen miles (24 km) southeast of Penuel and Karkor is likely to be found in the Wadi Sirhan one hundred fifty miles (241 km) from Jubeihat.[11]

Roles in the Story

This grand avalanche of place names does two things in the scenes that witness the defeat of the invading easterners. First, it confirms that the days of invading Israel's fields are over. The invaders no longer have plunder on their minds but flight from the land. Second, the place names that whisk by one after the other accelerate the pace of the story and give us a taste of the desperate, headlong flight of the enemy that signaled their complete defeat. If there were any questions about

10. Block, "Judges," 161.

11. Rainey and Notley, *Sacred Bridge*, 139.

whether one God was enough, this stunning victory of Israel leaves no doubt.

SUKKOTH AND PENIEL

In this story full of places names, two stand out because they are mentioned most frequently. Sukkoth is mentioned seven times (Judg 8:5, 6, 8, 14, 15, 16) and Penuel three times (8:8, 9, 17).

LOCATIONS

Both towns are located on the east side of the Jordan River. Sukkoth is linked historically to the archaeological site Tell Deir Allah.[12] Here, Jacob built shelters (סֻכֹּת, *sukkoth*) near a ford in the Jabbok River (Gen 32:22; 33:17) and the town was subsequently assigned to the Transjordan holdings of Gad (Josh 13:27). Nearby Peniel was also given its name by Jacob (Gen 32:22, 30). Its archaeological identification is likely Tell edh-Dhahab esh-Sharqi about five miles (8 km) up the Jabbok River canyon from the Jordan River.[13]

ROLES IN THE STORY

These two towns have three things in common (8:4–9, 13–17). Gideon approached both with a request for food to refresh his three hundred soldiers who were in hot pursuit of the fleeing invaders (8:4–5, 8). Both towns refused to help using language more akin to what we would expect of non-Israelites than those in league with Gideon (8:6, 8). Third, Gideon returned to punish both towns after he was successful in defeating the fleeing Midianites (8:13–17).

So, why do these towns merit such frequent mention? Their attitude toward Gideon and his mission illustrates the ongoing problem of tribal cohesion. This problem surfaces briefly in the mention of Ephraim (7:24; 8:1–2) but the attitude of Sukkoth and Peniel is particularly troubling because they represent tribes on the east side of the Jordan River. I believe the fundamental responsibility of the Transjordan tribes was safeguarding the tribes west of the Jordan River from eastern invasion. The Jordan River is an effective border but a more modest barrier to eastern invasion. As we see in the case with Israel's arrival in the region following their time in the wilderness, invasion of the Levant typically began by first securing the Transjordan.[14] Consequently, the most important role for the Transjordan tribes was safeguarding the eastern frontier and so securing the wellbeing of their countrymen who lived west of the Jordan River. The problem is presumed earlier in the story when we learn that the western tribes were facing invasion by desert nomads from the east but now it is highlighted by the repeated references to these locations and their failure to help Gideon, even when he was on the cusp of pushing out the eastern invaders.

OPHRAH

LOCATION

The final moments of Gideon's story return us to where the story began, in Ophrah (Judg 8:27–32).

12. Block, "Judges," 161.

13. Rainey and Notley, *Sacred Bridge*, 139.

14. George Adam Smith, *The Historical Geography of the Holy Land* (London: Hodder and Stoughton, 1897; repr., London: Forgotten Books, 2012), 576.

ROLES IN THE STORY

This geographic shift helps mark the end of the story and could well have marked the successful conclusion of it—a return to the town first convinced that one God is enough. Instead, Ophrah marks a return to an old pattern of thinking. The Israelites asked Gideon to be their king and establish a dynasty (8:22). Gideon sidestepped this request but then did something which was curious and troubling. He took forty-three pounds of gold plunder and made an ephod (8:27). Presumably, there was already a cultic ephod at the tabernacle in Shiloh (Exod 39:2–5). Was this to compete with the original? Was it a replica meant to remind Israel to seek the Lord? We don't know Gideon's intentions but there is no ambiguity about how others in Ophrah viewed it. "All Israel prostituted themselves by worshiping it there, and it became a snare to Gideon and his family" (8:27) And after Gideon was buried in Ophrah, "the Israelites again prostituted themselves to the Baals" (8:32–33).

The story of Gideon has taken us many places. But as when we return to Ophrah, the place the story began, it becomes clear that we have not gotten anywhere. Although the Lord had used Gideon to excise the invaders, Israel quickly forgot the Lord and all he had done through Gideon. The return to Ophrah marks the geographic close of the story and a return to a way of thinking that the story was meant to eliminate. We see Israel right back where they were at the start of the story, doing evil in the eyes of the Lord.

CONCLUSION

The biblical author uses some forty-three different place names in telling the story of Gideon. They are not tangential but integral to the way the story is told. The writer uses geography to shock us with Israel's apostasy, to encourage us by demonstrating that one God is enough, to animate the pace of the storytelling, and to give us insight into the problem of eastern invasion. No matter where we go, we see that one God is enough, if your God is the Lord. But sadly, our return to Ophrah marks a return to a very different perspective, one Israel had at the start of the story. When we return to Ophrah at the end of the story, it as if we had never left.

BIBLIOGRAPHY

Aharoni, Yohanan. *The Land of the Bible: A Historical Geography.* Translated by Anson F. Rainey. Rev. and enl. ed. Philadelphia: Westminster, 1979.

Beck, John A. "Gideon, Dew, and the Narrative-Geographical Shaping of Judges 6:33–40." *Bibliotheca Sacra* 165 (2008): 28–32.

Block, Daniel I. "Judges." *ZIBBCOT* 2: 94–241.

Butler, Trent C. *Joshua.* WBC. Nashville: Thomas Nelson, 2009.

Howard, David, Jr. *An Introduction to the Old Testament Historical Books.* Chicago: Moody, 1993.

Rainey, Anson F., and R. Steven Notley. *The Sacred Bridge: Carta's Atlas of the Biblical World.* Jerusalem: Carta, 2006.

Rasmussen, Carl G. *Zondervan Atlas of the Bible.* Grand Rapids: Zondervan, 2010.

Schneider, Tammi J. *Judges.* Berit Olam. Collegeville, MN: The Liturgical Press, 2000.

Smith, George Adam. *The Historical Geography of the Holy Land.* London: Hodder and Stoughton, 1897. Repr., London: Forgotten Books, 2012.

CHAPTER 25

EVIDENCE OF EARLY ISRAEL? A SOCIO-SPATIAL ANALYSIS OF THE "FOUR-ROOM" HOUSE IN CONTEXT

Judg 8–11, 17–20; Ruth 1–2

Douglas R. Clark and Monique D. Roddy

KEY POINTS

- Iron I in the southern Levant (c. 1200–1000 BC, the time of the biblical judges) featured common architectural and artifactual traditions across both sides of the Jordan River.
- Iron I "four-room" houses, with three long rooms and one broad room on the ground floor, are found in the southern Levant on both sides of the Jordan River.
- As seen in the archaeological record, Iron I "four-room" houses were well suited to the demands of hill country pastoral and agricultural subsistence in the southern Levant.
- Village domestic architecture in Iron I informs our understanding of social structures, activities, and identity.
- It is virtually impossible to distinguish ethnic identities on the basis of architecture in the southern Levant during Iron I.

INTRODUCTION

Readers often encounter the word "house" in the biblical record, even if with a variety of meanings, some physical and others metaphorical, and often as passing references in otherwise focused narratives. Interest in domestic architecture and furnishings is much more a modern concern, one which is informed by archaeology and helps create the backdrop to the biblical stories. While we do not learn a lot about physical houses in the Bible, archaeology is incredibly helpful in fleshing out the form and function of houses, how their inhabitants lived and survived in them, what the inhabitants ate, whom they worshiped, how they adorned themselves, and their family dynamics. With this wealth of information, we can read the biblical narratives with an enriched comprehension of the lives of the biblical characters. This essay will focus specifically on the houses of the early Iron Age (Iron I, c. 1200–1000 BC), a period depicted in the biblical book of Judges.

Iron I followed on the heels of seismic geopolitical and cultural tumult in the southern Levant at the end of the Late Bronze Age. As part of the dramatically shifting landscape and emerging existential realities, major changes appeared in the archaeological record, demonstrating several discontinuities (and some lines of continuity) between: (1) established, primarily urban Canaanite material culture on coastal plains and in intermontane valleys, and (2) an explosion of hundreds of small, mostly rural settlements in the hill country of both sides of the Jordan. It is during this period of transition and change in the highlands that archaeologists have observed the beginnings of new cultural traditions in the architecture, such as pillared or "three-room" or "four-room" buildings, economic structures, and other traceable remains of lifeways. The label "four-room" building or house is used to describe the ground floor footprint or floor plan of these structures: three adjacent parallel long rooms normally separated by rows of pillars or posts, with an entrance on one end and a broad room at the other, oriented perpendicularly to the long rooms (see Building B below in the figure "Iron I Neighborhood at Tall al-ʿUmayri" for a good example). These rooms can be subdivided, and the buildings can have a second story, but they are still called "four-room" structures.

It is also during this period that scholars find biblical and archaeological evidence for the beginnings of people groups who ultimately, in time, become well-documented tribal and state entities known from the Iron II period (c. 1000 to 500 BC): Israel, Judah, Ammon, Moab, and Edom. While some call these groups in the Iron I period proto-Israelites, proto-Ammonites, etc., the goal of this article is to explore the Iron I dynamics on their own terms and not on the basis of later historical observations which can, synchronically and diachronically, prejudge our labels for contemporary tribal entities and skew how we approach and seek to understand them.[1]

How, then, do early Iron I artifacts and architecture in the southern Levant, in particular "four-room" buildings, inform our understanding of how inhabitants lived, survived, thrived in the small, rural villages where most of these structures are found? What biblical, archaeological, and theoretical data exist that can help us answer these questions satisfac-

1. So also the familiar term "Transjordan," which privileges the text-derived perspective from west of the Jordan River. Thus, we simply use the descriptive terms west and east of the Jordan River. Shennan treats the larger issue of reading later, including our own, worlds into the past: "The importance of ethnic issues and conflicts of interest in the modern world at least partly explains and justifies our interest in them in the past. Unfortunately, in investigating these questions, as with so many others, we have tended to create the past in our own image" (Steven J. Shennan, "Introduction: Archaeological Approaches to Cultural Identity," in *Archaeological Approaches to Cultural Identity*, ed. Steven J. Shennan [London: Unwin Hyman, 1989], 1–32).

torily, based on available critically ascertained and analyzed sources? And what does it mean, in our attempts to respond to these questions, to apply "socio-spatial" analysis to ancient houses, urban settings, and wider geographical areas? Definitions for "socio-spatial," while general and somewhat varied among sources, indicate a theoretical approach to understanding sociological aspects of (mostly urban) spaces, how built infrastructure and society interact, and relational attributes within a space perspective.[2] We hope to understand how people groups in ancient communities interacted with the architecture around them and how they made use of the spaces available to them. This helps us understand better how they organized themselves socially and even consider how these spaces may have shaped society.

Biblical material depicting the Iron I period includes primarily the books of Joshua, Judges, and Ruth, even though, in final form, they all derive from later times. The Hebrew word for "house," *bayt* (בַּיִת), appears in these three books a total of one hundred times: twenty-five in Joshua, sixty-eight in Judges, and seven in Ruth. Of these references, over half, approximately fifty-five, denote domestic buildings, while the remaining occurrences suggest either the house of God or a familial or other relational category. One might expect these texts to provide at least some insights into houses and house construction and use. Unfortunately, the biblical material offers precious little about what these structures must have looked like, how they functioned socially, or what it took to construct one or a small village of them. Normally, the texts simply mention a house or houses in passing. We do read in this material of doors (Judg 3:23–25; 11:31; 19:22–27), a threshold (Judg 19:27), a household shrine (Judg 17–18), and an adjoining street (Judg 19:15–20), but this type of reference is rare. Otherwise, we are dependent on archaeological and anthropological resources for answers to our questions about domestic structures and their functions.

The archaeological and architectural data are voluminous for pillared, three-room (typically three long rooms and no broad room), and four-room structures in the Iron I hill country east and west of the Jordan River.[3] Scores of these domestic buildings been discovered and excavated across the southern Levant from the Iron I period, with hundreds across the entire Iron Age, mostly in the central hill country west of the Jordan River.[4] An equal measure of scholars have written about them, thus creating a massive stockpile of literature conveying various theories about numerous aspects of the buildings and what we can learn from them about their socio-spatial dynamics and ethnic diagnostics, and about social identity and enculturated mental templates of those who built and inhabited them.[5]

2. See Giorgio Osti, "Socio-spatial Relations: An Attempt to Move Space Near Society," *Poliarchie/Polyarchies* 4 (2015): 6.

3. See Shmuel Givon, "The Three-Roomed House from Tel Harassim, Israel," *Levant* 31 (1999): 173–77.

4. See the now dated summary by Chang-Ho Ji, "A Note on the Four-Room House in Palestine," *Orientalia* 66 (1997): 387–413.

5. For just a few examples, see Assaf Yasur-Landau, "Under the Shadow of the Four-Room House: Biblical Archaeology Meets Household Archaeology in Israel," in *Historical*

The history of this architectural form stretches from the late thirteenth century through the sixth century BC.[6] One of the earliest (late thirteenth century) and certainly the best preserved four-room house in the southern Levant was excavated by Douglas Clark at Tall al-Umayri, Jordan, part of the Madaba Plains Project.[7]

Biblical Archaeology and the Future: The New Pragmatism, ed. Thomas E. Levy (London: Equinox, 2010); Avraham Faust and Shlomo Bunimovitz, "The Four Room House: Embodying Iron Age Israelite Society," *NEA* 66 (2003): 22–31; James W. Hardin, "Understanding Houses, Households, and the Levantine Archaeological Record," in *Household Archaeology in Ancient Israel and Beyond*, ed. Assaf Yasur-Landau, Jennie R. Ebeling, and Laura B. Mazow (Leiden: Brill, 2011); Ann Killebrew, *Biblical Peoples and Ethnicity: An Archaeological Study of Egyptians, Canaanites, Philistines, and Early Israel 1300–1100 B.C.E.* (Atlanta: Society of Biblical Literature), 2005.

6. There is documentation for two, perhaps three Late Bronze Age "three-room" buildings (without the fourth, the "broad" room) in the Shephelah, which some see as precursors to Iron I pillared or three- and four-room houses. Givon states, "It is possible to see the three-roomed houses from Tel Harassim, Tel Batash and Tel Lachish, from the fourteenth century BC, and four-roomed houses from the Iron Age of Israel. It is obvious now that the origin of this architectural principle came from Canaanite culture ... [this idea] 'should strengthen the view which sees the material culture of the early Israelites as deriving from the Canaanite cultural environment'" (Givon, "Three-Roomed House," 173–77). For the early treatments of four-room houses, see Yigal Shiloh, "The Four Room House: Its Situation and Function in the Israelite City," *IEJ* 20 (1970): 180–90; Shiloh, "Elements in the Development of Town Planning in the Israelite City," *IEJ* 28 (1978): 36–51; Shiloh, "The Casemate Wall, the Four Room House and the Early Planning in the Israelite City," *BASOR* 268 (1987): 3–15.

7. For an overview of the Madaba Plains Project's work at Tall al-Umayri, see Larry G. Herr, Douglas R. Clark, and Kent Bramlett, "From the Stone Age to the Middle Ages in Jordan: Digging up Tall al-'Umayri," *NEA* 72 (2009): 68–97; for the seasonal excavation reports published in the Madaba Plains Project series, see Larry T. Geraty, Larry G. Herr, Øystein S. LaBianca, and Randall W. Younker, eds., *Madaba Plains Project 1:The 1984 Season at Tell el-'Umeiri and Vicinity and Subsequent Studies* (Berrien Springs, MI: Andrews University Press, 1989); Larry G. Herr, Larry T. Geraty, Øystein S. LaBianca, and Randall W. Younker, eds., *Madaba Plains Project 2: The 1987 Season at Tell el-'Umeiri and Vicinity and Subsequent Studies* (Berrien Springs, MI: Andrews University Press, 1991); Larry G. Herr, Larry T. Geraty, Øystein S. LaBianca, Randall W. Younker, and Douglas R. Clark, eds., *Madaba Plains Project 3: The 1989 Season at Tell el-'Umeiri and Vicinity and Subsequent Studies* (Berrien Springs, MI: Andrews University Press, 1997); Larry G. Herr, Douglas R. Clark, Larry T. Geraty, Øystein S. LaBianca, and Randall W. Younker, eds., *Madaba Plains Project 4: The 1992 Season at Tall al-'Umayri and Subsequent Studies* (Berrien Springs, MI: Andrews University Press, 2000); Larry G. Herr, Douglas R. Clark, Larry T. Geraty, Øystein S. LaBianca, and Randall W. Younker, eds., *Madaba Plains Project 5: The 1994 Season at Tall al-'Umayri and Subsequent Studies* (Berrien Springs, MI: Andrews University Press, 2002); Larry G. Herr, Douglas R. Clark, Larry T. Geraty, Randall W. Younker, and Øystein S. LaBianca, eds., *Madaba Plains Project 6: The 1996 and 1998 Seasons at Tall al-'Umayri and Subsequent Studies* (Berrien Springs, MI: Andrews University Press, 2014); Larry G. Herr, Douglas R. Clark, and Lawrence T. Geraty, eds., *Madaba Plains Project 7: The 2000 Season at Tall al-'Umayri and Subsequent Studies* (Riverside, CA: La Sierra University Center for Near Eastern Archaeology; Winona Lake, IN: Eisenbrauns, 2017); Larry G. Herr, Douglas R. Clark, and Lawrence T. Geraty, eds., *Madaba Plains Project 8: The 2002 Season at Tall al 'Umayri and Subsequent Studies* (Riverside, CA: La Sierra University Center for Near Eastern Archaeology; Winona Lake, IN: Eisenbrauns, 2019); Larry G. Herr, Douglas R. Clark, and Lawrence T. Geraty, eds., *Madaba Plains Project 9: The 2004 Season at Tall al-'Umayri and Subsequent Studies* (Riverside, CA: La Sierra University Center for Near Eastern Archaeology; Winona Lake, IN: Eisenbrauns, 2020).

Iron I Four-Room House at Umayri

Because of its chronological position at the very beginning of the Iron I period and, more importantly, because of its remarkable state of preservation, the Umayri four-room building will serve as the type-site for this article.[8] The structure was buried beneath seven feet (2 m) of second-story mudbrick debris, which totally encapsulated the entire structure and all durable remains inside.

We will first describe the Umayri structure, exploring socio-spatial features that characterized it during its construction, occupation, and demise. Second, we place it in the wider context of its neighborhood, analyzing household dynamics and the social identity of its inhabitants, region, and the southern Levant. Finally, we ask questions about ethnic metrics and diagnostics and what we can (and can't) know about ethnicity at this point in the region's architectural history. These steps will provide the archaeological background for domestic life in the early Iron Age which will help Bible readers understand and appreciate not only the architecture of houses but also the social dynamics of their inhabitants.

8. Tall al-Umayri also revealed a second Iron I four-room house in Field H from around fifty years after the destruction of the early Iron I neighborhood of Building B. Its construction technique and footprint varied significantly from the earlier example.

THE FOUR-ROOM HOUSE AT UMAYRI

As the figure "Iron I Neighborhood at Tall al-Umayri" below illustrates, the Umayri four-room structure (Building B) boasts two floors.[9] The thickness of the ground floor walls and, in particular the seven feet (2 m) of overlying mudbrick destruction debris, argue for a second floor over the entire trapezoidal ground floor footprint of roughly twenty-six-by-thirty-three feet (8 x 10 m). The three parallel long rooms and perpendicular broad room represent the classic four-room building design, a house plan utilized for over six centuries. The building abutted the perimeter wall on its west, its broad room creating a casemate double-wall line, which continued through Building A to the south, but no further along the remaining three adjacent buildings (C, D, and tentatively E) of this neighborhood.

The parallel long rooms were partitioned by two rows of flat stone bases embedded in the earth floor, which most likely supported wooden posts, as there was no evidence of stone pillars. The southern long room (B2C, see painting of the "'Four-Room' Building at Tall al-Umayri" below) was paved with cobblestones. The central long room (B2B) maintained a beaten earth floor consisting of thin, compact layers, and the northern long room (B2A) revealed small sections of pavement. In the broad room, approximately one third of the floor was stone-paved and the remainder beaten earth. Two post bases, one on either side of the broad room where the stone paving and dirt floors met, evidently supported two additional wooden posts.

Stone walls were dry-laid nearly three feet (1 m) in thickness on the south and north sides of the structure, but the western wall, also serving as the town's perimeter wall, was over five feet (1.5 m) thick. Virtually none of the nearly two hundred artifacts retrieved were discovered on the floor surfaces of the three long rooms, but the broad room contained almost one hundred ceramic vessels, the majority of which were large, collared pithoi (i.e., storage jars). Half of these had been on the ground floor, the other half having fallen directly from the second story. Because only one of the artifacts recovered from the building was found on the ground floor, nearly all remains from daily life in this building indicated human activity on the second story.

Two additional features of the Umayri four-room house deserve mention. The first, to be discussed more fully below, is the line of adjacent neighborhood build-

---

9. For more details of the house, see Monique D. Vincent, "Households, Communities, and Dimensions of Social Identity in the Early Iron Age at Tall al-'Umayri, Jordan," in *No Place Like Home: Ancient Near Eastern Houses and Households*, ed. Laura Battini, Aaron Brody, and Sharon R. Steadman (Oxford: Archaeopress, 2022); also, the preliminary excavation reports in Douglas R. Clark, "Field B: The Western Defense System," in Geraty, Herr, LaBianca, and Younker, *Madaba Plains Project* 1, 244–57; Clark, "Field B: The Western Defense System," in Herr, Geraty, LaBianca, and Younker, *Madaba Plains Project* 2, 53–73; Clark, "Field B: The Western Defense System," in Herr, Geraty, LaBianca, and Younker, *Madaba Plains Project* 3, 53–98; Clark, "Field B: The Western Defense System" in Herr, Clark, Geraty, Younker, and LaBianca, *Madaba Plains Project* 4, 59–94; Clark, "Field B: The Western Defense System," in Herr, Clark, Geraty, Younker, and LaBianca, *Madaba Plains Project* 5, 48–116; Clark, "Field B: The Western Defense System and Northwestern Domestic Area," in Herr, Clark, Geraty, Younker, and LaBianca, *Madaba Plains Project* 6, 77–185.

ings, all sharing common dividing walls. Second, dwellers constructed a massive midden or refuse pit five feet (1.5 m) from the house, measuring over sixteen feet long by nine feet wide and eight feet deep (5 m long by 3 m wide and 2 m deep). This huge disposal pit must have served the entire neighborhood, given its size. Depositions and ash layers indicated dumping primarily from the west, likely deriving from the four-room house and those nearby. Contents included thousands of pottery sherds and animal bones, over eighty percent from the edible portions of sheep and goats.

Construction materials for the building itself included unworked field stones for ground-level walls and floors, wooden support posts and ceiling/roof cross-members on both floors, reeds to support the mud and plaster of floors and roof, sun-dried mudbricks for the second story, and plaster for the walls, floors, and roof. Mass, volume, and density measurements of construction materials revealed a total weight of the Umayri four-room building, from the ground up, of over four hundred tons (363 metric tons). The demands of building construction during the Iron I period, which fell on householders and neighbors, were severe and required intensive labor investments with no protections from serious accident or injury.[10]

The artifactual assemblages in the Umayri building unequivocally represented a domestic context set in an agro-pastoral subsistence economy. Because virtually all artifacts except those in the broad room ground floor fell from the second story, it is also clear that domestic life—food preparation, consumption, some storage, use of textiles implements, and cultic functions—all happened upstairs. Without any evidence of stone stairways, we assume ladder access.

While challenging to determine in some of the building's rooms, space utilization was apparent in at least some places. The paved south-side, ground floor long-room floor (B2C) indicated small cattle stabling, most likely sheep and goats predominantly, given the high percentage of these bones in the massive midden east of the building. Householders later expanded the use of paved surfaces, first by the construction of a small animal enclosure in an emerging courtyard east of the building, then with yet another expansion, doubling the enclosure's size and capacity, thus allowing for the enlargement of herd size and enhancement of economic potential. How much of a role the north-side long room (B2A) played in animal husbandry is not clear, as only fragmentary sections of cobble paving appeared.

The central long room (B2B) left no clues as to its function; there were no artifacts found on its surface. It does appear likely, however, from the 0.33–0.39 feet (0.10–0.12 m) of compact earth layers of flooring material that it could have been laid intentionally, but it would not have served stabling functions well, as paved areas more easily handle liquid animal waste. It also indicates a roof covering the entire building rather than the presence of an open central courtyard,

10. See Douglas R. Clark, "Bricks, Sweat and Tears: The Human Investment in Constructing a 'Four-room' House," *NEA* 66.1–2 (2003): 34–43; Douglas R. Clark, Larry G. Herr, and Gloria A. London, "This Old House: Daily Life in Ancient Israel and Jordan," *Spectrum Magazine* 32.4 (2004): 13–23.

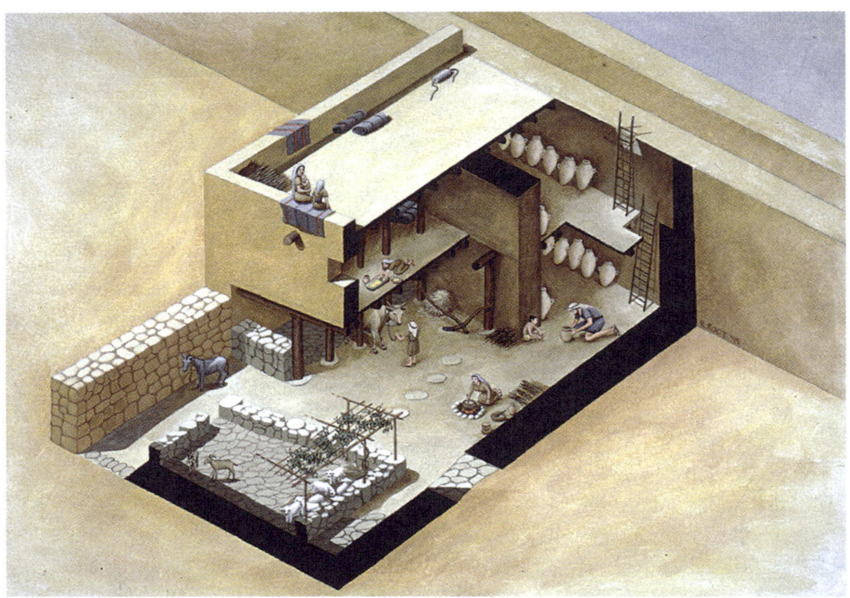

"Four-Room" Building at Tall al-Umayri

given the potential for interior flooding during often heavy winter rains.[11]

Thus, the three long rooms of the ground floor functioned not for human occupation, but for animal and, presumably, agricultural resources. One would assume, if humans inhabited this part of the building, there would be the presence of at least a few artifacts on the floor surfaces. Instead, there was only one, a grindstone tool, and this in a structure entirely buried and preserved in destruction debris. This scenario matches well the observations of Lawrence Stager: "The pillared house ... was first and foremost a successful adaptation to farm life: the ground floor had space allocated for food processing, small craft production, stabling, and storage; the second floor was suitable for dining, sleeping, and other activities. ... Its longevity attests to its continuing suitability not only to the environment ... but also for the socioeconomic unit housed in it—for the most part, rural families who farmed and raised livestock."[12]

The ground-level broad room presented a different picture. Its floor surfaces, paved and dirt, were utilized in

11. Netzer notes, "There are considerable difficulties in defining the central space in this group of buildings as an open-air courtyard, even though that is the considered opinion of most archaeologists" (Ehud Netzer, "Domestic Architecture in the Iron Age," in *The Architecture of Ancient Israel from the Prehistoric to the Persian Period*, ed. Aharon Kempinsky and Ronny Reich [Jerusalem: Israel Exploration Society, 1992], 196).

12. Lawrence E. Stager, "The Archaeology of the Family in Ancient Israel," *BASOR* 260 (1985): 17. See also Netzer, "Domestic Architecture," 193–201; John S. Holladay, "House, Israelite," *ABD* 3:308–18.

their entirety for storage of dry food supplies, including lentils, barley, wheat, and garbanzos.[13] While the excavation process and pressing timeframe to complete the clearance operation before the end of the 1994 season prevented a detailed mapping of all the collared pithoi and other mostly storage vessels, it was clear that storage capacity was divided between first and second-story floors.

Space utilization of the second floor can only be partially reconstructed. Artifacts found in the collapsed debris included basalt grindstone tools involved in food processing, spindle whorls involved in textile production, and other small items of everyday use, such as lamps and a bead. These artifacts represent a focus on producing the necessities for everyday life: food and clothing. A hematite weight, often associated with commerce and administration, and the lower legs and feet (as well as a peg mount) of a bronze Baal statue, likely used in a cultic context, were found in the house. The house, along with the entire village, came to an inglorious end due to a military assault evidenced by massive layers of burned debris across the site. Five bronze points found in the broad room of the four-room house add weight to this conclusion. Also in the room were the disarticulated and burned bone fragments of five individuals who were likely killed on the second floor or roof and then their bodies were cremated in the massive fire that brought the house down and preserved it.

The large number of grindstone artifacts found in every village house came primarily from the debris fallen from the upper stories and roofs of the structures. It is possible that the Iron Age women took their tools to their roofs in order to grind grain in a semi-communal location. Carol Meyers notes that grinding grain for bread was "the most time-consuming part of a woman's workload," requiring at least two hours each day for a nuclear family of six.[14] Rooftops, as spaces visible between houses where women could gather, may have provided a way for village women to socialize and interact, while carrying out their endless chores.[15] The use of rooftops for cultic and storage activities has been noted before, as well as the social aspect as a place especially for women.[16]

13. Use of these nearly one hundred total vessels for liquids seems highly unlikely given their porosity, which would be especially problematic with so many vessels located in such close proximity to each other.

14. Carol Meyers, *Rediscovering Eve: Ancient Israelite Women in Context* (Oxford: Oxford University Press, 2013), 130.

15. Meyers discusses this as a way of empowering village women through "informal networks" (Meyers, *Rediscovering Eve*, 139–46).

16. See Ronny Reich, "Building Materials and Architectural Elements in Ancient Israel," in Kempinski and Reich *Architecture of Ancient Israel*, 14; P. M. Michèle Daviau, "Family Religion: Evidence for the Paraphernalia of the Domestic Cult," in *The World of the Aramaeans II: Studies in History and Archaeology in Honour of Paul-Eugene Dion*, ed. P. M. Michèle Daviau, John W. Wevers, and Michael Weigl (Sheffield: Sheffield Academic, 2001), 200; Charles Wilson, *Peasant Life in the Holy Land* (London: J. Murray, 1906), 69–70; Carol Kramer, *Village Ethnoarchaeology: Rural Iran in Archaeological Perspective* (New York: Academic Press, 1982), 88, 111; Clifford Geertz, Hildred Geertz, and Lawrence Rosen, *Meaning and Order in Moroccan Society: Three Essays in Cultural Analysis* (Cambridge: Cambridge University Press, 1979), 62, 321.

General descriptions of four-room structures exist which, while not comprehensive, do capture basic functions. Typical is this one from William Dever:

> These pillar-courtyard houses would have made ideal farmhouses, easily sheltering anywhere from five individuals (the usual estimate for a nuclear family) to ten or more (an extended family). A cluster of several such pillar-courtyard houses, with a population of several dozen, would make up the typical village that we have seen in the Iron I settlements already described (fig. 3.14). The courtyard, whether roofed or not, often had a *tabun* (oven) that would have been used for food preparation, the supplies close at hand in the back room. The side rooms could have been stables, easily mucked out, the dung used as fuel. The rising heat would have helped to warm the rooms on the upper floor, where the family probably shared meals and other communal activities, as well as sleeping. The roof would have been used in good weather for drying foodstuffs.[17]

While Dever's reconstruction recommends a central courtyard in four-room houses, the one at Umayri consisted of two full stories covering the entire space of 0.02 acres (80 m^2), a conclusion supported by the massive amount of fallen wall and roof debris and the virtual absence of artifacts on the ground floor of the building. Otherwise, the recovered material culture at Umayri matches well Dever's description and analysis. Given Dever's assessment and the evidence from Umayri, one now needs to explore the houses in terms of spatial analysis like that of Ellen Pader. If Pader is correct, herein lies the socio-spatial significance of these houses:

> Thus, to understand the power of domestic space as a social construct, one must look beyond ritual action and grand cosmological belief systems and into the practical actions of daily life. As I will demonstrate, including the spatial dimensions of everyday actions in one's ethnographic research is imperative for understanding social change.[18]

It is also the case that change occurs constantly: "Like society, spatial relations are continually reproduced and reinterpreted in their use. If spatiality were to remain stagnant, which is hardly likely, social life itself would be inconceivable."[19] Pader's linkage of socio-spatial analysis to the activities of everyday life is especially well illustrated in the Umayri four-

17. William Dever, *Beyond the Texts: An Archaeological Portrait of Ancient Israel and Judah* (Atlanta: SBL Press, 2017), 171.

18. Ellen-J. Pader, "Spatiality and Social Change: Domestic Space Use in Mexico and the United States," *American Ethnologist*, 20.1 (1993): 114. Pader also notes, "Given the almost limitless ways of manipulating domestic space, choices in the end are predicated upon a creative adaptation of the actual built form in conjunction with one's deeply enculturated conceptual framework" (Pader, "Spatiality," 132).

19. Pader, "Spatiality," 115.

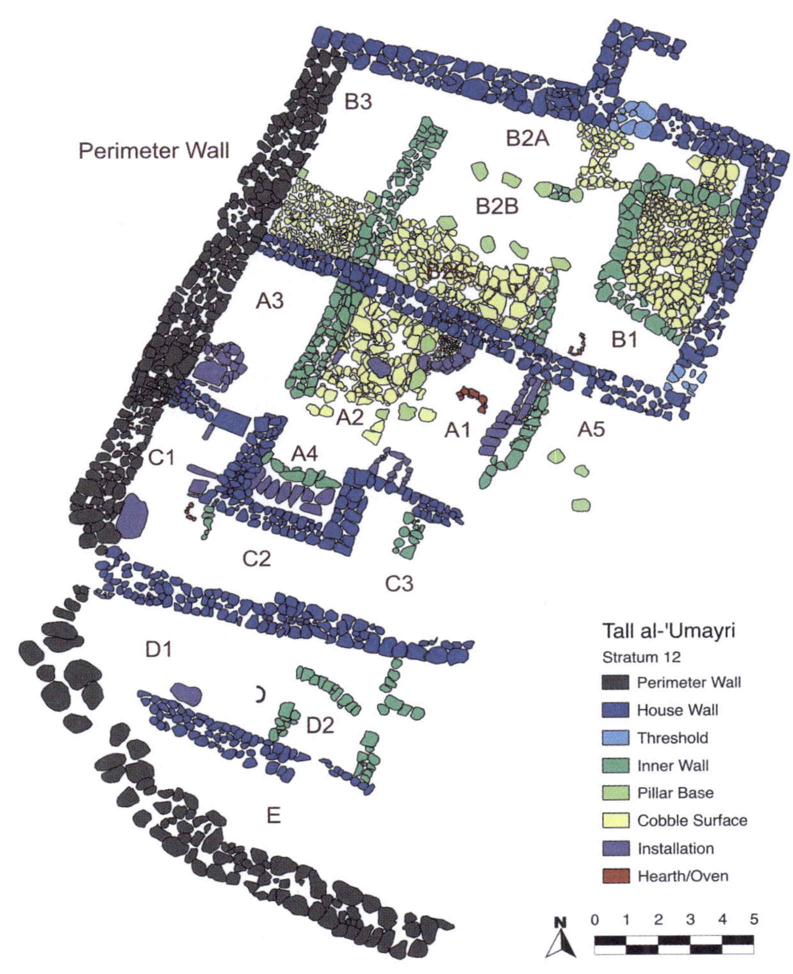

Iron I Neighborhood at Tall al-Umayri, Topographic Drawing

room building, given how much we can know from this extremely well-preserved structure, about artifact distribution, space utilization, and social identity. Unfortunately, the short lifespan of the Umayri house (c. 30–40 years), makes difficult any kind of analysis of changing spatial relations.

THE UMAYRI FOUR-ROOM HOUSE IN CONTEXT

Socio-spatial and geospatial dynamics surrounding four-room structures derive not only from households themselves, as observed above, but also from village neighborhoods, regional, and larger geographical areas.

1) THE VILLAGE NEIGHBORHOOD

On the community level, which at Umayri is represented by a partial picture of four, possibly five, structures along the western stretch of the village's perimeter wall, it is possible to step back and consider how everyday practices would have created opportunities for interactions between and among villagers.[20] Factors that may have worked to divide the community include differences in house construction and the quantity and quality of the objects each house contained, as well as the amount of storage each household maintained. These differences were stark. Buildings B and A were both constructed using wooden posts to roof wider, larger spaces, while Buildings C and D were narrow, linear structures two-thirds to half the size of their neighbors. Buildings B and A also contained a greater diversity and number of artifacts than their neighbors, including objects involved in administration and ritual such as weights used in trading goods and figurines used in the cult. The greatest inequality was in storage capacity, as Building B could have held over twice the amount of grain and other stored commodities as its neighbors. Building B held over seventy-four pithoi, while the others contained thirty-two or eighteen pithoi. On top of these material differences, the houses' architecture also worked to divide them, with shared solid walls separating each house. These economic and physical separations may have presented significant barriers to community life.

However, other factors may have worked to unite the community. Efforts that would have required everyone to participate for the greater communal good may have worked to counteract divisions. Shared activities may have included constructing the village's perimeter wall and houses, as well as communal ritual events centered on a cultic corner in Building A. Villagers may have also reduced the risks of a rural economy by building supportive relationships, sharing equipment, such as the olive crusher/roof roller found in Building B, and labor between households to care for their flocks and fields as suggested by ethnographic models for rotational herd duty.[21]

2) REGIONAL IRON I SITES WITH DOMESTIC ARCHITECTURE

In spite of the problem of limited excavation over much of Jordan, there is extensive information about complete or nearly complete houses at five to seven sites containing certain Iron I domestic structures: Khirbat al-Mudayna Aliya (eight exca-

---

20. This discussion of community practices is part of Vincent's unpublished dissertation—Monique D. Vincent, "Households, Communities, and Dimensions of Social Identity in the Early Iron Age at Tall al-ʿUmayri," (PhD diss., University of Chicago, 2016). For other early Iron Age sites, see Bruce Routledge, "Seeing through Walls: Interpreting Iron Age I Architecture at Khirbat al-Mudayna al-ʿAliya," *BASOR* 319 (August 2000): 37–70. See also Benjamin Porter, *Complex Communities: The Archaeology of Early Iron Age West-Central Jordan* (Tucson: University of Arizona Press, 2013). He deals with the Umayri pottery production as part of his larger discussion of identity in the early Iron Age.

21. Patty J. Watson, *Archaeological Ethnography in Western Iran* (Tuscon: University of Arizona Press, 1979), 94–97, 231; Siegfried Hirsch, *Sheep and Goats in Palestine* (Tel Aviv: Palestine Economic Society, 1933), 33; William Lancaster and Fidelity Lancaster, "Limitations on Sheep and Goat Herding in the Eastern Badia of Jordan: An Ethno-archaeological Enquiry," *Levant* 23 (1991), 136.

vated pillared houses out of 35–40 houses total), Tall Lahun (15 four-room/pillared buildings out of fifty to sixty buildings), Tall al-Umayri (the best preserved four-room house in the Levant, plus one from a few decades later), Tall al-Fukhar (one mostly preserved), Khirbat al-Mudayna Muarradja, and possibly Tall Madaba and Tall Ziraa.[22] General Iron I domestic housing found at Sahab, Dayr Alla, Pella, Rusayfa, Irbid, and Jarash is more fragmentary, but present. Many unknowns remain about structures from Tall Abu al-Kharaz, Tall Mazar, Tall as-Saidiyah and Tall Fidayn. Some potential exists at the sites of Ard al-Haureb/WHS 226, Ad-Dayr, Abu al-Kharaqa Qasr, Khirbat al-Mudayna ala al-Mujib, Arair, Araq al-Amir, Khirbat Umm ad-Dananir, Dhahab ash-Sharqiya, Dhahab al-Gharbiya, Tall al-Hamma, Tall Ghazala, Tall al-Maqbara, Tall Irbid, and Quwaylba (Abila), but the extent of excavation and/or limited reporting have left us with incomplete information. To this point, the remains in all of these examples of Iron I structures show them to be domestic in nature; nothing in the cultural deposits suggests otherwise. Clearly, more excavation is needed to recover the remains of what must be many more examples of this kind of housing from the early Iron Age, especially in Jordan. Thus, the regional context of Umayri's four-room house offers a partial picture of Iron I domestic housing and socio-spatial relationships among them, due in part to limited excavations and few sociological analyses.

3) Southern Levantine Iron I Dynamics

Socio-spatial or geospatial relationships more broadly conceived to include the entire southern Levant, home to virtu-

22. Unpublished results from research during a CAORC fellowship at the American Center of Oriental Research, 2002, by Douglas R. Clark; Vincent, "Households, Communities, and Dimensions"; Bruce Routledge, "Village Foundation and Community Formation in Iron I Transjordan," in *Proceedings of the Third International Congress on the Archaeology of the Ancient Near East, Paris 2002*, ed. Jean-Claude Margueron, Pierre de Miroschedji and Jean-Paul Thalmann (Winona Lake, IN: Eisenbrauns, 2005), 4.

ally all pillared and four-room structures during the Iron I, reveal several common features across the region. Generally speaking, these shared characteristics include:

1. survival subsistence economies
2. combined agricultural and pastoral economic pursuits
3. challenging hill country environments for the most part in which to survive (to say nothing of prospering)
4. an explosion of small mostly hill country sites and settlements numbering in the hundreds on both sides of the Jordan River
5. mostly very small settlements and villages and a few towns, many of the small settlements populated by a few families (most villages undefended in the west and many with defenses in the east)
6. rather basic domestic architecture, including pillared/four-room buildings, which were well adapted to an agro-pastoral economy, for the most part in the hill country on both sides of the Jordan River
7. relatively common ceramic traditions, mostly utilitarian
8. geopolitical realities favorable to rural development, given the regional power vacuum
9. tribal societal structures and cultic diversity
10. socio-economic conditions, if we accept Mazar's assessment (even if dated), characterized by nonurban social structures and egalitarian relationships[23]

These common southern Levantine contextual characteristics illustrate what made the four-room houses widely utilized but also help provide a more-broadly based explanation of shared features and cultural expression. Thus, in the context of Levantine environmental, economic, and social forces at work across the region, one can begin to address the larger issue of ethnicity and ethnic divisions.

THE QUESTION OF ETHNICITY

These common cultural features speak convincingly of the challenge of attempting to draw too precisely the lines of distinction between and among ethnic groups. The archaeological evidence presents a consistent picture across the region of family and tribal units struggling to eke out an existence in harsh conditions. The four-room structures formed part of a survival strategy practiced widely without regard to or connection with a discernible ethnic entity. In the words of Israel Finkelstein, "In sum, pottery and architectural forms in Iron I sites on both sides of the Jordan River reflect environmental, social, and eco-

23. Mazar writes, "This was a nonurban, sedentary population of small communities, each numbering several dozens of people who subsisted on farming and herding. It appears to have been an egalitarian society, striving for a livelihood in the difficult environmental conditions of the forested mountains and semiarid regions of Palestine" (Amihai Mazar, *Archaeology of the Land of the Bible 10,000–586 B.C.E.* [New York: Doubleday, 1990], 354).

nomic traits of the settlers. They tell us nothing about ethnicity."[24]

While many identify a number of cultural features arising at the transition between the Late Bronze Age and early Iron I, including four-room buildings, as "Israelite," does the evidence justify such a step? Answers to this question depend on how one defines ethnic groups and diagnostics, as well as how one applies them to the available data and timeframe. A number of scholars, including Dever, follow Fredrik Barth's definition of an ethnic group as a people who,

> (1) are largely biologically self-perpetuating; (2) share a fundamental, recognizable, relatively uniform set of cultural values, including language, realized in cultural forms; (3) constitute a partly independent "interaction sphere"; (4) have a membership that defines itself, as well as being defined by others, as a category distinct from other categories of the same order; and (5) perpetuate their self-identity both by developing rules for maintaining ethnic boundaries as well as for participating in inter-ethnic social encounters.[25]

An outgrowth of decades of attempting to apply proposed ethnic criteria to excavated Iron I data has produced several diagnostic categories by which some have sought to identify "Israel." Among these are: 1) the absence of pig bones, 2) the presence of agricultural terraces, 3) collared pithoi, 4) casemate walls, and 5) pillared/four-room buildings, among others. As recent research has indicated, however, none of these diagnostics, taken individually or collectively, can be used conclusively to designate ethnic identity in the Iron I hill country on either side of the Jordan. Abridged, here are representative notations from several spokespersons on the above five diagnostic categories with the addition of a sixth explaining general remarks on the use of ethnic diagnostics:

1) Pig Bones

Sapir-Hen: "As new data are accumulated, the alleged association of pigs' presence and absence with a site's ethnicity in the Iron Age becomes more ambiguous. ... From the above, it is clear that pigs cannot serve as an ethnic marker in the Late Bronze and Iron Ages of the southern Levant, and that the attitude towards pigs should be combined with other data in order to understand the emergence of early identity and 'ethnos.'"[26]

2) Terraces

London: "Terrace farming is not evidence of ethnic identity; it is evidence of a means to cultivate hilly terrain."[27]

---

24. Israel Finkelstein, "Ethnicity and the Origin of the Iron I Settlers in the Highlands of Canaan: Can the Real Israelites Stand Up?," *BA* 59 (1996): 206.

25. Dever, *Beyond the Texts*, 212. Compare with Fredrik Barth, *Ethnic Groups and Boundaries* (Boston: Little, Brown, 1969).

26. Lidar Sapir-Hen, "Food, Pork Consumption, and Identity in Ancient Israel," *NEA* 82.1 (2019): 58.

27. Gloria London, "A Comparison of Two Contemporaneous Lifestyles of the Late Second Millennium B.C.," *BASOR* 273 (1989): 48. Elsewhere, London notes, "In contrast, the terrace builders were neither Late Bronze Age urbanites nor nomads, but 'local village

3) COLLARED PITHOI

Bloch-Smith: "Early Israelites likely perceived their distinctiveness not in the pillared house and collar-rim storejar (or if they did, they failed to record it or identify the features' subsequent import) but in the [previously discussed contra-Philistine characteristics of] short beard, refraining from eating pork, circumcision and military inferiority."[28]

London: "Large collar rim store jars thus may be said to symbolize a system of storage and economics, not an ethnic entity."[29]

Raban: "Summing up the available data concerning the geographical, topographic, and site-type context within which collared-rim pithoi have been found, one becomes confused. The geographical, or spatial, distribution does not correspond to any ethnic framework, nor to a socio-economic one."[30]

4) CASEMATE WALLS AND
5) PILLARED BUILDINGS

Eitam: "Several architectural elements were attributed solely to the Israelite settlers, for instance the use of pillars, the

farmers, long since adapted to natural conditions in Cana'an'" (London, "Four-Room Structures at Late Bronze/Iron I Hill Country Workstations," in *The Near East in the Southwest: Essays in Honor of William G. Dever*, ed. Beth Alpert Nakhai [Boston: American Schools of Oriental Research, 2003], 70.

28. Elizabeth Bloch-Smith, "Israelite Ethnicity in Iron I: Archaeology Preserves What Is Remembered and What Is Forgotten in Israel's History," *JBL* 122 (2003): 415.

29. London, "Comparison," 44. London also notes that "Ceramic chronologies and typologies are misused, however, when challenged to provide evidence of ethnic identity" (London, "Comparison," 47). Similarly, Killebrew writes, "Thus, I tentatively propose that the mode of production used to produce the collared pithos, with its diverse procurement of raw materials and clay preparation, may indicate the existence of several workshops. ... I suggest production by itinerant potters who traveled from village to village in the region, perhaps in addition to pithos manufacture in a local workshop or workshops. ... Production of collared pithoi by itinerant potters may also explain the very close similarities between some Iron I assemblages, such as those from Tell el-'Umeiri in Transjordan and the sites from the Manasseh region in the hill country. The appearance of similar incisions on rims or handles from sites in Transjordan and Cisjordan may also be an indication of specific, perhaps itinerant, potters or workshops" (Ann Killebrew, "The Collared Pithos in Context: A Typological, Technological, and Functional Reassessment," in *Studies in the Archaeology of Israel and Neighboring Lands in Memory of Douglas L. Esse*, ed. Samuel R. Wolff [Atlanta: American Schools of Oriental Research, 2001], 389).

30. Avner Raban, "Standardized Collared-Rim Pithoi and Short Lived Settlements," in Wolff, *Studies in the Archaeology of Israel*, 500. Raban also states, "Summing up all the archaeological data and the technical facts concerning the collared-rim pithoi of the southern Levant during the early phases of the Iron Age, the following conclusions may be deduced [out of six in total]: (1) This container was a product of a long-lasting tradition of pottery making and was manufactured by professional potters in order to meet very specific and highly standardized administrative demands... . (3) Its spatial distribution does not fit any territorial boundary, either of a single ethnic, socioeconomic, political, or topographic unit" (Raban, "Standardized Collared-Rim Pithoi," 506–7). See also Douglas L. Esse, "The Collared Store Jar: Scholarly Ideology and Ceramic Typology," *SJOT* 2 (1991): 99–116; Larry Herr, "The History of the Collared Pithos at Tell el-'Umeiri, Jordan," in Wolff, *Studies in the Archaeology of Israel*, 237–50; Moawiyah Ibrahim, "The Collared-Rim Jar of the Early Iron Age," in *Archaeology in the Levant: Essays for Kathleen Kenyon*, ed. Roger Moorey and Peter Parr (Warminster: Aris & Phillips, 1978), 116–26; Killebrew, "Collared Pithos," 377–98; Esse, "Collared Store Jar," 99–116.

three and four room houses and the casemate structure. Following our method it seems that these elements evolved from a specific mode of life and geographical conditions and not from a specific ethnic origin … ."[31]

Gadot: "If anything, these articles have called for caution when evaluating the expression of identity through material culture. … By observing the different components that make up the highlander's material culture, scholars have questioned their use as ethnic markers. Four-room houses, collared-rim pithoi, and pig avoidance have been discussed and their status as identity markers have been found dubious at best. … As a result, the search for early Israel has moved from searching for identity markers to analyzing the formation of social complexity."[32]

6) ETHNIC DIAGNOSTICS IN GENERAL

Hill: [as part of conclusions] "First, social networks may be just as important in describing ethnicity as material culture, since material culture can be shared by several ethnic groups."[33]

Bloch-Smith: "… not a single feature of those settlements may be conclusively identified as exclusively 'Israelite.' Aside from the founding of new settlements in territory allegedly settled by Israel, nothing decisively links the new settlements to Merenptah's Israel or biblical Israel."[34]

Dever: "The *reality*—now at last revealed to us by independent archaeological investigation—is that the 'Proto-Israelite' settlers in the hill country were largely indigenous, displaced Canaanites, *i.e.*, subsistence farmers. … They were not propelled by a new ideology nor Yahwistic fervor, 'but simply by the economic necessities of colonizing the highland frontier.'"[35]

Sergi: "Archaeologically speaking, Finkelstein's conclusion brought with it an important archaeological observation: Material culture may only reflect the subsistence economy and the social mode of life of the highlands' population and not its ethnic identity (Finkelstein 1988, 270–85; 1996). … The fact is that the material remains of the newly sedentarized population in Transjordan and in the Negev Highlands (Iron I–IIA)—regions that saw the rise of the Ammonite, Moabite, and Edomite polities—are similar to those characterizing Cisjordan, where

31. David Eitam, "The Settlement of Nomadic Tribes during the 11th Century B.C.," in *Society and Economy in the Eastern Mediterranean (c. 1500–1000 B.C.)*, ed. Michael Heltzer and Edward Lipinski (Leuven: Uitgeverij Peeters, 1988), 328. For another interpretation, particularly for the Iron II Period, see Faust and Bunimovitz, "Four Room House," 22–33; Faust, *Israel's Ethnogenesis: Settlement, Interaction, Expansion and Resistance* (London: Equinox, 2006), 71–84.

32. Yigal Gadot, "The Iron I Settlement Wave in the Samaria Highlands and Its Connection with the Urban Centers," *NEA* 82.1 (2019): 35.

33. Carol W. Hill, "Who is What? A Preliminary Enquiry into Cultural and Physical Identity," in *Archaeological Approaches to Cultural Identity*, ed. Steven J. Shennan (London: Unwin Hyman, 1989), 240.

34. Bloch-Smith, *Israelite Identity*, 402.

35. William Dever, "Cultural Continuity, Ethnicity in the Archaeological Record, and the Question of Israelite Origins," *Eretz-Israel* 24 (1993): 24–25. Also see William Dever, "Ceramics, Ethnicity, and the Question of Israel's Origin," *BA* 58 (1995): 200–13.

the Israelite and Judahite polities were established."[36]

CONCLUSION

In summary, what we primarily have in the Iron I hill country on both sides of the Jordan are artifacts and architecture not tied to identifiable ethnic entities. These features, including the famous four-room house, indicate domestic structures extremely well suited to hill country agrarian and pastoral subsistence economies that were constructed for the survival of families living at times under severe environmental stress. For this reason, the basic house plan for these domestic structures persisted for six hundred years, making them one of the most resilient architectural footprints from the ancient Near Eastern world. Perhaps we should begin thinking of them more neutrally as southern Levantine hill country four-room houses which served their inhabitants well and then were adopted and adapted by emerging tribal and state groups. By doing so, we capture a more realistic perspective on how peoples of the Bible lived during this important period.[37]

BIBLIOGRAPHY

Barth, Fredrik. *Ethnic Groups and Boundaries*. Boston: Little Brown, 1969.

Bloch-Smith, Elizabeth. "Israelite Ethnicity in Iron I: Archaeology Preserves What Is Remembered and What Is Forgotten in Israel's History." *JBL* 122 (2003): 401–25.

Clark, Douglas R. "Bricks, Sweat and Tears: The Human Investment in Constructing a 'Four-room' House." *NEA* 66.1–2 (2003): 34–43.

———. "Field B: The Western Defense System." Pages 244–57 in *Madaba Plains Project 1: The 1984 Season at Tell el-'Umeiri and Vicinity and Subsequent Studies*. Edited by Lawrence T. Geraty, Larry G. Herr, Øystein S.

36. Omer Sergi, "The Formation of Israelite Identity in the Central Canaanite Highlands in the Iron Age I–IIA," *NEA* 82.1 (2019): 42.

37. A concluding postscript (Clark): As co-author with Larry Herr of an article in *BAR* several years ago, sometimes cited as confirming our support of "Israelite" identity for Umayri Iron I finds, I admit to serious unease (see Larry Herr and Douglas Clark, "Excavating the Tribe of Reuben: A Four-Room House Provides a Clue to Where the Oldest Israelite Tribe Settled," *BAR* 27.2 [2001]: 36–47, 64–66). We have always been nervous about the article's title, which surprised us when it appeared, making more by far of the Umayri four-room house than we intended. While the "Reubenite Hypothesis" of Frank Cross is intriguing, we recognize the problems of associating later Israelite tribal names with premonarchic social structures. We don't know what Umayri's inhabitants called themselves or how they aligned themselves socially through family and kinship relationships during a chaotic period in the region. Nor does Reuben figure strongly in later textual traditions. Weingart notes, "No important player in the history of Israel is identified as a Reubenite and the texts do not hint at any significant Reubenite clan within the kingdom of Israel" (Kristin Weingart, "'All These Are the Twelve Tribes of Israel': The Origins of Israel's Kinship Identity," *NEA* 82.1 [2019]: 28). Dever also comments on this very point: "That picture complements the model of Proto-Israelites advanced here from the other side of the Jordan (below). The early Transjordanian people were contemporary Proto-Ammonites and Proto-Moabites—not the progenitors of either archaeological or biblical Israel in the early Iron I Period" (Dever, *Beyond the Texts*, 206–7). Thus, while the quest for links between Umayri's Iron I remains and "Israelite" ethnic markers lacks persuasive evidence, the presence of four-room and pillared buildings in mostly small hillcountry rural settlements governed by local tribal social structures fits the data well.

LaBianca, and Randall W. Younker. Berrien Springs, MI: Andrews University Press, 1989.

———. "Field B: The Western Defense System." Pages 53–73 in *Madaba Plains Project 2: The 1987 Season at Tell el-'Umeiri and Vicinity and Subsequent Studies*. Edited by Larry G. Herr, Lawrence T. Geraty, Øystein S. LaBianca, and Randall W. Younker. Berrien Springs, MI: Andrews University Press, 1992.

———. "Field B: The Western Defense System." Pages 53–98 in *Madaba Plains Project 3: The 1989 Season at Tell el-'Umeiri and Vicinity*. Edited by Larry G. Herr, Lawrence T. Geraty, Øystein S. LaBianca, and Randall W. Younker. Berrien Springs, MI: Andrews University Press, 1997.

———. "Field B: The Western Defense System." Pages 59–94 in *Madaba Plains Project 4: The 1992 Season at Tall al-'Umayri and Subsequent Studies*. Edited by Larry G. Herr, Douglas R. Clark, Lawrence T. Geraty, Randall W. Younker, and Øystein S. LaBianca. Berrien Springs, MI: Andrews University Press, 2000.

———. "Field B: The Western Defense System." Pages 48–116 in *Madaba Plains Project 5: The 1994 Season at Tall al-'Umayri and Subsequent Studies*. Edited by Larry G. Herr, Douglas R. Clark, Lawrence T. Geraty, Randall W. Younker, and Øystein S. LaBianca. Berrien Springs, MI: Andrews University Press, 2002.

———. "Field B: The Western Defense System and Northwestern Domestic Area." Pages 77–185 in *Madaba Plains Project 6: The 1996 and 1998 Seasons at Tall al-'Umayri and Subsequent Studies*. Edited by Larry G. Herr, Douglas R. Clark, Lawrence T. Geraty, Randall W. Younker, and Øystein S. LaBianca. Berrien Springs, MI: Andrews University Press, 2014.

Clark, Douglas R., Larry G. Herr, and Gloria A. London. "This Old House: Daily Life in Ancient Israel and Jordan." *Spectrum Magazine* 32.4 (2004): 13–23.

Daviau, P. M. Michèle. "Family Religion: Evidence for the Paraphernalia of the Domestic Cult." Pages 199–239 in *The World of the Aramaeans II: Studies in History and Archaeology in Honour of Paul-Eugene Dion*. Edited by P. M. Michèle Daviau, John W. Wevers, and Michael Weigl. Sheffield: Sheffield Academic, 2001.

Dever, William. *Beyond the Texts: An Archaeological Portrait of Ancient Israel and Judah*. Atlanta: SBL Press, 2017.

———. "Ceramics, Ethnicity, and the Question of Israel's Origin." *BA* 58 (1995): 200–213.

———. "Cultural Continuity, Ethnicity in the Archaeological Record, and the Question of Israelite Origins." *Eretz-Israel* 24 (1993): 22–33.

Eitam, David. "The Settlement of Nomadic Tribes during the 11th Century B.C." Pages 313–40 in *Society and Economy in the Eastern Mediterranean (c. 1500–1000 B.C.)*. Edited by Michael Heltzer and Edward Lipinski. Leuven: Uitgeverij Peeters, 1988.

Esse, Douglas L. "The Collared Store Jar: Scholarly Ideology and Ceramic Typology." *SJOT* 2 (1991): 99–116.

Faust, Avraham. *Israel's Ethnogenesis: Settlement, Interaction, Expansion and Resistance*. London: Equinox, 2006.

Faust, Avraham, and Shlomo Bunimovitz. "The Four Room House: Embodying Iron Age Israelite Society." *NEA* 66 (2003): 22–33.

———. "Ethnicity and the Origin of the Iron I Settlers in the Highlands of Canaan: Can the Real Israelites Stand Up?" *BA* 59 (1996): 198–212.

Gadot, Yigal. "The Iron I Settlement Wave in the Samaria Highlands and Its Connection with the Urban Centers." *NEA* 82.1 (2019): 32–41.

Geertz, Clifford, Hildred Geertz, and Lawrence Rosen. *Meaning and Order in Moroccan Society: Three Essays in Cultural Analysis*. Cambridge: Cambridge University Press, 1979.

Geraty, Larry T., Larry G. Herr, Øystein S. LaBianca, and Randall W. Younker, eds. *The 1984 Season at Tell el-'Umeiri and Vicinity and Subsequent Studies*. Berrien Springs, MI: Andrews University Press, 1989.

Givon, Shmuel. "The Three-Roomed House from Tel Harassim, Israel." *Levant* 31 (1999): 173–77.

Hardin, James W. "Understanding Houses, Households, and the Levantine Archaeological Record." Pages 9–25 in *Household Archaeology in Ancient Israel and Beyond*. Edited by Assaf Yasur-Landau, Jennie R. Ebeling, and Laura B. Mazow. Leiden: Brill, 2011.

Herr, Larry. "The History of the Collared Pithos at Tell el-'Umeiri, Jordan." Pages 237–50 in *Studies in the Archaeology of Israel and Neighboring Lands in Memory of Douglas L. Esse*. Edited by Samuel R. Wolff. Atlanta: American Schools of Oriental Research, 2001.

Herr, Larry and Douglas Clark. "Excavating the Tribe of Reuben: A Four-Room House Provides a Clue to Where the Oldest Israelite Tribe Settled." *BAR* 27.2 (2001): 36–47, 64–66.

Herr, Larry G., Douglas R. Clark, and Kent Bramlett. "From the Stone Age to the Middle Ages in Jordan: Digging up Tall al-'Umayri." *NEA* 72 (2009): 68–97.

Herr, Larry G., Larry T. Geraty, Øystein S. LaBianca, and Randall W. Younker, eds. *Madaba Plains Project 1: The 1984 Season at Tell el-'Umeiri and Vicinity and Subsequent Studies*. Berrien Springs, MI: Andrews University Press, 1989.

———, eds. *Madaba Plains Project 2: The 1987 Season at Tell el-'Umeiri and Vicinity and Subsequent Studies*. Berrien Springs, MI: Andrews University Press, 1991.

———, eds. *Madaba Plains Project 3: The 1989 Season at Tell el-'Umeiri and Vicinity and Subsequent Studies*. Berrien Springs, MI: Andrews University Press, 1997.

Herr, Larry G., Douglas R. Clark, Larry T. Geraty, Øystein S. LaBianca, and Randall W. Younker, eds. *Madaba Plains Project 4: The 1992 Season at Tall al-'Umayri and Subsequent Studies*. Berrien Springs, MI: Andrews University Press, 2000.

———, eds. *Madaba Plains Project 5: The 1994 Season at Tall al-'Umayri and Subsequent Studies*. Berrien Springs, MI: Andrews University Press, 2002.

———, eds. *Madaba Plains Project 6: The 1996 and 1998 Seasons at Tall al-'Umayri and Subsequent Studies*. Berrien Springs, MI: Andrews University Press, 2014.

Herr, Larry G., Douglas R. Clark, and Larry T. Geraty, eds. *Madaba Plains Project 7: The 2000 Season at Tall al-'Umayri and Subsequent Studies*. Riverside, CA: La Sierra University Center for Near Eastern Archaeology and Winona Lake, IN: Eisenbrauns, 2017.

———, eds. *Madaba Plains Project 8: The 2002 Season at Tall al-ʿUmayri and Subsequent Studies*. Riverside, CA: La Sierra University Center for Near Eastern Archaeology and Winona Lake, IN: Eisenbrauns, 2019.

———, eds. *Madaba Plains Project 9: The 2004 Season at Tall al-ʿUmayri and Subsequent Studies*. Riverside, CA: La Sierra University Center for Near Eastern Archaeology and Winona Lake, IN: Eisenbrauns, 2020.

Hill, Carol W. "Who is What? A Preliminary Enquiry into Cultural and Physical Identity." Pages 233–41 in *Archaeological Approaches to Cultural Identity*. Edited by Steven J. Shennan. London: Unwin Hyman, 1989.

Hirsch, Siegfried. *Sheep and Goats in Palestine*. Tel Aviv: Palestine Economic Society, 1933.

Holladay, John S. "House, Israelite." *ABD* 3:308–18.

Ibrahim, Moawiyah. "The Collared-Rim Jar of the Early Iron Age." Pages 116–26 in *Archaeology in the Levant: Essays for Kathleen Kenyon*. Edited by Roger Moorey and Peter Parr. Warminster: Aris & Phillips, 1978.

Ji, Chang-Ho. "A Note on the Four-Room House in Palestine." *Orientalia* 66 (1997): 387–413.

Killebrew, Ann. *Biblical Peoples and Ethnicity: An Archaeological Study of Egyptians, Canaanites, Philistines, and Early Israel 1300–1100 B.C.E.* Atlanta: Society of Biblical Literature, 2005.

———. "The Collared Pithos in Context: A Typological, Technological, and Functional Reassessment." Pages 377–98 in *Studies in the Archaeology of Israel and Neighboring Lands in Memory of Douglas L. Esse*. Edited by Samuel R. Wolff. Atlanta: American Schools of Oriental Research, 2001.

Kramer, Carol. *Village Ethnoarchaeology: Rural Iran in Archaeological Perspective.* New York: Academic Press, 1982.

Lancaster, William and Fidelity Lancaster. "Limitations on Sheep and Goat herding in the Eastern Badia of Jordan: An Ethno-archaeological Enquiry." *Levant* 23 (1991): 125–38.

London, Gloria. "A Comparison of Two Contemporaneous Lifestyles of the Late Second Millennium B.C." *BASOR* 273 (1989): 37–55.

———. "Four-Room Structures at Late Bronze/Iron I Hill Country Workstations." Pages 69–84 in *The Near East in the Southwest: Essays in Honor of William G. Dever*. Edited by B. Alpert Nakhai. Boston: American Schools of Oriental Research, 2003.

Mazar, Amihai. *Archaeology of the Land of the Bible 10,000–586 B.C.E.* New York: Doubleday, 1990.

Meyers, Carol. *Rediscovering Eve: Ancient Israelite Women in Context.* Oxford: Oxford University Press, 2013.

Netzer, Ehud. "Domestic Architecture in the Iron Age." Pages 193–201 in *The Architecture of Ancient Israel from the Prehistoric to the Persian Period*. Edited by Aharon Kempinsky and Ronny Reich. Jerusalem: Israel Exploration Society, 1992.

Osti, Giorgio. "Socio-spatial Relations: An Attempt to Move Space Near Society." *Poliarchie/Polyarchies* 4 (2015): 6–24.

Pader, Ellen-J. "Spatiality and Social Change: Domestic Space Use in Mexico and the United States." *American Ethnologist* 20.1 (1993): 114–37.

Porter, Benjamin. *Complex Communities: The Archaeology of Early Iron Age West-Central Jordan.* Tucson: University of Arizona Press, 2013.

Raban, Avner. "Standardized Collared-Rim Pithoi and Short-Lived Settlements." Pages 493–518 in *Studies in the Archaeology of Israel and Neighboring Lands in Memory of Douglas L. Esse*. Edited by Samuel R. Wolff. Atlanta: American Schools of Oriental Research, 2001.

Reich, Ronny. "Building Materials and Architectural Elements in Ancient Israel." Pages 1–16 in *The Architecture of Ancient Israel from the Prehistoric to the Persian Period*. Edited by Aharon Kempinsky and Ronny Reich. Jerusalem: Israel Exploration Society, 1992.

Routledge, Bruce. "Seeing through Walls: Interpreting Iron Age I Architecture at Khirbat al-Mudayna al-'Aliya." *BASOR* 319 (2000): 37–70.

———. "Village Foundation and Community Formation in Iron I Transjordan." In *Proceedings of the Third International Congress on the Archaeology of the Ancient Near East, Paris 2002*. Edited by Jean-Claude Margueron, Pierre de Miroschedji, and Jean-Paul Thalmann. Winona Lake, IN: Eisenbrauns, 2005.

Sapir-Hen, Lidar. "Food, Pork Consumption, and Identity in Ancient Israel." *NEA* 82.1 (2019): 52–59.

Sergi, Omer. "The Formation of Israelite Identity in the Central Canaanite Highlands in the Iron Age I–IIA." *NEA* 82.1 (2019): 42–51.

Shennan, Steven J. "Introduction: Archaeological Approaches to Cultural Identity." Pages 1–32 in *Archaeological Approaches to Cultural Identity*. Edited by Steven J. Shennan. London: Unwin Hyman, 1989.

———, ed. *Archaeological Approaches to Cultural Identity*. London: Unwin Hyman, 1989.

Shiloh, Yigal. "The Casemate Wall, the Four Room House and the Early Planning in the Israelite City." *BASOR* 268 (1987): 3–15.

———. "Elements in the Development of Town Planning in the Israelite City." *IEJ* 28 (1978): 36–51.

———. "The Four Room House: Its Situation and Function in the Israelite City." *IEJ* 20 (1970): 180–90.

Stager, Lawrence E. "The Archaeology of the Family in Ancient Israel." *BASOR* 260 (1985): 1–35.

Vincent, Monique D. "Households, Communities, and Dimensions of Social Identity in the Early Iron Age at Tall al-'Umayri." PhD diss., University of Chicago, 2016.

———. "Households, Communities, and Dimensions of Social Identity in the Iron Age at Tall al-'Umayri, Jordan." In *No Place Like Home: Ancient Near Eastern Houses and Households*. Edited by Laura Battini, Aaron Brody, and Sharon Steadman. Ancient Near Eastern Archaeology Series. Oxford: Archaeopress, 2022.

Watson, Patty J. *Archaeological Ethnography in Western Iran*. Tucson: University of Arizona Press, 1979.

Weingart, Kristin. "'All These Are the Twelve Tribes of Israel': The Origins of Israel's Kinship Identity." *NEA* 82.1 (2019): 24–31.

Wilson, Charles. *Peasant Life in the Holy Land*. London: J. Murray, 1906.

Yasur-Landau, Assaf. "Under the Shadow of the Four-Room House: Biblical Archaeology Meets Household Archaeology in Israel." Pages 142–55 in *Historical Biblical Archaeology and the Future: The New Pragmatism*. Edited by Thomas E. Levy. London: Equinox, 2010.

CHAPTER 26

BETWEEN REALITY AND IDEOLOGY: REVISITING THE ISRAELITE ETHOS OF EGALITARIANISM AND SIMPLICITY

Judg 9; 1 Sam 8:7–20

Avraham Faust

KEY POINTS

- From the first phase of its ethnogenesis in the highlands of Canaan during the late thirteenth century BC, Israelite society had a strong ethos of what can be labeled as "simplicity" and/or "egalitarianism."
- This ethos served the settlers as a demarcating feature, differentiating them from some of their neighbors.
- The ethos was manifested in various biblical texts, as well as in different material traits including aversion to decorating pottery, aversion to the use of imported pottery, use of limited ceramic repertoire, aversion to temples and a priestly class, and more.
- These features cannot be attributed to the poor "simple life" of the highland villages during the Iron I, as such a "simple life" would not have prevented the settlers from, for example, using natural caves for burial or from decorating their pottery. A "simple life" also cannot explain the prevalence of such traits in the relatively hierarchical Iron II society.
- The ethos remained an important feature of large segments of Israelite society until its destruction by the Assyrian and Babylonian empires in the later Iron II. While the way some of these traits were used or manipulated changed, the ethos prevailed, and was now expressed also by the extreme rarity of built temples and royal inscriptions—of which, so far, none have been unearthed—both in stark contrast to other nearby societies.

INTRODUCTION

What do negative views of kingship, limited ceramic repertoire, rarity of burials, lack of royal inscriptions, the space syntax of the typical dwelling, and the use of simple, undecorated pottery all have in common?

All these traits, along with a few others, seem to be manifestations of an underlying ethos, an ethos that is alternatingly called "simplicity," "egalitarianism," or even a "primitive democracy."[1] Why do scholars think that this ethos existed in the first place? Why did it evolve? When was it adopted, and how was it developed and changed over the years? Or, perhaps, this ethos never existed, and the traits discussed are simply a manifestation of the harsh and difficult realities of living in the remote highlands of ancient Israel thousands of years ago? All these issues continue to be discussed and are of great importance for our comprehension of the processes that accompanied Israel's emergence and can even enhance our understanding of their origins.

The first part of this article will briefly review the history of research into this issue, and this will be accompanied by a discussion of some of this ethos's manifestations. This will be followed by a short review of the possible explanations for these manifestations and whether they reflect an ideology or simply resulted from the "simple life" in the highlands. The final part of this chapter will synthesize the data and examine how these various traits were developed, adopted, and modified in the course of ancient Israel's history, from the initial phase of their settlement into the highlands in the late thirteenth century BC, until the demise of the kingdoms of Israel and Judah in the late eighth and early sixth centuries, respectively. This chapter will conclude with a brief summary.

BACKGROUND: ISRAEL'S EGALITARIAN ETHOS

A BRIEF HISTORY OF RESEARCH

The mere existence of an ethos of simplicity and egalitarianism, or of what some scholars originally termed a "primitive democracy," was observed decades ago by biblical scholars belonging to differ-

1. The ethos discussed in this article is expressed, often subtly, in many biblical texts and Israel's material culture. Since we are discussing an ethos, and not laws or explicit instructions, it can usually only be understood within a broad context, and it is difficult, even misleading, to pinpoint to a specific biblical chapter or verse. For example, while the final editing of the book of Judges is pro-Davidic and promonarchic, this can be seen not only in the various texts but even in the structure of the book and its geographical organization. For example, in Judg 9, the story of Abimelek mocks the kingship but is still preserved, highlighting the persistence of this ethos even at a late stage. The ethos can also be seen in the importance of the prophetic work and its protestation against injustices and often even against the king (e.g., throughout the book of Jeremiah). The ethos is also expressed, indirectly, in the mere existence of various institutions, like the *edah* (עֵדָה, "assembly, congregation") (e.g., Judg 21:13; 1 Kgs 12:20) and the *zeqenim* (זְקֵנִים, "elders") or in Samuel's speech in 1 Sam 8:7–20 in which he outlines the negative consequences of kingship. On the whole, however, it would be misleading to discuss specific texts as it would greatly belittle the ethos's prevailing position within the biblical corpus, and it is better to look at the ethos manifestations within its broader context.

ent schools and streams of thought.[2] This ethos was seen as expressed in various biblical passages like 1 Sam 8:7–20, when Samuel warns Israel about the "hazards" or disadvantages of having a king, or the story of Abimelek in Judg 9, as well as in biblical institutions like the *edah* ("assembly, congregation"; e.g., Judg 21:13; 1 Kgs 12:20).[3] These passages were preserved despite the pro-Davidic (and hence promonarchic) and pro-priestly editing that reworked the text, and probably deleted some segments, attesting to the importance and perseverance of this ethos. Wolf, for example, noted that "[T]he period of the 'Judges' in Israel may reflect [a] decadent democracy," adding that "the evidence ... is such that the conviction cannot be avoided that some sort of democracy prevailed in ancient Israel."[4] Gordis argued that "the positive democratic spirit which actuated in its earliest period never died in Israel and, through the Bible, entered the fabric of western civilization."[5] Finally, Cross stated, "... there is a strong ... Patriarchal-egalitarian anti-feudal polemic in early Israel, which appears to be authentic, grounded in history."[6] Similar views were expressed also by Speiser, Shapira, Lods, Humphrey, Mendenhall, Gottwald, Lenski, and more recently also by Sparks, Berman, and Shapira.[7] Special credit should be given to the Norman Gottwald, whose

2. The terms "egalitarianism" and "simplicity" are based on the way we view this ethos as outsiders from a great cultural and chronological distance, and it is likely the ancients would have phrased it somewhat differently. The term "primitive democracy" is apparently under the influence of studies on Mesopotamia, like Thorkild Jacobsen, "Primitive Democracy in Ancient Mesopotamia," *JNES* 2 (1943): 159–72; see also Henri Frankfort et al., *The Intellectual Adventure of Ancient Man: An Essay on Speculative Thought in the Ancient Near East* (Chicago: Chicago University Press, 1946); Clifford C. Lamberg-Karlovsky, "The Near Eastern 'Breakout' and the Mesopotamian Social Contract," *Symbols: Newsletter of the Peabody Museum and Department of Anthropology* (1985): 8–11, 23–24; Gil Stein, "Economy, Ritual and Power in 'Ubaid Mesopotamia," in *Chiefdoms and Early States in the Near East: The Organizational Dynamics of Complexity*, ed. Gil Stein and Mitchell S. Rothman (Madison: Prehistory Press, 1994), 35–46; John N. Postgate, *Early Mesopotamia, Society and Economy at the Dawn of History* (London: Routledge, 1992), 80–81; for a more cautious approach, see Daniel E. Fleming, *Democracy's Ancient Ancestors: Mari and Early Collective Governance* (Cambridge: Cambridge University Press, 2004). The discussion of the situation in Mesopotamia, however, exceeds the scope of the present paper.

3. C. Umhau Wolf, "Traces of Primitive Democracy in Ancient Israel," *JNES* 6 (1947): 98–108.

4. Wolf, "Traces of Primitive Democracy," 98, 108.

5. Robert Gordis, "Primitive Democracy in Ancient Israel," in *Poets, Prophets and Sages, Essays in Biblical Interpretation*, ed. Robert Gordis (London: Bloomington, 1971), 56–57.

6. Frank Moore Cross, "Reuben, First-Born of Jacob," *ZAW* 100 Sup (1988): 62.

7. Ephraim Avigdor Speiser, "The Manner of the Kings," in *The World History of the Jewish People: Judges*, ed. Benjamin Mazar (Jerusalem: Masada, 1971), 3:280–87; Amnon Shapira, "'He Appointed Judges in the Land in all the Fortified Towns of Judah' (2 Chron. 19:45)—An Expression of the Separation of Powers in Israel," *Judea and Samaria Research Studies* 7 (1998): 233–43 [Hebrew]; Adolphe Lods, *Israel, from Its Beginning to the Middle of the Eighth Century* (New York: A. A. Knauf, 1932); Sarah C. Humphreys, *Anthropology and the Greeks* (London: Routledge and Kegan Paul, 1978); George E. Mendenhall, "The Hebrew Conquest of Palestine," *BA* 25 (1962): 66–87; Norman K. Gottwald, *The Tribes of Yahweh* (New York: Orbis Books, 1979); Gerhard Lenski, "Review of N. K. Gottwald, *The Tribes of Yahweh*," *Religious Studies Review* 6 (1980): 275–78; and more recently also by Kenton L. Sparks, "The Egalitarian Spirit in Biblical

work brought the importance of ancient Israelite egalitarianism to the fore.[8]

Admittedly, some of these studies were somewhat naïve and simplistic, as most did not differentiate between social reality and ideology—a major distinction to be elaborated below—and many have discussed the Iron I (from around the beginning of the thirteenth to the early tenth century BC), although hardly any text can be safely dated to this era. Still, it is clear that there is something in the data that drove these scholars to the conclusion that ancient Israel was egalitarian and even formed a primitive democracy.

These text-based studies were gradually accompanied by more materially oriented research, like Albright and Kelso, who were probably influenced by the previous bible-oriented works. Later scholars, such as Dever, Bunimovitz and Yasur-Landau, and others (below), who rely directly on the material record, would largely concur.[9] Thus, Albright wrote:

> [I]f we survey the archaeology of the period of the Judges, we cannot help but be struck by the extraordinary simplicity and lack of cultural sophistication which we find in the twelfth and eleventh centuries. The contrast between the well-constructed Canaanite foundations and drainage systems of the thirteenth century and the crude piles of stone, without benefit of drainage, which replace them in the twelfth century, especially in Bethel, can scarcely be exaggerated.[10]

Dever noted that "[T]here does appear to be kind of primitive democracy reflected in the settlements and the remains of their material culture."[11] In a purely archaeological vein, Bunimovitz and Yasur-Landau examined the Iron I ceramic assemblages and noted that the "poorness and isolation reflected in the Israelite assemblage" might reflect an ideology.[12] The distinction between an egalitarian social reality and a corresponding ideology, as well as which of these is reflected in the period's archaeological record, is important and has been discussed at some length by the present author.[13]

Law," *Sapientia Logos* 1 (2008): 99–121; Joshua A. Berman, *Created Equals: How the Bible Broke with Ancient Political Thought* (Oxford: Oxford University Press, 2008) [Hebrew]; Amnon Shapira, *Democratic Values in the Hebrew Bible* (Tel-Aviv: Hakibbutz Hameuchad, 2009).

8. Gottwald, *The Tribes of Yahweh*, 1979.

9. William Foxwell Albright, *The Archaeology of Palestine* (Harmondsworth: Penguin, 1961), 119; James L. Kelso, *The Excavation at Bethel (1934–1960)* (Cambridge, MA: American Schools of Oriental Research, 1968), 48; William G. Dever, "How to Tell a Canaanite from an Israelite?," in *The Rise of Ancient Israel*, ed. Hershel Shanks (Washington: Biblical Archaeology Society, 1992), 26–56; Shlomo Bunimovitz and Asaf Yasur-Landau, "Philistine and Israelite Pottery: A Comparative Approach to the Question of Pots and People," *TA* 23 (1996): 88–101.

10. Albright, *The Archaeology of Palestine*, 119.

11. Dever, "How to Tell a Canaanite from an Israelite?," 54.

12. Bunimovitz and Yasur-Landau, "Philistine and Israelite Pottery," 96.

13. E.g., Avraham Faust, *Israel's Ethnogenesis: Settlement, Interaction, Expansion and Resistance* (London: Equinox, 2006); Faust, "How Were the Israelites Buried: The Lack of Iron Age I Burial Sites in the Highlands in Context," in *In the Highlands Depth: Ephraim Range and Binyamin*, ed. Aharon Tavger, Zohar Amar, and Miriam Billig (Bethel: Midreshet Harei Gofna,

Israel's Egalitarianism Across Time: A Preliminary Note

The clearest material evidence for this ethos is found in the Iron I highland villages, and this is the data that is commented on by most archaeologists. Most of these traits, however, persisted throughout the Iron Age and are clearly evident in the later, complex and stratified settlements of the Iron Age II (c. tenth to sixth centuries BC), revealing one of ancient Israel's most distinctive and long-lasting features. I will elaborate on the significance of this observation at some length below, as it indicates that the traits presented here do not necessarily reflect an egalitarian society—which some claimed was true for the Iron I—as the Iron II society was highly stratified. Rather than an egalitarian reality, the various traits reveal certain dispositions and approaches, or in other words, an ethos. This distinction will be discussed at some length below, but this explains why throughout this article, I refer to an ethos of egalitarianism and simplicity.[14] In order to appreciate this distinction, however, I will first present the evidence.

Ancient Israelite Egalitarianism and Its Manifestations

This article focuses on the material aspects of the evidence, but given that the first suggestions that ancient Israel was a "primitive democracy" were raised by biblical scholars, I point to the objection to the institution of kingship. This objection is expressed in various biblical genres (sometimes even in books that were heavily edited by pro-Davidic editors), such as the story of Gideon, and especially of his son, Abimelek, in the book of Judges (Judg 9).[15] These stories not only object to the monarchy, but even mock it, as can be seen even by the name "Abimelek," "my father is king," that was given to this extremely negative figure who aspired to become a king. Similar views can be seen in Samuel's speech in 1 Sam 8:7–20 in which he outlines the negative consequences of kingship. The description of various institutions like the *edah*, which, in theory, relegated some authority to the common people (e.g., Judg 21:13; 1 Kgs 12:20), suggest that the power of the king was not (or at least was not viewed as) absolute.[16] Various other critical approaches, expressed by the prophets and perhaps even their mere existence, are also in line with the suggested ethos.[17] The historicity of the various events is irrelevant, since the texts apparently reflect an approach that was accepted by, or made sense to, large segments of the society and helped in the preservation of this approach.[18] These, along

2011), 12–32; Faust, "Decoration Versus Simplicity: Pottery and Ethnic Negotiations in Early Israel," *Ars Judaica* 9 (2013): 7–18.

14. For the distinction between such terms and actual reality in ancient Israel, see also Sparks, "The Egalitarian Spirit." See also comments below regarding the United States and Classical Athens.

15. See also, e.g., Yairah Amit, *The Book of Judges: The Art of Editing* (Jerusalem: Bialik Institute, 1992), 92–104.

16. Wolf, "Traces of Primitive Democracy."

17. E.g., Hemchand Gossai, *Justice, Righteousness and the Social Critique of the Eighth-Century Prophets* (New York: Lang, 1993); Bruce V. Malchow, *Social Justice in the Hebrew Bible* (Collegeville: Liturgical Press, 1996); Berman, *Created Equals*, 70–73

18. See Philip J. King and Lawrence E. Stager, *Life in Biblical Israel* (Louisville: Westminster John Knox, 2001), 7; Keith Hopkins, "Novel Evidence for Roman Slavery," *Past and Present*

with the influence of similar ideas about Mesopotamia, gave rise to the idea that ancient Israel was a primitive democracy.[19]

Our focus in this review, however, is on the material expressions of this ethos. For the sake of brevity, I will not describe the history of archaeological research into each phenomenon. Instead, I will briefly review a number of relevant material characteristics that show that such an ethos was indeed operating in ancient Israel. The chronological aspects and development of this ethos will be discussed in the synthetic part of this article.

Tradition of Not Decorating Pottery

A well-known characteristic of Iron Age highland pottery, in particular, and the pottery in the kingdoms of Israel and Judah, in general, is the extreme rarity of decoration.[20] This avoidance was practiced already in the Iron I, when Israelite pottery was extremely simple, although some of Israel's neighbors did use decorated pottery; for example, in nearby Philistia.[21] The use of undecorated pottery continued and is perhaps even much more noticeable in the Iron II, when not only did many of the nearby polities/cultures, such as Phoenicia and Cyprus, Edom, Philistia, perhaps Ammon and others, used decorated pottery, sometimes extensively, but Israelite society was clearly stratified.[22] Not only is the contrast striking, but when decoration on pottery is used to convey messages

---

138 (1993): 3–27; Jacob Burckhardt, *The Greeks and Greek Civilization* (New York: St. Martin's Press, 1998).

19. E.g., Jacobsen, "Primitive Democracy."

20. Gabriel Barkay, "The Iron Age II–III," in *The Archaeology of Israel*, ed. Amnon Ben-Tor (New Haven: Yale University Press, 1992), 354; Yohanan Aharoni, *The Archaeology of the Land of Israel* (Philadelphia: Westminster, 1982), 177; Hendricus J. Franken and Margarete L. Steiner, *Excavations in Jerusalem 1961–1967, Volume II* (London: Oxford University Press, 1990), 91; William G. Dever, "Ceramics, Ethnicity, and the Questions of Israel's Origins," *BA* 58.4 (1995): 205; Dever, "Ceramics, Syro-Palestinian Ceramics of the Neolithic, Bronze and Iron Ages," in *OEANE*, 1:465; Nancy L. Lapp, "Pottery, Pottery Chronology of Palestine," *ABD* 5:442; Amihai Mazar, "The Iron Age I," in *The Archaeology of Israel*, ed. Amnon Ben-Tor (New Haven: Yale University Press, 1992), 290; Elizabeth Bloch-Smith and Beth Alpert Nakhai, "A Landscape Comes to Life: The Iron I Period," *NEA* 62 (1999): 76; Faust, "Decoration versus Simplicity," 7–18. Slip and burnish are not regarded as decoration.

21. E.g., Trude Dothan, *The Philistines and Their Material Culture* (New Haven: Yale University Press and the Israel Exploration Society, 1982); David Ben-Shlomo, *Decorated Philistine Pottery: An Archaeological and Archaeometric Study* (Oxford: Archaeopress, 2006); Trude Dothan and Alexander Zukerman, "A Preliminary Study of the Mycenaean IIIC:1 Pottery Assemblages from Tel Miqne-Ekron and Ashdod," *BASOR* 333 (2004): 1–54.

22. For Israelite pottery, see Barkay, "The Iron Age II–III," 354; Aharoni, *The Archaeology of the Land of Israel*, 177; Franken and Steiner, *Excavations in Jerusalem 1961–1967, Volume II*, 91; Dever, "Ceramics, Syro-Palestinian Ceramics of the Neolithic, Bronze and Iron Ages," 465; Nancy L. Lapp, "Pottery, Pottery Chronology of Palestine," *ABD* 5:442; Faust, "Decoration versus Simplicity," 7–18. For Phoenicia and Cyprus, see Nicola Schreiber, *The Cypro-Phoenician Pottery of the Iron Age* (Leiden: Brill, 2003) (an example would be "Black on Red" pottery). For Edomite pottery, also called Busayra Ware, see Amihai Mazar, "The Israelite Settlement in Canaan in the Light of Archaeological Excavations," in *Biblical Archaeology Today—1984: Proceedings of the International Congress on Biblical Archaeology, Jerusalem, April 1984*, ed. Janet Amitai (Jerusalem: Israel Exploration Society, 1985). For Philistine, or Ashdod Ware, see Ben-Shlomo, *Decorated Philistine Pottery*. For Ammon, see Craig W. Tyson, *The Ammonites: Elites,*

Jars from Tel Eton

of various sorts, the lack of any decoration is a very suitable channel not only for a message of difference, but specifically for transmitting a message of egalitarianism and simplicity.[23] We can demonstrate this phenomenon by the "Governor's Residency" (Building 101) at Iron II Tel Eton. The ground floor of this large structure covered some 0.06 acres (225 m^2), and ashlar stones were embedded in the corners and doorways.[24] The wealth of the inhabitants was expressed also in the finds within the structure, which included some two hundred complete pottery vessels, including dozens of storage jars, many of which were discovered with their contents, and clearly indicate that large quantities of surpluses were stored in this large dwelling. Wealth is indicated also by the presence of cedars and even in the diet of the inhabitants that included high quality foods (e.g., a high percentage of wild animals among the faunal remains). Still, not a single vessel, out of the nearly two hundred pottery vessels unearthed in the building, was decorated! This clearly exemplifies the phenomenon discussed here and I will return to this example below.

Although a full discussion of the question of style is beyond the scope of the present paper, I would like to mention, as an illuminative example, a similar phenomenon of lack of decoration,

Empires, and Sociopolitical Change (1000–500 BCE) (London: Bloomsbury, 2014), 52–53. For others, see also Faust, *Israel's Ethnogenesis*, 41–48.

23. Nicholas David, Judy Sterner, and Kodzo Gavua, "Why Pots are Decorated," *Current Anthropology* 29.3 (1988): 365–89; Faust, *Israel's Ethnogenesis*, with additional references.

24. E.g., Avraham Faust et al., "The Birth, Life and Death of an Iron Age House at Tel 'Eton, Israel," *Levant* 49.2 (2017): 136–73.

even if in a completely different time and place.[25] Ivor Noël Hume noticed that the earliest English delftware produced in London was typically elaborately decorated, but after the English Civil War potters began to produce undecorated, plain vessels.[26] Only after the Restoration in 1660 did decorated pottery become popular again. Deetz summarized this trend: "Puritan attitudes toward decoration of everyday objects might have had an effect on the delftware industry in the London area in the form of a reduction of the amount of decorated pottery before the Restoration."[27] He furthermore attributes the lack of decoration on various artifacts in Anglo-America to Puritan attitudes.[28] It seems to me that the situation in Iron Age Israel was similar, and that we are witnessing a process in which an ethos is responsible for the "simple" pottery and for the lack of decoration.

Rarity of Imported Pottery

Another well-known Israelite ethnic trait is the extreme rarity of imported pottery in Israelite sites.[29] This trait is much more significant in the Iron II, following the resumption of trade in the eastern Mediterranean, but is manifested in the Iron I by the almost total absence of Philistine pottery in the highlands.[30] Indeed, imported pottery is extremely rare and is often missing altogether in Iron II Israelite sites, despite extensive evidence for trade in the very same sites (as was suggested in the past for various sites and regions, e.g., the Beersheba-Arad valleys in the seventh century BC).[31] I will exemplify it, again, with the "Governor's Residency" at Tel

25. E.g., David, Sterner, and Gavua, "Why Pots are Decorated"; Avraham Faust, "Burnished Pottery and Gender Hierarchy in Iron Age Israelite Society," *Journal of Mediterranean Archaeology* 15.1 (2002): 53–73; and many others.

26. Ivor Noël Hume, *A Guide to Artifacts of Colonial America* (New York: Knopf, 1974), 108.

27. James Deetz, *In Small Things Forgotten: An Archaeology of Early American Life* (New York: Anchor, 1996), 81.

28. Deetz, *In Small Things Forgotten*, 81–82.

29. E.g., Dever, "Ceramics, Ethnicity, and the Questions of Israel's Origins," 204; Lapp, "Pottery, Pottery Chronology of Palestine," 5:442; Dever, "Ceramics, Syro-Palestinian Ceramics of the Neolithic, Bronze and Iron Ages," 465; Bloch-Smith and Alpert Nakhai, "A Landscape Comes to Life," 76; Faust, *Israel's Ethnogenesis*; Faust, "Trade, Ideology and Boundary Maintenance in Iron Age Israelite Society," in *A Holy Community*, ed. Marcel Purthuis and Joshua Schwartz (Leiden: Brill, 2006), 17–35; Faust, "Decoration versus Simplicity."

30. In most highland sites, not a single Philistine sherd was uncovered—not even body sherds. In a number of cases a few sherds were discovered, but one should note that since even body sherds of this decorated pottery are easily identified, their number should be compared to the total number of body sherds uncovered in these periods, suggesting that the percentage was practically zero. Even at Tell en-Nasbeh, where it appears that many dozens of such sherds were uncovered (mainly body sherds of course; Dothan, *The Philistines*, 54; and see also Kyle Keimer, "New Light from Iron Age I Tell en-Nasbeh" [paper presented at the American Schools of Oriental Research Annual Meeting, Denver, CO, 14–17 November 2018]) the percentage is for all practical purposes zero, since the large site was excavated almost in its entirety, and hence the total number of body sherds from the relevant phases was at least hundreds of thousands, if not millions.

31. Faust, *Israel's Ethnogenesis*, 49–64; see also Nili Liphshitz and Gideon Biger, "Cedar of Lebanon (*Cedrus Libani*) in Israel during Antiquity," *IEJ* 41 (1991): 167–75.

Eton.[32] Although cedars were discovered in the building, indicating wealth and participation in international trade, and despite additional evidence for affluence, not even one of the nearly two hundred complete pottery vessels unearthed in the building was imported. The rarity of imported pottery therefore seems to reflect the same ethos of simplicity.

Pottery Repertoire

Much had been written about the continuity of pottery forms from the Late Bronze Age to the Iron Age.[33] It is clear, however, that the ceramic repertoire in the Iron I settlement sites in the highlands is extremely limited when compared to both Iron I lowlands and the Late Bronze Age throughout the entire region.[34] It is interesting to quote Bunimovitz and Yasur-Landau, who, after observing the isolated nature of the highland assemblage and its "poorness," raised the possibility that this is a "hint at *ideological* behavior."[35] While the issue was not elaborated on, it is clear that in contrast to a rich assemblage, a limited repertoire can easily be used to convey messages of simplicity and egalitarianism. Notably, unlike most other traits discussed in this section, the limited ceramic repertoire was characteristic only of the Iron I, and it grew in the Iron II, reflecting some social changes discussed below.

Extreme Rarity of Temples

The absence of temples in the Iron I highland villages is also very noticeable. While temples are abundant during the Late Bronze Age, practically everywhere, they disappear from the archaeological record of the Iron Age highlands.[36] It should be stressed that this cannot be attributed to the rural nature of the highland sites, as temples in villages existed in many periods, both before and after the Iron I.[37] Furthermore, temples are absent not only from the Iron I–II highland vil-

32. Faust et al., "The Birth, Life and Death of an Iron Age House at Tel ʿEton, Israel."

33. E.g., William G. Dever, "Cultural Continuity, Ethnicity in the Archaeological Record, and the Question of Israelite Origins," *Eretz-Israel* 24 (1993); Dever, "Ceramics, Ethnicity."

34. E.g., Albright, *The Archaeology of Palestine*, 119; Douglas L. Esse, "The Collared Store Jar: Scholarly Ideology and Ceramic Typology," *SJOT* 2 (1991): 109; Esse, "The Collared Pithos at Megiddo: Ceramic Distribution and Ethnicity," *JNES* 51 (1992): 94–95; Dever, "Ceramics, Ethnicity," 204–5; Mazar, "The Iron Age I," 290–92; King and Stager, *Life in Biblical Israel*, 139.

35. Bunimovitz and Yasur-Landau, "Philistine and Israelite Pottery," 96. Emphasis in original.

36. E.g., for the Late Bronze Age, Rivka Gonen, "The Late Bronze Age," in Ben-Tor, *Archaeology of Israel*, 222–32; Amihai Mazar, "Temples of the Middle and Late Bronze Age and the Iron Age," in *The Architecture of Ancient Israel from the Prehistoric to the Persian Period*, ed. Aharon Kempinsky and Ronny Reich (Jerusalem: Israel Exploration Society, 1992); Shlomo Bunimovitz, "The Late Bronze Age," in *Introduction to the Archaeology of the Land of Israel: from the Neolithic to Alexander's Conquests*, ed. Avraham Faust and Hayah Katz (Raʿanana: The Open University of Israel, 2019), 2:11–107 [Hebrew]; Aaron Greener, "Archaeology and Religion in Late Bronze Age Canaan," *Religions* 10.4 (2019): 258. E.g., for the Iron I, Bloch-Smith and Alpert Nakhai, "A Landscape Comes to Life," 76; Mazar, "The Iron Age I," 298.

37. E.g., at Nahal Rephaim, Tel Kitan, Manahat, Tell el-Hayyat, and others, and see Avraham Faust, "The Rural Community in Ancient Israel during the Iron Age II," *BASOR*

lages, but also from most cities in Iron II Israel and Judah.[38] The extreme rarity of temples and, probably, temple personnel (it is likely that there were local priests, etc.) suggests an egalitarian ideology that rejected overt signs of hierarchy.[39]

Lack of Royal Inscriptions

A phenomenon that was little discussed in the past is the lack of royal inscriptions in the kingdoms of Israel and Judah. It must be stressed that the territories of the kingdoms of Israel and Judah have been excavated much more extensively than any other polity in the region and have indeed yielded much larger quantities of finds of various sorts, for example ostraca.[40] When one examines the quantity of royal inscriptions, however, the situation changes dramatically. Although not abundant in any polity, all the kingdoms in the region yielded such inscriptions, with the exception of Israel and Judah.[41] This is a strange pattern in which the polities that have been excavated much more intensively than all the others and whose finds are much more numerous are lacking royal inscriptions. Evidence for writing is relatively abundant, of course, so it cannot be claimed that illiteracy is the cause for the pattern.[42]

This pattern cannot be an accident, as the large number of excavations indicates, and in accordance with the above-mentioned traits, it appears that the society under discussion did not generally approve of this genre.[43]

---

317 (2000): 6, 14; "The Canaanite Village: Social Structure of Middle Bronze Age Rural Communities," *Levant* 37 (2005): 112, 116, 119, for additional references.

38. Avraham Faust, "The Archaeology of the Israelite Cult: Questioning the Consensus," *BASOR* 360 (2010): 23–35; Faust, "Israelite Temples: Where Was Israelite Cult Not Practiced and Why," *Religions* 10.2 (2019): 106 (online publication).

39. Dever, "Ceramics, Ethnicity," 205.

40. E.g., Shmuel Ahituv, *Handbook of Ancient Hebrew Inscriptions from the Period of the First Commonwealth and the Beginning of the Second Commonwealth* (Jerusalem: Bialik Institute, 1992) [Hebrew].

41. For non-Israelite royal inscriptions, see Seymour Gitin, Trude Dothan, and Joseph Naveh, "A Royal Dedicatory Inscription from Ekron," *IEJ* 47 (1997): 1–16; Avraham Biran and Joseph Naveh, "An Aramaic Stele Fragment from Tel Dan," *IEJ* 43 (1993): 81–98; Biran and Naveh, "The Tel Dan Inscription: A New Fragment," *IEJ* 45 (1995): 1–18; P. Kyle McCarter, *Ancient Inscriptions: Voices from the Biblical World* (Washington DC: Biblical Archaeology Society, 1996), 84–96, and many others. E.g., Nadav Na'aman, *The Past that Shapes the Present: The Creation of Biblical Historiography in the Late First Temple Period and After the Downfall* (Jerusalem: Yeriot, 2002), 94; William W. Hallo, "Introduction: The Bible and the Monuments" (*COS* 2:xxiii–xxvi); Gary Rendsburg, "No Stelae, No Queens: Two Issues Concerning the Kings of Israel and Judah," in *The Archaeology of Difference: Gender, Ethnicity, Class and the "Other" in Antiquity: Studies in Honor of Eric M. Meyers*, ed. Douglas R. Edwards and C. Thomas McCollough (Boston: American Schools of Oriental Research, 2007). The Siloam Inscription, despite the nice script, does not even mention the king and cannot be regarded as royal in this sense.

42. I expect that a few royal inscriptions would be found in the future in some places, for example in non-Israelite regions of the kingdom of Israel, and perhaps also in palatial contexts. The general pattern, however, is clear, and such future discoveries are not likely to affect the overall picture.

43. See Stein, "'Ubaid Mesopotamia"; Richard E. Blanton, "Beyond Centralization: Steps toward a Theory of Egalitarian Behavior," in *Archaic States*, ed. Gary M. Feinman and Joyce

Rarity of Burials

Surprisingly, hardly any Iron Age burials are known in the highlands prior to the eighth century BC.[44] This stands in sharp contrast to the Late Bronze Age in all parts of the country (highlands and lowlands) and to an extent the Iron Age I–IIA lowlands.[45] Tombs and burials are an important channel for the transmission of messages of social difference and status, and they certainly served this purpose in the Late Bronze Age.[46] There are several reasons for the wide range of Late Bronze Age burials of which social hierarchy is only one, but the Iron I lacks even the "multiple cave burials" that characterized the highland throughout most of the second millennium BC, breaking a tradition that prevailed through wide segments of Canaanite society for almost eight hundred years.[47] Even if a few Iron I burials are identified in the highlands,[48] the general pattern is striking: during the Late Bronze Age the highlands were only sparsely settled but many tombs are known, while during the Iron I the area was filled with settlements but such burials are practically absent.[49] Clearly,

---

Marcus (Santa Fe: Institute of Advanced Studies, 1998), 162, for a similar interpretation in a different context.

44. See already Ron Tappy, "Did the Dead Ever Die in Biblical Judah?," *BASOR* 298 (1995): 65–66; David Ilan, "Burial Sites," in *OEANE*, 1:385; David Ilan, "Tombs," in *OEANE*, 5:220; Gabriel Barkay, "Burial Caves and Burial Practices in Judah in the Iron Age," in *Graves and Burial Practices in Israel in the Ancient Periods*, ed. Itamar Singer (Jerusalem: Yad Ben-Zvi, 1994), 160 n. 211 [Hebrew]; William G. Dever, *Who Were the Israelites and Where Did They Come From?* (Grand Rapids: Eerdmans, 2003); for an extended discussion see Raz Kletter, "People Without Burials? The Lack of Iron Age Burials in the Central Highlands of Palestine," *IEJ* 52 (2002): 28–48; Avraham Faust, "Mortuary Practices, Society and Ideology: The Lack of Highlands Iron Age I Burials in Context," *IEJ* 54 (2004): 174–90; Faust, "How Were the Israelites Buried?"

45. For the Late Bronze Age, see e.g., Rivka Gonen, *Burial Patterns and Cultural Diversity in Late Bronze Age Canaan* (Winona Lake, IN: Eisenbrauns, 1992); Gonen, "The Late Bronze Age," 240–45. For the Iron Age, see Elizabeth Bloch-Smith, *Judahite Burial Practices and Beliefs About the Dead* (Sheffield: Sheffield Academic, 1992); Kletter, "People Without Burials?"; see also Gunnar Lehmann and Oz Varoner, "Early Iron Age Tombs in Northern Israel Revisited," *TA* 45 (2018): 235–72.

46. E.g., Rivka Gonen, "The Late Bronze Age," in Ben-Tor, *Archaeology of Israel*, 222–232; Amihai Mazar, "Temples of the Middle and Late Bronze Age and the Iron Age," in Kempinsky and Reich, *Architecture of Ancient Israel*; Shlomo Bunimovitz, "The Late Bronze Age," 11–107 [Hebrew]; Aaron Greener, "Archaeology and Religion in Late Bronze Age Canaan," *Religions* 10.4 (2019): 258. For the Bronze Age specifically, see Shlomo Bunimovitz, "On the Edge of Empires—the Late Bronze Age (1500–1200 BCE)," in *The Archaeology of Society in the Holy Land*, ed. Thomas E. Levy (London: Leicester University, 1995), 326.

47. Gonen, "The Late Bronze Age," 245; Bunimovitz, "On the Edge of Empires," 331.

48. Elizabeth Bloch-Smith, "Resurrecting the Iron I Dead," *IEJ* 54 (2004): 77–91; see also David Livingstone, "A Middle Bronze Age II and Iron Age I Tomb (No. 65) at Khirbet Nisya," *'Atiqot* 43 (2002): 17–35.

49. Gonen, *Burial Patterns*; Gonen, "The Late Bronze Age," 240–45; see now also Irina Eisenstadt, Khaled Arabas, and Zur Ablas, "A Late Bronze Age Burial Cave at Zawata," in *Burial Caves and Sites in Judea and Samaria from the Bronze and Iron Ages*, ed. Hananya Hizmi and Alon De-Groot (Jerusalem: Staff Officer of Archaeology—Civil Administration of Judea and Samaria and Israel Antiquities Authority, 2004); Yuval Peleg and Irina Eisenstadt, "A Late Bronze Age Tomb at Hebron (Tell Rumeideh)," in Hizmi and De Groot, *Burial Caves*; Yuval

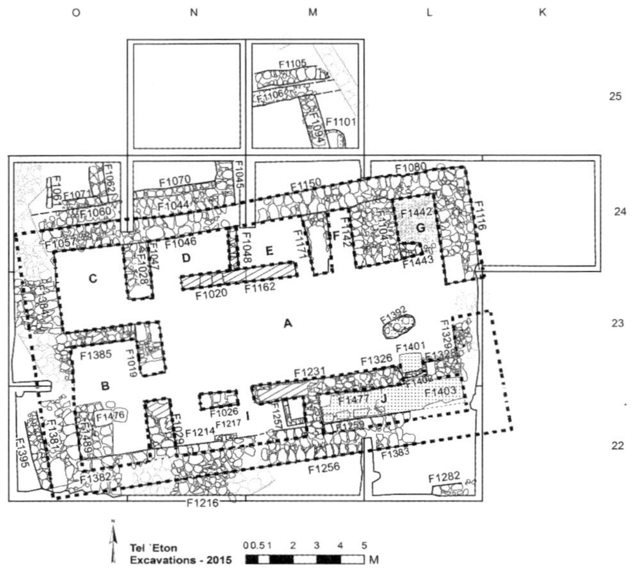

Floor Plan of Four-Room House at Tel Eton

most individuals during this period were buried in simple inhumations, but the lack of any observable burials is a clear reflection of an egalitarian ideology and exhibits a sharp contrast to Late Bronze Age Canaanite traditions.[50] As burials have an important social role, they are a chief vehicle through which such an ideology can be expressed.

It is important to reiterate that this pattern covers not only the Iron I but continues deep into the Iron II. Thus, hardly any tombs are known from the kingdom of Israel, while in Judah tombs (burial caves, known as the Judahite tomb) began to appear *en-masse* in the second half of the eighth century.[51] The new development will be briefly discussed below, but

Peleg, "Early Roman Farmhouse and Late Bronze Age Burial Cave East of Otniel," in Hizmi and De Groot, *Burial Caves*.

50. Faust "Mortuary Practices, Society and Ideology"; Faust, "How Were the Israelites Buried?"

51. The very few such tombs unearthed in the territories of the kingdom of Israel could have been early manifestations of this phenomenon, preceding the Assyrian conquest by a few years, or (and perhaps even more likely), evidence of Judahite presence or expansion in the late eighth or seventh century BC. The reasons for the emergence of the Judahite tomb are briefly mentioned below but are irrelevant to the present discussion. See Avraham Faust and Shlomo Bunimovitz, "The Judahite Rock-Cut Tomb: Family Response at a Time of Change," *IEJ* 58 (2008): 150–70.

it must be stressed that, despite the new trend, which also reflected socio-economic stratification, even the new burial caves retain the egalitarian ethos by the apparent equal treatment of the interred, regardless even of age or gender differences.[52]

In this case, too, it is clear that the simple burials do not necessarily reflect a simple society, since Iron II society in the kingdom of Israel, for example, was very hierarchical. Below we will elaborate on a few examples in which, due to ideological reasons, complex and stratified societies used simple inhumations.[53]

Four-Room House (The Longitudinal Four-Space House)

As claimed elsewhere, an egalitarian ideology is reflected in the plan of the four-room house, which is perhaps better called the longitudinal four-space house.[54] This can be seen most clearly in an analysis of movement (i.e., access analysis) within this house. Despite the complexity of the plan and the number of rooms, which is often very large, this plan enables easy access to every room, and is lacking any hierarchy in the structuring of the rooms. Unlike in other dwellings, there are hardly any movement restrictions, and once in the central room, one can go directly to any desired space.[55] This seems very much in line with an ideology of egalitarianism.

POORNESS OR EXPRESSION OF IDEOLOGY? A DISCUSSION

What can we learn from the above? We have seen that some scholars, including

52. Gabriel Barkay, "Burial Caves and Dwellings in Judah during Iron Age II: Sociological Aspects," in *Material Culture, Society and Ideology, New Directions in the Archaeology of the Land of Israel*, ed. Avraham Faust and Aren Maier (Ramat Gan: Bar-Ilan University, 1999), 96–102 [Hebrew]; Avraham Faust, *The Archaeology of Israelite Society in Iron Age II* (Winona Lake, IN: Eisenbrauns, 2012); Barkay, "Burial Caves and Dwellings in Judah during Iron Age II," 97.

53. Peter Metcalf and Richard Huntington, *Celebrations of Death: The Anthropology of Mortuary Ritual* (Cambridge: Cambridge University Press, 1991), 134; Pearson, "Mortuary Practices."

54. Shlomo Bunimovitz and Avraham Faust, "Ideology in Stone: Understanding the Four Room House," *BAR* 28 (2002): 32–41, 59–60; Shlomo Bunimovitz and Avraham Faust, "Building Identity: The Four Room House and the Israelite Mind," in *Symbiosis, Symbolism and the Power of the Past: Canaan, Ancient Israel and Their Neighbors from the Late Bronze Age through Roman Palestine*, ed. William G. Dever and Seymour Gitin (Winona Lake, IN: Eisenbrauns, 2003), 411–23; Avraham Faust and Shlomo Bunimovitz, "The Four Room House: Embodying Iron Age Israelite Society," *NEA* 66 (2003): 22–33; Avraham Faust and Shlomo Bunimovitz, "The House and the World: The Israelite House as a Microcosm," in *Family and Household Religion: Toward a Synthesis of Old Testament Studies, Archaeology, Epigraphy, and Cultural Studies*, ed. Rainer Albertz et al. (Winona Lake, IN: Eisenbrauns, 2014), 143–64.

55. See various plans in Ayelet Gilboa, Ilan Sharon, and Jeffrey R. Zorn, "An Iron Age Canaanite/Phoenician Courtyard House at Tel Dor: A Comparative Architectural and Functional Analysis," *BASOR* 372 (2014): 39–80; Avraham Faust, "Between the House of the Father and the House of the Lord: Privacy and Purity in the Israelite Dwelling and the Israelite Temple," in *Contextualizing Jewish Temples*, ed. Tova Ganzel and Shalom Holtz (Leiden: Brill, 2020), 65–84.

Iron II Four-Space House at Horvat Haroah

myself, argue that these traits reflect an ancient Israelite ethos of simplicity and/or egalitarianism. Others claim that this is more than just ideology, and that ancient Israel was a simple, egalitarian society that perhaps even actually practiced a sort of "primitive democracy." As some of these claims were raised as an explicit criticism of the suggestion that ancient Israel had an egalitarian ethos, it is worth paying them a few words.

Could it be that the finds simply reflect the harshness of life in the remote highland villages? Kletter, for example, claimed that the use of simple inhumation unearthed in the Iron I highlands reflect the poorness of the population that used these tombs, which did not have the means for a more elaborate burial or to use grave goods.[56] This is now echoed by Guillaume, who noted that the "egalitarian culture ... was the consequence of life in the highlands" and the conditions imposed by "natural environment on human societies," concluding that " the material culture of early Israel reflects ... the economic reality of the Iron Age I."[57] This dichotomy is also reflected in the name of his article: "Poor

56. Kletter, "People Without Burials?"; Some of these claims are repeated also in Raz Kletter, "Water from a Rock: Archaeology, Ideology, and the Bible," *SJOT* 30 (2016): 161–84, which, for example, ignores the fact that what he calls "Iron II" tombs (p. 164) do not exist in the Iron IIA (and probably also most of the Iron IIB), hence undermining his entire argument. I elaborate on Kletter's article below.

57. Philippe Guillaume, "Poor by Necessity or by Choice? Ancient Israelite Egalitarianism," in *The Land of Canaan in the Late Bronze Age*, ed. Lester L. Grabbe (London: Bloomsbury, 2016), 106.

by Necessity or by Choice?" The suggestion that the above-described traits are simply a reflection of a poor society is not only simplistic in its understanding of culture, a point I develop below, but is also problematic on additional factual and conceptual levels.

First, we should note that there are no truly egalitarian societies, as all appear to make some distinctions based at the very least on gender and age.[58] Second, while it is true that some simple societies are relatively egalitarian (if we disregard age and gender), the highland society cannot be equated with, say Neolithic societies, and was clearly more complex.[59] I should also note that even when reality is relatively egalitarian, this does not negate an egalitarian ideology, to say the least, and the dichotomy is simplistic and even a false one.[60] These are important methodological issues that cast a dark shadow over the above suggestions. Indeed, a mere dichotomy between functionalism and symbolism is problematic.[61] But this is only the beginning.

More significant in refuting the suggestion that Israelite society was so "simple" that it did not decorate its pottery or leave visible burials is the realization that even much simpler societies, even societies such as Neolithic societies that were not in contact with complex ones, often produced decorated pottery and had visible burials with grave goods.[62] Hence, a simple life does not account for the simple pottery or burials. Moreover, even if we will accept, for the sake of argument, the claim that the Iron I society was so poor and could not afford grave goods or to hew caves in the rock, why did the population not use natural caves for burial, as was practiced in earlier epochs? We can check one phenomenon after the other, and see that none reflect a poor society, even in the Iron I.

Furthermore, the above suggestions are problematic not only conceptually but also factually, as they ignore the fact that almost all the above discussed characteristics were typical not only of the Iron I—a period during which it could

58. E.g., Thomas Hylland Eriksen, *Small Places, Large Issues: An Introduction to Social and Cultural Anthropology*, 4th ed. (London: Pluto Press, 2015), 155–57.

59. For the Iron I Israel, see for example Nils Peter Lemche, *Ancient Israel* (Leiden: Brill, 1985); Israel Finkelstein, "The Emergence of the Monarchy in Israel: The Environmental and Socio-Economic Aspects," *JSOT* 44 (1989): 43–74; for agricultural societies in general, see Patrick Nolan and Gerhard Lenski, *Human Societies: An Introduction to Macrosociology*, 11th ed. (London: Paradigm, 2009), 137–75; Eriksen, *Small Places, Large Issues*, 256.

60. E.g., James C. Scott, *The Art of Not Being Governed: An Anarchist History of Upland Southeast Asia* (New Haven: Yale University Press, 2009), with many examples.

61. E.g., Ian Hodder and Scott Hutson, *Reading the Past*, 3rd ed. (Cambridge: Cambridge University Press, 2003), 71.

62. E.g., Edward B. Banning, "The Neolithic Period: Triumphs of Architecture, Agriculture and Art," *NEA* 61 (1998): 223–25; see also Gary A. Wright, "Social Differentiation in the Early Natufian," in *Social Archaeology, Beyond Subsistence and Dating*, ed. Charles L. Redman et al. (New York: Academic Press, 1978), 201–23; Anna Belfer-Cohen, "Rethinking Social Stratification in the Natufian Culture: The Evidence From Burial," in *The Archaeology of Death in the Ancient Near East*, ed. Stuart Campbell and Anthony Green (Oxford: Oxbow, 1995), 9–16; Dani Nadel, "The Visibility of Prehistoric Burials in the Southern Levant: How Rare are the Upper Paleolithic/Early Epipaleolithic Graves?," in Campbell and Green, *Archaeology of Death*, 1–8.

be claimed that that society was simple—but also of the Iron II. Iron II society was complex and hierarchical, and there is plenty of evidence for trade, expressed for example in large quantities of cedars unearthed at many sites, and wealth, expressed, for example, in the palaces and large residencies unearthed at many cities.[63] Still, decorated and imported pottery are practically missing from the wealthy residencies, royal inscriptions are practically absent from Israel and Judah, and burial caves are missing in most regions until the eighth century, i.e., almost throughout the entire existence of the kingdom of Israel, and more. At this time, it is impossible to suggest that the finds reflect poorness, hence disproving the claim that the finds reflect a poor society.[64]

---

63. E.g., Lipschitz and Biger, "Cedar of Lebanon (*Cedrus Libani*) in Israel during Antiquity"; Nili Lipschitz, *Timbers in Ancient Israel: Dendroarchaeology and Dendrochronology* (Tel Aviv: Tel Aviv University, 2007); see also Avraham Faust and Ehud Weiss, "Judah, Philistia, and the Mediterranean World: Reconstructing the Economic System of the Seventh Century B.C.E.," *BASOR* 338 (2005): 71–92; Ronny Reich, "Palaces and Residences in the Iron Age," in Kempinsky and Reich, *Architecture of Ancient Israel*, 202–22.

64. Kletter's article "Water from a Rock" is problematic on many grounds, as he misunderstands not only the nature of the data (above) but also the concept of an ethos (or ideology). He also misrepresents my views, for example by attributing to me an ideology of purity rather than practice (a distinction that he fails to grasp), and more. Among the dozens of drawbacks to his paper are his failure to acknowledge that local pottery can be decorated (p. 165), that purity is a universal concern (throughout the paper, and especially pp. 168–169), his failure to realize that some types of material can be avoided while others can be used (see his argument on p. 165), his misquote of my argument (p. 165) regarding the relations between the Priestly writings and the material record, as I suggested that the texts reflect or assume reality rather than produced it. His claim that any separate room would be sufficient to serve the purity needs (p. 165) ignores (1) the fact that should an "outer" room be in use by a pure individual, this would prevent the impure individuals from entering "inner" rooms, even if some of them were empty (whereas the shallow tree form of the four-room house allow them to enter every empty room), and (2) the egalitarian ethos. The claim that the fact that "the division of work between women and men in ancient Israel was not 'egalitarian'" (p. 164) contradicts my argument, exhibits Kletter's complete misunderstanding of the entire discourse, and is wrong on two accounts: first of all, I repeatedly claimed that society was not egalitarian—only that it had such an ethos. Even if his statement was correct, this tallies nicely with my argument. Moreover, even egalitarian societies distinguish on the basis of age and gender, and exhibit what is often called "a sexual division of labor" (e.g., Eriksen, *Small Places, Large Issues*, 155–75). His quote from Randall McGuire ("Dialogues with the Dead: Ideology and the Cemetery," in *The Recovery of Meaning: Historical Archaeology in the Eastern United States*, ed. Mark P. Leone and Parker B. Potter, Jr. [Washington and London: Smithsonian Institution Press, 1988]), and the entire discussion on p. 164 is puzzling as it precisely proves my point—that burials can (and in this case did) represent ideology and not reality. McGuire, notes that "Culture and ideology lie at the heart of this discourse" ("Dialogues with the Dead," 474), which is precisely my argument (contra Kletter). Note that McGuire uses the word "ideology" in this context, as Kletter devotes a lengthy (but confused) discussion to the topic and refers to the same author (in another publication) as if he is saying otherwise. These are simply a few minor examples from less than two pages of his article, and there are dozens more such examples. What is important is that even if we disregard Kletter's rhetoric, multiple misrepresentations and misunderstandings of both the data and the discourse, and dozens of errors, the major points addressed in the body of the article clearly refute Kletter's arguments.

IDEOLOGY AND THE MATERIAL WORLD

Indeed, Kletter's, Guillaume's, and others' assertion that the simple finds reflect a simple reality is naïve theoretically and reflect a dated approach that assumes direct connection between social reality and the archaeological record. This is similar to the ideas that were prevalent in the 1960s and 1970s, during the heyday of the "New Archaeology" (i.e., "processual archaeology"). According to this view burials, for example, reflect social reality, and an analysis of burials will expose all segments of society.[65] It is agreed by most scholars today, however, that this simple and direct equation of behavior and social structure is too simplistic. While there are examples in which burial can serve as an index of ranking, there are also numerous instances in which this is not true, and hence such cannot be assumed.

This misunderstanding seems to be at the heart of the above views, and it is therefore worth briefly developing. Thus, although the archaeological record is a result of past behavior, there is an element that could stand between the record left by this behavior and the actual structure of the society that produced the record—that is, ideas and beliefs, or what we may term as an ideology or a social ethos. Academic discussions of ideology often take a Marxist perspective, viewing ideology as masking or naturalizing exploitative situations. According to Giddens, the term refers to "Shared ideas or beliefs which serve to justify the interests of the dominant groups. Ideologies are found in all societies in which there are systematic and engrained inequalities between groups. The concept of ideology connects closely with that of power, since ideological systems serve to legitimize the differential power which groups hold."[66] Hodder and Hutson concluded that ideologies function in three ways: (1) representing sectorial interests as universal, (2) denying contradiction, and (3) making the existing situation seem natural—this how things should be.[67]

Other scholars tend to use a broader definition and stress the importance of worldviews.[68] From such a broad perspective, an "ethos" can be referred to as, in the words of Kroeber, "what would constitute disposition or character in an individual ... . The ethos includes the direction in which a culture is oriented, the things it aims at, prizes and endorses."[69] As such, an ethos is similar to systems of values, and it "deals with qualities that pervade the whole culture." Boehm believes that an ethos "is directly reflected in idealized statements about how people should or should not behave

65. E.g., Lewis R. Binford, *An Archaeological Perspective* (New York: Seminar, 1972).

66. Anthony Giddens, *Sociology* (Cambridge: Polity Press, 1993), 742.

67. Hodder and Hutson, *Reading the Past*, 85.

68. E.g., Heather Burke, "Ideology and the Material Culture of Life and Death," in *Historical Archaeology*, ed. Martin Hall and Stephen W. Silliman (Oxford: Blackwell, 2006), 128–46; see also Deetz, *In Small Things Forgotten*; Paul Shackel, "Craft to Wage Labor: Agency and Resistance in American Historical Archaeology," in *Agency in Archaeology*, ed. Marcia-Anne Dobres and John Robb (London: Routledge, 2000), 232–46.

69. Alfred Louis Kroeber, *Anthropology* (New York: Harcourt, Brace and Company, 1948), 294.

or be."[70] All these ideas and dispositions influence behavior and hence, the material record that past behaviors produced. One way or the other, it is clear that the material world does not just "reflect" social reality, and is often informed by the way reality is perceived, whether as a tool of the elite to justify, for example, stratification, or as reflecting deep rooted worldviews.

While quite a few examples of instances in which ideology influenced behaviors, resulting in a pattern that is different from social reality were briefly mentioned earlier (e.g., pottery in England during the Civil War), I would like to elaborate on this issue, continuing with burials as a case study. Examples where ideology or beliefs influence patterns of burials, resulting in a discrepancy between social reality and its supposedly material representation, are multiple. In the case of the Sakalawa of Madagascar, for example, major differentiations in society are reflected in tombs. Due, however, to complex symbolism within the society, kings are excluded from the hierarchy, having the "poorest" tombs.[71] The social structure that can be reconstructed on the basis of the material remains of burials alone therefore presents a very distorted picture, unless the symbolism ("ideology") is exposed and analyzed.[72] While this example is sufficient to exemplify the problematic nature of the equation "social reality=archaeological record," the following examples, which have close similarities to our case study, can strengthen this observation.

In a classical work, Metcalf and Huntington wrote that "the Kings of Saudi Arabia are buried with Spartan simplicity, their only monuments being rough piles of stones."[73] This resulted from the fact that "[I]n some of the stricter sects of Islam a conscious effort is made to stress the 'leveling' aspect of death."[74] This is a striking case, as we are witnessing an extremely simple burial in a highly stratified society. Actual behavior (i.e., the "simple" burial) does not correspond to social reality, which is highly stratified, and this discrepancy can easily be seen materially: simple tombs versus elaborated and stratified architecture. This discrepancy results from the fact that the burials do not reflect social reality as such, but an ideology or ethos, the latter intervening between "reality" and the archaeological record produced by the society. In the Saudi case, the simple burials result not from an egalitarian or poor reality but from an ideology, or religious perspectives about death.

Pearson's classical study of Cambridge cemeteries is an additional example that is relevant for the present study.[75] Here, too, the simple burials that are present do not reflect a simple or egalitarian society; the society in Britain, Cambridge included, was highly stratified. The simple burials resulted from changes in beliefs regarding religion, science,

70. Christopher Boehm, "Egalitarian Behavior and Reverse Dominance Hierarchy [and Comments and Reply]," *Current Anthropology* 34 (1993): 233.

71. Bloch, "Tombs and States," 144.

72. The archaeological implications of this example are discussed explicitly by Bloch, "Tombs and States," 145–46.

73. Metcalf and Huntington, *Celebrations of Death*, 134.

74. Metcalf and Huntington, *Celebrations of Death*, 134.

75. Pearson, "Mortuary Practices."

hygiene, etc.[76] Moreover, the only social groups that had more elaborate tombs—a rare phenomenon—were Gypsies, who were ranked low on the social scale.[77] Again, a simple analysis of the graves will not present us with social reality, unless the beliefs and ideas behind the system are deciphered.[78]

Hodder therefore wrote, "[B]urial ritual may be used as part of an ideology which faithfully represents and mirrors aspects of a living society, but it is equally possible that the ideology may be concerned with distorting, obscuring, hiding or inverting particular forms of social relationships."[79] he adds, "[A] lack of patterned role differentiation in death does not ... necessarily imply a 'mobile' society or one that is *relatively egalitarian*, since in the context of mortuary ritual distinct social differentiations may be denied or obscured (as in the case of the modern Church of England ...)."[80] In other words, in many cases what seem to be simple burials do not reflect the status of the dead or even of their living kin, but may be expressions of religious beliefs regarding the dead or other forms of ideology.[81]

The gap between reality and ideology can be seen not only in burial, of course. Let us recall the United States, where, until a few decades ago, African Americans and other minorities were not fully equals, but a democratic ethos was still quite present.[82] The same can be said of Classical Athens, where the majority of the population did not enjoy the benefits of the Athenian democracy.[83]

As Lemche noted, "instead of speaking of egalitarian societies it would be more appropriate to speak of societies which are dominated by an egalitarian ideology," adding that "this would allow for the fact that a society whose ideology is egalitarian need not in fact be

76. Pearson, "Mortuary Practices," 110–12.

77. Pearson, "Mortuary Practices," 104.

78. Archaeological examples are many; see for example the rarity and poorness of Latin burials in the sixth to fifth centuries BC, which was also attributed to social attitudes, an ethos, and perhaps even actual legislation. E.g., Guy Bradley, "Investigating Aristocracy in Archaic Rome and Central Italy: Social Mobility, Ideology and Cultural Influences," in *Aristocracy in Antiquity: Redefining Greek and Roman Elites*, ed. Nick Fisher and Hans van Wees (Swansea: The Classical Press of Whales, 2015), 98, and references. See also McGuire, "Dialogues with the Dead," which reveals similar patterns and show that culture and ideology are at the heart of the discourse.

79. Ian Hodder, *The Present Past: An Introduction to Anthropology for Archaeologists* (New York: Pica Press, 1982), 152; see also Feldore McHugh, *Theoretical and Quantitative Approaches to the Study of Mortuary Practice* (Oxford: Archaeopress, 1999), 17.

80. McHugh, *Mortuary Practice*, 152; emphasis added.

81. See also McGuire, "Dialogues with the Dead."

82. E.g., Robert V. Remini, *The Legacy of Andrew Jackson: Essays on Democracy, Indian Removal, and Slavery* (Baton Rouge: Louisiana University Press, 1988), 96–102, 110; see also John J. Macionis, *Sociology* (Tel Aviv: Open University of Israel, 1999), 69 [Hebrew].

83. E.g., Ian Morris, "An Archaeology of Equalities? The Greek City-States," in *The Archaeology of City-States: Cross-Cultural Approaches*, ed. Deborah L. Nichols and Thomas H. Charlton (Washington DC: Smithsonian Institution Press, 1997), 95–97.

egalitarian."[84] And as noted above, similar ideologies are well-known in a variety of contexts and circumstances, and have received a great deal of attention.[85] It is therefore quite clear that the various examples presented in this article reflect an ethos and not a reality. A society can be highly hierarchical, but some aspects of material culture will not reveal this hierarchy; others, of course, will.

Thus, while the term "primitive democracy" is anachronistic at best, the evidence does not suggest that the society was poor, but that it had an ideological component, or an ethos, that influenced its material culture.[86] Rather, than a "primitive democracy," an ethos of simplicity and/or egalitarianism is a more appropriate interpretation for the data at hand, although it is possible that perhaps a more accurate term will be suggested in the future.

This ethos was quite prevalent during both the Iron I and II, but why did it develop or why was it adopted? What can we say about this ethos, beyond noting its mere existence?

THE ETHOS IN HISTORICAL PERSPECTIVE

The evidence presented above, along with previous research on Israel's ethnogenesis and Israelite society, enables us to reconstruct the way the ethos developed and attained its central position, as well as the changes it experienced over time and the transformations of some of the discussed traits. The question of Israel's ethnogenesis has received a great deal of scholarly attention.[87] While not the place for a detailed discussion, in the following I refer to a number of issues that were raised in the past and seem relevant for understanding the adoption of this ethos and its development.[88]

The settlement process in the highlands on both sides of the Jordan River was apparently initiated in the second

---

84. Lemche, *Ancient Israel*, 223. In fact, Lemche also questions the existence of egalitarian ideology in the Israelite society (277, 407).

85. See also Boehm, "Egalitarian Behavior and Reverse Dominance Hierarchy [and Comments and Reply]"; Christopher Boehm, *Hierarchy in the Forest: The Evolution of Egalitarian Behavior* (Cambridge, MA: Harvard University Press, 1999); Shackel, "Craft to Wage Labor"; Blanton, "Beyond Centralization"; Scott, *The Art of Not Being Governed*.

86. For a critical analysis, see Fleming, *Democracy's Ancient Ancestors*.

87. E.g., Robert D. Miller, "Identifying Earliest Israel," *BASOR* 333 (2004):55–68; Elizabeth Bloch-Smith, "Israelite Ethnicity in Iron I: Archaeology Preserves What is Remembered and What is Forgotten in Israel's History," *JBL* 122 (2003): 401–25; Dever, *Who Were the Israelites*; Anne E. Killebrew, *Biblical Peoples and Ethnicity: An Archaeological Study of Egyptians, Canaanites, Philistines, and Early Israel 1300–1100 B.C.E.* (Atlanta: Society of Biblical Literature, 2005); Ralph Hawkins, *How Israel Became a People* (Nashville: Abingdon Press, 2013); Faust, *Israel's Ethnogenesis*; Faust, "The Emergence of Israel and Theories of Ethnogenesis," in *Blackwell Companion to Ancient Israel*, ed. Susan Niditch (Oxford: Blackwell, 2016), 155–73; Avraham Faust, "Israel's Birth," in *The Oxford Illustrated History of the Holy Land*, ed. Hugh G. M. Williamson and Robert G. Hoyland (Oxford: Oxford University Press, 2018), 4–32.

88. Especially in Faust, *Israel's Ethnogenesis*; Faust, "The Emergence of Iron Age Israel: On Origins and Habitus," in *Israel's Exodus in Transdisciplinary Perspective: Text, Archeology, Culture, and Geoscience*, ed. Thomas E. Levy, Thomas Schneider, and William. H. C. Propp (New York: Springer, 2015)," 467–82.

half of the thirteenth century BC.[89] This is the time when the Egyptian Empire strengthened its hold over Canaan, and it appears as if the empire's policy forced some groups out of the imperial zones of interaction located at the periphery of the more densely settled regions and pushed them into the sparsely settled highlands, where they settled down.[90] The process was therefore accompanied by hostile relations between Egyptian administration with their Canaanite vassals in the city-states on the one hand, and the highland settlers on the other hand. This process had two outcomes that are important for our purposes. First, the highland settlers negotiated their identity against the Egyptian Empire and the Canaanite city states, and this, as discussed below, had a major impact on the traits that

89. Faust, *Israel's Ethnogenesis*, 159–160; see also Israel Finkelstein, *The Archaeology of the Israelite Settlement* (Jerusalem: Israel Exploration Society, 1988), 320–21.

90. E.g., Eliezer Oren, "'Governor's Residencies' in Canaan under the New Kingdom: A Case Study of Egyptian Administration," *Journal of the Society for the Study of Egyptian Antiquities* 14 (1984): 37–56; Itamar Singer, "Merneptah's Campaign to Canaan and the Egyptian Occupation of the Southern Coastal Plain of Palestine in the Ramesside Period," *BASOR* 269 (1988): 1–10; Shlomo Bunimovitz, "Socio-Political Transformations in the Central Hill Country in the Late Bronze–Iron I Transition," in *From Nomadism to Monarchy: Archaeological and Historical Aspects of Early Israel*, ed. Israel Finkelstein and Nadav Na'aman (Jerusalem: Yad Ben Zvi, 1994), 172–202; Shlomo Bunimovitz, "'Canaan is Your Land and its Kings are Your Servants': Conceptualizing the Late Bronze Age Egyptian Government in the Southern Levant," in *The Social Archaeology of the Levant: From Prehistory to the Present*, ed. Assaf Yasur-Landau, Eric H. Cline, and Yorke M. Rowan (Cambridge: Cambridge University Press, 2019), 265–79; Ellen Morris, *Ancient Egyptian Imperialism* (Medford: Wiley Blackwell, 2018); Bunimovitz, "Socio-Political Transformations"; Faust, *Israel's Ethnogenesis*.

were chosen to symbolize their identity and define a boundary with the lowland system. We should also note that the relations between the two sides were vastly asymmetrical and such relations between groups typically result in the creation of groups with ethnic consciousness rather than simpler forms of identity.[91] It is likely that the group that was created in the process, regardless of the "origin" of its various components, is the Israel that is mentioned in the Merenptah Stele.[92]

Some of the various highland groups that merged into Israel came from a pastoral background. While this is not agreed by all, most scholars would agree that at least a small segment came from such background, and many consider this to be an important component of the population.[93] This component, however, was most likely relatively egalitarian. The "combined" highland group, Israel, used this basic characteristic (which was most likely also shared by others local highland components) to demarcate the difference between itself and the hierarchical groups with which they interacted.[94] They, therefore, defined themselves as "simple" and "egalitarian" in contrast to the highly stratified and diverse Canaanite society.[95] This is when this ethos became an integral part of the settlers' sense of identity. At this time, they avoided the use of imported or decorated pottery and even the elaborate burials that were prevalent and played an important social role in Canaanite society at the time. Decorated and imported wares, as well as burials, were part of the non-verbal communication of Canaanite society in the Late Bronze Age and were used to convey differences that were

---

91. See John Comaroff and Jean Comaroff, *Ethnography and Historical Imagination* (Boulder: Westview Press, 1992); Faust, *Israel's Ethnogenesis;* Scott, *The Art of Not Being Governed.*

92. Faust, *Israel's Ethnogenesis;* Faust, "The Emergence of Israel and Theories of Ethnogenesis," and references.

93. See Donald B. Redford, *Egypt, Canaan, and Israel in Ancient Times* (Princeton: Princeton University Press, 1992); Anson F. Rainey, "Israel in Merenptah Inscription and Reliefs," *IEJ* 51 (2001): 57–75; Thomas E. Levy and Augustin F. C. Holl, "Migrations, Ethnogenesis, and Settlement Dynamics: Israelites in Iron Age Canaan and Shuwa-Arabs in the Chad Basin," *Journal of Anthropological Archaeology* 21 (2002): 83–118; Thomas E. Levy, Russell B. Adams, and Adolfo Muniz, "Archaeology and the Shasu Nomads: Recent Excavations in the Jabal Himdat Firdan, Jordan," in *Le-David Maskil: A Birthday Tribute to David Noel Freedman*, ed. Richard Elliot Friedman and William H. C. Propp (Winona Lake, IN: Eisenbrauns, 2004), 63–89; Faust, *Israel's Ethnogenesis;* Faust, "Iron Age Israel"; Kenton L. Sparks, *Ethnicity and Identity in Ancient Israel* (Winona Lake, IN: Eisenbrauns, 1998); Kenton L. Sparks, "Religion, Identity and the Origins of Ancient Israel," *Religion Compass* 1 (2007): 587–614; Joseph Livni, "Testing Competing Archaeological Theories of Israel's Origins Using Computational Techniques," *Archeologia e Calcolatori* 28 (2017): 109–28; see also Erez Ben-Yosef, "A False Contrast? On the Possibility of an Early Iron Age Nomadic Monarchy in the Arabah (Early Edom) and Its Implications to the Study of Ancient Israel," in *From Nomadism to Monarchy? "The Archaeology of the Settlement Period" Thirty Years Later*, ed. Ido Koch, Oded Lipschits, and Omer Sergi (University Park, PA: Eisenbrauns, 2023).

94. Faust, *Israel's Ethnogenesis;* Faust, "Emergence of Israel"; see also Faust, "An Imperial Encounter: The Egyptian Empire in Canaan, Highland Ethnogenesis, and the Transformation of History," in *Power and Identity at the Margins of the Ancient Near East*, ed. Sara Mohr and Shane M. Thompson (Boulder, CO: University Press of Colorado, 2023).

95. See Scott, *The Art of Not Being Governed*, 327, 329.

Late Bronze Age Pottery from Taanach

important to the various groups that comprised this society. Complete avoidance of imported and decorated wares, and the use of simple burials, transmitted an even stronger message of difference, highlighting the effectiveness of the ethos at large. The lack (or extreme rarity) of temples, and the limited ceramic repertoire are also in line with this ethos. The highland settlers formed a relatively simple group, and at this stage the gap between the ethos that the group adopted and reality was not very stark.

During the twelfth century BC, the Egyptian Empire withdrew from the land of Israel. The Egyptian-Canaanite city-state system that characterized the Late Bronze Age was weakened, and while many cities continued to exist, and even prospered, the lowland system lost its influence in the highlands. At this point, the highland settlers had little interaction with the people of the lowlands. We may assume that at this stage the ethos continued to characterize the highland society even if it became less stressed, and the gap between it and social reality was probably still limited.

As the eleventh century progressed, however, the highland population once again confronted a powerful external "other"— the Philistines. By that time, the Philistines had an economic interest in various regions of Judah, and probably also southern Samaria and elsewhere. This strong external pressure led the highlanders to stress the boundaries between themselves and the Philistine "other." In the new ethnic negotiation that ensued, many of the former relevant traits were re-negotiated and were vetted with new meanings. Dominant among these was the ethos of simplicity and egalitarianism, as it highlighted the differences between the highlanders and the highly stratified Philistine society whose members lived in large, stratified cities and used elaborate sets of decorated pottery, etc. The use of undecorated pottery, the avoidance of imported pot-

Iron I Philistine Drinking Bowl from Ashkelon

tery, the avoidance of temples, etc., were therefore all imbued with new meaning.[96]

The interaction with the Philistines, along with other processes, led to growing social complexity and eventually to the creation of the state in ancient Israel regardless of the exact timing. The latter gradually expanded, bringing larger areas under Israelite control.[97] This led to some changes, and for our purposes I should note that one of the changes was the enlargement of the ceramic repertoire.[98] Such changes are to be expected and the larger assemblage was used to convey messages in various daily activities and "ceremonies," as society became more and more stratified.[99] The ethos, however, continued to prevail and most of its manifestations persisted even as society became highly stratified, as

96. New components that were deemed appropriate in the new context, like circumcision and the avoidance of pork which also highlighted difference with the Philistines, were adopted at this time as markers, even if not invented then; Faust, *Israel's Ethnogenesis;* Faust, "Israel's Birth."

97. E.g., Avraham Faust, "The 'United Monarchy' on the Ground: The Disruptive Character of the Iron I–II Transition and the Nature of Political Transformations," *Jerusalem Journal of Archaeology* 1 (2021): 15–67, and references.

98. E.g., Aharoni, *The Archaeology of the Land of Israel*, 239; Finkelstein, *The Archaeology of the Israelite Settlement*, 274; Orna Zimhoni, *Studies in the Iron Age Pottery of Israel: Typological, Archaeological and Chronological Aspects* (Tel Aviv: Tel Aviv University, 1997), 170; Hendricus J. Franken, *A History of Pottery and Potters in Ancient Jerusalem: Excavations by K. M. Kenyon in Jerusalem, 1961–1967* (London: Equinox, 2005), 76.

99. Roland de Vaux, *Ancient Israel: Its Life and Institutions* (New York: McGraw Hill, 1965); Henoch Reviv, *The Society in the Kingdoms of Israel and Judah* (Jerusalem: Bialik Institute, 1993) [Hebrew]; Dever, "Ceramics, Ethnicity"; Faust, *Israelite Society.*

can be seen clearly in the avoidance of imports, in the rarity of decoration, and the growing popularity of the longitudinal four-space house (becoming a standardized form at this stage), as well as in the extreme rarity of temples and lack of royal inscriptions. Since Israelite society had this strong ethos of egalitarianism and simplicity, all these were preserved, forming unique features of the Israelites, and subsequently marking them as different from other peoples.

Society is always dynamic, and in the late eighth century we witness another change with the adoption of noticeable burials in Judah in the form of the Judahite tombs. Still, not only did all other existing manifestations of the ethos continue (i.e., the rarity of decoration, avoidance of imports, use of four-room houses, lack of royals inscriptions, etc.), but this development, while indirectly reflecting stratification, was apparently not developed to convey hierarchy as such, but was rather a result of other social changes related to the growing insecurities of this era and the threat posed on the traditional extended families which comprised the backbone of the Judahite society.[100] Indeed, it appears that by the equal treatment of those interred within the tombs, this ideology continued to be a dominating feature.[101]

Despite the inevitable changes, however, most manifestations of the ethos we defined here as expressing egalitarianism and simplicity continued throughout the existence of Israel and Judah. The rarity of temples, avoidance of decoration on pottery and of the use of imported pottery, as well as the dominant position of the longitudinal four-space house, exhibit one of Israel's most important features: its long-lasting ethos of simplicity and egalitarianism, some evidence of which continues into later epochs.

SUMMARY

From the first phase of its ethnogenesis in the highlands of Canaan during the late thirteenth century BC, Israelite society had a strong ethos of what scholars label as "simplicity" and/or "egalitarianism," which served the settlers as a demarcating feature, differentiating them from their neighbors.[102] The ethos was manifested in various material traits including an aversion to decorating pottery, an aversion to the use of imported pottery, the use of limited ceramic repertoire, an aversion to temples and a priestly class, and more. These features cannot be attributed to the poor "simple life" of the highland villages during the Iron I, as this did not prevent them from, for example, using natural caves for burial, or from decorating their pottery as practiced by much simpler societies, and also because "simple life" cannot explain the prevalence of the above traits in the Iron II. While life in these Iron I villages was indeed simple, it was ideology that dictated a behavior that was not necessitated by this reality even then, let alone later, in the Iron II.

The significance of this ideology and the growing gap between ideology and social reality are expressed in the

100. Faust and Bunimovitz, "The Judahite Rock-Cut Tomb"; see also Faust, *Israelite Society*.

101. Barkay, "Burial Caves and Dwellings in Judah during Iron Age II," 97. We should also remember that not all Judahites adopted the new form of burial and many, probably not only the poor, continued to bury in simple inhumations.

102. See Scott, *The Art of Not Being Governed*.

Iron II as society became more complex. Although the way some of these traits were used or manipulated changed with the evolving circumstances, the ethos prevailed, and even became more expressed as the Israelites avoided (completely or almost completely) the use of royal inscriptions and the use of built temples—both in stark contrast to other nearby societies. Thus, despite the changes in the way some traits were used, like the adoption of a larger ceramic repertoire in the Iron IIA, or of the use of burial caves in the late Iron IIB, the bold manifestation of this ethos remains, as far as most of the traits are concerned, a distinctive feature of Israelite society until its devastation in the late eighth (Israel) and early sixth (Judah) century by the Assyrian and Babylonian empires, and the subsequent collapse of society, with some traits persisting even into the Second Temple period.

BIBLIOGRAPHY

Aharoni, Yohanan. *The Archaeology of the Land of Israel*. Philadelphia: Westminster, 1982.

Ahituv, Shmuel. *Handbook of Ancient Hebrew Inscriptions from the Period of the First Commonwealth and the beginning of the Second Commonwealth*. Jerusalem: Bialik Institute, 1992 [Hebrew].

Albright, William Foxwell. *The Archaeology of Palestine*. Harmondsworth: Penguin, 1961.

Amit, Yairah. *The Book of Judges: The Art of Editing*. Jerusalem: Bialik Institute, 1992 [Hebrew].

Banning, Edward B. "The Neolithic Period: Triumphs of Architecture, Agriculture and Art." *NEA* 61 (1998): 188–237.

Barkay, Gabriel. "Burial Caves and Burial Practices in Judah in the Iron Age." Pages 96–164 in *Graves and Burial Practices in Israel in the Ancient Periods*. Edited by Itamar Singer. Jerusalem: Yad Ben-Zvi, 1994 [Hebrew].

———. "Burial Caves and Dwellings in Judah during Iron Age II: Sociological Aspects." Pages 96–102 in *Material Culture, Society and Ideology, New Directions in the Archaeology of the Land of Israel*. Edited by Avraham Faust and Aren Maier. Ramat Gan: Bar-Ilan University, 1999 [Hebrew].

———. "The Iron Age II–III." Pages 302–73 in *The Archaeology of Israel*. Edited by Amnon Ben-Tor. New Haven: Yale University Press, 1992.

Belfer-Cohen, Anna. "Rethinking Social Stratification in the Natufian Culture: The Evidence from Burial." Pages 9–16 in *The Archaeology of Death in the Ancient Near East*. Edited by Stuart Campbell and Anthony Green. Oxford: Oxbow, 1995.

Ben-Shlomo, David. *Decorated Philistine Pottery: An Archaeological and Archaeometric Study*. Oxford: Archaeopress, 2006.

Ben-Yosef, Erez. "A False Contrast? On the Possibility of an Early Iron Age Nomadic Monarchy in the Arabah (Early Edom) and Its Implications to the Study of Ancient Israel." In *From Nomadism to Monarchy? "The Archaeology of the Settlement Period" Thirty Years Later*. Edited by Ido Koch, Oded Lipschits, and Omer Sergi. University Park, PA: Eisenbrauns, 2023.

Berman, Joshua A. *Created Equals: How the Bible Broke with Ancient Political Thought*. Oxford: Oxford University, 2008.

Binford, Lewis R. *An Archaeological Perspective*. New York: Seminar, 1972.
Biran, Avraham, and Joseph Naveh. "An Aramaic Stele Fragment from Tel Dan." *IEJ* 43 (1993): 81–98.
———. "The Tel Dan Inscription: A New Fragment." *IEJ* 45 (1995): 1–18.
Blanton, Richard E. "Beyond Centralization: Steps Toward a Theory of Egalitarian Behavior." Pages 135–72 in *Archaic States*. Edited by Gary M. Feinman and Joyce Marcus. Santa Fe: Institute of Advanced Studies, 1998.
Bloch, Maurice. "Tombs and States." Pages 137–47 in *Mortality and Immortality: The Anthropology and Archaeology of Death*. Edited by Sarah C. Humphreys and Helen King. London: Academic Press, 1981.
Bloch-Smith, Elizabeth. "Israelite Ethnicity in Iron I: Archaeology Preserves What is Remembered and What is Forgotten in Israel's History." *JBL* 122 (2003): 401–25.
———. *Judahite Burial Practices and Beliefs About the Dead*. Sheffield: Sheffield Academic Press, 1992.
———. "Resurrecting the Iron I Dead." *IEJ* 54 (2004): 77–91.
Bloch-Smith, Elizabeth, and Beth Alpert Nakhai. "A Landscape Comes to Life: The Iron I Period." *NEA* 62 (1999): 62–127.
Boehm, Christopher. "Egalitarian Behavior and Reverse Dominance Hierarchy [and Comments and Reply]." *Current Anthropology* 34 (1993): 227–54.
———. *Hierarchy in the Forest: The Evolution of Egalitarian Behavior*. Cambridge, MA: Harvard University Press, 1999.
Bradley, Guy. "Investigating Aristocracy in Archaic Rome and Central Italy: Social Mobility, Ideology and Cultural Influences." Pages 85–124 in *Aristocracy in Antiquity: Redefining Greek and Roman Elites*. Edited by Nick Fisher and Hans van Wees. Swansea: The Classical Press of Wales, 2015.
Bunimovitz, Shlomo. "'Canaan is Your Land and its Kings are Your Servants': Conceptualizing the Late Bronze Age Egyptian Government in the Southern Levant." Pages 265–79 in *The Social Archaeology of the Levant: From Prehistory to the Present*. Edited by Assaf Yasur-Landau, Eric H. Cline, and Yorke M. Rowan. Cambridge: Cambridge University, 2019.
———. "On the Edge of Empires—the Late Bronze Age (1500–1200 BCE)." Pages 320–31 in *The Archaeology of Society in the Holy Land*. Edited by Thomas E. Levy. London: Leicester University Press, 1995.
———. "The Late Bronze Age." Pages 11–107 in *Introduction to the Archaeology of the Land of Israel: from the Neolithic to Alexander's Conquests*. Volume 2. Edited by Avraham Faust and Hayah Katz. Ra'anana: The Open University of Israel, 2019 [Hebrew].
———. "Socio-Political Transformations in the Central Hill Country in the Late Bronze-Iron I Transition." Pages 172–202 in *From Nomadism to Monarchy: Archaeological and Historical Aspects of Early Israel*. Edited by Israel Finkelstein and Nadav Na'aman. Jerusalem: Yad Ben Zvi, 1994.
Bunimovitz, Shlomo, and Avraham Faust. "Building Identity: The Four Room House and the Israelite Mind." Pages 411–23 in *Symbiosis, Symbolism and the Power of the Past: Canaan, Ancient Israel and Their Neighbors from the Late Bronze Age through*

Roman Palestine. Edited by William G. Dever and Seymour Gitin. Winona Lake, IN: Eisenbrauns, 2003.

———. "Ideology in Stone: Understanding the Four Room House." *BAR* 28 (2002): 32–41, 59–60.

Bunimovitz, Shlomo, and Asaf Yasur-Landau, "Philistine and Israelite Pottery: A Comparative Approach to the Question of Pots and People." *TA* 23 (1996): 88–101.

Burckhardt, Jacob. *The Greeks and Greek Civilization*. New York: St. Martin's Press, 1998.

Burke, Heather. "Ideology and the Material Culture of Life and Death." Pages 128–46 in *Historical Archaeology*. Edited by Martin Hall and Stephan W. Silliman. Oxford: Blackwell, 2006.

Comaroff, John, and Jean Comaroff. *Ethnography and Historical Imagination*. Boulder: Westview Press, 1992.

Cross, Frank Moore. "Reuben, First-Born of Jacob." *ZAW* 100 Sup (1988): 46–65.

David, Nicholas, Judy Sterner, and Kodzo Gavua. "Why Pots are Decorated." *Current Anthropology* 29.3 (1988): 365–89.

de Vaux, Roland. *Ancient Israel: Its Life and Institutions*. New York: McGraw Hill, 1965.

Deetz, James. *In Small Things Forgotten: An Archaeology of Early American Life*. New York: Anchor, 1996.

Dever, William G. "Ceramics, Ethnicity, and the Questions of Israel's Origins." *BA* 58.4 (1995): 200–213.

———. "Ceramics, Syro-Palestinian Ceramics of the Neolithic, Bronze and Iron Ages." *OEANE* 1:459–65.

———. "Cultural Continuity, Ethnicity in the Archaeological Record, and the Question of Israelite Origins." *Eretz-Israel* 24 (1993): 22–33.

———. "How to Tell a Canaanite from an Israelite?" Pages 26–56 in *The Rise of Ancient Israel*. Edited by Hershel Shanks. Washington: Biblical Archaeology Society, 1992.

———. *Who Were the Israelites and Where Did They Come From?* Grand Rapids: Eerdmans, 2003.

Dothan, Trude. *The Philistines and Their Material Culture*. New Haven: Yale University and the Israel Exploration Society, 1982.

Dothan, Trude, and Alexander Zukerman. "A Preliminary Study of the Mycenaean IIIC:1 Pottery Assemblages from Tel Miqne-Ekron and Ashdod." *BASOR* 333 (2004):1–54.

Eisenstadt, Irina, Khaled Arabas, and Zur Ablas. "A Late Bronze Age Burial Cave at Zawata." Pages 77–106 in *Burial Caves and Sites in Judea and Samaria from the Bronze and Iron Ages*. Edited by Hananya Hizmi and Alon De-Groot. Jerusalem: Staff Officer of Archaeology—Civil Administration of Judea and Samaria and Israel Antiquities Authority, 2004.

Eriksen, Thomas Hylland. *Small Places, Large Issues: An Introduction to Social and Cultural Anthropology*. 4th ed. London: Pluto Press, 2015.

Esse, Douglas L. "The Collared Pithos at Megiddo: Ceramic Distribution and Ethnicity." *JNES* 51 (1992): 81–103.

———. "The Collared Store Jar: Scholarly Ideology and Ceramic Typology." *SJOT* 2 (1991): 99–116.

Faust, Avraham. "The Archaeology of the Israelite Cult: Questioning the Consensus." *BASOR* 360 (2010): 23–35.

———. *The Archaeology of Israelite Society in Iron Age II*. Winona Lake, IN: Eisenbrauns, 2012.

———. "Between the House of the Father and the House of the Lord: Privacy and Purity in the Israelite Dwelling and the Israelite Temple." Pages 65–84 in *Contextualizing Jewish Temples*. Edited by Tova Ganzel and Shalom Holtz. Leiden: Brill, 2020.

———. "Burnished Pottery and Gender Hierarchy in Iron Age Israelite Society." *Journal of Mediterranean Archaeology* 15.1 (2002): 53–73.

———. "The Canaanite Village: Social Structure of Middle Bronze Age Rural Communities." *Levant* 37 (2005): 105–25.

———. "Decoration Versus Simplicity: Pottery and Ethnic Negotiations in Early Israel." *Ars Judaica* 9 (2013): 7–18.

———. "The Emergence of Iron Age Israel: On Origins and Habitus." Pages 467–82 in *Israel's Exodus in Transdisciplinary Perspective: Text, Archeology, Culture, and Geoscience*. Edited by Thomas E. Levy, Thomas Schneider, and William. H. C. Propp. New York: Springer, 2015.

———. "The Emergence of Israel and Theories of Ethnogenesis." Pages 155–73 in *Blackwell Companion to Ancient Israel*. Edited by Susan Niditch. Oxford: Blackwell, 2016.

———. "How Were the Israelites Buried?: The Lack of Iron Age I Burial Sites in the Highlands in Context." Pages 12–32 in *The Highlands Depth: Ephraim Range and Binyamin*. Edited by Aharon Tavger, Zohar Amar, and Miriam Billig. Bethel: Midreshet Harei Gofna, 2011.

———. "An Imperial Encounter: The Egyptian Empire in Canaan, Highland Ethnogenesis, and the Transformation of History." Pages 14–41 in *Power and Identity at the Margins of the Ancient Near East*. Edited by Sara Mohr and Shane M. Thompson. Boulder, CO: University Press of Colorado, 2023.

———. *Israel's Ethnogenesis: Settlement, Interaction, Expansion and Resistance*. London: Equinox, 2006.

———. "Israel's Birth." Pages 4–32 in *The Oxford Illustrated History of the Holy Land*. Edited by Hugh G. M. Williamson and Robert G. Hoyland. Oxford: Oxford University Press, 2018.

———. "Israelite Temples: Where Was Israelite Cult Not Practiced and Why." *Religions* 10.2 (2019): 106.

———. "Mortuary Practices, Society and Ideology: The Lack of Highlands Iron Age I Burials in Context." *IEJ* 54 (2004): 174–90.

———. "The Rural Community in Ancient Israel during the Iron Age II." *BASOR* 317 (2000): 17–39.

———. "Trade, Ideology and Boundary Maintenance in Iron Age Israelite Society." Pages 17–35 in *A Holy Community*. Edited by Marcel Purthuis and Joshua Schwartz. Leiden: Brill, 2006.

———. "The 'United Monarchy' on the Ground: The Disruptive Character of the Iron I–II Transition and the Nature of Political Transformations." *Jerusalem Journal of Archaeology* 1 (2021): 15–67.

Faust, Avraham, and Shlomo Bunimovitz. "The Four Room House: Embodying Iron Age Israelite Society." *NEA* 66 (2003): 22–33.

———. "The House and the World: The Israelite House as a Microcosm." Pages 143–64 in *Family and Household Religion: Toward a Synthesis of Old Testament Studies, Archaeology, Epigraphy, and Cultural Studies*. Edited by Rainer Albertz, Beth Alpert Nakhai,

Saul M. Olyan and Rüdiger Schmitt. Winona Lake: Eisenbrauns, 2014.
———."The Judahite Rock-Cut Tomb: Family Response at a Time of Change." *IEJ* 58 (2008): 150–70.
Faust, Avraham, and Ehud Weiss. "Judah, Philistia, and the Mediterranean World: Reconstructing the Economic System of the Seventh Century B.C.E." *BASOR* 338 (2005): 71–92.
Faust, Avraham, Hayah Katz, Yair Sapir, Assaf Avraham, Ofer Marder, Guy Bar-Oz, Ehud Weiss, et al. "The Birth, Life and Death of an Iron Age House at Tel 'Eton, Israel." *Levant* 49 (2017): 136–73.
Finkelstein, Israel. *The Archaeology of the Israelite Settlement*. Jerusalem: Israel Exploration Society, 1988.
———. "The Emergence of the Monarchy in Israel: The Environmental and Socio-Economic Aspects." *JSOT* 44 (1989): 43–74.
Fleming, Daniel E. *Democracy's Ancient Ancestors: Mari and Early Collective Governance*. Cambridge: Cambridge University Press, 2004.
Franken, Hendricus J. *A History of Pottery and Potters in Ancient Jerusalem: Excavations by K.M. Kenyon in Jerusalem, 1961–1967*. London: Equinox, 2005.
Franken, Hendricus J. and Margarete L. Steiner. *Excavations in Jerusalem 1961–1967, Volume II*. London: Oxford University Press, 1990.
Frankfort, Henri, Henriëtte. A. Frankfort, John A. Wilson, Thorkild Jacobsen, and William A. Irwin. *The Intellectual Adventure of Ancient Man: An Essay on Speculative Thought in the Ancient Near East*. Chicago: Chicago University Press, 1946.
Giddens, Anthony. *Sociology*. Cambridge: Polity Press, 1993.
Gilboa, Ayelet, Ilan Sharon, and Jeffrey R. Zorn. "An Iron Age Canaanite/Phoenician Courtyard House at Tel Dor: A Comparative Architectural and Functional Analysis." *BASOR* 372 (2014): 39–80.
Gitin, Seymour, Trude Dothan, and Joseph Naveh. "A Royal Dedicatory Inscription from Ekron." *IEJ* 47 (1997): 1–16.
Gonen, Rivka. *Burial Patterns and Cultural Diversity in Late Bronze Age Canaan*. Winona Lake: Eisenbrauns, 1992.
———. "The Late Bronze Age." Pages 211–57 in *The Archaeology of Israel*. Edited by Amnon Ben-Tor. New Haven: Yale University Press, 1992.
Gordis, Robert. "Primitive Democracy in Ancient Israel." Pages 45–60 in *Poets, Prophets and Sages, Essays in Biblical Interpretation*. Edited by Robert Gordis. London: Bloomington, 1971.
Gossai, Hemchand. *Justice, Righteousness and the Social Critique of the Eighth-Century Prophets*. New York: Lang, 1993.
Gottwald, Norman K. *The Tribes of Yahweh*. New York: Orbis Books, 1979.
Greener, Aaron. "Archaeology and Religion in Late Bronze Age Canaan." *Religions* 10.4 (2019): 258.
Guillaume, Philippe. "Poor by Necessity or by Choice? Ancient Israelite Egalitarianism." Pages 102–11 in *The Land of Canaan in the Late Bronze Age*. Edited by Lester L. Grabbe. London: Bloomsbury, 2016.
Hallo, William W. "Introduction: The Bible and the Monuments." Pages xxi–xxvi in *Monumental Inscriptions from the Biblical World*. Vol. 2 of *The Context of the Scripture*. Leiden: Brill, 2003.

Hawkins, Ralph. *How Israel Became a People*. Nashville: Abingdon Press, 2013.
Hodder, Ian. *The Present Past: An Introduction to Anthropology for Archaeologists*. New York: Pica Press, 1982.
Hodder, Ian, and Scott Hutson. *Reading the Past*. 3rd ed. Cambridge: Cambridge University, 2003.
Hopkins, Keith. "Novel Evidence for Roman Slavery." *Past and Present* 138 (1993): 3–27.
Humphreys, Sarah C. *Anthropology and the Greeks*. London: Routledge and Kegan Paul, 1978.
Ilan, David. "Burial Sites." *OEANE* 1:384–86.
———. "Tombs." *OEANE* 1:218–21.
Jacobsen, Thorkild. "Primitive Democracy in Ancient Mesopotamia." *JNES* 2 (1943): 159–72.
Keimer, Kyle. "New Light from Iron Age I Tell en-Nasbeh." Paper Presented at the American Schools of Oriental Research Annual Meeting. Denver, CO, 14–17 November 2018.
Kelso, James L. *Excavation at Bethel (1934–1960)*. Cambridge, MA: American Schools of Oriental Research, 1968.
Killebrew, Ann E. *Biblical Peoples and Ethnicity: An Archaeological Study of Egyptians, Canaanites, Philistines, and Early Israel 1300–1100 B.C.E.* Atlanta: Society of Biblical Literature, 2005.
King, Philip J., and Lawrence E. Stager. *Life in Biblical Israel*. Louisville: Westminster John Knox, 2001.
Kletter, Raz. "People Without Burials? The Lack of Iron Age Burials in the Central Highlands of Palestine." *IEJ* 52 (2002): 28–48.
———. "Water from a Rock: Archaeology, Ideology, and the Bible." *SJOT* 30 (2016): 161–84.
Kroeber, Alfred Louis. *Anthropology*. New York: Harcourt, Brace and Company, 1948.
Lamberg-Karlovsky, Clifford C. "The Near Eastern 'Breakout' and the Mesopotamian Social Contract." *Symbols: Newsletter of the Peabody Museum and Department of Anthropology* (1985): 8–11, 23–24.
Lapp, Nancy L. "Pottery, Pottery Chronology of Palestine." *ABD* 5:433–44.
Lehmann, Gunnar, and Oz Varoner. "Early Iron Age Tombs in Northern Israel Revisited." *TA* 45 (2018): 235–72.
Lemche, Nils Peter. *Ancient Israel*. Leiden: Brill, 1985.
Lenski, Gerhard. "Review of N.K. Gottwald, The Tribes of Yahweh." *Religious Studies Review* 6 (1980): 275–78.
Levy, Thomas E., Russell B. Adams, and Adolfo Muniz. "Archaeology and the Shasu Nomads: Recent Excavations in the Jabal Himdat Firdan, Jordan." Pages 63–89 in *Le-David Maskil: A Birthday Tribute to David Noel Freedman*. Edited by Richard Elliot Friedman and William H. C. Propp. Winona Lake, IN: Eisenbrauns, 2004.
Levy, Thomas E., and Augustin F. C. Holl. "Migrations, Ethnogenesis, and Settlement Dynamics: Israelites in Iron Age Canaan and Shuwa-Arabs in the Chad Basin." *Journal of Anthropological Archaeology* 21 (2002): 83–118.
Lipschitz, Nili. *Timbers in Ancient Israel: Dendroarchaeology and Dendrochronology*. Tel Aviv: Tel Aviv University, 2007.
Lipschitz, Nili, and Gideon Biger. "Cedar of Lebanon (*Cedrus Libani*) in Israel during Antiquity." *IEJ* 41 (1991): 167–75.
Livingstone, David. "A Middle Bronze Age II and Iron Age I Tomb (No. 65)

at Khirbet Nisya." *'Atiqot* 43 (2002): 17–35.

Livni, Joseph. "Testing Competing Archaeological Theories of Israel's Origins Using Computational Techniques." *Archeologia e Calcolatori* 28 (2017): 109–28.

Lods, Adolphe. *Israel, from Its Beginning to the Middle of the Eighth Century*. New York: A. A. Knauf, 1932.

Macionis, John J. *Sociology*. Tel Aviv: Open University of Israel, 1999 [Hebrew].

Malchow, Bruce V. *Social Justice in the Hebrew Bible*. Collegeville: Liturgical Press, 1996.

Mazar, Amihai. "The Iron Age I." Pages 258–301 in *The Archaeology of Israel*. Edited by Amnon Ben-Tor. New Haven: Yale University Press, 1992.

———. "The Israelite Settlement in Canaan in the Light of Archaeological Excavations." Pages 61–71 in *Biblical Archaeology Today—1984: Proceedings of the International Congress on Biblical Archaeology, Jerusalem, April 1984*. Edited by Janet Amitai. Jerusalem: Israel Exploration Society, 1985.

———. "Temples of the Middle and Late Bronze Age and the Iron Age." Pages 161–87 in *The Architecture of Ancient Israel from the Prehistoric to the Persian Period*. Edited by Aharon Kempinsky and Ronny Reich. Jerusalem: Israel Exploration Society, 1992.

McCarter, P. Kyle. *Ancient Inscriptions: Voices from the Biblical World*. Washington D. C.: Biblical Archaeology Society, 1996.

McGuire, Randall H. "Dialogues with the Dead: Ideology and the Cemetery." Pages 435–80 in *The Recovery of Meaning: Historical Archaeology in the Eastern United States*. Edited by Mark P. Leone and Parker B. Potter, Jr. Washington and London: Smithsonian Institution Press, 1988.

McHugh, Feldore. *Theoretical and Quantitative Approaches to the Study of Mortuary Practice*. Oxford: Archaeopress, 1999.

Mendenhall, George E. "The Hebrew Conquest of Palestine." *BA* 25 (1962):66–87.

Metcalf, Peter, and Richard Huntington. *Celebrations of Death: The Anthropology of Mortuary Ritual*. Cambridge: Cambridge University Press, 1991.

Miller, Robert D. "Identifying Earliest Israel." *BASOR* 333 (2004): 55–68.

Morris, Ellen. *Ancient Egyptian Imperialism*. Medford: Wiley Blackwell, 2018.

Morris, Ian. "An Archaeology of Equalities? The Greek City-States." Pages 91–105 in *The Archaeology of City-States: Cross-Cultural Approaches*. Edited by Deborah L. Nichols and Thomas H. Charlton. Washington D. C.: Smithsonian Institution Press, 1997.

Na'aman, Nadav. *The Past that Shapes the Present: The Creation of Biblical Historiography in the Late First Temple Period and After the Downfall*. Jerusalem: Yeriot, 2002.

Nadel, Dani. "The Visibility of Prehistoric Burials in the Southern Levant: How Rare are the Upper Paleolithic/ Early Epipaleolithic Graves?" Pages 1–8 in *The Archaeology of Death in the Ancient Near East*. Edited by Stuart Campbell and Anthony Green. Oxford: Oxbow, 1995.

Hume, Ivor Noël. *A Guide to Artifacts of Colonial America*. New York: Knopf, 1974.

Nolan, Patrick, and Gerhard Lenski. *Human Societies: An Introduction*

to Macrosociology. 11th ed. London: Paradigm, 2009.
Oren, Eliezer. "'Governor's Residencies' in Canaan under the New Kingdom: A Case Study of Egyptian Administration." *Journal of the Society for the Study of Egyptian Antiquities* 14 (1984): 37–56.
Pearson, Michael Parker. *The Archaeology of Death and Burial*. Sparkford: Sutton Publishing Limited and J. H. Haynes & Co. Ltd, 2000.
———. "Mortuary Practices, Society and Ideology: An Ethnoarchaeological Case Study." Pages 99–113 in *Symbolic and Structural Archaeology*. Edited by Ian Hodder. Cambridge: Cambridge University Press, 1982.
Peleg, Yuval. "Early Roman Farmhouse and Late Bronze Age Burial Cave East of Otniel." Pages 260–84 in *Burial Caves and Sites in Judea and Samaria from the Bronze and Iron Ages*. Edited by Hananya Hizmi and Alon De-Groot. Jerusalem: Staff Officer of Archaeology—Civil Administration of Judea and Samaria and Israel Antiquities Authority, 2004.
Peleg, Yuval, and Irina Eisenstadt. "A Late Bronze Age Tomb at Hebron (Tell Rumeideh)." Pages 231–59 in *Burial Caves and Sites in Judea and Samaria from the Bronze and Iron Ages*. Edited by Hananya Hizmi and Alon De-Groot. Jerusalem: Staff Officer of Archaeology—Civil Administration of Judea and Samaria and Israel Antiquities Authority, 2004.
Postgate, John N. *Early Mesopotamia, Society and Economy at the Dawn of History*. London: Routledge, 1992.
Rainey, Anson F. "Israel in Merenptah Inscription and Reliefs." *IEJ* 51 (2001): 57–75.
Redford, Donald B. *Egypt, Canaan, and Israel in Ancient Times*. Princeton: Princeton University Press, 1992.
Reich, Ronny. "Palaces and Residences in the Iron Age." Pages 202–22 in *The Architecture of Ancient Israel from the Prehistoric to the Persian Period*. Edited by Aharon Kempinski and Ronny Reich. Jerusalem: Israel Exploration Society, 1992.
Remini, Robert V. *The Legacy of Andrew Jackson: Essays on Democracy, Indian Removal, and Slavery*. Baton Rouge: Louisiana University Press, 1988.
Rendsburg, Gary. "No Stelae, No Queens: Two Issues Concerning the Kings of Israel and Judah." Pages 95–107 in *The Archaeology of Difference: Gender, Ethnicity, Class and the 'Other' in Antiquity: Studies in Honor of Eric M. Meyers*. Edited by Douglas R. Edwards and C. Thomas McCollough. Boston: American Schools of Oriental Research, 2007.
Reviv, Henoch. *The Society in the Kingdoms of Israel and Judah*. Jerusalem: Bialik Institute, 1993 [Hebrew].
Schreiber, Nicola. *The Cypro-Phoenician Pottery of the Iron Age*. Leiden: Brill, 2003.
Scott, James C. *The Art of Not Being Governed: An Anarchist History of Upland Southeast Asia*. New Haven: Yale University Press, 2009.
Shackel, Paul A. "Craft to Wage Labor: Agency and Resistance in American Historical Archaeology." Pages 232–46 in *Agency in Archaeology*. Edited by Marcia-Anne Dobres and John Robb. London: Routledge, 2000.
Shapira, Amnon. *Democratic Values in the Hebrew Bible*. Tel Aviv: Hakibbutz Hameuchad, 2009 [Hebrew].
———. "'He Appointed Judges in the Land in all the Fortified Towns of

Judah' (2 Chron. 19:45)—an Expression of the Separation of Powers in Israel." *Judea and Samaria Research Studies* 7 (1998): 233–43 [Hebrew].

Singer, Itamar. "Merneptah's Campaign to Canaan and the Egyptian Occupation of the Southern Coastal Plain of Palestine in the Ramesside Period." *BASOR* 269 (1988): 1–10.

Sparks, Kenton L. "The Egalitarian Spirit in Biblical Law." *Sapientia Logos* 1 (2008): 99–121

———. *Ethnicity and Identity in Ancient Israel*. Winona Lake, IN: Eisenbrauns, 1998.

———. "Religion, Identity and the Origins of Ancient Israel." *Religion Compass* 1 (2007): 587–614.

Speiser, Ephraim Avigdor. "The Manner of the Kings." Pages 280–87 in vol. 3 of *The World History of the Jewish People: Judges*. Edited by Benjamin Mazar. Jerusalem: Masada.

Stein, Gil. "Economy, Ritual and Power in 'Ubaid Mesopotamia." Pages 35–46 in *Chiefdoms and Early States in the Near East: The Organizational Dynamics of Complexity*. Edited by Gil Stein and Mitchell S. Rothman. Madison: Prehistory Press, 1994.

Tappy, Ron. "Did the Dead Ever Die in Biblical Judah?" *BASOR* 298 (1995): 59–68.

Tyson, Craig W. *The Ammonites: Elites, Empires, and Sociopolitical Change (1000–500 BCE)*. London: Bloomsbury, 2014.

Wolf, C. Umhau. "Traces of Primitive Democracy in Ancient Israel." *JNES* 6 (1947): 98–108.

Wright, Gary A. "Social Differentiation in the Early Natufian." Pages 201–223 in *Social Archaeology, Beyond Subsistence and Dating*. Edited by Charles L. Redman, Mary Jane Berman, Edward V. Curtin, William T. Langhorne Jr., Nina M. Versaggi, and Jeffery C. Wanser. New York: Academic Press, 1978.

Zimhoni, Orna. *Studies in the Iron Age Pottery of Israel: Typological, Archaeological and Chronological Aspects*. Tel Aviv: Tel Aviv University, 1997.

CHAPTER 27

THE JEPHTHAH NARRATIVE IN ITS HISTORICAL-GEOGRAPHICAL CONTEXT

Judg 10:6–12:7

Elaine A. Phillips

KEY POINTS

- The region of Gilead on the east side of the Jordan River was prime geopolitical real estate
- Jephthah's attempt to negotiate with the Ammonite king as the result of Ammonite aggression into Gilead must be read in the context of Israel's prior history in Transjordan
- The theological components of the Jephthah narrative are reminders of God's presence, even in the unusual circumstances in which his covenant people find themselves

INTRODUCTION

When the Israelites who had settled in the region of Gilead east of the Jordan River experienced God's chastisement during the period of the judges, it was the hand of the Ammonites that afflicted them. There was a long history underlying this instance of Ammonite aggression, the response of the threatened Israelite tribes, and Jephthah's attempts at negotiating with the Ammonite ruler. When the king rebuffed Jephthah's appeal, Jephthah rehearsed the narrative of Israel's conquest of Transjordan to demonstrate that the Ammonite king's claims were false. Because these contested regions were eminently desirable, they were frequently caught in the vice of surrounding political entities vying for control.

The geographical data interfaces with the theological components of the narrative. Prior to engaging in battle against

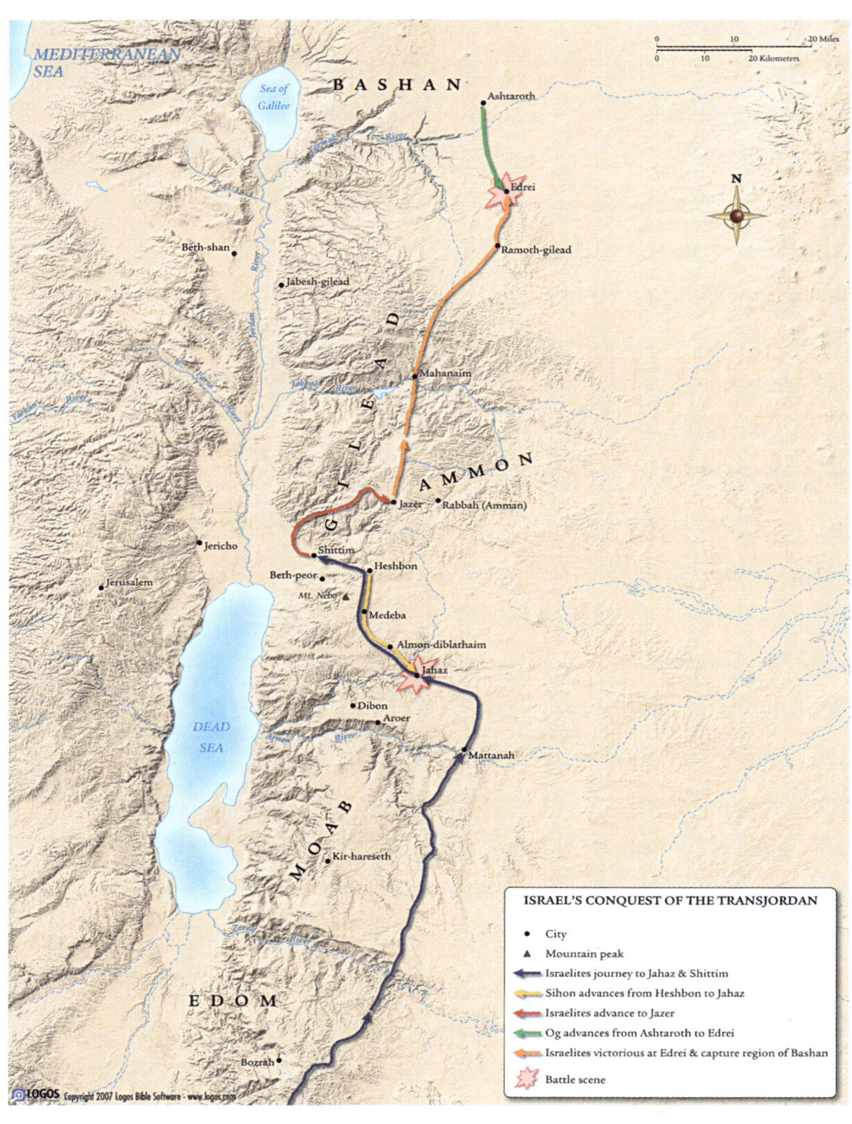

the Israelites' formidable oppressors in this contested area, Jephthah made a vow commensurate with the task before him. The nature and fulfillment of that vow are subject to a range of interpretive options, some of which are elucidated by insights from the cultural backdrop.

THE GEOPOLITICAL BACKDROP

The key issues here will be the regions of central Transjordan that were particularly attractive, the centers of control in these regions, and the flexible boundaries of the ethnic groups that attempted to dominate them.

Arnon River Flowing Through a Canyon

GEOGRAPHICAL FEATURES AND SPHERES OF POLITICAL CONTROL IN TRANSJORDAN

There are four major river systems that define significant regions and regional control in Transjordan.[1] From north to south, they are the Yarmuk, Jabbok, Arnon, and Zered.[2] Both the Jabbok and the Arnon figure in the Jephthah narrative. At first glance, the Jabbok might be

1. See George Adam Smith, *The Historical Geography of the Holy Land* (London: Hodder & Stoughton, 1894; repr., London: Fontana Library, 1966), 335–42; A. Denis Baly, *The Geography of the Bible*, rev. ed. (New York: Harper and Row, 1974), 210–13, 219–25; Yohanan Aharoni, *The Land of the Bible: A Historical Geography*, trans. Anson F. Rainey, rev. and enl. ed. (Philadelphia, Westminster, 1979), 36–40; Carl G. Rasmussen, *Zondervan Atlas of the Bible*, rev. ed. (Grand Rapids: Zondervan, 2010), 57–63.

2. The modern name of the Arnon is the Mujib; the Zered is Wadi Zarqa.

expected to serve as a natural boundary, separating the expanse to the north from the area to the south. Its course, however, is more complicated. It cuts west to east through the higher elevation known as the Dome of Gilead (or Upper Gilead), then loops to the south, swinging quite close to the city of Rabbah, and turning yet again toward the west. Rabbah was the hub of the small Ammonite kingdom. Segments of the Jabbok that make this loop served as borders of sorts, although permeable (see Num 21:24).

The river Arnon separates geopolitical Moab to its south from the Medeba Plateau, also known as the *mishor* (מִישׁוֹר; see Josh 13:9, 16). A sizable wadi, called Wadi Heidan, branches northeast from the Arnon toward the *mishor*. It softens the sense of a definitive boundary at the deep Arnon canyon and, instead, opens the *mishor* to intrusion from the south. The *mishor* continues to the east as it merges with the eastern desert lands. To the west are rugged cliffs adjacent to the Sea of Salt (Dead Sea).

The Dome of Gilead was inviting. The cenomanian limestone bedrock results in good soils and springs, the higher elevation means significant rainfall, and the western slopes of Gilead are agriculturally productive. There is no distinct topographical feature that separates the southern fringe of Gilead from Ammon to the southeast or the *mishor* to the south.

These features increased the likelihood of incursion into both Gilead and the *mishor*. Both regions became targets as nearby kings extended their control as far as they could. Prior to the Israelites' arrival, Sihon, king of the Amorites in Heshbon, controlled half of Gilead, the eastern Arabah from the Sea of Kinnereth to the Sea of Salt and southward below the slopes of Pisgah (Josh 12:2–3), as well as all of the cities that were in the *mishor* (Josh 13:17–21). He had previously wrested control of the entire region north of the Arnon from the king of Moab (Num 21:26). Sometime in the distant past, Moabites had apparently driven out a group known as the Emites (Deut 2:10–11).

The north-south travel route, called the King's Highway (Num 20:17; 21:22), connected major cities and population centers. Notable among these cities in central Transjordan were Aroer, Medeba, Heshbon, and Jazer.[3] Travelers moving farther north encountered Ramath Mizpah, Ramoth Gilead, and Edrei.[4]

ISRAELITE CONQUEST AND SETTLEMENT OF TRANSJORDAN

After crossing the Zered Valley and camping alongside the Arnon (Num 21:12–13; Deut 2:13), Israel encountered Sihon, king of the Amorites, and Og, king of Bashan (Num 21:21–35; see also Deut 2:26–37). The definitive battle between the Israelites and Og took place at Edrei (Num 21:33–35; Deut 3:1–10).

---

3. Jazer was west of Rabbah (in Ammon) although the prominence of Rabbah is indicated by the number of ancient routes that converged there. See the map of central Transjordan.

4. Although it is not identified with certainty, Ramath Mizpah seems to have been near the Jabbok in the Dome of Gilead. Place names often reflected characteristic geographical features. Mizpah comes from the Hebrew word *mitspeh* (מִצְפֶּה) which means to "look out" or "keep watch," suggesting a raised location. There are multiple places capturing this feature: Mizpah of Moab (1 Sam 22:3); Mizpah in Benjamin (1 Sam 7:16; 10:17); and this one in Gilead (Judg 10:17; 11:11,34). Likewise, *ram* (רָם) means "high" or "elevated." Both elements of this name suggest the place had strategic significance.

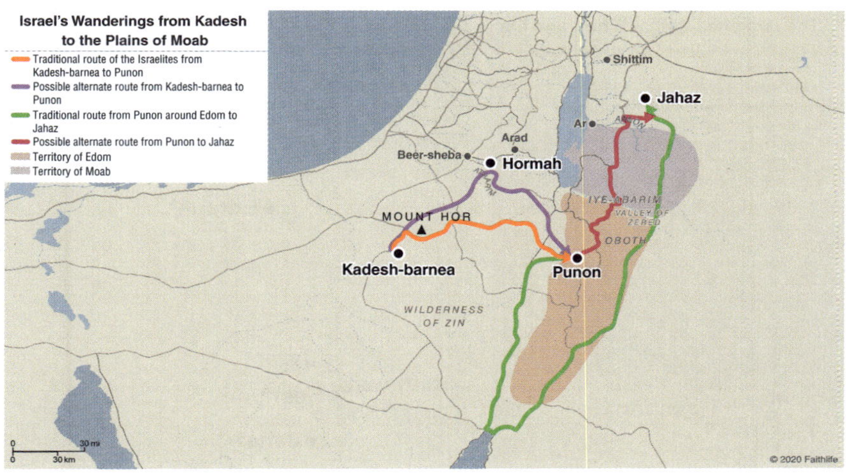

Victories over these two kings gave the Israelites extensive territory in Transjordan, and the tribes of Reuben, Gad, and the half-tribe of Manasseh, stepped up to lay claim (Num 32). At the time, they requested specifically the *mishor* (32:3) and Gilead (32:26). Once settled, the *mishor* and Gilead were loosely under the control of both Reuben and Gad; the Jordan Valley north to the Sea of Kinnereth was settled by half the Manassites (Deut 3: 12–17; Josh 13:8–31). Little did they know these would be perilous regions for centuries to follow; threats to Israel's security often came from the east and northeast. This started already in the period of the judges and only got worse. For example, Gideon faced Midianites (Judg 6–7), the judge immediately prior to Jephthah, Jair, served in Gilead (10:3–5), and Ehud dealt with a coalition of Moabites, Ammonites, and Amalekites, all coming to Benjamin from the east (3:12–14).[5]

The potentially ambiguous boundaries in these regions are evident in the textual indicators regarding the Ammonites in particular. In the initial conquest narrative, we learn that Israel took king Sihon's land "from the Arnon to the Jabbok, to the Ammonites, because the border of the Ammonites was strong" (Num 21:24).[6] Deuteronomy 3:16 indicates that the Reubenites and Gadites were given territory from the Gilead to the Arnon and to the Jabbok; the last served as a border for the Ammonites. This description may refer to the part of the Jabbok that actually curved southeast, south, and then circled slightly back west. Israel was not to take any of the Ammonite territory (Deut 2:19), but just what this meant seems to have been subject to change.

5. In 732 BC, Tiglath-Pileser III took the two and a half tribes into exile (1 Chr 5:26; 2 Kgs 15:29), and the territories became Assyrian provinces. See Anson F. Rainey and R. Steven Notley, *The Sacred Bridge: Carta's Atlas of the Biblical World* (Jerusalem: Carta, 2006), 229–32.

6. Unless otherwise indicated, all translations are the author's own.

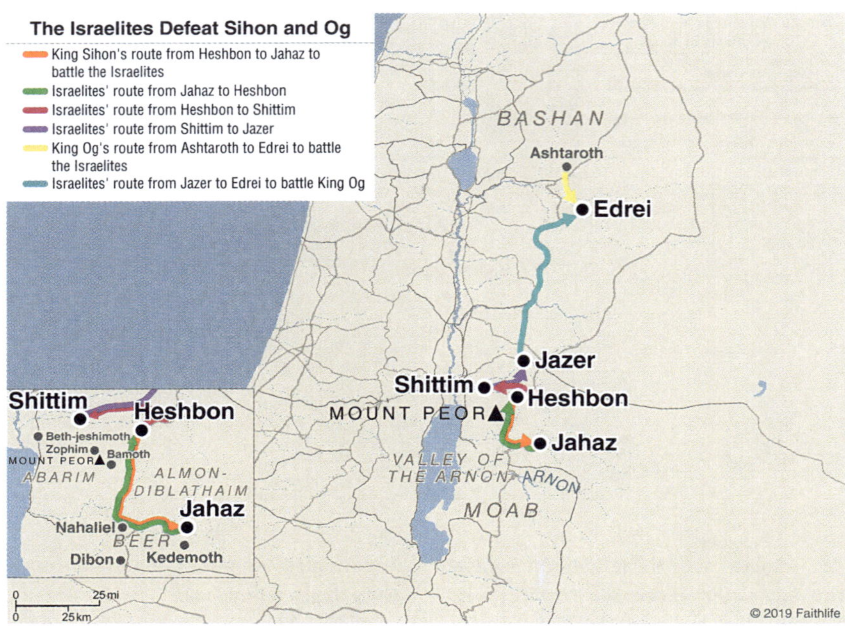

Joshua 12:2 also names the Jabbok River as a border of the Ammonites. This description echoes part of the description of Sihon's former territorial holdings (Num 21:24); the defining points are "from Aroer on the edge of the Arnon" to the Jabbok. In between was half of Gilead. The comprehensive three-tribe description in Josh 13:10 indicates that their holdings went out to the boundary of Ammonite territory.[7] Nevertheless, Josh 13:25–28 notes that Moses gave all the towns of Gilead and half the land of the Ammonites, up to Aroer, which was opposite Rabbah, as an inheritance to Gad.[8] The later record in 1 Chronicles inserts a note in regard to tribal mobility; the Gadites lived in Bashan, but also in Gilead and the pasturelands of Sharon (1 Chr 5:11–16).[9]

Reuben's parcel included all the towns on the *mishor*, the entire realm of Sihon (Josh 13:16–21). Again, the later perspective of 1 Chronicles notes that

7. Moses' review of the land apportionment indicated that Reuben and Gad together received the territory north of the Arnon and up to half of Gilead. The rest of Gilead and all of Bashan went to the half tribe of Manasseh. In this context we also learn that Jair had taken a good portion of the Bashan, resulting in the name Havvoth Jair ("villages/settlements of Jair"), and that Moses gave Gilead to Makir, the most significant descendant of Manasseh (Deut 3:12–17).

8. The southernmost city noted is Heshbon, but the Gadites ranged as far north as Ramath Mizpah and Mahanaim with claims in the Arabah stretching as far north as the shore of the Kinnereth. The towns of Succoth and Zaphon are also mentioned.

9. This is the Sharon of eastern Palestine (Smith, *Historical Geography*, 353). The word "Sharon" comes from the same root as *mishor* (ישׁר, *yshr*), indicating a flat area.

TRIBAL DISTRIBUTION
OF PALESTINE
City
Mountain
Territory shared by the tribes
of Judah and Simeon
0 15 30 Miles
0 15 30 Kilometers
MEDITERRANEAN
SEA
N
Damascus
Mt. Hermon
Pharpar River
Litani River
Ijon
Tyre
Dan
ASHER
Kedesh
Yiron
Lake Huleh
Merom
Hazor
EAST
MANASSEH
Acco
NAPHTALI
Cabul
Sea of Galilee
Hannathon
Rimmon
ZEBULUN
Daberath
Yarmuk River
Jokneam
Mt. Tabor
Sarid
Chesulloth
Edrei
Megiddo
ISSACHAR
Taanach
Jezreel
Beth-shan
Ramoth-gilead
Ibleam
Mt. Gilboa
Dothan
Jabesh-gilead
WEST
MANASSEH
Jordan
Socoh
Samaria
Mt. Ebal
Succoth
Pirathon
Shechem
Mt. Gerizim
Mahanaim
Jabbok River
Aphek
Tappuah
Janoah
Joppa
Shiloh
GAD
EPHRAIM
River
Lod
Rabbah (Amman)
DAN
Upper Beth-horon
Bethel
Jericho
Jabneel
Gezer
Mizpah
Shittim
Aijalon
Gibeon
Heshbon
Kiriath-Jearim
Adummim
Beth-hoglah
Bezer
Ashdod
Ekron
Beth-shemesh
Jerusalem
BENJAMIN
Mt. Nebo
Medeba
Gath
Bethlehem
Ashkelon
REUBEN
Beth-zur
Hebron
Gaza
Dibon
JUDAH
En-gedi
DEAD SEA
Aroer
Gerar
Ziklag
Eshtemoa
Arnon River
Besor
Sharuhen
Beersheba
Arad
Brook
Hormah
SIMEON
Kir-hareseth
Zered River
Tamar
Bozrah
Kadesh-barnea

Reuben occupied land up to the edge of the desert that extends to the Euphrates, the entire region east of Gilead, because the livestock had increased in Gilead (1 Chr 5:9–10). This suggests movement far to the east of any boundary the Jabbok might have marked.

The half-tribe of Manasseh was farther north. The regions under their control included all of Bashan, but also half of Gilead (Josh 13:30–31). The sixty cities of Havvoth Jair in Bashan are noted. This is particularly interesting since thirty towns in Gilead were called Havvoth Jair after the thirty sons of Jair, the judge (Judg 10:3–5).[10] Just as the eastern and southern boundaries of Gilead were fluid, so too was the northern boundary as it phased into Bashan.

This conclusion is strengthened by the indication already in Numbers that the descendants of Makir, son of Manasseh, went to Gilead and captured it, driving out the Amorites. Thus, Moses gave Gilead to the clan of Makir (Num 32:39–40).[11] The area was likely named after a descendant of Manasseh through the Makir clan.[12] The Gilead clan itself was extensive (Num 26:29–33) and likely populated a good portion of the region. At the same time, Gadites were also there, along with Reubenites (Josh 22:9–15; 1 Chr 5:11–16). In the aftermath of the Jephthah incident, when the Ephraimites realized they had been robbed of the honor of participating in the defeat of the Ammonites, they insulted the Gileadites by declaring them escapees from Ephraim and Manasseh (Judg 12:4). It seems that Gilead had become a miniature melting pot for the two and a half tribes (Josh 22:9–15).

Just as King Sihon had flexed his geopolitical muscle across invisible and flexible boundaries, so also the unnamed Ammonite king in Judges 10–12 attempted the same thing several centuries later. That sets the stage for the narrative of Jephthah, but first, a theological connection is necessary.

THEOLOGY AND GEOGRAPHY: REPEATED APOSTASY BROUGHT HOSTILITY FROM NEIGHBORING PEOPLES

During the period of the judges, the Israelites spiraled down into one idolatrous disaster after another. In response, the Lord used neighboring people groups to bring judgment upon them. When the people cried out in despair, the Lord sent judges to rescue them from oppression. Sadly, their repentance was short-lived, and the grim pattern repeated itself over and over again, looping progressively into more heinous idolatry with each successive incident (e.g., Judg 2:10–18).

It is against this wider backdrop that the individual narrative of Jephthah must be read. The surrounding nations are identified in conjunction with their

10. See Smith, *Historical Geography*, 355–56.

11. In this context, we again read of Jair capturing settlements and calling the whole enclave Havvoth Jair (Num 32:41).

12. Gilead either seems to have been a repeated family name, or the genealogical indicators are quite compressed. Manasseh was one of Joseph's sons; that would have been some four hundred years earlier. First Chronicles 7:14–18 indicates a son of Manasseh was Makir, father of Gilead.

gods, to which Israel had devoted themselves.[13] They had become entrapped by the Canaanite Baals and Ashtoreths, as well as the gods of Aram, Sidon, Moab, Ammon, and the Philistines (10:6). Rather than becoming a podium from which blessing would go forth (Gen 12:2–3), they caved in under the influence of the surrounding cultures.

JEPHTHAH IN CONTEXT

Because the Israelites had abandoned the Lord again, he sold them into the hands of the Philistines and the Ammonites. That meant severe pressure from both west and east, but the focus of this event is on the Ammonites, who were engaging in expansionist moves, both southwest from their center at Rabbah to the Medeba Plateau (*mishor*), as well as northwest into Gilead. In each case, these were regions the Israelites had taken after defeating King Sihon (Deut 2:31–37). Gilead was the Ammonites' initial target. Growing even more aggressive, the Ammonites also crossed the Jordan to fight against the tribes of Judah, Benjamin, and Ephraim, penetrating into the very heartland of Israel (Judg 10:8–9).

In desperation, the Israelites cried out to the Lord and also summoned Jephthah, a renegade mighty warrior from the extended family of Gilead, to return home to Gilead and help.[14] By that time, the Ammonites were camped in Gilead while the Israelites were assembled at Mizpah.[15]

Once Jephthah agreed to serve as the Israelites' commander in the forthcoming conflict with the Ammonites, he first sent a delegation to negotiate, asking why the king had come to fight in *Israel's* land (11:12). The Ammonite king responded with the accusation that Israel had taken *his* land "from the Arnon to the Jabbok to the Jordan" when they came up from Egypt (11:13). As previously discussed, that territorial description was accurate. It also meant that the Ammonite king was laying expansionist claims to the *mishor* and part of Gilead.

Jephthah's response included a summary of the journey of the Israelites from Kadesh to the Arnon, specifically noting that the Arnon was the boundary of Moab (11:18). From there the Israelites sent to Sihon requesting permission to pass through (11:19). It was to Sihon's detriment that he refused as it meant he lost his whole domain to Israel, specifically "from the Arnon to the Jabbok and from the desert to the Jordan" (11:21–22). As we have noted, where that desert began is uncertain. Jephthah pressed the point home. When Israel took over this land, it was because God had driven out the Amorites. Furthermore, Israel had inhabited the major centers of Heshbon and Aroer, as well as cities all along the Arnon, for three hundred years. If it really had been the land

13. It is not a coincidence that Jephthah's mother was a prostitute (Judg 11:1); her life was a distillation of the spiritual state of the whole of Israel.

14. He had been disinherited by his half-brothers and had fled to live in "a good [טוֹב, *tov*] land." It was close enough that his family, cognizant of his potential, summoned him when they needed him.

15. It is uncertain whether this is the Mizpah in Gilead (10:17; 11:29) or the Mizpah on the central plateau of Benjamin. If the latter, the inhabitants of Gilead had been temporarily forced west across the Jordan in the face of the Ammonite aggression.

of the Ammonites, they should have addressed the matter considerably earlier (11:23–26).

The unnamed Ammonite king ignored Jephthah's appeal. Thus, Jephthah crossed through Gilead and Manasseh, presuming those two designations overlap. From Mizpah of Gilead, he went over to fight with the Ammonites, taking twenty towns from Aroer to Abel Keramim, and subduing them (11:29–33). That, however, is not the whole of the story.

THEOLOGICAL ADDENDUM

As Jephthah advanced against the Ammonites, he made a vow to the Lord, the contents of which have troubled readers and commentators for centuries. How are we to understand this vow? What would have prompted him, as the Spirit rushed upon him, to vow to offer up to the Lord as a whole offering whoever first came out of the door of his house, should he return victorious (11:29–31)?[16]

There are several possible lenses through which to view this narrative. Given the configuration of the Israelite four-room house from that general time period, Jephthah may have been expecting an animal to emerge from the open central courtyard.[17] To his horror, his daughter, an only child, was the first to appear. In that circumstance, what then prompted him to *keep* the vow (11:35)? Was he so overwhelmed with the seriousness of vows as articulated in the Torah that he would offer a human life (Num 30)? Was this possibly combined with the syncretism and superstition of the wider culture? Whatever the case, the text indicates he did as he had vowed (Judg 11:39) after she had two months to mourn because she would never marry.

Several additional considerations may, however, re-shape our interpretation.[18] The circumstances prompting the vow in the first place were such that offering an animal, the fare of most offerings, would hardly seem sufficient. The inhabitants of Gilead had been shattered and subjugated for eighteen years (10:8); we might expect something more dramatic than a single animal. If, on the other hand, Jephthah had intended to appeal for divine

16. There has been considerable discussion regarding what precisely Jephthah expected. See George Foote Moore, *Judges*, ICC (New York: Charles Scribner's Sons, 1895), 304–5, for a summary of changing Jewish and Christian interpretations through the centuries. *Wehayah hayyotse asher yetse middalthe vethi liqrathi* (וְהָיָה הַיּוֹצֵא אֲשֶׁר יֵצֵא מִדַּלְתֵי בֵיתִי לִקְרָאתִי) is rendered literally as "the one coming out who will come out from the doors of my house to meet me." Elsewhere, *liqrathi* (לִקְרָאתִי), "to meet me," is only used of persons. Thus, we might interpret "whoever comes out" as referring to a person here as well. Further, the Hebrew word for the object of Jephthah's action is *olah* (עוֹלָה), the root of which means "to go up." The accompanying and related verbal form means "cause to go up." This offering in its entirety would be given up to the Lord. The sacrificial *animals* that were so designated were slaughtered and burned in their entirety on the altar (Lev 1:2–9).

17. The four-room "pillared house" was a characteristic Israelite structure by the eleventh century BC (Amihai Mazar, *Archaeology of the Land of the Bible: 10,000–586 BCE* [New York: Doubleday, 1992], 340–44). Animals would have been kept on the first floor of these homes and in the central courtyard. See, however, note 16. Reading the clause quoted above as "whatever comes out to meet me" would be unusual.

18. I am indebted to Gordon P. Hugenberger, "A Living Sacrifice: Judges 11:29–40," https://www.parkstreet.org/media/HugenbergerSeries, for summarizing the details of this interpretation.

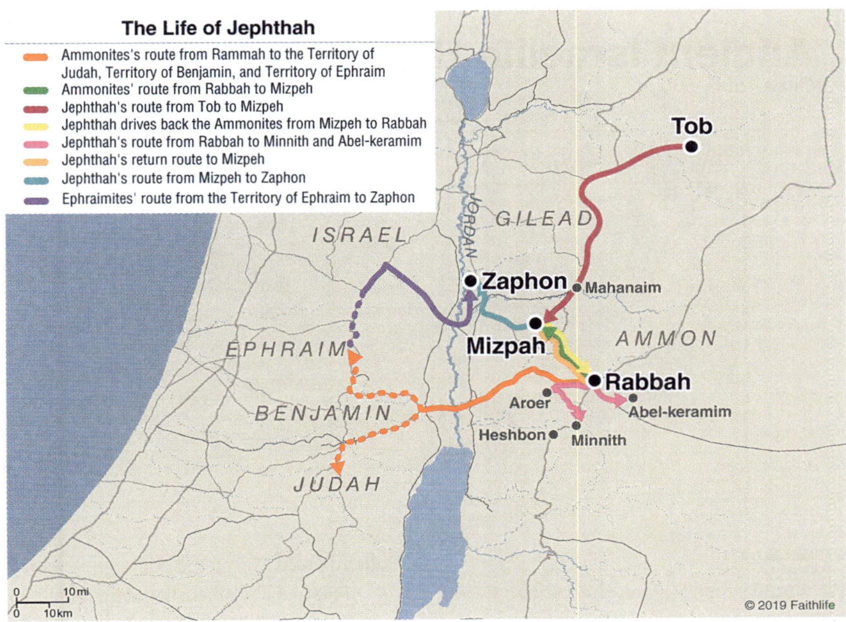

help by means of a human sacrifice, performing that rite *prior* to the battle may have seemed the more efficacious move.[19]

Perhaps Jephthah, in fact, was expecting a person to come out "to meet me" (11:30). This would have been a customary part of victory celebrations as women came out dancing (1 Sam 18:6). Would Jephthah have been prepared to offer up a servant girl from his household? Figuratively, yes. Understood this way, the objective of Jephthah's vow was to consecrate a person to whole-hearted service at the tent of meeting. There are precedents for this interpretation in that women served at the entrance to the tent of meeting (Exod 38:8), and the Levites were lifted up as wave offerings before the Lord (Num 8:13–14, 20–23); they were entirely the Lord's.[20] Thus, it would be with Jephthah's only daughter. She would be given entirely to the Lord, similar to Hannah's giving Samuel to the Lord's service (1 Sam 1). Why, then, would they mourn? Because she would never have a traditional life of marriage and family, and because this would mean the end of Jephthah's line. Notably, the end of the narrative simply states that Jephthah did to her as he had vowed (Judg 11:39); it does not say he offered her up as an offering.

19. While the circumstances are obscure, several centuries later, the king of Moab performed a similar chilling slaughter (2 Kgs 3:26–27).

20. The emphasis that his only daughter "was a virgin" and "would never marry" (11:38–39) fits within this context. An instance of heinous abuse of female servants appears in 1 Sam 2:22. This principle is echoed in Rom 12:1.

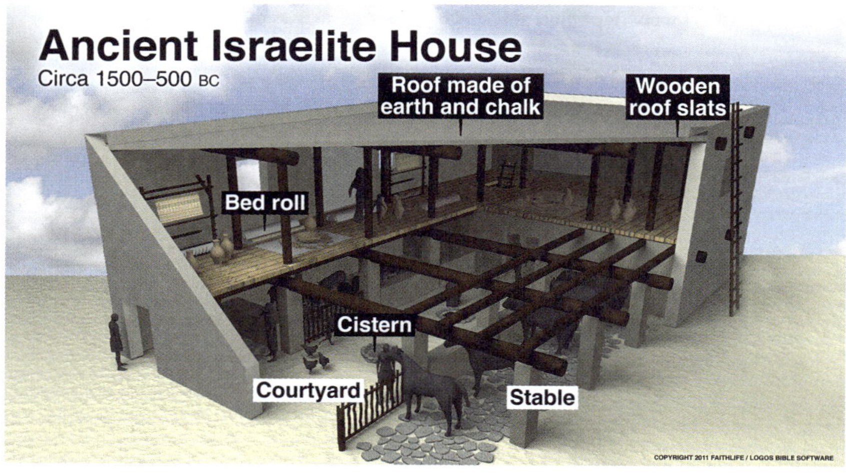

AFTERMATH

We would presume that the tribes on the west side of the Jordan would have been grateful for the deliverance effected by Jephthah, but that was not how it went, at least for the tribe of Ephraim. It seems not having a part in the process of deliverance was an affront to their honor. In a huff, they crossed the Jordan at Zaphon on the north side of the Jabbok near Succoth, confronted Jephthah, threatening to burn his house down, and added an insult regarding the social status of the Gileadites for good measure (Judg 12:1–4).

Ironically, the insult was to call the Gileadites "escapees" from Ephraim who were now mingled among the people of Ephraim and Manasseh. In true measure for measure fashion, the Ephraimites trying to find their way back across the Jordan were called "escapees" (Judg 12:4–5). Jephthah's response was harsh. He regrouped his men from Gilead, and they struck down the men from Ephraim. In order to prevent the Ephraimites from escaping back across the Jordan, they captured the fords and then put each man to a dialect test (12:5–6). Apparently on the west side of the Jordan, they did not pronounce the "sh" sound and *shibboleth* (שִׁבֹּלֶת) came out as *sibboleth* (סִבֹּלֶת).[21] The consequences of this dialectic difference were disastrous for any Ephraimites who could not manage the correct pronunciation.[22]

---

21. In fifteen of the nineteen occurrences of *shibboleth* in the Hebrew Bible, the word means "ear of grain." Many of these are in Gen 41 in conjunction with Pharaoh's dreams. The word also appears in Ps 69:2[MT 69:3], 69:15 [MT 69:16] and Isa 27:12 where the contexts suggest "torrents" or "courses of water," a meaning that fits in this Judges context. Hendel has summarized the various proposed interpretations of this dialectic difference. Rather than presuming a distinct dialect, he suggested that the phoneme was heard differently on the east side of the Jordan, which was influenced by their Ammonite neighbors. See Ronald S. Hendel, "Sibilants and *šibbōlet* (Judges 12:6)," *BASOR* 301 (1996): 69–75.

22. Whether *eleph* (אֶלֶף) means "thousand" in this context or the possible "clan leader" is another discussion. The demise of 42,000 Ephraimites seems a bit high. See Colin J.

CONCLUSION

Reviewing this narrative through geographical lenses adds richness and reality to our understanding of the messiness of conflict, especially conflict that has long historical roots—as most do. The land of Gilead was agriculturally productive, ideal for grazing, and less protected by natural barriers. Its geographical openness meant that boundaries would have been flexible at best and porous in times of outright conflict. The Ammonite kingdom to the east, in a more precarious position in terms of subsistence agriculture, continued to cast a covetous eye on Gilead, particularly against the backdrop of the past "golden age." Tragically, this would not be the end of their aggression against Gilead (Amos 1:13). An additional dark shadow behind this narrative is the ambiguous undercurrent of skewed cultic practices, perhaps absorbed from the immediate neighbors.

BIBLIOGRAPHY

Aharoni, Yohanan. *The Land of the Bible: A Historical Geography.* Translated by Anson F. Rainey. Rev. and enl. ed. Philadelphia: Westminster, 1979.

Baly, A. Denis. *The Geography of the Bible.* Rev. ed. New York: Harper and Row, 1974.

Hendel, Ronald S. "Sibilants and *šibbōlet* (Judges 12:6)." *BASOR* 301 (1996): 69–75.

Hugenberger, Gordon P. "A Living Sacrifice: Judges 11:29–40." https://www.parkstreet.org/media/HugenbergerSeries.

Humphreys, Colin J. "How Many People Were in the Exodus from Egypt?," *Science and Christian Belief* 12.1 (2000): 17–34.

Mazar, Amihai. *Archaeology of the Land of the Bible: 10,000–586 BCE.* New York: Doubleday, 1992.

Moore, George Foote. *Judges.* ICC. New York: Charles Scribner's Sons, 1895.

Rainey, Anson F., and R. Steven Notley. *The Sacred Bridge: Carta's Atlas of the Biblical World.* Jerusalem: Carta, 2006.

Rasmussen, Carl G. *Zondervan Atlas of the Bible.* Rev. ed. Grand Rapids: Zondervan, 2010.

Smith, George Adam. *The Historical Geography of the Holy Land.* London: Hodder & Stoughton, 1894. Repr., London: Fontana Library, 1966.

Humphreys, "How Many People Were in the Exodus from Egypt?" *Science and Christian Belief* 12.1 (2000): 17–34.

CHAPTER 28

SAMSON VERSUS THE PHILISTINES IN THE SHEPHELAH

Judg 13–16

Elaine A. Phillips

KEY POINTS

- The geographical region of the Shephelah (foothills) of Judah was a buffer zone between God's people living in the hill country and the more cosmopolitan and threatening populations on the coastal plain.
- In the time of Samson, God used the Philistines in the coastal plain to bring judgment on the wayward Israelites.
- The Philistines took advantage of the valleys cutting through the Shephelah to exert their control over the Israelites in Judah.
- God used Samson's attraction to Philistine women to bring judgment on the Philistines.

INTRODUCTION

With the Samson narrative, we see the ongoing significance of the Shephelah, the western lower foothills of the mountainous spine running primarily north-south through most of the land.[1] It served as the buffer zone between God's people settled in the hill country of Judah, and whatever foreign, more cosmopolitan, and potentially hostile people that inhabited the coastal plain. Increasingly during the period of the judges and into the early monarchy, those hostile people were the Philistines. They had already made an appearance in Judg 11 as a thorn in the flesh of the loose tribal confederation.

1. The Hebrew word *shphl* (שׁפל) means to be "low" and suggests that this designation was given to the region by those living in the higher hills, looking out over it. The meaning of word is illustrated by Isa 40:4, "every mountain and hill be made *low*." The elevation of the Shephelah is about half that of the hill country to the east.

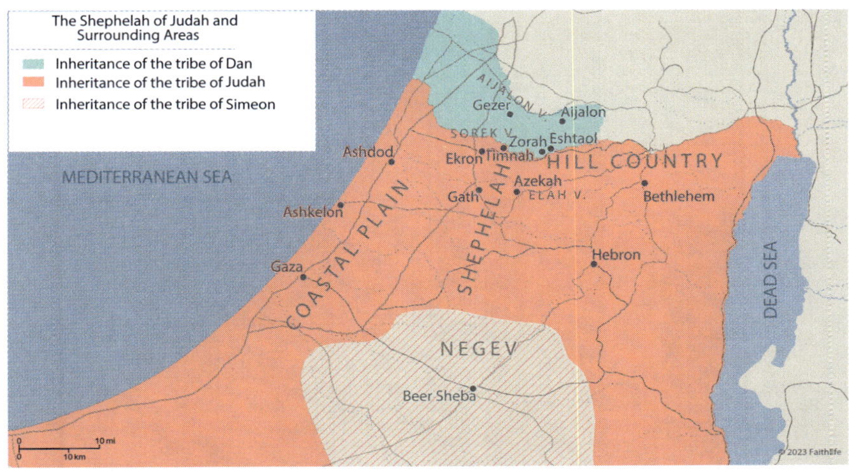

With the Samson narrative, their presence is front and center.

The recurring themes in the book of Judges are the downward spiral of God's covenant people into idolatry, the consequences of their disobedience as God used their geopolitical neighbors to chastise them, their repentance, and God's deliverance through individual judges. The final major judge, Samson, lived at the edge of the geopolitical and cultural interface between his traditional Israelite upbringing and the allure of the "big city."

Geography and Geopolitics

There are few locations that are so strategically critical as the Shephelah for understanding how biblical events unfolded in that geographical context. Positioned between the hill country to the east and the open sweep of international traffic through the coastal plain, its multiple, natural avenues into the protected communities in the hills practically invited invasion.

Hill Country Tribal Allotments

When the tribes settled in the land, the allotments for Judah, Benjamin, and Ephraim were in the central hill country. The relatively rugged topography meant they enjoyed a greater degree of security against attacks from outside. The good terra rosa soil and the abundance of springs, both products of the hard cenomanian limestone bedrock, shaped the agrarian lives of these tribes.[2] They also were dependent on the Lord for the blessings of rain and dew (Deut 11:11–17).

The Tribe of Dan in the Shephelah

Members of the tribe of Dan, on the other hand, found themselves in a much more precarious place. Their allotted portion abutted the northwest corner of Judah, was west of Benjamin, and bordered part of Ephraim to the north and east. That meant they were squarely in the northern Shephelah, sandwiched in between Israelites in the hill country and, in the period of the judges, the Philistines in

2. Yohanan Aharoni, *The Land of the Bible: A Historical Geography*, trans. and ed. Anson F. Rainey, rev. and enl. ed. (Philadelphia: Westminster, 1979), 11–12.

Shephelah and the Hill Country of Judah

the coastal plain. These low hills of the Shephelah are separated from the hill country by a continuous valley, called a "fosse" by the preeminent nineteenth century historical geographer, George Adam Smith; it follows the contours of the rugged range to the east.[3] Once enemy forces penetrated to the eastern side of the Shephelah, they had to determine how to access the rugged hills. There were few continuous ridges that served as invasion routes into the hill country proper.[4]

In addition, the Shephelah itself was cut through by east-west valleys, providing means of access as far as the "fosse." In the unfolding of biblical history, the three northernmost of these figured prominently as gateways toward the heartland. They are, from north to south, the Aijalon, Sorek, and Elah valleys. The tribal area of Dan included cities primarily in the Aijalon Valley with some also adjacent to the Sorek Valley (Josh 19:40–47); the Sorek is central to the Samson narrative.[5] The Shephelah was

3. Smith's label was well-chosen; invading forces repeatedly were stopped at this point. George Adam Smith, *The Historical Geography of the Holy Land* (London: Hodder & Stoughton, 1894; repr., London: Fontana Library, 1966), 146–47.

4. One of the notable ridges leading into the hills was the Husan ridge, reaching the central high country near Bethlehem. This diagonal valley between the Shephelah of Judah and the Judean hill country distinguished this region from Samaria to the north where the foothills were much more accessible. See Smith, *Historical Geography*, 145–46.

5. Josh 19:47 is a later note regarding the loss of the Shephelah tribal allotment and the resettlement of Dan at Leshem (Laish in Judg 18:7–29). From the outset, the Danites were prevented by the Amorites from laying hold of the cities in the plain (Judg 1:34). We will address

Aijalon Valley

a buffer zone as it was constantly under stress from both sides.

Because the underlying bedrock of the Shephelah is a combination of soft limestone and chalk, the low hills are not fertile agricultural areas. The valleys, on the other hand, have benefited from millennia of alluvial soils washing into them with grains among the primary crops.

PHILISTINE THREAT FROM THE COASTAL PLAIN

Between the low, rolling foothills of the Shephelah and the shores of the Mediterranean Sea is the coastal plain, sweeping from the promontory of Mount Carmel almost uninterrupted to the sands of northern Sinai. The two most significant sections of the coastal plain are the Sharon Plain, south of Mount Carmel, and the Philistine plain, our main area of interest. The demarcation point between the Sharon Plain and the Philistine plain was the Yarkon River, with its headwaters at the crucial site of Aphek. The Yarkon itself was an obstacle to traffic so Aphek became an important location to control.[6]

At the time of the judges, the Philistines had settled into the southern part of the coastal plain, defined primarily by their Pentapolis of cities: the coastal cities of Ashkelon, Gaza, and Ashdod; inland were Gath and Ekron. Ashkelon was the main Philistine harbor as there was a

the migration of the tribe further, as it no doubt had to do with pressure both from the Philistines to the west, as well as, possibly, pressure from the larger tribe of Judah. For example, the towns Zorah and Eshtaol are noted as given to both Judah (Josh 15:33) and Dan (Josh 19:40).

6. Aharoni, *Land of the Bible*, 49. Ideally, the tribal allotment of Dan extended as far north as the "waters of Yarkon" and the area facing Joppa (Josh 19:40–46).

break in the sand dunes at that point.[7] The Philistines held sway as far north as the Yarkon.

Along the coastline were ridges of calcified sandstone, kurkar, that impeded water run-off from the western slopes of the hill country out to the sea, creating swamps in significant parts of the coastal plain. Nevertheless, the rich alluvial soils allowed the grain-based agriculture to flourish.[8] This is reflected in the fact that the chief god of the Philistines, Dagon, was possibly associated with grain and corn (Judg 16:23; 1 Sam 5:1–12; 1 Chr 10:10).[9]

International traffic moved either very close to the sea or hugged the foothills to keep out of the swamps. The two inland cities of the Philistines, Gath and Ekron, were on the branch of the international route nearest these foothills. Millennia of commercial and military expeditions traversed this route on one branch or the other. It was marked by cosmopolitan populations, larger cities, and foreign powers seeking access into the interior of the country. Overall, the agricultural productivity along with the travel routes, made the Philistine plain prized real estate.

Our understanding of Philistine culture has been enriched by archaeological work at major Philistine cities. They were assuredly a foreign cultural entity originating in the Aegean, indicated by distinctive Aegean pottery, cult objects, and architecture.[10] The matter of pork consumption is an additional distinguishing feature. Prior to approximately 1200 BC (the beginning of Iron Age I), pork was a minimal part of the diet in the coastal plain cities. However, data from the two Philistine cities of Ekron and Ashkelon indicate that pork consumption increased at that chronological juncture. This is in marked contrast to contemporaneous Israelite settlements in the hill country where evidence of pig consumption continued to be almost entirely absent.[11] Assessment of the pottery is likewise helpful as Philistine pottery also appears in assemblages in Beth Shemesh, suggesting cultural mixing at this border location on the eastern (defensive) end of the Sorek Valley.[12] This is an important

7. Aharoni, *Land of the Bible*, 25, 48–49.

8. Anson F. Rainey and R. Steven Notley, *The Sacred Bridge: Carta's Atlas of the Biblical World* (Jerusalem: Carta, 2006), 38.

9. The worship of this deity (also called Dagan) was widespread in parts of Mesopotamia as reflected in texts from Mari. Dagan also played a minor role in Ugaritic religious practices. Likely neither of those contexts would have focused on grain products. Possibly the Philistines adopted this popular ANE figure, tailoring it to fit their context. J. E. Healey, "Dagon," in *DDD*, 216. See also John H. Walton, *Ancient Near Eastern Thought and the Old Testament: Introducing the Conceptual World of the Hebrew Bible* (Grand Rapids: Baker, 2006), 338–39.

10. Amihai Mazar, *Archaeology of the Land of the Bible: 10,000–586 B.C.E.* (New York: Doubleday, 1992), 308–28; Rainey and Notley, *Sacred Bridge*, 130; Ann E. Killebrew, *Biblical Peoples and Ethnicity: An Archaeological Study of Egyptians, Canaanites, Philistines, and Early Israel, 1300–1100 B.C.E.* (Atlanta: Society of Biblical Literature, 2005), 14–16; 206–30.

11. Killebrew, *Biblical Peoples*, 219; Avraham Faust, *Israel's Ethnogenesis: Settlement, Interaction, Expansion, and Resistance* (London: Equinox: 2006), 35–37.

12. The conclusions of the lead excavators, see Shlomo Bunimovitz and Zvi Lederman, *Tel Beth-Shemesh: A Border Community in Judah. Renewed Excavations 1990–200: The Iron Age* (Winona Lake, IN: Eisenbrauns, 2016).

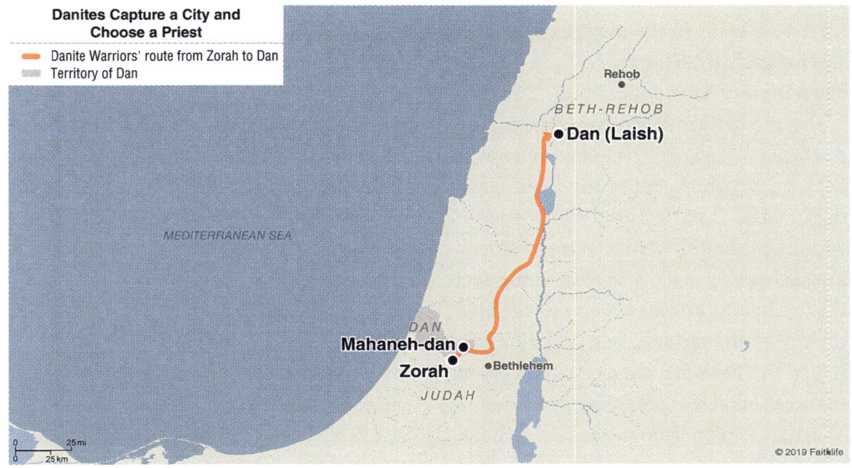

backdrop as we read of Philistine incursions into Israelite heartlands. We know from the biblical text that the Philistines held the upper hand in regard to military might because they controlled iron production and hence, more advanced weaponry (1 Sam 13:19–22).

Zorah, the hometown of Samson, rested on the slope overlooking the Sorek Valley just north of Beth Shemesh. Timnah (Tel Batash) was in the Sorek Valley west of Beth Shemesh and near the Philistine plain. Evidence of Philistine presence during the period of the judges appears in Stratum V (Iron Age I; 1200–1000 BC) at Timnah.[13]

THEMATIC ARRANGEMENT OF THE BOOK OF JUDGES—AND WHY IT MATTERS

The migration of the tribe of Dan to the northernmost part of the land is recorded in Judg 18. The reason stated for their attempt to resettle is that they had not yet come into an inheritance among the tribes, and thus they set out to explore additional options (18:1–2). Their key scouts, five in number, came from the towns of Zorah and Eshtaol, names we encounter in conjunction with the Samson narrative. After their first foray, they returned with a good report and persuaded six hundred fighting men to join them in attacking the unsuspecting town of Laish.[14] As they began the trek north, they stopped just west of Kiriath Jearim, a town on the boundary of Judah. Their camping spot was given the name Mahaneh Dan, meaning the "camp of Dan" (18:12).

This is an important datum as we think more broadly about the arrangement of the book of Judges. It is possible that this migration included only part of the tribe of Dan, and that it occurred

13. George L. Kelm and Amihai Mazar, "Three Seasons of Excavations at Tel Batash: Biblical Timnah," *BASOR* 248 (1982): 15–19.

14. En route, they also high-handedly took the idols and priest of an Ephraimite named Micah, a move that would have repercussions for centuries to come as they established a worship site at Dan (Judg 18:30–31).

relatively early in the period defined by the judgeships. Several considerations contribute to this conclusion. The first is the most significant for the Samson narrative. We learn that as Samson was growing up, the spirit of the Lord began "to stir him" (לְפַעֲמוֹ, *lephaamo*) while he was in Mahaneh Dan, between Zorah and Eshtaol (13:25). Add this to the fact that only six hundred men constituted the group that attacked Laish and established the new city named Dan. Perhaps the rest stayed in their original tribal allotment, even though they were hard-pressed from all sides. If so, they were part of the cultural context into which Samson was born.

This would mean that the book of Judges is arranged thematically rather than chronologically, the main point being to demonstrate that the people were more than ready for a king.[15] As each successive judge appeared, he was thrust into situations of worsening idolatry, and the stage was being set for the king who would be chosen. That would suggest that the events of Judg 17–21 occurred earlier, prior to the Samson narrative (Judg 13–16).[16] The Philistines were the major enemy both for Samson and for the Israelites as they transitioned to the monarchy. The Samson narrative thus closes the period of the judges and overlaps chronologically with 1 Samuel and the story of a more obedient Nazirite—the prophet Samuel.

SAMSON CHOOSES THE COASTAL PLAIN LIFESTYLE

The narrative of Samson's extraordinary birth is couched in the tragic description: "the Israelites again did evil in the eyes of the LORD" (Judg 13:1).[17] This time, the length of their servitude was forty years (13:1). The geographical indicators place the characters in the troubled circumstances that would have been affecting the tribe of Dan, such as Samson's father being from Zorah and a member of the "family of Dan" (מִשְׁפַּחַת הַדָּנִי, *mishpahat haddani*; 13:2).[18] The Philistines exerted increasing pressure, not only squeezing Dan, but also pressuring the western flank of the tribe of Judah. We get windows into the reality of the situation when Samson began his foray into

15. Thus, the repeated refrain at the end: "there was no king in Israel; everyone did what was right in his own eyes" (17:6; 18:1; 19:1; 21:25). The full expression (17:6 and 21:25) bookends these last five chapters.

16. Bolstering this understanding of Judges as not necessarily in chronological order are several additional data points. First, grandsons of Moses (18:30) and Aaron (20:28) were ministering. If this means "son of" and not "descendant," the general time frame would have to be closer to the beginning rather than the end of the period. Second, not one of the major judges (chs. 4–16) was from Judah. That is not surprising since Judah was more isolated and not under attack by foreigners to the degree Manasseh, Dan, and Ephraim were. In the last four chapters, however, Judah shows up in key incidents. They were required to lead the fight against Benjamin, important in the future aligning of tribes behind David and Saul. Bethlehem in Judah was important in the major incidents in the last five chapters and was the location for most of the book of Ruth. This is important for the connection to David established in the book of 1 Samuel. The tribe of Ephraim has some degree of prominence as well; it was the major tribe of the north after the kingdom fractured.

17. All Scripture translations are the author's.

18. The same term is used in Judg 18:2 with regard to the representatives of Danite clans sent to explore for another piece of inheritance.

the Philistine world. The equivalent of a parenthetical remark indicates that the Lord was planning to use Samson to confront the Philistines because at that time, they were ruling over Israel (14:4).[19] Somewhat later, the Philistines went up to camp in Judah in order to take Samson prisoner, and the Judahites, declaring that the Philistines were rulers over them, handed Samson over (15:9–13).

GREAT EXPECTATIONS AND THE NAZIRITE VOW

Whereas previous judges had armies with which to fight, Samson would be entirely on his own against the might of the Philistines. That is why such extraordinary and dramatic persons and events surrounded Samson's entrance on stage: the appearance and actions of the angel of the Lord, the name "wonderful" (פֶּלְאִי, *pheli;* 13:18; see Isa 9:6 [MT 9:5]), the sacrifice consumed in flames as the Lord ascended, and the rigors of the Nazirite vow (Judg 13). These would assure divine assistance in what appeared to be an impossible task. The people were to expect miraculous deliverance with this kind of prelude.

When the angel of the Lord first encountered Manoah's wife, the angel announced to this barren woman that she would have a son. The miraculous birth was a signal of a momentous event on the horizon.[20] The angel gave her very specific instructions (Judg 13:3–5). She was not to drink wine, nor was she to eat anything unclean lest that uncleanness be transferred to her unborn son. The same restrictions would be true for him once he was born. In particular, he could not cut his hair. The long hair was the specific sign that the person was called and set apart by God to accomplish God's purposes (Num 6).[21] In this case, the angel of the Lord declared that Samson was destined to begin the deliverance of Israel from the powerful domination of the Philistines (13:5). Even with all that fanfare, Samson would only affect the beginning of the conflict with the Philistines. The strife would continue well into the time of Saul and David.

In the first report that Samson's mother gave to her husband, Manoah, she left out the bit about taking on the Philistines and added that her son would be a Nazirite from the womb "until the day of his death" (13:7). When Manoah prayed for confirmation and instruction, the angel appeared again to the woman as she was out in the field. Manoah joined her, and all of the subsequent interaction between the parents-to-be and God's messenger took place in the field (13:8–23). Manoah was assured that his wife had heard correctly. The messenger deflected Manoah's request for his name, saying that it was in the realm of mystery—"wonderful" (13:17–18). Their

19. This would continue to be the case well into the time of Saul. The famed incident with Jonathan and his armor-bearer took place as the Philistines had penetrated well through the heartland of the tribe of Benjamin to the eastern edge of the central Benjamin plateau (1 Sam 13–14).

20. This motif—a child born to a barren woman—signaled God's intervention for God's purposes: Sarah, Rebekah, Rachel, and later Hannah would all bear significant sons.

21. In none of the iterations of the regulations did the angel of the Lord repeat the prohibition found in Num 6 regarding no contact with dead bodies. Perhaps that was assumed, but Samson did transgress the letter of the law as he left a trail of corpses behind him! In addition, he poked around the carcass of a lion he had earlier killed (Judg 14:5–9).

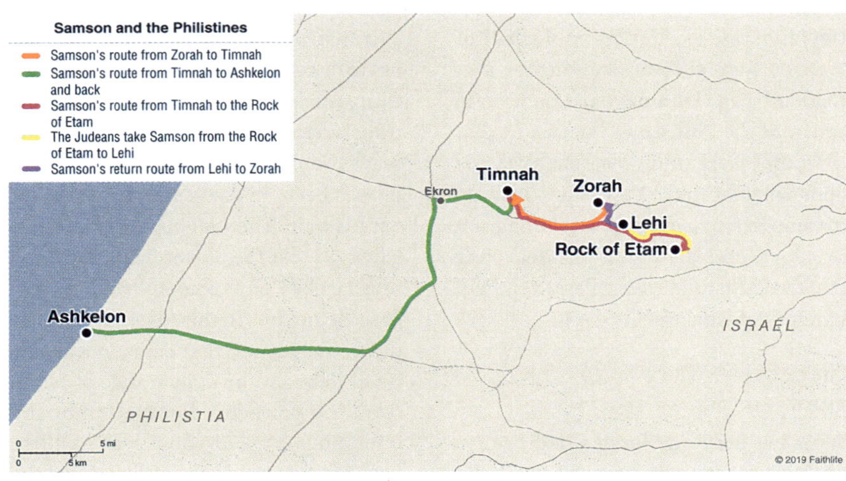

burnt and grain offerings were, however, accepted, and they *saw* the angel of the Lord ascend in the flames of the altar (13:19–20). Falling on their faces was the appropriate response in the face of seeing God. Manoah's terror and understandable presumption that they would die was calmed by his wife's logic. Why would God communicate so carefully with them only to kill them at the end (13:23)? After the drama, we learn she gave birth to the boy. As Samson grew, the Lord blessed him, and the Lord's Spirit was present with him (13:24–25).

THE ALLURE OF THE BIG CITY

The very next sentence begins "and Samson went down to Timnah" (14:1). The implications are multi-faceted. His hometown was Zorah, perched on the northern slope of the Sorek Valley with the rugged hill country just to the east. Timnah was farther west where the Sorek Valley broadens and swings around toward Ekron, one of the five Philistine cities. It is apparent that the influence of the larger city had crept to the smaller towns roundabout, and Samson was "going down" toward it. The Philistine culture offered severe temptations to Samson; he was characteristically venturing into the cosmopolitan context from his more traditional background. In Timnah, he was captivated by the sight of a Philistine woman, a source of utter dismay to his parents (14:3). This pattern would continue.

In the meantime, the narrative of the cross-cultural wedding is infused with geographical details. As Samson travelled with his father and mother into culturally threatening territory, their path took them past the vineyards of Timnah. From one of them a lion emerged to attack Samson. At this point, his parents fade into the background; they apparently did not see Samson tear it in two pieces using only his hands (14:5–6). While there are no lions in Israel today, the creature is no stranger in the Old Testament narratives.[22] The fact that there are multiple

22. On the disappearance of lions in Palestine, see George Cansdale, *Animals of Bible Lands* (Exeter, UK: Paternoster Press, 1970), 106–8. The ecological environment has shifted

Hebrew words to represent lion indicates they were well-known.[23] Later in 1 Samuel, David declared to Saul that the Lord had delivered him from the "hand" of the lion and the bear (1 Sam 17:33–37) as he was guarding his father's flocks in the wilderness.

Samson kept the report of his victory over the lion from his parents. Only some time later, when they all went back to Timnah for the festivities, did he turn aside, find bees and honey in the unclean carcass, and offer the delicacy to his unsuspecting parents (14:8–9). The presence of bees suggests sufficient wild flowers in the area. The whole situation was the basis for Samson's riddle to the thirty fellows who joined his wedding party (14:12–14).[24] Samson clearly had the upper hand in this until his bride-to-be was threatened by the fellows, who said they would burn her and her father's household to death if she did not give them the answer (14:15). Sadly, that is what they eventually did (15:6) after an interval replete with drama. The young woman cajoled Samson into divulging the answer to his riddle, which she promptly handed along, being driven by self-preservation (14:16–17). Their triumphant response to the riddle signaled to Samson that he had been betrayed; his bitter rejoinder may have been a thinly veiled accusation of sexual aggression against his bride-to-be (14:18).[25]

Samson's Vengeance and the Purposes of God

Enraged at the duplicity and empowered by the Spirit, Samson headed for Ashkelon, a good twenty-five miles (40 km) south and west across the Philistine plain. There, by killing thirty men of Ashkelon, he acquired the thirty outfits and changes of clothing to make good on the riddle-wager. He returned to Timnah, paid up, and stormed home. The young woman was given to one of his attending companions (14:19–20).

The cycle of vengeance ratcheted up. The next episode occurred at the time of the wheat harvest, a major crop of the Sorek Valley. When Samson discovered his bride had been handed off to another man by her own father, he let loose in standing grain three hundred foxes whose tails were tied together and lit on fire, serving as torches in the dry fields (15:1–5). That would have been late spring or early summer, and the first

---

due to increased human settlement over the centuries. The Crusader period is the last recorded killing of lions in Palestine; some were sighted in Syria in the mid-nineteenth century.

23. The most common Hebrew words are *aryeh* (אַרְיֵה, "lion") and *kephir* (כְּפִיר, "young lion"), accompanied by *gur* (גּוּר), which refers to a cub or lion pup.

24. Riddles served as entertainment in the ancient world, making discourse in a variety of contexts more engaging as the audience followed clues to the mystery that were posed in the realm of the ordinary. See James L. Crenshaw, "Riddles," *ABD* 5:723–25. It sounds as if these thirty companions may have been assigned to Samson's entourage; it happened "when they saw him" (14:11), and who "they" were is not specified. Perhaps something about his appearance was sufficiently threatening that the Philistines determined to take no chances with him and, under the guise of wedding attendants, were going to keep him under guard. Immediately thereafter, Samson posed the riddle: "from the one who eats has come forth food; and from the strong has come forth sweetness."

25. The expression "plowed with my heifer" might be interpreted in that manner.

of the significant harvest was utterly destroyed. But that was not all; the vineyards and olive groves also went up in flames. These represent the primary produce of the land: grain, new wine, and oil. We see them repeatedly in the statements of covenant blessings as well as the prophetic pronouncements with regard to Israel (e.g., Deut 11:14; Hos 2:8; Joel 1:10; 2:19; Hag 1:11), and they were equally vital for the Philistines as well. Thus, Samson's revenge struck at the heart of the agricultural economy of the area.

The Philistine response was brutal and struck at Samson's heart. They carried through on the earlier threat to burn his wife along with her father (15:6). He retaliated mightily and then went down to hide in a cleft of the rock (סְעִיף סֶלַע, *seiph sela*) of Etam.[26] It seems that Samson was headed back toward his own people with this move. He ended up in Judah's territory where the western edge of the hill country was riddled with caves in the limestone.[27]

The Philistines knew how to apply the pressure; after all, they had been subjugating the Israelites for forty years. Thus, they advanced up into the hill country of Judah and established a military presence sufficient to scare the men of Judah into handing Samson over. The Judahites were wary enough of Samson to go after him with good backup (15:9–12).[28] No doubt Samson deemed this a serious betrayal as he was led from the rock of Etam back up to the Philistine encampment at Lehi.

The Philistine's position at Lehi (לֶחִי, *lehi*) carried an ironic twist. This time when the Spirit empowered Samson, he seized the (fresh) jawbone of a donkey (לְחִי-חֲמוֹר, *lehi hamor*) and struck a whole troop of Philistines with it (15:14–15).[29] Then he made up a taunt song (15:16), mocking the heaps of corpses (חֲמוֹר חֲמֹרָתָיִם, *hamor hamoratayim*) that he had slaughtered with the jawbone of a *hamor* (חֲמוֹר). While the Hebrew word *hamor* means "donkey," a second meaning is "heap." In Samson's mockery, the jawbone of a single donkey has wreaked sufficient havoc to create "heaps of heaps." The second word in the expression (*hamoratayim*) is called a "dual form." The whole indicates the superlative.

The commemorative names arising from this episode, and the one forthcoming, suggest that Samson's exploits began to acquire their own epic quality.[30] This was, after all, happening in the tribal territory of Judah, and Samson had just delivered them. Immediately after he trounced that batch of Philistines, he was extremely thirsty. Although the time frame for the events in Judg 15 is not specified, this series of vicious exchanges began with the wheat harvest, and we might speculate that it spiraled out of

---

26. The idiom "leg [or hip] upon thigh" (שׁוֹק עַל-יָרֵךְ, *shoq al-yarek*) is used only here.

27. Hiding in a cave would not be unusual. David did the same thing later when he was on the run from both Saul and the Philistine king, Achish; he hid in the cave at Adullam (1 Sam 22:1).

28. The number three thousand is best understood as three troops, with a "troop" being somewhere between seven and twelve men. The Hebrew word *eleph* (אֶלֶף), which often means "thousand," can also mean "clan" or "troop." The latter fits well in this context.

29. As before, the Hebrew word is *eleph*, which may mean "one thousand" or could also refer to a troop of soldiers.

30. Ramat-Lehi: "hill of the jawbone."

Samson Slays a Thousand Men

control quite quickly. That would suggest his high energy activity was accompanied by the summer heat. It is no wonder he needed water; claiming he might die of thirst was not necessarily hyperbole. In response, God broke open a hollow place at Lehi, water poured forth, and once Samson had drunk the water, he revived (וַיֶּחִי, *vayyehi*).[31] The spring came to be known as "the spring of the one who calls out" (15:18–19).[32] There is a narrative pause at this point; the author indicates that the name persisted in the local lore at least until the writing of the text. Even in the shadow of Philistine power, Samson then judged Israel for twenty years (15:20).

In his early tumultuous years, Samson seems to have rejected everything that defined him as an Israelite and instead

31. The similarity in sound between *yehi* and *lehi* ought not be missed.

32. There are echoes of Moses (Exod 17:1–7; Num 20:2–13) as water poured from the rock when Samson called out.

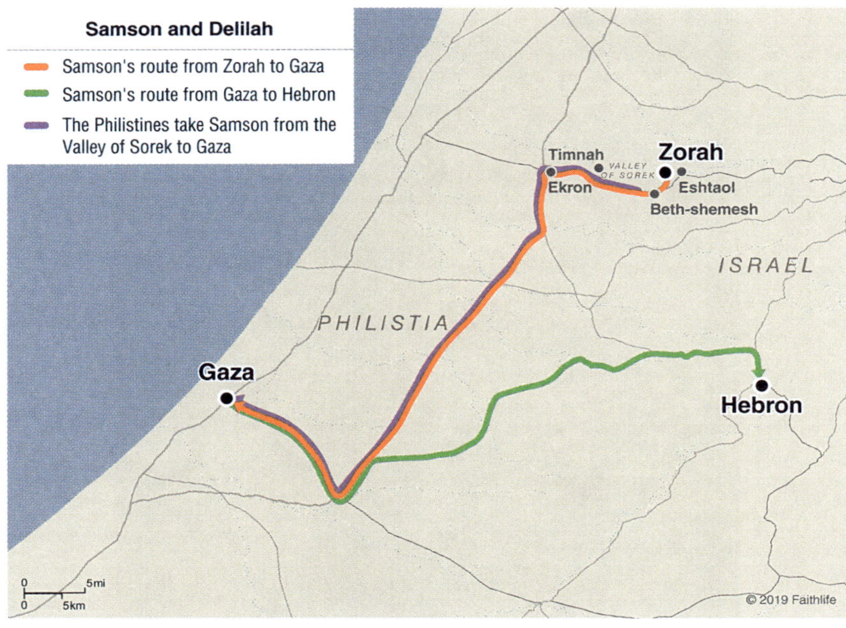

wreaked havoc of his own design on every adversary who arose. Nevertheless, God sovereignly used those character flaws to effect his own purposes. What a tangled web of solemn commands, good intentions, and deliberate disobedience, all securely under God's sovereign design!

A FINAL SHAMING TACTIC

After an undefined period of time, Samson went to Gaza where he chose to spend the night with a prostitute. The place was surrounded by people planning to apprehend him in the morning, but that did not stop Samson from demolishing the city's defense, the city gate, and carting the whole assemblage up to the hill opposite Hebron. This was no small ascent; Gaza is at sea level, while Hebron is about two thousand five hundred feet (762 m) above sea level, and at distance of nearly forty miles (64 km). Hebron was the chief city of Judah; Samson's arrival with the city gates of Gaza was essentially an announcement that the enemy was temporarily vulnerable and had been humiliated (16:1–3).

HEADING HOME

We do not know where Samson went in the interval after the Gaza incident. He next surfaced in the Sorek Valley (16:4). Perhaps he was trying to head back toward his roots and his home in his own faltering way. Delilah lived in the same general area as Samson's first wife—just down the valley from the tribal inheritance of Dan from which Samson hailed. Sadly, he did not make it home before he succumbed—once more—to his propensity for Philistine women.

Delilah was the object of his insatiable desire; she was also a mercenary. Enticed with the prospect of a substantial amount of easy money (16:5), Delilah attempted three times to cajole him into divulging

Samson Puts Down the Pillars

the secret of his strength that had gained him so much notoriety.[33] She was in the perfect place to become a rich woman. For his part, Samson lied to her initially, setting her up to appear a fool. Nevertheless, as she continued to pester him, his third response got closer to the truth. Finally, he told her about the Nazirite vow and the significance of his uncut hair (16:6–17). Perhaps by that time, he was weary of the trajectory of his always-public life. It had boiled down to sex, violence, and being perpetually hunted.

Samson seemed to demonstrate an odd combination of resignation and presumption as he continued to take God's presence with him for granted. Even after explaining to Delilah the consequences of using a razor on his head, he allowed himself to be lulled to sleep—perhaps respite in the midst of the constant tumult—and then thought that when Delilah warned him, he would be able to respond powerfully as before. It was with horror that he realized that his God-given strength had left him (16:19–20).

The Philistines took their prize back down to Gaza, perhaps a statement of reprisal after he had ripped their gates apart. Blinded, bound, enslaved, and humiliated, he was at his lowest point, but his hair began to grow (16:21–22). Recall that Manoah's wife reported the angel of the Lord saying that Samson would be a Nazirite until his death (13:7).

In the world view of the Philistines, their god (Dagon) had delivered their archenemy over to them—finally. That warranted a celebration in the temple to Dagon with Samson as the entertainment.

33. The eleven hundred shekels of silver may have been a standard figure. It shows up in the next chapter as the amount of silver the scoundrel, Micah, stole from his mother. Note the literary parallel with the three days of the first wedding feast when his first wife sobbed and pleaded with him to tell the riddle. This too was a riddle of sorts.

The text says he "performed" (יְשַׂחֵק/יְצַחֵק, *yesaheq/yetsaheq*) for them, and what a finale it was (16:25)!

SAMSON MEETS HIS END

No doubt the Israelites felt Samson's previous triumphs were short-lived when the Philistines had him bound in chains in Gaza. Certainly, the Philistines were bragging: "Our god has delivered into our hand our enemy, the one who has laid waste our land and multiplied our slain" (16:24). To the people of Judah, Samson's capture would have signaled continued oppression. No doubt they were cowering in the hill country settlements fearing further invasive maneuvers.

Then with one last act, still in the spirit of vengeance, Samson brought down the entire temple of Dagon on the Philistines' heads. He knew he would die in the process. His only care was to make a final devastating swipe in revenge for their having blinded him (16:28–30).

When his family came to retrieve his body and take it home for burial—the final event in Samson's tragic life—the narrative mentions his brothers and his father's whole family, but not his mother (16:31). It's a sad parallel: she was nameless at the beginning of the story, and absent at the end. This is out of the ordinary for the rest of the book of Judges in which women are unusually prominent. Perhaps this narrative silence is the only possible representation of a mother's response to such a violent death—the last blow after years of heartbreak and sorrow.

CONCLUSION

Set on its geopolitical stage, this narrative is replete with ironies and reversals. On the one side of the set are small Israelite towns perched in the protected hill country. On the other are the culturally dominant cities chock-full of temptations. In the center of the stage is the Shephelah, the buffer zone between these geopolitically and culturally disparate entities.

As a Nazirite, Samson was called to live a life of contrast to the wider culture, but he found the provincial traditional values stifling. Instead, he headed out for the excitement of those big cities, succumbing to the allure of Philistine culture. This is where we find him, wreaking havoc on the Philistines as he pursues women and revenge, spiraling steadily downward. Nevertheless, from the narrator's more distant perspective, God's sovereign purposes were not thwarted. Samson judged Israel twenty years, preventing the Philistines from further incursions into the tribe of Judah for that time. Samson's life ended in shame but, in ways that seem unfathomable to us, his vengeful spirit and weakness for women were the very means God used to break the Philistines' iron hold.

BIBLIOGRAPHY

Aharoni, Yohanan. *The Land of the Bible: A Historical Geography.* Translated and edited by Anson F. Rainey. Rev. and enl. ed. Philadelphia: Westminster, 1979.

Baly, A. Denis. *The Geography of the Bible.* Rev. ed. New York: Harper and Row, 1974.

Bunimovitz, Shlomo, and Zvi Lederman. *Tel Beth-Shemesh: A Border Community in Judah. Renewed Excavations 1990–200: The Iron Age.* Winona Lake, IN: Eisenbrauns, 2016.

Cansdale, George. *Animals of Bible Lands.* Exeter, UK: Paternoster Press, 1970.

Crenshaw, James L. "Riddles." *ABD* 5:723–25.

Faust, Avraham. *Israel's Ethnogenesis: Settlement, Interaction, Expansion, and Resistance.* London: Equinox: 2006.

Healey, J. E. "Dagon." *DDD*, 216–19.

Kelm, George L., and Amihai Mazar. "Three Seasons of Excavations at Tel Batash: Biblical Timnah." *BASOR* 248 (1982): 1–36.

Killebrew, Ann E. *Biblical Peoples and Ethnicity: An Archaeological Study of Egyptians, Canaanites, Philistines, and Early Israel, 1300–1100 B.C.E.* Atlanta: Society of Biblical Literature, 2005.

Mazar, Amihai. *Archaeology of the Land of the Bible: 10,000–586 B.C.E.* New York: Doubleday, 1992.

Rainey, Anson F., and R. Steven Notley. *The Sacred Bridge: Carta's Atlas of the Biblical World.* Jerusalem: Carta, 2006.

Smith, George Adam. *The Historical Geography of the Holy Land.* London: Hodder & Stoughton, 1894. Repr., London: Fontana Library, 1966.

Walton, John H. *Ancient Near Eastern Thought and the Old Testament: Introducing the Conceptual World of the Hebrew Bible.* Grand Rapids: Baker, 2006.

CHAPTER 29

ANCIENT DAN IN ITS GEOGRAPHICAL, ARCHAEOLOGICAL, AND BIBLICAL CONTEXTS

Judg 17–18; 1 Kgs 12:26–33

Jonathan S. Greer

KEY POINTS

- Geographically, the city of Dan is located at the Ain Leddan Spring, the largest water source in the region and the main source of the Jordan River, and at the cross-roads of important international routes.
- In the Bible, the tribe of Dan is said to have migrated north and conquered the peaceful city of Laish (or Leshem), where they established a shrine and renamed the city Dan (Judg 17–18). Later, Jeroboam I established a temple to Yahweh with a golden calf there (1 Kgs 12:26–33), and the city marked the northern boundary of the kingdom of Israel throughout most of its history.
- Archaeologically, the site is best known for the discovery of the Tel Dan Stela, providing our earliest mention of King David outside the Bible and likely also mentioning the assassination of Jehoram and Ahaziah, related to Jehu's coup in 1 Kgs 9–10. Other important finds include an arched mudbrick gate from the eighteenth century BC and the best example of an Israelite royal temple ever discovered.

INTRODUCTION

The city of Dan plays a prominent role in the story of ancient Israel, described in the Bible in a way that—along with Bethel—parallels the portrayal of Jerusalem. Both Dan (and Bethel) in the north and Jerusalem in the south are connected with stories from the premonarchic period, and both rise to important heights as religious centers during the days of the Israelite

The Zoilos Inscription from the Hellenistic Phase of the Sacred Precinct at Tel Dan

divided kingdom. Yet, in the case of Dan and Bethel, the stories are tainted by accusations of idolatry and the infamous "sin of Jeroboam son of Nebat" (see, e.g., 1 Kgs 16:26, 31; 22:52 [MT 22:53]; 2 Kgs 3:3; 10:29; 13:2, 11; 14:24; 15:9, 18, 24, 28; 23:15) that led to the conquest of the Northern Kingdom by the Neo-Assyrian empire in 722 BC. This essay aims to explore the geographic and archaeological contexts of ancient Dan in order to better understand the biblical portrayal of this important city and its role in the larger story of ancient Israel.

THE GEOGRAPHICAL SETTING OF ANCIENT DAN

The artificial mound of Tell el-Qadi (Arabic for "Mound of the Judge") was first identified as biblical Dan for the western world in 1838 through the exploration of Edward Robinson, and this identification has not convincingly been challenged since.[1] The 1976 discovery of the Hellenistic Zoilos inscription dedicated "to the God who is in Dan," found in the temple area at the site, confirmed this identification.[2]

1. Edward Robinson and Eli Smith, *Biblical Researches in Palestine, Mount Sinai and Arabia Petræa: A Journal of Travels in the Year 1838* (Boston: Crocker and Brewster; London: John Murray, 1841), 3:350–52. For a refutation of potential challenges, see Andrew R. Davis, "Tel Dan in Its Northern Cultic Context" (PhD diss., Johns Hopkins University, 2010), 44 n. 8.

The Arabic toponym may be related to the Hebrew name of the city semantically, as *dan* (דָן, "Dan"), means "judge." On the exception of this instance, see Yoel Elitzur, *Ancient Place Names in the Holy Land: Preservation and History* (Winona Lake, IN: Eisenbrauns, 2004), 208.

2. Avraham Biran, "'To the God Who is in Dan,'" in *Temples and High Places in Biblical Times: Proceedings of the Colloquium in Honor of the Centennial of Hebrew Union College-Jewish Institute*

The city of Dan exists because of water—lots of water—as is evident even today. The site sits adjacent to, and in fact around, the Ain Leddan Spring. This spring is the largest in the Middle East and the most abundant of the three sources of the Jordan River, discharging 66,043,013,090 gal. (250 million m³) of water annually, more than twice the output of the nearby Banias Spring.[3] These waters, fed by runoff and snowmelt from Mount Hermon and supplemented by some twenty to thirty inches (51–76 cm) of rainfall per year, have long attracted inhabitants who harnessed these resources for drinking and agriculture. The site is situated on the northern edge of the Huleh Valley, part of the northern branch of the Great Rift Valley, beyond the extent of the ancient swamplands. It is surrounded by rich soil types, including brown, terra rosa, and alluvial soils.[4]

Biblical texts note that the earlier name of the site was Leshem (לֶשֶׁם, *leshem*; Josh 19:47) or Laish (לַיִשׁ, *layish*; Judg 18:7, 27, 29), and several documents from the ancient Near East attest to the city by variations of this name. Such include mention in the later corpus of the Execration Texts from Egypt (as *ȝwsy* = *lēsi*) and in the archives of Mari from Syria (as *lawišim* or *layišim*), both dating to the eighteenth century BC, as well as in the fifteenth century BC conquest list of Thutmose III (as *rwś* = *lawiśa*).[5] Later sources, too, know of the site and identify it with biblical Dan, such as Josephus, as well as both Eusebius and Jerome, who place it four miles (6 km) from Banias.[6]

Other biblical references to this city include possible mention of it as the furthest extent of the boundary of Canaan in Gen 10:19 (if לָשַׁע [*lasha*] may be read *layish* [Laish]) and several references to it by its later name Dan, the first instance being the place unto which Abraham pursued the captors of Lot (Gen 14:14).[7] Other texts mention the city as a landmark of the northern border (2 Sam 24:6; Jer 8:16; Ezek 48:1; see also Deut 33:22). This is especially clear in the stock phrase designating the monarchic boundaries of "all Israel" from "Dan to Beersheba" in the Deuteronomistic History (Judg 20:1; 1 Sam 3:20; 2 Sam 3:10; 17:11; 24:2, 15; 1 Kgs 4:25 [MT 5:5]; see also Deut 34:1) or from "Beersheba to Dan" in the Chronicler's history (1 Chr 21:2; 2 Chr 30:5).[8]

---

of Religion, Jerusalem, 14–16 March 1977, ed. Avraham Biran (Jerusalem: Nelson Glueck School of Biblical Archaeology, 1981), 142–51.

3. F. D. Por, et al., "River Dan, Headwater of the Jordan, an Aquatic Oasis of the Middle East," *Hydrobiologia* 134 (1986): 121–40; D. Gil'ad and J. Bonne, "The Snowmelt of Mt. Hermon and Its Contribution to the Sources of the Jordan River," *Journal of Hydrology* 114 (1990): 1–15.

4. *MAB*, 59, map 17.

5. See Abraham Malamat, "Syro-Palestinian Destinations in a Mari Tin Inventory," *IEJ* 21 (1971): 35–36; see also Anson F. Rainey and R. Steven Notley, *The Sacred Bridge: Carta's Atlas of the Biblical World*, 2nd ed. (Jerusalem: Carta, 2014), 58 and 72.

6. Note that Josephus identifies the site as *Daphnē* (Daphnae) in *J.W.* 4.1.1, though all commentators agree that he means *Danē* (Dan) given the context of his discussion and reference to the spring and to Jeroboam's golden calf. See, e.g., Robinson and Smith, *Biblical Researches*, 3:352 n. 1. See also, Robinson and Smith, *Biblical Researches*, 3:351 n. 4. Eusebius, *Onom.* 369/76:6.

7. As queried by Rainey and Notley, *Sacred Bridge*, 34.

8. For more on this stock phrase, see John A. Beck, "'From Dan to Beersheba': A Geographical Analysis of the Recurring Expression of Israel's Monarchy," in this volume.

Local and International Routes Associated with Ancient Dan

Such geographic references in ancient Near Eastern and biblical texts attest to the importance of the city, presumably due to its perennial spring, and this, along with other features of the landscape, made it an essential destination on major routes that flowed throughout the region (see map below). These highways included the so-called great trunk road, or international highway, that ran from Egypt to Mesopotamia, an important branch of which followed the western edge of the Huleh Valley from Hazor to avoid the swamplands, then crossed above Lake Huleh through Dan on its way to Damascus. The road from Tyre, known in the Bible as "the Way of the Sea" (Isa 9:1 [MT 8:23]), joined by a road that merged in from Sidon to avoid the higher peaks of the Lebanon mountains directly to its east, also ran through Dan.[9] This connected Dan not only to the

9. Rainey and Notley, *Sacred Bridge*, 12.

Phoenician heartland but also to the vast networks of Mediterranean Sea trade. In fact, Dan served as a gateway for all goods from the western shipping lanes landing in Tyre, the most important port on the Levantine coast, as they flowed east toward Mesopotamia. The site also guarded the eastern edge of the Beqa Valley to its north and marked traffic running between the Lebanon and Anti-Lebanon mountains, on to Syria through Baalbek. This strategic location would have resulted in opportunities for heavy taxation, perhaps alluded to in reference to Dan as "a snake by the roadside, a viper along the path" in the Song of Jacob (Gen 49:17).[10]

DAN AS A HOLY CITY

The religious significance of Dan is also evident from the earliest times, no doubt related to the importance of the spring as attested in Ugaritic texts from the thirteenth century BC.[11] Early archaeological evidence, too, includes what may be an *in antis*, or *migdal* (מִגְדָּל), temple from the Middle Bronze Age (MB IIA; c. eighteenth century BC) built directly above the spring.[12] An Egyptian-styled figurine of a deity in a smiting pose, likely dating to the second half of the second millennium BC, was also discovered close to the spring prior to scientific excavations.[13] During the first phase of Iron Age II occupation (c. tenth/ninth century BC), a massive temple complex was established directly on top of the earlier MB IIA structure and expanded to include a courtyard, altar, and other cultic installations, as will be discussed in greater detail below. This later temple remained in use throughout the Iron Age II (tenth/ninth–sixth century BC), and into the Persian (sixth to fourth century BC), Hellenistic (fourth to first century BC), and early Roman (first century BC to first century AD) periods as well.[14]

The Bible, too, indicates the religious significance of Dan in Israelite tradition as seen in a foundation story describing the dubious conquest of the site and the installation of a shrine serviced by a descendent of Moses (Judg 17–18), and in descriptions of the later revival of the site as a royal temple and pilgrimage site under Jeroboam I, equipped with its own priesthood and festival calendar (1 Kgs 12:28–33) discussed below. Later Jewish apocalyptic texts, such as 1 Enoch (chs. 12–16; see, especially, 13:7) and the Testament of Levi (chs. 2–7), also attest to its enduring religious importance well into the Hellenistic period.[15]

---

10. So Avraham Biran, *Biblical Dan* (Jerusalem: Israel Exploration Society; Hebrew Union College-Jewish Institute of Religion, 1994), 135.

11. René Dussaud, "Cultes cananéens aux sources du Jourdain, d'après les textes de Ras Shamra," *Syria* 17 (1936): 283–95.

12. David Ilan, "A Middle Bronze Age 'Migdal' Temple at Tel Dan? [Hebrew with English Abstract]," *Eretz-Israel (Stager volume)* 33 (2018): 25–33.

13. Biran, *Biblical Dan*, 159–61.

14. Biran, *Biblical Dan*, 165–233.

15. Charles Clermont-Ganneau, "Le Mont Hermon et son dieu d'après une inscription inédite," *Recueil d'Archéologio Orientale* 5 (1903): 346–66; George W. E. Nickelsburg, "Enoch, Levi, and Peter: Recipients of Revelation in Upper Galilee," *JBL* 100 (1981): 575–600; John Francis Wilson, *Caesarea Philippi: Banias, the Lost City of Pan* (London: I. B. Tauris & Co Ltd, 2004), 72–73. Note, however, that some scholars have suggested Shechem as a setting for

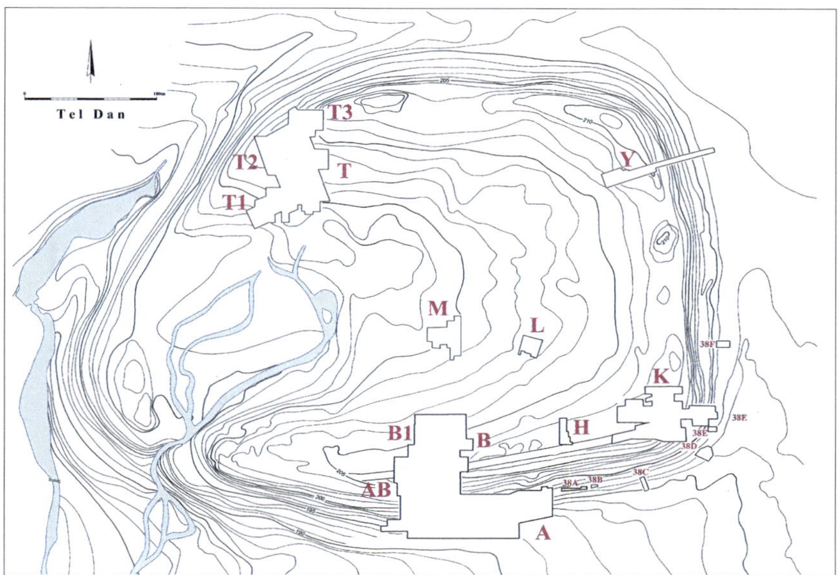

Archaeological Site Plan of Tel Dan

Archaeological Investigation of Tel Dan

Following a brief exploratory investigation by Ze'ev Yeivin of the Israel Department of Antiquities and Museums in 1963, excavation of the site began as a salvage operation in 1966–67 under the direction of Avraham Biran from the Nelson Glueck School of Biblical Archaeology (NGSBA) of the Hebrew Union College-Jewish Institute of Religion in Jerusalem. The dig continued under Biran's direction until 2003 and was resumed under the direction of David Ilan and Yifat Thareani, also of the NGSBA. It is still an active excavation site at the time of this writing.[16]

The mound of Tel Dan itself encompasses some fifty acres (202,343 m^2) with a roughly rectangular shape on the eastern side and tapered contours on the western side due to the spring. The tel rises nearly sixty-six feet (20 m) above the surrounding plain due to the remains of the massive MB IIA ramparts that encircle the site, forming a crater-like depression on the interior that drops to about thirty-three feet (10 m) lower than the peak of the rampart.

Levi as discussed, with references, in Susan Ackerman, "E-Dan," *Journal of Ancient Near Eastern Religions* 13 (2013): 157 n. 13.

16. See https://www.teldanexcavations.com and also http://ngsba.org/excavations/tel-dan/. Further information on the archaeological excavations described in the following paragraphs may be found in *NEAEHL* 1:323–32 and 5:1686–89, as well as in Biran, *Biblical Dan*. Much of the discussion follows Biran, except where noted, though the dating and interpretation of many aspects of the excavation are currently under reevaluation.

Middle Bronze Mudbrick Gate at Tel Dan

To date, seven excavation areas have been opened across the site (see site plan above): Area A that includes the gate area and exterior plaza on the south side of the mound; Area B on the interior of the southern edge of the rampart, with a combined Area AB that spans the area between A and B; Area M in the center of the tel; Area L to its east that has now expanded to include an area even further to its east; a small section cut known as Area H; Area K containing the MB IIA gate complex; Area Y crosscutting the rampart in the northeast; and Area T focused on the Iron Age II temple complex, with T1 expanding to the west, and T2 and T3 exposing the northwestern edge of the rampart.

One small trench in Area B, forty-three feet (13 m) below the surface, and another probe in Area T confirmed human habitation in the Pottery-Neolithic period, dated to the beginning of the fifth millennium BC. Because the next evidence for extensive settlement at the site comes from the Early Bronze Age II–III (c. 3000–2300 BC), the excavators hypothesize an occupational gap, though much of the tel remains unexcavated.

A large city was established during the Early Bronze Age (c. 2700 BC) as evidenced in widespread pottery throughout the site and architectural elements that were incorporated in the construction of the later Middle Bronze rampart. This city continued for some three hundred years and was followed by a period of decline marked by scant remains. In the MB IIA (early second millennium BC), the city again rose in prominence, as seen in a number of tombs and their associated grave goods and especially in the construction of the rampart. This plaster-covered *glacis* was built around a twenty-one feet (6.5 m) thick stone core and stood some thirty-three feet (10 m) high with an external base that is estimated to have extended at least

Charioteer Vase from Tel Dan

eighty-nine feet (27 m). The associated mid-eighteenth-century BC mudbrick gate, consisting of a three-course archway flanked by two towers, was preserved to a height of twenty-three feet (7 m) and was over forty-nine feet (15 m) wide. It remains the earliest intact mudbrick archway in the world.

After destructions at the end of the Middle Bronze Age, the site again rose in prominence during the Late Bronze Age, as is suggested by metal work from the sixteenth–fifteenth centuries BC, as well as material interactions with Egypt and the broader Mediterranean world in the LB II period (fourteenth–thirteenth centuries BC). The wealth of this period may be seen most clearly in a number of tombs, especially the so-called "Mycenaean tomb," an inter-generational tomb that included the remains of some forty individuals along with imported Mycenaean vessels, such as a notable "charioteer vase," Cypriot vessels, including *bilbils*, and exotic artifacts of alabaster, bronze, hippopotamus tusk, ivory, silver, and gold. Another important find from this period is a plaque depicting a male dancer with a lute wearing a mask and short tunic.

The transition to the Iron Age I (c. 1200) is marked by some evidence of destruction followed by the disappearance of imported wares and the presence of a large number of storage pits scattered throughout the site in dense clusters, especially in Area B (Stratum VI). The material culture, too, exhibits several changes, while certain local ceramic forms were maintained. Large concentrations of *pithoi* (large store jars for grain, oil, wine, and water) were found with the pits, both the Galilean type that is associated with other northern sites of this time and the collared-rim type that is sometimes connected with the arrival

Iron Age I *Pithoi* from Tel Dan

of the Israelites, although some dispute this association.[17] Slightly later (Stratum V, twelfth to early eleventh century BC), a third type of storage vessel, the handmade Phoenician *pithos,* appears and smaller vessels become more prevalent, coinciding with the construction of stone and mudbrick houses and the presence of some Philistine pottery and other elements of Sea Peoples culture, such as an Aegean-styled shrine. Extensive evidence of a metallurgical industry, including several crucibles, blow pipes, and fuel concentrations, were also uncovered in these phases and continued into the following IVB phase (late eleventh to early tenth century BC). This later phase is marked by the reconstruction of previously destroyed architecture and the appearance of Phoenician bichrome and slipped and burnished wares, pottery typical of the tenth/ninth century BC.

Faunal evidence also supports the archaeological interpretation of these periods of the Iron Age I as a less-settled "nomadic" habitation following the collapse of the Late Bronze Age city, which then became a settlement of increased socioeconomic complexity in the Iron Age II. This may be seen in the proportions of cattle, high percentages of which correlate to agricultural intensification and sedentism, compared to sheep and goats, present in larger numbers among nomadic populations. At Dan, the high percentage of cattle drops significantly

17. See Ann E. Killebrew, *Biblical Peoples and Ethnicity: An Archaeological Study of Egyptians, Canaanites, Philistines, and Early Israel 1300–1100 B.C.E.* (Atlanta: Society of Biblical Literature, 2005), 177–81 for an overview with references.

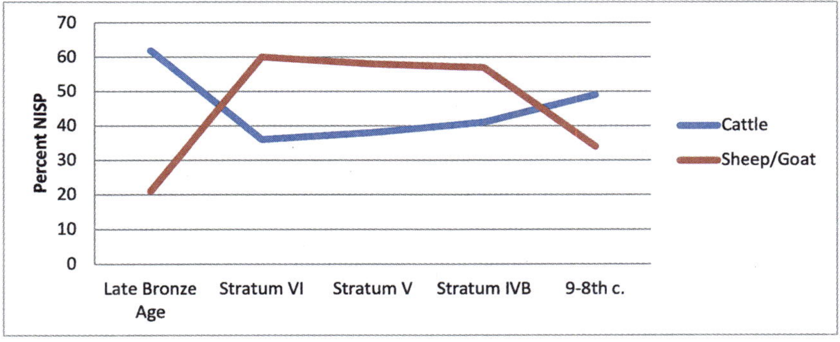

Relative Abundance of Cattle and Sheep/Goats over Time, Percentage of Number of Individual Specimens

with the transition from the Late Bronze Age to the Iron Age and then slowly rises in Iron Age II.[18]

During Iron Age II, from the late tenth/ninth century through the mid-eighth century, urbanization at the site continued, and a new system of fortifications was installed in stages evidenced most clearly in the gate system on the southern slope of the mound. There is some evidence for construction at the beginning of the period, but the most extensive fortifications are dated to the ninth and eighth centuries BC and were built in at least two phases. The massive basalt gates of the first phase featured a nearly thirteen feet (4 m) threshold, four chambers, benches, proto-Aeolic capitals, and a raised podium with column bases that may have been for a throne or, more likely, for an image or monument of some sort, such as a stela.

In fact, it is in the broad plaza outside the gate complex where fragments of the famous ninth-century BC Tel Dan Stela were found in secondary use (i.e., reused for pavement and walls in a later phase), detailing the military exploits of an Aramaean king, almost certainly Hazael, in which he claims to have killed a "king of Israel" and a "[ki]ng of the House of David," thus providing our earliest reference to David in an extra-biblical source within a few generations of his reign.[19] Though the inscription is broken in each case where the names are mentioned, based on what remains, these two kings may confidently be identified as Jehoram of Israel and Ahaziah of Judah. Also in this plaza stood at least one cultic

18. See Jonathan S. Greer, Deirdre N. Fulton, and Paula Wapnish, "The Animal Bone Remains," in *Dan IV: The Iron Age I Settlement: The Avraham Biran Excavations 1966–1999*, ed. David Ilan (Jerusalem: Hebrew Union College-Jewish Institute of Religion, 2020), 571–85; see also, Baruch Rosen, "Subsistence Economy of Stratum II," in *'Izbet Sartah: An Early Iron Age Site Near Rosh Ha'Ayin, Israel*, ed. Israel Finkelstein (Oxford: Archaeopress, 1986), 156–85; Paula Wapnish and Brian Hesse, "Faunal Remains From Tel Dan: Perspectives on Animal Production at a Village, Urban, and Ritual Center," *Archaeozoologia* 4.2 (1991): 9–86.

19. See George Athas, *The Tel Dan Inscription: A Reappraisal and a New Interpretation* (Sheffield: Sheffield Academic, 2003), for bibliography and discussion.

Tel Dan Stele

installation, as well as the eighth-century BC *huṣṣot*, a complex of buildings perhaps for commerce or lodging, in which two bronze plaques with religious scenes were discovered, one with a deity on the back of a calf.[20]

In the second phase of the eighth century BC, the direction of approach was reoriented some and an additional upper gate was added. A series of at least four groups of five standing stones were also discovered along the approach, as well as a cache of more than three hundred juglets in the later part of this phase, suggesting the religious importance of this dramatic route through the city, one that was maintained well into the Assyrian period (seventh century BC) and beyond.[21]

20. For discussion and potential relationship to calf iconography in the cult of Jeroboam, see Jonathan S. Greer, *Dinner at Dan: Biblical and Archaeological Evidence for Sacred Feasts at Iron Age II Tel Dan and Their Significance* (Leiden: Brill, 2013), 22–24; Mark S. Smith, "Counting Calves At Bethel," in *"Up to the Gates of Ekron": Essays on the Archaeology and History of the Eastern Mediterranean in Honor of Seymour Gitin*, ed. Sidnie White Crawford, et al. (Jerusalem: The W. F. Albright Institute of Archaeological Research; The Israel Exploration Society, 2007), 387–88; Tallay Ornan, "The Lady and the Bull: Remarks on the Bronze Plaque from Tel Dan," in *Essays on Ancient Israel in Its Near Eastern Context: A Tribute to Nadav Na'aman*, ed. Yairah Amit, et al. (Winona Lake, IN: Eisenbrauns, 2006), 297–312.

21. Avraham Biran, "Sacred Spaces: Of Standing Stones, High Places and Cult Objects at Tel Dan," *BAR* 24.5 (1998): 38–45, 70; David Ilan and Jonathan S. Greer, "A Pilgrimage to Iron Age II Tel Dan," *Advances in Ancient Biblical and Near Eastern Research* 1.3 (2021): 143–90.

Reconstructed Altar at Tel Dan

Such religious interest, no doubt, centered on the temple complex discovered in Area T. Above the spring, on top of the remains of the proposed *migdal* temple of the MB IIA, stood a large cultic precinct at least 197 feet (60 m) long by 148 feet (45 m) wide.[22] It was characterized by side chambers (only the western section of which has been excavated), flanking a large podium on the north upon which an elaborate superstructure was most likely built. In the center of the precinct stood an installation functioning as an altar, one horn of which was discovered, allowing for a reconstruction that suggests an altar with a base of 51 square feet (4.75 m^2) that stood 10 feet (3 m) high—the largest altar discovered anywhere in the region.

The precinct went through at least three major phases of construction (see figure below), though the complex as a whole was in a constant state of reuse and renovation. The first phase (Stratum IVA) consisted of smaller structures, ovens, an olive press, and water installations in the courtyard. Replete were numerous cultic elements including decorative "snake *pithoi*," incense stands, and seven-spouted oil lamps. The second phase (Stratum III) was also rich in religious artifacts and saw extensive renovation with the introduction of a more symmetrical layout and the use of wooden beams and fine ashlar

22. On continuity of holy space, see Jonathan S. Greer, "How Do You Define Cultic Context?," in *The Five-Minute Archaeologist in the Southern Levant*, ed. Cynthia Shafer-Elliot (Sheffield: Equinox, 2016), 178–81.

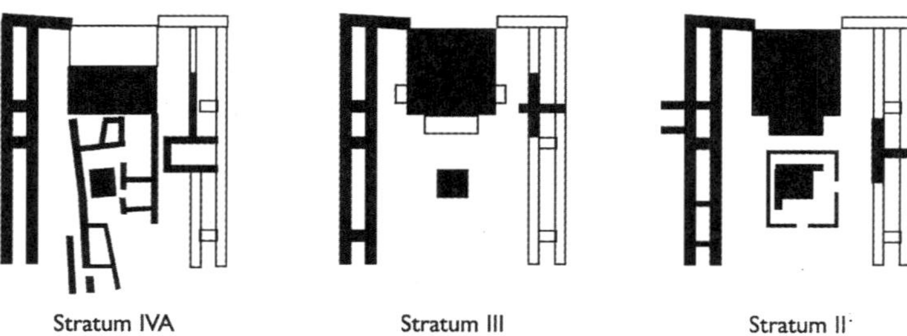

Architectural Phases at Area T Tel Dan

masonry installed in the header-stretcher style typical of ninth-century "Omride" monumental structures, the construction of which left a hard-packed "yellow floor" of travertine. In the mid-eighth-century BC phase, a temenos wall was added around the altar, and stairs were installed on the eastern and southern faces.[23] A destruction in the latter part of the eighth century BC sealed a number of cultic artifacts from Stratum II, most notably those of the so-called "altar room" consisting of a bronze bowl, three iron shovels, and a pot filled with ash next to a small altar base. Large concentrations of animal bones were also recovered in each phase. The precinct was rebuilt after the destruction and remained in use through the Hellenistic and early Roman periods when further features, including several water installations, were added.

The site as a whole suffered a massive mid-eighth-century BC destruction, perhaps as a result of an earthquake, with possible further destruction by the campaign of Tiglath-Pileser III in 733–32 BC.[24] Yet, the city enjoyed a resurgence in the seventh century BC following the domination of Assyria. During this period, domestic structures and public buildings of stone were constructed along well-planned streets, and settlement seems to have expanded to encompass the whole of the site. The site remained occupied through the brief Babylonian period, into the Persian period, and flourished again in the Hellenistic and early Roman period, before dwindling later in the Roman period.

THE BIBLICAL STORY OF ANCIENT DAN IN CONTEXT

Aside from passing geographic references mentioned above, the city of Dan first enters the biblical narrative with a description of the migration of the tribe of Dan to its northern location. Dan's original allotment had been a small section of the Shephelah and the coastal plain between the traditional boundaries of Ephraim and Judah (Josh 19:40–46), perhaps centered in the Sorek Valley as reflected in the story of Samson—the most famous Danite (Judg 13–16).

According to the biblical narrative, after being confined to the hill country

23. The dating of the stairs and the temenos wall is currently being reevaluated.

24. Though not explicitly mentioned in Assyrian records or the Bible, it may be implied (2 Kgs 15:29).

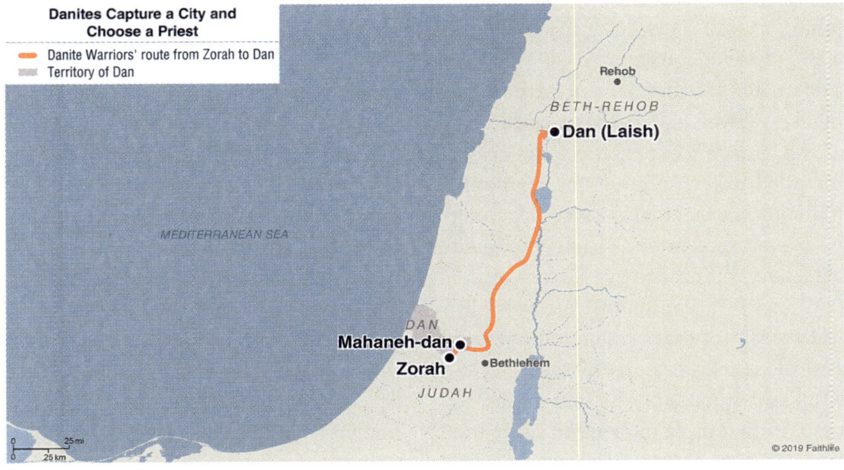

by the "Amorites" (Judg 1:34), the Danites took matters into their own hands. They traveled north to carve out a territory within the traditional allotment of Naphtali by slaughtering the peaceful and unsuspecting inhabitants of Laish and renaming the city Dan (Judg 18).[25] The story intersects with another story of a certain Micah in the hill country of Ephraim who established a shrine, perhaps at Bethel, with a silver image and other cultic paraphernalia, including an *ephod* (אֵפוֹד) and *teraphim* (תְּרָפִים), and installed as priest one of his sons and then later a young Levite from Bethlehem in Judah (Judg 17).[26] This priest, later identified as Jonathan, son of Gershom, son of Moses (Judg 18:30), was kidnapped by the Danites on their northern migration and later installed in the sanctuary of the conquered city.[27] Jonathan and his descendants served at the Danite shrine "until the time of the captivity of the land," presumably until the Assyrian annexation of 732 BC, though the image was said to have been in use only while "the house of God was in Shiloh" (Judg 18:30).[28]

Though the story is negative in its portrayal of the Danites and the foundation of the city of Dan, it is somewhat ambiguous in the portrayal of the religion of the Danites and the nature of their sanctuary. Consider the following: the names of the key figures, Micah and

25. For a detailed discussion of Judg 17–18, see Jason S. Bray, *Sacred Dan: Religious Tradition and Cultic Practice in Judges 17–18* (New York: T&T Clark, 2006).

26. Baruch Halpern, "Levitic Participation in the Reform Cult of Jeroboam I," *JBL* 95 (1976): 36–37.

27. The Leningrad Codex adds a suspended *nun* to intentionally change the name to Manasseh, likely to distance the name of Moses from apparent idolatry. The name Moses is preserved in other Hebrew manuscripts, as well as in certain manuscripts of the LXX, the Vulgate, and the Syro-Hexapla.

28. Also note another early reference to the cultic importance of Dan in LXX 2 Sam 20:18 remembering times when one would inquire at Abel, "and at Dan."

Jonathan, are Yahwistic; the image is made of silver consecrated for Yahweh; Micah, his mother, and Jonathan all invoke Yahweh in blessings; and the use of the "image" ceases before the ark is installed in Jerusalem. Such elements highlight the fact that the stories of Judg 17–18 were not intended to provide an objective, comprehensive history of the Danites but rather to illustrate the political anarchy of the premonarchic period and to cast aspersions (even if somewhat ambiguous) on the foundation of the Danite temple in order to serve the theological purposes of the larger story.

That said, some elements of the larger story do exhibit historical resonance. For example, the migration of the Danites fits the broader picture of the period following the collapse of the Late Bronze Age c. 1200 BC and the withdrawal of Egypt from the Levant. During this time, local entities often made up of multiethnic populations, as has been suggested for Iron Age I Dan, rose in prominence while maintaining certain elements of Egyptian infrastructure and culture through their inhabitants.[29]

With the arrival of the Sea Peoples soon after 1200 BC, some local entities were drawn into conflict while others integrated with the newcomers, as reflected in the Samson stories that describe both skirmishes and extensive commingling (and marriage) with the Philistines. Such may also be reflected in the cryptic reference in Judg 5:17 to the Danites "sojourning among the ships," perhaps a reference to economic affiliation with seafaring peoples on the coastal plain in the earliest period or with those of the Phoenician coast after the migration.[30] Some have also suggested a possible identification with the Danuna known from Greek sources.[31] Notably, a number of cultural elements of the Sea Peoples have been found in the Iron I strata of Tel Dan, including Philistine bichrome pottery, so-called "Ashdoda" figurine elements, and even what may be a small Aegean-styled shrine.[32]

While recent analyses suggest more cautious conclusions, Biran proposed a connection between the arrival of the Danites and the material culture of Stratum VI, especially the clusters of pits and the appearance of collared-rim store jars.[33] This suggestion may find some resonance in the discontinuity with the preceding strata in terms of diet and a near absence of pig remains, though this is

---

29. David Ilan, "Northeastern Israel in the Iron Age I: Cultural, Socioeconomic and Political Perspectives" (Ph.D. thesis, Tel Aviv University, 1999); Ilan, ed., *Dan IV: The Iron Age I Settlement: The Avraham Biran Excavations 1966–1999* (Jerusalem: Hebrew Union College-Jewish Institute of Religion, 2020).

30. For a southern connection, see Lawrence E. Stager, "The Song of Deborah: Why Some Tribes Answered the Call and Others Did Not," *BAR* 15.1 (1989): 63–64, and for a northern connection see Rainey and Notley, *Sacred Bridge*, 138–39.

31. So Yigael Yadin, "'And Dan, Why Did He Remain in Ships' (Judges V, 17)," *African Journal of Biblical Studies* 1 (1968): 9–23, but see the critique of Rainey and Notley, *Sacred Bridge*, 110, based primarily on the lack of reference in the Onomasticon of Amenope.

32. See further discussion in Ilan, *Dan IV*, 565–68.

33. See Biran, *Biblical Dan*, 125–46; note his connection with the metallurgy and biblical descriptions of artisans in Exod 31:6; 35:34; 38:23; and 2 Chr 2:13 on pp. 147–51.

a complicated matter with various possible interpretations.[34] Regardless, the collapse of the wealthy Late Bronze Age civilization followed by the introduction of new elements of material culture and a radically different settlement pattern suggest major social change. The archaeological trend of increasing social complexity and political hierarchy that follows this shift has also been related to ancient Israel and the rise of the monarchy.[35] The boundary lists mentioned above may relate to this period.

Dan again plays a prominent role in the biblical story in the cultic reforms of Jeroboam I (1 Kgs 12:26–33), following the secession of the northern tribes from the Solomonic monarchy. Jeroboam is said to have established a temple at Dan and another at Bethel, intending to rival Jerusalem, and installed golden calves in each that "became a sin" (1 Kgs 12:30) and were remembered as a central theological reason for the destruction of the Northern Kingdom (see, most clearly, 2 Kgs 17:21–23). Yet again, as observed in the Danite foundation story, the biblical texts preserve a somewhat ambiguous portrayal of the cult at Dan and clearly suggest that the temples were built to venerate Yahweh.[36] Further, a company of prophets associated with Elijah and Elisha are said to reside in Bethel but do not denounce the calf (2 Kgs 2:2–3), and Jehu, even in his Yahwistic reforms and eradication of Baalism, apparently leaves the calves intact (2 Kgs 10:29).

Geographically, Jeroboam's choice for the placement of his two temples at Bethel and Dan (1 Kgs 12:29) has significance in marking out the northern and southern boundaries of his kingdom, with Bethel strategically located on the ancestral ridge route just before one would cross over to Judah on the way to Jerusalem. Such locations may have also served political purposes by moving the temples away from his capital in Shechem, and, in the case of Dan, by reinvesting the north with a certain degree of power tied to the priesthood—especially significant after Solomon's neglect of the region.[37] Religiously, too, both Dan and Bethel were imbued with significance tied to ancestral traditions, especially in the case of Bethel (Gen 12:8; Gen 28:10–22; Gen 31:13; Judg 20:26–28), and the calves as a pair may have together represented

34. See Greer, Fulton, and Wapnish, "Animal Bone Remains," and, more specifically, Jonathan S. Greer, "Prohibited Pigs and Prescribed Priestly Portions: Zooarchaeological Remains from Tel Dan and Questions Concerning Ethnicity and Priestly Traditions in the Hebrew Bible," in *Food Taboos and Biblical Prohibitions: Reassessing Archaeological and Literary Perspectives*, ed. Peter Altmann, Anna Angelini, and Abra Spiciarich (Tübingen: Mohr Siebeck, 2020), 73–85.

35. Biran, *Biblical Dan*, 134–46.

36. See further Jonathan S. Greer, "The Cult at Dan: Aramean or Israelite?," in *Wandering Arameans: Arameans Outside Syria—Textual and Archaeological Perspectives*, ed. Angelika Berlejung, Aren Maeir, and Andreas Schüle (Wiesbaden: Harrasowitz, 2017), 3–18. That the golden calf was intended as an image associated with Yahweh in the parallel story of Exodus 32 is clear in Aaron's declaration of a "feast of Yahweh" (Exod 32:5) as discussed in Greer, *Dinner at Dan*, 25–26; see also Gary N. Knoppers, "Aaron's Calf and Jeroboam's Calves," in *Fortunate the Eyes That See: Essays in Honor of David Noel Freedman in Celebration of His Seventieth Birthday*, ed. Astrid B. Beck, et al. (Grand Rapids: Eerdmans, 1995), 92–104.

37. So Halpern, "Levitic Participation," 31–42, and also Wesley I. Toews, *Monarchy and Religious Institution in Israel Under Jeroboam I* (Atlanta: Scholars Press, 1993).

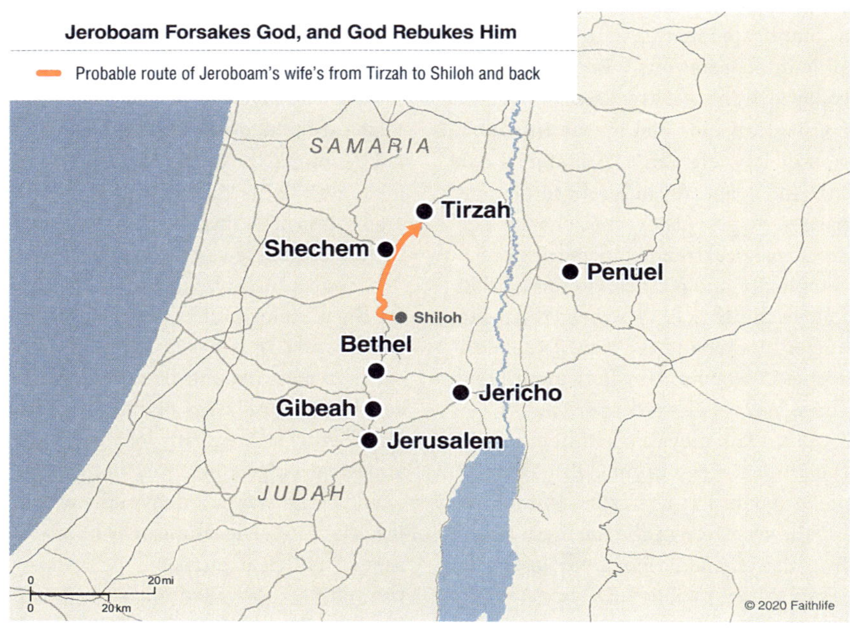

the throne of Yahweh overarching the whole of the Northern Kingdom.[38]

Archaeology has been especially helpful in illuminating the temple at Dan described in the biblical texts that remained in use throughout the Iron Age II and beyond. These discoveries may further explain some of the ambiguities in the biblical text in that much of the architecture, artifacts, and animal bone remains are congruent with what is known of Yahwistic worship in the Bible.[39] For example, the bowl, shovels, and ash pot mentioned above in the "altar room" of Stratum II coordinate with a remarkable degree of detail to priestly "altar kits" described in the Bible.[40] Of special note is the bowl, identified as a *mizraq* (מִזְרָק) (see drawing below), that would have been used for catching the blood of the sacrificial animal. Several statistically significant trends observed in the faunal analysis, too, may be interpreted as archaeological signatures of ritual practices described in Lev 1–7, such as indications that right-sided limb portions were set aside for priests.[41] Indeed, such discoveries help to explain the denouncement of Amos, addressed to northern Yahwists, that implies "orthodox" worship devoid

38. Halpern, "Levitic Participation," 32 n. 5.

39. Greer, *Dinner at Dan*; Andrew R. Davis, *Tel Dan in Its Northern Cultic Context* (Atlanta: SBL Press, 2013); Ackerman, "E-Dan," 153–87.

40. Jonathan S. Greer, "An Israelite *Mizrāq* at Tel Dan?," *BASOR* 358 (2010): 27–45.

41. Greer, *Dinner at Dan*, and in its broader context, Jonathan S. Greer, "The 'Priestly Portion' in the Hebrew Bible: Its Ancient Near Eastern Context and Its Implications for the Composition of P," *JBL* 138 (2019): 263–84.

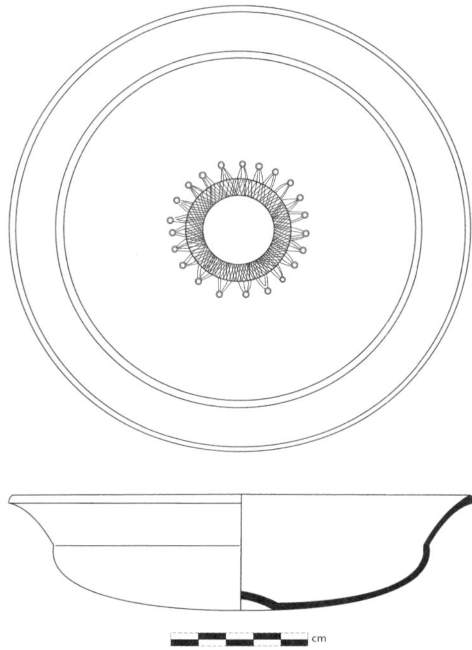

A Bronze Bowl from the "Altar Room" at Tel Dan Interpreted as an Israelite *Mizraq*

of ethical living (see Amos 5:21–24; 8:14 mentions Dan explicitly). Thus, the ambiguity in some of the biblical portrayals may stem from the fact that, although Dan and Bethel rivaled Jerusalem and included the problematic calf icons, they were still Yahwistic temples.

Several decades after Jeroboam, the city of Dan was then said to have been conquered by Ben-Hadad of Aram-Damascus. Ben-Hadad's invasion was in response to Asa of Judah's plea to attack Baasha of Israel and thus relieve pressure from their border war in the central Benjamin plateau (1 Kgs 15:16–20). This may correlate to the destruction of Stratum IVA, though the precise dating of these layers is still under investigation. The following phase (Stratum III), exhibiting the most extensive renovation discussed above, was attributed to Ahab by Biran and, though not certain, makes some sense given the current dating of the remains and the power of this northern king expressed not only in the Bible, but also in the Mesha Stela and Assyrian accounts of the battle of Qarqar.[42]

While debate continues as to the extent and duration of the Aramaean presence at the site, their influence is seen most clearly in the Tel Dan Stela marking an Aramaean victory.[43] The apparent claim

42. Biran, *Biblical Dan*, 184–91; 246–47.

43. Contrast Eran Arie, "Reconsidering the Iron Age II Strata at Tel Dan: Archaeological and Historical Implications," *TA* 35 (2008): 6–64, with Greer, "Cult at Dan," 3–18; Yifat Thareani,

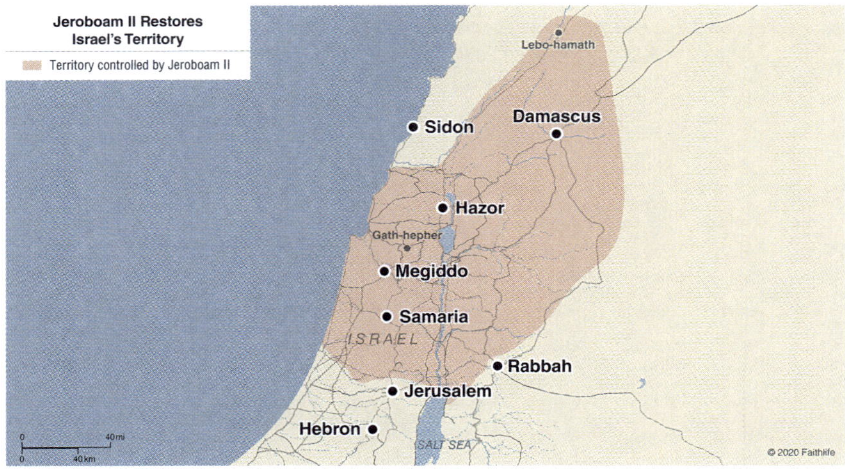

inferred from the stela that Hazael killed Jehoram and Ahaziah correlates to the story of the coup of Jehu in the biblical account (2 Kgs 9–10), with Jehu perhaps acting on behalf of Hazael (note 2 Kgs 10:32–33).[44] Archaeological evidence, in fact, suggests the presence of various ethnic groups at this time, including Israelite, Phoenician, and "Aramaean" peoples.[45] Regardless of political or ethnic affiliation, the inhabitants would have most likely identified themselves first as Danites, and worship at the sanctuary likely remained focused on Yahweh.[46]

Later, 2 Kgs 14:25 describes how Jeroboam II expanded the northern boundary past Dan in the first half of the eighth century BC. The archaeological evidence of this time affirms an Israelite presence via the discovery of several seal impressions bearing Hebrew personal names, some of which are Yahwistic. Most notable in this respect are two impressions bearing the name Immadi-yaw, a northern Yahwistic name meaning "Yahweh is with me" (compare the name Immanu-el, meaning "God is with us"). The site as a whole shows evidence of flourishing, and changes in

"Archaeology of an Imagined Community: Tel Dan in the Iron Age IIa," in *Researches on Israel and Aram: Autonomy, Interdependence and Related Issues. Proceedings of the First Annual RIAB Center Conference, Leipzig, June 2016*, ed. Angelika Berlejung and Aren Maeir (Tübingen: Mohr Siebeck, 2019), 263–76.

44. William M. Schniedewind, "Tel Dan Stela: New Light on Aramaic and Jehu's Revolt," *BASOR* 302 (1996): 75–90.

45. So Yifat Thareani, "Enemy at the Gates? The Archaeological Visibility of the Aramaeans at Dan," in *In Search of Aram and Israel: Politics, Culture and Identity*, ed. Izaak de Hulster, Manfred Oeming, and Omer Sergi (Tübingen: Mohr Siebeck, 2016), 169–97, and on the problematic nature of defining "Aramaeans" and identifying markers in material culture, also see K. Lawson Younger, *A Political History of the Arameans: From Their Origins to the End of Their Polities* (Atlanta: SBL Press, 2016).

46. For ethnicity, see Thareani, "Enemy at the Gates," 169–97. For religion, see Greer, "Cult at Dan," 3–18.

the sacred precinct suggest an increasing hierarchy.[47]

The enduring archaeological presence at the site discussed above may resonate, whether historically or as a literary trope, with later texts that speak of Israelites as far as Dan in the time of Hezekiah (2 Chr 30:5) and of Dan as a northern outpost heralding the invasion of the Babylonians (Jer 4:15; 8:16).

CONCLUSION

The history of Tel Dan is rooted in its geography. Its story was birthed in the waters of the Ain Leddan Spring and grew along the trade routes as attested by layer upon layer of archaeological remains. The biblical traditions are silhouetted against and imbedded within this geographic context and shaped by the ebb and flow of the struggles of peoples competing for its natural resources and strategic location. But the biblical stories have the greater purpose of describing the relationship of Yahweh and Israel, a complicated relationship marred by the counter-cult of Jeroboam but oriented by hope expressed in the words of Amos 9 describing the restoration of the Northern Kingdom.

The memory of Dan as a holy city endured into the Second Temple period, as may be suggested in the location of the vision of 1 Enoch, and the sacred nature of the region may provide a backdrop for depictions of Jesus' ministry in northern regions in New Testament times.[48] The hope of the restoration of the north, likewise, endured as expressed and expanded in James's citation of Amos 9:11–12 at the Jerusalem Council (Acts 15:16–18). Thus, the city of Dan casts a long shadow from the far north and played an important role in the story of ancient Israel and its relationship with Yahweh from its beginnings and beyond expressed in the Bible.

BIBLIOGRAPHY

Ackerman, Susan. "E-Dan." *Journal of Ancient Near Eastern Religions* 13 (2013): 153–87.

Arie, Eran. "Reconsidering the Iron Age II Strata at Tel Dan: Archaeological and Historical Implications." *TA* 35 (2008): 6–64.

Athas, George. *The Tel Dan Inscription: A Reappraisal and a New Interpretation*. Sheffield: Sheffield Academic, 2003.

Biran, Avraham. *Biblical Dan*. Jerusalem: Israel Exploration Society/Hebrew Union College-Jewish Institute of Religion, 1994.

———. "Sacred Spaces: Of Standing Stones, High Places and Cult Objects at Tel Dan." *BAR* 24.5 (1998): 38–45, 70.

———. "'To the God Who is in Dan.'" Pages 142–51 in *Temples and High Places in Biblical Times: Proceedings of the Colloquium in Honor of the Centennial of Hebrew Union College-Jewish Institute of Religion, Jerusalem, 14–16 March 1977*. Edited by Avraham Biran. Jerusalem: Nelson Glueck School of Biblical Archaeology, 1981.

47. See Davis, *Tel Dan*, especially 172–73, and Jonathan S. Greer, "Power to Unite and Power to Divide: Sacred Feasting and Social Change at Iron II Tel Dan," in *Feasting in the Archaeology and Texts of the Bible and the Ancient Near East*, ed. Peter Altmann and Janling Fu (Winona Lake, IN: Eisenbrauns, 2014), 117–25, on social change represented in the archaeology of the sacred precinct.

48. See, e.g., Nickelsburg, "Enoch, Levi, and Peter," 575–600.

Bray, Jason S. *Sacred Dan: Religious Tradition and Cultic Practice in Judges 17–18*. New York: T&T Clark, 2006.

Clermont-Ganneau, Charles. "Le Mont Hermon et son dieu d'après une inscription inédite." *Recueil d'archéologie orientale* 5 (1903): 346–66.

Davis, Andrew R. "Tel Dan in Its Northern Cultic Context." PhD diss., Johns Hopkins University, 2010.

———. *Tel Dan in Its Northern Cultic Context*. Atlanta: SBL Press, 2013.

Dussaud, René. "Cultes cananéens aux sources du Jourdain, d'après les textes de Ras Shamra." *Syria* 17 (1936): 283–95.

Elitzur, Yoel. *Ancient Place Names in the Holy Land: Preservation and History*. Winona Lake, IN: Eisenbrauns, 2004.

Gil'ad, D., and J. Bonne. "The Snowmelt of Mt. Hermon and Its Contribution to the Sources of the Jordan River." *Journal of Hydrology* 114 (1990): 1–15.

Greer, Jonathan S. "The Cult at Dan: Aramean or Israelite?" Pages 3–18 in *Wandering Arameans: Arameans Outside Syria: Textual and Archaeological Perspectives*. Edited by Angelika Berlejung, Aren Maeir, and Andreas Schüle. Wiesbaden: Harrasowitz, 2017.

———. *Dinner at Dan: Biblical and Archaeological Evidence for Sacred Feasts at Iron Age II Tel Dan and Their Significance*. Leiden: Brill, 2013.

———. "How Do You Define Cultic Context?" Pages 178–81 in *The Five-Minute Archaeologist in the Southern Levant*. Edited by Cynthia Shafer-Elliot. Sheffield: Equinox, 2016.

———. "An Israelite *Mizrāq* at Tel Dan?" *BASOR* 358 (2010): 27–45.

———. "Power to Unite and Power to Divide: Sacred Feasting and Social Change at Iron II Tel Dan." Pages 117–25 in *Feasting in the Archaeology and Texts of the Bible and the Ancient Near East*. Edited by Peter Altmann, and Janling Fu. Winona Lake, IN: Eisenbrauns, 2014.

———. "The 'Priestly Portion' in the Hebrew Bible: Its Ancient Near Eastern Context and Its Implications for the Composition of P." *JBL* 138 (2019): 263–84.

———. "Prohibited Pigs and Prescribed Priestly Portions: Zooarchaeological Remains from Tel Dan and Questions Concerning Ethnicity and Priestly Traditions in the Hebrew Bible." Pages 73–85 in *Food Taboos and Biblical Prohibitions: Reassessing Archaeological and Literary Perspectives*. Edited by Peter Altmann, Anna Angelini, and Abra Spiciarich. Tübingen: Mohr Siebeck, 2020.

Greer, Jonathan S., Deirdre N. Fulton, and Paula Wapnish. "The Animal Bone Remains." Pages 571–85 in *Dan IV: The Iron Age I Settlement: The Avraham Biran Excavations 1966–1999*. Edited by David Ilan. Jerusalem: Hebrew Union College-Jewish Institute of Religion, 2020.

Halpern, Baruch. "Levitic Participation in the Reform Cult of Jeroboam I." *JBL* 95 (1976): 31–42.

Ilan, David, ed., *Dan IV: The Iron Age I Settlement: The Avraham Biran Excavations 1966–1999*. Jerusalem: Hebrew Union College-Jewish Institute of Religion, 2020.

———. "A Middle Bronze Age 'Migdal' Temple at Tel Dan?" *Eretz-Israel* 33 (2018): 25–37 [Hebrew with English Abstract].

———. "Northeastern Israel in the Iron Age I: Cultural, Socioeconomic and

Political Perspectives." PhD diss., Tel Aviv University, 1999.

Ilan, David, and Jonathan S. Greer. "A Pilgrimage to Iron Age II Tel Dan." *Advances in Ancient Biblical and Near Eastern Research* 1.3 (2021): 143–90.

Killebrew, Ann E. *Biblical Peoples and Ethnicity: An Archaeological Study of Egyptians, Canaanites, Philistines, and Early Israel 1300–1100 B.C.E.* Atlanta: Society of Biblical Literature, 2005.

Knoppers, Gary N. "Aaron's Calf and Jeroboam's Calves." Pages 92–104 in *Fortunate the Eyes That See: Essays in Honor of David Noel Freedman in Celebration of His Seventieth Birthday*. Edited by Astrid B. Beck, Andrew H. Bartlet, Paul R. Raabe, and Chris A. Franke. Grand Rapids: Eerdmans, 1995.

Malamat, Abraham. "Syro-Palestinian Destinations in a Mari Tin Inventory." *IEJ* 21 (1971): 31–38.

Nickelsburg, George W. E. "Enoch, Levi, and Peter: Recipients of Revelation in Upper Galilee." *JBL* 100 (1981): 575–600.

Ornan, Tallay. "The Lady and the Bull: Remarks on the Bronze Plaque from Tel Dan." Pages 297–312 in *Essays on Ancient Israel in Its Near Eastern Context: A Tribute to Nadav Na'aman*. Edited by Yairah Amit, Ehud Ben Zvi, Israel Finkelstein, and Oded Lipschits. Winona Lake, IN: Eisenbrauns, 2006.

Por, F. D., H. J. Bromley, Ch. Dimentman, G. N. Herbst, and R. Ortal. "River Dan, Headwater of the Jordan, an Aquatic Oasis of the Middle East." *Hydrobiologia* 134 (1986): 121–40.

Rainey, Anson F., and R. Steven Notley. *The Sacred Bridge: Carta's Atlas of the Biblical World*. 2nd ed. Jerusalem: Carta, 2014.

Robinson, Edward, and Eli Smith. *Biblical Researches in Palestine, Mount Sinai and Arabia Petræa: A Journal of Travels in the Year 1838*. 3 Vols. Boston: Crocker and Brewster, 1841.

Rosen, Baruch. "Subsistence Economy of Stratum II." Pages 156–85 in *'Izbet Sartah: An Early Iron Age Site near Rosh Ha'Ayin, Israel*. Edited by Israel Finkelstein. Oxford: Archaeopress, 1986.

Schniedewind, William M. "Tel Dan Stela: New Light on Aramaic and Jehu's Revolt." *BASOR* 302 (1996): 75–90.

Smith, Mark S. "Counting Calves at Bethel." Pages 82–94 in *"Up to the Gates of Ekron": Essays on the Archaeology and History of the Eastern Mediterranean in Honor of Seymour Gitin*. Edited by Sidnie White Crawford, Amnon Ben-Tor, J. P. Dressel, William G. Dever, Amihai Mazar, and Joseph Aviram. Jerusalem: The W. F. Albright Institute of Archaeological Research; The Israel Exploration Society, 2007.

Stager, Lawrence E. "The Song of Deborah: Why Some Tribes Answered the Call and Others Did Not." *BAR* 15.1 (1989): 50–64.

Thareani, Yifat. "Archaeology of an Imagined Community: Tel Dan in the Iron Age IIa." Pages 263–76 in *Researches on Israel and Aram: Autonomy, Interdependence and Related Issues. Proceedings of the First Annual Riab Center Conference, Leipzig, June 2016*. Edited by Angelika Berlejung and Aren Maeir. Tübingen: Mohr Siebeck, 2019.

———. "Enemy at the Gates? The Archaeological Visibility of the Aramaeans at Dan." Pages 169–97 in *In Search of Aram and Israel: Politics,*

Culture and Identity. Edited by Izaak de Hulster, Manfred Oeming, and Omer Sergi. Tübingen: Mohr Siebeck, 2016.

Toews, Wesley I. *Monarchy and Religious Institution in Israel Under Jeroboam I*. Atlanta: Scholars Press, 1993.

Wapnish, Paula, and Brian Hesse. "Faunal Remains from Tel Dan: Perspectives on Animal Production at a Village, Urban, and Ritual Center." *Archaeozoologia* 4.2 (1991): 9–86.

Wilson, John Francis. *Caesarea Philippi: Banias, the Lost City of Pan*. London: I. B. Tauris & Co Ltd., 2004.

Yadin, Yigael. "'And Dan, Why Did He Remain in Ships' (Judges V, 17)." *African Journal of Biblical Studies* 1 (1968): 9–23.

Younger, K. Lawson, Jr. *A Political History of the Arameans: From Their Origins to the End of Their Polities*. Atlanta: SBL Press, 2016.

CHAPTER 30

"FROM DAN TO BEERSHEBA": A GEOGRAPHICAL ANALYSIS OF THE RECURRING EXPRESSION OF ISRAEL'S MONARCHY

Judg 20:1; 1 Sam 3:20; 2 Sam 3:10; 17:11; 24:2, 15; 1 Kgs 4:25; 1 Chr 21:2; 2 Chr 30:5

John A. Beck

KEY POINTS

- Dan and Beersheba have geographic realities and connotations that differ sharply from one another.
- Dan and Beersheba are joined into a geographic merism that communicates the notion of the ideal territory in a variety of literary contexts.

INTRODUCTION

The expression "from Dan to Beersheba" (מִדָּן וְעַד־בְּאֵר שָׁבַע, *middan wead-beer shava*; Judg–2 Kgs) or "from Beersheba to Dan" (מִבְּאֵר שֶׁבַע וְעַד־דָּן, *mibbeer sheva wead-dan*; 1–2 Chr) occurs nine times within the historical narrative of Judges through 2 Chronicles.[1] Like other local expressions, it has both descriptive and rhetorical power in those contexts. To appreciate its function more fully, we will explore the following questions: where are Dan and Beersheba and what characterizes them? What connotations are linked to each indi-

1. The Chronicler arrestingly reverses the expected order, replacing "Dan to Beersheba" with "Beersheba to Dan." This reversal is evident even when the writer is reporting the same quotation of David given in the parallel account (e.g., 2 Sam 24:2 and 1 Chr 21:2). The most likely reason for the inversion in Chronicles has to do with its southern perspective. Beersheba is mentioned first because it is closer to the homeland of the storytelling while Dan is more remote. See Louis C. Jonker, *1 & 2 Chronicles*, Understanding the Bible Commentary Series (Grand Rapids: Baker, 2013), 137.

vidually? How do these two locations function descriptively and rhetorically when linked in this geographic merism? How does this geographic merism function within the literary contexts in which it is deployed? In the end, we will see that the biblical authors put this expression to work when speaking of something they viewed as ideal, such as the ideal military muster, the ideal geopolitical kingdom, or the ideal religious restoration. We will also see that other geographical expressions are substituted for it when less-than-ideal situations are in view.

OCCURRENCES OF "FROM DAN TO BEERSHEBA" OR "FROM BEERSHEBA TO DAN"

Verse	***Phrase***	***Initial Descriptor***	***Literary Context***
Judg 20:1	"from Dan to Beersheba"	All the people of Israel	Military muster
1 Sam 3:20	"from Dan to Beersheba"	All Israel	Religious reformation
2 Sam 3:10	"from Dan to Beersheba"	Israel and Judah	Geopolitical designation
2 Sam 17:11	"from Dan to Beersheba"	All Israel	Military muster
2 Sam 24:2	"from Dan to Beersheba"	All the tribes of Israel	Military muster
2 Sam 24:15	"from Dan to Beersheba"	The people	Military muster
1 Kgs 4:25 (MT 5:5)	"from Dan to Beersheba"	Judah and Israel	Geopolitical designation
1 Chr 21:2	"from Beersheba to Dan"	Israel	Military muster
2 Chr 30:5	"from Beersheba to Dan"	All Israel	Religious reformation

THE GEOGRAPHY AND CONNOTATIONS OF DAN AND BEERSHEBA

We begin with the geographic parts of this merism before assembling them into the whole. We will consider the geographic realities of Dan and Beersheba as well as the connotations associated with each.

DAN

Dan is identified with the fifty-acre archaeological site of Tel el-Qadi at the southern base of majestic Mount Hermon.[2] This 9,232-foot (2,814 m) mountain is particularly effective at amassing rain and snow from the atmosphere which then flows into the tributary system that forms the Upper Jordan River. The Dan

2. For further discussion of the site and its archaeological remains, see LaMoine F. DeVries, *Cities of the Biblical World* (Peabody, MA: Hendrickson, 1997), 163–68.

Aerial View of Dan

Stream is one of the main tributaries. It rushes alongside the city of Dan, flowing at the phenomenal rate of 2,100 gallons per second (8 m³ per second). This abundant supply of water joins with rich local soils to create one of the lushest ecosystems in Israel, one in which both agriculture and pastoralism could flourish. It is today, as the Danites described it, "a land that lacks nothing whatever" (Judg 18:10).[3]

Dan's access to water and agricultural richness are further complimented by its role in superintending international travel. Mount Hermon to the north and the wetlands of the Huleh Basin to the south pinch together at Dan, allowing only a narrow passageway. Through this bottleneck, merchants and armies traveled between Damascus and Hazor or Tyre.[4] It was the perfect place to collect tariffs on those trade goods, and a critical location for resisting invasion of Israel from the north. According to the prophet Jeremiah, when one heard the enemy horses snorting at Dan, the entire land trembled, aware that such an invasion would quickly lead to Israel's interior (Jer 8:16).

For the biblical authors who have an interest in Israel's spiritual wellbeing, Dan carries negative connotations. Its stories persistently speak of Dan as the place of unfaithfulness that promoted misunderstanding of who God is. We see this unfaithfulness from the start as the tribe of Dan abandoned their divinely assigned land parcel (Josh 19:40–48) and seized land around Laish, land that was previously

3. All biblical quotations are from the New International Version (NIV) unless otherwise noted.

4. David A. Dorsey, *The Roads and Highways of Ancient Israel* (Baltimore: Johns Hopkins University Press, 1991), 157–59.

Aerial View of Beersheba

assigned to another tribe (Judg 18:7–10). This action cast the founding of the city of Dan (formerly Laish) in a very negative light on its own. The negative connotations associated with Dan are further enhanced when these same Danites seized the personal priest, ephod, household gods, and idol from the home of Micah in Ephraim's hill country. They took this religious apparatus with them to their new city of Dan, establishing a tribal worship center that stood in tension with the national sanctuary at Shiloh (Judg 18:11–31). If all this was not bad enough, things got worse after the time of Solomon. When the kingdom divided, Jeroboam tried to prevent reunification of the kingdom under David by building alternative worship sites for his Northern Kingdom at Bethel and Dan (1 Kgs 12:25–33). The worship of the golden calves in these locations became the great "sin of Jeroboam" that influenced all the northern kings that followed, infused their subjects with a misunderstanding of God, and precipitated the exile of the Northern Kingdom (2 Kgs 17:21–23). Dan resided in a rich, influential place but the Bible provides no story involving Dan that casts it in a positive light. Dan is a place of apostasy that persistently promoted misunderstanding of who God was.

Beersheba

Archaeologically, Beersheba is identified with Tell es-Saba (Arabic), also known as Tel Sheva (Hebrew).[5] The city was founded in the central Negev basin after the time of Abraham and his family who dug wells in this area (Gen 21:5, 30; 26:22–33). When those wells were contested by other local clans, an agreement was struck that produced the future name of the city, Beersheba meaning "well of the oath," or "well of the seven" (Gen 21:31; 26:33). At every geographic turn,

5. For further discussion of the site and its archaeological remains, see DeVries, *Cities*, 150–55.

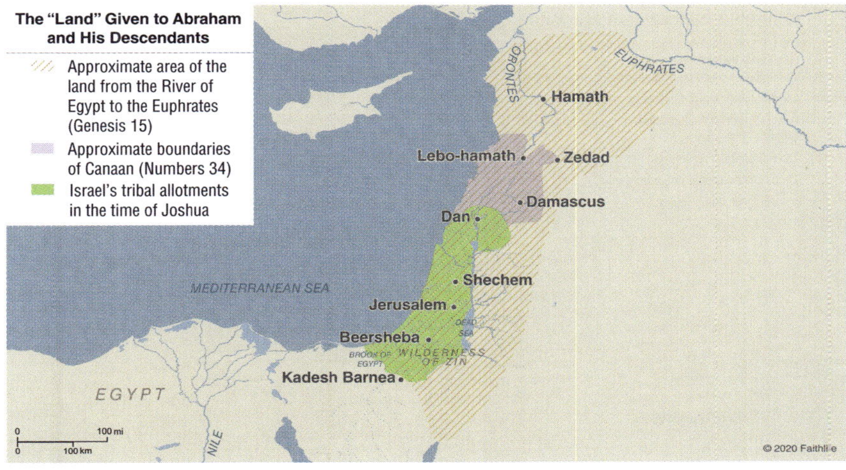

this basin lacked the qualities of Dan in the north. Two seasonal streams (wadis) passed alongside the site, and wells dug in these stream beds and underground cisterns promised access to water, but the rains came less frequently here and in uncertain amounts, leaving those watercourses dry much of the year (Ps 126:4). The loess soil of the basin had the nutrients to grow grain but because the soil is high in quartz, the crystals rise to the soil surface during rain and deflect rather than absorb the precious rainfall. All in all, life was more precarious here than in Dan, making Beersheba a place where pastoralism rather than agriculture was the primary lifestyle of its residents.[6] However, like Dan, Beersheba sat at a natural crossroads. Trade goods moving between Petra and the seaport of Gaza transited this basin and a ridge running north to Hebron created the connection between Hebron in Judah's hill country and the Way to Shur that traveled south to Egypt.[7]

The biblical authors leave us with more positive feelings about Beersheba, not because of its ecosystem but because of its stories.[8] As Abraham's family established themselves in the promised land, Beersheba played a significant role.[9] Abraham, Isaac, and Jacob all worshiped here (Gen 21:33; 26:25; 46:1), and it is where Jacob gave a powerful demonstration of his faith. He resisted leaving the promised land even though a severe famine gripped the land and his long-lost son Joseph had invited him to come and live in Egypt,

6. For more on the Negev, see *MAB*, 48.

7. Dorsey, *Roads and Highways*, 200.

8. This perspective yielded to more negative connotations during the divided kingdom. See Amos 5:5; 8:14.

9. Paul H. Wright, *Greatness Grace and Glory: Carta's Atlas of Biblical Biography* (Jerusalem: Carta, 2008), 11.

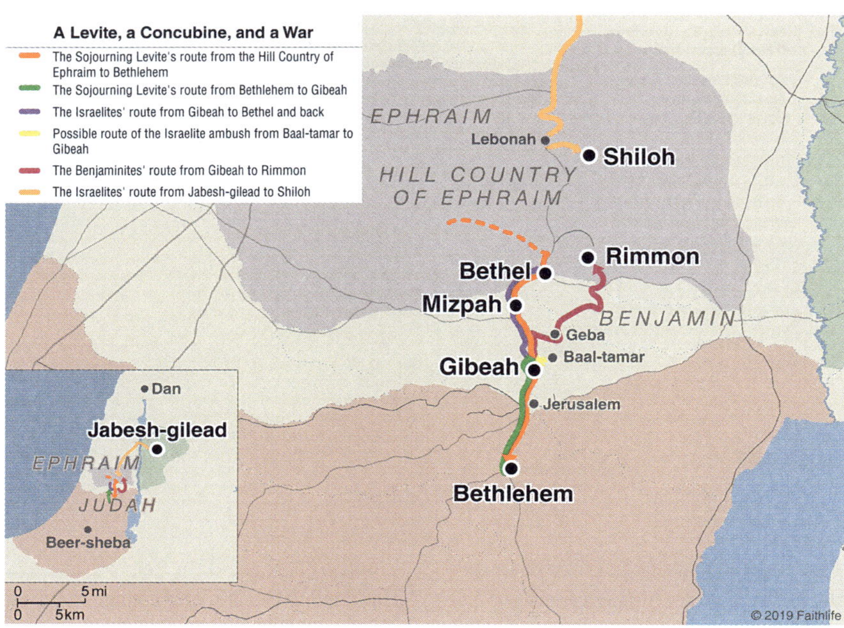

leaving only when the Lord assured him of return (Gen 46:1–6).[10]

GEOGRAPHIC MERISM AND ITS CONNOTATIONS

Dan and Beersheba each bring their own geographic realities and connotations to the stories in which they appear. Our focus now turns to how they unite to create meaning in the merism, "from Dan to Beersheba."

MERISM

A merism is a figure of speech that takes two well-known, contrasting elements and links them grammatically with a conjunction to put emphasis on the entirety that resides between those contrasting elements.[11] We find this figure of speech in the very first verse of the Bible where the text reports that the Lord created "the heavens and the earth" (Gen 1:1). We also meet a merism in the very last chapter of the Bible where Jesus calls himself "the Alpha and the Omega" (Rev 22:13).

Our expression is such a geographic merism. Dan and Beersheba contrast sharply from one another in many ways. Geographically, Dan and Beersheba are the major cities located on the north-

10. For a more complete discussion of the topic, see John A. Beck, *Discovery House Bible Atlas* (Grand Rapids: Discovery House, 2015), 59–62.

11. For more on this figure of speech as it appears in the Bible, see Alexander M. Honeyman, "Merismus in Biblical Hebrew," *JBL* 71 (1952):11–18; Ethelbert W. Bullinger, *Figures of Speech Used in the Bible Explained and Illustrated* (Grand Rapids: Baker, 1968), 435.

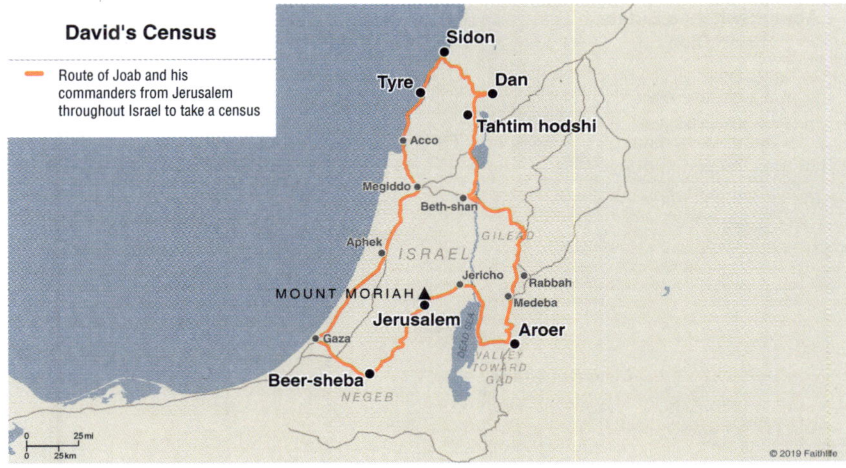

ern and southern borders of this land.[12] Hydrologically, they represent the extremes of the rain-rich north (Dan) and the rain-impoverished south (Beersheba). In terms of human geography, they contrast the focus on agriculture and pastoralism. Theologically, they connote apostasy and faithfulness to the Lord. Consequently, at more than one level, Dan and Beersheba represent the polar extremes that stand in sharp contrast to one another when mentioned separately, but when joined by a conjunction, they become a geographical merism that emphatically marks the entirety of the promised land.

CONNOTATIONS

But what connotations does this merism bring to its literary contexts? This is a question that needs to be answered for two reasons. From the chart above, you can see that each use of the merism is preceded by a geographic descriptor that already denotes the entirety of the land. That makes the merism redundant unless it functioned beyond the scope of denotation. We also need to consider how it differs from other geographic merisms that could have been used in its place to describe the extent of the land, such as, "the Wadi of Egypt to the great river, the Euphrates" (Gen 15:18; 1 Kgs 4:21).

So, what is the contribution of our merism? In contrast to alternate expressions, "from Dan to Beersheba" marks Israel's area of settlement rather than its broader sphere of influence.[13] More importantly, the selection of the expression "from Dan to Beersheba" harkens back to the land promise given to Abraham (Gen 12:1, 7). As Genesis reports Abraham's movement through the promised land, it follows his journey from Dan to Beersheba (Gen 14:14; 22:19). These travel details anticipate our merism and provide the background we need to see our expres-

12. Anson F. Rainey and R. Steven Notley, *The Sacred Bridge: Carta's Atlas of the Biblical World* (Jerusalem: Carta, 2006), 36.

13. Rainey and Notley, *Sacred Bridge*, 36.

sion as marking the ideal territory: the one divinely promised to Abraham's family.[14]

LITERARY CONTEXTS

What remains is to consider the literary contexts in which this expression occurs. We find it marking the ideal territory in three literary contexts: military muster, geopolitical designation, and religious restoration. Finally, we will call attention to places where we would expect the expression to be used but was not because the ideal state did not exist.

MILITARY MUSTER

The first time the merism occurs is in Judg 20:1. In a book dominated by stories that highlight the lack of tribal cooperation, the merism marks a moment of national unity akin to that known from the stories in Joshua.[15] The tribal militia gathers from all the tribes except Benjamin to address an outrageous act the likes of which had not been seen even among the tragic stories in Judges (19:22–30). At this moment, "all the people of Israel" gather to address the Benjamin problem, marked as the ideal muster by our expression "from Dan to Beersheba."

We find the same connotation at work in 2 Sam 17:11. Here, Hushai offers advice to Absalom, the son of King David, who had driven his father from the throne in Jerusalem. At this vulnerable moment when David and his men were "weak and weary" (17:2), Absalom had been advised to quickly pursue and wipe out his father's forces. Hushai wanted to buy David time to escape and recover, so he used our geographic merism to play on the vanity of Absalom. He urges Absalom to gather soldiers in ideal fashion, "from Dan to Beersheba," before continuing the pursuit of David.

Ironically, this merism comes back to haunt the story of David in 2 Sam 24:2, 15. David directed Joab to take an ill-advised census "from Dan to Beersheba" in

14. Beck, *Bible Atlas*, 53; Richard H. Hess, "Joshua," *ZIBBCOT* 2:215.
15. Trent C. Butler, *Judges*, WBC (Nashville: Thomas Nelson, 2009), 440.

order to determine the number he could muster for a militia when needed. Given that the Lord had proved his ability to save by many or few (Judg 7:2), the Lord punished this apparent vanity with a plague that killed thousands of potential soldiers "from Dan to Beersheba."[16] The ideal army was compromised by a plague that ironically struck the places from which the ideal army would be gathered.

GEOPOLITICAL DESIGNATION

The merism also occurs in geopolitical designations. When Saul's son, Ish-Bosheth, had a falling out with his general, Abner, the general told Ish-Bosheth that he was now ready to throw his support behind David. The civil war that followed Saul's death divided the kingdom, leaving the ideal state out of reach. Now Abner promised that he would "establish David's throne over Israel and Judah from Dan to Beersheba" (2 Sam 3:10).

Similarly, when the Lord established David's son Solomon as king of Israel, this king's success is articulated in many ways including this one: "During Solomon's lifetime Judah and Israel, from Dan to Beersheba, lived in safety" (1 Kgs 4:25). The ideal had been achieved.

RELIGIOUS RESTORATION

In two instances, the merism describes the gathering of people during times of religious restoration in Israel. The first occasion comes at the close of the troubled period of the judges. Even the sanctuary at Shiloh had been corrupted by the immoral acts of the high priest's sons (1 Sam 2:12–25). When no one was listening to the Lord, Samuel was doing so without even knowing it at first

16. The Lord directed Israel to take a census prior to entering the promised land (Num 1:1–54), which included enumeration of those eligible for military service (1:3). Although that appears to serve as a precedent for David's census, there must have been a problem with his motivation, a problem like hubris. This would explain both David's contrition and the divine judgement. His general, Joab, saw it and tried to talk David out of it, suggesting the census was not necessary from the military's point of view (2 Sam 24:3).

(1 Sam 3:1–14). He became the prophet who would lead Israel toward religious restoration. The return towards the ideal is marked, in part, using our merism: "And all Israel from Dan to Beersheba recognized that Samuel was a prophet of the LORD" (1 Sam 3:20).

The expression also occurs during the restoration championed by King Hezekiah (2 Kgs 18:1–8; 2 Chr 29:1–31:1). His reign was preceded by the dark and difficult days Israel faced under King Ahaz, whose list of religious failings is both extensive and shocking (2 Kgs 16:1–18; 2 Chr 28:1–4, 22–25). His legacy of spiritual apostasy was countered by the reforms of King Hezekiah, who purified the temple and called for a national celebration of Passover (2 Kgs 18:4; 2 Chr 29:1–31:1). Even though most of the Northern Kingdom's residents had been removed by the Assyrian conquest, Hezekiah reached beyond his own political boundaries of Judah. He sent a proclamation "throughout Israel, from Beersheba to Dan, calling people to come to Jerusalem and celebrate the Passover to the LORD, the God of Israel" (2 Chr 30:5).[17] Once again, the choice of our merism helps to conjure recollection of the ideal religious festival that extended to the old borders of the promised land.

ABSENT WITH CAUSE

The final category we consider is not one in which our merism is used but one in which it is absent. If "from Dan to Beersheba" marks the ideal, then we would expect it to be absent from narratives in which the biblical author felt the ideal was not being reached. Consider again the listing of texts in the chart above. While the expression appears in stories related to Samuel, Saul, David, and Solomon, it all but disappears as the biblical authors report on the realities of the divided kingdom. The one exception that stands out is the last we spoke of, during the time of King Hezekiah (2 Chr 30:5). In this case, the exception

17. Here again the order of the proper names is reversed, likely to represent a Southern Kingdom point of view.

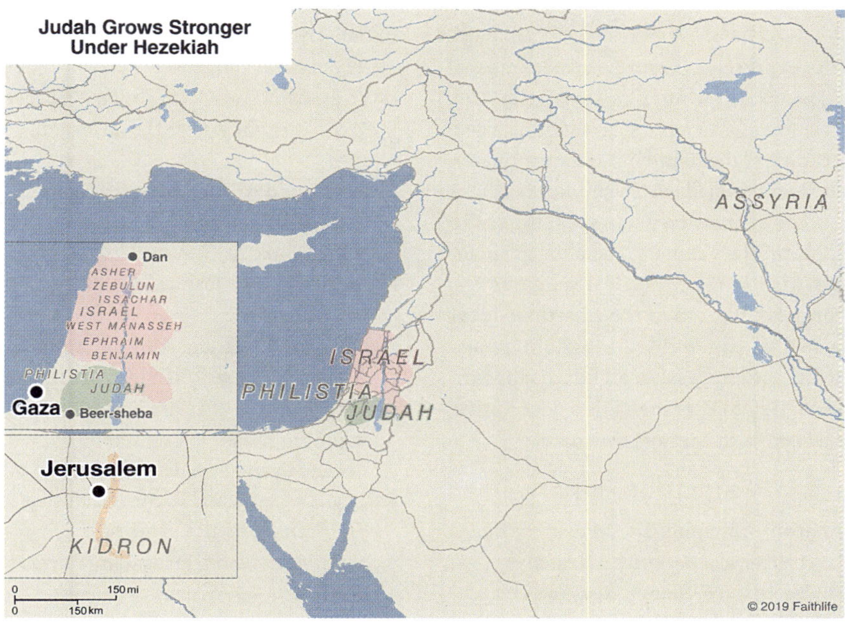

fits the overall storytelling strategy of the chronicler that idealizes the Davidic family and legacy. But generally speaking, the expression is absent from the block of divided kingdom stories because the ideal state, the one extending from Dan to Beersheba, did not exist.

In fact, we have a striking substitute for our expression offered in the report on the division of the united monarchy. Rehoboam succeeded his father Solomon and traveled to Shechem in order to secure the support of the northern tribes. Instead, he divided the once united monarchy (1 Kgs 11:43–12:24). Jeroboam became the first king of the northern kingdom of Israel but was concerned that if his subjects went to Jerusalem to worship at the temple, it would animate an interest in reuniting the kingdom under David's dynasty (1 Kgs 12:27). He responded by developing a distinct religious system for his own subjects that included the installation of high places at Bethel and Dan (1 Kgs 12:28–30). In doing so, he appears to have followed the ancient Near Eastern tradition of establishing sanctuaries at cities that marked the borders of the land, Dan over against Aram and Bethel over against Judah.[18] In doing so, he established a new geographic merism to support the reach of his new kingdom. It was not one that reached from Dan to Beersheba but from Dan to Bethel (1 Kgs 12:29; 2 Kgs 10:29). This highlights just how all-encompassing the Northern Kingdom's regression into polytheist thinking had become. Dan is no longer balanced by Beersheba but bolstered by Bethel.

18. Yohanan Aharoni, *The Land of the Bible: A Historical Geography*, trans. Anson F. Rainey, rev. and enl. ed. (Philadelphia: Westminster, 1979), 379.

CONCLUSION

The expression "from Dan to Beersheba" appears in nine places in the Old Testament. We have seen that it is a geographical merism that communicates the territorial ideal. The biblical authors use the expression when speaking of the ideal military muster, the ideal geopolitical kingdom, or the ideal religious restoration. But when the less-than-ideal world of the divided kingdom comes to be, the expression all but disappears. "From Dan to Beersheba" is a descriptive merism with connotative force.

BIBLIOGRAPHY

Aharoni, Yohanan. *The Land of the Bible: A Historical Geography.* Translated by Anson F. Rainey. Rev. and enl. ed. Philadelphia: Westminster, 1979.

Beck, John A. *Discovery House Bible Atlas.* Grand Rapids: Discovery House, 2015.

Bullinger, Ethelbert W. *Figures of Speech Used in the Bible Explained and Illustrated.* Grand Rapids: Baker, 1968.

Butler, Trent C. *Judges.* WBC. Nashville: Thomas Nelson, 2009.

DeVries, LaMoine F. *Cities of the Biblical World.* Peabody, MA: Hendrickson, 1997.

Dorsey, David A. *The Roads and Highways of Ancient Israel.* Baltimore: Johns Hopkins University Press, 1991.

Hess, Richard H. "Joshua." *ZIBBCOT* 2:2–94

Honeyman, Alexander M. "Merismus in Biblical Hebrew." *JBL* 71 (1952): 11–18.

Jonker, Louis C. *1 & 2 Chronicles.* Understanding the Bible Commentary Series. Grand Rapids: Baker, 2013.

Rainey, Anson F., and R. Steven Notley, *The Sacred Bridge: Carta's Atlas of the Biblical World.* Jerusalem: Carta, 2006.

Wright, Paul H. *Greatness Grace and Glory: Carta's Atlas of Biblical Biography*. Jerusalem: Carta, 2008.

CHAPTER 31

THE BOOK OF RUTH: A SOCIO-SPATIAL ANALYSIS OF MOAB AND BETHLEHEM

Ruth 1–4

Victor H. Matthews

> KEY POINTS
>
> - While physical space matters, the biblical narrative sometimes uses it for metaphorical purposes.
> - The journey from Bethlehem to Moab by Elimelech's household in each case represents movement from death to life.
> - Each locale in Bethlehem adds significance to the social transformation of Naomi and Ruth.
> - The threshing floor and the city gate provide legal settings designed to resolve the issue of inheritance and the future of the two widows.

INTRODUCTION

As Michel de Certeau states, "Every story is a travel story—a spatial practice."[1] The book of Ruth intentionally takes the audience on a series of journeys, both physical and cultural. Given the lack of detail, the storyteller assumes the ancient audience is familiar with the physical geography associated with the route taken or chooses to set aside as irrelevant the difficulties presented to the travelers. However, that leaves modern readers the task of extrapolating what obstacles the characters may have faced along the way. There is also no hint in the story of political or cultural barriers that would have prevented Elimelech and his household from emigrating to Moab and arranging

1. Michel de Certeau, *The Practice of Everyday Life* (Berkeley: University of California Press, 1984), 115.

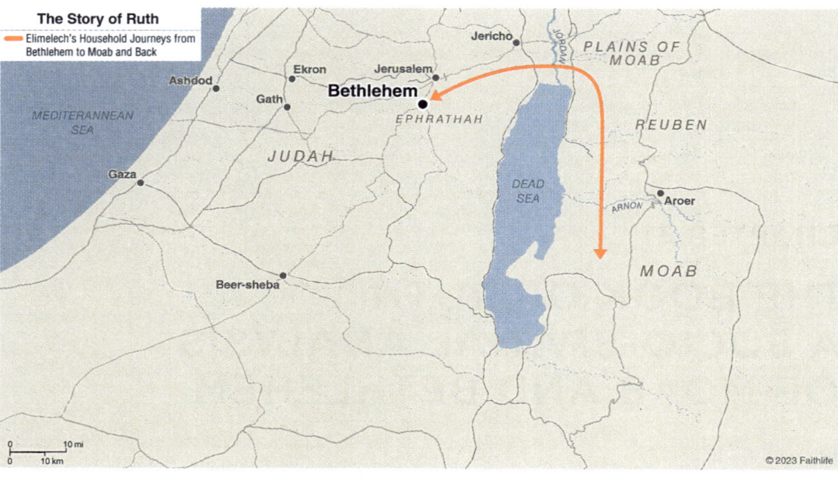

marriages for his sons. That "cultural blindness" or neutrality removes a measure of reality from the story since there is a great deal of anti-Moabite sentiment in the biblical narrative (Num 25:1–2; Judg 3:12–14).[2] However, it may reflect, as the story of Jacob and his sons moving to Goshen (Gen 46) indicates, that the movement of small groups of people from one area to another in times of climatic crisis was not unusual in the ancient Near East and may even have been welcomed as a source of itinerant labor (see Gen 12:10).

STAGE ONE: FROM BETHLEHEM TO MOAB

When a place no longer functions as hospitable, for whatever reason, it loses its sense of being considered a "home." In this story, Bethlehem, ironically the "House of Bread," experiences a famine. The village is situated on the eastern ridge of the central hill country in the "rain shadow" and consequently receives less annual rainfall than the areas to the west and north. An environmental crisis, such as a drought in Judah, would certainly result in a famine there, while the Transjordanian plateau could still receive enough rainfall to maintain its harvests.[3] Thus, the story's initial premise that drives the household of Elimelech to seek another, more accommodating place, in Moab would seem to be both sound and logical to the audience.[4] It does hinge, however, on a choice. Elimelech could have chosen to seek a better life in another Israelite village less effected by the drought/famine but instead chooses to go to Moab.[5]

2. Katherine D. Sakenfeld, *Ruth*, Interpretation (Louisville, KY: John Knox, 1999), 19.

3. Frederic Bush, *Ruth/Esther*, WBC (Dallas: Word Books, 1996), 61–62.

4. Note the parallel with David using Moab as a refuge for his family during his "outlaw period" and struggle with Saul (1 Sam 22:3–4). P. Kyle McCarter Jr., *I Samuel*, AB (New York: Doubleday, 1980), 359, sees the connection here based on David's genealogy through Ruth (Ruth 4:17–22) as the basis for David's overture to the unnamed king of Moab.

5. An interesting parallel to the story of the Levite and his concubine in Judg 19:11–15.

The basic itinerary for the journey to Moab involves traveling northeast from Bethlehem, just five miles (8 km) southwest of Jerusalem, around the northern end of the Dead Sea and then continuing east to cross the Jordan River at some point, a task not too difficult in a time of drought.[6] It would have been an interesting detail if the storyteller had included the place where they crossed the Jordan River, especially if it was at Mizpah where Joshua lead the Israelites into Canaan (Josh 4).

Once in Transjordan the family would then turn south through territory ascribed to the tribe of Reuben (Josh 13:15–23), although there is no mention of any stops or people encountered. Eventually, if they continued directly south, they would have reached the lip of the Arnon River/Gorge (Wadi Mujib) that bisects the plateau east-west and marks the northern boundary with Moab (Num 21:13). The distance from rim to rim of the river's gorge is approximately three miles (5 km) across and varies in depth from one thousand three hundred to two thousand three hundred feet (396–701 m). The only way to avoid this topographical feature is to travel several miles further east to the King's Highway where travelers can bypass the gorge's rim before continuing south. Since the biblical account does not tell us where in Moab the family eventually settled, the journey could be between thirty and sixty miles (48–97 km) and would have taken between seven and ten days to complete on foot.

The only aspect of the story that suggests that Elimelech's household was welcomed, or at least accepted into the Moabite community is the marriages arranged for his two sons. That does indicate that intermarriage was not an issue for either party and that, for a time at least, Moab was a place that could be considered "home." What changes after an unspecified number of years is the death of the male members of the household. Once again, there is a situation that places the household on the brink of extinction. It is not surprising, therefore, that the female remnant of Elimelech's household decides to make the return journey back to Bethlehem.

STAGE TWO: FROM MOAB TO BETHLEHEM

At that point in the narrative and in the face of such a personal tragedy and economic ruin, the thought of "home" or the "proper place" reemerges. Ruth and Naomi, experience multiple changes in their identity as they face a change in place. Britt points to the "killing off" of the men as a necessary literary element "for the story to proceed."[7] However, there is more here at stake for Naomi than a simple homecoming. Rather than lose her cultural identity and be absorbed into "foreign space" inhabited by strangers, she chooses to leave Moab and retrace

6. It is possible that a southern route could have been taken. Going around the southern end of the Dead Sea would have required a longer journey, but it would have eliminated two significant barriers to travel—the Jordan River crossing and the Wadi Mujib (Nahal Arnon) crossing.

7. Brian Britt, "Death, Social Conflict, and the Barley Harvest in the Hebrew Bible," *Journal of Hebrew Scriptures* 5 (2005): art. 14, p. 10, https://doi.org/10.5508/jhs.2005.v5.a15.

Aroer and the King's Highway from the South Rim of Wadi Mujib

her steps to familiar ground.[8] Ruth has the opposite problem. She will have to reshape her identity gradually so that when she reaches Bethlehem, the people will eventually stop referring to her as the Moabite (1:22; 2:2, 6, 21; 4:5; 4:10) and accept her as an honored woman "like Rachel and Leah" (4:11) and as Boaz's wife (4:13).[9]

At some point in the journey home, in what can only be termed liminal space since it is a non-specified location, Naomi provides an opportunity for her Moabite daughters-in-law to make the choice to retain their cultural identity and return to Moab while she goes on to Bethlehem. The conversation at this critical stage in their trek highlights a major theme in the book—transformation of personal identity.[10] Each character must decide who they are, who they will become, and then seek recognition from their community of that defined identity. It seems that Orpah makes the easier choice returning to her "proper" place (Ruth 1:11–15), while Ruth declares her willingness to leave her cultural background behind, remain with Naomi, and face a future that encompasses a difficult transition for her and for the people in Bethlehem (1:16–17).[11]

8. Dana N. Fewell, "Space for Moral Agency in the Book of Ruth," *JSOT* 40 (2015): 82.

9. Unless otherwise indicated, Scripture quotations are from the New Revised Standard Version (NRSV).

10. Victor H. Matthews, "The Determination of Social Identity in the Story of Ruth," *BTB* 36 (2006): 51–53.

11. See Philip F. Esler, "'All That You Have Done ... Has Been Fully Told to Me': The Power of Gossip and the Story of Ruth," *JBL* 137 (2018): 655–56, for what is entailed in Ruth's decision to embark on an "ethnic translation" from Moabite to Israelite.

STAGE THREE: SEARCH FOR IDENTITY AND PLACE IN BETHLEHEM

Even though their journey is done once they return to Judah, travel (in space and socially) continues to be a dominant factor in the narrative once the two women settle in Bethlehem. While Naomi remains at home, presumably the house she and Elimelech had once inhabited, Ruth moves about to various locations and participates in a series of transformative encounters. While some of these places are specified locations within the environs of the village (i.e., field and threshing floor), others like Elimelech's and Boaz's houses are assumed details in the story. Each plays its part in the narrative as either a staging area or a place associated with physical labor, business, or legal disputation. There are logical links between these places since they represent the range of activities and movement that would be expected to occur in a village setting.[12] The chart below provides a guide to these locations, their social function, and their role in the story.

NARRATIVE FUNCTION OF LOCATIONS IN BETHLEHEM

Location	**Function**	**Role in Story**
Elimelech's House (assumed)	Dwelling place	Place to return and meet with Naomi who remains here
Boaz's field	Productive land	Site where Ruth works and meets Boaz
Threshing Floor	Processing grain/ legal and business associations	Site where Ruth entreats Boaz to serve as their [her & Naomi's] levir
City Gate	Gathering place for elders	Site where Boaz, before witnesses, questions the "other" levir and assumes responsibility for Ruth and Naomi
Boaz's house (assumed)	Dwelling place	Place where Ruth and Boaz conceive Obed

Although it is assumed in the story that Naomi and Ruth are occupying a house, most likely the one tied to Elimelech's estate in Bethlehem, there is never an explicit mention or description of that dwelling. It is possible that it was a typical four-room house commonly found in Iron Age Israelite villages, and that would have provided plenty of space for the two women.[13] However, because they lack any animals or means of making a living, the house along with Elimelech's "parcel of land" (Ruth 4:3) would be subject to "redemption" by the kinsman redeemer as a means of supporting the widows, at least until an heir for Ruth's deceased husband could reclaim his inheritance. Thus, the house serves as a physical base

12. Fewell, "Space for Moral Agency," 81–82.

13. Avraham Faust, "The Four Room House: Embodying Iron Age Israelite Society," *NEA* 66 (2003): 22–31.

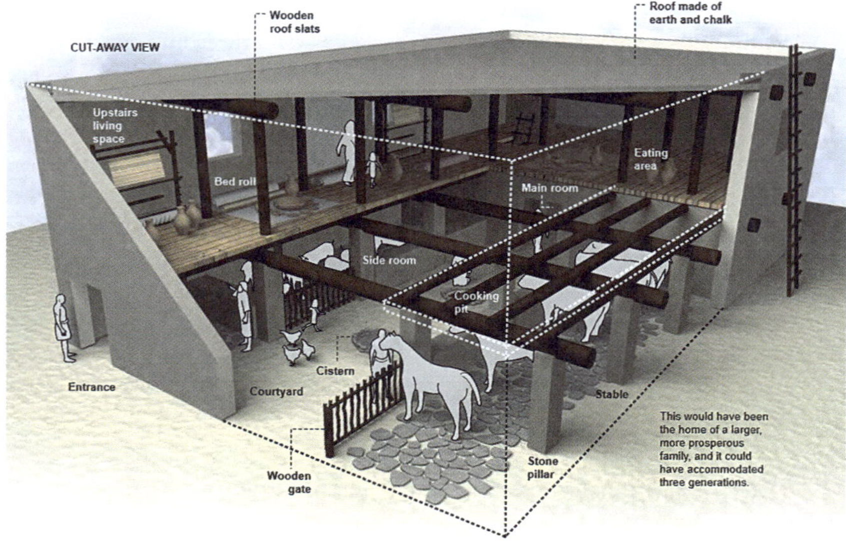

Ancient Israelite House

For more than 600 years—circa 1500 BC–500 BC—nearly all Israelite houses were built with the same distinctive layout. While surrounding cultures used other house plans, the Israelites even used this one for wealthy homes and public buildings. Its usage disappeared during the Babylonian exile.

---

from which Naomi sends Ruth to work in the fields and to meet with Boaz at the threshing floor.

Since Naomi and Ruth arrive in Bethlehem "at the beginning of the barley harvest" (1:22), which is in early summer and about four weeks before the wheat harvest, the stage is set for Ruth to take the opportunity to go into the fields and glean behind the harvesters. The time cue is also an indicator that the famine has ended, and normal life can resume for the inhabitants of the village. Although the storyteller indicates that Naomi is aware of the kinship relationship with Boaz, the text states that Ruth does not intentionally go to his field, only that "as it happens," she found herself in the section that belonged to him (2:3). Her subsequent diligence in gathering more than her due as a gleaner not only brings attention to a humanitarian statute (Lev 19:9–10; Deut 24:19–22), but further demonstrates how personal initiative is a necessary component in ensuring a basic existence for herself and Naomi.[14] The extent to which Ruth is rewarded by her own efforts and the generosity of a likely besotted Boaz suggests just how bountiful the fields have

14. David Baker, "To Glean or Not to Glean … ," *Expository Times* 117 (2006): 406–10.

now become and presages Ruth's future fertility as a wife.[15]

The next logical step or physical link in the story takes place on the village threshing floor. Following the harvest, the sheaves of grain are brought to this communal facility for processing (see Mic 4:12). It would have occupied a flat, circular bit of ground adjacent to the fields. A threshing sled pulled by oxen would crush the stalks (2 Sam 24:21–22; Amos 1:3), and the workers would rely upon a prevailing wind to blow away the chaff when winnowing forks cast the crushed stalks of grain into the air (Ruth 3:2; Jer 15:7).

Since the men, who had worked hard all day, slept beside their heaps of grain to guard their share of the harvest, the strategy that Naomi and Ruth use to confront Boaz here makes sense for several reasons. To begin with, the threshing floor over time took on the additional connotation as a place where business and law are transacted.[16] At Naomi's direction, Ruth washes and dresses (Ruth 3:3), waits until the men had eaten and were asleep, and lays as a penitent at Boaz's feet. All these actions serve as preparation for her request that he physically and metaphorically "spread his cloak" over her and take on the responsibility of the next-of-kin (3:9). Place is critical in this situation since it adds a greater solemnity to Ruth's request and to Boaz's response based on his interpretation of inheritance and kin law (3:11–12). While some see this scene as primarily a seduction or overt sexual encounter, the use of the threshing floor as the "court setting" moves it more in the direction of a legal plea.[17] It also coincides with Boaz's statement that he is aware of Ruth's "loyalty" (3:10), presumably based on testimony he has received from people within the Bethlehem community.[18]

STAGE FOUR: LEGAL RESOLUTION IN SIGNIFICANT SPACE

Completing the series of narrative and spatial links is Boaz's use of the city gate. The gate area is a defined zone made authoritative by regular social practice and as such is an instrument of social and political control. It is thus the appropriate place in which to discuss the legal status of Naomi and Ruth and the disposition of Elimelech's estate. As was the case when Ruth and Naomi target the threshing floor as the strategic zone for their plan, Boaz employs a tactic that is designed to use this space as a forum for socio-legal control disputation.[19] He deliberately goes to this significant spot because it serves as the

15. See Jeff Hayes, "Intentional Ambiguity in Ruth 4.5: Implications for Interpretation of Ruth," *JSOT* 41 (2016): 176, for an evaluation of the various opinions on Boaz's reaction to Ruth's gleaning in his fields.

16. Andrew Tobolowsky, "Where Doom is Spoken: Threshing Floors as Places of Decision and Communication in Biblical Literature," *Journal of Ancient Near Eastern Religions* 16 (2016): 114; Victor H. Matthews, "Physical Space, Imagined Space, and 'Lived Space' in Ancient Israel," *BTB* 33 (2003): 13.

17. Yitzhak Berger, "Ruth and the David-Bathsheba Story: Allusions and Contrasts," *JSOT* 33 (2009): 450. See also Bush, *Ruth/Esther*, 165, for arguments against this approach.

18. Esler, "Power of Gossip," 664.

19. Setha M. Low and Denise Lawrence-Zúñiga, "Locating Culture," in *The Anthropology of Space and Place: Locating Culture*, ed. Setha M. Low and Denise Lawrence-Zúñiga (Malden, MA: Blackwell, 2003), 30.

A Threshing Floor

In the ancient world, farmers used threshing floors to separate grain from its inedible husk (chaff) by beating it with a flail or walking animals on it—sometimes while towing a threshing sledge. Sledges were fitted with flint teeth to dehusk the grain more quickly. Other workers would turn the grain over so that it would be evenly threshed by the sledge.

"city hall" of the village culture. It is the appropriate place where matters of law that concern the well-being of the community are to be presented (see Deut 21:19; 22:15). By stationing himself there, Boaz signals that he intends to call a meeting of the elders and thus initiates a recognized social strategy to raise an important legal proposition.

Once in place, Boaz waits for the players to appear as they pass on their way to and from the village. He first calls on the "kinsman redeemer" to sit with him and then gathers a group of ten elders. They will serve as witnesses to the legal discourse and provide a stamp of approval once consensus is achieved. Boaz lays out the situation in stages, first announcing that it is Naomi's intention to sell the land that had belonged to "our kinsman" Elimelech (Ruth 4:4). Once against the story is tied to space and the right of redemption that would keep land within the extended kinship group, just as it is when the prophet Jeremiah is asked to redeem the field of his deceased cousin Hanamel (Jer 32:7).

Having received the initial assurance that the next of kin would redeem Elimelech's field, Boaz's next statement amends his announcement by revealing that the redeemer would also be "acquiring Ruth" with the expectation that he would raise up an heir for the deceased man and thus, set up a sequence of events that would, in the end, deprive him of the ownership of the field (4:5).[20] Staging this event in the gate before witnesses gives Boaz the legal pathway to declare his claim to Ruth and Elimelech's estate (4:9–11), and sets up the final scene in which she gives birth to a son, who will be the ancestor of David (4:13, 18–22).

CONCLUSION

Following a series of journeys, some through physical space and some through the cultural channels, Naomi and Ruth obtain economic stability and the recognition by the community in Bethlehem of their acquired identities. They have emerged from death to life and set up the future through their genealogical connection to King David. The story ends with all the characters in their proper place and at rest, for now.

BIBLIOGRAPHY

Baker, David. "To Glean or Not to Glean ... ." *Expository Times* 117 (2006): 406–10.

Berger, Yitzhak. "Ruth and the David-Bathsheba Story: Allusions and Contrasts." *JSOT* 33 (2009): 433–52.

Britt, Brian. "Death, Social Conflict, and the Barley Harvest in the Hebrew Bible." *Journal of Hebrew Scriptures* 5 (2005): art. 14, pp. 1–29. https://doi.org/10.5508/jhs.2005.v5.a15.

Bush, Frederic. *Ruth/Esther*. WBC. Dallas: Word Books, 1996.

de Certeau, Michel. *The Practice of Everyday Life*. Berkeley: University of California Press, 1984.

Esler, Philip F. "'All That You Have Done ... Has Been Fully Told to Me': The Power of Gossip and the Story of Ruth." *JBL* 137 (2018): 645–66.

Faust, Avraham. "The Four Room House: Embodying Iron Age Israelite Society." *NEA* 66 (2003): 22–31.

Fewell, Dana N. "Space for Moral Agency in the Book of Ruth." *JSOT* 40 (2015): 79–96.

Hayes, Jeff. "Intentional Ambiguity in Ruth 4.5: Implications for Interpretation of Ruth." *JSOT* 41 (2016): 159–82.

Low, Setha M., and Denise Lawrence-Zúñiga. "Locating Culture." Pages 1–30 in *The Anthropology of Space and Place: Locating Culture*. Edited by Setha M. Low and Denise Lawrence-Zúñiga. Malden, MA: Blackwell, 2003.

Matthews, Victor H. "The Determination of Social Identity in the Story of Ruth." *BTB* 36 (2006): 49–54.

———. "Physical Space, Imagined Space, and 'Lived Space' in Ancient Israel." *BTB* 33 (2003): 12–20.

McCarter, P. Kyle, Jr. *I Samuel*. AB. New York: Doubleday, 1980.

Sakenfeld, Katherine D. *Ruth*. Interpretation. Louisville, KY: John Knox, 1999.

Tobolowsky, Andrew. "Where Doom is Spoken: Threshing Floors as Places of Decision and Communication in Biblical Literature." *Journal of Ancient Near Eastern Religions* 16 (2016): 95–120.

20. Efforts to characterize Boaz as a trickster or a comic, ineffectual character in this scene (see Hayes, "Intentional Ambiguity," 173–75) degrade the systematic nature of his strategy.

CONTRIBUTORS

Barry J. Beitzel (PhD, Dropsie University) is professor emeritus of Old Testament and Semitic Languages at Trinity Evangelical Divinity School in Deerfield, Illinois. He obtained a postdoctorate in ancient Near Eastern geography from the Université de Liège, Belgium, and has engaged in post-doctoral archaeological work through UCLA in eastern Syria. He is the author of *Where Was The Biblical Red Sea? Examining the Ancient Evidence* (Lexham) and *The New Moody Atlas of the Bible*. His publications on Near Eastern geography have appeared in a variety of monographs and journals from *Biblical Archaeology Review* and *The Bulletin of the American Schools of Oriental Research* to *Iraq: The British Institute for the Study of Iraq*. His maps appear in *National Geographic*, *The Biblical World: An Illustrated Atlas*, *The Holman Bible Atlas*, *The NIV Study Bible*, *The ESV Study Bible*, and in several monographs.

John A. Beck (PhD, Trinity International University) has taught courses in Hebrew and Old Testament at various colleges and universities for more than twenty-five years. During that time, he has been teaching field studies in Israel, Jordan, and Egypt that explore the relationship between geography, culture, and the way the biblical authors express themselves. Beck spends most of his year writing books and documentaries. He is a permanent adjunct faculty member at Jerusalem University College in Israel. His books include: *The Basic Bible Atlas*, *Zondervan Dictionary of Biblical Imagery*, *The Baker Illustrated Guide to Everyday Life in Bible Times*, *The Discovery House Bible Atlas*, *The Baker Book of Bible Charts, Maps, and Time Lines*, and *The Holy Land for Christian Travelers*. He has also released the book and documentary resources *Along the Road: How Jesus Used Geography to Tell God's Story* and *Land without Borders: How God Guides You Through the Wilderness*. He is the host of the film series *The Holy Land—Connecting the Land with Its Stories*.

Douglas R. Clark (PhD, Vanderbilt University), has taught at Southwestern Adventist University, Walla Walla University, and La Sierra University, having also held administrative positions at Walla Walla and La Sierra universities, as well as being Executive Director of the American Schools of Oriental Research (ASOR, now the American Society of Overseas Research) in Boston for two years. Clark is partially retired and living on the Olympic Peninsula in Washington State, continues to serve as Director of the Center for Near Eastern Archaeology at La Sierra University in Riverside, California which, with a dedicated support team, he established in 2012. He also directs the Madaba Plains Project at Tall al-'Umayri, Jordan (in research and publication phases), where he has worked since the project's inception in 1984. He has authored, edited, or co-edited sixteen volumes (with one more in press) and 200+ articles, and has made 200+

presentations worldwide. Some of his recent volumes include The Madaba Plains Project: Forty Years of Archaeological Research into Jordan's Past, for which he was lead editor and an author (published by Equinox, Sheffield, UK, in 2011) and seasonal volumes in the Madaba Plains Project, 'Umayri series (the most recent one, volume 10, published in 2022 by Eisenbrauns, an imprint of Pennsylvania State University Press), for which he has been co-editor and author.

S. Cameron Coyle (PhD, Southwestern Baptist Theological Seminary) is an adjunct professor of Old Testament at Southwestern Baptist Theological Seminary in Fort Worth, Texas. He has academic training in both archaeology and biblical studies, including extensive archaeological field work at and around the site of Tel Gezer, Israel, with the Tel Gezer Excavation Project and the Gezer Regional Survey Project. At Tel Gezer, he supervised the excavations of Field E, a broad exposure of the Iron Age IIA Israelite city, including a large administrative building adjacent to Gezer's well-known "Solomonic Gate." He has published on archaeological and biblical topics in the *Israel Exploration Journal*, *Hadashot Arkheologiyot*, and elsewhere.

Brian Donnelly-Lewis (PhD, UCLA) is an independent scholar living in Wisconsin. He has published articles on the Hebrew Bible and Northwest Semitic inscriptions in the *Journal of Biblical Literature*, *BASOR*, *Journal for Semitics*, and *Semitica*.

Avraham (Avi) Faust (PhD, Bar-Ilan University), is professor of archaeology at the Department of General History, Bar-Ilan University. He received his degrees from Bar-Ilan University and also studied in the University of Oxford (visiting graduate student) and Harvard (post-doc). He is directing the excavations at Tel 'Eton in the Judean Shephelah and the survey in its vicinity, and "The National Knowledge Center on the History and Heritage of Jerusalem and its Environs," and serves as an editor of the *Jerusalem Journal of Archaeology* and *Qadmoniot*. He authored more than 200 publications, covering various aspects of the region's archaeology from the Early Bronze Age to the Byzantine period, with a special focus on Iron Age society. Among the books he authored are *Israel's Ethnogenesis: Settlement, Interaction, Expansion and Resistance* (Equinox/Routledge, 2006), *The Archaeology of the Israelite Society in the Iron Age II* (Eisenbrauns, 2012), *Judah in the Neo-Babylonian Period: The Archaeology of Desolation* (The Society of Biblical Literature, 2012), *The Settlement History of Ancient Israel: A Quantitative Analysis* (Rennert Center for Jerusalem Studies, 2015 [in Hebrew]) (with Zeev Safrai) and *The Neo-Assyrian Empire in the Southwest: Imperial Domination and its Consequences* (Oxford University Press).

Benjamin A. Foreman (PhD, University of Aberdeen) lived in Israel for nearly twenty years and served as a faculty member at the Israel extension of The Master's University (IBEX), where he taught historical geography and biblical history. He also travels to Hungary on a yearly basis and is a guest lecturer of Manners and Customs and Psalms at the Word of Life Bible Institute. He has participated in several archaeological digs in Israel and is the author of *Animal Metaphors and the People of Israel in the Book of Jeremiah* (Vandenhoeck & Ruprecht). He currently lives in Boise, Idaho.

Jonathan S. Greer (PhD, The Pennsylvania State University) is visiting Professor of Archaeology at Grand Valley State University (Michigan, USA). He is an archaeologist and biblical scholar with research interests in ancient Israelite religion, sacrifice, and feasting. His Ph.D. focused on Hebrew Bible, ancient Near Eastern studies, and archaeology. He and was formerly Professor of Old Testament and Director of the Hesse Archaeological Laboratory at Grand Rapids Theological Seminary. He is the Associate Director of excavations at Tel Dan, Israel (www.teldanexcavations.com) and has published a number of works on the relationship of the Bible to the ancient world.

Michael G. Hasel (PhD, University of Arizona) is professor of Near Eastern Studies and Archaeology and founding Director of the Institute of Archaeology and Lynn H. Wood Archaeological Museum at Southern Adventist University where he has taught since 1998. He has lectured on five continents. He has contributed to, edited or written over twenty books, including *Domination and Resistance: Egyptian Military Activity in the Southern Levant, 1185 BC*; *Military Practice and Polemic: Israel's Laws of Warfare in Near Eastern Perspective*; *In the Footsteps of King David: Revelations from and Ancient Biblical City*; *The Promise: God's Everlasting Covenant*; "Exodus" in the *Andrews Bible Commentary* and *Jerusalem: An Archaeological Guide*. He has excavated twelves sites in Cyprus, Jordan, and Israel and co-directed expeditions to Khirbet Qeiyafa, Socoh, Hazor, and Lachish.

Michelle Knight (PhD, Wheaton College) is associate professor of Old Testament and Semitic Languages at Trinity Evangelical Divinity School. She has a PhD from Wheaton College with an emphasis in Old Testament and biblical theology. Her canonical specialty is the Former Prophets; her teaching and research focus especially on the books of Joshua and Judges, in which she trains students to read the Hebrew text carefully, with theological attentiveness and literary sophistication. She is the author of *The Prophet's Anthem: The Song of Deborah and Barak in the Narrative of Judges* and has worked and written extensively on the Song of Deborah and Barak from Judges 5.

J. Carl Laney (ThD, Dallas Theological Seminary), who is now retired, served as Professor of Biblical Literature at Western Seminary in Portland, Oregon from 1977 to 2018. Laney was introduced to the land of the Bible in 1973 during his studies at Jerusalem University College (formerly the Institute of Holy Land Studies). Since that experience he has given special attention to the geographical, cultural, and historical background of the Bible, writing his ThM, thesis at Western Seminary on "The Geopolitics of the Judean Hill Country" and his ThD dissertation at Dallas Theological Seminary on "Selective Geographical Problems in the Life of Christ." Laney's studies in Israel have included excavations at Tel Qasile, Tel Jezreel, and Bethsaida. Since 1992 he has been taking students to Israel to participate in the short-term program at the Jerusalem University College. Laney's book, *Concise Bible Atlas: A Geographical Survey of Bible History*, is published by Hendrickson. His self-published books, including *The Story of Israel*, *Laney's Israel Guide*, and *Essential Bible Background* available on Amazon.

Aren M. Maeir (PhD, Hebrew University of Jerusalem) studied archaeology and

Jewish History at the Hebrew University of Jerusalem, and completed his PhD in archaeology in 1997. From 1991 he has taught archaeology at Bar-Ilan University (in Ramat-Gan, Israel), at the Martin (Szusz) Department of Land of Israel Studies and Archaeology. He serves as the Head of the Institute of Archaeology at Bar-Ilan University, directs the Tell es-Safi/Gath Archaeological Project (gath.wordpress.com), co-directs the Minerva Center for the Relations between Israel and Aram in Biblical Times (aramisrael.org), directs the Ingeborg Rennert Center for Jerusalem Studies (Bar-Ilan University), co-edits the Israel Exploration Journal, and is a corresponding member of the German Archaeological Institute.

Victor H. Matthews (PhD, Brandeis University) is the dean of the College of Humanities and Public Affairs and professor of religious studies at Missouri State University in Springfield, Missouri, where he has taught for thirty years. He is the author of numerous books, including *The History of Bronze and Iron Age Israel* (Oxford University Press), *The Cultural World of the Bible: An Illustrated Guide to Manners and Customs* (Baker Academic), *The Hebrew Prophets and Their Social World* (Baker Academic), and *Studying the Ancient Israelites: A Guide to Sources and Methods* (Baker Academic). He is co-author with Don C. Benjamin of *Old Testament Parallels: Laws and Stories from the Ancient Near East* (Paulist Press) and *The Social World of Ancient Israel 1250–587 B.C.E.* (Hendrickson) and co-author with John H. Walton and Mark W. Chavalas of the *IVP Bible Background Commentary: Old Testament* (InterVarsity Press).

Chris McKinny (PhD, Bar-Ilan University). His dissertation focused on the historical geography and archaeology of the town lists of Judah and Benjamin in the book of Joshua. Chris is also a senior staff member of the Tel Burna Archaeological Project (biblical Libnah) in which capacity he has contributed a wide-range of peer-reviewed articles, conference papers, and popular essays. Besides being involved in several other writing and research projects, Chris is author of *My People as Your People: A Textual and Archaeological Analysis of the Reign of Jehoshaphat* (Peter Lang), of the forthcoming monograph *The Tribal Allotments of Judah and Benjamin in the Book of Joshua: A Historical Geography* (Eisenbrauns), and is co-author with Mark D. Janzen of the forthcoming *The Route of the Exodus: The Historical Geography of the Exodus and Wilderness Wanderings* (Lexham). He also co-edited *Tell It in Gath: Studies in the History and Archaeology of Israel: Essays in Honor of Aren M. Maeir on the Occasion of his Sixtieth Birthday* with Itzhaq Shai, Jeffrey R. Chadwick, Louise A. Hitchcock, Amit Dagan, and Joe Uziel (Zaphon) and *The Late Bronze and Early Iron Ages of Southern Canaan* with Aren M. Maeir and Itzhaq Shai (DeGruyter). In addition, he currently serves as an adjunct faculty member at Texas A&M University-Corpus Christi, The Master's University (IBEX), and William Jessup University.

Thomas Middlebrook (PhD, Trinity Evangelical Divinity School) is the Assistant Professor of Old Testament at A.W. Tozer Theological Seminary (Simpson University) in Redding, CA. As a student of the Bible, Dr. Middlebrook focus on the literary beauty, the ancient culture, and the physical settings of the Bible. Outside of contributions to the *Lexham Geographic Commentary* Series, he has presented at ASOR, ETS, and at

UW-Madison's *Emerging Voices in Samuel Studies*, written several scholarly reviews, and contributed to online forums, including the Center for BioEthics and Human Dignity. His current research is a grant-funded project focusing on communication theory relating to comic book Bibles.

Steven M. Ortiz (PhD, University of Arizona) is professor of archaeology at Lipscomb University and director of the Lanier Center for Biblical Archaeology. He was formerly director of the Tandy Institute for Archaeology at Southwestern Baptist Theological Seminary where he was professor of archaeology and biblical backgrounds. (This program was eliminated in 2020.) He is the principal investigator and co-director of the Tel Gezer Excavation Project and is now a senior staff member at Tel Burna. He was on the Old Testament team who wrote the study notes for the *ESV Archaeology Study Bible* (Crossway). He is co-author with Seymour Gitin and Trude Dothan of the forthcoming excavation report *Tel Miqne-Ekron Excavations 1994–1996, Fields IVNE/NW and VSE/SW: The Iron Age II, Late Philistine Temple Complex* (Tel Miqne-Ekron Final Field Reports Series). Ortiz's research and publications focus on the archaeology of David and Solomon, Iron Age I and II transition, and the border relations between Judah and Philistia.

Elaine A. Phillips (PhD, Dropsie College for Hebrew and Cognate Learning) is Distinguished Professor of Biblical Studies (retired) at Gordon College in Wenham, Massachusetts, where she taught from 1993 to 2020. She studied and taught at the Institute for Holy Land Studies, now Jerusalem University College (JUC), from 1976–1979 and is adjunct faculty with JUC, serving as a field instructor for the three week course in Historical and Geographical Settings of the Bible. In addition to field study in Israel, her areas of interest and scholarly writing include the books of Exodus and Esther, biblical wisdom literature, and hermeneutics. Her book length commentary on Esther is included in *The Expositor's Bible Commentary*, revised edition, edited by Tremper Longman III and David Garland (Zondervan). She is the author of *With God Nothing Is Impossible* (Deep River), tracing narratives of key women in the Bible as their stories unfolded in the promised land, and *An Introduction to Reading Biblical Wisdom Texts* (Hendrickson), designed for inquisitive laypersons.

Monique D. (Vincent) Roddy (PhD, University of Chicago) is Associate Professor of History at Walla Walla University. She is Publications Manager for the Center for Near Eastern Archaeology at La Sierra University, where she is an editor on the Madaba Plains Project - Tall al-'Umayri excavation volumes. The most recent monograph, *MPP 10: The 2006 Season at Tall al-'Umayri and Subsequent Studies*, was published in 2022 with Penn State University Press. Dr. Roddy is co-director of the Balu'a Regional Archaeological Project, which excavates at Khirbat al-Balu'a in Jordan. Her research there focuses on household archaeology, especially of the Iron II or Moabite period. Recent publications include articles on the "The Qasr at Balu'a" (2023) and "Households, Communities, and Dimensions of Social Identity in the Iron Age at Tall al-'Umayri, Jordan" (2022), the latter on the Early Iron Age Stratum 12 settlement at 'Umayri that is the focus of the discussion in this volume.

Aubrey Taylor McClain (PhD, Bar-Ilan University) is assistant professor of theology and Shapiro Fellow for Jewish-Christian Studies at Greenville University in Greenville, Illinois. She has also served as a member of the faculty for Jerusalem University College in Jerusalem, where she received her MA in Biblical History and Geography. Having lived in Israel for the better part of ten years, she taught dozens of field courses on the historical geography of the Bible for university and seminary students from all over the world. She has also lectured at the Tantur Ecumenical Institute in Jerusalem and led educational tours of Israel for lay audiences. Interested in how space can be used for communicative effect, her work makes use of historical geography, the social sciences, and literary approaches to the Bible.

Paul H. Wright (PhD, Hebrew Union College) is president of Jerusalem University College/Institute of Holy Land Studies. He has lived full time in Jerusalem since 1997, where he has taught classes in biblical historical geography and on the cultural backgrounds of the Bible to thousands of students in Israel. He has published numerous books on topics related to the landed context of the Bible with the Israeli publisher Carta and is the author of the *Rose Then and Now Bible Map Atlas* and the *Holman Illustrated Guide to Biblical Geography*.

SUBJECT AND AUTHOR INDEX

SCRIPTURE INDEX

Old Testament

Genesis

Exodus

Leviticus

Numbers

Deuteronomy

Joshua

Judges

Ruth

1 Samuel

2 Samuel

1 Chronicles

New Testament

Deuterocanonical Books

ANCIENT SOURCES INDEX

Ancient Near Eastern Texts

Egyptian Texts

Mesopotamian Texts

West-Semitic Texts

Old Testament Pseudepigrapha

Dead Sea Scrolls

Ancient Jewish Writers

Rabbinic Works

Early Christian Writings

Greco-Roman Texts

IMAGE ATTRIBUTION

Page 10. Aerial View of Shiloh from the East. Image by Bill Schlegel. Copyright Bill Schlegel/BiblePlaces.com. Used by permission.

Page 11. View of the Tabernacle Plateau at Shiloh. Image by A.D. Riddle. Copyright A.D. Riddle/BiblePlaces.com. Used by permission.

Page 24. The Elevation of Palestine. Image by Barry J. Beitzel. Copyright 2009 Barry J. Betizel The Moody Bible Institute of Chicago. Used by permission.

Page 25. Aerial View of Adam. Image by Todd Bolen. Copyright Todd Bolen/ BiblePlaces.com. Used by permission.

Page 26. Tel es-Sultan, Jericho. Image by Todd Bolen. Copyright Todd Bolen/ BiblePlaces.com. Used by permission.

Page 39. Aerial View of the Ascent of Adummim and Wadi Qelt near Jericho. Image by Bill Schlegel. Copyright Bill Schlegel/BiblePlaces.com. Used by permission.

Page 40. Aeriel View of Modern-Day Jericho. Image by Barry J. Beitzel. Copyright 2014 Faithlife / Logos Bible Software. Used by permission.

Page 50. Aerial View of Et-Tell and Deir Dibwan from the West. Image by Bill Schlegel. Copyright Bill Schlegel/BiblePlaces.com. Used by permission.

Page 57. Shechem Between Mount Gerizim and Mount Ebal. Image by Todd Bolen. Copyright Todd Bolen/BiblePlaces.com. Used by permission.

Page 58. Altar on Mount Ebal. Image by Bill Schlegel. Copyright Bill Schlegel/ BiblePlaces.com. Used by permission.

Page 60. Aerial View of Shechem from the North. Image by Bill Schlegel. Copyright Bill Schlegel/BiblePlaces.com. Used by permission.

Page 67. Aerial View of Gibeon and the Central Benjaminite Plateau. Image by Bill Schlegel. Copyright Bill Schlegel/BiblePlaces.com. Used by permission.

Page 73. Relief of Tiglath-Pileser III with His Foot on the Neck of an Enemy. Image by Todd Bolen. Copyright Todd Bolen/BiblePlaces.com. Used by permission.

Page 79. Aerial View of Hazor. Image by Bill Schlegel. Copyright Bill Schlegel/ BiblePlaces.com. Used by permission.

Page 81. Aerial View of Excavations at Dor. Image by Bill Schlegel. Copyright Bill Schlegel/BiblePlaces.com. Used by permission.

Page 91. Late Bronze Palace Mudbricks at Hazor. Image by Todd Bolen. Copyright Todd Bolen/BiblePlaces.com. Used by permission.

Page 102. Jericho (Tell es-Sultan) Mudbrick Wall. Image by Todd Bolen. Copyright Todd Bolen/BiblePlaces.com. Used by permission.

Page 184. Iron IIA Cooking Jug from Tell es-Safi/Gath. Image by Aren M. Maier. Copyright Aren M. Maier/Logos User. Used by permission.

Page 185. Monolithic Two-horned Stone Altar from Tell es-Safi/Gath In Situ in a Late Iron IIA Temple in Area D West, Lower City of Tell es-Safi/Gath. Image by Aren M. Maier. Copyright Aren M. Maier/Logos User. Used by permission.

Page 201. Portion of Pottery Timeline Featuring Iron Age I Philistine Decorated Sherds. Image by Todd Bolen. Copyright Todd Bolen/BiblePlaces.com. Used by permission.

Page 204. Illustration of Land Battle of Ramesses III and Sea Peoples from Medinet Habu. Image by Guiseppe Angelelli. Public Domain.

Page 205. Relief Illustrating Sea Peoples Engaged in Sea Battle with Ship from Medinet Habu. Image by Todd Bolen. Copyright Todd Bolen/BiblePlaces.com. Used by permission.

Page 206. Model of Iron I Settlement in Ephraim and Manasseh. Image by Chris McKinny. Copyright Chris McKinny/BiblePlaces.com. Used by permission.

Page 209. Samaria Ostraca, Early 8th Century BC. Image by Todd Bolen. Copyright Todd Bolen/BiblePlaces.com. Used by permission.

Page 225. Aerial View of the Jordan River and Surrounding Hills near Nahal Jabok. Image by Todd Bolen. Copyright Todd Bolen/BiblePlaces.com. Used by permission.

Page 242. Distributoin of Land in Kufr Al-Ma according to Descent Group-1960. Image by Richard T. Antoun. From Richard T. Antoun, Diagram of a Jordanian Arab Village, in Arab Village: A Social Structural Study of a Trans-Jordanian Peasant Community, (Bloomington, IN: Indiana University Press, 1972).

Page 248. Tribal Alottments of Judah and Benjamin. Image by Chris McKinny. Copyright Chris McKinny. Used by permission.

Page 252. Map: The Elevation of Palestine with Annotations. Image by Barry J. Beitzel. Copyright 2009 Barry J. Betizel The Moody Bible Institute of Chicago. Used by permission.

Page 261. Shephelah and the Hill Country of Judah East of Lachish. Image by Todd Bolen. Copyright Todd Bolen/BiblePlaces.com. Used by permission.

Page 265. Aerial View of Tel Megiddo. Image by Itamar Grinberg. Liscended under CC BY-SA 2.0 (https://creativecommons.org/licenses/by-sa/2.0/). Via Wikimedia Commons.

Page 266. Aerial View of Gibeon and the Central Benjaminite Plateau. Image by Bill Schlegel. Copyright Bill Schlegel/BiblePlaces.com. Used by permission.

Page 268. Aerial View of the Negev East of Beersheba. Image by Todd Bolen. Copyright Todd Bolen/BiblePlaces.com. Used by permission.

Page 272. Statue of Pharaoh Merenptah at the Egyptian Museum in Cairo. Image by A.D. Riddle. Copyright A.D. Riddle/BiblePlaces.com. Used by permission.

Page 273. Detail of the Merenptah Stele Discovered in 1896 by Sir William Flinders Petrie. Image by A.D. Riddle. Copyright A.D. Riddle/BiblePlaces.com. Used by permission.

Page 275. Merenptah's Reliefs at the Cour de la Cachette, Karnak. Image by Todd Bolen. Copyright Todd Bolen/BiblePlaces.com. Used by permission.

Page 278. Detail of the Name "Israel" on the Merenptah Stela. Image by A.D. Riddle. Copyright A.D. Riddle/BiblePlaces.com. Used by permission.

Page 279. The Hymnic Poetic Unit of the Merenptah Stela Pertaining to Canaan. Image by Michael G. Hasel. Copyright Michael G. Hasel. Used by permission.

Page 281. The Grammatical Structure in the Hymnic-Poetic Unit. Image by Michael G. Hasel. Copyright Michael G. Hasel. Used by permission.

Page 292. Aerial View of Shiloh Excavations. Image by Bill Schlegel. Copyright Bill Schlegel/BiblePlaces.com. Used by permission.

Page 294. Shiloh and the Surrounding Hill Country. Image by Todd Bolen. Copyright Todd Bolen/BiblePlaces.com. Used by permission.

Page 295. Fields near Shechem. Image by Todd Bolen. Copyright Todd Bolen/BiblePlaces.com. Used by permission.

Page 297. Model of Iron I Settlement in Ephraim and Manasseh. Image by Chris McKinny. Copyright Chris McKinny/BiblePlaces.com. Used by permission.

Page 304. Bethel, Modern Day Beitin. Image by Daniel Warner. Copyright 2004 The Virtual Bible. Used by permission.

Page 317. Mount Tabor (Left) and Hill of Moreh (Right) in the Jezreel Valley, View from the West. Image by Bill Schlegel. Copyright Bill Schlegel/BiblePlaces.com. Used by permission.

Page 318. Harod Valley and Mount Moreh from Mount Gilboa. Image by Todd Bolen. Copyright Todd Bolen/BiblePlaces.com. Used by permission.

Page 320. Tel Akko. Image by Barry J. Beitzel. Copyright 2014 Faithlife /Logos Bible Software.

Page 322. Tel Dan. Image by Barry J. Beitzel. Copyright 2014 Faithlife/Logos Bible Software.

Page 324. Tel Dan Stele. Image by Reuben Evans, Branson Anderson. Copyright 2016 Faithlife/Logos Bible Software.

Page 331. Possible Libnah, Tel Burna, from the Northwest. Image by Todd Bolen. Copyright Todd Bolen/BiblePlaces.com. Used by permission.

Page 332. Section of the Medeba Map Showing "Jethor, also Jethera." Image by Todd Bolen. Copyright Todd Bolen/BiblePlaces.com. Used by permission.

Page 336. Aerial View of 2018 Excavations at Beth Shemesh. Image by Bill Schlegel. Copyright Bill Schlegel/BiblePlaces.com. Used by permission.

Page 338. Aerial View of Gibeon. Image by Barry J. Beitzel. Copyright 2014 Faithlife/Logos Bible Software.

Page 340. Aerial View of Beth Horon. Image by Barry J. Beitzel. Copyright 2014 Faithlife/Logos Bible Software.

Page 353. Aerial View of Jokneam Excavations. Image by Bill Schlegel. Copyright Bill Schlegel/BiblePlaces.com. Used by permission.

Page 377. Dead Sea and Mountains of Moab. Image by Sarti Design, Faith Based Expeditions, Richard Myers, Shaun Goodman. Copyright 2011 Logos Bible Software.

Page 385. Aerial View of Jezebel Valley with Megiddo Pass, Mounts Tabor and Moreh in Background. Image by Bill Schlegel. Copyright Bill Schlegel/BiblePlaces.com. Used by permission.

Page 386. Hazor Lower City. Image by Todd Bolen. Copyright Todd Bolen/BiblePlaces.com. Used by permission.

Page 389. Mount Tabor. Image by Todd Bolen. Copyright 2009 Todd Bolen/BiblePlaces.com. Used by permission.

Page 393. Jael Smote Sisera, and Slew Him (Tissot). Image by James Tissot. Public Domain.

Page 397. Cuneiform Letter to Ibni-Addu, King of Hazor. Image by A.D. Riddle. Copyright A.D. Riddle/BiblePlaces.com. Used by permission.

Page 402. Kishon River near Mount Carmel. Image by Daniel Warner. Copyright 2004 The Virtual Bible. Used by permission.

Page 415. Mount Hermon. Image by Barry J. Beitzel. Copyright 2014 Faithlife/Logos Bible Software.

Page 416. Aerial View of Masada. Image by Barry J. Beitzel. Copyright 2014 Faithlife/Logos Bible Software.

Page 419. Granite Casing on Menkaure's Pyramid at Giza. Image by Barry J. Beitzel. Copyright 2014 Faithlife/Logos Bible Software.

Page 420. Aerial View of the Judean Wilderness. Image by Barry J. Beitzel. Copyright 2014 Faithlife/Logos Bible Software.

Page 422. Cenomanian Limestone. Image by A.D. Riddle. Copyright A.D. Riddle/BiblePlaces.com. Used by permission.

Page 422. Eocene Chalk in the Shephelah, Capped with Nari Limestone. Image by A.D. Riddle. Copyright A.D. Riddle/BiblePlaces.com. Used by permission.

Page 422. Grain Mill Made of Basalt. Image by Barry J. Beitzel. Copyright 2014 Faithlife/Logos Bible Software.

Page 427. Ein Harod, Spring of Gideon, at the Foot of Mount Gilboa. Image by Todd Bolen. Copyright Todd Bolen/BiblePlaces.com. Used by permission.

Page 429. Jezreel Valley with the Hill of Moreh in Background. Image by Todd Bolen. Copyright Todd Bolen/BiblePlaces.com. Used by permission.

Page 437. Iron I Four-Room House at Umayri. Image by Douglas Clark. Copyright Douglas Clark. Used with permission.

Page 440. "Four-room" Building at Tall al-Umayri. Image by Rhonda Root. Copyright Rhonda Root. Used by permission.

Page 443. Iron I Neighborhood at Tall al-Umayri, Topographic Drawing. Image by Monique Roddy. Copyright Monique Vincent. Used by permission.

Page 461. Jars from Tel Eton. Image by Tel 'Eton Expedition. Copyright Tel 'Eton Expedition. Used with permission.

Page 466. Floor Plan of Four-Room House at Tel Eton. Image by Tel 'Eton Expedition. Copyright Tel 'Eton Expedition. Used with permission.

Page 468. Iron II Four-space House at Horvat Haroah. Image by A.D. Riddle. Copyright A.D. Riddle/BiblePlaces.com. Used by permission.

Page 477. Late Bronze Pottery from Taanach. Image by Todd Bolen. Copyright Todd Bolen/BiblePlaces.com. Used by permission.

Page 478. Iron I Philistine Drinking Bowl from Ashkelon. Image by Todd Bolen. Copyright Todd Bolen/BiblePlaces.com. Used by permission.

Page 491. Arnon River Flowing Through Canyon. Image by Barry J. Beitzel. Copyright 2014 Faithlife/Logos Bible Software.

Page 504. Shephelah and the Hill Country of Judah, East of Lachish. Image by Todd Bolen. Copyright Todd Bolen/BiblePlaces.com. Used by permission.

Page 505. Aijalon Valley. Image by Daniel Frese. Copyright Daniel Frese/BiblePlaces.com. Used by permission.

Page 513. Samson Slays a Thousand Men. Image by James Tissot. Public Domain.

Page 515. Samson Puts Down the Pillars. Image by James Tissot. Public Domain.

Page 519. The Zoilos Inscription from the Hellenistic Phase of the Sacred Precinct at Tel Dan. Image by William Krewson. Copyright William Krewson/Bibleplaces.com. Used by permission.

Page 521. Map: Local and International Routes Associated with Ancient Dan. Image by Nelson Glueck. Copyright /Courtesy of Nelson Glueck School of Biblical Archaeology.

Page 523. Archaeological Site Plan of Tel Dan. Image by Nelson Glueck. Copyright / Courtesy of Nelson Glueck School of Biblical Archaeology. Revised Version of a copyrighted map.

Page 524. Middle Bronze Mudbrick Gate at Tel Dan. Image by Todd Bolen. Copyright Todd Bolen/BiblePlaces.com. Used by permission.

Page 525. Charioteer Vase from Tel Dan. Image by Todd Bolen. Copyright Todd Bolen/BiblePlaces.com. Used by permission.

Page 526. Iron Age I Pithoi from Tel Dan. Image by Chris McKinny. Copyright Chris McKinny/BiblePlaces.com. Used by permission.

Page 527. Relative Abundance of Cattle and Sheep/Goats over Time, Percentage of Number of Individual Specimens. Image by J.S. Greer. Copyright Jonathan S. Greer. Used with permission.

Page 528. Tel Dan Stele. Image by Reuben Evans, Branson Anderson. Copyright 2016 Faithlife/Logos Bible Software.

Page 529. Reconstructed Altar at Tel Dan. Image by David A. deSilva. Copyright 2016 David A. deSilva/Logos Bible Software.

Page 530. Architectural Phases at Area T Tel Dan (drawn by J. S. Greer After Images in Biran, Biblical Dan, 182, 188, 205, respectively). Image by J. S. Greer. Copyright Jonathan S. Greer. Used with permission.

Page 535. A Bronze Bowl from the "Altar Room" at Tel Dan Interpreted as an Israelite Mizraq (Drawn by J. S. Greer after Images in Avraham Biran, "The Dancer from Dan, the Empty Tomb and the Altar Room," IEJ 36 (1986): 186, fig. 15). Image by J. S. Greer. Copyright Jonathan S. Greer. Used with permission.

Page 543. Aerial View of Dan. Image by Ferrell Jenkins. Copyright Ferrell Jenkins/BiblePlaces.com. Used with permission.

Page 544. Aerial View of Beersheba. Image by Todd Bolen. Copyright Todd Bolen/BiblePlaces.com. Used by permission.

Page 556. Aroer and the King's Highway from the South Rim of Wadi Mujib. Image by A.D. Riddle. Copyright A.D. Riddle/BiblePlaces.com. Used by permission.

PROJECT STAFF

EDITORIAL STAFF

Douglas Mangum, managing editor
Amy Balogh, academic editor
Lynsey Stepan, assistant editor
Jessica Parks, media editor
Iker Flores, media editor

INFORMATION ARCHITECTURE

Sean Boisen
Jeremy Thompson

MAP DESIGN

Ben Vander Woude

PRODUCTION STAFF

Katy Smith
Mandi Newell
David Bomar
Abigail Stocker

COVER DESIGN

Bryan Hintz